500 FRUIT RECIPES

A DELICIOUS COLLECTION OF FRUITY SOUPS, SALADS, COOKIES, CAKES, PASTRIES, PIES, TARTS, PUDDINGS, PRESERVES AND DRINKS, SHOWN IN 500 PHOTOGRAPHS

EDITED BY FELICITY FORSTER

greene&golden

This edition is published by greene&golden
an imprint of Anness Publishing Ltd, Blaby Road
Wigston, Leicestershire LE18 4SE; info@anness.com

www.annesspublishing.com

If you like the images in this book and would like to investigate using them for publishing, promotions or advertising, please visit our website www.practicalpictures.com for more information.

Publisher: Joanna Lorenz
Senior Editor: Felicity Forster
Production Controller: Pirong Wang

© Anness Publishing Ltd 2012

A CIP catalogue record for this book is available from the British Library.

PUBLISHER'S NOTE
Although the advice and information in this book are believed to be accurate and true at the time of going to press, neither the authors nor the publisher can accept any legal responsibility or liability for any errors or omissions that may have been made nor for any inaccuracies nor for any loss, harm or injury that comes about from following instructions or advice in this book.

NOTES
Bracketed terms are intended for American readers.
For all recipes, quantities are given in both metric and imperial measures and, where appropriate, in standard cups and spoons. Follow one set of measures, but not a mixture, because they are not interchangeable.

Standard spoon and cup measures are level.
1 tsp = 5ml, 1 tbsp = 15ml, 1 cup = 250ml/8fl oz.
Australian standard tablespoons are 20ml.
Australian readers should use 3 tsp in place of 1 tbsp for measuring small quantities.
American pints are 16fl oz/2 cups. American readers should use 20fl oz/2.5 cups in place of 1 pint when measuring liquids.

Electric oven temperatures in this book are for conventional ovens. When using a fan oven, the temperature will probably need to be reduced by about 10–20°C/20–40°F. Since ovens vary, you should check with your manufacturer's instruction book for guidance.

The nutritional analysis given for each recipe is calculated per portion (i.e. serving or item), unless otherwise stated. If the recipe gives a range, such as Serves 4–6, then the nutritional analysis will be for the smaller portion size, i.e. 6 servings. The analysis does not include optional ingredients, such as salt added to taste.

Medium (US large) eggs are used unless otherwise stated.

Main front cover image shows Meringue Cake with Raspberries – for recipe, see page 171.

Contents

Introduction

Fruit offers an amazing variety of colours, textures, scents and flavours, and there is nothing like the sight of a glorious display of fruit in a market to lift the spirits and whet the appetite. Fruit is not only good for the soul; it is a supremely healthy food, bursting with energy-giving natural sugars, vitamins and minerals. When energy

levels are low, a few grapes, a banana or an apple can revitalize in moments.

Most fruit can be eaten raw, just as it is (be sure to wash it first), although some varieties may need peeling. Nothing beats a simple dessert of perfectly ripe juicy fruit, perhaps served with a scoop or two of vanilla ice cream or a dollop of cream, or with some good cheese. Fruits can either be served on their own, or used to create sweet and savoury dishes of infinite variety, from pies, puddings, cakes and muffins to ice creams, mousses, soufflés and pavlovas. You could easily base an entire meal on fruit without repeating any colours, textures or flavours. The meal might begin with the classic combination of pears and Stilton, or a refreshing fruit

soup, followed by roast duck with prunes and apples, then a platter of cheese, fresh and dried fruit and nuts, and finally a tropical fruit salad, a bowl of bright red berries or a lemon tart.

Fruit is enormously rewarding to cook with and is very versatile. Almost all fruits complement each other, so you can create all manner of interesting combinations. Although the recipes in this book focus more on the use of fruits in sweet dishes, they have an important role to play in savouries too. Tart fruits such as gooseberries, rhubarb and cranberries cut the richness of fatty fish such as mackerel, and can also enhance the sometimes plain flavour of poultry. Dried fruits are used extensively in North African and Middle Eastern cooking – the combination of meat and sweet, sticky dates, prunes or dried apricots is superb. Most fruits also marry well with

exotic spices, such as cinnamon, ginger and vanilla, and even those fruits that are relatively bland can be lifted by the addition of a squeeze of lemon or lime juice.

Fruits are no longer the seasonal produce they once were. Nowadays, thanks to sophisticated transportation methods, all types of fruit from every country are available almost all year round. The result of this is that we no longer need to wait with eager anticipation for a particular fruit to come into season. So strawberries, raspberries and peaches have ceased to be exclusively summer treats, but can be bought in almost any season, although they will never taste as good as when freshly picked, and are still always at their best and cheapest in the summer.

The ideal time to buy fruit is when it is fully ripe and at its peak. The exceptions are fruits such as bananas and pears – these ripen quickly and should therefore be bought at different stages of maturity so that they are not all ready at the same time. You are most likely to find top-quality fruits in markets and shops that have a quick turnover of fresh produce, preferably with a daily delivery. Although most fruits are now available almost year-round, they are best and cheapest when in season in the country of origin. Only buy as much fruit as you need at one time so that it remains fresh and appetizing.

For some fruits, the only preparation needed is washing or wiping with a damp cloth; others must be peeled or skinned, cored, stoned or seeded. Always wash fruit just before using and, if necessary, cut away any bruised or damaged parts. Most fruits can be cooked in a variety of ways. Apples and pears, stone fruits, figs, rhubarb and even grapes can be stewed or poached, either whole, halved or in segments. Any firm fruits can be grilled, with or without sugar. Tropical fruits such as bananas and pineapple are particularly good for grilling; for desserts, they can be cut into wedges or chunks and threaded on to skewers to make kebabs. Peaches, nectarines, apricots and plums can be baked whole or in halves, wedges or slices according to type. All fruits can be microwaved with excellent results, although the skins on some, such as plums, may not soften sufficiently in the short cooking time, and whole fruits such as apples should be scored to prevent them from bursting. Many fruits can be sautéed and tossed in hot butter until lightly browned all over. And finally, you can deep-fry fruits such as apples, bananas and pineapple to make fritters.

The hundreds of different kinds of fruit can be divided into four main categories: 'pome' fruits of the apple and pear families; citrus fruits such as oranges, lemons and limes; stone fruits such as peaches, apricots, plums and cherries; and soft fruits such as strawberries, raspberries and blueberries. In addition, there are the 'one-offs' that do not fit into the other categories. These include melons, grapes, figs, rhubarb (which is actually a vegetable but is always treated as an honorary fruit), and tropical fruits such as bananas, mango, papaya and passion fruit. The recipes within each chapter of this book follow this basic order.

Whether you are looking for a healthy breakfast drink, a refreshing fruit salad, a tasty teatime cookie, an exotic main course meal, a warming slice of pie, a decadent dinner party dessert or a festive fruit cake for Christmas, you are sure to find an inspirational idea in this colourful volume of 500 fabulous fruit recipes.

To make the most of the different types of fruit, there are certain preparation techniques that are useful. Firm fruits often simply need peeling and coring, while stone fruits need their skins immersed in boiling water before peeling, and their stones (pits) removed. Tropical fruits, such as pineapple and mango, have their own special techniques, as shown here.

Fruit should be stored at the bottom of the refrigerator or in the salad crisper, making sure it is kept away from any uncooked meat. For some fruits, the only preparation needed is washing or wiping with a damp cloth. You should wash fruit only just before using – gently rub under running water, or rinse and drain in a colander. This is especially important for fruits that are served raw. Some fruits must then be peeled, cored, stoned (pitted) or seeded before use.

Peeling Firm Fruit
Some firm fruits, such as eating apples and pears, can be served raw without peeling. For cooking, peeling is often necessary. Pare off the skin as thinly as possible to avoid losing the valuable nutrients under the skin.

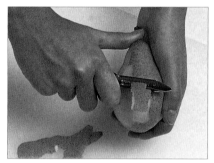

1 To peel fruit, first wash it, and then pat it dry by using kitchen paper. Use a small, sharp paring knife or a vegetable peeler to pare off the skin in long, thin vertical strips all round the fruit, making sure that you cut into the fruit as thinly as possible. Pears, in particular, are best peeled by this method.

2 Alternatively, for apples, thinly peel all round the fruit in a spiral.

Coring Firm Fruit
1 To core whole apples and pears, place the sharp edge of a corer over the stem end of the fruit.

2 Press the corer down firmly into the fruit, and then twist it slightly; the core, complete with all of the pips (seeds), should come away in the centre of the corer. Push out the corer from the handle end to remove the complete core cleanly.

Segmenting Firm Fruit

1 Halve the fruit lengthways, then cut it into quarters or segments.

2 Cut out the central core and pips (seeds) using a small, sharp knife, taking care not to cut yourself as you work the knife towards you.

Peeling Citrus Fruit
It is very important to remove all of the bitter white pith that lies just beneath the rind of citrus fruits.

1 To peel firm-skinned fruits, hold the fruit over a bowl to catch the juice, and use a sharp knife to cut off the rind.

2 For loose-skinned fruit, such as tangerines, pierce the skin with your forefinger at the stalk end, and peel off the rind. Pull off all the white shreds adhering to the fruit.

Segmenting Citrus Fruit

1 Using a small serrated knife, cut down between the membranes enclosing the segments, then ease out the flesh.

Grating Citrus Fruit

1 For finely grated rind, grate the fruit against the fine face of a grater. Remove only the coloured rind; if you grate too deeply into the peel, you will be in danger of including the bitter white pith.

2 For thinly pared strips of rind, use a cannelle knife (zester) or vegetable peeler, then cut into shreds if necessary.

Decorating with Citrus Fruit

1 To make thick julienne strips of rind, cut lengthways using a cannelle knife.

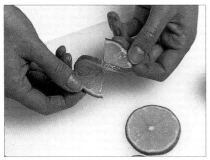

2 To make twists, slice the fruits thinly, cut to the centre, then twist the ends in opposite directions to make an S-shape.

Peeling Soft Fruit

Fruits such as peaches, nectarines and apricots can be peeled with a sharp paring knife, but this may waste some of the delicious flesh. It is better to loosen the skins first by dipping them briefly in boiling water.

1 To remove the skins quickly and cleanly from peaches, nectarines and apricots, start by making a tiny nick in the skin, using the point of a sharp knife. This is done in order to help the skins spring off the flesh when the fruits are immersed in boiling water. Take care when you are handling the soft fruit, as the flesh can be easily damaged by clutching the fruit too firmly.

2 Cover with boiling water and leave for 15–30 seconds, depending on the ripeness of the fruit. Remove the fruit with a slotted spoon and peel off the skin, which should come away easily.

Removing Stones (Pits) and Seeds

1 Cut all round the fruit through the seam. Twist the halves in opposite directions, then lever out the stone (pit).

2 To pit cherries, simply place a cherry in a cherry stoner and then push the bar firmly into the fruit. The pit will be neatly ejected.

3 To remove the seeds from grapes, first cut the grapes in half, and then pick out the tiny pips using the tip of a small sharp knife.

4 To remove either papaya or melon seeds, you should first cut the fruit in half using a sharp knife, and then neatly scoop out all of the seeds with a spoon.

Preparing a Pineapple

1 Cut away the top and base of the pineapple. Then cut down the sides, removing all the dark 'eyes', but leaving the pineapple in a good shape.

2 Cut the pineapple into thin slices and, with an apple corer, remove the hard central core.

Preparing a Mango
1 Cut vertically down each side of the stone (pit). Taking the two large slices, cut the flesh into a criss-cross pattern down to (but not through) the skin.

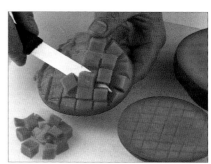

2 Press each half inside out, then cut the mango cubes away from the skin.

Cook's Tips
• *Some fruits, such as apples, pears and bananas, quickly oxidize and turn brown when exposed to the air. To prevent discoloration, brush cut fruits with lemon juice. Alternatively, acidulate a bowl of cold water by stirring in the juice of half a lemon. Drop the cut fruits into the bowl immediately after preparing.*
• *Do not wash fruit before storing, but only when you are ready to use it.*
• *Do not refrigerate unripe fruit; keep it at room temperature or in a cool, dark place.*
• *Refrigerate fragile fruits, such as berries, in a single layer on a paper-lined tray.*

Apple Soup with Mixed Vegetables

This delicious and unusual soup makes the most of freshly picked apples.

Serves 6
45ml/3 tbsp oil
1 kohlrabi, diced
3 carrots, diced
2 celery sticks, diced
1 green (bell) pepper, seeded and diced
2 tomatoes, diced
2 litres/3^1/2 pints/9 cups chicken stock
6 large green apples
45ml/3 tbsp plain (all-purpose) flour
150ml/^{1}/4 pint/^{2}/3 cup double (heavy) cream
15ml/1 tbsp sugar
30–45ml/2–3 tbsp lemon juice
salt and freshly ground black pepper
lemon wedges and crusty bread, to serve

1 Heat the oil in a large pan. Add the kohlrabi, carrots, celery, green pepper and tomatoes and fry for 5–6 minutes to soften.

2 Pour in the chicken stock, bring to the boil, then reduce the heat and simmer for about 45 minutes.

3 Meanwhile, peel and core the apples, then chop into small cubes. Add to the pan and simmer for a further 15 minutes.

4 In a bowl, mix together the flour and cream, then pour slowly into the soup, stirring well, and bring to the boil. Add the sugar and lemon juice before seasoning. Serve immediately with lemon wedges and crusty bread.

Cook's Tip
Firm, sweet-sour eating apples are ideal for this soup as they hold their shape and complement the vegetable mixture. For a vegetarian version, use vegetable stock. For a meaty variation, dice and fry some firm meaty sausage, such as ham sausage, kabanos or salami, and use to garnish the soup before serving.

Parsnip & Apple Soup

Choose a sharp apple juice to complement the sweetness of the parsnips and the warmth of the spices in this tempting soup.

Serves 4–6
25g/1oz/2 tbsp butter
1 onion, finely chopped
1 garlic clove, finely chopped
500g/1^1/4lb parsnips, thinly sliced
5ml/1 tsp curry paste or powder
300ml/^{1}/2 pint/1^1/4 cups apple juice
600ml/1 pint/2^1/2 cups vegetable stock
300ml/^{1}/2 pint/1^1/4 cups milk
salt and ground black pepper
thick natural yogurt, to serve
chopped fresh herbs such as mint or parsley, to serve

1 Melt the butter in a large pan and add the onion, garlic and parsnips. Cook gently, without browning, for about 10 minutes, stirring often.

2 Add the curry paste or powder and cook, stirring, for 1 minute. Pour in the apple juice and stock and bring to the boil. Reduce the heat, cover the pan and simmer gently for about 20 minutes or until the parsnips are soft.

3 Process or blend the soup until smooth and return it to the rinsed-out pan. Stir in the milk and season to taste with salt and pepper. Reheat the soup gently, without boiling, and serve topped with a spoonful of yogurt and a sprinkling of herbs.

Variations
• *Omit the curry paste or powder and season the soup with a little cinnamon and freshly grated nutmeg, adding it at the beginning of cooking to give an integrated, mellow flavour.*
• *Instead of apple juice, peel, core and finely chop 4 eating apples and cook them with the onion. Replace the juice with extra stock.*
• *Add a fruity garnish to the soup – core and thinly slice a red-skinned eating apple and sprinkle over the soup before adding the chives.*
• *Garnish with toasted cashew nuts and chives.*

Apple Soup Energy 278kcal/1159kJ; Protein 2.4g; Carbohydrate 24.8g, of which sugars 18.8g; Fat 19.5g, of which saturates 9.2g; Cholesterol 34mg; Calcium 63mg; Fibre 4.6g; Sodium 54mg.
Parsnip and Apple Energy 130kcal/548kJ; Protein 3.4g; Carbohydrate 18.5g, of which sugars 12.6g; Fat 5.3g, of which saturates 2.9g; Cholesterol 12mg; Calcium 101mg; Fibre 4g; Sodium 56mg.

Juniper & Apple Soup

This is an example of the savoury fruit soups that are popular throughout northern Europe. The apple and juniper flavours are particularly Norwegian. Here it's the berries that are being used, not the fresh young shoots.

Serves 4

15ml/1 tbsp juniper berries
4 green cardamom pods
3 whole allspice
1 small cinnamon stick
bunch of fresh parsley
30ml/2 tbsp olive oil
3 cooking apples, peeled, cored and diced
2 celery sticks, finely chopped
2 shallots, chopped
2.5cm/1in piece fresh root ginger, finely chopped
1 litre/1¾ pints/4 cups light chicken stock
250ml/8fl oz/1 cup cider
250ml/8fl oz/1 cup double (heavy) cream
75ml/5 tbsp Armagnac (optional)
salt and ground black pepper
chopped fresh parsley, to garnish

1 Put the juniper berries, cardamom pods, allspice and cinnamon stick in a piece of muslin (cheesecloth) and tie together with string. Tie the parsley together.

2 Heat the oil in a pan, add the apples, celery, shallots and ginger, and season with salt and pepper. Place a piece of dampened baking parchment on top, cover the pan and cook gently for 10 minutes. Discard the parchment.

3 Add the stock and cider and stir well. Add the spices and parsley. Bring the soup slowly to the boil, then lower the heat and cover the pan. Simmer for 40 minutes, until the apples are reduced to a pulp and the vegetables are soft. Remove the spices and parsley.

4 Pour the soup into a food processor or blender and blend until smooth. Then pass it through a sieve (strainer) into a clean pan. Reheat, stirring occasionally, until boiling. Reduce the heat or turn it off, so that the soup barely simmers, then stir in the cream and Armagnac, if using. Taste the soup and add salt and pepper if necessary. Ladle the soup into bowls and serve hot, garnished with parsley.

Curried Apple Soup

South-east Asian food has become popular in Norway, the home of this apple soup, and the coconut milk in this recipe replaces the traditional cream.

Serves 4

50g/2oz/4 tbsp butter
2 shallots, finely chopped
1 cooking apple, peeled, cored and chopped
10ml/2 tsp curry paste
30ml/2 tbsp plain (all-purpose) flour
1.25 litres/2¼ pints/5½ cups chicken or beef stock
400ml/14fl oz can unsweetened coconut milk
salt and ground black pepper

For the garnish

60ml/4 tbsp double (heavy) cream or coconut milk
chopped fresh parsley

1 Melt the butter in a pan, add the shallots and cook gently for about 5 minutes until softened but not coloured. Add the apple, season with salt and pepper and cook for another 2 minutes, until the apple is slightly softened.

2 Stir in the curry paste and flour, and cook over low heat, stirring, for 1–2 minutes, without colouring. Remove from the heat and gradually stir in the stock to form a smooth sauce.

3 Return the pan to the heat and bring to the boil, stirring all the time; cook until the soup thickens. Reduce the heat and simmer gently for 10 minutes.

4 Stir in the coconut milk. Check the seasoning, adding salt and pepper if necessary. Pour the soup into bowls and serve with a swirl of cream or coconut milk in each portion. Add chopped parsley to garnish.

Cook's Tips

• For a smooth soup, blend the soup in a blender or food processor before reheating and serving.
• For a lower-fat version, use reduced-fat coconut milk and swirl a little natural (plain) yogurt into the soup instead of cream.

Juniper and Apple Energy 406kcal/1677kJ; Protein 1.4g; Carbohydrate 8.5g, of which sugars 8.1g; Fat 39.2g, of which saturates 21.7g; Cholesterol 86mg; Calcium 48mg; Fibre 1.2g; Sodium 29mg.
Curried Apple Soup Energy 195kcal/812kJ; Protein 1.7g; Carbohydrate 14.3g, of which sugars 7.6g; Fat 15g, of which saturates 9.2g; Cholesterol 37mg; Calcium 66mg; Fibre 1.3g; Sodium 200mg.

Kohlrabi, Apple & Caraway Soup

The apples in this kohlrabi soup give the dish a delightfully sweet edge. You could use other fruits and berries in the recipe, including apricot, cherry, plum, gooseberries and redcurrants. Depending on their preparation, they can have a savoury emphasis or a much sweeter one.

Serves 4–6
10g/¼oz/½ tbsp butter
1 kohlrabi, diced
2 carrots, diced
2 celery sticks, diced
1 yellow (bell) pepper,
    seeded and diced
1 tomato, diced
1.5 litres/2½ pints/6¼ cups
    vegetable stock
800g/1¾lb crisp, green
    eating apples, peeled
15ml/1 tbsp sugar
2.5ml/½ tsp ground
    caraway seeds
45ml/3 tbsp sour cream
1 small bunch parsley,
    leaves chopped
salt and ground black pepper

1 Put the butter in a large pan and melt over medium heat. Add the diced vegetables and sauté for 3–4 minutes, or until soft. Season to taste.

2 Add the vegetable stock and bring to the boil, then reduce the heat to low and simmer for 1 hour.

3 Grate the apples and add to the simmering soup, followed by the sugar and the caraway seeds. Cook for a further 15 minutes and adjust the seasoning.

4 Stir in the sour cream and sprinkle with the parsley. Serve hot.

> **Cook's Tips**
> • Kohlrabi survives frost very well and can be stored over a long period in a suitable cool, dark storage area.
> • Kohlrabi bulbs are available in white and purple varieties – the white ones have much more flavour when they are small. Purple kohlrabi tends to have a spicier taste.

Pear & Roquefort Soup

Like most fruit-based soups, this is served in small portions. It makes an unusual and seasonal starter for an autumn dinner party.

Serves 4
30ml/2 tbsp sunflower oil
1 onion, chopped
3 pears, peeled, cored
    and chopped
400ml/14fl oz/1⅔ cups
    vegetable stock
2.5ml/½ tsp paprika
juice of ½ lemon
175g/6oz Roquefort cheese
salt and ground black pepper
watercress sprigs, to garnish

For the caramelized pears
50g/2oz/¼ cup butter
2 pears, halved, cored and
    cut into wedges

1 Heat the oil in a pan. Add the onion and cook for 4–5 minutes until soft. Add the pears and stock, then bring to the boil. Cook for 8–10 minutes, until the pears are very soft. Stir in the paprika, lemon juice, cheese and seasoning.

2 Cool the soup slightly before puréeing it in a food processor or blender until smooth. Pass the soup through a fine sieve (strainer) and return it to the pan.

3 To make the caramelized pears, melt the butter in a frying pan and add the pears. Cook for 8–10 minutes, turning occasionally, until golden and beginning to caramelize.

4 Reheat the soup gently, then ladle into small, shallow bowls. Add a few caramelized pear wedges to each portion. Garnish with tiny sprigs of watercress and serve at once.

> **Cook's Tip**
> Pears discolour quickly when peeled, so prepare them at the last minute. Adding the peeled fruit to a bowl of cold water with a little lemon juice added helps to prevent them from turning brown. This is not so important for the soup, but the caramelized pears should not be discoloured before cooking.

Kohlrabi Energy 104kcal/442kJ; Protein 1.6g; Carbohydrate 18.1g, of which sugars 17.9g; Fat 3.4g, of which saturates 1.9g; Cholesterol 8mg; Calcium 69mg; Fibre 4.6g; Sodium 44mg.
Pear and Roquefort Energy 381kcal/1579kJ; Protein 10.1g; Carbohydrate 21.8g, of which sugars 20.9g; Fat 28.7g, of which saturates 15.6g; Cholesterol 59mg; Calcium 246mg; Fibre 4.7g; Sodium 616mg.

Tomato & Peach Soup

American-style soups, made from the clear juices extracted from vegetables or fruits and referred to as 'water' soups by chefs, provide the inspiration for this recipe.

Serves 6

1.5kg/3–3¹/₂lb ripe peaches, peeled, stoned and cut into chunks
1.2kg/2¹/₂lb beef tomatoes, peeled and cut into chunks
30ml/2 tbsp white wine vinegar
1 lemon grass stalk, crushed and chopped
2.5cm/1in fresh root ginger, grated
1 bay leaf
150ml/¹/₄ pint/²/₃ cup water
18 tiger prawns (jumbo shrimp), shelled with tails on and deveined
olive oil, for brushing
salt and ground black pepper
handful of fresh coriander (cilantro) leaves and 2 vine-ripened tomatoes, peeled, seeded and diced, to garnish

1 Purée the peaches and tomatoes in a food processor or blender. Stir in the vinegar and seasoning. Line a large bowl with muslin (cheesecloth). Pour the purée into the bowl, gather up the ends of the muslin and tie tightly. Suspend over the bowl and leave at room temperature for 3 hours or until about 1.2 litres/2 pints/5 cups juice have drained through.

2 Meanwhile, put the lemon grass, ginger and bay leaf into a pan with the water, and simmer for 5–6 minutes. Set aside to cool. Strain the mixture into the tomato and peach juice and chill for at least 4 hours.

3 Using a sharp knife, slit the prawns down their curved sides, cutting about three-quarters of the way through and keeping their tails intact. Open them out flat.

4 Heat a griddle or frying pan and brush with a little oil. Sear the prawns for 1–2 minutes on each side, until tender and slightly charred. Pat dry on kitchen paper to remove any remaining oil. Cool, but do not chill.

5 Ladle the soup into bowls and place three prawns in each. Add torn coriander leaves and diced tomato to each bowl.

Iced Melon Soup

Use different varieties of melon for this cool soup and ice sorbet to create subtle contrast. Try a mix of Charentais and Ogen or cantaloupe and Galia.

Serves 6–8

2.25kg/5–5¹/₄lb very ripe melon
45ml/3 tbsp orange juice
30ml/2 tbsp lemon juice
mint leaves, to garnish

For the melon and mint sorbet

25g/1oz/2 tbsp sugar
120ml/4fl oz/¹/₂ cup water
2.25kg/5–5¹/₄lb very ripe melon
juice of 2 limes
30ml/2 tbsp chopped fresh mint

1 To make the melon and mint sorbet, put the sugar and water into a pan and heat gently until the sugar dissolves. Bring to the boil and simmer for 4–5 minutes, then remove from the heat and leave to cool.

2 Halve the melon. Scrape out the seeds, then cut it into large wedges and cut the flesh out of the skin. Weigh about 1.5kg/3¹/₂lb melon.

3 Purée the melon in a food processor or blender with the cooled syrup and lime juice.

4 Stir in the mint and pour the melon mixture into an ice-cream maker. Churn, following the manufacturer's instructions, or until the sorbet is smooth and firm. Alternatively, pour the mixture into a suitable container and freeze until icy around the edges. Transfer to a food processor or blender and process until smooth. Repeat the freezing and processing two or three times or until smooth and holding its shape, then freeze until firm.

5 To make the chilled melon soup, prepare the melon as in step 2 and purée it in a food processor or blender. Pour the purée into a bowl and stir in the orange and lemon juice. Place the soup in the fridge for 30–40 minutes, but do not chill it for too long as this will dull its flavour.

6 Ladle the soup into bowls and add a large scoop of the sorbet to each. Garnish with mint leaves and serve at once.

Iced Melon Energy 150kcal/639kJ; Protein 3g; Carbohydrate 35g, of which sugars 35g; Fat 1g, of which saturates 0g; Cholesterol 0mg; Calcium 82mg; Fibre 5.1g; Sodium 136mg.
Tomato and Peach Energy 217kcal/922kJ; Protein 22g; Carbohydrate 25g, of which sugars 25g; Fat 4g, of which saturates 1g; Cholesterol 195mg; Calcium 111mg; Fibre 8.3g; Sodium 276mg.

Lentil & Apricot Soup

This beautiful orange-coloured soup is delightfully light and elegant. Lentils are excellent soup components, and can also be used for stuffing, in salads and in terrines. Dried apricots are a Turkish touch that blend beautifully with the red lentils. The soup is bright orange and almost luminous when cooked.

Serves 4

45ml/3 tbsp olive oil
1 large onion, finely chopped
3 garlic cloves, finely chopped
50g/2oz/¼ cup ready-to-eat
  dried apricots, chopped
300g/11oz/scant 1½ cups split
  red lentils
1 litre/1¾ pints/4 cups vegetable
  stock or water
3 medium tomatoes, peeled
  and chopped, or use
  canned tomatoes
2.5ml/½ tsp ground cumin
handful of thyme leaves
juice of 1 lemon
salt and ground black pepper
handful of flat leaf parsley,
  leaves chopped, to garnish

1 Heat the oil in a large, heavy pan over medium heat. Add the onion, garlic and dried apricots. Sauté, stirring, for 10 minutes, or until the onions are soft. Add the lentils and stock, and bring to the boil.

2 Reduce the heat, cover and simmer for 20–30 minutes, or until the lentils are soft and tender.

3 Add the tomatoes, cumin and thyme, and simmer for a further 15 minutes.

4 Spoon the soup into a food processor or blender and purée in batches until smooth. Return the purée to the pan and add the lemon juice, salt and pepper to taste. Sprinkle liberally with the parsley, and serve hot.

> **Cook's Tip**
> To peel the tomatoes easily, plunge them into boiling water for 30 seconds, then refresh in cold water. Peel away the skins.

Chilled Cherry Soup

Soups made from seasonal fruits are a favourite Central European treat. Cherry soup, one of the glories of the Hungarian table, is also a Jewish speciality, often served during the festival of Shavuot when dairy foods are traditionally feasted upon. It is served with sour cream – and the test is whether you can resist that extra spoonful!

Serves 6

1kg/2¼lb fresh, frozen or canned
  sour cherries, such as Morello
  or Montmorency, pitted
175–250g/6–9oz/about 1 cup
  sugar, to taste
1–2 cinnamon sticks, each about
  5cm/2in long
750ml/1¼ pints/3 cups dry
  red wine
5ml/1 tsp almond extract,
  or to taste
250ml/8fl oz/1 cup single
  (light) cream
250ml/8fl oz/1 cup sour cream
  or crème fraîche

1 Add the pitted cherries, 250ml/8 fl oz/1 cup water, sugar, cinnamon and wine in a large pan. Bring to the boil, reduce the heat and simmer for 20–30 minutes, until the cherries are tender. Remove from the heat and pour into a bowl.

2 Stir the almond extract into the soup and leave until cool. Then cover and chill.

3 In a bowl, stir a few tablespoons of single cream into the sour cream or crème fraîche to thin it down, then stir in the rest until the mixture is smooth. Stir half the cream into the soup and chill until ready to serve. Chill the remaining cream.

4 To serve, ladle the soup into small bowls and swirl in the remaining cream.

> **Variation**
> When plums are in season, use them instead of cherries.

Lentil and Apricot Energy 377kcal/1589kJ; Protein 20.2g; Carbohydrate 55.4g, of which sugars 13.2g; Fat 9.8g, of which saturates 1.4g; Cholesterol 0mg; Calcium 97mg; Fibre 6.9g; Sodium 42mg.
Chilled Cherry Energy 484Kcal/2037kJ; Protein 3.7g; Carbohydrate 64.1g, of which sugars 64.1g; Fat 16.3g, of which saturates 10.3g; Cholesterol 48mg; Calcium 125mg; Fibre 1g; Sodium 53mg.

Danish Dried Fruit Soup

Throughout Scandinavia, soups made with dried fruit used to be especially welcome during the long, dark winter months when fresh fruit was unavailable. Any combination of dried fruit can be used in this recipe; pears and peaches are a modern addition, but are faithful to the soup's northern European heritage.

115g/4oz/¹⁄₂ cup prunes
115g/4oz/¹⁄₂ cup dried apples
115g/4oz/¹⁄₂ cup dried peaches
115g/4oz/¹⁄₂ cup dried pears
15ml/1 tbsp lemon zest
7.5cm/3in cinnamon stick
5 whole cloves
40g/1¹⁄₂oz/¹⁄₄ cup quick-cook
   tapioca
250ml/8fl oz/1 cup double
   (heavy) cream

Serves 6–8
50g/2oz/¹⁄₄ cup currants
50g/2oz/¹⁄₄ cup sultanas
   (golden raisins)
115g/4oz/¹⁄₂ cup dried apricots

1 Chop all the dried fruit and place in a large pan together with 1 litre/1¾ pints/4 cups water. Cover, and leave to stand for at least 2 hours or overnight.

2 Stir the lemon zest, cinnamon stick, cloves and tapioca into the dried fruit mixture. Bring to the boil, cover and simmer gently for 1 hour, stirring occasionally.

3 Remove the pan from the heat. Remove the cinnamon stick and discard. Let the fruit mixture cool slightly.

4 Beat the double cream until soft peaks form. Serve the warm fruit soup with a dollop of cream in each bowl.

Cook's Tip
It is important to soak the dried fruits before using, to restore their moisture. Leaving them in water overnight will soften their texture without losing their flavour.

Red Berry Soup with Cream

Some call this ruby-red berry soup Denmark's national dessert. Utterly simple to prepare, it can be made using a blend of various red berries. Currants and raspberries are traditional, but raspberries and strawberries, red and blackcurrants, or currants and cherries are also delightful. Served cold with a swirl of cream in each bowl, the soup is sweet and tangy.

Serves 6
400g/14oz redcurrants
450g/1lb raspberries
100–150g/3¾–5oz/¹⁄₂–¾ cup
   sugar (depending on the
   sweetness of the fruit)
550ml/18fl oz/2¹⁄₂ cups
   blackcurrant juice
45ml/3 tbsp cornflour
   (cornstarch)
250ml/8fl oz/1 cup double
   (heavy) cream
10ml/2 tsp vanilla sugar
raspberries, to decorate

1 Put the berries, sugar and 500ml/17fl oz/generous 2 cups of the blackcurrant juice into a pan and add 750ml/1¼ pints/ 3 cups water. Bring the mixture to the boil and cook over a medium-high heat for 3 minutes. Pour the fruit and juice through a sieve (strainer) set over a pan. Use a wooden spoon to press through as much berry juice as possible.

2 In a small bowl, mix the cornflour with the remaining blackcurrant juice. Stir this mixture into the berry juice. Place the pan over a medium heat and bring the juice to the boil, stirring, until it thickens slightly.

3 Pour the cream into a bowl and stir in the vanilla sugar. Pour the soup into individual bowls and spoon 30ml/2 tbsp cream into each bowl, swirling it slightly. Sprinkle each bowl with a few raspberries and serve.

Cook's Tip
Chopped, fresh rhubarb blended with berries can also be used to make this dish. Potato flour can be substituted for cornflour, but do not boil the soup after adding it, or it will become rubbery.

Dried Fruit Soup Energy 305kcal/1277kJ; Protein 2.7g; Carbohydrate 37.4g, of which sugars 31.5g; Fat 17.1g, of which saturates 10.4g; Cholesterol 43mg; Calcium 51mg; Fibre 4g; Sodium 17mg.
Red Berry Soup Energy 383kcal/1606kJ; Protein 3.1g; Carbohydrate 44g, of which sugars 37.1g; Fat 23g, of which saturates 14.1g; Cholesterol 57mg; Calcium 84mg; Fibre 3.6g; Sodium 25mg.

Beetroot & Cranberry Soup

Although it sounds complex, this soup is ridiculously easy to make. The sweet, earthy flavour of fresh, cooked beetroot is combined with zesty orange and tart cranberry.

Serves 4
350g/12oz cooked beetroot (beet), roughly chopped
grated rind and juice of 1 orange
600ml/1 pint/2½ cups unsweetened cranberry juice
450ml/¾ pint/scant 2 cups Greek (strained plain) yogurt
a little Tabasco
4 slices brioche
60ml/4 tbsp mascarpone
salt and ground black pepper

For the garnish
sprigs of mint
cooked cranberries

1 Purée the beetroot with the orange rind and juice, half the cranberry juice and the yogurt in a blender until smooth.

2 Press the purée through a sieve (strainer) into a clean bowl. Stir in the remaining cranberry juice, Tabasco and salt and pepper to taste. Chill for at least 2 hours.

3 Preheat the grill (broiler). Using a large pastry cutter, stamp a round out of each slice of brioche and toast until golden. Ladle the soup into bowls and top each with brioche and mascarpone. Garnish with mint and fresh cranberries.

> **Variation**
> Raspberries are superb with beetroot (beet). Use raspberry juice instead of the cranberry juice and add a few fresh raspberries for the garnish.

> **Cook's Tip**
> If the oranges you use are a little tart, add a pinch or two of caster (superfine) sugar to the soup.

Prawn & Pineapple Broth

This simple dish is often served as an appetite enhancer because of its hot and sour flavour. It is also popular as a tasty accompaniment to plain rice or noodles. A nice touch is to serve the broth in a hollowed-out pineapple, which has been halved lengthways. It looks great and contributes to the fruity flavour.

Serves 4
30ml/2 tbsp vegetable oil
15–30ml/1–2 tbsp tamarind paste
15ml/1 tbsp sugar
450g/1lb raw prawns (shrimp), peeled and deveined
4 thick fresh pineapple slices, cored and cut into bitesize chunks
salt and ground black pepper
fresh coriander (cilantro) and mint leaves, to garnish
steamed rice or plain noodles, to serve (optional)

For the spice paste
4 shallots, chopped
4 fresh red chillies, seeded and chopped
25g/1oz fresh root ginger, peeled and chopped
1 lemon grass stalk, chopped
5ml/1 tsp shrimp paste

1 Make the spice paste. Using a mortar and pestle or a food processor or blender, grind the shallots, chillies, ginger and lemon grass to a paste. Add the shrimp paste and mix well.

2 Heat the oil in a wok or heavy pan. Stir in the spice paste and fry until fragrant. Stir in the tamarind paste and the sugar, then pour in 1.2 litres/2 pints/5 cups water. Mix well and bring to the boil. Reduce the heat and simmer for 10 minutes. Season the broth with salt and pepper.

3 Add the prawns and pineapple to the broth and simmer for 4–5 minutes, or until the prawns are cooked. Using a slotted spoon, lift the prawns and pineapple out of the broth and divide them among four warmed bowls. Ladle over some of the broth and garnish with coriander and mint leaves. The rest can be served separately as a drink, or spooned over steamed rice or plain noodles, if you want to transform this into a slightly more substantial dish.

Beetroot Soup Energy 365kcal/1544kJ; Protein 13.9g; Carbohydrate 63.7g, of which sugars 40.5g; Fat 8g, of which saturates 1.9g; Cholesterol 18mg; Calcium 316mg; Fibre 1.7g; Sodium 331mg.
Prawn and Pineapple Energy 192kcal/808kJ; Protein 20.4g; Carbohydrate 14.2g, of which sugars 13.9g; Fat 6.4g, of which saturates 0.8g; Cholesterol 219mg; Calcium 111mg; Fibre 1.3g; Sodium 216mg.

Spiced Mango Soup

Mangoes may seem an unusual choice for a savoury soup, but this is actually a delicious invention by Chutney Mary's, an Anglo-Indian restaurant in London. It is best when served chilled. Gram flour, or chickpea flour, also known as besan, is available from Asian stores.

Serves 4

2 ripe mangoes
15ml/1 tbsp gram flour
120ml/4fl oz/½ cup natural
 (plain) yogurt
900ml/1½ pints/3¾ cups cold
 or chilled water
2.5ml/½ tsp grated fresh
 root ginger
2 fresh red chillies, seeded and
 finely chopped
30ml/2 tbsp olive oil
2.5ml/½ tsp mustard seeds
2.5ml/½ tsp cumin seeds
8 curry leaves
salt and ground black pepper
fresh mint leaves, shredded,
 to garnish natural (plain)
 yogurt, to serve

1 Peel the mangoes, remove the stones and cut the flesh into chunks. Purée in a food processor or blender until smooth. Pour into a pan and stir in the gram flour, yogurt, water, ginger and chillies.

2 Bring the ingredients slowly to the boil, stirring occasionally. Simmer for 4–5 minutes until thickened slightly, then set aside off the heat.

3 Heat the oil in a frying pan over medium to low heat. Add the mustard seeds and cook for a few seconds until they begin to pop, then add the cumin seeds.

4 Add the curry leaves and then cook for 5 minutes. Stir the spice mixture into the soup, return it to the heat and cook for 10 minutes.

5 Press through a sieve (strainer), if you like, then season to taste. Leave the soup to cool completely, then chill for at least 1 hour.

6 Ladle the soup into bowls, and top each with a dollop of yogurt. Garnish with shredded mint leaves and serve.

Pomegranate Broth

Clear and refreshing, this Persian soup is usually served as a sophisticated palate cleanser between courses, or as a light appetizer at the start of a meal. Sour pomegranates are often available in Middle Eastern stores.

Serves 4

5–6 sour or sweet pomegrantes
1.2 litres/2 pints/5 cups clear
 chicken stock
juice of 1 lemon, if using sweet
 pomegranates
seeds of 1 sweet pomegranate
salt and ground black pepper
fresh mint leaves, to garnish

1 For 150ml/¼ pint/⅔ cup juice, you will need 5–6 sour pomegranates. Cut the pomegranates in half and extract the juice by turning the fruit on a stainless-steel, glass or wooden lemon squeezer.

2 Pour the stock into a pan and bring to the boil. Lower the heat, and stir in the pomegranate juice and lemon juice if using sweet pomegranates. Bring the stock back to the boil.

3 Reduce the heat again and stir in half the pomegranate seeds, then season the broth to taste and turn off the heat.

4 Ladle the broth into warmed bowls. Sprinkle the remaining pomegranate seeds into the bowls. Garnish with mint leaves and serve.

Variation
Try unsweetened white grape juice and water, mixed half and half, instead of the stock. Cool and chill before adding the seeds. This can also be served for dessert: open freeze small scoops of whipped cream until firm and add to each portion.

Cook's Tip
Do not use any metal other than stainless steel for squeezing, or it will cause the juice to discolour and taste unpleasant.

Spiced Mango Soup Energy 83kcal/354kJ; Protein 3g; Carbohydrate 14.4g, of which sugars 12.7g; Fat 2g, of which saturates 0.5g; Cholesterol 0mg; Calcium 72mg; Fibre 2g; Sodium 28mg.
Pomegranate Broth Energy 62kcal/260kJ; Protein 2g; Carbohydrate 3.9g, of which sugars 2.3g; Fat 4.4g, of which saturates 0.4g; Cholesterol 0mg; Calcium 14mg; Fibre 0.6g; Sodium 205mg.

Pears & Stilton

Stilton is the classic British
blue cheese, but you could
use other blue cheeses.
Comice pears are a good
choice for this dish, but for
a dramatic colour contrast,
select the excellent Red
Williams pear.

Serves 4
4 ripe pears, lightly chilled
75g/3oz blue Stilton

50g/2oz curd (farmer's)
  cheese
ground black pepper
watercress sprigs or rocket
  (arugula), to garnish

For the dressing
45ml/3 tbsp light olive oil
15ml/1 tbsp lemon juice
10ml/2 tsp toasted
  poppy seeds
salt and ground black pepper

1 First make the dressing: place the olive oil and lemon juice,
poppy seeds and seasoning in a screw-top jar and then shake
together until emulsified.

2 Cut the pears in half lengthways, then scoop out the cores
and cut away the calyx from the rounded end.

3 Beat together the Stilton, curd cheese and a little pepper.
Divide this mixture among the cavities in the pears.

4 Shake the jar containing the dressing to mix it again,
then spoon it over the pears. Serve garnished with some
watercress sprigs or rocket leaves.

Variation
Other blue cheese to try in place of the Stilton include
Gorgonzola, Roquefort, Danish blue and Dolcelatte.

Cook's Tip
Place unripe pears in a brown paper bag to speed up
the ripening process. If you need to slow down the speed
of ripening, keep the pears in the refrigerator.

Cheese-stuffed Pears

These autumn pears, made
in the slow cooker, make
a sublime dish with their
scrumptious creamy
topping. If you don't have a
large slow cooker, choose
short squat pears rather
than long, tapering ones, so
that they will fit in one layer.

Serves 4
50g/2oz/¼ cup ricotta cheese
50g/2oz/¼ cup dolcelatte cheese

15ml/1 tbsp honey
½ celery stick, finely sliced
8 green olives, pitted and
  roughly chopped
4 dates, stoned (pitted) and
  cut into thin strips
pinch of paprika
2 medium barely ripe
  pears
150ml/¼ pint/²⁄₃ cup fresh
  apple juice
mixed salad leaves, to serve
  (optional)

1 Place the ricotta cheese in a bowl and crumble in the
dolcelatte. Add the honey, celery, olives, dates and paprika
and mix together well until creamy and thoroughly blended.

2 Halve the pears lengthways. Use a melon baller or teaspoon
to remove the cores and make a hollow for the filling.

3 Divide the ricotta filling equally between the pears, packing
it into the hollow, then arrange the fruit in a single layer in the
ceramic cooking pot.

4 Pour the apple juice around the pears, then cover with the
lid. Cook on high for 1½–2 hours, or until the fruit is tender.
(The cooking time will depend on the ripeness of the pears.)

5 Remove the pears from the slow cooker and brown them
under a hot grill (broiler) for a few minutes. Serve with mixed
salad leaves, if you like.

Cook's Tip
These pears go particularly well with slightly bitter and peppery
leaves, such as chicory and rocket (arugula). Try them tossed in
a walnut oil dressing.

Pears and Stilton Energy 243kcal/1007kJ; Protein 7.2g; Carbohydrate 15.5g, of which sugars 15.5g; Fat 17.2g, of which saturates 6.4g; Cholesterol 21mg; Calcium 109mg; Fibre 3.5g; Sodium 208mg.
Cheese-stuffed Pears Energy 236kcal/992kJ; Protein 6.9g; Carbohydrate 35.6g, of which sugars 35.6g; Fat 8.2g, of which saturates 5.0g; Cholesterol 24mg; Calcium 141mg; Fibre 4.1g; Sodium 261mg.

Pears with Cashel Blue Cream & Walnuts

The cheese Cashel Blue is the perfect partner to the ripe, juicy pears that start to appear in grocery stores in autumn – and it is now widely available from specialist cheese suppliers.

Serves 6
115g/4oz fresh cream cheese
75g/3oz Cashel Blue cheese
30–45ml/2–3 tbsp single
 (light) cream
115g/4oz/1 cup roughly
 chopped walnuts

6 ripe pears
15ml/1 tbsp lemon juice
mixed salad leaves, such as frisée,
 oakleaf lettuce and radicchio
6 cherry tomatoes
sea salt and ground black pepper
walnut halves and sprigs of
 fresh flat leaf parsley,
 to garnish

For the dressing
juice of 1 lemon
a little finely grated lemon rind
pinch of caster (superfine) sugar
60ml/4 tbsp olive oil

1 Mash the cream cheese and Cashel Blue cheese together in a mixing bowl with a good grinding of black pepper, then blend in the cream to make a smooth mixture. Add 25g/1oz/¼ cup chopped walnuts and mix to distribute evenly. Cover and chill.

2 Peel and halve the pears and scoop out the core. Put them into a bowl of water with the lemon juice to prevent them from browning. To make the dressing, whisk the lemon juice, lemon rind, caster sugar and olive oil together in a bowl and season with salt and pepper to taste.

3 Arrange a bed of salad leaves on six plates – shallow soup plates are ideal – add a tomato to each and sprinkle over the remaining chopped walnuts.

4 Drain the pears well and pat dry with kitchen paper, then turn them in the prepared dressing and arrange, hollow side up, on the salad leaves. Divide the Cashel Blue mixture between the six halved pears and spoon the rest of the dressing over the top. Garnish each pear with a walnut half and a sprig of fresh flat leaf parsley.

Mixed Melon & Orange Salsa

A combination of two very different melons gives this salsa an exciting flavour and texture. It is ideal for a hot summer's day in the garden. Try it with some thinly sliced Parma ham or smoked salmon.

Serves 10
1 small orange-fleshed melon,
 such as Charentais
1 large wedge watermelon
2 oranges
Parma ham or smoked salmon,
 to serve

1 Quarter the orange-fleshed melon and scoop out all the seeds. Use a large, sharp knife to cut off the skin. Dice the melon flesh.

2 Pick out the seeds from the watermelon, then remove the skin. Dice the flesh into small chunks.

3 Use a zester to pare long strips of rind from both oranges. Halve the oranges and squeeze out all their juice, using a hand juicer if you have one.

4 Mix both types of melon and the orange rind and juice together in a large bowl. Chill in the refrigerator for about 30 minutes and serve.

Cook's Tips
• *When buying melons, avoid any with soft spots, lacerations or other blemishes on the skin.*
• *Store whole melons in the refrigerator if possible and use within a week. If the melon is too large for your refrigerator, keep it in a cool, dark place.*
• *Wrap cut pieces of melon, refrigerate and use within a day or so.*

Variation
Other types of melon can be used for this salsa. You could try cantaloupe, Galia or Ogen.

Pears with Cashel Energy 243kcal/1007kJ; Protein 7.2g; Carbohydrate 15.5g, of which sugars 15.5g; Fat 17.2g, of which saturates 6.4g; Cholesterol 21mg; Calcium 109mg; Fibre 3.5g; Sodium 208mg.
Mixed Melon Salsa Energy 58kcal/250kJ; Protein 1.1g; Carbohydrate 13.5g, of which sugars 13.5g; Fat 0.4g, of which saturates 0.1g; Cholesterol 0mg; Calcium 30mg; Fibre 0.9g; Sodium 25mg.

Orange, Tomato & Chive Salsa

Fresh chives and large, sweet oranges provide a very cheerful combination of flavours in this tangy dish. An unusual salsa, this is a very good accompaniment for grilled meats, such as lamb or pork kebabs. It also tastes good with grilled halloumi.

Serves 4
2 large, sweet oranges
1 ripe beefsteak tomato,
    or 2 plum tomatoes
bunch of fresh chives
1 garlic clove
30ml/2 tbsp extra virgin olive oil
    or grapeseed oil
sea salt

1 Slice the base off one orange so that it will stand firmly on a chopping board. Using a large sharp knife, remove the peel by slicing from the top to the bottom of the orange. Prepare the second orange in the same way.

2 Working over a bowl, segment each orange in turn. Slice towards the middle of the fruit, and slightly to one side of a segment, and then gently twist the knife to release the orange segment. Repeat. Squeeze any juice from the remaining membrane so that it falls into the bowl.

3 Roughly chop the orange segments and add them to the bowl with the collected orange juice.

4 Halve the tomato and use a teaspoon to scoop the seeds into the bowl. With a sharp knife, finely dice the flesh and add to the oranges and juice in the bowl.

5 Hold the bunch of chives neatly together and use a pair of kitchen scissors to snip them into the bowl.

6 Thinly slice the garlic and stir it into the orange mixture. Pour over the olive oil, season with sea salt and stir well to mix.

7 Serve the salsa in the bowl in which it was made, or spoon into four individual bowls. It can also be spooned into the empty orange shells for serving. This involves slightly more difficult preparation, but looks very effective.

Fruit & Nut Coleslaw

A delicious and nutritious mixture of crunchy vegetables, fruit and nuts, tossed together in a mayonnaise dressing.

Serves 6
225g/8oz white cabbage
1 large carrot
175g/6oz/ ³⁄₄ cup ready-to-eat
    dried apricots
50g/2oz/ ¹⁄₂ cup walnuts

50g/2oz/ ¹⁄₂ cup hazelnuts
115g/4oz/ ²⁄₃ cup raisins
30ml/2 tbsp chopped
    fresh parsley
105ml/7 tbsp mayonnaise
75ml/5 tbsp natural (plain)
    yogurt
salt and ground black pepper
fresh chives, to garnish

1 Finely shred the cabbage and coarsely grate the carrot. Place both in a large mixing bowl.

2 Roughly chop the dried apricots, walnuts and hazelnuts. Stir them into the cabbage and carrot mixture with the raisins and chopped parsley.

3 In a separate bowl, mix together the mayonnaise and yogurt and season to taste with salt and pepper.

4 Add the mayonnaise mixture to the cabbage mixture and toss together to mix. Cover and set aside in a cool place for at least 30 minutes before serving, to allow the flavours to mingle. Garnish with a few fresh chives and serve.

Variations
• For a salad that is lower in fat, use low-fat natural (plain) yogurt and reduced-calorie mayonnaise.
• Instead of walnuts and hazelnuts, use flaked almonds and chopped pistachios.
• Omit the dried apricots and add a cored and chopped, unpeeled eating apple.
• Substitute other dried fruit or a mixture for the apricots – try nectarines, peaches or prunes.

Orange Salsa Energy 91kcal/380kJ; Protein 1.3g; Carbohydrate 9.3g, of which sugars 9.3g; Fat 5.7g, of which saturates 0.8g; Cholesterol 0mg; Calcium 49mg; Fibre 2g; Sodium 7mg.
Fruit Coleslaw Energy 309kcal/1285kJ; Protein 4.3g; Carbohydrate 19.1g, of which sugars 18.8g; Fat 24.5g, of which saturates 2.9g; Cholesterol 13mg; Calcium 72mg; Fibre 2.5g; Sodium 103mg.

Grape & Walnut Raita

Refreshing raitas are served to cool the effect of hot curries. Cucumber and mint raita is the best known combination. Here is a refreshing fruit and nut version, which is particularly good with beef curries.

Serves 4
350ml/12fl oz/1½ cups
   natural (plain) yogurt
75g/3oz seedless grapes
50g/2oz/½ cup shelled
   walnuts
2 firm bananas

5ml/1 tsp granulated sugar
salt
5ml/1 tsp freshly ground
   cumin seeds
1.5ml/¼ tsp freshly roasted
   cumin seeds, chilli powder
   or paprika, to garnish

1 Place the yogurt in a chilled bowl and add the grapes and walnuts.

2 Slice the bananas directly into the bowl and fold in gently before they turn brown.

3 Add the sugar, salt and ground cumin, and gently mix together.

4 Chill, and just before serving, sprinkle on the cumin seeds, chilli powder or paprika.

> **Variations**
> • Instead of grapes, try kiwi fruit, peaches or nectarines.
> • Almonds or hazelnuts can be used instead of or as well as the walnuts.
> • For Coconut and Raisin Raita, coarsely grate half a fresh coconut by hand or using a food processor. Mix in a bowl with 225g/8oz natural (plain) yogurt and 2.5ml/½ tsp sugar. Stir in 25g/1oz chopped fresh coriander (cilantro) or mint, and add salt to taste. Transfer to a serving bowl.

Sultana & Cashew Pilau

The secret of a perfect pilau is to wash the rice thoroughly, then soak it briefly. This softens and moistens the grains, enabling the rice to absorb moisture during cooking, which results in fluffier rice.

Serves 4
600ml/1 pint/2½ cups hot
   chicken or vegetable stock
generous pinch of saffron threads
50g/2oz/¼ cup butter
1 onion, chopped

1 garlic clove, crushed
2.5cm/1in piece cinnamon
   stick
6 green cardamom pods
1 bay leaf
250g/9oz/1⅓ cups basmati
   rice, soaked in water for
   20–30 minutes
50g/2oz/⅓ cup sultanas
   (golden raisins)
15ml/1 tbsp vegetable oil
50g/2oz/½ cup cashew nuts
naan bread and tomato and
   onion salad, to serve

1 Pour the hot chicken stock into a jug (pitcher). Stir in the saffron threads and set aside.

2 Heat the butter in a pan and fry the onion and garlic for 5 minutes. Stir in the cinnamon stick, cardamoms and bay leaf and cook for 2 minutes.

3 Drain the rice and add to the pan, then cook, stirring, for 2 minutes more. Pour in the saffron stock and add the sultanas. Bring to the boil, stir, then lower the heat, cover and cook gently for 10 minutes or until the rice is tender and all the liquid has been absorbed.

4 Meanwhile, heat the oil in a wok, karahi or large pan and fry the cashew nuts until browned. Drain on kitchen paper, then sprinkle the cashew nuts over the rice. Serve with naan bread and tomato and onion salad.

> **Cook's Tip**
> Saffron powder can be used instead of saffron threads, if you prefer. Dissolve it in the hot stock.

Grape and Walnut Energy 219kcal/917kJ; Protein 8g; Carbohydrate 23g, of which sugars 22g; Fat 11g, of which saturates 2g; Cholesterol 10mg; Calcium 197mg; Fibre 2.4g; Sodium 73mg.
Sultana and Cashew Energy 477kcal/2002kJ; Protein 8g; Carbohydrate 69g, of which sugars 11g; Fat 21g, of which saturates 8g; Cholesterol 27mg; Calcium 197mg; Fibre 2.7g; Sodium 380mg.

Devils on Horseback

This is a popular savoury dish that can be served either as an appetizer or at the end of a lavish dinner. The tasty morsels will go down a treat at any gathering. They can be served on crisp, fried bread instead of buttered toast, if you prefer.

Serves 4
16 pitted prunes
fruit chutney, such as mango
8 rindless rashers (strips) of
*   streaky (fatty) bacon*
8 small slices of bread
butter, for spreading

1 Preheat the oven to 200°C/400°F/Gas 6. Ease open the prunes and spoon a small amount of the fruit chutney into each cavity.

2 Lay the streaky bacon rashers on a chopping board, slide the back of a knife along each one to stretch it out and then cut each in half crossways.

3 Wrap a piece of bacon around each prune, secure with a cocktail stick (toothpick) and place on a baking sheet. (Alternatively, omit the cocktail sticks and lay them close together on the baking sheet so that they won't unroll in the oven.)

4 Place the wrapped prunes into the hot oven for about 8–10 minutes until the bacon is just cooked through.

5 Meanwhile, toast the bread. When the bacon is cooked, butter the hot toast and top each piece with a bacon-wrapped prune. Serve immediately.

Variations
• *Instead of filling the prunes with fruit chutney, why not try some other ingredients. If you prefer, the prunes can be stuffed with pâté, olives, whole almonds, or nuggets of cured meat.*
• *For an adult version, soak the prunes in a glass of red wine for 3–4 hours before stuffing and wrapping with the bacon.*

Figs with Prosciutto & Roquefort

In this easy, stylish dish, figs and honey balance the richness of the ham and cheese. Serve with warm bread for a simple appetizer before any rich main course.

Serves 4
8 fresh figs
75g/3oz prosciutto
45ml/3 tbsp clear honey
75g/3oz Roquefort cheese
ground black pepper

1 Preheat the grill (broiler). Quarter the figs and place on a foil-lined grill rack. Tear each slice of prosciutto into two or three pieces. Crumple the pieces of prosciutto and place them on the foil beside the figs. Brush the figs with 15ml/1 tbsp of the clear honey and cook under the grill until lightly browned.

2 Crumble the Roquefort cheese and divide among four plates, setting it to one side. Add the honey-grilled figs and ham, and pour over any cooking juices caught on the foil. Drizzle the remaining honey over the figs, ham and cheese, and serve seasoned with plenty of ground black pepper.

Variations
• *Any thinly sliced cured ham, such as Westphalian, Bayonne, Culatello or Serrano, can be used instead of prosciutto.*
• *The figs could be replaced with fresh pears. Slice 2 ripe but firm dessert pears in quarters and remove the cores. Toss in olive oil and cook on a hot ridged grill or griddle pan for 2 minutes on each side. Drizzle balsamic vinegar over and cook for 1 minute more until nicely coloured.*

Cook's Tip
Fresh figs are a delicious treat, whether you choose dark purple, yellowy green or green-skinned varieties. When they are ripe, you can split them open with your fingers to reveal the soft, sweet flesh full of edible seeds. They also taste great stuffed with goat's cheese.

Devils on Horseback Energy 309kcal/1303kJ; Protein 14.7g; Carbohydrate 41.7g, of which sugars 18.3g; Fat 10.4g, of which saturates 3.5g; Cholesterol 30mg; Calcium 75mg; Fibre 3.6g; Sodium 1132mg.
Figs Energy 326kcal/1378kJ; Protein 10.7g; Carbohydrate 57.4g, of which sugars 57.4g; Fat 7.5g, of which saturates 3.8g; Cholesterol 25mg; Calcium 324mg; Fibre 6.9g; Sodium 512mg.

Fried Plantains

These simple and tasty tropical treats from the Caribbean are the perfect accompaniment to highly spiced and seasoned foods. Their sweet flavour provides an interesting contrast to savoury meat dishes.

Serves 4

4 ripe plantains
75g/3oz/6 tbsp butter
10ml/2 tsp vegetable oil
strips of spring onion (scallion)
  and red (bell) pepper,
  to garnish

1 Peel the plantains, cut them in half lengthways, then cut them in half again. Melt the butter with the oil in a large frying pan.

2 Add the plantains to the pan in a single layer and fry for 8–10 minutes, turning halfway through. Drain on kitchen paper. Spoon into a heated dish and garnish with strips of spring onion and red pepper. Serve immediately.

Variation
Fried plantains are very good on their own, or with a generous scoop of sour cream, crème fraîche or thick yogurt, but also taste great with black beans. Soak 450g/1lb/2½ cups black turtle beans in water overnight. On the next day, drain the beans and put them in a pan. Cover with cold water. Add a 115g/4oz piece of gammon or uncooked ham and a bay leaf. Bring to the boil, then simmer and cook for 1 hour or until the beans are tender. In a separate pan, fry 2 crushed garlic cloves in 30ml/2 tbsp oil until aromatic. Add two ladles of cooked beans and fry for 2–3 minutes, breaking up the beans. Tip the refried beans back into the pan and season. Simmer gently for 10 minutes, then serve.

Cook's Tip
Ripe plantains have dark, almost black skins. Do not use green, under-ripe plantains, which are very hard and which will not soften, no matter how long you cook them for.

Stir-fried Pineapple with Ginger

This dish makes an interesting accompaniment to grilled meat or strongly flavoured fish such as tuna or swordfish. If the idea seems strange, think of it as resembling a fresh mango chutney, but with pineapple as the principal ingredient.

2 garlic cloves, finely
  chopped
2 shallots, finely chopped
5cm/2in piece fresh root
  ginger, peeled and
  finely shredded
30ml/2 tbsp light soy sauce
juice of ½ lime
1 large fresh red chilli, seeded
  and finely shredded

Serves 4
1 pineapple
15ml/1 tbsp vegetable oil

1 Trim and peel the pineapple. Cut out the core and dice the flesh into small pieces.

2 Heat the oil in a wok or frying pan. Stir-fry the garlic and shallots over a medium heat for 2–3 minutes, until golden. Do not let the garlic burn or the dish will taste bitter.

3 Add the pineapple. Stir-fry for about 2 minutes, or until the pineapple cubes start to turn golden on the edges.

4 Add the ginger, soy sauce, lime juice and shredded chilli.

5 Toss the mixture together until well mixed. Cook over a low heat for a further 2 minutes. Serve the pineapple as an accompaniment.

Variations
• *This dish also tastes excellent if peaches or nectarines are substituted for the diced pineapple. Use three or four, depending on their size.*
• *Instead of using light soy sauce, you could try Worcestershire sauce mixed with a little water.*
• *Experiment with different types and colours of fresh chilli.*

Fried Plantains Energy 205kcal/861kJ; Protein 1.2g; Carbohydrate 29.5g, of which sugars 5.8g; Fat 10g, of which saturates 5.5g; Cholesterol 21mg; Calcium 11mg; Fibre 1.3g; Sodium 65mg.
Stir-fried Pineapple Energy 110kcal/467kJ; Protein 1g; Carbohydrate 20.8g, of which sugars 20.8g; Fat 3.2g, of which saturates 0.3g; Cholesterol 0mg; Calcium 37mg; Fibre 2.4g; Sodium 538mg.

Apple & Beetroot Salad with Red Leaves

Bitter salad leaves are complemented by sweet-flavoured apples and juicy beetroot in this side salad.

Serves 4
50g/2oz/⅓ cup whole unblanched almonds
2 red apples, cored and diced
juice of ½ lemon
115g/4oz/4 cups red salad leaves, such as lollo rosso, oakleaf and radicchio

200g/7oz pre-cooked beetroot (beet) in natural juice, sliced

For the dressing
30ml/2 tbsp olive oil
15ml/1 tbsp walnut oil
15ml/1 tbsp red or white wine vinegar
salt and ground black pepper

1 Toast the almonds in a dry frying pan for 2–3 minutes until golden brown, tossing frequently to prevent them burning.

2 Meanwhile, make the dressing. Put the olive and walnut oils, vinegar and salt and pepper in a bowl or screw-top jar. Stir or shake thoroughly to combine.

3 Toss the apples in lemon juice to prevent them browning, then place in a large bowl and add the salad leaves, beetroot and almonds. Pour over the dressing and toss gently to disperse the ingredients evenly.

> **Cook's Tips**
> • Try to use fresh, raw beetroot (beet) if it is available. Cooking fresh beetroot is surprisingly easy – the important thing is not to puncture the skin before cooking, otherwise the bright red juice will leak out. To prepare fresh beetroot, trim off most of the leafy stalks, then wash and cook the unpeeled roots in boiling water for 1–2 hours, depending on size.
> • Red fruits and vegetables have high levels of vitamins C and E, and beta carotene.

Beetroot, Apple & Potato Salad

This salad is from Finland, where it is known as rosolli. It is served on Christmas Eve, just as the festive excitement mounts. The sweet apple and beetroot are the perfect partner for potatoes, pickled gherkins and eggs.

Serves 4
1 apple
3 cooked potatoes, finely diced

2 large gherkins, finely diced
3 cooked beetroot (beets), finely diced
3 cooked carrots, finely diced
1 onion, finely chopped
500ml/17fl oz/generous 2 cups double (heavy) cream
3 hard-boiled eggs, roughly chopped
15ml/1 tbsp chopped fresh parsley
salt and ground white pepper

1 Cut the apple into small dice. Place the pieces into a large bowl and add the diced potatoes, gherkins, beetroot, carrots and onion. Season the ingredients with plenty of salt and ground black pepper.

2 Carefully mix together all the ingredients in the bowl until they are well combined. Spoon the mixture into individual serving bowls.

3 Place the double cream into a separate bowl. Add any juice from the diced beetroot into the cream to give it additional flavour and an attractive pinkish colour. Stir well until the juice and cream are thoroughly combined.

4 Spoon the beetroot cream over the chopped vegetables and apple. Sprinkle the chopped eggs and parsley over the top of each portion before serving.

> **Variation**
> Stir in ½ finely chopped salted herring fillet or 2 finely chopped anchovy fillets to the mixture with the parsley to add an extra dimension to the dish. Omit the added salt if you add the fish, as they will be salty themselves.

Apple and Beetroot Energy 216kcal/895kJ; Protein 4.1g; Carbohydrate 9.5g, of which sugars 8.8g; Fat 18.2g, of which saturates 1.9g; Cholesterol 0mg; Calcium 54mg; Fibre 2.7g; Sodium 58mg.
Beetroot Potato Salad Energy 717kcal/2959kJ; Protein 8.5g; Carbohydrate 11g, of which sugars 10.2g; Fat 71.5g, of which saturates 42.9g; Cholesterol 314mg; Calcium 114mg; Fibre 2.3g; Sodium 132mg.

Waldorf Rice Salad

Waldorf Salad takes its name from the Waldorf Hotel in New York, where it was first made. The rice makes this dish slightly more substantial than usual. It can be served as an accompaniment, or as a main meal for two.

Serves 2–4

115g/4oz/generous ½ cup white
   long grain rice
1 red apple
1 green apple
60ml/4 tbsp lemon juice
3 celery sticks

2–3 slices thick cooked ham
90ml/6 tbsp good quality
   mayonnaise, preferably
   home-made
60ml/4 tbsp soured cream
generous pinch of saffron,
   dissolved in 15ml/1 tbsp
   hot water
10ml/2 tsp chopped
   fresh basil
15ml/1 tbsp chopped
   fresh parsley
several romaine or iceberg
   lettuce leaves
50g/2oz/½ cup walnuts,
   roughly chopped
salt and ground black pepper

1 Cook the rice in plenty of boiling salted water until tender. Drain and set aside in a bowl to cool.

2 Cut the apples into quarters, remove the cores and finely slice one red and one green apple quarter. Place the slices in a bowl with half the lemon juice and reserve for the garnish. Peel the remaining apple quarters and cut into fine sticks. Place in a separate bowl and toss with another 15ml/1 tbsp of the fresh lemon juice.

3 Cut the celery into thin strips. Roll up each slice of ham, slice finely and add to the apple sticks, with the celery.

4 Mix together the mayonnaise, soured cream and saffron water. Stir in salt and pepper to taste. Stir into the rice with the herbs. Add the apple and celery and the remaining lemon juice.

5 Arrange the lettuce leaves around the outside of a salad bowl and pile the rice and apple mixture into the centre. Scatter with the chopped walnuts and garnish with fans of the apple slices.

Watercress & Pear Salad

A refreshing light salad, this dish combines peppery watercress, soft juicy pears and a tart dressing. Dunsyre Blue cheese has a sharp flavour with a crumbly texture.

Serves 4

2 bunches watercress, thoroughly
   washed and trimmed
2 ripe pears
salt and ground black pepper

For the dressing
25g/1oz Dunsyre Blue cheese
30ml/2 tbsp walnut oil
15ml/1 tbsp lemon juice

1 To make the dressing, crumble the Dunsyre Blue into a bowl, then mash into the walnut oil, using a fork.

2 Whisk in the lemon juice to create a thickish mixture. Add a little more cheese to thicken it further, if necessary. Season.

3 Arrange a pile of watercress on the side of four plates.

4 Peel and slice the two pears, then place the pear slices to the side of the watercress, allowing half a pear per person.

5 Drizzle the dressing over the salad. The salad is best served immediately at room temperature. If you want to chill it for a while, take it out of the refrigerator 30 minutes before serving, and only add the dressing at the last minute.

Cook's Tips
• Choose ripe Comice or similar pears that are soft and juicy.
• If you want to get this dish ready in advance, peel and slice the pears, then rub with some lemon juice; this will prevent them from discolouring so quickly.

Variation
For a milder, tangy dressing, use Dolcelatte cheese instead.

Waldorf Rice Salad Energy 523kcal/2178kJ; Protein 24.7g; Carbohydrate 32.4g, of which sugars 9.3g; Fat 32.9g, of which saturates 6.4g; Cholesterol 84mg; Calcium 111mg; Fibre 3.2g; Sodium 1331mg.
Watercress and Pear Salad Energy 106kcal/442kJ; Protein 2.3g; Carbohydrate 7.6g, of which sugars 7.6g; Fat 7.6g, of which saturates 1.8g; Cholesterol 5mg; Calcium 81mg; Fibre 2g; Sodium 91mg.

Salad with Watermelon & Feta Cheese

The combination of sweet and juicy watermelon with salty feta cheese was inspired by the Turkish tradition of eating watermelon with salty white cheese in the hot summer months. It is ideal for a cold appetizer.

Serves 6–8
30–45ml/2–3 tbsp extra virgin
   olive oil
juice of ½ lemon
5ml/1 tsp vinegar of choice
sprinkling of fresh thyme
pinch of ground cumin
4 large slices of
   watermelon, chilled
1 frisée lettuce, core removed
130g/4½oz feta cheese,
   preferably sheep's milk feta,
   cut into bitesize pieces
handful of lightly toasted
   pumpkin seeds
handful of sunflower seeds
10–15 black olives

1 Pour the extra virgin olive oil, lemon juice and vinegar into a bowl or jug (pitcher).

2 Add the fresh thyme and ground cumin to the bowl or jug, and whisk until the ingredients are well combined. Set the dressing aside until you are ready to serve the salad.

3 Cut the rind off the watermelon and remove as many seeds as possible from inside the fruit. Cut the flesh into bitesize triangular-shaped chunks.

4 Put the lettuce leaves in a salad bowl, pour over the dressing and toss together. Arrange the leaves on a serving dish or individual plates and top with the watermelon pieces, feta cheese, pumpkin and sunflower seeds and black olives. Serve the salad immediately.

Cook's Tip
Use plump black Mediterranean olives, such as kalamata, for this recipe, or other shiny, dry-cured black olives.

Melon & Prosciutto Salad

Sections of cool fragrant melon wrapped with slices of air-dried ham make a delicious salad appetizer. If strawberries are in season, serve with a savoury-sweet strawberry salsa.

Serves 4
1 large cantaloupe, Charentais
   or Galia melon
175g/6oz prosciutto or Serrano
   ham, thinly sliced

For the salsa
225g/8oz/2 cups strawberries
5ml/1 tsp caster
   (superfine) sugar
30ml/2 tbsp groundnut (peanut)
   or sunflower oil
15ml/1 tbsp orange juice
2.5ml/½ tsp finely grated
   orange rind
2.5ml/½ tsp finely grated fresh
   root ginger
salt and ground black pepper

1 Halve the melon and scoop the seeds out with a spoon. Cut the rind away with a paring knife, then slice the melon thickly. Chill until ready to serve.

2 To make the salsa, hull the strawberries and cut them into large dice. Place in a small mixing bowl with the sugar and crush lightly to release the juices.

3 Add the oil, orange juice, rind and ginger and mix until all the ingredients are combined. Season to taste with salt and pepper.

4 Arrange the sliced melon on a serving plate, lay the ham over the top and serve with a bowl of salsa, handed round separately for diners to help themselves.

Cook's Tip
Prosciutto means 'ham' in Italian, and is a term generally used to describe seasoned, salt-cured and air-dried hams. Parma ham is the most famed prosciutto. Italian prosciuttos are designated prosciutto cotto, or cooked, and prosciutto crudo, or raw – although edible due to curing. They are labelled according to the place of origin, such as prosciutto di Parma and prosciutto di San Daniele. Buy it in supermarkets and Italian delicatessens.

Salad with Watermelon Energy 256kcal/1006kJ; Protein 7.7g; Carbohydrate 12.9g, of which sugars 11.6g; Fat 19.7g, of which saturates 6.2g; Cholesterol 23mg; Calcium 165mg; Fibre 1.4g; Sodium 616mg.
Melon Salad Energy 147kcal/614kJ; Protein 9.2g; Carbohydrate 12.2g, of which sugars 12.2g; Fat 7.1g, of which saturates 1.2g; Cholesterol 25mg; Calcium 29mg; Fibre 1.1g; Sodium 568mg.

Prawn, Melon & Chorizo Salad

This is a rich and colourful fruity seafood salad. It tastes best when made with fresh prawns.

Serves 4
450g/1lb/4 cups cooked
   white long grain rice
1 avocado
15ml/1 tbsp lemon juice
½ small Galia melon,
   cut into wedges
15g/½oz/1 tbsp butter
½ garlic clove

115g/4oz raw prawns (shrimp),
   peeled and deveined
25g/1oz chorizo sausage,
   finely sliced
flat leaf parsley, to garnish

For the dressing
75ml/5 tbsp natural (plain)
   yogurt
45ml/3 tbsp mayonnaise
15ml/1 tbsp olive oil
3 fresh tarragon sprigs
freshly ground black pepper

1 Put the cooked rice in a large salad bowl.

2 Peel the avocado and cut it into chunks. Place in a mixing bowl and toss lightly with the lemon juice. Slice the melon off the rind, cut the flesh into chunks, and add to the avocado.

3 Melt the butter in a small pan and gently fry the garlic for 30 seconds. Add the prawns and cook for about 3 minutes until evenly pink. Add the chorizo and stir-fry for 1 minute more.

4 Tip the mixture into the bowl with the avocado and melon chunks. Mix lightly, then leave to cool.

5 Make the dressing by mixing together all the ingredients in a food processor or blender. Stir half of the mixture into the rice and the remainder into the prawn and avocado mixture. Pile the salad on top of the rice. Chill for about 30 minutes before serving, garnished with flat leaf parsley sprigs.

Cook's Tip
Select a ripe and flavourful, but not overly soft, avocado, so that the chunks retain their shape and do not colour the dressing.

Halloumi & Grape Salad

Sweet, juicy grapes really complement the distinctive salty flavour of halloumi cheese in this delectable warm salad from Cyprus.

Serves 4
150g/5oz mixed green
   salad leaves
75g/3oz seedless green grapes
75g/3oz seedless black grapes
250g/9oz halloumi cheese

45ml/3 tbsp olive oil
fresh young thyme leaves or dill,
   to garnish

For the dressing
60ml/4 tbsp olive oil
15ml/1 tbsp lemon juice
2.5ml/½ tsp caster
   (superfine) sugar
15ml/1 tbsp chopped fresh
   thyme or dill
salt and ground black pepper

1 To make the dressing, mix together the olive oil, lemon juice and sugar. Season with salt and pepper to taste. Stir in the thyme or dill and set aside.

2 Toss together the salad leaves and the green and black grapes, then transfer to a large serving plate.

3 Thinly slice the cheese. Heat the oil in a large frying pan. Add the cheese and fry briefly until turning golden on the underside. Turn the cheese with a fish slice or metal spatula and cook the other side until golden.

4 Arrange the cooked cheese slices on top of the salad. Pour over the dressing and toss to combine. Garnish with thyme or dill and serve immediately.

Cook's Tips
• *Most supermarkets sell ready-mixed bags of prepared salad leaves, which are ideal for use in this recipe. Experiment with various combinations to find the lettuce flavours that you like best. A mix of rocket (arugula), spinach and watercress is good, or try a mix with fresh herbs included.*
• *Halloumi cheese is now widely available from most large supermarkets and Greek delicatessens.*

Prawn Salad Energy 414kcal/1734kJ; Protein 10.8g; Carbohydrate 44.6g, of which sugars 8.8g; Fat 22.6g, of which saturates 5.8g; Cholesterol 75mg; Calcium 102mg; Fibre 1.5g; Sodium 236mg.
Halloumi and Grape Energy 365kcal/1513kJ; Protein 12.2g; Carbohydrate 7.2g, of which sugars 7.2g; Fat 32.2g, of which saturates 11.4g; Cholesterol 36mg; Calcium 250mg; Fibre 0.8g; Sodium 250mg.

Carrot & Orange Salad

This classic fruit and
vegetable combination
makes a wonderful, fresh-
tasting salad. It makes a
great first-course dish
for the winter months,
and it is also particularly
good with hot or cold
poultry dishes.

Serves 4
450g/1lb carrots
2 large oranges
15ml/1 tbsp olive oil
30ml/2 tbsp lemon juice
pinch of sugar (optional)
30ml/2 tbsp chopped pistachio
  nuts or toasted pine nuts
salt and ground black pepper

1 Peel the carrots, if necessary, and grate them into a large
serving bowl.

2 Cut a slice off the top and bottom of one orange. Place
the orange upright on a chopping board and cut off the skin,
taking care to remove all the bitter white pith.

3 Repeat with the second orange, reserving any juice.

4 Working over a bowl to catch the juices, cut between the
membranes to release the orange segments.

5 Whisk together the olive oil, lemon juice and reserved
orange juice in a bowl. Season with a little salt and pepper
to taste, and add sugar, if you like.

6 Toss the orange segments together with the carrots and
pour the dressing over.

7 Sprinkle the salad with the pistachio nuts or pine nuts
before serving.

> **Cook's Tip**
> *If the carrots are very young and fresh, then they shouldn't
> need peeling – a thorough wash with a scrubbing brush will
> be sufficient. The older the carrots get, the tougher their skin
> will be, and they will need peeling before grating.*

Asparagus & Orange Salad

This is a slightly unusual
combination of ingredients
with a simple dressing based
on good-quality olive oil.

Serves 4
*225g/8oz asparagus, trimmed
  and cut into 5cm/2in lengths*

2 large oranges
*2 well-flavoured tomatoes,
  cut into eighths*
50g/2oz cos lettuce leaves
*30ml/2 tbsp extra virgin
  olive oil*
2.5ml/½ tsp sherry vinegar
salt and ground black pepper

1 Cook the asparagus in boiling, salted water for 3–4 minutes,
until just tender. The cooking time may vary according to the
size of the asparagus stems. Drain and refresh under cold water,
then leave on one side to cool.

2 Grate the rind from half one orange and reserve.

3 Cut a slice off the top and bottom of one orange to reveal
the flesh. Place the orange upright on a board and, using a small
sharp knife, cut off the skin, taking care to remove all the bitter
white pith. Repeat with the second orange, reserving any juice.

4 Holding one orange over a bowl to catch the juices, cut
between the membrane to release the segments. Repeat with
the second orange. Reserve the juices.

5 Put the asparagus, orange segments, tomatoes and lettuce
in a salad bowl.

6 Mix together the oil and vinegar, and add 15ml/1 tbsp of the
reserved orange juice and 5ml/1 tsp of the grated rind. Season
with salt and pepper to taste. Just before serving, pour the
dressing over the salad and mix gently to coat the ingredients.

> **Cook's Tip**
> *Take care not to overcook the asparagus; it should still be quite
> firm when you bite into it. Overcooked spears will lose not only
> their flavour, but also many of their healthy nutrients.*

Asparagus and Orange Salad Energy 92kcal/384kJ; Protein 2.6g; Carbohydrate 7.2g, of which sugars 7.1g; Fat 6.1g, of which saturates 0.9g; Cholesterol 0mg; Calcium 46mg; Fibre 2.4g; Sodium 8mg.
Carrot and Orange Salad Energy 137kcal/571kJ; Protein 2.9g; Carbohydrate 15.9g, of which sugars 15.1g; Fat 7.3g, of which saturates 1.1g; Cholesterol 0mg; Calcium 72mg; Fibre 4.4g; Sodium 72mg.

Fennel, Orange & Rocket Salad

This light and refreshing salad is ideal to serve with spicy or rich foods. Zesty orange blends perfectly with the delicate flavour of fennel and the peppery rocket.

Serves 4
2 oranges, such as Jaffa, Shamouti
  or blood oranges
1 fennel bulb
115g/4oz rocket (arugula)
  leaves
50g/2oz/¹/₃ cup black olives

For the dressing
30ml/2 tbsp extra-virgin
  olive oil
15ml/1 tbsp balsamic vinegar
1 small garlic clove, crushed
salt and ground black pepper

1 Using a vegetable peeler, pare off strips of rind from the oranges, leaving the pith behind, then cut the pared rind into thin julienne strips. Blanch the strips in boiling water for a few minutes. Drain and set aside.

2 Cut a slice off the top and bottom of one orange. Place the orange upright on a board and cut off the skin, taking care to remove all the bitter white pith. Repeat with the second orange, reserving any juice. Slice the oranges into thin rounds.

3 Trim the fennel bulb, then cut in half lengthwise and slice across the bulb as thinly as possible, preferably in a food processor fitted with a slicing disc or using a mandolin.

4 Combine the slices of orange and fennel in a serving bowl and toss with the rocket leaves.

5 To make the dressing, mix together the oil, vinegar and garlic and season with salt and pepper to taste. Pour over the salad, toss together well and leave to stand for a few minutes. Sprinkle with the black olives and julienne strips of orange.

> **Variation**
> For a twist in flavour, substitute minneolas for the oranges.

Orange & Red Onion Salad with Cumin

Cumin and mint give this refreshing, quick-to-prepare salad a very Middle-Eastern flavour. Small, seedless oranges are most suitable, if available, as they will involve less preparation than larger oranges.

Serves 6
6 oranges
2 red onions
15ml/1 tbsp cumin seeds
5ml/1 tsp coarsely ground
  black pepper
15ml/1 tbsp chopped fresh mint
90ml/6 tbsp olive oil
salt
fresh mint sprigs and pitted black
  olives, to garnish

1 Slice the oranges thinly, catching any juices. Holding each orange slice in turn over a bowl, cut round with scissors to remove the peel and pith. Reserve the juice.

2 Peel the red onions, keeping them whole, and then thinly slice them and separate into rings.

3 Arrange the orange and onion slices in layers in a shallow dish, sprinkling each layer with cumin seeds, black pepper, chopped mint, olive oil and salt to taste. Pour over the reserved orange juice.

4 Toss the salad to ensure the ingredients are coated and leave to marinate in a cool place for about 2 hours. Garnish with the fresh mint sprigs and sprinkle over the pitted black olives, and serve immediately.

> **Cook's Tip**
> Whole cumin seeds are available from large supermarkets and Asian food stores. Store them in a cool, dark place in an airtight jar and use within a few months of buying, otherwise they will begin to lose their excellent flavour – the same applies to most other dried spices and herbs in the kitchen.

Orange Salad Energy 199kcal/825kJ; Protein 1.6g; Carbohydrate 11.52g, of which sugars 11.3g; Fat 16.6g, of which saturates 2.4g; Cholesterol 0mg; Calcium 68mg; Fibre 2.3g; Sodium 7mg.
Fennel Salad Energy 113kcal/469kJ; Protein 2.5g; Carbohydrate 9.9g, of which sugars 9.8g; Fat 7.3g, of which saturates 1g; Cholesterol 0mg; Calcium 116mg; Fibre 3.9g; Sodium 332mg.

Orange Chicken Salad

Orange segments are the perfect partner for tender chicken in this tasty rice salad. To appreciate all the flavours fully, serve the salad at room temperature.

Serves 4
3 large seedless oranges
175g/6oz/scant 1 cup long grain rice
475ml/16fl oz/2 cups water

175ml/6fl oz/³⁄₄ cup vinaigrette
10ml/2 tsp strong Dijon mustard
2.5ml/¹⁄₂ tsp caster (superfine) sugar
450g/1lb cooked chicken, diced
45ml/3 tbsp chopped fresh chives
75g/3oz/³⁄₄ cup almonds or cashew nuts, toasted
salt and ground black pepper
mixed salad leaves, to serve

1 Pare one of the oranges thinly, removing only the zest, not the bitter white pith. Put the orange rind in a pan and add the rice. Pour in the water, add a pinch of salt and bring to the boil. Cover and cook the rice over a very low heat for about 15 minutes, or until the rice is tender and all the water has been absorbed.

2 Meanwhile, peel the oranges, removing all the white pith. Working over a plate to catch the juices, separate them into segments. Add the orange juice to the vinaigrette with the mustard and sugar, whisking to combine. Check the seasoning.

3 When the rice is cooked, remove it from the heat and discard the pieces of orange rind. Spoon the rice into a bowl, let it cool slightly, then add half the dressing. Toss well, then set aside to cool completely.

4 Add the chicken, chives, toasted nuts and orange segments to the cooled rice. Pour over the remaining dressing and toss gently to combine. Serve on a bed of mixed salad leaves.

Cook's Tip
To make a simple vinaigrette, whisk 45ml/3 tbsp wine vinegar with 120ml/8 tbsp extra-virgin olive oil and season well.

Chicken & Banana Maryland Salad

Grilled chicken, sweetcorn, bacon, banana and salad leaves combine in a sensational main-course salad. Serve with jacket potatoes and extra bacon, if you like.

Serves 4
4 boneless chicken breast portions
oil, for brushing
225g/8oz rindless unsmoked bacon
4 corn on the cob, husks removed
45ml/3 tbsp soft butter (optional)

4 ripe bananas, peeled and halved
4 firm tomatoes, halved
1 escarole or round (butterhead) lettuce
1 bunch watercress
salt and ground black pepper

For the dressing
75ml/5 tbsp groundnut (peanut) oil
15ml/1 tbsp white wine vinegar
10ml/2 tsp maple syrup
10ml/2 tsp prepared mild mustard

1 Preheat the grill (broiler). Season the chicken breasts with salt and pepper, brush with oil and grill (broil) for 15 minutes, turning once. Grill the bacon for 8–10 minutes, or until crisp.

2 Bring a large pan of salted water to the boil and cook the corn on the cob for 20 minutes. For extra flavour, brush the corn cobs with butter and brown under the grill.

3 Grill the bananas and tomatoes for 6–8 minutes; you can brush these with butter too if you wish.

4 To make the dressing, combine the oil, vinegar, maple syrup and mustard with 15ml/1 tbsp water in a screw-top jar and shake well to combine.

5 Separate the lettuce leaves and put into a large bowl. Pour over the dressing and toss well. Distribute the salad leaves between four individual plates.

6 Slice the chicken and arrange over the salad leaves, together with the bacon, banana, sweetcorn and tomatoes.

Orange Chicken Energy 729kcal/3035kJ; Protein 36.3g; Carbohydrate 47.5g, of which sugars 12g; Fat 34g, of which saturates 5.6g; Cholesterol 79mg; Calcium 150mg; Fibre 4.2g; Sodium 561mg.
Chicken and Banana Energy 659kcal/2768kJ; Protein 50.9g; Carbohydrate 56.4g, of which sugars 37.1g; Fat 27.1g, of which saturates 7g; Cholesterol 135mg; Calcium 51mg; Fibre 4.2g; Sodium 1319mg.

Duck Salad with Orange Sauce

The rich, gamey flavour of duck is enhanced by warm orange and spices, while crisp croûtons add crunch.

Serves 4
1 small orange, sliced thickly
2 boneless duck breasts
150ml/¼ pint/⅔ cup dry white wine
5ml/1 tsp ground coriander seeds
2.5ml/½ tsp ground cumin or fennel seeds
30ml/2 tbsp sugar
juice of ½ small lime or lemon
45ml/3 tbsp garlic oil
75g/3oz thickly sliced day-old bread, crusts removed and cut into short fingers
½ escarole lettuce
½ frisée lettuce
30ml/2 tbsp sunflower or groundnut (peanut) oil
salt and cayenne pepper
4 sprigs fresh coriander (cilantro), to garnish

1 Put the orange slices in a small pan. Cover with water, bring to the boil and simmer for 5 minutes to remove the bitterness. Drain the orange slices and set aside.

2 Pierce the skin of the duck breasts diagonally with a small knife. Rub the skin with salt. Heat a heavy frying pan (skillet) and cook the breasts for 20 minutes, turning once, until they are medium-rare. Transfer them to a warm plate and cover.

3 Heat the sediment in the frying pan until it begins to caramelize. Add the wine and stir to loosen the sediment. Add the coriander, cumin or fennel seeds, sugar and orange slices.

4 Boil quickly and reduce to a coating consistency. Sharpen with the lime or lemon juice and season to taste with salt and cayenne. Transfer the sauce to a bowl, cover and keep warm.

5 Heat the garlic oil in a heavy frying pan and brown the bread fingers. Season with salt, then turn out on to kitchen paper.

6 Moisten the salad leaves with oil and arrange on plates. Slice the duck breasts diagonally and divide between the plates. Spoon on the orange sauce, scatter with the croûtons and garnish with a sprig of fresh coriander. Serve warm.

Strawberry & Smoked Venison Salad

The combination of strawberries, balsamic vinegar and smoked venison creates a perfect *ménage à trois*. The tang of the vinegar sets off the sweetness of the strawberries, which must be ripe, and adds a fruity contrast to the rich, dry, smoky venison.

Serves 4
12 ripe Scottish strawberries
2.5ml/½ tsp caster (superfine) sugar
5ml/1 tsp balsamic vinegar
8 thin slices of smoked venison
mixed salad leaves

For the dressing
10ml/2 tsp olive oil
5ml/1 tsp balsamic vinegar
splash of strawberry wine (optional)
salt and ground black pepper

1 Slice the strawberries vertically into three or four pieces then place in a bowl with the sugar and balsamic vinegar. Leave for 30 minutes.

2 Meanwhile, make the dressing. Place the olive oil and balsamic vinegar in a small bowl and whisking together with the wine, if using. Add salt and ground black pepper to taste.

3 Cut the smoked venison into little strips. Mix the salad leaves together, then toss with the dressing.

4 Divide the salad between four plates and sprinkle with the strawberries and venison.

> **Cook's Tips**
> • Suitable salad leaves include lollo rosso for colour, rocket (arugula) and lamb's lettuce (corn salad) for a peppery flavour and colour, and Little Gem (Bibb) for crunch.
> • The sugar brings out the moisture in the strawberries, which combines with the balsamic vinegar to creates a lovely shiny coat. Do not leave them to stand for too long, as they can become tired-looking – 30 minutes is about right.

Duck Salad Energy 231kcal/971kJ; Protein 17.3g; Carbohydrate 13.3g, of which sugars 4.5g; Fat 11.1g, of which saturates 1.7g; Cholesterol 83mg; Calcium 68mg; Fibre 1.5g; Sodium 185mg.
Strawberry and Venison Energy 116Kcal/486kJ; Protein 11.6g; Carbohydrate 3.1g, of which sugars 3.1g; fat 6.8g, of which saturates 1.2g; Cholesterol 25mg; Calcium 16mg; Fibre 0.6g; Sodium 31mg.

Goat's Cheese & Fig Salad

Fresh figs, walnuts, goat's cheese and couscous make a tasty salad, full of texture. The dressing has no vinegar, depending instead on the acidity of the goat's cheese.

Serves 4

175g/6oz/1 cup couscous
30ml/2 tbsp toasted buckwheat
1 egg, hard-boiled (hard-cooked)
30ml/2 tbsp chopped parsley
60ml/4 tbsp olive oil
45ml/3 tbsp walnut oil

115g/4oz rocket (arugula) leaves
½ frisée lettuce
175g/6oz crumbly white goat's cheese
50g/2oz/½ cup broken walnuts, toasted
4 ripe figs, trimmed and almost cut into four (leave the pieces joined at the base)

1 Place the couscous and toasted buckwheat in a bowl, cover with boiling water and leave to soak for 15 minutes. Place in a sieve (strainer) to drain off any remaining water, then spread out on a metal tray and allow to cool.

2 Shell the hard-boiled egg and grate finely. Toss the grated egg, parsley, couscous and buckwheat together in a bowl.

3 Combine the olive and walnut oils and use half to moisten the couscous mixture.

4 Toss the salad leaves in the remaining oil and distribute between four large serving plates. Pile the couscous mixture into the centre of each plate and crumble the goat's cheese over the top. Scatter with toasted walnuts, place a fig in the centre of each plate and serve immediately.

Cook's Tip
Goat's cheeses vary in strength, from the youngest, which are soft and mild, to strongly-flavoured, mature cheeses, which have a firm and crumbly texture. The crumbly varieties are best suited to salads.

Devilled Ham & Pineapple Salad

This tasty salad, with its crunchy almond topping, can be prepared quickly using store-cupboard items.

Serves 4

225g/8oz wholewheat penne
150ml/¼ pint/⅔ cup natural (plain) yogurt
15ml/1 tbsp cider vinegar
5ml/1 tsp wholegrain mustard
large pinch of caster (superfine) sugar
30ml/2 tbsp hot mango chutney

115g/4oz cooked lean ham, cubed
200g/7oz can pineapple chunks, drained
2 celery sticks, chopped
½ green (bell) pepper, seeded and diced
15ml/1 tbsp toasted flaked almonds, chopped roughly
salt and ground black pepper
crusty bread, to serve

1 Cook the pasta in a large pan of lightly salted boiling water according to the packet instructions, until *al dente*. Drain and rinse thoroughly. Leave to cool.

2 To make the dressing, mix the yogurt, vinegar, mustard, sugar and mango chutney together. Season with salt and pepper.

3 Add the pasta to the dressing and toss lightly, then transfer it to a serving dish.

4 Add the ham, pineapple, celery and green pepper. Sprinkle toasted almonds over the top of the salad.

Variations
• *Although ham and pineapple are a well known and popular combination, don't be afraid to experiment with different ingredients. For example, chicken and fresh mango would be perfect with this dressing, or you could use left-over roast lamb with fresh apricots.*
• *Aim for soft, mellow fruits rather than apples or citrus, so that you still get the lovely juicy sweetness to contrast with the crisp nuts and celery.*

Goat's Cheese and Fig Energy 581kcal/2410kJ; Protein 17g; Carbohydrate 35.9g, of which sugars 13.3g; Fat 41.9g, of which saturates 11.4g; Cholesterol 88mg; Calcium 189mg; Fibre 3.5g; Sodium 301mg.
Devilled Ham Energy 311kcal/1319kJ; Protein 15.3g; Carbohydrate 55.5g, of which sugars 15.5g; Fat 4.7g, of which saturates 0.8g; Cholesterol 17mg; Calcium 115mg; Fibre 3.2g; Sodium 402mg.

Hot Coconut Prawn & Papaya Salad

This colourful seafood salad is tossed in a creamy, gently spiced coconut and lime dressing to provide a light meal, full of wonderfully exotic flavours.

Serves 4–6
225g/8oz raw or cooked tiger prawns (jumbo shrimp), peeled with tails intact
2 ripe papaya
1 firm tomato
225g/8oz mixed salad leaves, such as cos, romaine or Little Gem (Bibb) lettuce, Chinese leaves or young spinach
3 spring onions (scallions), shredded
1 small bunch fresh coriander (cilantro), shredded
1 large fresh chilli, seeded and sliced

For the dressing
15ml/1 tbsp creamed coconut
30ml/2 tbsp boiling water
90ml/6 tbsp vegetable oil
juice of 1 lime
2.5ml/½ tsp hot chilli sauce
10ml/2 tsp fish sauce (optional)
5ml/1 tsp sugar

1 To make the dressing, place the creamed coconut in a screw-top jar and add the boiling water, vegetable oil, lime juice, chilli sauce, fish sauce, if using, and sugar. Shake well and set aside, but do not refrigerate.

2 If using raw prawns, place them in a pan and cover with water. Bring to the boil and simmer for 2 minutes until the prawn have turned opaque. Drain and set aside.

3 To prepare the papayas, cut each in half from top to bottom and remove the black seeds with a teaspoon. Peel away the outer skin and cut the flesh into even pieces.

4 Cut the tomato in half, then remove the seeds and discard. Roughly chop the tomato flesh.

5 Place the salad leaves in a bowl. Add the prawns, papaya, tomato, spring onions, coriander and sliced chilli. Pour over the dressing and toss lightly. Serve immediately.

Mango, Tomato & Red Onion Salad

This salad makes a delicious appetizer. The under-ripe mango blends well with the tomato.

Serves 4
1 firm under-ripe mango
2 large tomatoes or 1 beefsteak tomato, sliced
½ red onion, sliced into rings
½ cucumber, peeled and thinly sliced
chopped chives, to garnish

For the dressing
30ml/2 tbsp vegetable oil
15ml/1 tbsp lemon juice
1 garlic clove, crushed
2.5ml/½ tsp hot pepper sauce
salt and ground black pepper

1 Using a sharp knife or peeler, remove the skin from the mango, then cut and slice the flesh into bitesize pieces.

2 Arrange the mango, tomatoes, onion and cucumber on a large serving plate.

3 Make the dressing. Blend the oil, lemon juice, garlic, pepper sauce and seasoning in a blender or food processor, or shake vigorously in a small screw-top jar.

4 Spoon the dressing over the salad. Garnish with the chopped chives and serve.

Cook's Tip
When cutting a mango, first peel the skin off with a sharp knife or peeler. Next, cut the fleshy cheeks from each side. Trim carefully around the fruit, following the curvature of the stone (pit), to remove all the flesh. You will end up with the stone, two cheeks and two thinner strips of fruit, which can then be sliced.

Mango Salad Energy 116kcal/482kJ; Protein 1g; Carbohydrate 11g, of which sugars9g; Fat 8g, of which saturates 1g; Cholesterol 0mg; Calcium 25mg; Fibre 2.6g; Sodium 17mg.
Hot Coconut Prawn Energy 201kcal/837kJ; Protein 8.1g; Carbohydrate 12.7g, of which sugars 12.6g; Fat 13.4g, of which saturates 2.9g; Cholesterol 73mg; Calcium 88mg; Fibre 3.6g; Sodium 84mg.

Aromatic Apples with Spicy Pilaff

Vegetables and fruit stuffed with an aromatic pilaff are a great favourite. This recipe is for apples, but you can easily use it to stuff vegetables.

Serves 4

4 cooking apples, or any firm,
    sour apple of your choice
30ml/2 tbsp olive oil
juice of ½ lemon
10ml/2 tsp sugar
salt and ground black pepper

For the filling
30ml/2 tbsp olive oil
a little butter
1 onion, finely chopped

2 garlic cloves
30ml/2 tbsp pine nuts
30ml/2 tbsp currants, soaked in
    warm water for 5–10 minutes
    and drained
5–10ml/1–2 tsp ground cinnamon
5–10ml/1–2 tsp ground allspice
5ml/1 tsp sugar
175g/6oz/scant 1 cup short
    grain rice, thoroughly rinsed
    and drained
1 bunch each of fresh flat leaf
    parsley and dill, finely chopped

To serve
1 tomato
1 lemon
a few fresh mint or basil leaves

1 Make the filling. Heat the oil and butter in a pan, stir in the onion and garlic and cook until softened. Add the pine nuts and currants and cook for 5 minutes. Mix in the spices, sugar and rice. Pour in water to cover the rice – roughly 1–2cm/½–¾in above the grains – and bring to the boil. Season, then simmer for 10–12 minutes, until almost all the water has been absorbed.

2 Toss in the herbs and turn off the heat. Cover the pan with a dry dish towel and the lid, and leave the rice to steam for 5 minutes. Preheat the oven to 200°C/400°F/Gas 6.

3 Cut the stalk ends off the apples and keep to use as lids. Core each apple, removing enough flesh to create a cavity. Pack spoonfuls of the rice into the apples. Replace the lids and stand the apples in a small baking dish.

4 Mix together 100ml/3½fl oz/scant ½ cup water with the oil, lemon juice and sugar. Pour over and around the apples, then bake for 30–40 minutes, until the apples are tender. Serve with a tomato and lemon garnish and mint or basil leaves.

Roasted Courgettes & Peaches

This recipe combines fruit and vegetables to make a colourful medley that is baked rather than deep-fried or grilled. Serve with warm, crusty bread, or as an accompaniment to grilled, broiled or barbecued meats and poultry.

Serves 4

2 courgettes (zucchini)
2 yellow or red (bell) peppers,
    seeded and cut into wedges

120ml/4fl oz/½ cup olive oil
4–6 plum tomatoes
2 firm peaches, peeled, halved
    and stoned (pitted), then
    cut into wedges
30ml/2 tbsp pine nuts
salt and ground black pepper

For the yogurt sauce
500g/1¼lb/2¼ cups thick
    and creamy natural
    (plain) yogurt
2–3 garlic cloves, crushed
juice of ½ lemon

1 Preheat the oven to 200°C/400°F/Gas 6. Using a vegetable peeler or a small, sharp knife, peel the courgettes lengthways in stripes like a zebra, then halve and slice them lengthways, or cut into wedges.

2 Place the courgettes and peppers in a baking dish, preferably an earthenware one. Drizzle the oil over them and sprinkle with salt, then bake in the oven for 20 minutes.

3 Take the dish out of the oven and turn the vegetables in the oil, then mix in the tomatoes and peaches. Bake for another 20–25 minutes, until everything is nicely browned.

4 Meanwhile, make the yogurt sauce. In a bowl, beat the yogurt with the garlic and lemon juice. Season with salt and ground black pepper and set aside, or chill in the refrigerator until needed.

5 Dry-roast the pine nuts in a small, heavy pan until they turn golden brown and give off a nutty aroma. Remove from the heat.

6 When the roasted vegetables are ready, remove the dish from the oven and sprinkle the pine nuts over the top. Serve with the yogurt sauce.

Aromatic Apples Energy 382kcal/1595kJ; Protein 5g; Carbohydrate 54.1g, of which sugars 18.8g; Fat 16.5g, of which saturates 1.9g; Cholesterol 0mg; Calcium 26mg; Fibre 2.1g; Sodium 4mg.
Roasted Courgettes Energy 362kcal/1507kJ; Protein 11.7g; Carbohydrate 26.7g, of which sugars 26.3g; Fat 24.1g, of which saturates 3.7g; Cholesterol 2mg; Calcium 284mg; Fibre 4.8g; Sodium 120mg.

Pumpkin Stuffed with Apricot Pilaffs

Pumpkins make ideal cooking vessels, filled with tasty and aromatic fruity pilaffs.

Serves 4–6

1 medium-sized pumpkin
225g/8oz/generous 1 cup long
 grain rice, well rinsed
30–45ml/2–3 tbsp olive oil
15ml/1 tbsp butter
a fingerful of saffron threads
5ml/1 tsp coriander seeds
2–3 strips of orange peel, sliced
45–60ml/3–4 tbsp pistachio nuts

30–45ml/2–3 tbsp dried
 cranberries, soaked in
 boiling water for 5 minutes
 and drained
175g/6oz/¾ cup dried apricots,
 sliced or chopped
1 bunch of fresh basil,
 leaves loosely torn
1 bunch each of fresh coriander,
 mint and flat leaf parsley,
 coarsely chopped
salt and ground black pepper
lemon wedges and natural (plain)
 yogurt, to serve

1 Preheat the oven to 200°C/400°F/Gas 6. Wash the pumpkin and cut off the stalk end to use as a lid. Scoop all the seeds out. Replace the lid and bake the pumpkin on a baking tray for 1 hour.

2 Tip the rice into a pan and pour in just enough water to cover. Add a pinch of salt and bring to the boil, then lower the heat and partially cover the pan. Simmer for 10–12 minutes, until all the water has been absorbed.

3 Heat the oil and butter in a wide, heavy pan. Stir in the saffron, coriander seeds, orange zest, pistachios, cranberries and apricots, then toss in the cooked rice, making sure everything is well mixed, and season with salt and pepper. Turn off the heat, cover the pan with a dish towel and press the lid tightly on top. Leave the pilaff to steam for 10 minutes, then toss in the herbs.

4 Take the pumpkin out of the oven. Lift off the lid and spoon the pilaff into the cavity. Put the lid back on and put it back in the oven for about 20 minutes.

5 To serve, remove the lid and slice a round off the top of the pumpkin. Place the ring on a plate and spoon in some pilaff. Continue slicing and filling on individual plates until all the pumpkin and pilaff are used up. Serve with lemon wedges and yogurt.

Aubergine & Apricot Tagine

Spiced with coriander, cumin, cinnamon, turmeric and a dash of chilli sauce, this Moroccan-style stew makes a filling supper dish when served with couscous.

Serves 4

1 small aubergine (eggplant),
 cut into 1cm/½in dice
2 courgettes (zucchini),
 thickly sliced
60ml/4 tbsp olive oil
1 large onion, sliced
2 garlic cloves, chopped
150g/5oz/2 cups brown cap
 (cremini) mushrooms, halved

15ml/1 tbsp ground coriander
10ml/2 tsp cumin seeds
15ml/1 tbsp ground cinnamon
10ml/2 tsp ground turmeric
225g/8oz new potatoes,
 quartered
600ml/1 pint/2½ cups passata
 (bottled strained tomatoes)
15ml/1 tbsp tomato purée (paste)
15ml/1 tbsp chilli sauce
75g/3oz/⅓ cup ready-to-eat
 unsulphured dried apricots
400g/14oz/3 cups canned
 chickpeas, drained and rinsed
salt and ground black pepper
15ml/1 tbsp chopped fresh
 coriander (cilantro), to garnish

1 Sprinkle salt over the aubergine and courgettes and leave for 30 minutes. Rinse and pat dry with a dish towel. Heat the grill (broiler) to high. Arrange the courgettes and aubergine on a baking tray and toss in 30ml/2 tbsp of the olive oil. Grill (broil) for 20 minutes, turning occasionally, until tender and golden.

2 Meanwhile, heat the remaining oil in a large heavy pan and cook the onion and garlic for 5 minutes until softened, stirring occasionally. Add the mushrooms and sauté for 3 minutes until tender. Add the spices and cook for 1 minute more, stirring, to allow the flavours to mingle.

3 Add the potatoes and cook for about 3 minutes, stirring. Pour in the passata, tomato purée and 150ml/¼ pint/⅔ cup water. Cover and cook for 10 minutes to thicken the sauce.

4 Add the aubergine, courgettes, chilli sauce, apricots and chickpeas. Season and cook, partially covered, for about 15 minutes until the potatoes are tender. Add a little extra water if the tagine becomes too dry. Sprinkle with chopped fresh coriander to serve.

Pumpkin Energy 345kcal/1443kJ; Protein 9.9g; Carbohydrate 50.1g, of which sugars 18.6g; Fat 12g, of which saturates 2.6g; Cholesterol 5mg; Calcium 299mg; Fibre 9.6g; Sodium 93mg.
Aubergine Energy 359kcal/1509kJ; Protein 13.9g; Carbohydrate 45g, of which sugars 19.3g; Fat 15g, of which saturates 2.1g; Cholesterol 0mg; Calcium 123mg; Fibre 9.7g; Sodium 597mg.

Fruit & Nut Couscous with Spices

In Morocco this dish of steamed couscous with dried fruit and nuts, topped with sugar and cinnamon, is served on special celebrations. It is often presented as a course on its own, just before the dessert, but it is delicious served with spicy tagines, or grilled or roasted meat.

Serves 6
500g/1¼lb medium couscous
600ml/1 pint/2½ cups
  warm water
5ml/1 tsp salt
pinch of saffron threads
45ml/3 tbsp sunflower oil
30ml/2 tbsp olive oil
a little butter
115g/4oz/½ cup dried apricots,
  cut into slivers
75g/3oz/½ cup dried dates,
  chopped
75g/3oz/generous ½ cup
  seedless raisins
115g/4oz/1 cup blanched
  almonds, cut into slivers
75g/3oz/¾ cup pistachio nuts
10ml/2 tsp ground cinnamon
45ml/3 tbsp sugar

1 Preheat the oven to 180°C/350°F/Gas 4. Put the couscous in a bowl. Mix the water, salt and saffron and pour the mixture over the couscous, stirring. Leave to stand for 10 minutes, or until the grains have plumped up and become tender. Add the sunflower oil and, using your fingers, rub it evenly through the couscous grains.

2 In a heavy pan, heat the olive oil and butter and stir in the apricots, dates, raisins, most of the almonds (reserving some to garnish the dish) and the pistachio nuts. Cook over a gentle heat until the raisins plump up, then tip the nuts and fruit into the couscous and toss together.

3 Tip the couscous into an ovenproof dish and cover with foil. Place in the oven for about 20 minutes, until heated through. Meanwhile, toast the reserved slivered almonds.

4 Pile the hot couscous in a mound on a large warmed serving dish and sprinkle with the cinnamon and sugar – these are traditionally added in vertical stripes down the mound of couscous. Sprinkle the toasted almonds over the top of the dish and serve immediately.

Tzimmes

This Jewish dish consists of baked vegetables and dried fruit, although sometimes fresh apples and pears are added. Some tzimmes also contain meat, and can be served either as a main meal or an accompaniment.

Serves 6
250g/9oz carrots, peeled
  and sliced
1 sweet potato, peeled and
  cut into chunks
1 potato, peeled and cut
  into chunks
pinch of sugar
25g/1oz/2 tbsp butter or
  30ml/2 tbsp rendered
  chicken fat or vegetable oil
1 onion, chopped
10 pitted prunes, halved
  or quartered
30–45ml/2–3 tbsp currants
5 dried apricots, roughly chopped,
  or 30ml/2 tbsp sultanas
  (golden raisins)
30ml/2 tbsp honey
5–10ml/1–2 tsp chopped fresh
  root ginger
1 cinnamon stick or 2–3 shakes
  of ground cinnamon
juice of ½ lemon
salt

1 Preheat the oven to 160°C/325°F/Gas 3. Put the carrots, sweet potato and potato into a pan of sugared and salted boiling water and cook until they are almost tender. Drain, reserving the cooking liquid, and set aside.

2 Heat the butter or oil in a flameproof casserole, add the onion and fry until softened. Add the cooked vegetables and enough of the cooking liquid to cover the vegetables completely, then add the remaining ingredients.

3 Cover the casserole with a lid and cook in the oven for about 40 minutes. Towards the end of cooking time, check the amount of liquid in the casserole. If there is too much liquid, remove the lid for the last 10–15 minutes.

Variation
To make a meat tzimmes, braise about 500g/1¼lb beef, cut into chunks, for 1–1½ hours until tender. In step 2 use oil, rather than butter, and add the meat to the pan with the vegetables.

Couscous Energy 576kcal/2403kJ; Protein 12.5g; Carbohydrate 73g, of which sugars 29.4g; Fat 27.8g, of which saturates 3.1g; Cholesterol 0mg; Calcium 102mg; Fibre 4.2g; Sodium 74mg.
Tzimmes Energy 143kcal/601kJ; Protein 1.9g; Carbohydrate 26.8g, of which sugars 15.9g; Fat 3.9g, of which saturates 2.3g; Cholesterol 9mg; Calcium 36mg; Fibre 2.9g; Sodium 55mg.

Fruity Stuffed Vegetables

Colourful peppers and tomatoes make perfect containers for various meat and vegetable stuffings. This rice and sultana version uses Mediterranean ingredients.

Serves 4

2 large ripe tomatoes
1 green (bell) pepper
1 yellow or orange (bell) pepper
60ml/4 tbsp olive oil, plus extra
   for sprinkling
2 onions, chopped
2 garlic cloves, crushed
50g/2oz/1/2 cup blanched
   almonds, chopped
75g/3oz/scant 1/2 cup long grain
   rice, boiled and drained
15g/1/2oz mint, roughly chopped
15g/1/2oz fresh parsley,
   roughly chopped
25g/1oz/2 tbsp sultanas
   (golden raisins)
45ml/3 tbsp ground almonds
salt and ground black pepper
chopped mixed fresh herbs,
   to garnish

1 Preheat the oven to 190°C/375°F/Gas 5. Cut the tomatoes in half and scoop out the pulp and seeds using a teaspoon. Leave the tomatoes to drain on kitchen paper with cut sides down. Roughly chop the tomato pulp and seeds.

2 Halve the peppers, leaving the stalks intact. Scoop out the seeds. Brush the peppers with 15ml/1 tbsp of the oil and bake on a baking tray for 15 minutes.

3 Place the peppers and tomatoes in an ovenproof dish and season with salt and pepper.

4 Fry the onions in the remaining oil for 5 minutes. Add the garlic and chopped almonds and fry for a further minute.

5 Remove the pan from the heat and stir in the rice, chopped tomatoes, mint, parsley and sultanas. Season well and spoon the mixture into the tomatoes and peppers.

6 Pour ⅔ cup boiling water around the tomatoes and peppers and bake, uncovered, for 20 minutes. Scatter with the ground almonds and sprinkle with a little extra olive oil. Return to the oven and bake for 20 minutes more, or until turning golden. Serve garnished with fresh herbs.

Sweet Potato & Prune Tagine

The fruit and vegetables in this succulent, syrupy tagine are chosen for their sweetness, and should be slightly caramelized. They are at their best when served with grilled meats, couscous or lots of warm, crusty bread, accompanied by a leafy, herb-filled salad.

Serves 4–6

45ml/3 tbsp olive oil
a little butter
25–30 pearl or button onions,
   blanched and peeled
900g/2lb sweet potatoes, peeled
   and cut into bitesize chunks
2–3 carrots, cut into bitesize
   chunks
150g/5oz/generous 1/2 cup
   ready-to-eat pitted prunes
5ml/1 tsp ground cinnamon
2.5ml/1/2 tsp ground ginger
10ml/2 tsp clear honey
450ml/3/4 pint/scant 2 cups
   vegetable stock
small bunch of fresh coriander
   (cilantro), finely chopped
small bunch of mint,
   finely chopped
salt and ground black pepper

1 Preheat the oven to 200°C/400°F/Gas 6. Heat the olive oil in a flameproof casserole with the butter and stir in the peeled onions. Cook the onions over medium heat for about 5 minutes until they are tender, then remove half the onions from the pan and set aside.

2 Add the sweet potatoes and carrots to the pan and cook until the vegetables are lightly browned. Stir in the prunes with the cinnamon, ginger and honey, then pour in the stock. Bring to the boil, season well, cover the casserole and transfer to the oven for about 45 minutes.

3 Stir in the reserved onions and bake for a further 10 minutes. Gently stir in the fresh coriander and mint, and serve the tagine immediately.

> **Cook's Tip**
> Sweet potatoes have dark red or orange skin and orange flesh with a flavour reminiscent of chestnuts. Buy fresh, firm specimens that do not 'give' when pressed.

Fruity Stuffed Vegetables Energy 234kcal/981kJ; Protein 5.7g; Carbohydrate 32.5g, of which sugars 14.5g; Fat 9.9g, of which saturates 1.2g; Cholesterol 0mg; Calcium 71mg; Fibre 3.6g; Sodium 14mg.
Sweet Potato Energy 388kcal/1638kJ; Protein 5.4g; Carbohydrate 74.8g, of which sugars 37.5g; Fat 9.6g, of which saturates 1.5g; Cholesterol 0mg; Calcium 129mg; Fibre 11g; Sodium 120mg.

Chicken Wings with Blood Oranges

The rub that gives the chicken wings their fiery flavour is based on a classic spice mix called harissa. It is often used in Middle Eastern or African dishes. Sweet-tart blood oranges are in season during the winter, and their bright red flesh gives a splash of vibrant colour to this dish. The juicy oranges also help to balance the heat of the spicy wings. Serve the oranges separately or on skewers with the chicken.

Serves 4
60ml/4 tbsp fiery harissa
30ml/2 tbsp olive oil
16–20 chicken wings
4 blood oranges, quartered
icing (confectioners') sugar
small bunch of fresh coriander
   (cilantro), chopped, to garnish
salt

1 Preheat the grill (broiler) to its hottest setting. Put the harissa in a small bowl with the olive oil and mix to form a loose paste. Add a little salt and stir to combine.

2 Brush the harissa mixture over the chicken wings so that they are well coated on all sides. Grill (broil) the wings over a medium heat for 5–8 minutes on each side, until cooked and a dark golden brown.

3 Once the wings begin to cook, dip the orange quarters lightly in icing sugar and grill them for a few minutes, until they are slightly burnt, but take care they do not become black and charred. Serve the chicken wings immediately with the oranges, sprinkled with a little chopped fresh coriander.

> **Variations**
> • If you prefer, you can use cherry tomatoes in place of the blood oranges in this recipe.
> • When blood oranges are out of season and not available, normal oranges can be used instead.

Apricot & Almond Stuffed Chicken

Couscous makes a light and simple base for this summery slow-cooker dish.

Serves 4
50g/2oz/¼ cup ready-to-eat
   dried apricots
150ml/¼ pint/⅔ cup orange juice
4 skinned chicken breast fillets
50g/2oz/⅓ cup instant couscous

150ml/¼ pint/⅔ cup boiling
   chicken stock
25g/1oz/¼ cup chopped
   toasted almonds
1.5ml/¼ tsp dried tarragon
1 egg yolk
30ml/2 tbsp orange marmalade
salt and ground black pepper
boiled or steamed basmati and
   wild rice, to serve

1 Put the apricots in a bowl and pour over the orange juice. Leave to soak while you prepare the remaining ingredients.

2 Cut a deep pocket horizontally in each chicken breast fillet, taking care not to cut all the way through. Put the fillets between two sheets of oiled clear film (plastic wrap), then gently beat with a rolling pin or mallet until slightly thinner.

3 Put the couscous in a bowl and spoon over 50ml/2fl oz/¼ cup of the stock. Leave to stand until all the stock has been absorbed.

4 Drain the apricots, reserving the juice, then stir them into the couscous along with the almonds and tarragon. Season with salt and pepper, then stir in enough egg yolk to bind the mixture.

5 Divide the stuffing between the chicken fillets, securing with cocktail sticks (toothpicks). Place the stuffed chicken fillets in the base of the ceramic cooking pot.

6 Stir the orange marmalade into the remaining hot stock until dissolved, then stir in the orange juice. Season with salt and pepper and pour over the chicken. Cover the pot and cook on high for 3–5 hours, or until the chicken is tender.

7 Remove the chicken from the sauce and keep warm. Transfer the sauce to a wide pan and boil rapidly until reduced by half. Carve the chicken into slices and arrange on plates. Spoon over the sauce and serve with basmati and wild rice.

Chicken Wings Energy 500kcal/2077kJ; Protein 44.8g; Carbohydrate 0g, of which sugars 0g; Fat 35.6g, of which saturates 8.9g; Cholesterol 196mg; Calcium 14mg; Fibre 0g; Sodium 132mg.
Apricot Stuffed Chicken Energy 379kcal/1604kJ; Protein 40.2g; Carbohydrate 38g, of which sugars 27g; Fat 8.5g, of which saturates 1.3g; Cholesterol 155mg; Calcium 61mg; Fibre 1.6g; Sodium 117mg.

Roasted Chicken with Grapes & Fresh Root Ginger

Oven-roasted chicken with a delicious blend of spices and sweet autumn fruit.

Serves 4

115–130g/4–4¹/₂oz fresh
　root ginger, grated
6–8 garlic cloves, roughly chopped
juice of 1 lemon
about 30ml/2 tbsp olive oil
2–3 large pinches of
　ground cinnamon
1–1.6kg/2¹/₄–3¹/₂lb chicken
500g/1¹/₄lb seeded red and
　green grapes
500g/1¹/₄lb seedless green grapes
5–7 shallots, chopped
about 250ml/8fl oz/1 cup
　chicken stock
salt and ground black pepper

1 Mix together half the ginger, the garlic, half the lemon juice, the oil, cinnamon and seasoning. Rub over the chicken and set aside.

2 Meanwhile, cut the red and green seeded grapes in half, remove the seeds and set aside. Add the whole green seedless grapes to the halved ones.

3 Preheat the oven to 180°C/350°F/Gas 4. Heat a heavy frying pan or flameproof casserole until hot. Remove the chicken from the marinade and cook in the pan until browned on all sides.

4 Put a few shallots into the chicken cavity with the garlic and ginger from the marinade and as many of the red and green grapes as will fit. Roast for 40–60 minutes, or until cooked.

5 Remove the chicken from the pan and keep warm. Pour off any oil from the pan, reserving any sediment in the base. Add the remaining shallots and cook for 5 minutes until softened.

6 Add half the remaining red and green grapes, the remaining ginger, the stock and any juices from the chicken and cook over medium-high heat until the grapes have reduced to a thick sauce. Season with salt, pepper and the remaining lemon juice.

7 Serve the chicken on a warmed serving dish, surrounded by the sauce and the reserved grapes.

Tagine of Poussins with Dates & Orange Flower Water

Dates and almonds are probably the most ancient culinary combination in Arab cuisines, married in sweet dishes or with lamb and chicken. For this type of tagine, the small birds can be cooked on top of the stove or in the oven. Quail, partridge, pheasant or pigeon can be used instead of poussins, if you like. Served with a traditional Moroccan salad and couscous, this makes a very special dinner party dish.

Serves 4

25g/1oz fresh root ginger, peeled
　and roughly chopped
2 garlic cloves
60ml/4 tbsp olive oil
juice of 1 lemon
30–45ml/2–3 tbsp clear honey
4 small poussins
350g/12oz/2 cups moist dried
　dates, stoned (pitted)
5–10ml/1–2 tsp ground cinnamon
15ml/1 tbsp orange flower water
knob (pat) of butter
30–45ml/2–3 tbsp blanched
　almonds
salt and ground black pepper

1 Using a mortar and pestle, crush the ginger with the garlic to form a paste. Mix the paste with the olive oil, lemon juice, honey and seasoning.

2 Place the poussins in a tagine or flameproof casserole and rub the paste all over them. Pour in a little water to cover the base of the dish and bring to the boil. Reduce the heat, cover and simmer for about 30 minutes, turning the poussins occasionally, until they are cooked through. Top up the water during cooking, if necessary.

3 Lift the poussins out of the tagine, transfer them to a plate, cover with foil and keep hot. Add the dates to the liquid in the tagine and stir in the cinnamon and orange flower water. Cook gently for about 10 minutes, or until the dates are soft and have absorbed the flavours of the sauce as well as some of the liquid.

4 Replace the poussins and cover the tagine to keep hot. Melt the butter in a separate pan and brown the almonds, then toss them over the poussins. Serve immediately.

Roasted Chicken Energy 454kcal/1891kJ; Protein 31.6g; Carbohydrate 19.5g, of which sugars 19.5g; Fat 28.1g, of which saturates 7.1g; Cholesterol 165mg; Calcium 28mg; Fibre 1g; Sodium 116mg.
Poussins Energy 672kcal/2816kJ; Protein 24g; Carbohydrate 70g, of which sugars 69g; Fat 35g, of which saturates 21g; Cholesterol 100mg; Calcium 92mg; Fibre 8.1g; Sodium 181mg.

Duck with Orange Sauce

The classic partnering of
duck with orange sauce
makes for a tasty festive dish.

Serves 2–3
2kg/4½lb duck 2 oranges
90g/3½oz/½ cup caster
(superfine) sugar

90ml/6 tbsp white wine vinegar
or cider vinegar
120ml/4fl oz/½ cup Grand
Marnier or other orange-
flavoured liqueur
salt and ground black pepper
watercress and orange slices,
to garnish

1 Preheat the oven to 150°C/300°F/Gas 2. Trim off all the
excess fat and skin from the duck and prick the skin all over
with a fork. Generously season the duck inside and out, and
tie the legs together with string to hold them in place.

2 Place the duck on a rack in a large roasting pan. Cover
tightly with foil and cook in the preheated oven for 1½ hours.
Remove the rind in wide strips from the oranges, then stack up
two or three strips at a time and slice into very thin julienne
strips. Squeeze the juice from the oranges and set it aside.

3 Place the sugar and vinegar in a pan and stir to dissolve
the sugar. Boil over high heat, without stirring, until the mixture
is a rich caramel colour. Remove the pan from the heat and
carefully add the orange juice, pouring it down the side of the
pan. Swirl the pan to blend, then bring back to the boil and
add the orange rind and liqueur. Simmer for 2–3 minutes.

4 Remove the duck from the oven and pour off all the fat from
the pan. Raise the oven temperature to 200°C/400°F/Gas 6.
Roast the duck, uncovered, for 25–30 minutes, basting three or
four times with the caramel mixture, until the duck is golden
brown and the juices run clear when the thigh is pierced.

5 Pour the juices from the cavity into the casserole and
transfer the duck to a carving board. Cover loosely with foil and
leave to stand for 10–15 minutes. Pour the roasting juices into
the pan with the rest of the caramel mixture, skim off the fat
and simmer gently. Serve the duck with the orange sauce,
garnished with sprigs of watercress and orange slices.

Roast Duck Legs with Quince, Ginger, Honey & Cinnamon

The quince is a fruit of the
ancient world, recorded in
recipes from the Roman and
Arab empires that launched
invasions on vast tracts of
the Middle East and North
Africa. These scented fruit
that resemble large, hard
pears often feature with
lamb or rich poultry, as in
this typically Moroccan recipe.
When cooking, quinces fill
the air with their heady
scent and impart a fruity
honey flavour to the dish.

Serves 4
4 duck legs
30ml/2 tbsp olive oil
2 lemons
600ml/1 pint/2½ cups water
2 quinces, quartered, cored
and peeled
a little butter
25g/1oz fresh root ginger,
peeled and grated
10ml/2 tsp ground cinnamon
30ml/2 tbsp clear honey
salt and ground black pepper
small bunch of fresh coriander
(cilantro), chopped, to serve

1 Preheat the oven to 230°C/450°F/Gas 8. Rub the duck legs
with half the olive oil, season with salt and pepper, and place on
a rack in a roasting pan. Roast in the oven for about 30 minutes
until the skin is crisp and golden.

2 Squeeze the juice from ½ lemon and place in a pan. Add
the water and bring to the boil. Add the quince quarters and
simmer for about 15 minutes until tender. Drain and refresh,
then cut each quince quarter into slices. Heat the remaining
olive oil and butter in a frying pan and fry the quince slices until
brown. Remove from the pan, place in a dish and keep warm.

3 Take the duck out of the oven and pour 30ml/2 tbsp of the
duck fat into the pan in which the fruit was cooked. Stir in
the ginger and cook for 1 minute, then add the cinnamon,
honey and the remaining lemon juice. Pour in 30–45ml/
2–3 tbsp water and stir until it bubbles up to make a small
amount of sauce; remove from the heat.

4 Arrange the duck legs and quince slices on a plate and
spoon the sauce over them. Sprinkle with coriander and serve.

Duck with Orange Energy 280kcal/1181kJ; Protein 30.8g; Carbohydrate 23.8g, of which sugars 23.8g; Fat 10g, of which saturates 1.9g; Cholesterol 165mg; Calcium 48mg; Fibre 0.4g; Sodium 195mg.
Roast Duck Energy 328kcal/1369kJ; Protein 26g; Carbohydrate 10g, of which sugars 9g; Fat 21g, of which saturates 6g; Cholesterol 123mg; Calcium 42mg; Fibre 2.6g; Sodium 220mg.

Duck with Plum Sauce

This is a great autumn meal featuring a number of ingredients that are at their best this season: plums, celeriac and duck. The sharp plums cut the rich flavour of duck wonderfully well in this updated version of an old English dish. Duck is often considered to be a fatty meat, but modern breeding methods have made leaner ducks widely available. For an easy dinner party main course, serve the duck with creamy mashed potatoes and seasonal celeriac and steamed broccoli.

Serves 4

4 duck quarters
1 large red onion, finely chopped
500g/1¼lb ripe plums, stoned (pitted) and quartered
30ml/2 tbsp redcurrant jelly
creamy mashed potato, celeriac and broccoli, to serve (optional)
salt and ground black pepper

1 Prick the duck skin all over with a fork to release the fat during the cooking process and help give a crisp result, then place the portions in a heavy frying pan, skin side down.

2 Cook the duck pieces for about 8–10 minutes on each side, or until golden brown and cooked right through. Remove the duck from the frying pan using a slotted spoon and keep warm while you prepare the rest.

3 Pour away all but 30ml/2 tbsp of the duck fat, then stir-fry the onion for about 5 minutes, or until soft and golden. Add the plums and cook for another 5 minutes, stirring frequently. Add the jelly and mix well.

4 Replace the duck portions in the pan and cook for a further 5 minutes, or until thoroughly reheated. Season to taste with salt and pepper before serving.

> **Cook's Tip**
> *It is important that the plums used in this dish are very ripe, otherwise the mixture will be too dry and the sauce will be extremely sharp.*

Duck with Apricot & Honey

The summer months bring an abundance of apricots. They are often made into preserves, and used in savoury dishes such as this one, which uses apricot compote and jam with honey to make a fragrant glaze, giving a sweet complement to the duck.

Serves 4

1 large whole duck, about 1.8kg/4lb
3 thyme sprigs
4–5 parsley sprigs
3 rosemary sprigs
1 carrot, roughly chopped
1 celery stick
1 onion, halved
salt and ground black pepper

For the glaze

400g/14oz apricot compote
10ml/2 tsp clear honey
15ml/1 tbsp apricot jam
juice of 1 small lemon
juice of 1 small orange

1 Preheat the oven to 200°C/400°F/Gas 6. Prepare the duck by washing it well, then drying and seasoning it with salt and ground black pepper.

2 Put the herbs, carrot, celery and onion into the cavity. Put the duck in a roasting pan and, once the oven has reached its correct temperature, roast for 30 minutes.

3 Meanwhile, make the apricot and honey glaze. Pour the syrup from the apricot compote into a small pan and bring to a gentle boil, then simmer to reduce; this will take about 10 minutes.

4 Finely chop the apricots from the compote and set aside. Add the honey to the pan, with the apricot jam and the lemon and orange juice, and simmer for 3–5 more minutes. Season to taste with salt and pepper and add the chopped apricots.

5 Remove the duck from the oven, and pour the glaze all over the breast and legs, then return to the oven, and reduce the temperature to 180°C/350°F/Gas 4. Cook for a further 1–1½ hours, basting regularly with the cooking juices and glaze. The duck is ready to serve when the skin is crispy and becomes a deep golden colour.

Duck with Apricot Energy 210kcal/885kJ; Protein 25g; Carbohydrate 10g, of which sugars 10g; Fat 8.2g, of which saturates 2.7g; Cholesterol 135mg; Calcium 23mg; Fibre 0.5g; Sodium 145mg.
Duck with Plum Energy 894kcal/3755kJ; Protein 17.8g; Carbohydrate 110.8g, of which sugars 42.9g; Fat 45.5g, of which saturates 17.9g; Cholesterol 67mg; Calcium 170mg; Fibre 11.6g; Sodium 1052mg.

Duck with Damson & Ginger Sauce

This is a variation of salt duck, a traditional Welsh recipe that would be well suited to serving at the festive table. Simple pan-fried duck breast fillets go well with a fruit sauce too, as in this recipe with damsons and ground ginger.

Serves 4
250g/9oz fresh damsons
5ml/1 tsp ground ginger
45ml/3 tbsp sugar
10ml/2 tsp wine vinegar
  or sherry vinegar
4 duck breast fillets
15ml/1 tbsp oil
salt and ground black pepper

1 Put the damsons in a pan with the ginger and 45ml/3 tbsp water. Bring to the boil, cover and simmer gently for 5 minutes, or until the fruit is soft. Stir frequently and add a little extra water if the fruit looks as if it is drying out or sticking to the bottom of the pan.

2 Stir in the sugar and vinegar. Press the mixture through a sieve (strainer) to remove stones (pits) and skin. Taste the sauce and add more sugar, if necessary, and seasoning to taste.

3 Meanwhile, with a sharp knife, score the fat on the duck breast portions in several places without cutting into the meat. Brush the oil over both sides of the duck. Sprinkle a little salt and pepper on the fat side only.

4 Preheat a griddle pan or heavy frying pan. When hot, add the duck breast fillets, skin side down, and cook over medium heat for about 5 minutes or until the fat is evenly browned and crisp. Turn over and cook the meat side for 4–5 minutes. Lift out and leave to rest for 5–10 minutes.

5 Cut the duck fillets into slices on the diagonal and serve immediately, accompanied by the sauce.

Cook's Tip
Both the duck and the sauce are also good when served cold. Serve them with simple steamed winter vegetables.

Duck Sausages with Plum Sauce

Rich duck sausages are best baked in their own juices for 30 minutes. Creamy mashed sweet potatoes and spicy plum sauce are the perfect seasonal complements, and contrast well with the richness of the sausages.

Serves 4
8–12 duck sausages

For the sweet potato mash
1.5kg/3¼lb sweet potatoes,
  cut into chunks

25g/1oz/2 tbsp butter
60ml/4 tbsp milk
salt and ground black pepper

For the plum sauce
30ml/2 tbsp olive oil
1 small onion, chopped
1 small red chilli, seeded
  and finely chopped
450g/1lb plums, stoned (pitted)
  and chopped
30ml/2 tbsp red wine vinegar
45ml/3 tbsp clear honey

1 Preheat the oven to 190°C/375°F/Gas 5. Arrange the duck sausages in a single layer in a large, shallow ovenproof dish and bake, uncovered, for 25–30 minutes, turning the sausages two or three times during cooking, to ensure that they brown and cook evenly.

2 Meanwhile, put the sweet potatoes in a pan and pour in enough water to cover them. Bring to the boil, reduce the heat and simmer for 20 minutes, or until tender.

3 Drain and mash the sweet potatoes, then place the pan over a low heat. Stir frequently for about 5 minutes to dry out the mashed potatoes. Beat in the butter and milk, and season with salt and pepper.

4 Heat the oil in a frying pan and fry the onion and chilli gently for 5 minutes until the onion is soft and translucent. Stir in the plums, vinegar and honey, then simmer gently for 10 minutes.

5 Divide the freshly cooked sausages among four plates and serve immediately with the sweet potato mash and piquant plum sauce.

Duck with Damson Energy 275kcal/1157kJ; Protein 29.9g; Carbohydrate 17.5g, of which sugars 17.5g; Fat 12.5g, of which saturates 2.4g; Cholesterol 165mg; Calcium 39mg; Fibre 1.1g; Sodium 167mg.
Duck Sausages Energy 894kcal/3755kJ; Protein 17.8g; Carbohydrate 110.8g, of which sugars 42.9g; Fat 45.5g, of which saturates 17.9g; Cholesterol 67mg; Calcium 170mg; Fibre 11.6g; Sodium 1052mg.

Roast Duck with Prunes & Apples

This autumn dish features a roast duck stuffed with seasonal apples and prunes. Serve with roast potatoes, and braised red cabbage, or serve more simply with steamed cauliflower – another autumn favourite.

Serves 4

1 duck, about 1.8–2.5kg/4–5¹⁄₂lb, with giblets

150g/5oz pitted prunes, sliced
2 medium dessert apples, peeled and chopped
20g/³⁄₄oz fine breadcrumbs
475ml/16fl oz/2 cups hot chicken stock
small bay leaf
30ml/2 tbsp plain (all-purpose) flour
15ml/1 tbsp single (light) cream
salt and white pepper

1 Preheat the oven to 240°C/475°F/Gas 9. Rinse the duck and pat dry. Score the breast with a crosshatch pattern. Season well.

2 Toss the prunes and apples with the breadcrumbs in a bowl and spoon this mixture into the duck cavity, packing it firmly. Close the opening with skewers or sew up with fine string.

3 Pour 250ml/8fl oz/1 cup of the chicken stock into a roasting pan. Place the duck on a rack in the pan, breast side down, and cook for 20 minutes.

4 Put the giblets in a pan with 475ml/16fl oz/2 cups water and the bay leaf. Bring to a rolling boil for 20–30 minutes until reduced. Strain and set aside.

5 Lower the oven to 180°C/350°F/Gas 4. Turn the duck breast side up. Pour the remaining stock into the pan. Continue to cook for 40 minutes per kg/20 minutes per lb, until the juices run clear when the thickest part of the leg is pierced. Transfer to a serving dish and leave in a warm place for 10 minutes.

6 To make the gravy, pour off the fat from the roasting pan and whisk the flour into the remaining juices. Cook over medium heat for 2–3 minutes until light brown. Gradually whisk in the giblet stock and stir in the cream. Cook the gravy, stirring, for 3 minutes, pour into a sauceboat and serve with the duck.

Roast Grouse with Rowanberry & Wine Sauce

Autumn is the best time of year for enjoying game meats of all descriptions, particularly the various game birds on offer. As with venison, rowan jelly goes well with this autumn bird. Young grouse have very little fat on them, so bacon is used in this recipe to protect the breasts during the initial roasting.

Serves 2

2 young grouse
6 rashers (strips) bacon
2 sprigs of rowanberries or 1 lemon, quartered, plus 30ml/2 tbsp extra rowanberries (optional)
50g/2oz/¹⁄₄ cup butter
150ml/¹⁄₄ pint/²⁄₃ cup red wine
150ml/¹⁄₄ pint/²⁄₃ cup water
5ml/1 tsp rowan jelly
salt and ground black pepper

1 Preheat the oven to 200°C/400°F/Gas 6. Wipe the grouse with kitchen paper and place in a roasting pan. Lay the bacon over the breasts.

2 If you have rowanberries, place one sprig in the cavity of each grouse as well as a little butter. Otherwise put a lemon quarter in each cavity.

3 Roast the grouse in the preheated oven for 10 minutes, then remove the bacon and pour in the wine. Return to the oven for 10 minutes.

4 Baste the birds with the juices and cook for a further 5 minutes. Remove the birds from the pan and keep warm. Add the water and rowan jelly to the pan and simmer gently until the jelly melts. Strain into another pan, add the rowanberries, if using, and simmer until the sauce just begins to thicken. Season with salt and ground black pepper.

> **Cook's Tip**
> Grouse is traditionally served with bread sauce and game chips, but the Scottish oatmeal dish skirlie is excellent too.

Roast Duck Energy 663kcal/2757kJ; Protein 31.6g; Carbohydrate 24g, of which sugars 14.6g; Fat 49.6g, of which saturates 14g; Cholesterol 100mg; Calcium 55mg; Fibre 2.8g; Sodium 222mg.
Roast Grouse Energy 423kcal/1763kJ; Protein 43.8g; Carbohydrate 1.5g, of which sugars 1.5g; Fat 24g, of which saturates 10.8g; Cholesterol 51mg; Calcium 43mg; Fibre 0g; Sodium 902mg.

Pork with Cream & Apple Sauce

Tender noisettes of pork in a creamy leek and apple sauce make a great dinner party dish. Use the same white wine as the one you plan to serve with the meal, or you could try cider.

Serves 4
30ml/2 tbsp plain
    (all-purpose) flour
4 noisettes of pork, firmly tied
25g/1oz/2 tbsp butter
4 baby leeks, finely sliced
5ml/1 tsp mustard seeds,
    coarsely crushed

150ml/¼ pint/⅔ cup dry
    white wine
2 eating apples
150ml/¼ pint/⅔ cup double
    (heavy) cream
30ml/2 tbsp chopped
    fresh parsley
salt and ground black pepper
red cabbage and fried polenta,
    to serve

1 Place the flour in a bowl and add plenty of seasoning. Turn the noisettes in the flour mixture to coat them lightly and evenly on both sides.

2 Melt the butter in a heavy frying pan and cook the noisettes for 1 minute on each side, turning them with tongs.

3 Add the sliced leeks to the pan and cook for 3 minutes. Stir in the mustard seeds. Pour in the wine. Cook gently for 10 minutes, turning the pork occasionally. Peel the apples, remove the cores, cut in half and slice thinly.

4 Add the sliced apples and double cream to the pan and simmer for 3 minutes, or until the pork is fully cooked and the sauce is thick, rich and creamy. Taste for seasoning, add salt and pepper if needed, then stir in the chopped parsley and serve the pork at once with red cabbage and fried polenta.

> **Variation**
> *Use thin slices of pork fillet (tenderloin) for even faster cooking.*

Pork Escalopes with Apple & Potato Rösti

The juices from the pork cook into the seasonal apples and potatoes, giving the dish a wonderfully autumnal flavour.

Serves 4
2 large potatoes, finely grated
1 medium Bramley apple, grated
2 garlic cloves, crushed
1 egg, beaten
butter, for greasing

15ml/1 tbsp olive oil
4 large slices prosciutto
4 pork escalopes, about
    175g/6oz each
4 sage leaves
1 medium Bramley apple,
    cut into thin wedges
25g/1oz/2 tbsp unsalted
    (sweet) butter, diced
salt and ground black pepper
caramelized apple wedges,
    to serve

1 Preheat the oven to 200°C/400°F/Gas 6. Squeeze out all the excess liquid from the grated potatoes and apple. Thoroughly mix the grated ingredients together with the garlic, egg and seasoning.

2 Divide the potatoes into four portions and spoon each quarter on to a baking sheet that has been lined with foil and greased. Form a circle with the potatoes and flatten out slightly with the back of a spoon. Drizzle with a little olive oil. Bake for 10 minutes.

3 Meanwhile, lay the prosciutto on a clean surface and place a pork escalope on top. Lay a sage leaf and a quarter of the apple wedges over each escalope and top each piece with the butter. Wrap the prosciutto around each piece of meat, making sure it is covered completely.

4 Remove the potatoes from the oven, place each pork parcel on top of the potatoes and return the pan to the oven for about 20 minutes.

5 Carefully lift the pork and potatoes off the foil and serve at once with caramelized wedges of apple and any cooking juices on the side.

Pork with Cream Energy 415kcal/1724kJ; Protein 23.1g; Carbohydrate 8.8g, of which sugars 4.4g; Fat 29.5g, of which saturates 17.2g; Cholesterol 128mg; Calcium 45mg; Fibre 1.3g; Sodium 119mg.
Pork Escalopes Energy 396kcal/1659kJ; Protein 42.7g; Carbohydrate 19.2g, of which sugars 4.4g; Fat 16.9g, of which saturates 6.7g; Cholesterol 177mg; Calcium 29mg; Fibre 1.5g; Sodium 310mg.

Fried Pork & Apples

This is a very simple dish that turns an inexpensive cut of meat into a most enjoyable meal. It is ideal for a quick supper dish over the festive period.

Serves 4
600g/1¼lb lightly salted or
   fresh belly of pork, cut into
   thin slices

500g/1¼lb crisp eating apples
30ml/2 tbsp soft light brown sugar
salt and ground black pepper
chopped fresh parsley or chives,
   to garnish
boiled potatoes and a seasonal
   green vegetable, such as
   cabbage, Brussels sprouts
   or kale, to serve

1 Heat a large frying pan, without any oil or fat, until hot. Add the salted or fresh belly pork slices and fry over low heat for about 3–4 minutes each side, until golden brown. Season the pork slices with salt and pepper. Transfer to a warmed serving dish and keep warm.

2 Core the apples but do not peel, then cut the apples into rings. Add the apple rings to the frying pan and fry gently in the pork fat for about 3–4 minutes each side, until just beginning to turn golden and translucent.

3 Sprinkle the slices with the sugar and turn once more for a couple of minutes until the sugar side starts to caramelize.

4 Serve the pork slices with the apple rings. Accompany the pork with plain boiled potatoes and a green seasonal vegetable, garnished with fresh parsley.

> **Cook's Tips**
> • *This is a great dish to make the most of seasonal apples, which are at their best in the run-up to Christmas. Cut the rings to a depth of 5mm/¼in across the apple. Most apples will make about four rings for this dish.*
> • *Other seasonal vegetables that would go well in this recipe include beetroot (beet), carrots, cauliflower or leeks.*

Roast Pork, Apples & Glazed Potatoes

For this fruity pork and potato recipe, select a bone-in pork loin with the skin left on for the crackling.

Serves 8–10
2.25kg/5lb bone-in pork loin,
10ml/2 tsp mustard powder
15 whole cloves
2 bay leaves
900ml/1½ pints/3¾ cups water
175ml/6fl oz/¾ cup single (light)
   cream (optional)
salt and white pepper
braised red cabbage, to serve

For the glazed potatoes
900g/2lb small potatoes
50g/2oz/¼ cup caster
   (superfine) sugar
65g/2½ oz/5 tbsp butter

For the apples with redcurrant jelly
750ml/1¼ pints/3 cups water
115g/4oz/generous ½ cup
   soft light brown sugar
5ml/1 tsp lemon juice
4–5 tart apples, peeled, cored
   and halved
60–75ml/4–5 tbsp redcurrant jelly

1 Preheat the oven to 200°C/400°F/Gas 6. Score the pork skin and rub with the salt, pepper and mustard powder. Push the cloves and bay leaves into the skin. Place the pork, skin side up, on a rack in a roasting pan and cook for 1 hour, until the skin is crisp. Pour the water into the pan and cook for 30 minutes.

2 Boil the potatoes in salted water for 15–20 minutes, or until soft. Drain, peel and keep warm. Melt the sugar in a frying pan over low heat until it turns light brown. Add the potatoes and butter and cook for 6–8 minutes. Keep warm.

3 Bring the water for the apples to the boil in a pan and stir in sugar, lemon juice and apple halves. Lower the heat and simmer until the apples are just tender. Remove the apples and spoon 7.5ml/1½ tsp jelly into the hollow of each half. Keep warm.

4 Transfer the pork to a serving dish and rest for 15 minutes before carving. Make the gravy: pour the roasting pan juices into a pan and reduce over medium heat. Whisk in a little cream if you wish, and season. Remove the crackling. Serve the pork with the gravy, potatoes, apples and crackling.

Roast Pork Energy 654kcal/2735kJ; Protein 36.9g; Carbohydrate 39.5g, of which sugars 26.2g; Fat 39.9g, of which saturates 16.1g; Cholesterol 124mg; Calcium 36mg; Fibre 1.5g; Sodium 152mg.
Fried Pork Energy 645kcal/2676kJ; Protein 23.4g; Carbohydrate 19g, of which sugars 19g; Fat 53.4g, of which saturates 19.7g; Cholesterol 108mg; Calcium 21mg; Fibre 2g; Sodium 113mg.

Pork Sausages with Grapes

In the early autumn, when ripe grapes are plentiful, they make a delicious combination of flavours fried in a pan with rich pork sausages. Big, sweet, thick-skinned and firm white grapes are best for this dish, which is like the hot-weather version of sausages with beans or lentils. However, a mixture of white and red grapes will add more colour. Serve with roast potatoes and a green salad, if you like.

Serves 4

8 plump Italian sausages
10ml/2 tsp olive oil
30ml/2 tbsp water
8 handfuls firm grapes

1 Prick the sausages all over with a knife to allow the fat to run and the heat to permeate the sausage.

2 Put the oil and water in a large frying pan over a medium heat for 2 minutes.

3 Lay the sausages in the pan. Cook gently, turning frequently, for 10 minutes, or until cooked through.

4 Add the grapes. Cook until slightly caramelized, and then serve immediately.

Cook's Tips
• *Don't leave the sausages unattended in the frying pan during cooking – make sure you turn them often to ensure that they are cooked evenly and gently.*
• *Choose seedless varieties of grapes, and do not cook them for too long. They should become soft but not too broken up.*

Variation
Choose any type of Italian sausage for this recipe; instead of plain pork sausages, try those with flavourings such as fennel seeds, chilli, black pepper or garlic, for a more spicy dish.

Pork & Pineapple Coconut Curry

The heat of this curry balances out the sweetness of the pineapple, and the coconut cream and spices make it a smooth, fragrant dish. It takes very little time to cook, so is ideal for a quick supper before going out, or for a midweek family meal on a busy evening.

Serves 4
400ml/14fl oz can
    coconut milk
10ml/2 tsp Thai red curry paste
400g/14oz pork loin steaks,
    trimmed and thinly sliced
15ml/1 tbsp Thai fish sauce
5ml/1 tsp palm sugar or light
    muscovado (brown) sugar
15ml/1 tbsp tamarind juice,
    made by mixing tamarind
    paste with warm water
2 kaffir lime leaves, torn
1/2 medium pineapple, peeled
    and chopped
1 fresh red chilli, seeded and
    finely chopped

1 Pour the coconut milk into a bowl and let it settle, so that the cream rises to the surface. Scoop the cream into a measuring jug (cup). You should have about 250ml/8fl oz/1 cup. If necessary, add a little of the coconut milk.

2 Pour the measured coconut cream into a large pan and bring it to the boil.

3 Cook the coconut cream for about 10 minutes, until it separates, stirring frequently to prevent it from sticking to the base of the pan and scorching. Add the red curry paste and stir until well mixed. Cook, stirring occasionally, for about 4 minutes, until the paste is fragrant.

4 Add the sliced pork and stir in the fish sauce, sugar and tamarind juice. Cook, stirring constantly, for 1–2 minutes, until the sugar has dissolved and the pork is no longer pink.

5 Add the reserved coconut milk and the lime leaves. Bring to the boil, then stir in the pineapple. Reduce the heat and simmer gently for 3 minutes, or until the pork is fully cooked. Sprinkle over the chilli and serve.

Pork Sausages Energy 638kcal/2648kJ; Protein 16.3g; Carbohydrate 29.7g, of which sugars 17.5g; Fat 51.3g, of which saturates 18.7g; Cholesterol 71mg; Calcium 75mg; Fibre 1.5g; Sodium 1142mg.
Pork Curry Energy 187kcal/790kJ; Protein 22.2g; Carbohydrate 15.3g; of which sugars 15.3g; Fat 4.5g; of which saturates 1.6g; Cholesterol 63mg; Calcium 55mg; Fibre 1.2g; Sodium 449mg.

Spiced Lamb with Apricots

Inspired by Middle Eastern cooking, this fruity, spicy casserole is simple to make yet looks impressive.

Serves 4

115g/4oz ready-to-eat
    dried apricots
50g/2oz/scant ½ cup
    seedless raisins
2.5ml/½ tsp saffron threads
150ml/¼ pint/⅔ cup
    orange juice
15ml/1 tbsp red wine vinegar
30–45ml/2–3 tbsp olive oil
1.5kg/3–3½ lb leg of lamb,
    boned and diced
1 onion, chopped
2 garlic cloves, crushed
10ml/2 tsp ground cumin
1.25ml/¼ tsp ground cloves
15ml/1 tbsp ground coriander
25g/1oz/¼ cup plain
    (all-purpose) flour
600ml/1 pint/2½ cups lamb
    or chicken stock
45ml/3 tbsp chopped fresh
    coriander (cilantro)
salt and ground black pepper
saffron rice mixed with toasted
    almonds and chopped fresh
    coriander, to serve

1 Mix together the dried apricots, raisins, saffron, orange juice and vinegar in a bowl. Cover with clear film (plastic wrap) and leave to soak for 2–3 hours.

2 Preheat the oven to 160°C/325°F/Gas 3. Heat 30ml/2 tbsp oil in a large flameproof casserole over medium heat. Add the lamb, in batches, and cook, stirring frequently, for 5–8 minutes, until evenly browned. Remove and set aside.

3 Add a little more oil to the casserole, if necessary, and lower the heat. Add the onion and garlic and cook, stirring occasionally, for 5 minutes, until softened but not coloured.

4 Stir in the spices and flour and cook for 1–2 minutes more. Return the meat to the casserole. Stir in the stock, fresh coriander and the soaked fruit with its liquid. Season to taste with salt and pepper, then bring to the boil. Cover the casserole with a tight-fitting lid and simmer for 1½ hours (adding extra stock if necessary), or until the lamb is tender. Serve with saffron rice mixed with toasted almonds and fresh coriander.

Braised Lamb with Prunes

The warm flavours of bay leaves, cinnamon and cloves go very well with the sweetness of prunes in this dish of tender leg of lamb. Serve with either rice or boiled potatoes.

Serves 4

75ml/5 tbsp vegetable oil
1 large onion, finely chopped
30ml/2 tbsp plain
    (all-purpose) flour
600g/1lb 5oz boned
    leg of lamb, cut into
    5cm/2in cubes
200ml/7fl oz/scant 1 cup stock
    made from the lamb bones
15ml/1 tbsp caster
    (superfine) sugar
75ml/5 tbsp white wine
    vinegar
2 bay leaves
2.5ml/½ tsp ground cinnamon
pinch of ground cloves
200g/7oz/scant 1 cup
    ready-to-eat prunes
salt and ground black pepper

1 Heat the oil in a flameproof casserole, add the onion and sauté until lightly coloured.

2 Put the flour on a plate and season with salt and pepper. Add the meat and dust all over. Put the meat in the casserole and cook until browned on all sides.

3 Add the stock and simmer for 20–30 minutes, or until the sauce has slightly thickened.

4 Add the sugar, vinegar, bay leaves, cinnamon, cloves and prunes to the casserole. Bring to a boil, and simmer for a further 20 minutes, or until the meat is tender. Serve hot.

Cook's Tips
• A boned leg of lamb is quicker to cook than cuts of meat that include the bones, so the casserole does not need to cook for hours – the meat just needs to be cooked through.
• Choosing ready-to-eat prunes will ensure the best flavour for this dish, because they are deliciously tender and juicy.

Spiced Lamb Energy 765kcal/3192kJ; Protein 58.5g; Carbohydrate 27.5g, of which sugars 23.4g; Fat 47.5g, of which saturates 14.7g; Cholesterol 218mg; Calcium 53mg; Fibre 2.5g; Sodium 181mg.
Braised Lamb Energy 530kcal/2215kJ; Protein 32.3g; Carbohydrate 32.7g, of which sugars 25.2g; Fat 31g, of which saturates 9.3g; Cholesterol 114mg; Calcium 60mg; Fibre 4.1g; Sodium 137mg.

Veal with Grapes & Apricots

This recipe has many versions – this one, of Turkish and Bulgarian origin, is prepared using fresh summer fruits. It can also be made with dried fruits. The veal has to be marinated, so you need to start your preparations the day before.

Serves 4

15ml/1 tbsp clear honey
5ml/1 tsp grated fresh root ginger
5ml/1 tsp ground cinnamon
5ml/1 tsp ground black pepper
100ml/3½fl oz/scant ½ cup
   white wine

800g/1¾lb veal shoulder,
   cut into 3cm/1¼in cubes
45ml/3 tbsp olive oil
1 onion, chopped
1 cinnamon stick
30ml/2 tbsp black sesame seeds
115g/4oz seedless grapes,
   halved
115g/4oz fresh apricots,
   halved and stoned (pitted)

1 Using a large bowl, combine the honey, ginger, cinnamon, pepper and wine. Rub this mixture over the veal, then cover and let it marinate in the refrigerator overnight.

2 Drain the veal and set the marinade aside.

3 Heat the olive oil in a large sauté pan, and sauté the onion until just golden in colour, then add the veal cubes and brown evenly.

4 Add the reserved marinade, 300ml/½ pint/1¼ cups water and the cinnamon stick, and simmer for 30 minutes, or until the liquid has reduced by about half, and the veal is cooked.

5 Meanwhile, put the sesame seeds in a dry pan and toast over medium-high heat, tossing regularly, for 1 minute.

6 Add the grapes and apricot halves and simmer in the pan for a further 5–8 minutes. Serve immediately, sprinkled with the sesame seeds, and accompanied by plain rice.

Veal & Prune Stew

This hearty, rich stew is a delicious mixture of veal, prunes, lemon and cream. It would make a satisfying meal for friends and family over the festive season.

Serves 8

20 ready-to-eat pitted prunes
100ml/3½ oz/scant
   ½ cup brandy
2.5ml/½ tsp grated
   lemon rind
65g/2½oz/5 tbsp butter

600g/1lb 6oz braising veal, diced
200ml/7fl oz/scant 1 cup
   veal stock or water
30ml/2 tbsp lemon juice
1 thyme sprig
1 bay leaf
200ml/7fl oz/scant 1 cup
   whipping cream
5ml/1 tsp potato flour or
   cornflour (cornstarch)
salt and ground black pepper
chopped fresh parsley, to garnish
young peas, carrots and small
   new potatoes, to serve

1 Put the prunes in a bowl, add the brandy and lemon rind, cover and soak overnight.

2 Melt the butter in a pan, add the veal and cook over a medium heat, stirring frequently, for about 10 minutes, until evenly browned. Season and add the stock or water, lemon juice, thyme and bay leaf. Lower the heat, cover and simmer for 1 hour, or until tender.

3 Arrange the vegetables in a ring on a warm serving plate. Using a slotted spoon, transfer the veal to the centre of the plate and keep warm.

4 Bring the cooking liquid to the boil and reduce slightly, then stir in the cream. Remove and discard the thyme and bay leaf. Season the sauce with salt and pepper.

5 Mix the potato flour or cornflour with 15ml/1 tbsp cold water to a paste in a small bowl and stir into the sauce until thickened and smooth. Add the prunes with their soaking liquid and warm through.

6 Pour the sauce over the veal, sprinkle the vegetables with parsley and serve immediately.

Veal Grapes Energy 405kcal/1696kJ; Protein 44.7g; Carbohydrate 11.3g, of which sugars 9.6g; Fat 18.7g, of which saturates 3.7g; Cholesterol 168mg; Calcium 86mg; Fibre 1.3g; Sodium 226mg.
Veal Stew Energy 610kcal/2536kJ; Protein 34.4g; Carbohydrate 19.9g, of which sugars 18.7g; Fat 37.9g, of which saturates 22.4g; Cholesterol 213mg; Calcium 86mg; Fibre 3.5g; Sodium 286mg.

Citrus Beef Curry

This aromatic orange-and-lemon beef curry is not exceptionally hot, but it is full of flavour.

Serves 4

450g/1lb rump (round) steak
30ml/2 tbsp vegetable oil
30ml/2 tbsp medium curry paste
2 bay leaves
400ml/14fl oz/1²/₃ cups
   coconut milk
300ml/¹/₂ pint/1¹/₄ cups
   beef stock
30ml/2 tbsp lemon juice
grated rind and juice of
   ¹/₂ orange

15ml/1 tbsp granulated sugar
115g/4oz baby (pearl) onions,
   peeled but left whole
225g/8oz new potatoes, halved
115g/4oz/1 cup unsalted
   roasted peanuts, roughly
   chopped
115g/4oz fine green beans,
   halved
1 red (bell) pepper, seeded
   and thinly sliced
unsalted roasted peanuts,
   to garnish (optional)

1 Trim any visible fat from the beef and cut the meat into 5cm/2in strips.

2 Heat the vegetable oil in a large, heavy pan, add the medium curry paste and cook over medium heat for 30 seconds, stirring constantly.

3 Add the beef and cook, stirring, for 2 minutes until it is beginning to brown and is thoroughly coated with the spices.

4 Stir in the bay leaves, coconut milk, stock, lemon juice, orange rind and juice, and sugar. Bring to the boil, stirring frequently.

5 Add the onions and potatoes, then bring back to the boil, reduce the heat and simmer, uncovered, for 5 minutes.

6 Stir in the peanuts, beans and pepper and simmer for a further 10 minutes, or until the beef and potatoes are tender. Serve in shallow bowls, with a spoon and fork, to enjoy all the rich and creamy juices. Sprinkle with extra unsalted roasted peanuts, if you like.

Venison Tenderloins with Cherry Sauce

Served mainly in autumn or winter during the hunting season, venison's rich flavour and earthy taste have led to a revival in its popularity. Creamed parsnips go well with this colourful cherry-topped dish, together with some braised leeks.

Serves 4–6
2–2.5kg/4¹/₂–5¹/₂lb venison
   tenderloin
25g/1oz/2 tbsp butter, softened
250ml/8fl oz/1 cup water
salt and ground black pepper

For the sauce
250ml/8fl oz/1 cup cherry juice
120ml/4fl oz/¹/₂ cup water
25ml/1¹/₂ tbsp cornflour
   (cornstarch)
425g/15oz canned or frozen
   unsweetened pitted cherries
90g/3¹/₂oz/¹/₂ cup sugar,
   or to taste
salt

1 Preheat the oven to 230°C/450°F/Gas 8. Tie the venison at 2.5cm/1in intervals with fine string to hold its shape while roasting. Sprinkle with salt and pepper, and spread with butter.

2 Place the venison on a rack in a shallow roasting pan, and pour in the water. Cook in the hot oven for 20 minutes to brown the surface of the meat.

3 Lower the heat to 180°C/350°F/Gas 4. Continue to cook the tenderloin, basting at intervals with the pan juices, for a further 1¹/₄ hours, until barely pink in the centre (65°C/150°F on a meat thermometer). Leave the meat in a warm place to rest for 10 minutes before slicing.

4 Meanwhile, to make the sauce, bring the cherry juice to the boil in a pan over a medium-high heat. Whisk together the water and cornflour in a small bowl, and stir into the cherry juice. Cook the sauce, stirring constantly, until the mixture thickens. Stir in the cherries and bring the mixture back to the boil. Serve with the venison.

Citrus Beef Energy 471kcal/1974kJ; Protein 35g; Carbohydrate 29g, of which sugars 18g; Fat 25g, of which saturates 5g; Cholesterol 66mg; Calcium 93mg; Fibre 4.9g; Sodium 467mg.
Venison Energy 518kcal/2197kJ; Protein 74.6g; Carbohydrate 37.5g, of which sugars 33.7g; Fat 10.8g, of which saturates 4.8g; Cholesterol 176mg; Calcium 45mg; Fibre 0.4g; Sodium 220mg.

Fish with Tomato & Pomegranate Sauce

This is a tasty method for cooking any firm-fleshed fish, such as large sardines, sea bass, red snapper, grouper and trout. The inclusion of pomegranate molasses in the recipe is a Middle Eastern touch that adds a tangy, sour note to the sauce, as well as beautifully enriching the colour of the finished dish.

Serves 4
900g/2lb firm-fleshed fish fillets
45–60ml/3–4 tbsp olive oil
juice of 1 lemon
2–3 cloves garlic, finely chopped
4 tomatoes, skinned, seeded
  and chopped
15ml/1 tbsp pomegranate
  molasses
10ml/2 tsp sugar
sea salt and ground black pepper
small bunch of fresh parsley,
  finely chopped, to garnish

1 Preheat the oven to 180°C/350°F/Gas 4.

2 Arrange the fish in an ovenproof dish, rub with salt and pepper and pour over 30ml/2 tbsp olive oil and the lemon juice. Cover with foil and bake for about 25 minutes, until the fish is cooked.

3 Meanwhile, heat the rest of the oil in a heavy frying pan. Fry the garlic until it begins to colour, then add the tomatoes. Cook for 5 minutes, then stir in the pomegranate molasses with the sugar. Reduce the heat and cook gently until the sauce thickens. Season with salt and pepper. Keep warm until the fish is ready.

4 Arrange the fish on a serving dish, spoon the sauce over and around the fish, and sprinkle with the parsley.

Cook's Tip
Pomegranate molasses, sometimes sold as pomegranate syrup, is available from Middle Eastern stores and some specialist delicatessens and supermarkets.

Mackerel with Gooseberry Relish

This is a very healthy dish – mackerel is good for you, and the tart gooseberries give you a serving of fruit too. What more could you want from a main meal?

Serves 4
4 whole mackerel
60ml/4 tbsp olive oil

For the sauce
250g/9oz gooseberries
25g/1oz/2 tbsp soft light
  brown sugar
5ml/1 tsp wholegrain mustard
salt and ground black pepper

1 For the sauce, wash and trim the gooseberries, and then roughly chop them so there are some pieces larger than others.

2 Cook the gooseberries in a little water with the sugar in a small pan. A thick and chunky purée will form. Add the mustard, and season to taste with salt and ground black pepper.

3 Preheat the grill (broiler) to high and line the grill pan with foil. Using a sharp knife, slash the fish two or three times down each side, then season and brush with the olive oil.

4 Place the fish in the grill pan and grill (broil) for about 4 minutes on each side until cooked. You may need to cook them for a few minutes longer if they are particularly large. The slashes will open up to speed cooking, and the skin should be lightly browned. To check that they are cooked properly, use a small sharp knife to pierce the skin and check for uncooked flesh.

5 Place the mackerel on warmed plates and spread generous dollops of the gooseberry relish over them. Pass the remaining sauce around at the table.

Cook's Tip
Turn the grill (broiler) on well in advance, as the fish need a fierce heat to cook quickly. The foil lining in the grill pan is to catch the smelly drips; roll it up and throw it away afterwards.

Fish Energy 284kcal/1192kJ; Protein 41.7g; Carbohydrate 6.9g, of which sugars 6.9g; Fat 10.1g, of which saturates 1.5g; Cholesterol 104mg; Calcium 28mg; Fibre 0.8g; Sodium 149mg.
Mackerel Energy 576kcal/2390kJ; Protein 38.1g; Carbohydrate 8.4g, of which sugars 8.4g; Fat 43.5g, of which saturates 8.2g; Cholesterol 108mg; Calcium 43mg; Fibre 1.5g; Sodium 128mg.

Mackerel with Rhubarb Sauce

These fish are really at their best in early summer, just when rhubarb is growing strongly. The tartness of rhubarb offsets the richness of the oily fish to perfection.

Serves 4
4 whole mackerel, cleaned
25g/1oz/2 tbsp butter
1 onion, finely chopped
90ml/6 tbsp fresh white
  breadcrumbs
15ml/1 tbsp chopped fresh parsley
finely grated rind of 1 lemon

freshly grated nutmeg
1 egg, lightly beaten
melted butter or olive oil,
  for brushing
sea salt and ground black pepper

For the sauce
225g/8oz rhubarb (trimmed
  weight), cut in 1cm/½in lengths
25–50g/1–2oz/2–4 tbsp caster
  (superfine) sugar
25g/1oz/2 tbsp butter
15ml/1 tbsp chopped fresh
  tarragon (optional),
  to garnish

1 Ask the fishmonger to bone the mackerel, or do it yourself: open out the body of the fish, turn flesh side down and run your thumb firmly down the backbone – when you turn the fish over, the bones should lift out in a complete section.

2 Melt the butter in a pan and cook the onion gently for 5–10 minutes, until softened but not browned. Add the breadcrumbs, parsley, lemon rind, salt, pepper and grated nutmeg. Mix well, and then add the beaten egg to bind.

3 Divide the mixture among the four fish, wrap the fish over and secure with cocktail sticks (toothpicks). Brush with melted butter or olive oil. Preheat the grill (broiler) and cook under medium heat for about 8 minutes on each side.

4 Meanwhile, make the sauce: put the rhubarb into a pan with 75ml/2½fl oz/⅓ cup water, 25g/1oz/2 tbsp of the sugar and the butter. Cook over low heat until the rhubarb is tender. Taste for sweetness and add extra sugar if necessary, bearing in mind that the sauce needs to be quite sharp.

5 Serve the stuffed mackerel with the hot rhubarb sauce, garnished with a little of the fresh tarragon.

Pineapple Curry with Prawns & Mussels

The delicate sweet-and-sour flavour of this curry comes from the pineapple, and although it seems an odd combination, it is absolutely delicious. Use the freshest shellfish that you can find.

Serves 4–6
600ml/1 pint/2½ cups
  coconut milk
30ml/2 tbsp curry paste
15ml/1 tbsp granulated
  sugar

225g/8oz king prawns (jumbo
  shrimp), peeled and deveined
450g/1lb mussels, cleaned
  (see Cook's Tip)
175g/6oz fresh pineapple, finely
  crushed or chopped
2 bay leaves
2 fresh red chillies, chopped,
  and coriander (cilantro) leaves,
  to garnish

1 In a large pan, bring half the coconut milk to the boil and heat, stirring, until it separates.

2 Add the curry paste and cook until fragrant. Add the sugar and continue to cook for 1 minute.

3 Stir in the remainder of the coconut milk and bring back to the boil. Add the king prawns, mussels, chopped pineapple and bay leaves.

4 Reheat until boiling and then simmer for 3–5 minutes, until the prawns are cooked and the mussels have opened. Remove any mussels that have not opened and throw them away. Discard the bay leaves if you like. Serve the curry garnished with chopped red chillies and coriander leaves.

Cook's Tip
To clean mussels, scrub the shells with a stiff brush and rinse them under cold running water. Scrape off any barnacles and remove the 'beards' with a small knife. Rinse them well.

Mackerel Energy 728kcal/3034kJ; Protein 48.2g; Carbohydrate 27.5g, of which sugars 9.8g; Fat 48g, of which saturates 14.3g; Cholesterol 193mg; Calcium 129mg; Fibre 1.8g; Sodium 398mg.
Pineapple Curry Energy 102kcal/435kJ; Protein 10g; Carbohydrate 12g, of which sugars 11g; Fat 2g, of which saturates 0g; Cholesterol 83mg; Calcium 81mg; Fibre 0.4g; Sodium 318mg.

Apple & Elderflower Stars

These delicious, crumbly apple cookies are topped with a sweet yet very sharp icing. If packaged in a pretty box, they would make a delightful gift for someone special.

Makes about 18
115g/4oz/½ cup unsalted (sweet) butter, at room temperature, diced
75g/3oz/scant ½ cup caster (superfine) sugar
2.5ml/½ tsp mixed spice (apple pie spice)
1 large (US extra large) egg yolk
25g/1oz dried apple rings, finely chopped
200g/7oz/1¾ cups self-raising (self-rising) flour
5–10ml/1–2 tsp milk, if necessary

For the topping
200g/7oz/1¾ cups icing (confectioners') sugar, sifted
60–90ml/4–6 tbsp elderflower cordial
sugar, for sprinkling

1 Preheat the oven to 190°C/375°F/Gas 5. Lightly grease two baking sheets.

2 Beat together the butter and sugar until light and fluffy. Beat in the mixed spice and egg yolk. Add the chopped apple and flour and stir together well. The mixture should form a stiff dough but if it is too dry, add some milk.

3 Roll the dough out on a floured surface to 5mm/¼in thick. Using a star cookie cutter, stamp out the cookies.

4 Place on the baking sheets and bake for about 10–15 minutes, or until beginning to brown around the edges. Using a metal spatula, transfer the cookies to a wire rack to cool.

5 To make the topping, sift the icing sugar into a bowl and add just enough elderflower cordial to mix to a fairly thick but still pourable consistency.

6 When the cookies are completely cool, trickle the icing randomly over the stars. Immediately sprinkle with sugar and leave to set.

Orange Oaties

These are so delicious that it is difficult to believe that they are healthy too. As they are packed with flavour and are wonderfully crunchy, the whole family will love them.

Makes about 16
175g/6oz/¾ cup clear honey
120ml/4fl oz/½ cup orange juice
90g/3½oz/1 cup rolled oats, lightly toasted
115g/4oz/1 cup plain (all-purpose) flour
115g/4oz/generous ½ cup golden caster (superfine) sugar
finely grated rind of 1 orange
5ml/1 tsp bicarbonate of soda (baking soda)

1 Preheat the oven to 180°C/350°F/Gas 4. Line two baking sheets with baking parchment.

2 Put the honey and orange juice in a small pan and simmer over a low heat for 8–10 minutes, stirring occasionally, until the mixture is thick and syrupy. Remove the pan from the heat and set aside to cool slightly.

3 Put the oats, flour, sugar and orange rind into a bowl. Mix the bicarbonate of soda with 15ml/1 tbsp boiling water and add to the flour mixture, together with the honey and orange syrup. Mix well with a wooden spoon.

4 Place spoonfuls of the mixture on to the prepared baking sheets, spaced slightly apart, and bake for 10–12 minutes, or until golden brown.

5 Leave to firm up slightly on the baking sheets for 5 minutes, then using a metal spatula, carefully transfer the cookies to a wire rack and leave to cool completely.

Variation
For additional flavour and aroma, use orange blossom honey when making the orange syrup in step 2.

Apple and Elderflower Energy 157kcal/659kJ; Protein 1.4g; Carbohydrate 26.6g, of which sugars 18.1g; Fat 5.7g, of which saturates 3.4g; Cholesterol 25mg; Calcium 27mg; Fibre 0.4g; Sodium 42mg.
Orange Oaties Energy 110kcal/466kJ; Protein 1.5g; Carbohydrate 26.2g, of which sugars 16.6g; Fat 0.6g, of which saturates 0g; Cholesterol 0mg; Calcium 18mg; Fibre 0.6g; Sodium 4mg.

Date & Orange Oat Cookies

The fragrant aroma of orange permeates the whole kitchen when these cookies are baking in the oven. Orange is a classic partner with dates, and both add a richness to these healthy crumbly oat cookies.

Makes 25
150g/5oz/¾ cup soft dark
   brown sugar
150g/5oz/10 tbsp butter

finely grated rind of 1 unwaxed
   orange
150g/5oz/1¼ cups self-raising
   (self-rising) wholemeal
   (whole-wheat) flour
5ml/1 tsp baking powder
75g/3oz/⅔ cup medium oatmeal
75g/3oz/½ cup dried dates,
   roughly chopped

1 Preheat the oven to 180°C/350°F/Gas 4. Lightly grease two baking sheets.

2 Put the sugar and butter in a large bowl and beat together until light and fluffy. Stir in the orange rind.

3 In a separate bowl, sift the flour with the baking powder. Fold the flour mixture and then the oatmeal in to the butter and sugar mixture until well combined. Add the dates and mix well.

4 Place heaped tablespoonfuls of the mixture on to the prepared baking sheets, spacing them well apart to allow the mixture room for spreading. Bake in the oven for 15–20 minutes, until golden.

5 Leave the cookies to firm up slightly on the baking sheet for 1–2 minutes. Use a metal spatula to carefully transfer the cookies to wire racks and leave to cool completely. Store in an airtight container for 3–4 days.

Variation
Replace the dates with dried chopped apricots, raisins, sultanas (golden raisins) or figs.

Fruity Chocolate Cookie Cakes

The combination of spongy cookie, fruity preserve and dark chocolate makes irresistible eating. As cookies go, these are a little fiddly to make, but you will find that the finished resuts are worth the extra effort.

Makes 18
90g/3½oz/½ cup caster
   (superfine) sugar
2 eggs
50g/2oz/½ cup plain
   (all-purpose) flour
75g/3oz/6 tbsp orange
   marmalade or apricot jam
125g/4¼oz plain (semisweet)
   chocolate

1 Preheat the oven to 190°C/375°F/Gas 5. Lightly grease 18 patty tins (muffin pans), preferably non-stick.

2 Stand a mixing bowl in very hot water for a couple of minutes to heat through, keeping the inside of the bowl dry. Put the sugar and eggs in the bowl and whisk with a hand-held electric mixer until light and frothy and the beaters leave a ribbon trail when lifted. Sift the flour over the mixture and stir in gently using a large metal spoon.

3 Divide the sponge mixture among the patty tins. Bake for 10 minutes, until just firm and pale golden around the edges. Using a metal spatula, carefully lift from the sponges from the tins and transfer to a wire rack to cool.

4 Press the marmalade or jam through a sieve (strainer) to remove any rind or fruit pieces. Spoon a little of the smooth jam on to the centre of each sponge.

5 Break the chocolate into pieces and place in a heatproof bowl set over a pan of gently simmering water. Heat, stirring frequently, until melted and smooth.

6 Spoon a little chocolate on to the top of each cookie and spread to the edges, covering the jam completely. Once the chocolate has just started to set, very gently press it with the back of a fork to give a textured surface. Leave to set for at least 1 hour.

Date and Orange Energy 121kcal/508kJ; Protein 1.5g; Carbohydrate 17.4g, of which sugars 8.4g; Fat 5.5g, of which saturates 3.1g; Cholesterol 13mg; Calcium 17mg; Fibre 0.7g; Sodium 39mg.
Fruity Chocolate Energy 84kcal/353kJ; Protein 1.3g; Carbohydrate 14.7g, of which sugars 12.5g; Fat 2.6g, of which saturates 1.3g; Cholesterol 22mg; Calcium 12mg; Fibre 0.3g; Sodium 11mg.

Almond Orange Cookies

The combination of lard and almonds gives these traditional cookies a lovely short texture, so that they melt in the mouth, but you could use white cooking fat, if you like. Serve them whenever you have guests – they are perfect with coffee or hot chocolate.

Makes 36
250g/9oz/1½ cups lard, softened
125g/4½oz/generous ½ cup caster (superfine) sugar

2 eggs, beaten
grated rind and juice of 1 small orange
300g/11oz/2¾ cups plain (all-purpose) flour, plus extra for dusting
5ml/1 tsp baking powder
200g/7oz/1¾ cups ground almonds

For dusting
50g/2oz/½ cup icing (confectioners') sugar
5ml/1 tsp ground cinnamon

1 Preheat the oven to 200°C/400°F/Gas 6. Lightly grease two or three large baking sheets.

2 Place the lard in a large bowl and beat until light and fluffy. Gradually beat in the caster sugar.

3 Beat in the eggs, orange rind and juice until well combined, then sift over the flour and baking powder in batches and stir in after each addition. Add the almonds and bring together to form a dough.

4 Roll out on a lightly floured surface to 1cm/½in thick. Stamp out 36 rounds with a cookie cutter.

5 Lift the rounds on to the prepared baking sheets and bake for about 10 minutes, until golden. Leave on the baking sheets for 10 minutes to cool and firm slightly before transferring with a metal spatula to a wire rack to cool.

6 Place the wire rack over the baking sheet. Combine the icing sugar with the cinnamon and sift evenly over the cookies. Leave to cool completely.

Citrus Drops

These soft cake-like treats are deliciously tangy, with a zesty, crumbly base filled with sweet, sticky lemon or orange curd. The crunchy topping of almonds makes the perfect finish.

Makes about 20
175g/6oz/¾ cup unsalted (sweet) butter, at room temperature, diced
150g/5oz/¾ cup caster (superfine) sugar

finely grated rind of 1 large lemon
finely grated rind of 1 orange
2 egg yolks
50g/2oz/½ cup ground almonds
225g/8oz/2 cups self-raising (self-rising) flour
lemon and/or orange curd
milk, for brushing
flaked (sliced) almonds, for sprinkling

1 Preheat the oven to 160°C/325°F/Gas 3. Lightly grease two baking sheets.

2 In a large bowl, beat the butter and sugar together until light and fluffy, then stir in the citrus rinds.

3 Stir the egg yolks into the mixture, then add the ground almonds and flour and mix well.

4 Divide the mixture into 20 pieces and shape each into a smooth ball with your hands. Place on the baking sheets. Using the handle of a wooden spoon, make a hole in the centre of each cookie.

5 Put about 2.5ml/½ tsp lemon or orange curd into each hole and gently pinch the opening together with your fingers to semi-enclose the curd.

6 Brush the top of each cookie with milk and sprinkle with flaked almonds.

7 Bake for about 20 minutes, until pale golden brown. Leave to cool slightly on the baking sheets to firm up, then transfer to a wire rack using a metal spatula, and leave to cool completely.

Almond Orange Energy 148kcal/617kJ; Protein 2.3g; Carbohydrate 12.1g, of which sugars 5.6g; Fat 10.4g, of which saturates 3.1g; Cholesterol 17mg; Calcium 29mg; Fibre 0.7g; Sodium 5mg.
Citrus Drops Energy 157kcal/658kJ; Protein 2.1g; Carbohydrate 16.8g, of which sugars 8.2g; Fat 9.6g, of which saturates 4.9g; Cholesterol 39mg; Calcium 31mg; Fibre 0.6g; Sodium 55mg.

Candied Peel Crumble Cookies

Crumbly melt-in-the-mouth cookies, these incorporate candied peel, walnuts and white chocolate chips, and are coated with a zingy lemon glaze.

Makes about 24
175g/6oz/³⁄₄ cup unsalted
  (sweet) butter, at room
  temperature, diced
90g/3¹⁄₂oz/¹⁄₂ cup caster
  (superfine) sugar
1 egg, beaten
finely grated rind of 1 lemon

200g/7oz/1³⁄₄ cups self-raising
  (self-rising) flour
90g/3¹⁄₂oz/generous ¹⁄₂ cup
  candied peel, chopped
75g/3oz/³⁄₄ cup chopped walnuts
50g/2oz/¹⁄₃ cup white
  chocolate chips

For the glaze
50g/2oz/¹⁄₂ cup icing
  (confectioners') sugar,
  sifted
15ml/1 tbsp lemon juice
thin strips of candied peel,
  to decorate (optional)

1 Preheat the oven to 180°C/350°F/Gas 4. Lightly grease two baking sheets.

2 Put the butter and sugar in a large bowl and beat together until light and fluffy. Add the egg and beat well together.

3 Add the lemon rind and flour and stir together gently. Fold the candied peel, walnuts and chocolate chips into the mixture.

4 Place tablespoonfuls of the mixture, spaced slightly apart, on the baking sheets and bake in the oven for 12–15 minutes, until cooked but still pale in colour. Transfer the cookies to a wire rack using a metal spatula and to leave to cool completely.

5 For the glaze, put the icing sugar in a bowl and stir in the lemon juice. Spoon some glaze over each cookie. Decorate with candied peel, if using.

> **Variation**
> Replace the candied peel in the cookies with glacé (candied) cherries and decorate with a small piece of cherry on top.

Rosemary-scented Citrus Tuiles

These delicious crisp cookies are flavoured with tangy orange and lemon rind, and they are made beautifully fragrant with fresh rosemary – an unusual but winning combination.

Makes 18–20
50g/2oz/¹⁄₄ cup unsalted
  (sweet) butter, diced
2 egg whites

115g/4oz/generous ¹⁄₂ cup caster
  (superfine) sugar
finely grated rind of ¹⁄₂ lemon
finely grated rind of ¹⁄₂ orange
10ml/2 tsp finely chopped
  fresh rosemary
50g/2oz/¹⁄₂ cup plain
  (all-purpose) flour

1 Preheat the oven to 190°C/375°F/Gas 5. Lightly grease two baking sheets.

2 Melt the butter in a pan over a low heat. Remove the pan from the heat and leave to cool.

3 Whisk the egg whites until stiff, then gradually whisk in the sugar.

4 Fold the lemon and orange rinds, rosemary, flour and then the melted butter into the egg white mixture.

5 Place two large tablespoonfuls of the mixture on to a baking sheet. Spread each to a thin disc about 9cm/3¹⁄₂in in diameter. Bake for 5–6 minutes until golden.

6 Remove the baking sheet from the oven. Carefully lift the tuiles using a metal spatula, and drape them over a rolling pin. Transfer to a wire rack when set in a curved shape. Bake the rest of the mixture in the same way.

> **Cook's Tip**
> Don't be tempted to bake more than two tuiles at a time, or they will set firm before you have time to shape them.

Candied Peel Energy 150kcal/626kJ; Protein 1.8g; Carbohydrate 16.2g, of which sugars 9.8g; Fat 9.2g, of which saturates 4.4g; Cholesterol 23mg; Calcium 31mg; Fibre 0.5g; Sodium 61mg.
Rosemary-scented Citrus Tuiles Energy 51kcal/214kJ; Protein 0.6g; Carbohydrate 8g, of which sugars 6.1g; Fat 2.1g, of which saturates 1.3g; Cholesterol 5mg; Calcium 7mg; Fibre 0.1g; Sodium 22mg.

Coconut & Lime Macaroons

These pretty pistachio nut-topped cookies are crunchy on the outside and soft and gooey in the centre. The zesty lime topping contrasts wonderfully well with the sweetness of the coconut.

Makes 12–14
4 large (US extra large)
    egg whites
250g/9oz/3 cups desiccated
    (dry unsweetened
    shredded) coconut
150g/5oz/¾ cup sugar
10ml/2 tsp vanilla extract
25g/1oz/¼ cup plain
    (all-purpose) flour
115g/4oz/1 cup icing
    (confectioners') sugar, sifted
grated rind of 1 lime
15–20ml/3–4 tsp lime juice
about 15g/½oz/1 tbsp pistachio
    nuts, chopped

1 Preheat the oven to 180°C/350°F/Gas 4. Line two baking sheets with baking parchment.

2 Put the egg whites, desiccated coconut, sugar, vanilla extract and flour in a large, heavy pan. Mix well. Place over a low heat and cook for 6–8 minutes, stirring constantly to ensure it does not stick. When the mixture becomes the consistency of thick porridge (oatmeal), remove from the heat.

3 Place spoonfuls of the mixture in rocky piles on the lined baking sheets. Bake for 12–13 minutes, until golden. Leave to cool completely on the baking sheets.

4 To make the topping, put the icing sugar and lime rind into a bowl and add enough lime juice to give a thick pouring consistency. Place a spoonful of icing on to each macaroon and allow it to drip down the sides. Sprinkle over the pistachio nuts and serve.

Variation

If you prefer, make Coconut and Lemon Macaroons by substituting grated lemon rind and juice.

Apricot & Coconut Kisses

These tangy, fruity treats make a colourful addition to the tea table. Although they are easy to make and can be mixed and shaped in a matter of a few minutes, allow plenty of time for the apricots to soak and also for the cookies to chill before serving.

Makes 12
130g/4½oz/generous ½ cup
    ready-to-eat dried apricots
100ml/3½fl oz/scant ½ cup
    orange juice
40g/1½oz/3 tbsp unsalted
    (sweet) butter, at room
    temperature, diced
75g/3oz/¾ cup icing
    (confectioners') sugar,
    plus extra for dusting
90g/3½oz/generous 1 cup
    desiccated (dry unsweetened
    shredded) coconut,
    lightly toasted
2 glacé (candied) cherries,
    cut into wedges

1 Finely chop the dried apricots, then tip them into a bowl. Pour in the orange juice and leave to soak for about 1 hour, until all the juice has been absorbed.

2 In a large bowl, beat together the butter and sugar with a wooden spoon until pale and creamy. Gradually add the soaked apricots to the creamed butter and sugar mixture, beating well after each addition. Stir in the toasted coconut.

3 Lightly grease a small baking tray. Place teaspoonfuls of the coconut mixture on to the baking sheet, piling them up into little pyramids. Gently press the mixture together with your fingers to form neat shapes.

4 Top each cookie with a wedge of cherry. Chill in the refrigerator for about 1 hour until firm, then serve lightly dusted with icing sugar.

Cook's Tip

It is essential that all the orange juice has been absorbed by the apricots before adding them to the butter mixture, otherwise the cookies will be too moist to set properly.

Coconut and Lime Energy 198kcal/830kJ; Protein 2.3g; Carbohydrate 22.4g, of which sugars 21g; Fat 11.7g, of which saturates 9.6g; Cholesterol 0mg; Calcium 18mg; Fibre 2.6g; Sodium 29mg.
Apricot and Coconut Energy 115kcal/480kJ; Protein 1g; Carbohydrate 11.7g, of which sugars 11.7g; Fat 7.5g, of which saturates 5.7g; Cholesterol 7mg; Calcium 14mg; Fibre 1.7g; Sodium 25mg.

Apricot & Hazelnut Oat Cookies

These cookie-cum-flapjacks have a chewy, crumbly texture. They are sprinkled with apricots and toasted hazelnuts, but any combination of dried fruit and nuts can be used.

Makes 9
115g/4oz/1 cup self-raising (self-rising) flour, sifted
115g/4oz/1 cup rolled oats
75g/3oz/scant ½ cup chopped ready-to-eat dried apricots
115g/4oz/½ cup unsalted (sweet) butter
75g/3oz/scant ½ cup golden caster (superfine) sugar
15ml/1 tbsp clear honey

For the topping
25g/1oz/2 tbsp chopped ready-to-eat dried apricots
25g/1oz/¼ cup toasted and chopped hazelnuts

1 Preheat the oven to 160°C/325°F/Gas 3. Lightly grease a large baking sheet.

2 Put the flour, oats and chopped apricots in a large mixing bowl.

3 Put the butter, sugar and honey in a pan and cook over a gentle heat until the butter melts and the sugar dissolves, stirring the mixture occasionally. Remove the pan from the heat.

4 Pour the honey and sugar mixture into the bowl containing the flour, oats and apricots. Mix with a wooden spoon to form a sticky dough.

5 Divide the dough into nine pieces and place on the prepared baking sheet. Press into 1cm/½in thick rounds.

6 Scatter over the topping of apricots and hazelnuts and press into the dough. Bake the cookies for about 15 minutes, until they are golden and slightly crisp. Leave to cool on the baking sheet for 5 minutes, then transfer to a wire rack to cool completely.

Cherry Coconut Munchies

You'll find it hard to stop at just one of these munchies, which make a wonderful morning or afternoon treat. If you like, drizzle 25–50g/1–2oz melted chocolate over the cold munchies and leave to set before serving.

Makes 20
2 egg whites
115g/4oz/1 cup icing (confectioners') sugar, sifted
115g/4oz/1 cup ground almonds
115g/4oz/generous 1 cup desiccated (dry unsweetened shredded) coconut
few drops of almond extract
75g/3oz/⅓ cup glacé (candied) cherries, finely chopped

1 Preheat the oven to 150°C/300°F/Gas 2. Line two baking sheets with baking parchment.

2 Place the egg whites in a grease-free bowl and whisk until stiff peaks form.

3 Gently fold in the icing sugar using a metal spoon. Fold in the ground almonds, coconut and almond extract to form a sticky dough. Finally, fold in the chopped glacé cherries.

4 Place mounds on the baking sheets. Bake for 25 minutes. Allow to cool and set briefly on the baking sheets, then transfer to a wire rack.

Cook's Tips
• These cookies are at their best when just baked, but may be stored in an airtight container for up to 3 days.
• When whisking egg whites, avoid using a plastic bowl, as plastic scratches easily.

Variation
Use ground hazelnuts in place of the almonds and omit the almond extract.

Apricot and Hazelnut Energy 262kcal/1098kJ; Protein 3.7g; Carbohydrate 33.2g, of which sugars 14.4g; Fat 13.6g, of which saturates 6.8g; Cholesterol 27mg; Calcium 71mg; Fibre 2.1g; Sodium 130mg.
Cherry Coconut Energy 103kcal/431kJ; Protein 1.9g; Carbohydrate 9.3g, of which sugars 9.1g; Fat 6.8g, of which saturates 3.3g; Cholesterol 0mg; Calcium 20mg; Fibre 1.2g; Sodium 10mg.

Microwave Fruit & Nut Cookies

These irresistible cookies
make the best of familiar
flapjacks and old-fashioned,
chocolate-coated Florentines.

Makes 16
75g/3oz/6 tbsp butter
45ml/3 tbsp/¼ cup golden
   (light corn) syrup
115g/4oz/1¼ cups rolled oats

25g/1oz/2 tbsp soft brown sugar
25g/1oz/2 tbsp chopped
   mixed candied peel
25g/1oz/2 tbsp glacé
   (candied) cherries,
   coarsely chopped
25g/1oz/¼ cup hazelnuts,
   coarsely chopped
115g/4oz/⅔ cup plain
   (semisweet) chocolate

1 Lightly grease a 20cm/8in square microwave-proof
dish and line the base with a sheet of rice paper.

2 Place the butter and golden syrup in a microwave-proof
bowl and microwave on full (100 per cent) power for
1½ minutes until melted. Stir well together.

3 Add the oats, sugar, peel, cherries and hazelnuts and mix well.

4 Spoon the mixture into the dish and level the surface with the
back of a spoon. Microwave on full (100 per cent) power for
6 minutes, giving the dish a half turn every 2 minutes. Allow to
cool slightly, then cut into 16 fingers and place on a wire rack.

5 Break the chocolate into pieces and put in a microwave-
proof bowl. Microwave on full (100 per cent) power for
2–3 minutes, stirring twice, until melted and smooth.

6 Spread the chocolate over the tops of the cookies and mark
in a zig-zag pattern with the prongs of a fork. Leave to set.

Cook's Tip
*Rice paper is used for cooking in traditional recipes as well as
in microwave methods. It prevents mixtures, such as this sweet
oat base, from sticking by cooking on to them. When cooked,
the rice paper can be eaten with the biscuits or other items.*

Mini Florentines with Grand Marnier

Orange liqueur adds a note
of glorious luxury to these
ever-popular nut and dried
fruit cookies. These mini
versions would be delicious
with dessert or after-dinner
coffee and liqueurs.

Makes about 24
50g/2oz/¼ cup soft light
   brown sugar
15ml/1 tbsp clear honey

15ml/1 tbsp Grand Marnier
50g/2oz/¼ cup butter
40g/1½oz/⅓ cup plain
   (all-purpose) flour
25g/1oz/¼ cup hazelnuts,
   coarsely chopped
50g/2oz/½ cup flaked (sliced)
   almonds, chopped
50g/2oz/¼ cup glacé (candied)
   cherries, chopped
115g/4oz dark (bittersweet)
   chocolate, melted, for coating

1 Preheat the oven to 180°C/350°F/Gas 4. Line two or three
baking sheets with baking parchment.

2 Combine the sugar, honey, Grand Marnier and butter in a
small pan and melt over a low heat.

3 Remove the pan from the heat and tip in the flour, hazelnuts,
almonds and cherries. Stir well.

4 Spoon small heaps of the mixture on to the baking sheets.
Bake for about 10 minutes, until golden brown. Leave the
cookies on the baking sheets until the edges begin to harden
a little, then remove and cool on a wire rack.

5 Spread the melted chocolate over the underside of each
Florentine with a round-bladed knife. When the chocolate is
just beginning to set, drag a fork through to make wavy lines.
Leave to set completely.

Variation
*For an extra decoration, pour melted milk, plain (semisweet)
or white chocolate into a paper piping (pastry) bag, snip
off the end and pipe zig-zag lines over the plain side of
each Florentine.*

Microwave Cookies Energy 133kcal/555kJ; Protein 1.5g; Carbohydrate 15.7g, of which sugars 10.4g; Fat 7.5g, of which saturates 3.7g; Cholesterol 10mg; Calcium 14mg; Fibre 0.9g; Sodium 44mg.
Mini Florentines Energy 82kcal/342kJ; Protein 1g; Carbohydrate 8.6g, of which sugars 7.2g; Fat 4.9g, of which saturates 2g; Cholesterol 5mg; Calcium 13mg; Fibre 0.4g; Sodium 14mg.

Chocolate & Prune Cookies

When freshly baked, these cookies have a deliciously gooey centre. As they cool down, the mixture hardens slightly to form a firmer, fudge-like consistency.

Makes 18

150g/5oz/⅔ cup butter, at room temperature, diced
150g/5oz/¾ cup caster (superfine) sugar
I egg yolk
250g/9oz/2¼ cups self-raising (self-rising) flour
25g/1oz/¼ cup unsweetened cocoa powder
about 90g/3½oz plain (semisweet) chocolate, coarsely chopped

For the topping

50g/2oz plain (semisweet) chocolate
9 ready-to-eat prunes, halved

1 Preheat the oven to 190°C/375°F/Gas 5. Line two baking sheets with baking parchment.

2 Beat the butter and sugar together until light and creamy. Beat in the egg yolk. Sift over the flour and cocoa powder and stir in to make a firm yet soft dough.

3 Roll out a third of the dough on baking parchment. Using a 5cm/2in cookie cutter, stamp out 18 rounds and place them on the baking sheets. Sprinke the chopped chocolate in the centre of each cookie.

4 Roll out the remaining dough in the same way and, using a 7.5cm/3in round cookie cutter, stamp out 18 'lids'. Place the lids over the cookie bases and press the edges together to seal.

5 Bake for about 10 minutes, until the cookies have spread a little and are just firm to the touch. Leave them on the baking sheets for a few minutes to firm up, then, using a metal spatula, transfer to a wire rack to cool completely.

6 For the topping, melt the chocolate in a heatproof bowl set over a pan of gently simmering water. Dip the cut side of the prunes in the chocolate, then place one on top of each cookie. Spoon any remaining chocolate over the prunes.

Banana Cream Cookies

These delicious cookies are inspired by the classic childhood dessert, bananas and cream. The warm banana cookies are coated in crisp sugar-frosted cornflakes and, for the ultimate indulgence, they are delicious served warm drizzled with clear honey.

Makes about 24

2 eggs
250g/9oz/1¼ cups soft light brown sugar
5ml/1 tsp vanilla extract
100ml/3½fl oz/scant ½ cup sunflower oil
90g/3½oz/scant ½ cup crème fraîche
200g/7oz/1¾ cups plain (all-purpose) flour
200g/7oz/1¾ cups self-raising (self-rising) flour
50g/2oz/2½ cups frosted cornflakes
125g/4¼oz dried small bananas, chopped, or 2 bananas, peeled and chopped
icing (confectioners') sugar, sifted, for dredging

1 Put the eggs and sugar in a large bowl and whisk together until well blended. Stir in the vanilla extract.

2 Add the oil and crème fraîche and stir well to combine. Add the flours and mix thoroughly. (The mixture will be quite runny at this stage.) Cover with clear film (plastic wrap) and chill for about 30 minutes.

3 Preheat the oven to 180°C/350°F/Gas 4. Lightly grease two or three baking sheets.

4 Put the frosted cornflakes in a large bowl. Remove the cookie dough from the refrigerator and stir in the bananas.

5 Using a tablespoon, drop heaps of the cookie mixture into the cornflakes. Lightly toss so that each cookie is well coated, then remove and place on the prepared baking sheets. Flatten slightly with your fingertips.

6 Bake for 15–20 minutes, or until risen and golden brown and crispy. Transfer the cookies to a wire rack and dredge with sifted icing sugar. Serve while still warm.

Chocolate and Prune Energy 197kcal/825kJ; Protein 2.3g; Carbohydrate 26.4g, of which sugars 15.5g; Fat 9.8g, of which saturates 5.9g; Cholesterol 29mg; Calcium 33mg; Fibre 1.1g; Sodium 66mg.
Banana Cream Energy 159kcal/669kJ; Protein 2.5g; Carbohydrate 27.7g, of which sugars 13.1g; Fat 5g, of which saturates 1.5g; Cholesterol 20mg; Calcium 34mg; Fibre 0.6g; Sodium 29mg.

Apple Crumble & Custard Slices

These luscious apple slices are easy to make using ready-made sweet pastry and custard. Just think, all the ingredients of one of the world's most popular desserts – in a cookie.

Makes 16
350g/12oz ready-made
  sweet pastry dough
1 large cooking apple, about
  250g/9oz

30ml/2 tbsp caster
  (superfine) sugar
60ml/4 tbsp ready-made
  thick custard

For the crumble topping
115g/4oz/1 cup plain
  (all-purpose) flour
2.5ml/½ tsp ground cinnamon
60ml/4 tbsp sugar
90g/3½oz/7 tbsp unsalted
  (sweet) butter, melted

1 Preheat the oven to 190°C/375°F/Gas 5. Lightly grease a 28 × 18cm/11 × 7in shallow cake tin (pan).

2 Roll out the dough and use to line the base of the tin. Prick the dough with a fork, line with foil and baking beans and bake blind for about 10–15 minutes. Remove the foil and baking beans and return the pastry to the oven for another 5 minutes, until cooked and golden brown.

3 Meanwhile, peel, core and chop the apple. Place in a pan with the sugar. Heat gently until the sugar dissolves, then cover with a lid and cook gently for 5–7 minutes, until a thick purée is formed. Beat with a wooden spoon and set aside to cool.

4 Mix the cold apple with the custard. Spread over the pastry base in an even layer.

5 To make the crumble topping, put the flour, cinnamon and sugar into a bowl and pour over the melted butter. Stir thoroughly until the mixture forms small clumps. Sprinkle the crumble over the filling.

6 Return to the oven and bake for about 10–15 minutes, until the crumble topping is cooked and golden brown. Leave to cool in the tin, then slice into bars to serve.

Fruity Breakfast Bars

Instead of buying fruit and cereal bars from the supermarket, try making this quick and easy version – these are much tastier and more nutritious than most of the commercially made ones. They can be stored in an airtight container for up to four days.

Makes 12
270g/10oz/1¼ cups ready-made
  apple sauce
115g/4oz/½ cup ready-to-eat
  dried apricots, chopped

115g/4oz/¾ cup raisins
50g/2oz/¼ cup demerara
  (raw) sugar
50g/2oz/scant ½ cup
  sunflower seeds
25g/1oz/2 tbsp sesame seeds
25g/1oz/¼ cup pumpkin seeds
75g/3oz/scant 1 cup rolled oats
75g/3oz/¾ cup self-raising
  (self-rising) wholemeal
  (whole-wheat) flour
50g/2oz/⅔ cup desiccated
  (dry unsweetened
  shredded) coconut
2 eggs

1 Preheat the oven to 200°C/400°F/Gas 6. Lightly grease a 20cm/8in square shallow baking tin (pan) and line with baking parchment.

2 Put the apple sauce in a large bowl with the apricots, raisins, sugar and the sunflower, sesame and pumpkin seeds and stir together with a wooden spoon until thoroughly mixed.

3 Add the oats, flour, coconut and eggs to the fruit mixture and gently stir together until evenly combined.

4 Turn the mixture into the tin and spread to the edges in an even layer. Bake for about 25 minutes, or until golden and just firm to the touch.

5 Leave to cool in the tin, then lift out on to a board and cut into bars.

Cook's Tip
It's best to sift the flour before adding it to the mixture.

Apple Crumble Energy 196kcal/822kJ; Protein 2.1g; Carbohydrate 23.7g, of which sugars 8.1g; Fat 11g, of which saturates 4.9g; Cholesterol 15mg; Calcium 37mg; Fibre 0.9g; Sodium 124mg.
Fruity Breakfast Energy 207kcal/871kJ; Protein 4.9g; Carbohydrate 29.3g, of which sugars 19.2g; Fat 8.7g, of which saturates 3g; Cholesterol 32mg; Calcium 65mg; Fibre 2.8g; Sodium 24mg.

Sticky Marmalade Squares

These baked treats have a plain lower layer supporting a scrumptious nutty upper layer flavoured with orange and chunky marmalade. Cut into squares or bars – whichever you prefer.

Makes 24
350g/12oz/3 cups plain
  (all-purpose) flour
200g/7oz/scant 1 cup unsalted
  (sweet) butter, diced
150g/5oz/²/₃ cup light muscovado
  (brown) sugar
2.5ml/¹/₂ tsp bicarbonate of soda
  (baking soda)
1 egg, beaten
120ml/4fl oz/¹/₂ cup single
  (light) cream
50g/2oz/¹/₂ cup pecan
  nuts, chopped
50g/2oz/¹/₃ cup mixed
  (candied) peel
90ml/6 tbsp chunky marmalade
15–30ml/1–2 tbsp orange juice

1 Preheat the oven to 190°C/375°F/Gas 5. Line the base of a 28 × 18cm/11 × 7in tin (pan) with baking parchment.

2 Put the flour in a bowl and rub in the butter with your fingertips. Stir in the sugar and then spread half over the base of the prepared tin. Press down firmly. Bake for 10–15 minutes, until lightly browned. Leave to cool.

3 To make the filling, put the remaining flour mixture into a bowl. Stir in the bicarbonate of soda. Mix in the egg and cream, pecan nuts, peel and half the marmalade.

4 Pour the mixture over the cooled base Bake for 20–25 minutes, or until the filling is just firm and golden.

5 Put the remaining marmalade into a small pan and heat gently. Add just enough orange juice to make a spreadable glaze. Brush the glaze over the baked cookie mixture while it is still warm. Leave to cool. Cut into bars.

Variation
These bars would be just as delicious made with lemon, lime, grapefruit or mixed fruit marmalade instead of orange.

Chewy Orange Flapjacks

Flapjacks are about the easiest cookies to make and, with a little guidance, can be knocked up in minutes by even the youngest cooks. This chunky, chewy version is flavoured with orange rind, but you can substitute other fruits such as a handful of raisins, chopped prunes or apricots.

Makes 18
250g/9oz/generous 1 cup
  unsalted (sweet) butter
finely grated rind of 1 large
  orange
225g/8oz/²/₃ cup golden
  (light corn) syrup
75g/3oz/¹/₃ cup light muscovado
  (brown) sugar
375g/13oz/3³/₄ cups
  rolled oats

1 Preheat the oven to 180°C/350°F/Gas 4. Line the base and sides of a 28 × 20cm/11 × 8in shallow baking tin (pan) with baking parchment.

2 Put the butter, orange rind, syrup and sugar in a large pan and heat gently until the butter has melted.

3 Add the oats to the pan and stir to mix thoroughly. Tip the mixture into the tin and spread into the corners in an even layer.

4 Bake for 15–20 minutes, until just beginning to colour around the edges. (The mixture will still be very soft but will harden as it cools.) Leave to cool in the tin.

5 Lift the flapjack out of the tin in one piece and cut into fingers.

Cook's Tips
• *'Flapjack' is the British name for this traditional British cookie – in the United States, the term refers to pancakes. But whether you call them flapjacks or energy bars, these oaty treats are always delicious.*
• *Don't be tempted to overcook flapjacks; they'll turn crisp and dry, and will lose their lovely chewy texture.*

Chewy Orange Energy 241kcal/1007kJ; Protein 2.7g; Carbohydrate 29.5g, of which sugars 14.3g; Fat 13.2g, of which saturates 7.2g; Cholesterol 30mg; Calcium 18mg; Fibre 1.4g; Sodium 125mg.
Sticky Marmalade Energy 194kcal/809kJ; Protein 2.1g; Carbohydrate 22g, of which sugars 10.9g; Fat 11.4g, of which saturates 6.2g; Cholesterol 33mg; Calcium 36mg; Fibre 0.7g; Sodium 77mg.

Fruity Lemon Drizzle Bars

These tangy iced, spongy bars are great for popping in lunchboxes. Experiment with other filling combinations, such as orange, dried apricots and dried pineapple.

Makes 16
250g/9oz ready-made sweet
   shortcrust pastry dough
90g/3¼ oz/³⁄₄ cup self-raising
   (self-rising) flour
75g/3oz/³⁄₄ cup fine or
   medium oatmeal
5ml/1 tsp baking powder
130g/4½oz/generous ½ cup light
   muscovado (brown) sugar
2 eggs
150g/5oz/²⁄₃ cup unsalted
   (sweet) butter, at room
   temperature, diced
finely grated rind of 1 lemon
90g/3½oz/³⁄₄ cup sultanas
   (golden raisins)
150g/5oz/1¼ cups icing
   (confectioners') sugar
15–20ml/3–4 tsp lemon juice

1 Preheat the oven to 190°C/375°F/Gas 5 and place a baking sheet in the oven to heat through. Generously grease a 28 × 18cm/11 × 7in shallow baking tin (pan).

2 Roll out the dough thinly on a lightly floured, clean surface. Line the base of the baking tin, pressing the pastry up the sides.

3 Put the flour, oatmeal, baking powder, sugar, eggs, butter and lemon rind in a mixing bowl. Beat for 2 minutes with a hand-held electric whisk until pale and creamy. Stir in the sultanas.

4 Tip the filling into the pastry case (pie shell) and spread evenly. Place the tin on the heated baking sheet in the oven and bake for about 30 minutes, until pale golden and firm.

5 Put the icing sugar in a small bowl with enough lemon juice to mix to a thin paste, about the consistency of thin cream.

6 Using a teaspoon, drizzle the icing diagonally across the warm cake in thin lines. Leave to cool in the tin.

7 When the icing has set, use a sharp knife to cut the cake in half lengthways. Cut each half across into 8 even-size bars.

Apricot & Pecan Flapjacks

A tried-and-tested favourite made even more delicious by the addition of maple syrup, fruit and nuts. This is a real energy booster at any time of day – great for kids and adults alike.

Makes 10
150g/5oz/²⁄₃ cup unsalted
   (sweet) butter, diced
150g/5oz/²⁄₃ cup light
   muscovado (brown) sugar
30ml/2 tbsp maple syrup
200g/7oz/2 cups rolled oats
50g/2oz/½ cup pecan
   nuts, chopped
50g/2oz/¼ cup ready-to-eat
   dried apricots, chopped

1 Preheat the oven to 160°C/325°F/Gas 3. Lightly grease an 18cm/7in square shallow baking tin (pan).

2 Put the butter, sugar and maple syrup in a large heavy pan and heat gently, stirring occasionally, until the butter has melted. Remove from the heat and stir in the oats, nuts and apricots until thoroughly combined.

3 Spread evenly in the prepared tin and, using a knife, score the mixture into ten bars. Bake for about 25–30 minutes, or until golden.

4 Remove from the oven and cut through the scored lines. Leave until completely cold before removing from the tin.

Cook's Tip
Make sure that you stir the syrup mixture quite frequently to prevent it from sticking to the base of the pan.

Variations
• *You can substitute walnuts for the pecan nuts, if you like, although the nutty flavour won't be so intense.*
• *Try using different dried fruits instead of the apricots.*

Fruity Lemon Energy 272kcal/1141kJ; Protein 3.1g; Carbohydrate 37.3g, of which sugars 22.5g; Fat 13.3g, of which saturates 6.5g; Cholesterol 46mg; Calcium 42mg; Fibre 0.9g; Sodium 132mg.
Apricot and Pecan Energy 240kcal/1000kJ; Protein 3.2g; Carbohydrate 18.3g, of which sugars 3.7g; Fat 17.6g, of which saturates 8.1g; Cholesterol 32mg; Calcium 21mg; Fibre 1.9g; Sodium 98mg.

Granola Bars

A gloriously dense fruity, nutty and oaty mixture, packed with goodness and delicious too, these bars are an ideal snack and perfect to pack for a school lunch.

Makes 12
175g/6oz/³⁄₄ cup unsalted (sweet) butter, diced
150g/5oz/²⁄₃ cup clear honey
250g/9oz/generous 1 cup demerara (raw) sugar
350g/12oz/3 cups jumbo oats
5ml/1 tsp ground cinnamon
75g/3oz/³⁄₄ cup pecan nut halves
75g/3oz/generous ¹⁄₂ cup raisins
75g/3oz/¹⁄₃ cup ready-to-eat dried papaya, chopped
75g/3oz/¹⁄₃ cup ready-to-eat dried apricots, chopped
50g/2oz/¹⁄₂ cup pumpkin seeds
50g/2oz/scant ¹⁄₂ cup sunflower seeds
50g/2oz/¹⁄₄ cup sesame seeds
50g/2oz/¹⁄₂ cup ground almonds

1 Preheat the oven to 190°C/375°F/Gas 5. Line a 23cm/9in square cake tin (pan) with baking parchment.

2 Put the butter and honey in a large heavy pan and heat gently until the butter has melted and the mixture is completely smooth.

3 Add the demerara sugar to the pan and heat very gently, stirring constantly, until the sugar has completely dissolved. Bring the butter mixture to the boil and continue to boil for 1–2 minutes, stirring the mixture constantly until it has formed a smooth caramel sauce.

4 Add the remaining ingredients and mix together. Transfer the mixture to the tin and press down with a spoon. Bake for 15 minutes, until the edges turn brown.

5 Leave to cool, then chill for 1–2 hours. Turn out of the tin, peel off the parchment and cut into bars.

> **Variation**
> *You can use other dried fruits, such as mango and pear.*

Apricot Specials

These attractive bars taste great with tea, coffee or a cold drink, and fit the bill perfectly whenever you need a nutritious snack. They're surprisingly easy to make, too.

Makes 12
90g/3¹⁄₂oz/generous ¹⁄₃ cup soft light brown sugar
75g/3oz/³⁄₄ cup plain (all-purpose) flour
75g/3oz/6 tbsp unsalted (sweet) butter, chilled and diced

For the topping
150g/5oz/generous ¹⁄₂ cup ready-to-eat dried apricots
250ml/8fl oz/1 cup water
grated rind of 1 lemon
55g/2¹⁄₂oz/5 tbsp caster (superfine) sugar
10ml/2 tsp cornflour (cornstarch)
50g/2oz/¹⁄₂ cup chopped walnuts

1 Preheat the oven to 180°C/350°F/Gas 4.

2 In a bowl, combine the brown sugar and flour. Rub in the butter with your fingertips until the mixture resembles coarse breadcrumbs.

3 Spoon the flour and butter mixture into a 20cm/8in square baking tin (pan) and level the surface by pressing down with the back of a spoon. Bake for 15 minutes, until just set. Remove from the oven but leave the oven switched on.

4 To make the topping, put the apricots into a pan and pour in the measured water. Bring to the boil, then lower the heat and simmer for about 10 minutes, until soft. Strain, reserving the cooking liquid. Chop the apricots.

5 Return the apricots to the pan and add the lemon rind, caster sugar, cornflour, and 60ml/4 tbsp of the soaking liquid. Cook for 1 minute.

6 Cool slightly before spreading the topping over the base. Sprinkle over the walnuts and continue baking for 20 minutes more. Leave to cool in the tin before cutting into bars.

Apricot Specials Energy 169kcal/711kJ; Protein 1.8g; Carbohydrate 23.9g, of which sugars 18.3g; Fat 8.1g, of which saturates 3.5g; Cholesterol 13mg; Calcium 30mg; Fibre 1.1g; Sodium 41mg.
Granola Bars Energy 522kcal/2189kJ; Protein 8.4g; Carbohydrate 63.8g, of which sugars 40.9g; Fat 27.7g, of which saturates 8.9g; Cholesterol 31mg; Calcium 93mg; Fibre 4.3g; Sodium 108mg.

Almond-scented Chocolate Cherry Wedges

These cookies are a chocoholic's dream when made with the very best-quality chocolate. Erratically shaped, they are packed with crunchy cookies, juicy raisins and munchy nuts.

Makes about 15
50g/2oz ratafia biscuits (almond macaroons) or small amaretti
90g/3¹/₂oz shortcake biscuits (cookies)

150g/5oz/1 cup jumbo raisins
50g/2oz/¹/₄ cup natural glacé (candied) cherries, quartered
450g/1lb dark (bittersweet) chocolate (minimum 70 per cent cocoa solids)
90g/3¹/₂oz/scant ¹/₂ cup unsalted (sweet) butter, diced
30ml/2 tbsp amaretto liqueur (optional)
25g/1oz/¹/₄ cup toasted flaked (sliced) almonds

1 Line a baking sheet with baking parchment.

2 Put the ratafia biscuits in a large bowl. Break half of them into coarse pieces. Break the shortcakes into three or four pieces and add to the bowl. Add the raisins and glacé cherries and mix well.

3 Melt the chocolate and butter with the liqueur, if using, in a heatproof bowl set over a pan of gently simmering water, stirring until smooth and combined. Remove from the heat and set aside to cool slightly.

4 Pour the chocolate over the cookie mixture and toss lightly together until everything is coated in chocolate. Spread out over the prepared baking sheet.

5 Sprinkle over the almonds and push them in at angles so they stick well to the chocolate-coated cookies. Leave in a cool place until set.

6 When the mixture is completely cold and set, cut into long, thin triangles.

Nutty Marshmallow & Chocolate Squares

Unashamedly sweet, with chocolate, marshmallows, cherries, nuts and coconut, this recipe is a favourite for anyone with a sweet tooth.

Makes 9
200g/7oz digestive biscuits (graham crackers)
90g/3¹/₂oz plain (semisweet) chocolate

200g/7oz coloured mini marshmallows
150g/5oz/1¹/₄ cups chopped walnuts
90g/3¹/₂oz/scant ¹/₂ cup glacé (candied) cherries, halved
50g/2oz/²/₃ cup desiccated (dry unsweetened shredded) coconut
350g/12oz milk chocolate

1 Put the digestive biscuits in a plastic bag and, using a rolling pin, crush them until they are fairly small. Transfer the crumbs to a bowl.

2 Melt the plain chocolate in a heatproof bowl set over a pan of gently simmering water. Pour the melted plain chocolate over the broken biscuits and stir well.

3 Spread the mixture in the base of a 20cm/8in square shallow cake tin (pan).

4 Put the marshmallows, walnuts, cherries and coconut in a large bowl.

5 Melt the milk chocolate in a heatproof bowl set over a pan of gently simmering water. Pour the melted milk chocolate over the marshmallow and nut mixture and toss gently together until almost everything is coated. Spread the mixture over the chocolate base. Chill until set, then cut into squares.

Variation
Other nuts can be used instead of the walnuts – the choice is yours.

Almond Wedges Energy 288kcal/1206kJ; Protein 2.7g; Carbohydrate 34.6g, of which sugars 29.7g; Fat 16.4g, of which saturates 9.5g; Cholesterol 20mg; Calcium 31mg; Fibre 1.3g; Sodium 75mg.
Marshmallow Energy 603kcal/2523kJ; Protein 8.6g; Carbohydrate 69.7g, of which sugars 53.2g; Fat 34.1g, of which saturates 14.7g; Cholesterol 19mg; Calcium 133mg; Fibre 2.5g; Sodium 179mg.

Sultana & Cinnamon Chewy Bars

These spicy, chewy bars are hard to resist and make a great treat, especially for children and teenagers.

Makes 16
115g/4oz/½ cup butter
25g/1oz/2 tbsp light soft
   brown sugar
25g/1oz plain toffees
50g/2oz/¼ cup clear honey
175g/6oz/generous 1 cup
   sultanas (golden raisins)
10ml/2 tsp ground cinnamon
175g/6oz/6 cups crisped
   rice cereal

1 Lightly grease a shallow rectangular 23 × 28cm/9 × 11in cake tin (pan).

2 Place the butter, sugar, toffees and honey in a pan and heat gently until melted, stirring. Bring to the boil, then remove the pan from the heat.

3 Stir in the sultanas, cinnamon and crisped rice cereal and mix well. Transfer the mixture to the prepared tin and spread the mixture evenly, pressing it down firmly.

4 Leave to cool, then chill until firm. Cut into bars, and serve. Store the bars in an airtight container in the refrigerator.

Cook's Tip
Take care when melting the butter, sugar, toffees and honey, and stir constantly to prevent the mixture from catching.

Variation
For an extra-special treat, melt 75g/3oz plain (semisweet) or milk chocolate in a heatproof bowl over a pan of gently simmering water, then spread it over the cold crisped rice cereal mixture. Alternatively, using a teaspoon or a paper piping (pastry) bag, drizzle it decoratively over the mixture. Leave to set for about 1 hour before cutting into bars.

Spicy Fruit Slices

A double-layered sweet cookie in which the topping combines dried fruit, with grated carrot to keep it moist. It is a truly indulgent teatime treat.

Makes 12–16
90g/3½oz/7 tbsp butter
75g/3oz/scant ½ cup caster
   (superfine) sugar
1 egg yolk
115g/4oz/1 cup plain
   (all-purpose) flour
30ml/2 tbsp self-raising
   (self-rising) flour
30ml/2 tbsp desiccated
   (dry unsweetened
   shredded) coconut
icing (confectioners') sugar,
   for dusting

For the topping
30ml/2 tbsp ready-to-eat
   prunes, chopped
30ml/2 tbsp sultanas
   (golden raisins)
50g/2oz/½ cup ready-to-eat
   dried pears, chopped
25g/1oz/¼ cup walnuts,
   chopped
75g/3oz/¾ cup self-raising
   (self-rising) flour
5ml/1 tsp ground cinnamon
2.5ml/½ tsp ground ginger
175g/6oz/generous 1 cup
   grated carrots
1 egg, beaten
75ml/5 tbsp vegetable oil
2.5ml/½ tsp bicarbonate of soda
   (baking soda)
90g/3½oz/scant ½ cup
   muscovado sugar (molasses)

1 Preheat the oven to 180°C/350°F/Gas 4. Line a 28 × 18cm/11 × 7in shallow baking tin (pan) with baking parchment.

2 In a large mixing bowl, beat together the butter, sugar and egg yolk until smooth and creamy.

3 Stir in the plain flour, self-raising flour and coconut and mix together well. Press into the base of the prepared tin, using your fingers to spread the dough evenly.

4 Bake for about 15 minutes, or until firm to the touch and light golden brown.

5 To make the topping, mix together all the ingredients and spread over the cooked base. Bake for about 35 minutes, or until firm. Cool completely in the tin before cutting into bars or squares. Dust with icing sugar.

Sultana and Cinnamon Energy 145kcal/608kJ; Protein 1.1g; Carbohydrate 22.2g, of which sugars 12.8g; Fat 6.4g, of which saturates 3.9g; Cholesterol 16mg; Calcium 60mg; Fibre 0.3g; Sodium 122mg.
Spicy Fruit Slices Energy 228kcal/955kJ; Protein 2.7g; Carbohydrate 29.7g, of which sugars 13.9g; Fat 11.8g, of which saturates 3.8g; Cholesterol 25mg; Calcium 34mg; Fibre 1.1g; Sodium 55mg.

Chocolate & Prune Bars

Wickedly self-indulgent and very easy to make, these fruity chocolate bars will keep for 2–3 days in the refrigerator – if they don't all get eaten immediately. You could try adding different combinations of dried fruit.

Makes 12 bars
250g/9oz good-quality
  milk chocolate
50g/2oz/¼ cup butter
115g/4oz digestive biscuits
  (graham crackers)
115g/4oz/½ cup
  ready-to-eat prunes

1 Break the chocolate into small pieces and place in a heatproof bowl. Add the butter and place the bowl over a pan of gently simmering water until the butter and chocolate have melted. Stir to mix and set aside.

2 Put the digestive biscuits in a plastic bag and seal it, then crush them into small pieces with a rolling pin.

3 Coarsely chop the prunes and stir into the melted chocolate with the biscuits.

4 Spoon the chocolate and prune mixture into a 20cm/8in square cake tin (pan) and chill for 1–2 hours until set. Remove the cake from the refrigerator and cut into 12 bars.

Cook's Tip
Do not cover the bars with cling film (plastic wrap) when chilling, as condensation may spoil their texture.

Variations
• *Other dried fruits are also delicious in these bars. Try dried plums, which are not quite the same as prunes, and are usually made from golden rather than red varieties. Apricots would also be a good alternative in this recipe.*
• *For extra flavour, stir 1.5ml/¼ tsp freshly grated nutmeg or 2.5ml/½ tsp ground cinnamon into the chocolate mixture.*

Spiced Raisin Squares

Moist and aromatic, these tasty fruit bars make great any-time-of-day snacks, and are the perfect choice for a summer picnic basket.

Makes 30
115g/4oz/1 cup plain
  (all-purpose) flour
7.5ml/1½ tsp baking powder
5ml/1 tsp ground cinnamon
2.5ml/½ tsp freshly grated
  nutmeg

1.5ml/¼ tsp ground cloves
1.5ml/¼ tsp ground allspsice
200g/7oz/1½ cups raisins
115g/4oz/½ cup butter,
  at room temperature
90g/3½oz/½ cup caster
  (superfine) sugar
2 eggs
165g/5½oz/scant ½ cup
  black treacle (molasses)
50g/2oz/½ cup walnuts,
  chopped

1 Preheat the oven to 180°C/350°F/Gas 4. Line a 33 × 23cm/13 × 9in tin (pan) with baking parchment and lightly grease the surface.

2 Sift together the flour, baking powder, cinnamon, nutmeg, cloves and allspice into a bowl.

3 Place the raisins in another bowl and toss with a few tablespoons of the flour mixture.

4 In another bowl, beat the butter and sugar together until light and fluffy. Beat in the eggs, one at a time, then the treacle. Stir in the flour mixture, raisins and walnuts.

5 Spoon the mixture into the prepared tin and spread evenly with the back of the spoon. Bake for 15–18 minutes, until just firm to the touch. Leave to cool completely in the tin before cutting into bars or squares.

Variation
You could also make these spicy bars with chopped dried figs instead of raisins, and substitute either pistachio nuts or hazelnuts for the walnuts.

Chocolate Prune Energy 197kcal/826kJ; Protein 2.5g; Carbohydrate 21.7g, of which sugars 16.4g; Fat 11.8g, of which saturates 6.8g; Cholesterol 18mg; Calcium 59mg; Fibre 0.9g; Sodium 102mg.
Spiced Raisin Squares Energy 84kcal/353kJ; Protein 1.2g; Carbohydrate 11.4g, of which sugars 8.4g; Fat 4.1g, of which saturates 1.8g; Cholesterol 19mg; Calcium 43mg; Fibre 0.3g; Sodium 37mg.

Fruity Muesli Bars

These fruity muesli bars make an appetizing treat for a takeaway snack.

Makes 10–12
115g/4oz/½ cup butter
75g/3oz/⅓ cup soft light
 brown sugar
45ml/3 tbsp golden
 (light corn) syrup
150g/5oz/1¼ cups Swiss-style
 muesli (granola)
150g/2oz/½ cup rolled oats
5ml/1 tsp ground mixed spice
 (apple pie spice)
50g/2oz/⅓ cup sultanas
 (golden raisins)
50g/2oz/½ cup chopped
 ready-to-eat dried pears

1 Preheat the oven to 180°C/350°F/Gas 4. Lightly grease an 18cm/7in square cake tin (pan).

2 Put the butter, sugar and syrup in a pan and heat gently until melted, stirring.

3 Remove the pan from the heat and add the muesli, rolled oats, spice, sultanas and dried pears. Mix well with a wooden spoon until thoroughly combined.

4 Transfer the mixture to the prepared tin and level the surface, pressing down.

5 Bake for 20–30 minutes, until golden brown. Cool slightly into the tin, then mark into bars using a sharp knife.

6 When firm, remove the muesli bars from the tin and cool on a wire rack.

Variations
• A combination of rolled oats and oatmeal can be used instead of muesli (granola), for a delicious change.
• Try using different dried fruits instead of sultanas (golden raisins) and pears – papaya and mango for a tropical taste, cranberries and apple for a hint of autumn (fall), or apricots and dates for a Middle Eastern flavour.

Creamy Fig & Peach Squares

A sweet cream cheese and dried fruit filling with a hint of mint makes these cookies really special. They are ideal for quietening hunger pangs after school or work.

Makes 24
350g/12oz/3 cups plain
 (all-purpose) flour, plus extra
 for dusting
200g/7oz/scant 1 cup unsalted
 (sweet) butter, diced
1 egg, beaten
caster (superfine) sugar,
 for sprinkling

For the filling
500g/1¼lb/2½ cups ricotta
 cheese
115g/4oz/generous ½ cup
 caster (superfine) sugar
5ml/1 tsp finely chopped
 fresh mint
50g/2oz/⅓ cup ready-to-eat
 dried figs, chopped
50g/2oz/¼ cup ready-to-eat
 dried peaches, chopped

1 Preheat the oven to 190°C/375°F/Gas 5. Lightly grease a 33 × 23cm/13 × 9in Swiss roll tin (jelly roll pan) or shallow cake tin (pan).

2 Put the flour and butter into a bowl. Rub in the butter with your fingertips until the mixture resembles fine breadcrumbs. Add the egg and enough water to mix to a firm but not sticky dough.

3 Divide the dough into two and roll out one piece on a lightly floured surface to fit the base of the prepared tin. Place in the tin and trim.

4 To make the filling, put all the ingredients in a bowl and mix together. Spread over the pastry base.

5 Roll out the remaining dough and place on top of the filling. Prick lightly all over with a fork then sprinkle with caster sugar.

6 Bake for about 30 minutes, until light golden brown. Remove from the oven and sprinkle more caster sugar thickly over the top. Cool and cut into slices to serve.

Fruity Muesli Bars Energy 221kcal/927kJ; Protein 3.2g; Carbohydrate 32.1g, of which sugars 17.2g; Fat 9.8g, of which saturates 5.1g; Cholesterol 20mg; Calcium 32mg; Fibre 2g; Sodium 122mg.
Creamy Fig and Peach Energy 179kcal/747kJ; Protein 3.8g; Carbohydrate 18.8g, of which sugars 7.7g; Fat 10.3g, of which saturates 6.3g; Cholesterol 34mg; Calcium 32mg; Fibre 0.7g; Sodium 56mg.

Date & Honey Bars

Fresh dates are a good source of natural fibre, yet are kind and gentle on the digestive system. For a slightly different, more toffee flavour, replace the honey with real maple syrup.

Makes 16
175g/6oz/1 cup fresh dates, stoned and coarsely chopped
45ml/3 tbsp clear honey
30ml/2 tbsp lemon juice
150g/5oz/1¼ cups plain (all-purpose) flour
150ml/¼ pint/⅔ cup water
1.5ml/¼ tsp freshly grated nutmeg
115g/4oz/1 cup self-raising (self-rising) flour
25g/1oz/2 tbsp brown sugar
150g/5oz/1¼ cups rolled oats
175g/6oz/¾ cup unsalted (sweet) butter, melted

1 Preheat the oven to 190°C/375°F/Gas 5. Lightly grease the base of an 18cm/7in square cake tin (pan) and line with baking parchment.

2 Put the dates, honey, lemon juice, plain flour and measured water into a heavy pan. Gradually bring to the boil over a low heat, stirring constantly. Remove the pan from the heat and leave to cool.

3 Sift together the nutmeg and self-raising flour into another bowl and stir in the sugar, oats and melted butter until well combined. Spoon half the mixture into the prepared tin and spread it out evenly over the base with the back of the spoon, pressing down well.

4 Spread the date mixture over the top and finish with the remaining oat mixture, pressing evenly all over the surface with the back of a spoon. Bake for about 25 minutes until golden. Cool in the cake tin for 1 hour, then cut into bars.

> **Cook's Tip**
> To remove the stone (pit), split the date lengthways with a small sharp knife without cutting right through. Ease out the stone with the point of the knife.

Sticky Date & Apple Squares

Combining fresh and dried fruits gives these bars a wonderful texture and fabulous flavour – truly a winning partnership.

Makes 16
115g/4oz/½ cup butter
50g/2oz/4 tbsp soft dark brown sugar
50g/2oz/4 tbsp golden (light corn) syrup
115g/4oz/⅔ cup dried dates, chopped
115g/4oz/1⅓ cup rolled oats
115g/4oz/1 cup wholemeal (whole-wheat) self-raising (self-rising) flour
2 eating apples, peeled, cored and grated
5–10ml/1–2 tsp lemon juice
walnut halves, to decorate

1 Preheat the oven to 190°C/375°F/Gas 5. Line an 18–20cm/7–8in square or rectangle loose-based cake tin (pan).

2 Put the butter, sugar and golden syrup into a large pan and melt over a low heat, stirring occasionally, until smooth and thoroughly combined.

3 Add the dates and cook until they have softened. Gradually work in the oats, flour, apples and lemon juice until well mixed.

4 Spoon into the prepared tin and spread out evenly. Top with the walnut halves.

5 Bake for 30 minutes, then reduce the temperature to 160°C/325°F/Gas 3 and bake for 10–12 minutes more, until firm to the touch and golden.

6 Cut into squares or bars while still warm if you are going to eat them straightaway, or wrap in foil when nearly cold and keep for 1–2 days before eating.

> **Variation**
> Although not quite so sticky, these bars would also be delicious made with dried blueberries instead of dates.

Date and Honey Bars Energy 203kcal/853kJ; Protein 3g; Carbohydrate 27g, of which sugars 7.5g; Fat 10g, of which saturates 5.7g; Cholesterol 23mg; Calcium 34mg; Fibre 1.4g; Sodium 71mg.
Sticky Date Energy 150kcal/631kJ; Protein 1.9g; Carbohydrate 22g, of which sugars 11.3g; Fat 6.7g, of which saturates 3.8g; Cholesterol 15mg; Calcium 21mg; Fibre 1.1g; Sodium 56mg.

Date & Orange Slices

These tempting wholesome slices make tasty and chewy treats that will keep hunger at bay any time of the day.

Makes 16
350g/12oz/2⅓ cups stoned (pitted) dried dates, finely chopped
200ml/7fl oz/scant 1 cup freshly squeezed orange juice
finely grated rind of 1 orange

115g/4oz/1 cup plain (all-purpose) wholemeal (whole-wheat) flour
175g/6oz/1¾ cups rolled oats
50g/2oz/½ cup fine oatmeal
pinch of salt
175g/6oz/¾ cup butter
75g/3oz/⅓ cup soft light brown sugar
10ml/2 tsp ground cinnamon

1 Preheat the oven to 190°C/375°F/Gas 5. Lightly grease an 18 × 28cm/7 × 11in non-stick cake tin (pan).

2 Put the dates in a pan with the orange juice. Cover, bring to the boil and simmer for 5 minutes, stirring occasionally. Stir in the orange rind and set aside to cool completely.

3 Put the flour, oats, oatmeal and salt in a bowl and mix together. Lightly rub in the butter.

4 Stir in the sugar and cinnamon. Press half the oat mixture over the base of the prepared tin. Spread the date mixture on top and sprinkle the remaining oat mixture evenly over the dates to cover them completely. Press down lightly.

5 Bake for about 30 minutes, until golden brown.

6 Leave to cool slightly in the tin and mark into 16 bars, using a sharp knife. When firm, remove from the tin and cool completely on a wire rack.

> **Variation**
> *Ready-to-eat dried apricots or prunes used in place of the dates in this recipe make equally tasty slices.*

Lemon-iced Date Slices

Lemon-flavoured icing tops these scrumptious, low-fat bars, which are full of succulent fruit and crunchy seeds – the perfect mid-morning pick-me-up with a cup of tea or coffee.

Makes 12–16
175g/6oz/¾ cup light muscovado (brown) sugar
175g/6oz/1 cup ready-to-eat dried dates, chopped
115g/4oz/1 cup self-raising (self-rising) flour

50g/2oz/½ cup muesli (granola)
30ml/2 tbsp sunflower seeds
15ml/1 tbsp poppy seeds
30ml/2 tbsp sultanas (golden raisins)
150ml/¼ pint/⅔ cup natural (plain) low-fat yogurt
1 egg, beaten
200g/7oz/1¾ cups icing (confectioners') sugar, sifted
lemon juice
15–30ml/1–2 tbsp pumpkin seeds

1 Preheat the oven to 180°C/350°F/Gas 4. Line a 28 × 18cm/ 11 × 7in shallow baking tin (pan) with baking parchment.

2 In a bowl mix together the muscovado sugar, dates, flour, muesli, sunflower seeds, poppy seeds, sultanas, yogurt and beaten egg until thoroughly combined.

3 Spread in the tin and bake for about 25 minutes, until golden brown. Leave to cool.

4 To make the topping, put the icing sugar in a bowl and stir in just enough lemon juice to make a spreading consistency.

5 Spread the icing evenly over the baked date mixture and sprinkle generously with pumpkin seeds. Leave to set before cutting into squares or bars.

> **Variation**
> *Pumpkin seeds can sometimes be rather fibrous, so if you prefer, you could substitute other seeds, such as sesame, or flaked (sliced) almonds.*

Date and Orange Energy 241kcal/1011kJ; Protein 4g; Carbohydrate 36g, of which sugars 21g; Fat10g, of which saturates 6g; Cholesterol 23mg; Calcium 31mg; Fibre 3.2g; Sodium 101mg.
Lemon-iced Date Energy 211kcal/893kJ; Protein 3.6g; Carbohydrate 43.6g, of which sugars 35.5g; Fat 3.6g, of which saturates 0.5g; Cholesterol 12mg; Calcium 56mg; Fibre 1.3g; Sodium 18mg.

Hazelnut & Raspberry Bars

The hazelnuts make a superb sweet pastry which is baked with a layer of raspberry jam in the middle.

Makes 30
250g/9oz/2¼ cups hazelnuts
300g/10oz/2½ cups plain (all-purpose) flour
5ml/1 tsp mixed spice (apple pie spice)
2.5ml/½ tsp ground cinnamon
150g/5oz/1¼ cups golden icing (confectioners') sugar
15ml/1 tbsp grated lemon rind
300g/10oz/1¼ cups unsalted (sweet) butter, softened
3 egg yolks
350g/12oz/1¼ cups seedless raspberry jam

For the topping
1 egg, beaten
15ml/1 tbsp clear honey
50g/2oz/½ cup flaked (sliced) almonds

1 Grind the hazelnuts in a food processor and then put in a bowl. Sift in the flour, spices and icing sugar. Add the lemon rind and mix well, then add the butter and the egg yolks and, using your hands, knead until a smooth dough is formed. Wrap in clear film (plastic wrap) and chill for 30 minutes.

2 Preheat the oven to 200°C/400°F/Gas 6. Lightly grease a 33 × 23cm/13 × 9in Swiss roll tin (jelly roll pan).

3 Roll out half the dough and fit in the base of the tin. Spread the jam over the dough base. Roll out the remaining dough and place on top of the jam.

4 To make the topping, beat the egg and honey together and brush over the dough. Sprinkle the almonds evenly over the top.

5 Bake for 10 minutes, lower the oven temperature to 180°C/350°F/Gas 4. Bake for another 20–30 minutes until golden brown. Cool, then cut into bars.

> **Cook's Tip**
> Don't use ready-ground hazelnuts for these bars.

Chocolate Raspberry Macaroon Bars

Any other seedless jams, such as strawberry or plum, can be used instead of the raspberry in the topping for these flavour-packed bars.

Makes 16–18 bars
115g/4oz/½ cup unsalted (sweet) butter
50g/2oz/½ cup icing (confectioners') sugar
25g/1oz/¼ cup unsweetened cocoa powder
pinch of salt
5ml/1 tsp almond extract
150g/5oz/1¼ cups plain (all-purpose) flour

For the topping
150g/5oz/scant ½ cup seedless raspberry jam
15ml/1 tbsp raspberry-flavoured liqueur
175g/6oz/1 cup mini chocolate chips
175g/6oz/1½ cups finely ground almonds
4 egg whites
pinch of salt
200g/7oz/1 cup caster (superfine) sugar
2.5ml/½ tsp almond extract
50g/2oz/½ cup flaked (sliced) almonds

1 Preheat the oven to 160°C/325°F/Gas 3. Line a 23 × 33cm/9 × 13in cake tin (pan) with lightly greased foil.

2 In a bowl, beat together the butter, sugar, cocoa and salt. Add the almond extract and flour and stir until the mixture forms a crumbly dough. Turn the dough into the lined tin and smooth out. Prick with a fork. Bake for 20 minutes, until just set. Remove from the oven and increase the temperature to 190°C/375°F/Gas 5.

3 To make the topping, mix together the raspberry jam and liqueur in a bowl. Spread evenly over the chocolate crust, then sprinkle with chocolate chips.

4 In a food processor fitted with a metal blade, blend the almonds, egg whites, salt, sugar and almond extract until foamy. Pour over the raspberry layer. Sprinkle with flaked almonds.

5 Bake for 20–25 minutes, until the top is golden. Transfer to a wire rack to cool in the tin for 20 minutes. Remove to a wire rack to cool completely. Cut into bars.

Hazelnut and Raspberry Energy 231kcal/962kJ; Protein 2.9g; Carbohydrate 22.1g, of which sugars 14.3g; Fat 15.1g, of which saturates 5.9g; Cholesterol 41mg; Calcium 38mg; Fibre 1g; Sodium 66mg.
Chocolate Raspberry Energy 266kcal/1115kJ; Protein 4.5g; Carbohydrate 32.1g, of which sugars 26.6g; Fat 14.1g, of which saturates 5.7g; Cholesterol 16mg; Calcium 66mg; Fibre 1.2g; Sodium 79mg.

Fourth of July Blueberry Softbakes

These berry bakes are simply wonderful when eaten still warm from the oven. However, they are also good if allowed to cool and then packed for a traditional Independence Day picnic.

Makes 10
150g/5oz/1¼ cups plain
 (all-purpose) flour
7.5ml/1½ tsp baking powder

5ml/1 tsp ground cinnamon
50g/2oz/¼ cup unsalted
 (sweet) butter, at room
 temperature, diced
50g/2oz/¼ cup demerara
 (raw) sugar, plus extra
 for sprinkling
120ml/4fl oz/½ cup sour cream
90g/3½oz/scant 1 cup fresh
 blueberries
50g/2oz/½ cup semi-dried
 cranberries

1 Preheat the oven to 190°C/375°F/Gas 5. Line two baking sheets with baking parchment.

2 Sift together the flour, baking powder and cinnamon into a large mixing bowl. Add the diced butter and rub in with your fingers until the mixture resembles fine breadcrumbs. Stir in the demerara sugar.

3 Add the sour cream, blueberries and cranberries and stir until just combined.

4 Spoon ten mounds of the mixture, spaced well apart, on to the prepared baking sheets. Sprinkle with the extra demerara sugar and bake for about 20 minutes, or until golden and firm in the centre. Serve warm.

> **Variations**
> • For Thanksgiving, substitute fresh cranberries for the blueberries, and chopped preserved stem ginger for the semi-dried cranberries.
> • For Halloween, substitute chocolate chips and chopped almonds for the fruit.
> • For Christmas, substitute raisins for the blueberries, soaking them in rum for 20 minutes before use.

Tropical Fruit Slices

Densely packed dried exotic fruits make the filling for these deliciously moist bars. Vary the tropical fruits in different areas of the baking tray for differently tasting snacks from the same batch.

Makes 12–16
175g/6oz/1½ cups plain
 (all-purpose) flour, plus extra
 for dusting
90g/3½oz/generous ½ cup white
 vegetable fat (shortening)
60ml/4 tbsp apricot jam, sieved,
 or ready-made apricot glaze

For the filling
115g/4oz/½ cup unsalted
 (sweet) butter, softened
115g/4oz/generous ½ cup caster
 (superfine) sugar
1 egg, beaten
25g/1oz/¼ cup ground almonds
25g/1oz/2½ tbsp ground rice
300g/11oz/scant 2 cups
 ready-to-eat mixed dried
 tropical fruits, chopped

1 Preheat the oven to 180°C/350°F/Gas 4. Lightly grease a 28 × 18cm/11 × 7in tin (pan).

2 Sift the flour into a bowl and add the vegetable fat. Cut it into the flour, then rub in with your fingertips until the mixture resembles fine breadcrumbs. Gradually add just enough water to mix to a firm dough.

3 Roll out to a rectangle on a lightly floured surface and use to line the base of the prepared tin, trimming off any excess. Spread 30ml/2 tbsp of the apricot jam or glaze evenly over the dough base.

4 To make the filling, beat together the butter and sugar in a bowl until light and creamy. Beat in the egg, then stir in the ground almonds, ground rice and mixed fruits. Spread the mixture evenly in the tin.

5 Bake for about 35 minutes, until firm and golden. Remove from the oven and brush with the remaining apricot jam or glaze. Leave to cool completely in the tin before cutting into bars.

Fourth of July Energy 185kcal/775kJ; Protein 3.3g; Carbohydrate 25.2g, of which sugars 9.8g; Fat 8.4g, of which saturates 4.6g; Cholesterol 78mg; Calcium 48mg; Fibre 0.8g; Sodium 42mg.
Tropical Fruit Slices Energy 220kcal/921kJ; Protein 2.7g; Carbohydrate 26.9g, of which sugars 17.3g; Fat 12g, of which saturates 6g; Cholesterol 28mg; Calcium 41mg; Fibre 1.7g; Sodium 98mg.

Iced Apple Ring

A deliciously moist apple cake with a silky icing.

Makes one ring cake
675g/1½lb apples, peeled, cored and quartered
500g/1¼lb/generous 4½ cups caster (superfine) sugar
15ml/1 tbsp water
350g/12oz/3 cups plain (all-purpose) flour
9ml/1¾ tsp bicarbonate of soda (baking soda)
5ml/1 tsp ground cinnamon
5ml/1 tsp ground cloves
175g/6oz/generous 1 cup raisins
150g/5oz/1¼ cups chopped walnuts
225g/8oz/1 cup butter or margarine, at room temperature
5ml/1 tsp vanilla extract

For the icing
115g/4oz/1 cup icing (confectioners') sugar
1.5ml/¼ tsp vanilla extract
30–45ml/2–3 tbsp milk

1 Put the apples, 50g/2oz/¼ cup of the sugar and the water in a pan and bring to the boil. Simmer for 25 minutes, stirring occasionally to break up any lumps. Leave to cool. Preheat the oven to 160°C/325°F/Gas 3. Thoroughly butter and flour a 1.75 litre/3 pint/7½ cup tube tin (pan).

2 Sift the flour, bicarbonate of soda and spices into a bowl. Remove 30ml/2 tbsp of the mixture to another bowl and toss with the raisins and 115g/4oz/1 cup of the walnuts.

3 Cream the butter or margarine and remaining sugar together until light and fluffy. Fold in the apple mixture gently. Fold the flour mixture into the apple mixture. Stir in the vanilla extract and the raisin and walnut mixture. Pour into the tube tin. Bake until a skewer inserted in the centre comes out clean, about 1½ hours. Cool completely in the tin on a wire rack, then unmould on to the rack.

4 To make the icing, put the sugar in a bowl and stir in the vanilla extract and 15ml/1 tbsp milk. Add more milk until the icing is smooth and has a thick pouring consistency. Transfer the cake to a serving plate and drizzle the icing over the top. Sprinkle with the remaining nuts. Allow the icing to set.

Dorset Apple Cake

Serve this fruity apple cake warm, and spread slices with butter, if you like.

Makes one 18cm/7in round cake
225g/8oz cooking apples, peeled, cored and chopped
juice of ½ lemon
225g/8oz/2 cups plain (all-purpose) flour
7.5ml/1½ tsp baking powder
115g/4oz/½ cup butter, diced
165g/5½oz/¾ cup soft light brown sugar
1 egg, beaten
about 30–45ml/2–3 tbsp milk, to mix
2.5ml/½ tsp ground cinnamon

1 Preheat the oven to 180°C/350°F/Gas 4. Grease and line an 18cm/7in round cake tin (pan).

2 Toss the apple with the lemon juice and set aside. Sift the flour and baking powder together, then rub in the butter using your fingertips or a pastry cutter, until the mixture resembles breadcrumbs.

3 Stir in 115g/4oz/1 cup of the brown sugar, the apple and the egg, and mix well, adding sufficient milk to make a soft dropping consistency.

4 Transfer the batter to the prepared tin. In a bowl, mix together the remaining sugar and the cinnamon. Sprinkle over the cake mixture, then bake for 45–50 minutes, or until golden. Leave to cool in the tin for 10 minutes, then transfer to a wire rack to cool completely.

Cook's Tips
For successful cakes, remember these few golden rules:
• *Heat the oven to the correct temperature in plenty of time.*
• *Measure out the ingredients carefully.*
• *Use the correct size tins (pans), and prepare them before you start combining the ingredients.*

Iced Apple Energy 7054kcal/29678kJ; Protein 64g; Carbohydrate 1107g, of which sugars 838g; Fat 295g, of which saturates 127g; Cholesterol 482mg; Calcium 920mg; Fibre 4.7g; Sodium 3485mg.
Dorset Apple Energy 2436kcal/10244kJ; Protein 30.5g; Carbohydrate 368.6g, of which sugars 197.9g; Fat 103.7g, of which saturates 62.2g; Cholesterol 437mg; Calcium 495mg; Fibre 10.5g; Sodium 801mg.

Dutch Apple Cake

The apple topping makes this cake really moist. It is just as good hot as it is cold.

Makes 8–10 slices
250g/9oz/2¼ cups self-raising (self-rising) flour
10ml/2 tsp baking powder
5ml/1 tsp ground cinnamon
130g/4½oz/generous ½ cup caster (superfine) sugar
50g/2oz/¼ cup butter, melted

2 eggs, beaten
150ml/¼ pint/⅔ cup milk

For the topping
2 eating apples
15g/½oz/1 tbsp butter, melted
60ml/4 tbsp demerara (raw) sugar
1.5ml/¼ tsp ground cinnamon

1 Preheat the oven to 200°C/400°F/Gas 6. Grease and line a 20cm/8in round cake tin (pan). Sift the flour, baking powder and cinnamon into a large mixing bowl. Stir in the caster sugar. In a separate bowl, whisk the melted butter, eggs and milk together, then stir the mixture into the dry ingredients.

2 Pour the cake mixture into the prepared tin, smooth the surface, then make a shallow hollow in a ring around the edge of the mixture.

3 Make the topping. Peel and core the apples, slice them into wedges and slice the wedges thinly. Arrange the slices around the edge of the cake mixture, in the hollowed ring. Brush with the melted butter, then scatter the demerara sugar and ground cinnamon over the top.

4 Bake for 45–50 minutes or until the cake has risen well, is golden and a skewer inserted into the centre comes out clean.

5 Serve immediately, or remove from the tin, peel off the lining paper and cool on a wire rack before serving cold with cream.

> **Variation**
> Add a few seedless raisins to the sliced apples, if you like.

Spiced Apple Cake

As grated apple and dates give this cake a natural sweetness, it may not be necessary to add all the sugar.

Serves 8
225g/8oz/2 cups self-raising (self-rising) wholemeal (whole-wheat) flour
5ml/1 tsp baking powder
10ml/2 tsp ground cinnamon
175g/6oz/1 cup chopped dates

75g/3oz/scant ½ cup soft light brown sugar
15ml/1 tbsp pear and apple spread
120ml/4fl oz/½ cup apple juice
2 eggs, beaten
90ml/6 tbsp sunflower oil
2 eating apples, cored and grated
15ml/1 tbsp chopped walnuts

1 Preheat the oven to 180°C/350°F/Gas 4. Line and grease a 20cm/8in deep round cake tin (pan).

2 Sift the flour, baking powder and cinnamon into a mixing bowl, then mix in the dates and make a well in the centre.

3 Mix some of the sugar with the pear and apple spread in a small bowl. Gradually stir in the apple juice.

4 Add to the dry ingredients with the eggs, oil and apples. Mix thoroughly. Taste and add the rest of the sugar, if necessary.

5 Spoon into the prepared cake tin, sprinkle with the walnuts and bake for 60–65 minutes, or until a skewer inserted into the centre of the cake comes out clean.

6 Invert on a wire rack, remove the lining paper and leave to cool completely.

> **Cook's Tip**
> It is not necessary to peel the apples – the skin adds extra fibre to the cake, and softens on cooking.

Dutch Apple Cake Energy 225Kcal/951kJ; Protein 3.7g; Carbohydrate 40g, of which sugars 21.4g; Fat 6.8g, of which saturates 3.8g; Cholesterol 52mg; Calcium 105mg; Fibre 1g; Sodium 145mg.
Spiced Apple Cake Energy 282kcal/1186kJ; Protein 4.9g; Carbohydrate 42.8g, of which sugars 21.3g; Fat 11.3g, of which saturates 1.5g; Cholesterol 48mg; Calcium 60mg; Fibre 1.6g; Sodium 22mg.

Cranberry & Apple Ring

Tangy cranberries add an unusual flavour to this moist cake, which is best eaten very fresh.

Makes one ring cake
225g/8oz/2 cups self-raising (self-rising) flour
5ml/1 tsp ground cinnamon
75g/3oz/scant 1/2 cup light muscovado (brown) sugar
1 eating apple, cored and diced
75g/3oz/3/4 cup fresh or frozen cranberries
60ml/4 tbsp sunflower oil
150ml/1/4 pint/2/3 cup apple juice
cranberry jelly and apple slices, to decorate

1 Preheat the oven to 180°C/350°F/Gas 4. Lightly grease a 1 litre/1¾ pint/4 cup ring tin (pan) with oil.

2 Sift together the flour and ground cinnamon in a large bowl, then stir in the light muscovado sugar.

3 Toss together the diced apple and cranberries in a small bowl.

4 Stir the apple mixture into the dry ingredients, then add the oil and apple juice and beat together until everything is thoroughly combined.

5 Spoon the cake mixture into the prepared ring tin and bake for 35–40 minutes, or until the cake is firm to the touch.

6 Leave the cake in the tin for 5 minutes, then turn out on to a wire rack and leave to cool completely.

7 To serve, arrange apple slices over the cake and drizzle warmed cranberry jelly over the top.

Cook's Tip
This moist, tangy ring would be an ideal alternative to Christmas cake for those who do not like such dense, rich cakes. It would also be a good way of using up any left-over cranberries or cranberry jelly.

Pear & Cardamom Spice Cake

Fresh pears and cardamoms – a classic combination – are used together in this moist fruit and nut cake.

Makes one 20cm/8in round cake
115g/4oz/1/2 cup butter
115g/4oz/generous 1/2 cup caster (superfine) sugar
2 eggs, lightly beaten
225g/8oz/2 cups plain (all-purpose) flour
15ml/1 tbsp baking powder
30ml/2 tbsp milk
crushed seeds from 2 cardamom pods
50g/2oz/1/2 cup walnuts, finely chopped
15ml/1 tbsp poppy seeds
500g/1 1/4lb dessert pears, peeled, cored and thinly sliced
3 walnut halves, to decorate
clear honey, to glaze

1 Preheat the oven to 180°C/350°F/Gas 4. Grease and base-line a 20cm/8in round, loose-based cake tin (pan).

2 Cream the butter and sugar in a large bowl until pale and light. Gradually beat in the eggs.

3 Sift over the flour and baking powder, and fold in gently with the milk.

4 Stir in the cardamom seeds, chopped nuts and poppy seeds. Reserve one-third of the pear slices, and chop the remainder. Fold into the creamed mixture.

5 Transfer to the cake tin. Smooth the surface, making a small dip in the centre. Place the walnut halves in the centre of the cake and fan the reserved pear slices around the walnuts, covering the cake mixture.

6 Bake for 1¼–1½ hours, or until a skewer inserted into the centre comes out clean.

7 Remove the cake from the oven and brush with the honey. Leave in the tin for 20 minutes, then transfer to a wire rack to cool completely before serving.

Cranberry Energy 1565kcal/6610kJ; Protein 22.1g; Carbohydrate 280.7g, of which sugars 109.2g; Fat 47.2g, of which saturates 5.7g; Cholesterol 0mg; Calcium 371mg; Fibre 9.2g; Sodium 17mg.
Pear Energy 2781kcal/11648kJ; Protein 44.8g; Carbohydrate 348.8g, of which sugars 177g; Fat 143.8g, of which saturates 66.6g; Cholesterol 628mg; Calcium 592mg; Fibre 19.7g; Sodium 882mg.

Devil's Food Cake with Orange

Chocolate and orange always taste great together.

Makes one 23cm/9in round cake

50g/2oz/½ cup unsweetened cocoa powder
175ml/6fl oz/¾ cup boiling water
175g/6oz/¾ cup butter, at room temperature
350g/12oz/2 cups soft dark brown sugar
3 eggs
275g/10oz/2½ cups plain (all-purpose) flour

7.5ml/1½ tsp bicarbonate of soda (baking soda)
1.5ml/¼ tsp baking powder
120ml/4fl oz/½ cup sour cream
blanched orange rind shreds, to decorate

For the frosting

300g/11oz/scant 1½ cups caster (superfine) sugar
2 egg whites
60ml/4 tbsp orange juice concentrate
15ml/1 tbsp lemon juice
grated rind of 1 orange

1 Preheat the oven to 180°C/350°F/Gas 4. Line two 23cm/9in cake tins (pans) with baking parchment and grease the paper. In a bowl, mix the cocoa powder and water until smooth.

2 Cream the butter and sugar until light and fluffy. Add the eggs, one at a time, beating well after each addition. When the cocoa mixture is lukewarm, add to the butter mixture. Sift together the flour, bicarbonate of soda and baking powder twice. Fold into the cocoa mixture in three batches, alternating with the sour cream. Pour into the tins and bake until the cakes pull away from the sides, 30–35 minutes. Leave to cool in the tins for 15 minutes, then turn out on to a wire rack to cool completely.

3 To make the frosting, place all the ingredients in the top of a double boiler or in a heatproof bowl over a pan of simmering water. With an electric mixer, beat until the mixture holds soft peaks. Continue beating off the heat until thick enough to spread.

4 Sandwich the cake layers with frosting, then spread over the top and side. Decorate with orange rind shreds.

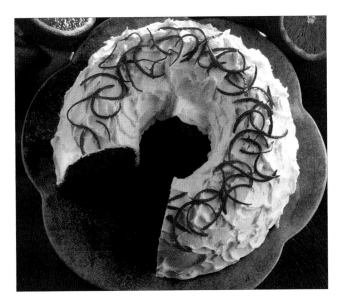

Chocolate & Orange Angel Cake

This light-as-air sponge with its fluffy icing is the answer to a cake-lover's prayer.

Makes one 20cm/8in ring cake

25g/1oz/¼ cup plain (all-purpose) flour
15g/½oz/2 tbsp unsweetened cocoa powder
15g/½oz/2 tbsp cornflour (cornstarch)
a pinch of salt

5 egg whites
2.5ml/½ tsp cream of tartar
115g/4oz/generous ½ cup caster (superfine) sugar
blanched and shredded rind of 1 orange, to decorate

For the icing

200g/7oz/1 cup caster (superfine) sugar
1 egg white

1 Preheat the oven to 180°C/350°F/Gas 4. Sift the flour, cocoa powder, cornflour and salt together three times.

2 Beat the egg whites in a large bowl until foamy. Add the cream of tartar, then whisk until soft peaks form.

3 Add the caster sugar to the egg whites a spoonful at a time, whisking after each addition. Sift a third of the flour and cocoa mixture over the meringue and gently fold in. Repeat twice more.

4 Spoon the mixture into a non-stick 20cm/8in ring mould and level the top. Bake for 35 minutes, or until springy when lightly pressed. Turn upside-down on to a wire rack and leave to cool in the tin. Carefully ease out of the tin.

5 To make the icing, put the sugar in a pan with 75ml/5 tbsp cold water. Stir over a low heat until dissolved. Boil until the syrup reaches soft ball stage (119°C/238°F on a sugar thermometer). Remove from the heat.

6 Whisk the egg white until stiff. Add the syrup in a thin stream, whisking all the time, until the mixture is very thick and fluffy.

7 Spread the icing over the top and sides of the cooled cake. Sprinkle the orange rind over the top of the cake and serve.

Devil's Food Energy 5459kcal/23002kJ; Protein 68.3g; Carbohydrate 906.2g, of which sugars 690.9g; Fat 199g, of which saturates 117.8g; Cholesterol 1016mg; Calcium 1038mg; Fibre 14.8g; Sodium 1983mg.
Chocolate and Orange Energy 1495kcal/6373kJ; Protein 24.1g; Carbohydrate 364.1g, of which sugars 329.6g; Fat 3.7g, of which saturates 2g; Cholesterol 0mg; Calcium 233mg; Fibre 2.6g; Sodium 535mg.

Orange & Walnut Swiss Roll

This unusual cake is tasty enough to serve alone, but you could also pour over some single (light) cream.

Makes one 23cm/9in long roll

4 eggs, separated
115g/4oz/generous ½ cup caster (superfine) sugar
115g/4oz/1 cup very finely chopped walnuts
a pinch of cream of tartar
a pinch of salt

icing (confectioners') sugar, for dusting

For the filling
300ml/½ pint/1¼ cups whipping cream
15ml/1 tbsp caster (superfine) sugar
grated rind of 1 orange
15ml/1 tbsp orange-flavoured liqueur

1 Preheat the oven to 180°C/350°F/Gas 4. Line a 30 × 23cm/ 12 × 9in Swiss roll tin (jelly roll pan) with baking parchment and grease the paper.

2 Beat the egg yolks and sugar until thick. Stir in the walnuts. In another bowl, beat the egg whites with the cream of tartar and salt until stiffly peaking. Fold into the walnut mixture.

3 Pour the mixture into the prepared tin and level the top. Bake for 15 minutes. Invert the cake on to baking parchment dusted with icing sugar. Peel off the lining paper. Roll up the cake with the sugared paper. Leave to cool.

4 For the filling, whip the cream until softly peaking. Fold in the caster sugar, orange rind and liqueur.

5 Unroll the cake. Spread with the filling, then re-roll. Chill. To serve, dust with icing sugar.

> **Cook's Tip**
> Rolling up the Swiss roll (jelly roll) while still warm ensures that it will re-roll around its cream filling when it is cold without cracking.

Chocolate Orange Battenberg Cake

A tasty variation on the traditional pink-and-white Battenberg cake. Use good-quality marzipan for the best flavour.

Makes one 18cm/7in long rectangular cake

115g/4oz/½ cup soft margarine
115g/4oz/½ cup caster (superfine) sugar
2 eggs, beaten

a few drops of vanilla extract
15g/½oz/1 tbsp ground almonds
115g/4oz/1 cup self-raising (self-rising) flour, sifted
grated rind and juice of ½ orange
15g/½oz/2 tbsp unsweetened cocoa powder, sifted
30–45ml/2–3 tbsp milk
1 jar chocolate and nut spread
225g/8oz white marzipan

1 Preheat the oven to 180°C/350°F/Gas 4. Grease and line an 18cm/7in square cake tin (pan) with baking parchment. Put a double piece of foil across the middle of the tin, to divide it into two equal oblongs.

2 Cream the margarine and sugar. Beat in the eggs, vanilla extract and almonds. Divide the mixture evenly into two halves.

3 Fold half of the flour into one half, with the orange rind and enough juice to give a soft dropping consistency. Fold the rest of the flour and the cocoa powder into the other half, with enough milk to give a soft dropping consistency. Fill the tin with the two mixes and level the top.

4 Bake for 15 minutes, reduce the heat to 160°C/325°F/Gas 3 and cook for 20–30 minutes, or until the top is just firm. Leave to cool in the tin for a few minutes. Turn out on to a board, cut each cake into two strips and trim evenly. Leave to cool.

5 Using the chocolate and nut spread, sandwich the cakes together, Battenberg-style.

6 Roll out the marzipan on a board lightly dusted with cornflour to a rectangle 18cm/7in wide and long enough to wrap around the cake. Wrap the paste around the cake, putting the join underneath. Press to seal.

Orange and Walnut Energy 2788kcal/11573kJ; Protein 48.6g; Carbohydrate 151.4g, of which sugars 150.6g; Fat 221.9g, of which saturates 88.3g; Cholesterol 1076mg; Calcium 465mg; Fibre 4g; Sodium 372mg.
Chocolate Orange Energy 716kcal/2993kJ; Protein 11.5g; Carbohydrate 77.2g, of which sugars 65g; Fat 42.3g, of which saturates 6.9g; Cholesterol 49mg; Calcium 163mg; Fibre 2.9g; Sodium 204mg.

Greek Honey & Lemon Cake

A wonderfully moist and tangy cake, you could ice it if you wished.

Makes one 19cm/7½in square cake
40g/1½oz/3 tbsp sunflower margarine
60ml/4 tbsp clear honey
finely grated rind and juice of 1 lemon
150ml/¼ pint/⅔ cup milk

150g/5oz/1¼ cups plain (all-purpose) flour
7.5ml/1½ tsp baking powder
2.5ml/½ tsp freshly grated nutmeg
50g/2oz/⅓ cup semolina
2 egg whites
10ml/2 tsp sesame seeds

1 Preheat the oven to 200°C/400°F/Gas 6. Lightly oil and base-line a 19cm/7½in square deep cake tin (pan).

2 Place the margarine and 45ml/3 tbsp of the honey in a pan and heat gently until melted.

3 Reserve 15ml/1 tbsp lemon juice, then stir in the rest with the lemon rind and milk.

4 Sift together the flour, baking powder and nutmeg, then beat in with the semolina. Whisk the egg whites until they form soft peaks, then fold evenly into the mixture.

5 Spoon into the cake tin and sprinkle with sesame seeds. Bake for 25–30 minutes, or until golden brown. Mix the reserved honey and lemon juice, and drizzle over the cake while warm. Cool in the tin, then cut into fingers to serve.

> **Cook's Tip**
> Baking powder is a useful raising agent for making cakes and is used with plain (all-purpose) flour. When mixed with a liquid, it forms a gas that causes the cake to rise. It also acts further when the cake is baked. Always check the use-by date on the packet and replace as necessary for successful baking.

Tangy Lemon Cake

The lemon syrup forms a crusty topping when it has completely cooled. Leave the cake in the tin until ready to serve.

Makes one 900g/2lb loaf
175g/6oz/¾ cup butter
175g/6oz/scant 1 cup caster (superfine) sugar

3 eggs, beaten
175g/6oz/1½ cups self-raising (self-rising) flour
grated rind of 1 orange
grated rind of 1 lemon

For the syrup
115g/4oz/generous ½ cup caster (superfine) sugar
juice of 2 lemons

1 Preheat the oven to 180°C/350°F/Gas 4. Grease a 900g/2lb loaf tin (pan).

2 Beat the butter and sugar together until light and fluffy, then gradually beat in the eggs.

3 Fold in the flour and the orange and lemon rinds.

4 Turn the cake mixture into the prepared cake tin and bake for 1¼–1½ hours, or until set in the centre, risen and golden.

5 Remove the cake from the oven, but leave it in the tin rather than turning out on to a wire rack.

6 To make the syrup, gently heat the sugar in a small pan with the lemon juice until the sugar has completely dissolved, then boil for 15 seconds.

7 Pour the syrup over the hot cake in the tin and leave to cool completely.

> **Cook's Tip**
> You can use a skewer to pierce holes over the cake's surface so that the syrup will drizzle through and soak into the cake. There will still be a crusty, sugary top, but the cake itself will be moist.

Tangy Lemon Energy 2849kcal/11927kJ; Protein 36.3g; Carbohydrate 331.9g, of which sugars 201.9g; Fat 162.6g, of which saturates 96.2g; Cholesterol 944mg; Calcium 830mg; Fibre 5.4g; Sodium 1912mg.
Greek Honey Energy 1307kcal/5510kJ; Protein 32.4g; Carbohydrate 208.7g, of which sugars 55.6g; Fat 43.8g, of which saturates 9.2g; Cholesterol 12mg; Calcium 474mg; Fibre 6.5g; Sodium 525mg.

Nutty Lemon & Apricot Cake

This fruit and nut cake is soaked in a tangy lemon syrup after baking to keep it really moist.

Makes one 23 x 13cm/ 9 x 5in loaf
175g/6oz/³/4 cup butter, softened
175g/6oz/1¹/2 cups self-raising (self-rising) flour
2.5ml/¹/2 tsp baking powder
175g/6oz/generous ³/4 cup caster (superfine) sugar
3 eggs, lightly beaten
finely grated rind of I lemon

175g/6oz/1¹/2 cups ready-to-eat dried apricots, finely chopped
75g/3oz/³/4 cup ground almonds
40g/1¹/2oz/6 tbsp pistachio nuts, chopped
50g/2oz/¹/2 cup flaked (sliced) almonds
15g/¹/2oz/2 tbsp whole pistachio nuts

For the syrup
45ml/3 tbsp caster (superfine) sugar
freshly squeezed juice of I lemon

1 Preheat the oven to 180°C/350°F/Gas 4. Grease and line a 23 x 13cm/9 x 5in loaf tin (pan) with baking parchment and grease the paper.

2 Place the butter in a large bowl. Sift over the flour and baking powder, then add the sugar, eggs and lemon rind.

3 Using an electric whisk or a wooden spoon, beat for 1–2 minutes, or until smooth and glossy, then stir in the apricots, ground almonds and chopped pistachio nuts.

4 Spoon the mixture into the loaf tin and smooth the surface. Sprinkle with the flaked almonds and the whole pistachio nuts.

5 Bake for 1¹/4 hours, or until a skewer inserted into the centre of the cake comes out clean. Check the cake after 45 minutes and cover with a piece of foil when the top is nicely browned. Leave the cake to cool in the tin.

6 To make the lemon syrup, gently dissolve the sugar in the lemon juice in a small pan over a low heat. Spoon the syrup over the cake. When the cake is completely cooled, turn it carefully out of the tin and peel off the lining paper.

Lemon Coconut Layer Cake

This is a delicious sweet treat with custard and coconut.

Makes one 20cm/8in cake
175g/6oz/1¹/2 cups plain (all-purpose) flour, sifted with 1.5ml/¹/4 tsp salt
7 eggs
350g/12oz/1³/4 cups caster (superfine) sugar
15ml/1 tbsp grated orange rind
grated rind of 1¹/2 lemons
juice of I lemon
65g/2¹/2oz/scant I cup desiccated (dry unsweetened shredded) coconut

15ml/1 tbsp cornflour (cornstarch)
120ml/4fl oz/¹/2 cup water
40g/1¹/2oz/3 tbsp butter

For the icing
75g/3oz/6 tbsp unsalted (sweet) butter
175g/6oz/1¹/2 cups icing (confectioners') sugar
grated rind of 1¹/2 lemons
30ml/2 tbsp lemon juice
200g/7oz/2¹/2 cups desiccated (dry unsweetened shredded) coconut

1 Preheat the oven to 180°C/350°F/Gas 4. Line and grease three 20cm/8in shallow round cake tins (pans) with baking parchment.

2 Place six of the eggs in a bowl set over a pan of hot water and beat until frothy. Beat in 225g/8oz/generous 1 cup sugar until the mixture doubles in volume. Remove from the heat. Fold in the orange rind, half the lemon rind, 15ml/1 tbsp of the lemon juice and the coconut. Sift over the flour mixture and gently fold in.

3 Divide between the cake tins. Bake for 20–25 minutes. Leave in the tins for 5 minutes, then cool on a wire rack.

4 Blend the cornflour with a little cold water to dissolve. Whisk in the remaining egg until blended. In a pan, mix the remaining lemon rind and juice, water, remaining sugar and butter. Bring to the boil. Whisk in the cornflour, return to the boil and whisk until thick. Remove, cover with clear film (plastic wrap) until cool.

5 Cream the butter and icing sugar. Stir in the lemon rind and enough lemon juice to obtain a spreadable consistency. Sandwich the cake layers with the lemon custard. Spread the icing over the top and sides. Cover with the coconut.

Lemon Coconut Energy 5225kcal/21906kJ; Protein 74.3g; Carbohydrate 659.5g, of which sugars 517.6g; Fat 274g, of which saturates 173.1g; Cholesterol 1927mg; Calcium 760mg; Fibre 20.4g; Sodium 1793mg.
Nutty Lemon Energy 4358kcal/18221kJ; Protein 80.6g; Carbohydrate 443.9g, of which sugars 305.8g; Fat 264g, of which saturates 105.8g; Cholesterol 944mg; Calcium 967mg; Fibre 29.1g; Sodium 1622mg.

Peach Roll

A slice of this peach sponge cake makes the perfect light treat for a summer afternoon tea in the garden.

Serves 6–8
3 eggs
115g/4oz/ generous ½ cup caster (superfine) sugar
75g/3oz/⅔ cup plain (all-purpose) flour, sifted
15ml/1 tbsp boiling water
90ml/6 tbsp peach jam
icing (confectioners') sugar, for dusting (optional)

1 Preheat the oven to 200°C/400°F/Gas 6. Line and grease a 30 x 20cm/12 x 8in Swiss roll tin (jelly roll pan).

2 Combine the eggs and sugar in a bowl. Beat with a hand-held electric whisk until thick and mousse-like: when the whisk is lifted a trail should remain on the surface of the mixture for at least 30 seconds.

3 Carefully fold in the flour with a large metal spoon, then add the boiling water in the same way.

4 Spoon the mixture into the prepared tin, spread evenly to the edges and bake for 10–12 minutes, or until the cake springs back when lightly pressed.

5 Spread a sheet of baking parchment on a flat surface and sprinkle it with caster sugar. Carefully invert the cake on top and peel off the lining paper.

6 Make a neat cut two-thirds of the way through the cake, about 1cm/½in from the short edge nearest you – this will make it easier for you to roll the sponge cake. Trim the remaining edges to give a neat finish to the cake.

7 Spread the cake with the peach jam and roll up quickly from the partially cut end. Hold in position for a minute, making sure the join is underneath.

8 Cool on a wire rack. Dust with icing sugar, if you like.

Gooseberry Cake

This fruity cake is delicious when served warm with a dollop of whipped cream.

Makes one 18cm/7in square cake
115g/4oz/½ cup butter
165g/5½oz/1⅓ cups self-raising (self-rising) flour
5ml/1 tsp baking powder
2 eggs, beaten
115g/4oz/generous ½ cup caster (superfine) sugar
5–10ml/1–2 tsp rose water
pinch of freshly grated nutmeg
115g/4oz jar gooseberries in syrup, drained, juice reserved
caster (superfine) sugar, to decorate
whipped cream, to serve

1 Preheat the oven to 180°C/350°F/Gas 4. Grease an 18cm/7in square cake tin (pan) and line the base and sides with baking parchment. Grease the paper.

2 Gently melt the butter in a pan, then transfer to a large bowl and allow to cool.

3 Sift together the flour and baking powder and add to the butter in the bowl.

4 Beat in the eggs, one at a time, the sugar, rose water and grated nutmeg, until you have a smooth batter.

5 Mix in 15–30ml/1–2 tbsp of the reserved gooseberry juice from the jar, then pour half of the batter mixture into the prepared tin. Sprinkle over the gooseberries and pour over the remaining batter mixture.

6 Bake for about 45 minutes, or until a skewer inserted into the centre of the cake comes out clean.

7 Leave in the tin for 5 minutes, then turn out on a wire rack, peel off the lining paper and allow to cool for a further 5 minutes.

8 Dredge with caster sugar and serve immediately with whipped cream, or leave the cake to cool completely before decorating.

Peach Roll Energy 252kcal/1069kJ; Protein 4g; Carbohydrate 57g, of which sugars 50g; Fat 3g, of which saturates 1g; Cholesterol 87mg; Calcium 32mg; Fibre 0.5g; Sodium 41mg.
Gooseberry Energy 2080kcal/8719kJ; Protein 30.1g; Carbohydrate 263.9g, of which sugars 138.2g; Fat 108.1g, of which saturates 63.3g; Cholesterol 626mg; Calcium 392mg; Fibre 7.3g; Sodium 857mg.

Cherry Batter Cake

This colourful tray bake looks pretty when cut into neat squares or fingers. Its unusual topping makes it especially tasty.

**Makes one 33 x 23cm/
13 x 9in cake**
225g/8oz/2 cups self-raising
  (self-rising) flour
5ml/1 tsp baking powder
75g/3oz/6 tbsp butter, softened
150g/5oz/scant 1 cup soft light
  brown sugar
1 egg, lightly beaten
150ml/¼ pint/⅔ cup milk

icing (confectioners') sugar,
  for dusting
whipped cream, to
  serve (optional)

For the topping
675g/1½lb jar black cherries
  or blackcurrants, drained
175g/6oz/¾ cup soft light
  brown sugar
50g/2oz/½ cup self-raising
  (self-rising) flour
50g/2oz/¼ cup butter, melted

1 Preheat the oven to 190°C/375°F/Gas 5. Grease and line a 33 x 23cm/13 x 9in Swiss roll tin (jelly roll pan) with baking parchment, and grease the paper.

2 To make the base, sift the flour and baking powder into a large bowl. Add the butter, sugar, egg and milk.

3 Beat until the mixture becomes smooth, then turn into the prepared tin and smooth the surface.

4 To make the topping, sprinkle the drained cherries or blackcurrants evenly over the batter mixture.

5 Mix together the brown sugar, flour and melted butter, and spoon evenly over the fruit.

6 Bake for 40 minutes, or until the top is golden brown and the centre is firm to the touch.

7 Leave to cool for 15 minutes in the tin, then turn out and leave on a wire rack to cool completely. Dust with icing sugar. Serve with whipped cream, if you like.

Pound Cake with Red Fruit

This orange-scented cake is good for tea, or served as a dessert with cream.

**Makes one 20 x 10cm/
8 x 4in cake**
450g/1lb/4 cups fresh raspberries,
  strawberries or pitted cherries,
  or a combination of any of these
175g/6oz/generous ¾ cup caster
  (superfine) sugar, plus 15–30ml/
  1–2 tbsp, plus extra for sprinkling
15ml/1 tbsp lemon juice

175g/6oz/1½ cups plain
  (all-purpose) flour
10ml/2 tsp baking powder
pinch of salt
175g/6oz/¾ cup unsalted
  (sweet) butter, softened
3 eggs
grated rind of 1 orange
15ml/1 tbsp orange juice

1 Reserve a few whole fruits for decorating. In a blender or food processor, process the fruit until smooth. Add 15–30ml/1–2 tbsp sugar and the lemon juice, and process again. Strain the sauce and chill.

2 Grease the base and sides of a 20 x 10cm/8 x 4in loaf tin (pan) and line the base with baking parchment. Grease the paper. Sprinkle with sugar and tip out any excess. Preheat the oven to 180°C/350°F/Gas 4.

3 Sift together the flour, baking powder and a pinch of salt. In another bowl, beat the butter until creamy. Add the sugar and beat until light and fluffy. Add the eggs, one at a time, beating well after each addition.

4 Beat in the orange rind and juice. Gently fold the flour mixture into the butter mixture in three batches, then spoon the mixture into the loaf tin and tap gently to release any air bubbles.

5 Bake for 35–40 minutes, or until the top is golden and it is springy to the touch. Leave the cake in its tin on a wire rack for 10 minutes, then remove the cake from the tin and cool for 30 minutes. Remove the paper and serve slices of cake with a little of the fruit sauce, decorated with the reserved fruit.

Cherry Energy 3770kcal/15932kJ; Protein 43g; Carbohydrate 686g, of which sugars 476.4g; Fat 114.4g, of which saturates 68.8g; Cholesterol 466mg; Calcium 890mg; Fibre 12.6g; Sodium 974mg.
Pound Energy 2927kcal/12264kJ; Protein 43.5g; Carbohydrate 341.9g, of which sugars 208.6g; Fat 164.1g, of which saturates 96.6g; Cholesterol 944mg; Calcium 569mg; Fibre 16.7g; Sodium 1301mg.

Jewel Cake

This pretty cherry-decorated cake is excellent served as a special teatime treat.

**Makes one 23 x 13cm/
9 x 5in cake**
115g/4oz/½ cup mixed glacé
(candied) cherries, halved,
washed and dried
50g/2oz/4 tbsp preserved stem
ginger in syrup, chopped,
washed and dried
50g/2oz/⅓ cup chopped mixed
(candied) peel
115g/4oz/1 cup self-raising
(self-rising) flour
75g/3oz/⅔ cup plain
(all-purpose) flour

25g/1oz/¼ cup cornflour
(cornstarch)
175g/6oz/¾ cup butter
175g/6oz/scant 1 cup caster
(superfine) sugar
3 eggs
grated rind of 1 orange

To decorate
175g/6oz/1½ cups icing
(confectioners') sugar,
sifted
30–45ml/2–3 tbsp freshly
squeezed orange juice
50g/2oz/¼ cup mixed glacé
(candied) cherries, chopped
25g/1oz/2½ tbsp mixed
(candied) peel, chopped

1 Preheat the oven to 180°C/350°F/Gas 4. Grease and line a 23 x 13cm/9 x 5in loaf tin (pan) and grease the paper.

2 Place the glacé cherries, stem ginger and mixed peel in a plastic bag with 25g/1oz/¼ cup of the self-raising flour and shake to coat evenly. Sift together the remaining flours and cornflour.

3 In a large bowl, beat together the butter and sugar until light and fluffy. Beat in the eggs, one at a time. Fold in the sifted flours with the orange rind, then stir in the dried fruit.

4 Transfer the mixture to the cake tin and bake for 1¼ hours, or until a skewer inserted into the centre comes out clean. Leave in the tin for 5 minutes, then cool on a wire rack.

5 For the decoration, mix the icing sugar with the orange juice until smooth. Drizzle the icing over the cake.

6 Mix together the glacé cherries and mixed peel, then use to decorate the cake. Allow the icing to set before serving.

Fruit & Nut Cake

A rich, fibrous fruit cake that matures with keeping. Omit the fruit and nut decoration from the top if you want to ice it for a Christmas cake.

Serves 12–14
175g/6oz/1½ cups self-raising
(self-rising) wholemeal
(whole-wheat) flour
175g/6oz/1½ cups self-raising
(self-rising) white flour
10ml/2 tsp mixed (apple pie) spice

15ml/1 tbsp apple and
apricot spread
45ml/3 tbsp clear honey
15ml/1 tbsp molasses
90ml/6 tbsp sunflower oil
175ml/6fl oz/¾ cup orange juice
2 eggs, beaten
675g/1½lb/4 cups luxury mixed
dried fruit
115g/4oz/½ cup glacé (candied)
cherries, halved
45ml/3 tbsp split almonds

1 Preheat the oven to 160°C/325°F/Gas 3. Line and grease a deep 20cm/8in cake tin (pan). Tie a band of newspaper around the outside of the tin and stand it on a pad of newspaper on a baking sheet.

2 Combine the flours in a mixing bowl. Stir in the mixed spice and make a well in the centre.

3 Put the apple and apricot spread in a small bowl. Gradually stir in the honey and molasses. Add to the bowl with the oil, orange juice, eggs and mixed fruit. Stir with a wooden spoon to mix thoroughly.

4 Scrape the mixture into the prepared tin and smooth the surface. Arrange the cherries and almonds in a decorative pattern over the top. Bake for 2 hours, or until a skewer inserted into the centre of the cake comes out clean. Turn on to a wire rack to cool, then remove the lining paper.

> **Cook's Tip**
> For a less elaborate cake, omit the cherries, chop the almonds roughly and sprinkle them over the top.

Jewel Energy 4369kcal/18404kJ; Protein 41.5g; Carbohydrate 726.1g, of which sugars 560.5g; Fat 164.9g, of which saturates 96.5g; Cholesterol 982mg; Calcium 1042mg; Fibre 11.5g; Sodium 2007mg.
Fruit and Nut Energy 327kcal/1384kJ; Protein 5.2g; Carbohydrate 63g, of which sugars 43.8g; Fat 7.8g, of which saturates 1g; Cholesterol 27mg; Calcium 94mg; Fibre 2.2g; Sodium 40mg.

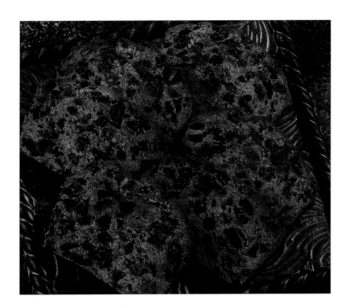

Light Fruit Cake

Dried fruit soaked in wine and rum gives this fruit cake an exquisite flavour. For the best taste, wrap it in foil and store it for a week before cutting.

**Makes two 23 x 13cm/
9 x 5in cakes**
225g/8oz/1 cup prunes
225g/8oz/1⅓ cups dates
225g/8oz/1 cup currants
225g/8oz/generous 1¼ cups
  sultanas (golden raisins)
250ml/8fl oz/1 cup dry
  white wine
250ml/8fl oz/1 cup rum
350g/12oz/3 cups plain
  (all-purpose) flour
10ml/2 tsp baking powder
5ml/1 tsp ground cinnamon
2.5ml/½ tsp freshly grated nutmeg
225g/8oz/1 cup butter,
  at room temperature
225g/8oz/generous 1 cup caster
  (superfine) sugar
4 eggs, lightly beaten
5ml/1 tsp vanilla extract

1 Stone (pit) the prunes and dates and chop finely. Place in a bowl with the currants and sultanas. Stir in the wine and rum and leave, covered, for 2 days. Stir occasionally.

2 Preheat the oven to 150°C/300°F/Gas 2 with a tray of hot water in the bottom. Line two 23 x 13cm/9 x 5in loaf tins (pans) with baking parchment and grease the paper.

3 Sift together the dry ingredients. Cream the butter and sugar together until light and fluffy. Gradually add the eggs and vanilla extract. Fold in the flour mixture in three batches, and finally fold in the dried fruit mixture and its liquid.

4 Divide the mixture between the prepared tins and bake until a skewer inserted into the centre comes out clean, about 1½ hours. Leave to stand for 20 minutes, then unmould the cake on to a wire rack to cool completely.

> **Variation**
> *You can use a combination of any dried fruit, such as apricots, figs and cranberries in place of the prunes and/or dates. You could also add glacé (candied) cherries.*

Rich Fruit Cake

Sweet sherry adds to the fruit and spices in this cake.

**Makes one 23 x 8cm/
9 x 3in cake**
150g/5oz/generous ½ cup currants
170g/6oz/generous 1 cup raisins
50g/2oz/½ cup sultanas
  (golden raisins)
50g/2oz/¼ cup glacé (candied)
  cherries, halved
45ml/3 tbsp sweet sherry
175g/6oz/¾ cup butter
200g/7oz/scant 1 cup soft dark
  brown sugar
2 eggs, at room temperature
200g/7oz/1¾ cups plain
  (all-purpose) flour
10ml/2 tsp baking powder
10ml/2 tsp each ground ginger,
  allspice, and cinnamon
15ml/1 tbsp golden (light
  corn) syrup
15ml/1 tbsp milk
55g/2oz/⅓ cup cut mixed
  (candied) peel
115g/4oz/1 cup chopped walnuts

For the decoration
120ml/4fl oz/scant ½ cup
  orange marmalade
crystallized citrus fruit slices
glacé (candied) cherries

1 A day in advance, combine the dried fruit and cherries in a bowl. Stir in the sherry, cover and soak overnight.

2 Preheat the oven to 150°C/300°F/Gas 2. Line and grease a 23 x 7.5cm/9 x 3in springform tin (pan) with baking parchment. Place a tray of hot water in the bottom of the oven.

3 Cream the butter and sugar. Beat in the eggs, one at a time. Sift the flour, baking powder and spices together three times. Fold into the butter mixture in three batches. Fold in the syrup, milk, dried fruit and liquid, mixed peel and walnuts.

4 Spoon into the prepared tin, spreading the mixture out so that there is a slight depression in the centre. Bake for about 2½–3 hours. Cover with foil when the top is golden to prevent over-browning. Cool in the tin on a rack. To decorate, melt the marmalade over a low heat, then brush over the top of the cake. Decorate the cake with the crystallized citrus fruit slices and glacé cherries.

Light Energy 5719kcal/24077kJ; Protein 75.8g; Carbohydrate 918.1g, of which sugars 689.5g; Fat 218.7g, of which saturates 8.5g; Cholesterol 951mg; Calcium 1232mg; Fibre 28.3g; Sodium 2664mg.
Rich Energy 4509kcal/18916kJ; Protein 28.3g; Carbohydrate 629.3g, of which sugars 628.5g; Fat 220.7g, of which saturates 95.2g; Cholesterol 363mg; Calcium 642mg; Fibre 14.6g; Sodium 1480mg.

Irish Whiskey Cake

This succulent fruit cake is drizzled with whiskey as soon as it comes out of the oven. It is both high in fibre and full of flavour.

Serves 10
115g/4oz/³⁄₄ cup sultanas
   (golden raisins)
115g/4oz/scant 1 cup raisins
115g/4oz/½ cup currants
115g/4oz/½ cup glacé
   (candied) cherries
175g/6oz/1¼ cups soft light
   brown sugar
300ml/½ pint/1¼ cups cold tea
1 egg, beaten
300g/11oz/2⅔ cups self-raising
   (self-rising) flour, sifted
45ml/3 tbsp Irish whiskey

1 Mix the sultanas, raisins, currants, cherries, sugar and tea in a large bowl. Leave to soak overnight until the tea has been absorbed.

2 Preheat the oven to 180°C/350°F/Gas 4. Line and grease a 1kg/2¼lb loaf tin (pan).

3 Add the egg and flour to the fruit mixture and beat thoroughly until well mixed.

4 Pour into the prepared tin and bake for 1½ hours or until a skewer inserted into the centre comes out clean.

5 Prick over the top of the cake with a skewer and drizzle over the whiskey while the cake is still hot.

6 Allow to stand for 5 minutes, then remove from the tin and cool completely on a wire rack.

Variation
For a tangy finish, drizzle with lemon icing. Mix the juice of 1 lemon with 225g/8oz/2 cup icing (confectioners') sugar and enough warm water for the icing to have a thin consistency. Drizzle the icing over the cooled cake and decorate with crystallized lemon slices, if you like.

Moist & Rich Christmas Cake

This festive cake can be made 4–6 weeks ahead.

Makes one 20cm/8in cake
225g/8oz/1⅓ cups sultanas
   (golden raisins)
225g/8oz/1 cup currants
225g/8oz/1⅓ cups raisins
115g/4oz/1 cup pitted and
   chopped prunes
50g/2oz/¼ cup halved glacé
   (candied) cherries
50g/2oz/⅓ cup mixed chopped
   (candied) peel
45ml/3 tbsp brandy or sherry
225g/8oz/2 cups plain
   (all-purpose) flour
pinch of salt
2.5ml/½ tsp ground cinnamon
2.5ml/½ tsp grated nutmeg
15ml/1 tbsp unsweetened
   cocoa powder
225g/8oz/1 cup butter
225g/8oz/1 cup brown sugar
4 large (US extra large) eggs
finely grated rind of 1 orange
50g/2oz/⅔ cup ground almonds
50g/2oz/½ cup chopped almonds

To decorate
60ml/4 tbsp apricot jam, warmed
450g/1lb ready-made
   almond paste
450g/1lb ready-to-roll
   fondant icing
225g/8oz ready-made royal icing

1 Put the dried fruits, cherries and peel in a bowl with the brandy or sherry, covered, overnight. The next day, grease a 20cm/8in round cake tin (pan) and line it with baking parchment.

2 Preheat the oven to 160°C/325°F/Gas 3. Sift together the flour, salt, spices and cocoa powder. Whisk the butter and sugar until fluffy and beat in the eggs, then mix in the orange rind, all the almonds, soaked fruits and liquid, and the flour mixture. Spoon into the cake tin and level the top. Bake for 3 hours. Cool in the tin on a wire rack for an hour, then turn out, leaving the paper on. When cold, wrap in foil and store.

3 Strain the apricot jam. Remove the paper from the cake, place on a cake board and brush it with apricot glaze. Cover with almond paste, then fondant icing. Pipe a border around the base of the cake with royal icing. Tie a ribbon around the sides.

4 From the trimmings, make a bell motif, leaves and holly berries. Dry for 24 hours. Attach all to the cake with a dab of royal icing. When dry, cover the cake and pack in an airtight container.

Irish Whiskey Energy 311kcal/1323kJ; Protein 4.4g; Carbohydrate 73g, of which sugars 50.1g; Fat 1.1g, of which saturates 0.2g; Cholesterol 19mg; Calcium 84mg; Fibre 1.7g; Sodium 23mg.
Moist and Rich Energy 8145kcal/34415kJ; Protein 74.4g; Carbohydrate 1528.9g, of which sugars 1385.8g; Fat 204.6g, of which saturates 105.4g; Cholesterol 1154mg; Calcium 1859mg; Fibre 38.1g; Sodium 2326mg.

Glazed Christmas Ring

Whole brazil nuts decorate this fabulous fruit-packed Christmas cake.

Makes one 25cm/10in ring cake

225g/8oz/generous 1⅓ cups sultanas (golden raisins)
175g/6oz/¾ cup raisins
175g/6oz/generous 1 cup currants
175g/6oz/1 cup dried figs, chopped
90ml/6 tbsp whisky
45ml/3 tbsp orange juice
225g/8oz/1 cup butter
225g/8oz/1cup dark soft brown sugar
5 eggs
250g/9oz/2¼ cups plain (all-purpose) flour
15ml/1 tbsp baking powder
15ml/1 tbsp mixed (apple pie) spice
115g/4oz/½ cup glacé (candied) cherries, chopped
115g/4oz/1 cup chopped brazil nuts
50g/2oz/⅓ cup chopped mixed (candied) peel
50g/2oz/½ cup ground almonds
grated rind and juice 1 orange
30ml/2 tbsp thick-cut orange marmalade

To decorate

150ml/¼ pint/⅔ cup thick-cut orange marmalade
15ml/1 tbsp orange juice
175g/6oz/¾ cup glacé (candied) cherries
115g/4oz/⅔ cup dried figs, halved
75g/3oz/½ cup whole brazil nuts

1 Put the dried fruits in a bowl, pour over 60ml/4 tbsp of the whisky and all the orange juice, and marinate overnight.

2 Preheat the oven to 160°C/325°F/Gas 3. Grease and line a 25cm/10in ring mould. Cream the butter and sugar. Beat in the eggs. Sift together the flour, baking powder and mixed spice. Fold into the egg mixture, alternating with the remaining ingredients, except the whisky. Transfer to the tin.

3 Bake for 1 hour, then reduce the oven temperature to 150°C/300°F/Gas 2 and bake for a further 1¾–2 hours.

4 Prick the cake all over and pour over the reserved whisky. Cool in the tin for 30 minutes, then transfer to a wire rack. Boil the marmalade and orange juice for 3 minutes. Stir in the fruit and nuts. Cool, then spoon over the cake and leave to set.

Flourless Fruit Cake

This makes the perfect base for a celebration fruit cake for anyone who needs to avoid eating flour.

Makes one 25cm/10in round cake

450g/1lb/1⅓ cups mincemeat
350g/12oz/2 cups dried mixed fruit
115g/4oz/½ cup ready-to eat dried apricots, chopped
115g/4oz/⅔ cup ready-to-eat dried figs, chopped
115g/4oz/½ cup glacé (candied) cherries, halved
115g/4oz/1 cup walnut pieces
225g/8oz/8–10 cups cornflakes, crushed
4 eggs, lightly beaten
410g/14½oz can evaporated milk
5ml/1 tsp mixed (apple pie) spice
5ml/1 tsp baking powder
mixed glacé (candied) fruits, chopped, to decorate (optional)

1 Preheat the oven to 150°C/300°F/Gas 2.

2 Grease a 25cm/10in round cake tin (pan), line the base and sides with a double thickness of baking parchment and grease the paper.

3 Put the mincemeat, dried mixed fruit, figs and glacé cherries into a large bowl. Beat together until well combined.

4 Add the walnut pieces and cornflakes. Stir in the eggs, evaporated milk, mixed spice and baking powder.

5 Turn into the cake tin and smooth the surface.

6 Bake for about 1¾ hours, or until a skewer inserted in the centre of the cake comes out clean.

7 Allow the cake to cool in the tin for 10 minutes, then turn out on to a wire rack, peel off the lining paper and leave to cool completely.

8 Once the cake has cooled, decorate with the chopped glacé fruits, if you like.

Glazed Energy 9132kcal/38385kJ; Protein 120.5g; Carbohydrate 1340.7g, of which sugars 1147.5g; Fat 380.9g, of which saturates 158.8g; Cholesterol 1431mg; Calcium 2500mg; Fibre 58.7g; Sodium 2368mg.
Flourless Energy 5252kcal/22194kJ; Protein 111.3g; Carbohydrate 939.6g, of which sugars 755.7g; Fat 142.5g, of which saturates 23.3g; Cholesterol 848mg; Calcium 2125mg; Fibre 35.8g; Sodium 3371mg.

Eggless Christmas Cake

This simple cake contains a wealth of fruit and nuts to give it that traditional Christmas flavour. It is decorated with large pieces of colourful glacé fruits.

Makes one 18cm/7in square cake

75g/3oz/½ cup sultanas (golden raisins)
75g/3oz/scant ½ cup raisins
75g/3oz/scant ½ cup currants
75g/3oz/scant ½ cup glacé (candied) cherries, halved
50g/2oz/⅓ cup mixed (candied) peel
250ml/8fl oz/1 cup apple juice
25g/1oz/2 tbsp toasted hazelnuts
30ml/2 tbsp pumpkin seeds
2 pieces preserved stem ginger in syrup, chopped
finely grated rind of 1 lemon
120ml/4fl oz/½ cup milk
50ml/2fl oz/¼ cup sunflower oil
225g/8oz/2 cups self-raising (self-rising) wholemeal (whole-wheat) flour
10ml/2 tsp mixed (apple pie) spice
45ml/3 tbsp brandy or dark rum
apricot jam, for brushing
glacé (candied) fruits, to decorate

1 Soak the sultanas, raisins, currants, cherries and mixed peel in the apple juice overnight.

2 Preheat the oven to 150°C/300°F/Gas 2. Grease and line an 18cm/7in square cake tin (pan).

3 Transfer the soaked fruit to a large bowl. Add the hazelnuts, pumpkin seeds, ginger and lemon rind to the fruit.

4 Stir in the milk and oil. Sift the flour and spice into another bowl, then add to the fruit mixture with the brandy or rum. Combine thoroughly.

5 Spoon the mixture into the prepared cake tin and bake for about 1½ hours, or until the cake is golden brown and firm to the touch.

6 Turn out and cool on a wire rack. Warm the apricot jam and sieve it. Brush over the cake to glaze it and decorate with glacé fruits.

Chocolate Date Cake

A recipe for a stunning date cake that tastes wonderful. Rich and gooey – it's a chocoholic's delight!

Serves 8

4 egg whites
115g/4oz/generous ½ cup caster (superfine) sugar
200g/7oz plain (semisweet) chocolate
175g/6oz/1 cup Medjool dates, stoned (pitted) and chopped
175g/6oz/1½ cups chopped walnuts or pecan nuts
5ml/1 tsp vanilla extract

For the frosting
200g/7oz/scant 1 cup fromage frais or ricotta cheese
200g/7oz/scant 1 cup mascarpone
a few drops of vanilla extract
icing (confectioners') sugar, to taste

1 Preheat the oven to 180°C/350°F/Gas 4. Grease and base-line a 20cm/8in springform tin (pan).

2 To make the frosting, mix together the fromage frais or ricotta and mascarpone, add a few drops of vanilla extract and icing sugar to taste, then set aside.

3 Whisk the egg whites until they form stiff peaks. Whisk in 30ml/2 tbsp of the caster sugar until the meringue is thick and glossy, then fold in the remainder.

4 Chop 175g/6oz of the chocolate. Carefully fold into the meringue with the dates, nuts and 5ml/1 tsp of the vanilla extract. Pour into the prepared tin, spread level and bake for about 45 minutes, or until risen around the edges.

5 Allow to cool in the tin for about 10 minutes, then unmould, peel off the lining paper and leave to cool completely. Swirl the frosting over the top of the cake.

6 Melt the remaining chocolate in a double boiler or in a heatproof bowl over a pan of simmering water. Spoon into a small paper piping (icing) bag and drizzle the chocolate over the cake. Chill before serving.

Eggless Energy 2366kcal/9987kJ; Protein 44.8g; Carbohydrate 393.4g, of which sugars 253.8g; Fat 68.1g, of which saturates 8.6g; Cholesterol 7mg; Calcium 628mg; Fibre 30.3g; Sodium 291mg.
Chocolate Date Energy 441kcal/1841kJ; Protein 10.2g; Carbohydrate 40.3g, of which sugars 39.9g; Fat 27.6g, of which saturates 9.1g; Cholesterol 14mg; Calcium 70mg; Fibre 1.8g; Sodium 45mg.

Almond & Raspberry Roll

This light and airy sponge cake is rolled up with a fresh cream and raspberry filling for a decadent teatime treat.

Makes one 23cm/9in long roll
3 eggs
75g/3oz/6 tbsp caster (superfine) sugar
50g/2oz/¹⁄₂ cup plain (all-purpose) flour
30ml/2 tbsp ground almonds
caster (superfine) sugar, for dusting
250ml/8fl oz/1 cup double (heavy) cream
225g/8oz/1¹⁄₃ cups fresh raspberries
16 flaked almonds, toasted, to decorate

1 Preheat the oven to 200°C/400°F/Gas 6. Grease a 33 x 23cm/13 x 9in Swiss roll tin (jelly roll pan) and line with baking parchment. Grease the paper.

2 Whisk the eggs and sugar in a heatproof bowl until blended. Place the bowl over a pan of simmering water and whisk until thick and pale.

3 Whisk off the heat until cool. Sift over the flour and almonds, and fold in gently.

4 Transfer to the prepared tin and bake for 10–12 minutes, until risen and springy to the touch.

5 Invert the cake in its tin on to baking parchment dusted with caster sugar. Leave to cool, then remove the tin and lining paper.

6 Reserve a little cream, then whip the remainder until it holds its shape. Fold in all but 8 raspberries and spread the mixture over the cooled cake, leaving a narrow border. Roll the cake up and sprinkle with caster sugar.

7 Whip the reserved cream until it just holds its shape, and spoon or pipe a line along the top of the roll in the centre. Decorate the cream with the reserved raspberries and toasted flaked almonds.

Banana Ginger Parkin

The combination of banana and ginger give a new slant to the traditional recipe for this delicious cake.

Makes 16–20 squares
200g/7oz/1¾ cups plain (all-purpose) flour
10ml/2 tsp bicarbonate of soda (baking soda)
10ml/2 tsp ground ginger
150g/5oz/1¼ cups medium oatmeal
50g/2oz/¹⁄₄ cup muscovado sugar (molasses)
75g/3oz/6 tbsp sunflower margarine
150g/5oz/3 tbsp golden (light corn) syrup
1 egg, beaten
3 ripe bananas, mashed
75g/3oz/³⁄₄ cup icing (confectioners') sugar
preserved stem ginger, to decorate (optional)

1 Preheat the oven to 160°C/325°F/Gas 3. Grease and line an 18 x 28cm/7 x 11in cake tin (pan).

2 Sift together the flour, bicarbonate of soda and ginger in a bowl, then stir in the oatmeal.

3 Melt the sugar, margarine and syrup in a pan over a low heat, then stir into the flour mixture.

4 Beat the egg and mashed bananas into the flour mixture until thoroughly combined. Spoon the mixture into the prepared tin and bake for about 1 hour, or until firm to the touch.

5 Leave the cake to cool in the tin for 5 minutes, then turn it out on to a wire rack and allow it to cool completely.

6 If you want to keep the cake for a few months, wrap it in foil and put it in an air-tight container without cutting it. If you want to eat it immediately, cut it into squares.

7 Make the icing when you want to serve the cake: sift the icing sugar into a bowl and stir in just enough water to make a smooth, runny icing. Drizzle the icing over each square of cake in a zigzag pattern and top with a piece of stem ginger, if you like.

Almond Energy 2166kcal/9012kJ; Protein 37.3g; Carbohydrate 133.9g, of which sugars 95g; Fat 169g, of which saturates 89.8g; Cholesterol 914mg; Calcium 446mg; Fibre 9.4g; Sodium 282mg.
Banana Ginger Energy 157kcal/662kJ; Protein 2.4g; Carbohydrate 29.2g, of which sugars 15.8g; Fat 4.2g, of which saturates 0.7g; Cholesterol 10mg; Calcium 25mg; Fibre 1g; Sodium 57mg.

Banana Coconut Cake

Slightly over-ripe bananas are best for this perfect coffee-morning cake topped with honey and coconut.

Makes one 18cm/7in square cake
115g/4oz/½ cup butter, softened
115g/4oz/generous ½ cup caster (superfine) sugar
2 eggs
115g/4oz/1 cup self-raising (self-rising) flour
50g/2oz/½ cup plain (all-purpose) flour
5ml/1 tsp bicarbonate of soda (baking soda)
120ml/4fl oz/½ cup milk
2 large bananas, peeled and mashed
75g/3oz/1 cup desiccated (dry unsweetened shredded) coconut, toasted

For the topping
25g/1oz/2 tbsp butter
30ml/2 tbsp clear honey
115g/4oz/2 cups shredded coconut

1 Preheat the oven to 190°C/375°F/Gas 5. Grease a deep 18cm/7in square cake tin (pan), line with baking parchment and grease the paper.

2 Beat the butter and sugar until smooth and creamy. Beat in the eggs, one at a time. Sift together the flours and bicarbonate of soda, sift half into the butter mixture and stir to mix.

3 Combine the milk and mashed banana, and beat half into the egg mixture. Stir in the remaining flour and banana mixtures and the toasted coconut. Transfer the batter to the cake tin and smooth the surface.

4 Bake for 1 hour, or until a skewer inserted into the centre of the cake comes out clean. Leave in the tin for 5 minutes, then turn out on to a wire rack, peel off the paper and leave to cool completely.

5 To make the topping, gently melt the butter and honey in a small pan. Stir in the shredded coconut and cook, stirring, for 5 minutes or until lightly browned. Remove from the heat and allow to cool slightly. Spoon the topping over the cake and allow to cool.

Chocolate Banana Cake

Fresh fruit is especially good for making a moist cake mixture. Here is a delicious sticky chocolate cake, moist enough to eat without the icing if you want to cut down on the calories.

Serves 8
225g/8oz/2 cups self-raising (self-rising) flour
45ml/3 tbsp reduced-fat unsweetened cocoa powder
115g/4oz/½ cup soft light brown sugar
30ml/2 tbsp malt extract
30ml/2 tbsp golden (light corn) syrup
2 eggs, beaten
60ml/4 tbsp skimmed milk
60ml/4 tbsp sunflower oil
2 large ripe bananas

For the icing
175g/6oz/1½ cups icing (confectioners') sugar, sifted
30ml/2 tbsp reduced-fat unsweetened cocoa powder, sifted
15–30ml/1–2 tbsp warm water

1 Preheat the oven to 160°C/325°F/Gas 3. Line and grease a deep 20cm/8in round cake tin (pan). Sift the flour into a mixing bowl with the cocoa powder. Stir in the sugar.

2 Make a well in the centre of the dry ingredients and add the malt extract, golden syrup, eggs, milk and oil. Mix well.

3 Mash the bananas thoroughly and stir them into the mixture until thoroughly combined.

4 Spoon the cake mixture into the prepared tin and bake for 1–1¼ hours, or until the centre of the cake springs back when lightly pressed.

5 Remove from the tin and turn on to a wire rack to cool.

6 To make the icing, put the icing sugar and cocoa in a mixing bowl and gradually add enough water to make a mixture thick enough to coat the back of a wooden spoon.

7 Pour over the top of the cake and ease to the edges, allowing the icing to dribble down the sides.

Chocolate Banana Energy 352kcal/1487kJ; Protein 6.5g; Carbohydrate 64.4g, of which sugars 41.9g; Fat 9.4g, of which saturates 2.3g; Cholesterol 48mg; Calcium 145mg; Fibre 2.3g; Sodium 233mg.
Banana Coconut Energy 3291kcal/13744kJ; Protein 43g; Carbohydrate 332.2g, of which sugars 201.8g; Fat 208.5g, of which saturates 144.6g; Cholesterol 686mg; Calcium 560mg; Fibre 24.4g; Sodium 1092mg.

Apple Crumble Cake

In the autumn, use windfall apples. When served warm with thick cream or custard, this cake works beautifully as a sweet, fruity dessert.

Serves 8–10
75g/3oz/⅔ cup self-raising
   (self-rising) flour
½ tsp ground cinnamon
40g/1½oz/3 tbsp butter
25g/1oz/2 tbsp caster
   (superfine) sugar

For the base
50g/2oz/¼ cup butter, softened
75g/3oz/6 tbsp caster
   (superfine) sugar

1 egg, beaten
115g/4oz/1 cup self-raising
   (self-rising) flour, sifted
2 cooking apples, peeled, cored
   and sliced
50g/2oz/⅓ cup sultanas
   (golden raisins)

To decorate
1 red dessert apple, cored,
   thinly sliced and tossed in
   lemon juice
25g/1oz/2 tbsp caster (superfine)
   sugar, sifted
pinch of ground cinnamon

1 Preheat the oven to 180°C/350°F/Gas 4. Grease a deep 18cm/7in springform tin (pan), line the base with baking parchment and grease the paper.

2 To make the topping, sift the flour and cinnamon into a mixing bowl. Rub the butter into the flour using your fingertips or a pastry cutter until it resembles breadcrumbs, then stir in the sugar. Set aside.

3 To make the base, put the butter, sugar, egg and flour into a bowl and beat for 1–2 minutes, or until smooth. Spoon into the prepared tin.

4 Mix together the apple slices and sultanas, and spread them evenly over the top. Sprinkle with the topping.

5 Bake for about 1 hour. Cool in the tin for 10 minutes before turning out on to a wire rack and peeling off the lining paper. Serve warm or cool, decorated with slices of red dessert apple and sprinkled with caster sugar and cinnamon.

Nut & Apple Gateau

Pecan nuts and apples give this gateau a beautiful texture and flavour.

**Makes one 23cm/9in
round cake**
115g/4oz/⅔ cup pecan nuts
   or walnuts, toasted
50g/2oz/½ cup plain
   (all-purpose) flour
10ml/2 tsp baking powder

1.5ml/¼ tsp salt
2 large cooking apples
3 eggs
225g/8oz/generous 1 cup caster
   (superfine) sugar
5ml/1 tsp vanilla extract
175ml/6fl oz/¾ cup
   whipping cream

1 Preheat the oven to 160°C/325°F/Gas 3. Line two 23cm/9in cake tins (pans) with baking parchment and grease the paper.

2 Finely chop the nuts. Reserve 25ml/1½ tbsp and place the remainder in a mixing bowl. Sift over the flour, baking powder and salt, and stir well.

3 Peel and core the apples. Cut into 3mm/⅛in dice, then stir into the flour mixture. Beat the eggs until frothy. Gradually add the sugar and vanilla extract, and beat until ribbon trails form when you lift the whisk out of the mixture, about 8 minutes. Fold in the flour mixture.

4 Pour the mixture into the prepared cake tins and bake until a skewer inserted into the centre comes out clean, about 35 minutes. Leave to stand in the tin for 10 minutes, then turn out on to a wire rack to cool.

5 Whip the cream until firm. Use half for the filling. Using a large star nozzle, pipe rosettes on the top and then sprinkle over the reserved nuts to finish.

> **Cook's Tip**
> *Toast the nuts on a foil-covered grill (broiling) pan under a hot grill (broiler) or in the oven until golden brown.*

Apple Crumble Energy 211kcal/890kJ; Protein 2.7g; Carbohydrate 33.7g, of which sugars 19.3g; Fat 8.3g, of which saturates 4.9g; Cholesterol 38mg; Calcium 42mg; Fibre 1.1g; Sodium 64mg.
Nut and Apple Energy 2807kcal/11741kJ; Protein 39.3g; Carbohydrate 303.2g, of which sugars 263.3g; Fat 168.6g, of which saturates 55.5g; Cholesterol 755mg; Calcium 454mg; Fibre 10.2g; Sodium 274mg.

Cinnamon & Apple Gateau

Make this lovely moist and fruity gateau as a guilt-free autumn teatime treat.

Serves 8

3 eggs
115g/4oz/½ cup caster (superfine) sugar
75g/3oz/¾ cup plain (all-purpose) flour
5ml/1 tsp ground cinnamon

For the filling and topping

4 large eating apples
15ml/1 tbsp water
60ml/4 tbsp clear honey
75g/3oz/½ cup sultanas (golden raisins)
2.5ml/½ tsp ground cinnamon
350g/12oz/1½ cups low-fat soft cheese
60ml/4 tbsp reduced-fat fromage frais or low-fat cream cheese
10ml/2 tsp lemon juice

1 Preheat the oven to 190°C/375°F/Gas 5. Line and grease a 23cm/9in shallow round cake tin (pan). Whisk the eggs and sugar until thick, then sift the flour and cinnamon over the surface and carefully fold in with a large metal spoon.

2 Pour into the prepared tin and bake for 25–30 minutes, or until the cake springs back when lightly pressed. Leave on a wire rack to cool completely.

3 To make the filling, peel, core and slice three of the apples and cook them in a covered pan with the water and half the honey until softened. Add the sultanas and cinnamon, stir well, replace the lid and leave to cool.

4 Put the soft cheese in a bowl with the fromage frais, the remaining honey and half the lemon juice; beat until smooth. Split the sponge cake in half, place the bottom half on a plate and drizzle over any liquid from the apples.

5 Spread with two-thirds of the cheese mixture, then top with the apple filling. Fit the top of the cake in place.

6 Swirl the remaining filling over the top of the sponge. Quarter, core and slice the remaining apple, dip the slices in the remaining lemon juice and use to decorate the edges.

Passion Cake

This cake is associated with Passion Sunday. The carrot and banana give it a rich, moist texture.

Makes one 20cm/8in round cake

200g/7oz/1¾ cups self-raising (self-rising) flour
10ml/2 tsp baking powder
5ml/1 tsp cinnamon
2.5ml/½ tsp freshly grated nutmeg
150g/5oz/10 tbsp butter, softened, or sunflower margarine
150g/5oz/generous 1 cup soft light brown sugar
grated rind of 1 lemon
2 eggs, beaten

2 carrots, coarsely grated
1 ripe banana, mashed
115g/4oz/¾ cup raisins
50g/2oz/½ cup chopped walnuts or pecan nuts
30ml/2 tbsp milk
6–8 walnuts, halved, to decorate
coffee crystal sugar, to decorate

For the frosting

200g/7oz/scant 1 cup cream cheese, softened
30g/1½oz/scant ⅓ cup icing (confectioners') sugar
juice of 1 lemon
grated rind of 1 orange

1 Line and grease a deep 20cm/8in round cake tin (pan). Preheat the oven to 180°C/350°F/Gas 4. Sift the flour, baking powder and spices into a bowl.

2 In another bowl, cream the butter or margarine and sugar with the lemon rind until it is light and fluffy, then beat in the eggs. Fold in the flour mixture, then the carrots, banana, raisins, chopped nuts and milk.

3 Spoon the mixture into the prepared cake tin, level the top and bake for about 1 hour, or until risen and the top is springy to the touch. Turn the tin upside down and allow the cake to cool in the tin for 30 minutes. Then turn out on to a wire rack and leave to cool completely. When cold, split the cake in half.

4 To make the frosting, cream the cheese with the icing sugar, lemon juice and orange rind, then sandwich the two halves of the cake together with half of the frosting. Spread the rest of the frosting on top and decorate with walnut halves and sugar.

Cinnamon and Apple Energy 239kcal/1010kJ; Protein 10.8g; Carbohydrate 39.9g, of which sugars 32.8g; Fat 5.8g, of which saturates 2.9g; Cholesterol 82mg; Calcium 97mg; Fibre 1.1g; Sodium 225mg.
Passion Energy 2643kcal/11041kJ; Protein 31.2g; Carbohydrate 279.3g, of which sugars 184.2g; Fat 163.7g, of which saturates 88.2g; Cholesterol 545mg; Calcium 488mg; Fibre 9g; Sodium 1088mg.

Pear & Polenta Cake

Polenta gives the light sponge topping and sliced pears a nutty corn flavour that complements the fruit perfectly. Serve as a dessert with custard or cream.

Makes 10 slices
butter or margarine,
  for greasing
175g/6oz/¾ cup golden caster
  (superfine) sugar

4 ripe pears
juice of ½ lemon
30ml/2 tbsp clear honey
3 eggs
seeds from 1 vanilla pod
  (bean)
120ml/4fl oz/½ cup
  sunflower oil
115g/4oz/1 cup self-raising
  (self-rising) flour
50g/2oz/⅓ cup instant polenta

1 Preheat the oven to 180°C/350°F/Gas 4. Generously grease and line a 21cm/8½in round cake tin (pan). Sprinkle 30ml/2 tbsp of the golden caster sugar over the base of the prepared tin.

2 Peel and core the pears. Cut them into chunky slices and toss in the lemon juice. Arrange them on the base of the prepared cake tin. Drizzle the honey over the pears and set aside.

3 Mix together the eggs, seeds from the vanilla pod and the remaining golden caster sugar in a bowl.

4 Beat the egg mixture until thick and creamy, then gradually beat in the oil. Sift together the flour and polenta and fold into the egg mixture.

5 Pour the mixture carefully into the tin over the pears. Bake for about 50 minutes or until a skewer inserted into the centre comes out clean. Cool in the tin for 10 minutes, then turn the cake out on to a plate, peel off the lining paper, invert and slice.

Cook's Tip
Use the tip of a small, sharp knife to scrape out the vanilla seeds. If you do not have a vanilla pod, use 5ml/1 tsp pure vanilla extract instead.

Upside-down Pear & Ginger Cake

This light spicy sponge, topped with glossy baked fruit and ginger, makes an excellent pudding.

Serves 6–8
900g/2lb can pear halves, drained
120ml/8 tbsp finely chopped
  preserved stem ginger
120ml/8 tbsp ginger syrup
  from the jar

175g/6oz/1½ cups self-raising
  (self-rising) flour
2.5ml/½ tsp baking powder
5ml/1 tsp ground ginger
175g/6oz/¾ cup soft light
  brown sugar
175g/6oz/¾ cup butter,
  softened
3 eggs, lightly beaten

1 Preheat the oven to 180°C/350°F/Gas 4. Base-line and grease a deep 20cm/8in round cake tin (pan).

2 Fill the hollow in each pear with half the chopped preserved stem ginger. Arrange, flat sides down, in the base of the cake tin, then spoon over half the ginger syrup.

3 Sift together the flour, baking powder and ground ginger. Stir in the sugar and butter, add the eggs and beat until creamy, about 1–2 minutes.

4 Spoon the mixture into the cake tin. Bake in the oven for 50 minutes, or until a skewer inserted in the centre of the cake comes out clean. Leave the cake in the tin for 5 minutes. Turn out on to a wire rack, peel off the lining paper and leave to cool completely.

5 Add the reserved ginger to the pear halves and drizzle over the remaining syrup.

Cook's Tip
Canned pears are ideal for this cake, but you can also core, peel and halve fresh pears, and then poach them until tender in a little white wine to cover, with 50g/2oz/ ½ cup sugar added.

St Clement's Cake

A tangy orange-and-lemon cake makes a spectacular centrepiece when decorated with fruits, silver dragées and fresh flowers.

Makes one 23cm/9in ring cake

175g/6oz/¾ cup butter
75g/3oz/scant ⅓ cup soft light brown sugar
3 eggs, separated
grated rind and juice of 1 orange and 1 lemon
150g/5oz/1¼ cups self-raising (self-rising) flour
75g/3oz/6 tbsp caster (superfine) sugar
15g/½oz/1 tbsp ground almonds
350ml/12fl oz/1½ cups double (heavy) cream
15ml/1 tbsp Grand Marnier
16 crystallized orange and lemon slices, silver dragées, sugared almonds and fresh flowers, to decorate

1 Preheat the oven to 180°C/350°F/Gas 4. Grease and flour a 900ml/1½ pint/3¾ cup ring mould.

2 Cream half the butter and all of the brown sugar until pale and light. Beat in the egg yolks, orange rind and juice and fold in 75g/3oz/⅔ cup flour.

3 Cream the remaining butter and the caster sugar in another bowl. Stir in the lemon rind and juice and fold in the remaining flour and the ground almonds. Whisk the egg whites until they form stiff peaks, and fold into the batter.

4 Spoon the two mixtures alternately into the prepared tin. Using a skewer or small spoon, swirl through the mixture to create a marbled effect. Bake for 45–50 minutes, or until risen, and a skewer inserted in the cake comes out clean. Cool in the tin for 10 minutes then transfer to a wire rack to cool.

5 Whip the cream and Grand Marnier together until lightly thickened. Spread over the cake and swirl a pattern over the icing with a metal spatula. Decorate the ring with the crystallized fruits, dragées and sugared almonds to resemble a jewelled crown. Arrange a few fresh flowers with their stems wrapped in foil in the centre.

Chestnut & Orange Roulade

A very moist roulade with a sweet and creamy filling – ideal to serve as an impressive low-fat dessert.

Serves 8

3 eggs, separated
115g/4oz/generous ½ cup caster (superfine) sugar
½ x 439g/15½ oz can unsweetened chestnut purée
grated rind and juice of 1 orange
icing (confectioners') sugar, for dusting

For the filling
225g/8oz/1 cup low-fat soft cheese
15ml/1 tbsp clear honey
1 orange

1 Preheat the oven to 180°C/350°F/Gas 4. Line and grease a 30 x 20cm/12 x 8in Swiss roll tin (jelly roll pan).

2 Whisk the egg yolks and sugar in a bowl until thick. Put the chestnut purée into a separate bowl. Whisk the orange rind and juice into the purée, then whisk into the egg mixture.

3 Whisk the egg whites until fairly stiff. Stir a spoonful into the chestnut mixture, then fold in the remaining egg whites.

4 Spoon the mixture into the prepared tin and bake for 30 minutes, or until firm. Cool for 5 minutes in the tin, then cover with a clean damp dish towel and leave until completely cold.

5 Meanwhile, make the filling. Put the soft cheese in a bowl with the honey. Finely grate the orange rind and add to the bowl. Using a sharp knife, cut away all the peel and pith from the orange. Cut the fruit into segments, cutting either side of the membrane so that you have only the flesh. Chop roughly and set aside. Add any juice to the bowl, then beat until smooth. Mix in the orange segments.

6 Sprinkle a sheet of baking parchment with icing sugar. Turn the roulade out on to the paper; peel off the lining paper. Spread the filling over the roulade and roll up like a Swiss roll (jelly roll). Transfer to a plate and dust with icing sugar.

St Clement's Energy 4486kcal/18629kJ; Protein 43.4g; Carbohydrate 281.3g, of which sugars 166.6g; Fat 358.8g, of which saturates 213.6g; Cholesterol 1424mg; Calcium 614mg; Fibre 5.8g; Sodium 1363mg.
Chestnut and Orange Energy 176kcal/741kJ; Protein 7.2g; Carbohydrate 28.1g, of which sugars 19.9g; Fat 5.1g, of which saturates 2.2g; Cholesterol 78mg; Calcium 64mg; Fibre 1.1g; Sodium 154mg.

Lemon Chiffon Cake

Tangy lemon mousse makes a delicious filling in this light cake, which is surprisingly low in saturated fat.

Serves 8
1 lemon sponge cake mix
lemon glacé icing
shreds of blanched lemon rind

For the filling
2 eggs, separated
75g/3oz/6 tbsp caster
    (superfine) sugar
grated rind and juice of
    1 small lemon
20ml/4 tsp water
10ml/2 tsp powdered gelatine
120ml/4fl oz/½ cup
    reduced-fat fromage frais
    or crème fraîche

1 Preheat the oven to 180°C/350°F/Gas 4. Line and grease a 20cm/8in loose-based cake tin (pan).

2 Add the sponge mixture and bake for 20–25 minutes, or until firm and golden. Cool on a wire rack, then split the cake in half. Return the lower half of the cake to the clean cake tin and set aside.

3 To make the filling, whisk the egg yolks, sugar, lemon rind and juice in a bowl until thick, pale and creamy. In a grease-free bowl, whisk the egg whites until they form soft peaks.

4 Sprinkle the gelatine over the water in a heatproof bowl. When the gelatine has become spongy, place the bowl over a pan of simmering water and dissolve the gelatine, stirring occasionally. Cool slightly, then whisk into the yolk mixture. Fold in the fromage frais.

5 When the mixture begins to set, fold in a generous spoonful of the egg whites to lighten it, then fold in the remaining whites.

6 Spoon the lemon mousse over the sponge in the cake tin. Set the second layer of sponge on top and chill until set.

7 Carefully transfer the cake to a serving plate. Pour the glacé icing over the cake and spread it evenly to the edges. Decorate with the lemon shreds.

Warm Lemon Syrup Cake

This delicious citrus cake is perfect as a winter dessert, served with poached pears.

Serves 8
3 eggs
175g/6oz/¾ cup butter, softened
175g/6oz/scant 1 cup caster
    (superfine) sugar
175g/6oz/1½ cups self-raising
    (self-rising) flour
50g/2oz/½ cup ground almonds

1.25ml/¼ tsp freshly
    grated nutmeg
50g/2oz/5 tbsp candied
    lemon peel, finely chopped
grated rind of 1 lemon
30ml/2 tbsp lemon juice
poached pears, to serve

For the syrup
175g/6oz/scant 1 cup caster
    (superfine) sugar
juice of 3 lemons

1 Preheat the oven to 180°C/350°F/Gas 4. Grease and base-line a deep, round 20cm/8in cake tin (pan).

2 Place the butter, sugar, flour and ground almonds in a large bowl. Add the nutmeg, chopped candied lemon peel and the lemon rind and juice. Beat for 2–3 minutes, until light and fluffy.

3 Tip the mixture into the prepared tin, spread level and bake for 1 hour, or until golden and firm to the touch.

4 To make the syrup, put the sugar, lemon juice and 75ml/5 tbsp water in a pan. Heat gently, stirring, until the sugar has dissolved, then boil, without stirring, for a further 1–2 minutes.

5 Turn out the cake on to a plate with a rim. Prick the surface of the cake all over with a fork, then pour over the hot syrup. Leave to soak for about 30 minutes. Serve the cake warm with thin wedges of poached pears.

Cook's Tip
To poach the pears, peel, core and quarter 450g/1lb pears. Place in a pan with 300ml/½ pint/1¼ cups water, 75g/3oz/ 6 tbsp sugar and a cinnamon stick. Simmer gently until just tender. Cool in the syrup.

Lemon Chiffon Energy 356kcal/1491kJ; Protein 6.7g; Carbohydrate 43.6g, of which sugars 29.8g; Fat 18.4g, of which saturates 4g; Cholesterol 118mg; Calcium 68mg; Fibre 0.6g; Sodium 227mg.
Warm Lemon Energy 490kcal/2056kJ; Protein 6.1g; Carbohydrate 67g, of which sugars 50.1g; Fat 23.9g, of which saturates 12.3g; Cholesterol 118mg; Calcium 92mg; Fibre 1.4g; Sodium 181mg.

Lemon Yogurt Ring

The glaze gives this dessert a refreshing finishing touch.

Serves 12
225g/8oz/1 cup butter,
  at room temperature
285g/10½oz/1½ cups caster
  (superfine) sugar
4 eggs, separated
10ml/2 tsp grated
  lemon rind
90ml/6 tbsp lemon juice
250ml/8fl oz/1 cup natural
  (plain) yogurt

275g/10oz/2½ cups plain
  (all-purpose) flour
10ml/2 tsp baking powder
5ml/1 tsp bicarbonate of soda
  (baking soda)
2.5ml/½ tsp salt

For the glaze
115g/4oz/1 cup icing
  (confectioners') sugar
30ml/2 tbsp lemon juice
45–60ml/3–4 tbsp natural
  (plain) yogurt

1 Preheat the oven to 180°C/350°F/Gas 4. Grease a 3 litre/5¼ pint/ 13¼ cup *bundt* or fluted tube tin and dust lightly with flour.

2 Cream the butter and caster sugar in a large bowl until light and fluffy. Add the egg yolks, one at a time, beating well after each addition. Add the lemon rind, juice and yogurt, and stir gently to incorporate.

3 Sift together the flour, baking powder and bicarbonate of soda. In another bowl, beat the egg whites and salt until they hold stiff peaks.

4 Fold the dry ingredients into the butter mixture, then fold in a spoonful of egg whites to lighten the mixture. Fold in the remaining egg whites.

5 Pour into the tin and bake until a skewer inserted in the centre comes out clean, about 50 minutes. Leave in the tin for 15 minutes, then turn out and cool on a wire rack.

6 To make the glaze, sift the icing sugar into a bowl. Stir in the lemon juice and just enough yogurt to make a smooth glaze. Set the cooled cake on the wire rack over a sheet of baking parchment. Pour over the glaze and allow to set.

Coconut Lime Gateau

Fresh lime and coconut give this gateau a fabulous flavour.

Makes one 23cm/9in round cake
225g/8oz/2 cups plain
  (all-purpose) flour
12.5ml/2½ tsp baking powder
1.5ml/¼ tsp salt
225g/8oz/1 cup butter,
  at room temperature
225g/8oz/generous 1 cup caster
  (superfine) sugar
grated rind of 2 limes

4 eggs
60ml/4 tbsp fresh lime juice
75g/3oz/1 cup desiccated
  (dry unsweetened
  shredded) coconut

For the frosting
450g/1lb/generous 2 cups
  granulated sugar
60ml/4 tbsp water
a pinch of cream of tartar
1 egg white, whisked until stiff

1 Preheat the oven to 180°C/350°F/Gas 4. Grease and base-line two 23cm/9in shallow round cake tins (pans). Sift together the flour, baking powder and salt.

2 Beat the butter until soft. Add the sugar and lime rind, and beat until pale and fluffy. Beat in the eggs, one at a time.

3 Gradually fold in the dry ingredients, alternating with the lime juice, then stir in two-thirds of the coconut.

4 Divide the mixture between the cake tins, level the tops and bake for 30–35 minutes. Cool in the tins on a wire rack for 10 minutes, then turn out and peel off the lining paper.

5 Bake the remaining coconut on a baking sheet until golden brown, stirring occasionally.

6 To make the frosting, heat the sugar, water and cream of tartar until dissolved, stirring. Boil to reach 120°C/250°F on a sugar thermometer. Remove from the heat and, when the bubbles subside, whisk in the egg white until thick.

7 Sandwich and cover the cake with the frosting. Sprinkle over the toasted coconut. Leave to set before serving.

Lemon Yogurt Energy 387kcal/1626kJ; Protein 5.8g; Carbohydrate 54.6g, of which sugars 37.1g; Fat 17.8g, of which saturates 10.5g; Cholesterol 104mg; Calcium 109mg; Fibre 0.7g; Sodium 160mg.
Coconut Energy 5859kcal/24634kJ; Protein 58g; Carbohydrate 886.4g, of which sugars 714.9g; Fat 256.6g, of which saturates 163.9g; Cholesterol 1241mg; Calcium 846mg; Fibre 17.3g; Sodium 1773mg.

Peach & Amaretto Cake

Try this delicious peach cake for dessert with reduced-fat fromage frais, or serve it solo for afternoon tea.

Serves 8
3 eggs, separated
175g/6oz/³⁄₄ cup caster
    (superfine) sugar
grated rind and juice of
    1 lemon
50g/2oz/¹⁄₂ cup semolina
40g/1¹⁄₂oz/scant ¹⁄₂ cup
    ground almonds

25g/1oz/¹⁄₄ cup plain
    (all-purpose) flour

For the syrup
75g/3oz/6 tbsp caster
    (superfine) sugar
90ml/6 tbsp water
30ml/2 tbsp amaretto liqueur
2 peaches or nectarines,
    halved and stoned (pitted)
60ml/4 tbsp apricot jam,
    sieved, to glaze

1 Preheat the oven to 180°C/350°F/Gas 4. Grease a 20cm/8in round loose-based cake tin (pan). Whisk the egg yolks, caster sugar, lemon rind and juice in a bowl until thick, pale and creamy, then fold in the semolina, almonds and flour until the mixture is smooth.

2 Whisk the egg whites in a grease-free bowl until fairly stiff. Using a metal spoon, stir a generous spoonful of the whites into the semolina mixture to lighten it, then fold in the remaining egg whites. Spoon into the prepared cake tin.

3 Bake for 30–35 minutes, then remove the cake from the oven and carefully loosen the edges. Prick the top with a skewer and leave to cool slightly in the tin.

4 Meanwhile, make the syrup. Heat the sugar and water in a small pan, stirring until dissolved, then boil without stirring for 2 minutes. Add the amaretto liqueur and drizzle slowly over the cake. Leave to cool in the tin.

5 Remove the cake from the tin and transfer it to a serving plate. Slice the peaches or nectarines and arrange them in concentric circles over the top of the cake. Brush the fruit with the glaze.

Coffee, Peach & Almond Daquoise

This peach treat has pretty layers of textures and flavours.

Makes one 23cm/9in gateau
5 eggs, separated
425g/15oz/generous 2 cups caster
    (superfine) sugar
15ml/1 tbsp cornflour (cornstarch)
175g/6oz/1¹⁄₂ cups ground
    almonds, toasted
135ml/4¹⁄₂fl oz/generous
    ¹⁄₂ cup milk

275g/10oz/1¹⁄₄ cups unsalted
    (sweet) butter, diced
45–60ml/3–4 tbsp coffee extract
2 x 400g/14oz cans peach halves
    in juice, drained
65g/2¹⁄₂oz/generous ¹⁄₂ cup flaked
    (sliced) almonds, toasted
icing (confectioners') sugar,
    for dusting
a few fresh mint leaves,
    to decorate

1 Preheat the oven to 150°C/300°F/Gas 2. Draw three 23cm/9in circles on to baking parchment and invert on to baking sheets.

2 Whisk the egg whites until stiff. Gradually whisk in 275g/10oz/scant 1¹⁄₂ cups of the sugar until thick and glossy. Fold in the cornflour and almonds. Using a 1cm/¹⁄₂in plain icing nozzle, pipe the meringue to cover the circles drawn on the paper. Bake for 2 hours. Turn on to wire racks to cool.

3 For the pastry cream, beat together the egg yolks and remaining sugar until thick and pale. Heat the milk in a small pan to boiling point and beat into the egg mixture. Return to the pan and heat until the mixture coats the back of a spoon. Strain into a large bowl and beat until lukewarm. Gradually beat in the butter until glossy. Beat in the coffee extract.

4 Trim the meringues and crush the trimmings. Reserve 3 peach halves, chop the rest. Divide the pastry cream between two bowls, and fold the peaches into one bowl with the crushed meringue. Use to sandwich the meringues together and place on a serving plate.

5 Ice the cake with the plain pastry cream. Cover the top with flaked almonds and dust generously with icing sugar. Thinly slice the reserved peaches and use to decorate the cake edge. Add some mint leaves.

Peach and Amaretto Energy 244kcal/1034kJ; Protein 4.7g; Carbohydrate 46.7g, of which sugars 39.4g; Fat 5g, of which saturates 0.8g; Cholesterol 71mg; Calcium 47mg; Fibre 0.9g; Sodium 32mg.
Coffee Energy 5984kcal/24978kJ; Protein 95.1g; Carbohydrate 560.1g, of which sugars 539.8g; Fat 390.1g, of which saturates 163.1g; Cholesterol 1546mg; Calcium 1190mg; Fibre 24.2g; Sodium 2237mg.

Apricot Brandy-snap Roulade

A magnificent combination of soft and crisp textures, this apricot-filled cake looks impressive but is actually very easy to prepare.

Makes one 33cm/13in long roll
4 eggs, separated
7.5ml/1½ tsp fresh orange juice
115g/4oz/generous ½ cup caster (superfine) sugar
175g/6oz/1½ cups ground almonds
4 brandy snaps, crushed, to decorate

For the filling
150g/5oz canned apricots, drained
300ml/½ pint/1¼ cups double (heavy) cream
25g/1oz/¼ cup icing (confectioners') sugar

1 Preheat the oven to 190°C/375°F/Gas 5. Base-line and grease a 33 × 23cm/13 × 9in Swiss roll tin (jelly roll pan).

2 Beat together the egg yolks, orange juice and sugar until thick and pale, about 10 minutes. Fold in the ground almonds.

3 Whisk the egg whites until they hold stiff peaks. Fold into the almond mixture, then transfer to the Swiss roll tin and smooth the surface.

4 Bake for 20 minutes, or until a skewer inserted into the centre comes out clean. Leave to cool in the tin, covered with a just-damp dish towel.

5 To make the filling, process the apricots in a blender or food processor until smooth. Whip the cream and icing sugar until it holds soft peaks. Fold in the apricot purée.

6 Spread the crushed brandy snaps over a sheet of baking parchment. Spread one-third of the cream mixture over the cake, then carefully invert it on to the brandy snaps. Peel off the lining paper.

7 Use the remaining cream mixture to cover the whole cake, then roll up the roulade from a short end, being careful not to disturb the brandy snap coating. Transfer the roulade to a serving dish.

Apricot & Orange Roulade

This sophisticated apricot and orange dessert tastes very good when served with a spoonful of thick yogurt or crème fraîche.

Makes one 33cm/13in long roll
4 egg whites
115g/4oz/generous ½ cup golden caster (superfine) sugar
50g/2oz/½ cup plain (all-purpose) flour
finely grated rind of 1 orange
45ml/3 tbsp orange juice

For the filling
115g/4oz/½ cup ready-to-eat dried apricots
150ml/¼ pint/⅔ cup orange juice

For the decoration
10ml/2 tsp icing (confectioners') sugar
shredded orange rind

1 Preheat the oven to 200°C/400°F/Gas 6. Base-line and grease a 33 × 23cm/13 × 9in Swiss roll tin (jelly roll pan).

2 Place the egg whites in a large bowl and whisk until they hold soft peaks. Gradually add the sugar, whisking well between each addition, until all of the sugar has been incorporated.

3 Fold in the flour, orange rind and juice. Spoon the mixture into the prepared tin and spread it evenly.

4 Bake the cake for 15–18 minutes, or until the sponge is firm and light golden in colour. Turn out on to a sheet of baking parchment and roll it up loosely from one short side. Leave to cool completely.

5 Roughly chop the apricots and place them in a pan with the orange juice. Cover and leave to simmer until most of the liquid has been absorbed. Purée the apricots in a food processor or blender until smooth.

6 Unroll the roulade and spread with the apricot mixture. Roll up. To decorate, arrange strips of paper diagonally across the roll, sprinkle lightly with icing sugar and then remove the paper. Sprinkle the top with orange rind.

Apricot Brandy Energy 3674kcal/15272kJ; Protein 69.4g; Carbohydrate 208.1g, of which sugars 193.9g; Fat 291.3g, of which saturates 114.1g; Cholesterol 1172mg; Calcium 809mg; Fibre 14.7g; Sodium 511mg.
Apricot and Orange Energy 1145kcal/4878kJ; Protein 29.1g; Carbohydrate 270.4g, of which sugars 232.3g; Fat 1.5g, of which saturates 0.1g; Cholesterol 0mg; Calcium 271mg; Fibre 9g; Sodium 427mg.

Plum Crumble Cake

This cake can also be made with the same quantity of apricots or cherries.

Serves 8–10
675g/1½lb red plums
150g/5oz/10 tbsp butter
  or margarine, at room
  temperature
150g/5oz/¾ cup caster
  (superfine) sugar
4 eggs, at room temperature
7.5ml/1½ tsp vanilla extract

150g/5oz/1¼ cups plain
  (all-purpose) flour
5ml/1 tsp baking powder

For the topping
115g/4oz/1 cup plain
  (all-purpose) flour
130g/4½oz/generous 1 cup soft
  light brown sugar
7.5ml/1½ tsp ground cinnamon
75g/3oz/6 tbsp butter, diced

1 Halve and stone (pit) the plums and set them aside.

2 Preheat the oven to 180°C/350°F/Gas 4. Using baking parchment, line a 25 × 5cm/10 × 2in tin (pan) and grease the paper.

3 To make the topping, combine the flour, light brown sugar and cinnamon in a bowl. Add the butter and rub in well using your fingertips or a pastry cutter until it resembles coarse breadcrumbs.

4 Cream the butter or margarine and sugar until light and fluffy. Beat in the eggs, one at a time. Stir in the vanilla. Sift the flour and baking powder into a bowl then fold into the creamed mixture in three batches.

5 Pour the batter into the prepared tin. Arrange the plums on top and sprinkle with the topping.

6 Bake until a skewer inserted in the centre comes out clean, about 45 minutes. Cool in the tin.

7 To serve, run a knife around the inside edge of the cake and invert on to a plate. Invert again on to a serving plate so that the topping is uppermost.

Autumn Fruit Dessert Cake

Greengages, plums or semi-dried prunes are delicious in this recipe. Serve with cream or ice cream.

Serves 6–8
115g/4oz/½ cup butter,
  softened
150g/5oz/¾ cup caster
  (superfine) sugar
3 eggs, beaten
75g/3oz/¾ cup ground hazelnuts
150g/5oz/1¼ cups chopped
  pecan nuts

50g/2oz/½ cup plain
  (all-purpose) flour
5ml/1 tsp baking powder
2.5ml/½ tsp salt
675g/1½lb/3 cups plums,
  greengages or
  semi-dried prunes
60ml/4 tbsp lime marmalade
15ml/1 tbsp lime juice
30ml/2 tbsp blanched almonds,
  chopped, to decorate

1 Stone (pit) the plums, greengages or prunes and set aside until they are needed.

2 Preheat the oven to 180°C/350°F/Gas 4. Grease a 23cm/9in round, fluted flan tin (tart pan).

3 Beat the softened butter and caster sugar until light and fluffy. Gradually beat in the eggs, alternating with the ground hazelnuts. Do not overbeat.

4 Stir in the pecan nuts, then sift and fold in the flour, baking powder and salt. Spoon into the tart tin.

5 Bake for 45 minutes, or until a skewer inserted into the centre comes out clean.

6 Arrange the fruit on the base. Return to the oven and bake for 10–15 minutes, or until the fruit has softened. Transfer to a wire rack to cool, then turn out.

7 Warm the marmalade and lime juice gently. Brush over the fruit, then sprinkle with the almonds.

8 Allow to set, then chill before serving.

Plum Crumble Energy 426kcal/1787kJ; Protein 5.7g; Carbohydrate 57g, of which sugars 36.8g; Fat 21.1g, of which saturates 12.4g; Cholesterol 124mg; Calcium 77mg; Fibre 1.9g; Sodium 168mg.
Autumn Fruit Energy 481kcal/2007kJ; Protein 7.1g; Carbohydrate 39g, of which sugars 33.7g; Fat 34.2g, of which saturates 9.7g; Cholesterol 102mg; Calcium 74mg; Fibre 3.2g; Sodium 122mg.

Chocolate & Fresh Cherry Gateau

Make this sophisticated cake for a special occasion.

Makes one 20cm/8in round cake
115g/4oz/½ cup butter
150g/5oz/¾ cup caster (superfine) sugar
3 eggs, lightly beaten
175g/6oz/1 cup plain (semisweet) chocolate chips, melted
60ml/4 tbsp Kirsch
150g/5oz/1¼ cups self-raising (self-rising) flour
5ml/1 tsp ground cinnamon
2.5ml/½ tsp ground cloves
350g/12oz fresh cherries, pitted and halved

45ml/3 tbsp morello cherry jam, warmed
5ml/1 tsp lemon juice

For the frosting
115g/4oz/⅔ cup plain chocolate chips
50g/2oz/¼ cup unsalted (sweet) butter
60ml/4 tbsp double (heavy) cream

To decorate
18 fresh cherries dipped in 75g/3oz/½ cup white chocolate chips, melted, and a few rose leaves, washed and dried

1 Preheat the oven to 160°C/325°F/Gas 3. Grease, base-line and flour a 20cm/8in round springform tin (pan).

2 Cream the butter and 115g/4oz/½ cup of the sugar until pale. Beat in the eggs. Stir in the chocolate and half the Kirsch. Fold in the flour and spices. Transfer to the tin and bake for 55–60 minutes. Cool for 10 minutes, then transfer to a wire rack.

3 For the filling, bring the cherries, the remaining Kirsch and sugar to the boil, cover, and simmer for 10 minutes. Uncover for a further 10 minutes until syrupy. Leave to cool.

4 Halve the cake horizontally. Cut a 1cm/½in deep circle from the middle of the base, leaving a 1cm/½in edge. Crumble this cake into the filling mixture and fill the cut-away depression.

5 Sieve the jam and lemon juice. Brush all over the cake. For the frosting, melt all the ingredients. Cool, pour over the cake. Decorate with chocolate-dipped cherries and leaves.

Black Forest Gateau

A perfect cherry gateau for a special tea party, or for serving as a sumptuous dinner party dessert.

Makes one 20cm/8in gateau
5 eggs
175g/6oz/scant 1 cup caster (superfine) sugar
50g/2oz/½ cup plain (all-purpose) flour
50g/2oz/½ cup unsweetened cocoa powder
75g/3oz/6 tbsp butter, melted

For the filling
75–90ml/5–6 tbsp Kirsch
600ml/1 pint/2½ cups double (heavy) cream
425g/15oz can black cherries, drained, pitted and chopped

To decorate
chocolate curls
15–20 fresh cherries, preferably with stems
icing (confectioners') sugar

1 Preheat the oven to 180°C/350°F/Gas 4. Base-line and grease two deep 20cm/8in round cake tins (pans).

2 Beat together the eggs and sugar for 10 minutes, or until thick and pale. Sift over the flour and cocoa powder, and fold in gently. Trickle in the melted butter and fold in gently.

3 Transfer the mixture to the cake tins. Bake for 30 minutes, or until springy to the touch.

4 Leave in the tins for 5 minutes, then turn out on to a wire rack, peel off the lining paper and leave to cool. Cut each cake in half horizontally and sprinkle with the Kirsch.

5 Whip the cream until softly peaking. Combine two-thirds of the cream with the chopped cherries. Place a layer of cake on a serving plate and spread with one-third of the filling. Repeat twice, and top with a layer of cake. Use the reserved cream to cover the top and side of the gateau.

6 Decorate the side of the gateau with chocolate curls, and place more in the centre of the top of the cake. Arrange fresh cherries around the edge and finally dredge the top with icing sugar.

Chocolate Energy 5172kcal/21630kJ; Protein 60.1g; Carbohydrate 587.6g, of which sugars 470.7g; Fat 287.9g, of which saturates 171.5g; Cholesterol 1022mg; Calcium 781mg; Fibre 16.6g; Sodium 1337mg.
Black Forest Energy 5386kcal/22373kJ; Protein 58.3g; Carbohydrate 316.8g, of which sugars 272.9g; Fat 423.1g, of which saturates 253.7g; Cholesterol 1934mg; Calcium 742mg; Fibre 10.1g; Sodium 1458mg.

Strawberry Gateau

It is difficult to believe that a luscious cake that tastes as delicious as this can be so low in fat. It is the perfect way to enjoy the first locally grown strawberries of the season.

Serves 6
2 eggs
75g/3oz/6 tbsp caster
    (superfine) sugar
grated rind of ¹/₂ orange
50g/2oz/¹/₂ cup plain
    (all-purpose) flour

For the filling
275g/10oz/1¹/₄ cups low-fat
    soft cheese
grated rind of ¹/₂ orange
30ml/2 tbsp caster
    (superfine) sugar
60ml/4 tbsp reduced-fat fromage
    frais or crème fraîche
225g/8oz/2 cups strawberries,
    halved and chopped
25g/1oz/¹/₄ cup chopped
    almonds, toasted

1 Preheat the oven to 190°C/375°F/Gas 5. Line a 30 × 20cm/12 × 8in Swiss roll tin (jelly roll pan) with baking parchment.

2 In a bowl, whisk the eggs, sugar and orange rind until thick and mousse-like, then lightly fold in the flour.

3 Turn into the prepared tin. Bake for 15–20 minutes, or until the surface is firm to the touch and golden.

4 Turn the cake out on to on a wire rack to cool. When cold, remove the lining paper.

5 Meanwhile, make the filling. In a bowl, mix the soft cheese with the grated orange rind, sugar and fromage frais until smooth. Divide the mixture between two bowls.

6 Add half the strawberries to one bowl. Cut the sponge horizontally into three equal pieces and sandwich together with the strawberry filling. Place the gateau on a serving plate.

7 Spread the plain filling over the top and sides of the cake. Press the toasted almonds over the sides and decorate the top with the remaining strawberry halves.

Strawberry Mint Sponge

This combination of summer fruit, fresh mint and ice cream will prove popular with everyone.

Makes one 20cm/8in round cake
6–10 fresh mint leaves, plus extra
    to decorate
175g/6oz/scant 1 cup caster
    (superfine) sugar
175g/6oz/³/₄ cup butter

175g/6oz/1¹/₂ cups self-raising
    (self-rising) flour
3 eggs
1.2 litres/2 pints/5 cups
    strawberry ice cream,
    softened
600ml/1 pint/2¹/₂ cups double
    (heavy) cream
30ml/2 tbsp mint liqueur
350g/12oz/3 cups
    fresh strawberries

1 Tear the fresh mint leaves into pieces, mix with the sugar, and leave overnight. Remove the leaves from the sugar the next day.

2 Preheat the oven to 190°C/375°F/Gas 5. Grease and line a 20cm/8in deep springform tin (pan).

3 Cream the butter and mint-flavoured sugar, add the flour, and then the eggs. Pour the mixture into the prepared tin.

4 Bake for 20–25 minutes, or until a skewer inserted in the centre comes out clean. Turn out on to a wire rack to cool completely. When cool, split into two layers.

5 Wash the cake tin and line with clear film (plastic wrap). Put the cake base back in the tin. Spread evenly with the softened ice cream, then cover with the top half of the cake. Freeze for 3–4 hours.

6 Whip the cream with the mint liqueur. Turn the cake out on to a serving plate and quickly spread a layer of whipped cream all over it, leaving a rough finish. Freeze until 10 minutes before serving.

7 Decorate the cake with the strawberries and place fresh mint leaves around it.

Strawberry Gateau Energy 305kcal/1288kJ; Protein 25.6g; Carbohydrate 35.7g, of which sugars 22.4g; Fat 7.6g, of which saturates 1.1g; Cholesterol 64mg; Calcium 163mg; Fibre 7.2g; Sodium 37mg.
Strawberry Mint Energy 7965kcal/33162kJ; Protein 86.7g; Carbohydrate 636.8g, of which sugars 480.7g; Fat 574.1g, of which saturates 340.9g; Cholesterol 1839mg; Calcium 2245mg; Fibre 9.3g; Sodium 2305mg.

Strawberry Shortcake Gateau

A light cookie-textured sponge cake forms the base of this port-marinated summertime dessert.

Makes one 20cm/8in round cake

225g/8oz/2 cups fresh
  strawberries, hulled
30ml/2 tbsp ruby port
225g/8oz/2 cups self-raising
  (self-rising) flour
10ml/2 tsp baking powder
75g/3oz/6 tbsp unsalted (sweet)
  butter, diced
40g/1½oz/3 tbsp caster
  (superfine) sugar
1 egg, lightly beaten
15–30ml/1–2 tbsp milk
melted butter, for brushing
250ml/8fl oz/1 cup double
  (heavy) cream
icing (confectioners') sugar,
  for dusting

1 Preheat the oven to 220°C/425°F/Gas 7. Grease and base-line two 20cm/8in shallow, round, loose-based cake tins (pans).

2 Reserve 5 strawberries, slice the remainder and marinate in the port for about 1–2 hours. Strain, reserving the port.

3 Sift the flour and baking powder into a bowl. Rub in the butter until the mixture resembles fine breadcrumbs and stir in the sugar. Work in the egg and 15ml/1 tbsp of the milk to form a soft dough, adding more milk if needed.

4 Knead briefly on a lightly floured surface and divide into two pieces. Roll out each piece, mark one into eight wedges, and transfer both to the prepared cake tins. Brush with a little melted butter and bake for 15 minutes. Cool in the tins for 10 minutes, then transfer to a wire rack to cool completely.

5 Cut the marked cake into wedges. Reserving a little cream for decoration, whip the remainder until it holds its shape, and fold in the reserved port and marinated strawberry slices. Spread over the round cake. Place the wedges on top tilting them at a slight angle, and dust with icing sugar.

6 Whip the remaining cream and use to pipe swirls on each wedge. Halve the reserved strawberries and decorate the cake.

Fresh Fruit Genoese

This beautifully decorated Italian classic can be made with any selection of seasonal fruits.

Serves 8–10
For the sponge
175g/6oz/1½ cups plain
  (all-purpose) flour
a pinch of salt
4 eggs
115g/4oz/generous ½ cup caster
  (superfine) sugar
90ml/6 tbsp orange-
  flavoured liqueur

For the filling and topping
60ml/4 tbsp vanilla sugar
600ml/1 pint/2½ cups double
  (heavy) cream
450g/1lb mixed fresh fruits
150g/5oz/1¼ cups chopped
  pistachio nuts
60ml/4 tbsp apricot jam,
  warmed and sieved

1 Preheat the oven to 180°C/350°F/Gas 4. Grease and line the base of a 20cm/8in springform cake tin (pan) with baking parchment.

2 Sift the flour and salt together three times, then set aside. Using an electric mixer, beat the eggs and sugar together for 10 minutes until thick and pale.

3 Fold the flour mixture gently into the egg and sugar mixture. Transfer the cake mixture to the prepared tin and bake for 30–35 minutes. Leave the cake in the tin for about 5 minutes, and then transfer to a wire rack, remove the paper and cool completely.

4 Cut the cake horizontally into two layers, and place one layer on a plate. Sprinkle both layers with liqueur.

5 To make the filling and topping, add the vanilla sugar to the cream and whisk until the cream holds soft peaks. Spread two-thirds of the cream over the cake base layer and top with half the fruit.

6 Top with the second layer and spread the top and sides with the remaining cream. Press the nuts around the sides, arrange the remaining fruit on top. Brush the fruit with the warmed apricot jam.

Strawberry Energy 2911kcal/12118kJ; Protein 34.4g; Carbohydrate 239.1g, of which sugars 67.7g; Fat 204.9g, of which saturates 124.7g; Cholesterol 694mg; Calcium 556mg; Fibre 9.4g; Sodium 610mg.
Fresh Fruit Energy 815kcal/3411kJ; Protein 8.5g; Carbohydrate 99.6g, of which sugars 85.9g; Fat 43g, of which saturates 21.8g; Cholesterol 158mg; Calcium 128mg; Fibre 2g; Sodium 132mg.

Fruit Gateau with Heartsease

This strawberry gateau would be lovely to serve as a dessert at a summer lunch party in the garden.

Makes one ring cake

90g/3½oz/scant ½ cup
  soft margarine
90g/3½oz/½ cup caster
  (superfine) sugar
10ml/2 tsp clear honey
150g/5oz/1¼ cups self-raising
  (self-rising) flour
2.5ml/½ tsp baking powder

30ml/2 tbsp milk
2 eggs
15ml/1 tbsp rose water
15ml/1 tbsp Cointreau

To decorate

16 heartsease pansy flowers
1 egg white, lightly beaten
caster (superfine) sugar
icing (confectioners') sugar
450g/1lb/4 cups strawberries
strawberry leaves

1 Preheat the oven to 190°C/375°F/Gas 5. Grease and lightly flour a ring mould. Put the soft margarine, sugar, honey, flour, baking powder, milk and eggs into a mixing bowl and beat well for 1 minute. Add the rose water and the Cointreau, and mix well.

2 Pour the mixture into the mould and bake for 40 minutes. Allow to stand for a few minutes, and then turn out on to a serving plate.

3 Crystallize the heartsease pansies by painting them with the lightly beaten egg white and sprinkling with caster sugar. Leave to dry thoroughly.

4 Sift icing sugar over the cake. Fill the centre of the ring with strawberries – if they will not all fit, place some around the edge. Decorate with the crystallized heartsease flowers and some strawberry leaves.

> **Cook's Tip**
> Rose water is distilled from rose petals and water, and it is not only useful for cakes but can also be added to ice creams and sorbets, jams, jellies, milk puddings and fruit salads.

Raspberry Meringue Gateau

A rich hazelnut meringue filled with cream and raspberries makes a delicious combination of different textures and tastes.

Serves 8

4 egg whites
225g/8oz/generous 1 cup caster
  (superfine) sugar
a few drops of vanilla extract
5ml/1 tsp malt vinegar
115g/4oz/1⅔ cup toasted
  chopped hazelnuts, ground

300ml/½ pint/1¼ cups double
  (heavy) cream
350g/12oz/2 cups raspberries
icing (confectioners') sugar,
  for dusting
raspberries and mint sprigs,
  to decorate

For the sauce

225g/8oz/1⅓ cups raspberries
45ml/3 tbsp icing
  (confectioners') sugar
15ml/1 tbsp orange liqueur

1 Preheat the oven to 180°C/350°F/Gas 4. Grease two 20cm/8in shallow round cake tins (pans) and line the bases with baking parchment.

2 Whisk the egg whites in a large bowl until they hold stiff peaks, then gradually whisk in the caster sugar a tablespoon at a time, whisking well after each addition.

3 Continue whisking the meringue mixture for a minute or two until very stiff, then fold in the vanilla extract, malt vinegar and the ground hazelnuts. Divide the meringue mixture between the prepared tins and spread level. Bake for 50–60 minutes, or until crisp. Remove the meringues from the tins and leave to cool on a wire rack.

4 Meanwhile, make the sauce. Purée the raspberries with the icing sugar and orange liqueur in a blender or food processor, then press the purée through a nylon sieve (strainer) to remove any pips. Chill the sauce until ready to serve.

5 Whip the cream until just thickened then fold in the raspberries. Sandwich the meringue rounds with the raspberry cream. Dust with icing sugar, and then decorate with fruit and mint. Serve the meringue with the sauce.

Fruit Gateau Energy 1586kcal/6630kJ; Protein 25.4g; Carbohydrate 180.3g, of which sugars 142.2g; Fat 86.1g, of which saturates 3.5g; Cholesterol 382mg; Calcium 294mg; Fibre 6.5g; Sodium 969mg.
Raspberry Energy 445kcal/1860kJ; Protein 6.1g; Carbohydrate 40.5g, of which sugars 40.3g; Fat 29.5g, of which saturates 13.3g; Cholesterol 51mg; Calcium 76mg; Fibre 2.7g; Sodium 61mg.

Pineapple & Apricot Cake

This is not a long-keeping fruit cake, but you can freeze it, well-wrapped in a sheet of baking parchment and then a piece of foil.

Makes one 18cm/7in square or 20cm/8in round cake
175g/6oz/³/4 cup unsalted (sweet) butter
150g/5oz/generous ³/4 cup caster (superfine) sugar
3 eggs, beaten
few drops vanilla extract

225g/8oz/2 cups plain (all-purpose) flour
1.5ml/¹/4 tsp salt
7.5ml/1¹/2 tsp baking powder
225g/8oz/1 cup ready-to-eat dried apricots, chopped
115g/4oz/¹/2 cup each chopped crystallized ginger and crystallized pineapple
grated rind and juice of ¹/2 orange
grated rind and juice of ¹/2 lemon
a little milk

1 Preheat the oven to 180°C/350°F/Gas 4. Double line an 18cm/7in square or 20cm/8in round cake tin (pan).

2 Cream the butter and sugar together until light and fluffy.

3 Gradually beat in the eggs with the vanilla extract, beating well after each addition.

4 Sift together the flour, salt and baking powder. Add a little of the flour with the last of the egg, then fold in the remainder.

5 Gently fold in the apricots, ginger and pineapple and the orange and lemon rinds, then add sufficient fruit juice and milk to give the batter a fairly soft dropping consistency.

6 Spoon the batter into the prepared cake tin and smooth the top with a wet spoon.

7 Bake for 20 minutes, then reduce the oven temperature to 160°C/325°F/Gas 3 and bake for a further 1¹/2–2 hours, or until a skewer inserted into the centre comes out clean.

8 Leave the cake to cool completely in the tin. Wrap in fresh paper before storing in an airtight tin.

Pineapple Upside-down Cake

Canned pineapple rings make this a useful and unusual cake to make with a few ingredients that you might already have in the kitchen cupboard.

Makes one 25cm/10in round cake
115g/4oz/¹/2 cup butter
200g/7oz/scant 1 cup soft dark brown sugar

450g/1lb canned pineapple slices, drained
4 eggs, separated
grated rind of 1 lemon
pinch of salt
115g/4oz/generous ¹/2 cup caster (superfine) sugar
75g/3oz/²/3 cup plain (all-purpose) flour
5ml/1 tsp baking powder

1 Preheat the oven to 180°C/350°F/Gas 4. Melt the butter in a 25cm/10in ovenproof cast-iron frying pan. Then reserve 15ml/1 tbsp butter. Add the brown sugar to the pan and stir to blend. Place the pineapple slices on top in one layer. Set aside.

2 Whisk together the egg yolks, reserved butter and lemon rind until well blended. Set aside.

3 Beat the egg whites and salt until they form stiff peaks. Gradually fold in the caster sugar, then the egg yolk mixture.

4 Sift the flour and baking powder together. Carefully fold into the egg mixture in three batches.

5 Pour the mixture over the pineapple. Bake until a skewer inserted in the centre comes out clean, about 30 minutes.

6 While still hot, invert on to a serving plate. Serve hot or cold.

> **Variation**
> For an apricot cake, replace the pineapple slices with 225g/8oz/1³/4 cups dried ready-to-eat apricots.

Pineapple Energy 3400kcal/14276kJ; Protein 52.3g; Carbohydrate 455.1g, of which sugars 283.7g; Fat 165.6g, of which saturates 96.3g; Cholesterol 944mg; Calcium 748mg; Fibre 25.9g; Sodium 1326mg.
Upside-down Energy 2858kcal/12025kJ; Protein 35.7g; Carbohydrate 443g, of which sugars 385.9g; Fat 117.7g, of which saturates 66.3g; Cholesterol 1006mg; Calcium 443mg; Fibre 4.6g; Sodium 1003mg.

Apple & Cinnamon Muffins

These fruity, spicy muffins are quick and easy to make and are perfect for serving for breakfast or tea. The appetizing aroma as they bake is out of this world.

Makes 6

1 egg, beaten
40g/1½oz/3 tbsp caster (superfine) sugar
120ml/4fl oz/½ cup milk
50g/2oz/¼ cup butter, melted

150g/5oz/1¼ cups plain (all-purpose) flour
7.5ml/1½ tsp baking powder
pinch of salt
2.5ml/½ tsp ground cinnamon
2 small eating apples, peeled, cored and finely chopped

For the topping

12 brown sugar cubes, coarsely crushed
5ml/1 tsp ground cinnamon

1 Preheat the oven to 200°C/400°F/Gas 6. Arrange 6 paper cases in a muffin tin (pan).

2 Mix the egg, sugar, milk and melted butter in a large bowl. Sift in the flour, baking powder, salt and cinnamon. Add the chopped apple and mix roughly.

3 Spoon the mixture into the prepared muffin cases. To make the topping, mix the crushed sugar cubes with the cinnamon. Sprinkle over the uncooked muffins.

4 Bake for 30–35 minutes, until well risen and golden brown on top. Transfer the muffins to a wire rack to cool, then serve.

> **Cook's Tip**
> Do not overmix the muffin mixture – it should still be slightly lumpy when spooned into the cases.

> **Variation**
> You can also make these muffins with pears or even quinces, both of which go well with cinnamon.

Apple & Cranberry Muffins

If you choose a really sweet variety of apple, it will provide a lovely contrast with the sharp flavour of the cranberries.

Makes 12

50g/2oz/¼ cup butter
1 egg
90g/3½oz/½ cup caster (superfine) sugar
grated rind of 1 large orange
120ml/4fl oz/½ cup freshly squeezed orange juice
150g/5oz/1¼ cups plain (all-purpose) flour

5ml/1 tsp baking powder
2.5ml/½ tsp bicarbonate of soda (baking soda)
5ml/1 tsp ground cinnamon
2.5ml/½ tsp freshly grated nutmeg
2.5ml/½ tsp ground allspice
1.5ml/¼ tsp ground ginger
pinch of salt
1–2 eating apples
150g/6oz/1½ cups cranberries
50g/2oz/¼ cup walnuts, chopped
icing (confectioners') sugar, for dusting (optional)

1 Preheat the oven to 180°C/350°F/Gas 4. Arrange 12 paper cases in a muffin tin (pan).

2 Melt the butter over a gentle heat. Set aside to cool.

3 In a large bowl, whisk the egg lightly. Add the melted butter and whisk to combine. Add the sugar, orange rind and juice. Whisk to blend, then set aside.

4 In a mixing bowl, sift together the flour, baking powder, bicarbonate of soda, cinnamon, nutmeg, allspice, ginger and salt. Set aside.

5 Make a well in the dry ingredients and pour in the egg mixture. With a spoon, stir until just blended.

6 Quarter, core and peel the apples. Chop coarsely. Add the apples, cranberries and walnuts, and stir to blend.

7 Fill the cases three-quarters full and bake for 25–30 minutes, until the tops spring back when touched lightly. Transfer to a rack to cool. Dust with icing sugar.

Apple and Cinnamon Energy 236kcal/995kJ; Protein 4.3g; Carbohydrate 38.2g, of which sugars 19.1g; Fat 8.5g, of which saturates 4.9g; Cholesterol 51mg; Calcium 74mg; Fibre 1.2g; Sodium 73mg.
Apple and Cranberry Energy 149kcal/624kJ; Protein 2.5g; Carbohydrate 20.4g, of which sugars 10.8g; Fat 6.9g, of which saturates 2.6g; Cholesterol 25mg; Calcium 30mg; Fibre 0.9g; Sodium 34mg.

Individual Apple Cakes

These delicate little cakes can be rustled up in next to no time for eating hot when visitors call. The quantities have been kept small because they really must be eaten while still fresh. To make more, simply double up on the measures.

Makes 8–10
125g/4½oz/generous 1 cup
self-raising (self-rising) flour,
plus extra for dusting

pinch of salt
65g/2½oz/5 tbsp butter,
diced
50g/2oz/4 tbsp demerara
(raw) or light muscovado
(brown) sugar
1 small cooking apple,
weighing about 150g/5oz
about 30ml/2 tbsp milk
caster (superfine) sugar,
for dusting

1 Sift the flour and salt into a mixing bowl. Add the butter and, with your fingertips, rub it into the flour until the mixture resembles fine breadcrumbs. Stir in the sugar.

2 Peel and grate the apple, discarding the core, and stir the apple into the flour mixture with enough milk to make a mixture that can be gathered into a ball of soft, moist dough. Work it slightly to make sure the flour is mixed in well.

3 Transfer to a lightly floured surface and roll out the dough to about 5mm/¼in thick. With a 6–7.5cm/2½–3in cookie cutter, stamp out rounds, gathering up the scraps and re-rolling them to make more rounds.

4 Heat a heavy frying pan over low to medium heat. Smear a little butter on the pan and cook in batches, for about 4–5 minutes on each side, or until golden and cooked through.

5 Lift on to a wire rack and dust with caster sugar. Serve warm.

Cook's Tip
Add a pinch of ground cinnamon or nutmeg to the flour.

Date & Apple Muffins

These spiced muffins are delicious and very filling. If possible, use fresh Medjool dates from Egypt, as they have sweet, dense flesh and a truly opulent flavour.

Makes 12
150g/5oz/1¼ cups self-raising
(self-rising) wholemeal
(whole-wheat) flour
150g/5oz/1¼ cups self-raising
(self-rising) flour

5ml/1 tsp ground cinnamon
5ml/1 tsp baking powder
25g/1oz/2 tbsp butter
75g/3oz/⅓ cup light muscovado
(brown) sugar
250ml/8fl oz/1 cup apple juice
30ml/2 tbsp pear and apple jam
1 egg, lightly beaten
1 eating apple
75g/3oz/½ cup chopped dates
15ml/1 tbsp chopped pecan nuts

1 Preheat the oven to 200°C/400°F/Gas 6. Arrange 12 paper cases in a muffin tin (pan).

2 Sift together both flours, the cinnamon and baking powder into a large bowl. Add the butter and rub it in with your fingertips until the mixture resembles fine breadcrumbs. Add the sugar and stir well to mix.

3 In a mixing bowl, stir a little of the apple juice with the pear and apple jam until smooth. Mix in the remaining apple juice, then add to the rubbed-in mixture with the beaten egg.

4 Quarter and core the apple, and peel it if you like, then chop the flesh finely. Add to the batter and stir in the dates. Divide the mixture among the muffin cases.

5 Sprinkle the chopped pecans on top. Bake for 20–25 minutes, until golden brown and firm in the middle. Transfer to a wire rack and serve while still warm.

Cook's Tip
If self-raising (self-rising) wholemeal (whole-wheat) flour is not available, use more self-raising (self-rising) white flour instead.

Individual Apple Cakes Energy 121kcal/508kJ; Protein 1.4g; Carbohydrate 16.5g, of which sugars 6.9g; Fat 6g, of which saturates 3.7g; Cholesterol 15mg; Calcium 26mg; Fibre 0.6g; Sodium 45mg.
Date and Apple Muffins Energy 158kcal/670kJ; Protein 3.2g; Carbohydrate 30.7g, of which sugars 11.7g; Fat 3.4g, of which saturates 0.3g; Cholesterol 16mg; Calcium 45mg; Fibre 1g; Sodium 25mg.

Apricot & Almond Cakes

What an utterly perfect combination. If they aren't eaten immediately, these fruity cakes will stay moist for several days if stored in an airtight container.

Makes 18
225g/8oz/2 cups self-raising
  (self-rising) flour
115g/4oz/½ cup light muscovado
  (brown) sugar
50g/2oz/⅓ cup semolina
175g/6oz/¾ cup ready-to-eat
  dried apricots, chopped
2 eggs
30ml/2 tbsp malt extract
30ml/2 tbsp clear honey
60ml/4 tbsp skimmed milk
60ml/4 tbsp sunflower oil
a few drops of almond extract
30ml/2 tbsp flaked
  (sliced) almonds

1 Preheat the oven to 160°C/325°F/Gas 3. Lightly grease a 28 × 18cm/11 × 7in shallow cake tin (pan) and line with baking parchment.

2 Sift the flour into a bowl and add the muscovado sugar, semolina, dried apricots and eggs. Add the malt extract, clear honey, milk, sunflower oil and almond extract. Mix well until smooth.

3 Turn the mixture into the prepared cake tin and spread to the edges. Smooth the top. Sprinkle the flaked almonds all over the surface in as even a layer as possible.

4 Bake for 30–35 minutes, until the centre of the cake springs back when lightly pressed.

5 Transfer the tin to a wire rack and leave to cool, then turn out the cake. Remove and discard the lining paper, place the cake on a board and cut it into 18 slices with a sharp knife, to serve.

> **Variation**
> You can substitute dried peaches or nectarines for the apricots; they both have an affinity with almonds.

Pear & Sultana Bran Muffins

These tasty muffins are best eaten freshly baked and served warm or cold, on their own, or spread with butter, jam or honey.

Makes 12
75g/3oz/¾ cup plain
  (all-purpose) wholemeal
  (whole-wheat) flour, sifted
50g/2oz/½ cup plain
  (all-purpose) white flour, sifted
50g/2oz/3 cups bran
15ml/1 tbsp baking powder
pinch of salt
50g/2oz/4 tbsp butter
50g/2oz/¼ cup soft light
  brown sugar
1 egg
200ml/7fl oz/scant 1 cup
  skimmed (low fat) milk
50g/2oz/⅓ cup ready-to-eat
  dried pears, chopped
50g/2oz/⅓ cup sultanas
  (golden raisins)

1 Preheat the oven to 200°C/400°F/Gas 6. Arrange 12 paper cases in a muffin tin (pan).

2 Mix together the flours, bran, baking powder and salt in a bowl. Set aside.

3 Gently heat the butter in a small pan until melted.

4 Mix together the melted butter, sugar, egg and milk.

5 Pour the butter mixture over the dry ingredients. Gently fold the ingredients together, only enough to combine. The mixture should look quite lumpy.

6 Fold in the dried pears and sultanas.

7 Spoon the mixture into the prepared muffin tins. Bake for 15–20 minutes, until well risen and golden brown. Turn out on to a wire rack to cool.

> **Cook's Tip**
> For a quick and easy way to chop dried fruit, chop with kitchen scissors.

Apricot and Almond Energy 140kcal/589kJ; Protein 3.1g; Carbohydrate 23.6g, of which sugars 11.9g; Fat 4.3g, of which saturates 0.6g; Cholesterol 21mg; Calcium 40mg; Fibre 1.2g; Sodium 13mg.
Pear and Sultana Bran Energy 121kcal/510kJ; Protein 3g; Carbohydrate 18.7g, of which sugars 9.8g; Fat 4.3g, of which saturates 2.4g; Cholesterol 25mg; Calcium 51mg; Fibre 2.2g; Sodium 42mg.

Dried Cherry Muffins

Cherries are always a great favourite, especially with children, so why not spoil the family and serve these scrumptious muffins freshly baked and still warm from the oven, smothered with butter and cherry jam. Dried cherries are full of antioxidants, and are a healthy food to eat.

Makes 16

250ml/8fl oz/1 cup natural (plain) yogurt
225g/8oz/1 cup dried cherries
115g/4oz/½ cup butter, softened
175g/6oz/scant 1 cup caster (superfine) sugar
2 eggs
5ml/1 tsp vanilla extract
200g/7oz/1¾ cups plain (all-purpose) flour
10ml/2 tsp baking powder
5ml/1 tsp bicarbonate of soda (baking soda)
pinch of salt

1 In a mixing bowl, combine the yogurt and dried cherries. Cover with clear film (plastic wrap) and leave to stand for about 30 minutes.

2 Preheat the oven to 180°C/350°F/Gas 4. Arrange 12 paper cases in a muffin tin (pan).

3 Beat together the butter and caster sugar in a bowl until light and fluffy. Add the eggs, one at a time, beating well after each addition until fully incorporated.

4 Add the vanilla extract and yogurt and cherry mixture and stir well until thoroughly mixed.

5 Sift the flour, baking powder, bicarbonate of soda and salt over the batter in batches. Gently fold in using a metal spoon after each addition.

6 Spoon the mixture into the prepared muffin tins, filling them about two-thirds full. Bake for 20 minutes, or until risen and golden and the tops spring back when touched lightly. Transfer to a wire rack to cool completely before serving or storing in an airtight container.

Apricot & Orange Muffins

Serve these fruity muffins freshly baked and warm.

Makes 8 large or 12 medium muffins

115g/4oz/1 cup cornmeal
75g/3oz/¾ cup rice flour
15ml/1 tbsp baking powder
pinch of salt
50g/2oz/4 tbsp butter, melted
50g/2oz/¼ cup light soft brown sugar
1 egg, beaten
200ml/7fl oz/scant 1 cup semi-skimmed (low-fat) milk
finely grated rind of 1 orange
115g/4oz/½ cup ready-to-eat dried apricots, chopped

1 Preheat the oven to 200°C/400°F/Gas 6. Arrange 12 paper cases in a muffin tin (pan).

2 Place the cornmeal, rice flour, baking powder and salt in a bowl and mix together.

3 Stir together the melted butter, sugar, egg, milk and orange rind, then pour the mixture over the dry ingredients. Fold the ingredients gently together. The mixture will look quite lumpy, which is correct, as over-mixing will result in heavy muffins.

4 Fold in the chopped dried apricots, then spoon the mixture into the prepared paper cases, dividing it equally among them.

5 Bake for 15–20 minutes, until the muffins have risen and are golden brown and springy to the touch. Turn them out on to a wire rack to cool.

6 Serve the muffins warm or cold, on their own or cut in half and spread with a little butter or low-fat spread. Store in an airtight container for up to 1 week or seal in plastic bags and freeze for up to 3 months.

Variation
Try substituting grapefruit rind for the orange, and the same quantity of chopped dried mango for the apricots.

Dried Cherry Muffins Energy 196kcal/825kJ; Protein 3.2g; Carbohydrate 32.1g, of which sugars 22.6g; Fat 7g, of which saturates 4g; Cholesterol 39mg; Calcium 67mg; Fibre 0.7g; Sodium 69mg.
Apricot and Orange Energy 136kcal/570kJ; Protein 3g; Carbohydrate 21g, of which sugars 9g; Fat 5g, of which saturates 3g; Cholesterol 29mg; Calcium 46mg; Fibre 2.2g; Sodium 193mg.

Raspberry Buttermilk Muffins

Low-fat buttermilk gives these muffins a light and spongy texture. Make them in the summer when fresh raspberries are at their seasonal best.

Makes 10–12

300g/11oz/2¾ cups plain
(all-purpose) flour
15ml/1 tbsp baking powder
115g/4oz/generous ½ cup caster
(superfine) sugar
1 egg
250ml/8fl oz/1 cup buttermilk
60ml/4 tbsp sunflower oil
150g/5oz/1 cup raspberries

1 Preheat the oven to 200°C/400°F/Gas 6. Arrange 10–12 paper cases in a muffin tin (pan).

2 Sift the flour and baking powder into a mixing bowl. Stir in the sugar, then make a well in the centre.

3 Mix the egg, buttermilk and sunflower oil together in a bowl, pour into the flour mixture and mix quickly until just combined.

4 Add the raspberries and lightly fold them into the mixture with a metal spoon until just combined. Spoon the mixture into the prepared paper cases, filling them about two-thirds full.

5 Bake for 20–25 minutes, until golden brown and firm in the centre. Transfer to a wire rack and serve warm or cold.

Cook's Tips

• As with other soft fruits – which can also be used in these delicious muffins – don't buy more raspberries than you require, as they deteriorate quickly, although they do freeze well. If they're sold in packs, make sure that there are no squashed ones underneath. Avoid soaking them in water when washing them; just wipe with damp kitchen paper.
• Raspberry muffins make a fabulous breakfast treat with butter and honey, and are great at teatime when served warm with raspberry jam and thickly whipped cream.

Raspberry Crumble Buns

Make these stylish muffins for a special occasion in the summer, when raspberries are bursting with flavour. For total luxury, serve like scones, with raspberry jam and cream.

Makes 12

175g/6oz/1½ cups plain
(all-purpose) flour
10ml/2 tsp baking powder
pinch of salt
5ml/1 tsp ground cinnamon
50g/2oz/¼ cup sugar
50g/2oz/¼ cup soft light
brown sugar
115g/4oz/½ cup butter, melted
1 egg
120ml/4fl oz/½ cup milk
225g/8oz/1⅓ cups fresh
raspberries
grated rind of 1 lemon

For the crumble topping

50g/2oz/½ cup pecan nuts,
finely chopped
50g/2oz/¼ cup soft dark
brown sugar
45ml/3 tbsp plain
(all-purpose) flour
5ml/1 tsp ground cinnamon
40g/1½oz/3 tbsp butter, melted

1 Preheat the oven to 180°C/350°F/Gas 4. Arrange 12 paper cases in a muffin tin (pan).

2 Sift the flour, baking powder, salt and cinnamon into a bowl. Stir in the sugars. Make a well in the centre.

3 Beat together the butter, egg and milk in a large bowl until light. Add the flour mixture to it and stir until just combined. Stir in the raspberries and lemon rind.

4 Spoon the batter into the muffin tins, filling them almost to the top.

5 To make the topping, mix the pecans, sugar, flour and cinnamon in a bowl. Stir in the melted butter.

6 Spoon a little of the crumble topping over the top of each muffin. Bake for about 25 minutes.

7 Transfer to a wire rack to cool slightly. Serve the muffins warm.

Raspberry Buttermilk Energy 132kcal/555kJ; Protein 4g; Carbohydrate 19g, of which sugars 5.7g; Fat 5g, of which saturates 2.7g; Cholesterol 42mg; Calcium 48mg; Fibre 1.5g; Sodium 45mg.
Raspberry Crumble Energy 225kcal/940kJ; Protein 2.7g; Carbohydrate 25.2g, of which sugars 14.1g; Fat 13.3g, of which saturates 7.3g; Cholesterol 45mg; Calcium 48mg; Fibre 0.9g; Sodium 93mg.

Blueberry Muffins

Light and fruity, these well-known American muffins are delicious at any time of day. Serve them warm for breakfast or brunch, or as a special teatime treat.

Makes 12

2 eggs
50g/2oz/4 tbsp butter, melted
175ml/6fl oz/³/₄ cup milk
5ml/1 tsp vanilla extract
5ml/1 tsp grated lemon rind
180g/6¹/₄oz/generous 1¹/₂ cups
    plain (all-purpose) flour
60g/2¹/₄oz/generous ¹/₄ cup sugar
10ml/2 tsp baking powder
pinch of salt
175g/6oz/1¹/₂ cups fresh
    blueberries

1 Preheat the oven to 200°C/400°F/Gas 6. Arrange 12 paper cases in a muffin tin (pan) or grease the tin.

2 In a bowl, whisk the eggs until blended. Add the melted butter, milk, vanilla and lemon rind, and stir to combine.

3 Sift the flour, sugar, baking powder and salt into a large bowl. Make a well in the centre and pour in the egg mixture. With a metal spoon, stir until the flour is just moistened.

4 Add the blueberries to the muffin mixture and gently fold in.

5 Spoon the batter into the muffin tin or paper cases, leaving enough room for the muffins to rise.

6 Bake for 20–25 minutes, until the tops spring back when touched lightly. Leave the muffins in the tin, if using, for 5 minutes before turning out on to a wire rack to cool.

> **Variation**
> *Muffins are delicious with all kinds of different fruits. Try out some variations using this basic muffin recipe. Replace the blueberries with the same weight of bilberries, blackcurrants, pitted cherries or raspberries.*

Chocolate Blueberry Muffins

Blueberries are one of the many fruits that combine deliciously with the richness of chocolate, while still retaining their own distinctive flavour. These muffins are best served warm.

Makes 12

115g/4oz/¹/₂ cup butter
75g/3oz plain (semisweet)
    chocolate, chopped
200g/7oz/scant 1 cup sugar
1 egg, lightly beaten
250ml/8fl oz/1 cup buttermilk
10ml/2 tsp vanilla extract
275g/10oz/2¹/₂ cups plain
    (all-purpose) flour
5ml/1 tsp bicarbonate of soda
    (baking soda)
175g/6oz/generous 1 cup fresh or
    thawed frozen blueberries
25g/1oz plain (semisweet)
    chocolate, melted, to decorate

1 Preheat the oven to 190°C/375°F/Gas 5. Arrange 12 paper cases in a muffin tin (pan).

2 Melt the butter and chocolate in a pan over a medium heat, stirring frequently until smooth. Remove from the heat and leave to cool slightly.

3 Stir the sugar, egg, buttermilk and vanilla extract into the melted chocolate mixture. Gently fold in the flour and bicarbonate of soda until just blended. (The mixture should be slightly lumpy.) Gently fold in the blueberries.

4 Spoon the batter into the paper cases. Bake for 25–30 minutes, until a skewer inserted in the centre comes out with just a few crumbs attached. Transfer the muffins to a wire rack.

5 To decorate, drizzle with the melted chocolate and serve warm or at room temperature.

> **Cook's Tip**
> *Do not keep the batter waiting once you have folded in the blueberries. Bake the muffins immediately or they won't rise very well during cooking.*

Blueberry Muffins Energy 236kcal/992kJ; Protein 4.9g; Carbohydrate 34.7g, of which sugars 12.4g; Fat 9.6g, of which saturates 5.6g; Cholesterol 54mg; Calcium 88mg; Fibre 1.4g; Sodium 82mg.
Chocolate Blueberry Energy 279kcal/1172kJ; Protein 4.1g; Carbohydrate 43.5g, of which sugars 25.4g; Fat 11g, of which saturates 6.6g; Cholesterol 38mg; Calcium 73mg; Fibre 1.2g; Sodium 75mg.

Cranberry & Chocolate Cakes

There is no doubt that the contrasting flavours of tangy, sharp cranberries and sweet chocolate were made for each other – and make simply fabulous cream-topped squares.

Makes 12
115g/4oz/¹/₂ cup unsalted (sweet) butter
60ml/4 tbsp unsweetened cocoa powder
215g/7¹/₂oz/scant 1 cup light muscovado (brown) sugar
150g/5oz/1¹/₄ cups self-raising (self-rising) flour, plus extra for dusting
2 eggs, beaten
115g/4oz/1 cup fresh or thawed frozen cranberries

For the topping
150ml/¹/₄ pint/²/₃ cup sour cream
75g/3oz/scant ¹/₂ cup caster (superfine) sugar
30ml/2 tbsp self-raising (self-rising) flour
50g/2oz/4 tbsp soft butter
1 egg, beaten
2.5ml/¹/₂ tsp vanilla extract
75ml/5 tbsp coarsely grated plain (semisweet) chocolate, for sprinkling

1 Preheat the oven to 180°C/350°F/Gas 4. Lightly grease an 18 × 25cm/7 × 10in cake tin (pan) and dust lightly with flour, shaking out any excess.

2 Combine the butter, cocoa powder and sugar in a pan and stir over a low heat until melted and smooth.

3 Remove the pan from the heat and stir in the flour and beaten eggs. Stir in the cranberries, then spread the mixture evenly in the prepared cake tin.

4 To make the topping, put the sour cream, sugar, flour, butter, beaten egg and vanilla extract into a bowl and beat well until smooth and thoroughly combined. Spoon the mixture into the tin and gently spread it evenly over the chocolate and cranberry base.

5 Sprinkle evenly with the coarsely grated chocolate and bake for about 40 minutes, or until risen and firm. Leave to cool completely in the tin, then cut into 12 squares.

Cranberry & Orange Muffins

These delicious muffins are perfect to eat at any time of day, and are a real energy boost for breakfast or as a lunchbox treat. Use fresh or frozen cranberries.

Makes 10–12
350g/12oz/3 cups plain (all-purpose) flour, sifted
15ml/1 tsp baking powder
pinch of salt
115g/4oz/generous ¹/₂ cup caster (superfine) sugar
2 eggs
150ml/¹/₄ pint/²/₃ cup milk
50ml/2fl oz/¹/₄ cup corn oil
finely grated rind of 1 orange
150g/5oz/1¹/₄ cups cranberries, thawed if frozen

1 Preheat the oven to 190°C/375°F/Gas 5. Arrange 10–12 paper cases in a muffin tin (pan).

2 Sift together the flour, baking powder and salt into a large bowl. Add the sugar and stir well to mix.

3 Lightly beat the eggs with the milk and corn oil in another bowl until thoroughly combined.

4 Make a well in the centre of the dry ingredients and pour in the egg mixture. Stir with a wooden spoon until blended to a smooth batter. Gently fold in the grated orange rind and cranberries with a metal spoon.

5 Divide the mixture among the paper cases and bake for about 25 minutes, until risen and golden. Transfer to a wire rack to cool and serve warm or cold.

Cook's Tip
The flared sides of a proper muffin tin (pan) increase the surface area, encouraging the dough to rise.

Variation
Replace half the cranberries with blueberries or raspberries.

Cranberry and Orange Energy 184kcal/780kJ; Protein 4.3g; Carbohydrate 34.4g, of which sugars 12.2g; Fat 4.3g, of which saturates 0.9g; Cholesterol 32mg; Calcium 66mg; Fibre 1.1g; Sodium 19mg.
Cranberry Chocolate Energy 343kcal/1439kJ; Protein 4.8g; Carbohydrate 42.9g, of which sugars 30.8g; Fat 18.2g, of which saturates 8.7g; Cholesterol 76mg; Calcium 63mg; Fibre 1.4g; Sodium 164mg.

Spiced Sultana Muffins

Sunday breakfasts will never be the same again, once you have tried these delicious sultana muffins. They are easy to prepare and take only a short time to bake.

Makes 6

75g/3oz/6 tbsp butter
1 small (US medium) egg
120ml/4fl oz/½ cup unsweetened coconut milk
150g/5oz/1¼ cups wholemeal (whole-wheat) flour
7.5ml/1½ tsp baking powder
5ml/1 tsp ground cinnamon
generous pinch of salt
115g/4oz/⅔ cup sultanas (golden raisins)

1 Preheat the oven to 190°C/375°F/Gas 5. Arrange 6 paper cases in a muffin tin (pan).

2 Beat the butter, egg and coconut milk in a bowl until well combined.

3 Sift the wholemeal flour, baking powder, ground cinnamon and salt over the beaten mixture. Fold in carefully, then beat well. Fold in the sultanas. Divide the mixture among the paper cases.

4 Bake for 20 minutes, or until the muffins have risen well and are firm to the touch. Cool slightly on a wire rack before serving.

> **Variation**
> The heath-conscious or those following a slimming plan can substitute the same quantity of low-fat spread for the butter. The finished muffins will still be utterly delicious, although not quite so rich in flavour.

> **Cook's Tip**
> These muffins taste equally good cold. They also freeze well, packed in freezer bags. To serve, leave them to thaw overnight, or defrost in a microwave, then warm them briefly in the oven.

Sunflower Sultana Scones

Traditional fruit scones are given a delightful new twist with a crunchy topping of sunflower seeds.

Makes 10–12

225g/8oz/2 cups self-raising (self-rising) flour, plus extra for dusting
5ml/1 tsp baking powder
25g/1oz/2 tbsp butter
30ml/2 tbsp golden caster (superfine) sugar
50g/2oz/⅓ cup sultanas (golden raisins)
30ml/2 tbsp sunflower seeds
150g/5oz/⅔ cup natural (plain) yogurt
about 30–45ml/2–3 tbsp milk

1 Preheat the oven to 230°C/450°F/Gas 8. Lightly grease a baking sheet.

2 Sift together the flour and baking powder into a bowl. Add the butter and rub it in with your fingertips until the mixture resembles fine breadcrumbs. Add the sugar, sultanas and half the sunflower seeds and stir well to mix.

3 Stir in the yogurt, then add just enough milk to mix to a soft but not wet dough.

4 Roll out on a lightly floured surface to about 2cm/¾in thick. Stamp out 6cm/2½in rounds with a floured cookie cutter and lift on to the baking sheet.

5 Brush the tops of the scones with milk and sprinkle with the reserved sunflower seeds.

6 Bake for 10–12 minutes, until well risen and golden brown. Transfer to a wire rack. Serve while still warm, split in half and spread with butter and jam.

> **Variation**
> You could substitute pumpkin seeds for the sunflower. Both are high in nutrients and have the essential crunch factor.

Spiced Sultana Energy 240kcal/1006kJ; Protein 4.9g; Carbohydrate 30.3g, of which sugars 14.9g; Fat 11.9g, of which saturates 6.9g; Cholesterol 58mg; Calcium 35mg; Fibre 2.6g; Sodium 114mg.
Sunflower Sultana Energy 121kcal/513kJ; Protein 3g; Carbohydrate 21.2g, of which sugars 6.9g; Fat 3.3g, of which saturates 0.6g; Cholesterol 0mg; Calcium 99mg; Fibre 0.8g; Sodium 97mg.

Oat & Raisin Muffins

Often the simplest things are the nicest, and that is the case with these flavour-packed fruit muffins.

Makes 12

75g/3oz/scant 1 cup rolled oats
250ml/8fl oz/1 cup buttermilk
115g/4oz/¹/₂ cup butter, at
  room temperature
90g/3¹/₂oz/generous ¹/₃ cup soft
  dark brown sugar
1 egg, at room temperature
115g/4oz/1 cup plain
  (all-purpose) flour
5ml/1 tsp baking powder
2.5ml/¹/₂ tsp bicarbonate of soda
  (baking soda)
pinch of salt
25g/1oz/2 tbsp raisins

1 In a bowl, combine the oats and buttermilk, and leave to soak for 1 hour.

2 Preheat the oven to 200°C/400°F/Gas 6. Arrange 12 paper cases in a muffin tin (pan).

3 In a bowl, cream the butter and sugar until light and fluffy. Beat in the egg.

4 Sift the flour, baking powder, bicarbonate of soda and salt into the butter mixture in batches. Alternate with batches of the oat mixture. Stir to combine after each addition. Fold in the raisins. Do not overmix.

5 Fill the prepared cups two-thirds full. Bake for about 20–25 minutes, until a skewer inserted in the centre comes out clean. Transfer to a rack to cool.

Cook's Tip
Buttermilk is made from skimmed milk fermented with a special culture under controlled conditions, resulting in an acidic product that helps dough to rise. If it is not available, add 5ml/1 tsp lemon juice or vinegar to milk and leave to stand for a few minutes until curdled.

Raisin Brownies

Adding dried fruit makes brownies a little more substantial, although no less moist and delicious. Try to find Californian or Spanish raisins for the best flavour and texture.

Makes 16

115g/4oz/¹/₂ cup butter, diced
50g/2oz/¹/₂ cup unsweetened
  cocoa powder
2 eggs
225g/8oz/generous 1 cup caster
  (superfine) sugar
5ml/1 tsp vanilla extract
40g/1¹/₂ oz/¹/₃ cup plain
  (all-purpose) flour
75g/3oz/³/₄ cup walnuts, chopped
65g/2¹/₂oz/¹/₂ cup raisins
icing (confectioners') sugar,
  for dusting

1 Preheat the oven to 180°C/350°F/Gas 4. Line a 20cm/8in square baking tin (pan) with baking parchment and grease the paper lightly.

2 Melt the butter in a small pan over a low heat. Remove from the heat and stir in the cocoa.

3 In a bowl, beat together the eggs, sugar and vanilla extract with an electric mixer until light and fluffy. Add the cocoa mixture and stir to blend.

4 Sift the flour over the cocoa mixture and fold in gently with a metal spoon. Add the walnuts and raisins, mixing them in gently, then scrape the mixture into the prepared tin.

5 Bake for about 30 minutes, until firm to the touch, being careful not to overbake.

6 Leave in the tin on a rack to cool completely. Cut into 5cm/2in squares and remove from the tin. Dust with sifted icing sugar before serving.

Variation
For an adult taste, try substituting rum for the vanilla.

Oat and Raisin Muffins Energy 177kcal/742kJ; Protein 3g; Carbohydrate 22.3g, of which sugars 10.4g; Fat 9.1g, of which saturates 5.2g; Cholesterol 37mg; Calcium 51mg; Fibre 0.8g; Sodium 77mg.
Raisin Brownies Energy 181kcal/759kJ; Protein 2.5g; Carbohydrate 20.4g, of which sugars 18.1g; Fat 10.5g, of which saturates 4.6g; Cholesterol 39mg; Calcium 26mg; Fibre 0.7g; Sodium 86mg.

Oat & Raisin Drop Scones

Serve these fruit scones at teatime or as a dessert with real maple syrup or honey. If you are feeling indulgent, add a spoonful of sour cream or crème fraîche.

Makes about 16
75g/3oz/³⁄₄ cup self-raising (self-rising) flour
pinch of salt
2.5ml/½ tsp baking powder
50g/2oz/scant ½ cup raisins
25g/1oz/¼ cup fine oatmeal
25g/1oz/2 tbsp caster (superfine) sugar
grated rind of 1 orange
2 egg yolks
7.5ml/1½ tsp unsalted (sweet) butter, melted
100ml/3½fl oz single (light) cream
100ml/3½fl oz/scant ½ cup water

1 Sift together the flour, salt and baking powder into a large mixing bowl.

2 Add the raisins, oatmeal, caster sugar and grated orange rind and stir well to mix. Gradually beat in the egg yolks, melted butter, cream and measured water until thoroughly combined into a creamy batter.

3 Lightly grease and heat a large frying pan or griddle and drop about 30ml/2 tbsp of batter at a time on to the pan or griddle to make six or seven small pancakes.

4 Cook over a medium heat until bubbles show on the scones' surface, then turn them over and cook for another 2 minutes until golden.

5 Transfer the scones to a plate and keep warm while cooking the remaining mixture. Serve warm.

> **Cook's Tip**
> *There are two secrets to making light-as-air drop scones. Firstly, do not leave the batter to stand once it has been mixed. The second is to heat the frying pan or griddle slowly until it is very hot before adding the batter.*

Hot Currant Cakes

Traditionally many cooks use half lard and half butter in this recipe. Serve the hot currant cakes warm or cold, as they are, or buttered.

Makes about 16
250g/9oz/2¼ cups plain (all-purpose) flour, plus extra for dusting
pinch of salt
7.5ml/1¼ tsp baking powder
125g/4½oz/½ cup butter, diced
100g/3½oz/½ cup caster (superfine) sugar, plus extra for dusting
75g/3oz/⅓ cup currants
1 egg
45ml/3 tbsp milk

1 Sift the flour, salt and baking powder into a large mixing bowl. Add the butter and, with your fingertips, rub it into the flour until it resembles fine breadcrumbs. Stir in the sugar and currants.

2 Lightly beat the egg and with a round-end knife and with a cutting action, stir it into the flour mixture with enough milk to gather the mixture into a ball of soft dough.

3 Transfer to a lightly floured surface and roll out to about 5mm/¼in thick. With a 6–7.5cm/2½–3in cookie cutter, stamp out rounds, gathering up the scraps and re-rolling to make more rounds.

4 Heat a heavy frying pan over medium to low heat. Smear a little butter or oil over the pan and cook the cakes, in small batches, for about 4–5 minutes on each side, or until they are slightly risen, golden brown and cooked through.

5 Transfer to a wire rack, dust with caster sugar on both sides and leave to cool.

> **Variation**
> *For a change, add a large pinch of mixed spice (apple pie spice) in step 1, or a little vanilla extract in step 2.*

Hot Currant Cakes Energy 128kcal/540kJ; Protein 4.1g; Carbohydrate 22.8g, of which sugars 1.3g; Fat 2.9g, of which saturates 1.4g; Cholesterol 29mg; Calcium 66mg; Fibre 0.9g; Sodium 29mg.
Oat and Raisin Energy 375kcal/1574kJ; Protein 5.6g; Carbohydrate 50g, of which sugars 23.2g; Fat 18.4g, of which saturates 9.6g; Cholesterol 57mg; Calcium 93mg; Fibre 1.8g; Sodium 129mg.

Prune Muffins

Muffins with prunes are nutritious as well as delicious, and perfect as a weekend breakfast treat. These are made with oil rather than butter, so they are very quick to mix.

Makes 12
1 egg
250ml/8fl oz/1 cup milk
50ml/2fl oz/¼ cup vegetable oil

50g/2oz/¼ cup sugar
30ml/2 tbsp soft dark
   brown sugar
225g/8oz/2 cups plain
   (all-purpose) flour
10ml/2 tsp baking powder
pinch of salt
1.5ml/¼ tsp grated nutmeg
150g/5oz/¾ cup cooked
   prunes, or ready-to-eat prunes,
   chopped

1 Preheat the oven to 200°C/400°F/Gas 6. Arrange 12 paper cases in a muffin tin (pan).

2 Break the egg into a mixing bowl and beat with a fork. Beat in the milk and oil.

3 Stir the sugars into the egg mixture. Set aside. Sift the flour, baking powder, salt and nutmeg into a mixing bowl. Make a well in the centre, pour in the egg mixture and stir. The batter should be slightly lumpy.

4 Gently fold the prunes into the batter until just evenly distributed. Spoon into the prepared muffin tins, filling them two-thirds full.

5 Bake for about 20 minutes, until golden brown. Leave to stand for 10 minutes before transferring to a wire rack. Serve warm or cold.

Cook's Tip
When cooking prunes, if there is time, soak them overnight in 400ml/14fl oz/1⅔ cups water, then bring to the boil with 5ml/1 tsp lemon juice and 30ml/2 tbsp caster (superfine) sugar, if you like. Simmer for about 10 minutes, until soft.

Date & Walnut Brownies

These date brownies are great for afternoon tea, but they also make a fantastic dessert. Reheat slices briefly in the microwave oven and serve with crème fraîche.

Makes 12
350g/12oz plain (semisweet)
   chocolate, broken into squares
225g/8oz/1 cup butter, diced
3 large (US extra large) eggs

115g/4oz/generous ½ cup caster
   (superfine) sugar
5ml/1 tsp vanilla extract
75g/3oz/¾ cup plain
   (all-purpose) flour, sifted
225g/8oz/1½ cups fresh dates,
   peeled, stoned (pitted)
   and chopped
200g/7oz/1¾ cups walnut pieces
icing (confectioners') sugar,
   for dusting

1 Preheat the oven to 190°C/375°F/Gas 5. Generously grease a 30 × 20cm/12 × 8in rectangular baking tin (pan) and line with baking parchment.

2 Put the chocolate squares and diced butter into a large heatproof bowl. Set the bowl over a pan of gently simmering water and heat gently until melted. Stir until smooth, then remove the bowl from the heat and leave to cool slightly.

3 In a separate bowl, beat together the eggs, sugar and vanilla. Beat into the chocolate mixture, then fold in the flour, dates and nuts. Pour into the tin.

4 Bake for 30–40 minutes, until firm and the mixture comes away from the sides of the tin. Cool in the tin, then turn out, remove the parchment and dust with icing sugar. Cut the brownies into bars or squares.

Cook's Tip
When melting the chocolate and butter, keep the water in the pan beneath simmering gently, but do not let it approach boiling point. Chocolate is notoriously sensitive to heat; it is vital not to let it get too hot, or it may stiffen into an unmanageable mass.

Prune Muffins Energy 190kcal/801kJ; Protein 3.7g; Carbohydrate 28.1g, of which sugars 10.7g; Fat 7.8g, of which saturates 1.2g; Cholesterol 17mg; Calcium 66mg; Fibre 1.3g; Sodium 17mg.
Date and Walnut Energy 504kcal/2097kJ; Protein 6.5g; Carbohydrate 39.9g, of which sugars 34.8g; Fat 36.5g, of which saturates 16g; Cholesterol 89mg; Calcium 54mg; Fibre 1.8g; Sodium 136mg.

Pineapple & Cinnamon Drop Scones

Making the batter with pineapple juice instead of milk cuts down on the amount of fat and adds a fruity piquancy to the flavour of these delicious drop scones.

Makes 24
115g/4oz/1 cup self-raising (self-rising) wholemeal (whole-wheat) flour
115g/4oz/1 cup self-raising (self-rising) white flour
5ml/1 tsp ground cinnamon
15ml/1 tbsp caster (superfine) sugar
1 egg
300ml/½ pint/1¼ cups pineapple juice
75g/3oz/½ cup semi-dried pineapple, chopped

1 Put the wholemeal flour in a mixing bowl. Sift in the white flour, add the cinnamon and caster sugar and mix together. Make a well in the centre. Add the egg with half of the pineapple juice to the well.

2 Gradually incorporate the flour to make a smooth batter, then beat in the remaining pineapple juice and stir in the chopped pineapple.

3 Heat a griddle, then lightly grease it. Drop tablespoons of the batter on to the surface, spacing them apart, and leave them until they bubble and the bubbles begin to burst.

4 Turn over the drop scones with a metal spatula and cook until the underside is golden brown. Continue to cook in successive batches.

> **Cook's Tips**
> • Drop scones do not keep well and are best eaten freshly cooked. In any case, they are especially delicious served hot.
> • If self-raising (self-rising) wholemeal (whole-wheat) flour is not readily available, use white self-raising flour instead.

Chocolate & Date Brownies

Dark and full of flavour, these fruity brownies are irresistible. They make a good teatime treat, or are perfect for accompanying a cup of coffee with friends.

Makes 20
150g/5oz/⅔ cup butter
150g/5oz/scant 1 cup stoned (pitted) dates, softened in boiling water, then drained and finely chopped
150g/5oz/1¼ cups self-raising (self-rising) wholemeal (whole-wheat) flour
10ml/2 tsp baking powder
60ml/4 tbsp unsweetened cocoa powder dissolved in 30ml/2 tbsp hot water
60ml/4 tbsp apple and pear spread
90ml/6 tbsp unsweetened coconut milk
50g/2oz/½ cup walnuts or pecan nuts, coarsely broken

1 Preheat the oven to 160°C/325°F/Gas 3. Lightly grease a 28 × 18cm/11 × 7in shallow baking tin.

2 Beat the butter and dates together in a bowl. Sift together the flour and baking powder into another bowl, then, using a flexible spatula, gradually fold the dry ingredients into the butter mixture in batches, alternating with the cocoa, apple and pear spread and coconut milk. Stir in the nuts.

3 Spoon the mixture into the prepared tin and smooth the surface with the back of the spoon.

4 Bake for about 45 minutes, or until a fine skewer inserted in the centre comes out clean. Cool for a few minutes in the tin, then cut into bars or squares. Using a metal spatula, transfer to a wire rack to cool completely.

> **Cook's Tip**
> You can use dried dates straight from the packet, but they are better softened first. Put them in a small pan and add water to cover. Bring to the boil, then lower the heat and simmer gently for about 5 minutes. Drain well and pat dry with kitchen paper before chopping.

Chocolate and Date Energy 285kcal/1189kJ; Protein 4.3g; Carbohydrate 26.3g, of which sugars 13.3g; Fat 9.8g, of which saturates 5.3g; Cholesterol 56mg; Calcium 38mg; Fibre 1.3g; Sodium 62mg.
Pineapple and Cinnamon Energy 48kcal/202kJ; Protein 1g; Carbohydrate 10g, of which sugars 3g; Fat 0g, of which saturates 0g; Cholesterol 10mg; Calcium 27mg; Fibre 0.9g; Sodium 32mg.

Banana Brownies

Bananas, powerhouses of energy and packed with nutrients yet very low in fat, not only make these brownies deliciously moist, but also a healthy option.

Makes 9

75ml/5 tbsp unsweetened cocoa powder
15ml/1 tbsp caster (superfine) sugar
75ml/5 tbsp milk

3 large bananas, mashed
175g/6oz/³⁄₄ cup soft light brown sugar
5ml/1 tsp vanilla extract
5 egg whites
75g/3oz/³⁄₄ cup self-raising (self-rising) flour
75g/3oz/³⁄₄ cup oat bran
15ml/1 tbsp icing (confectioners') sugar, for dusting

1 Preheat the oven to 180°C/350°F/Gas 4. Line a 20cm/8in square cake tin (pan) with baking parchment.

2 Blend the cocoa powder and caster sugar with the milk in a bowl. Add the bananas, soft brown sugar and vanilla extract.

3 In a large bowl, lightly beat the egg whites with a fork. Add the chocolate mixture and continue to beat well.

4 Sift the flour over the mixture and fold in with the oat bran. Pour the mixture into the prepared cake tin.

5 Bake for 40 minutes, or until the top is firm and crusty. Leave to cool completely in the tin before cutting into squares. Lightly dust the brownies with icing sugar before serving.

Variation
Adding dried fruit or fresh berries would make these brownies even more of a special treat without dramatically increasing the fat content. Good extras include 50g/2oz/ scant ½ cup raisins, 50g/2oz/⅓ cup dried sour cherries or cranberries or 50g/2oz/½ cup fresh blueberries or 50g/2oz/ ⅓ cup fresh raspberries.

Banana Gingerbread Slices

Bananas make this spicy bake delightfully moist. The flavour develops on keeping, so store the gingerbread for a few days before cutting into slices, if possible.

Makes 20 slices

275g/10oz/2½ cups plain (all-purpose) flour
5ml/1 tsp bicarbonate of soda (baking soda)
20ml/4 tsp ground ginger

10ml/2 tsp mixed spice (apple pie spice)
115g/4oz/⅔ cup soft light brown sugar
60ml/4 tbsp sunflower oil
30ml/2 tbsp black treacle (molasses)
30ml/2 tbsp malt extract
2 eggs
60ml/4 tbsp orange juice
3 ripe bananas
115g/4oz/⅔ cup raisins or sultanas (golden raisins)

1 Preheat the oven to 180°C/350°F/Gas 4. Lightly grease and line a 28 × 18cm/11 × 7in shallow baking tin (pan).

2 Sift the flour, bicarbonate of soda and spices into a mixing bowl. Place the sugar in the sieve (strainer) over the bowl, add some of the flour mixture and rub through with a spoon.

3 Make a well in the centre of the dry ingredients. Add the oil, treacle, malt extract, eggs and juice. Mix thoroughly.

4 Mash the bananas on a plate. Add the raisins or sultanas to the gingerbread mixture, then mix in the mashed bananas.

5 Scrape the mixture into the prepared baking tin. Bake for about 35–40 minutes, or until the centre of the gingerbread springs back when lightly pressed.

6 Leave to cool for 5 minutes, then turn out on to a wire rack to cool completely. Cut into 20 slices to serve.

Cook's Tip
If your brown sugar is lumpy, mix it with a little flour and it will be easier to sift.

Banana Brownies Energy 101kcal/426kJ; Protein 4.6g; Carbohydrate 16.6g, of which sugars 10.8g; Fat 2.2g, of which saturates 1.2g; Cholesterol 0mg; Calcium 31mg; Fibre 2.8g; Sodium 167mg.
Banana Gingerbread Energy 133kcal/563kJ; Protein 2.3g; Carbohydrate 25.9g, of which sugars 15.2g; Fat 3g, of which saturates 0.5g; Cholesterol 19mg; Calcium 37mg; Fibre 0.7g; Sodium 18mg.

Chunky Chocolate & Banana Muffins

Luxurious but not overly sweet, these muffins are simple and quick to make. Serve warm while the chocolate is still gooey.

Makes 12
90ml/6 tbsp semi-skimmed (low-fat) milk
2 eggs
150g/5oz/²⁄₃ cup unsalted (sweet) butter, melted
225g/8oz/2 cups plain (all-purpose) flour
pinch of salt
5ml/1 tsp baking powder
150g/5oz/¾ cup golden caster (superfine) sugar
150g/5oz plain (semisweet) chocolate, cut into large chunks
2 small bananas, mashed

1 Preheat the oven to 200°C/400°F/Gas 6. Arrange 12 paper cases in a muffin tin (pan).

2 Place the milk, eggs and melted butter in a bowl and whisk until combined.

3 Sift together the flour, salt and baking powder into a separate bowl. Add the sugar and chocolate to the flour mixture and stir to combine. Gradually stir in the milk mixture, but do not beat it. Fold in the mashed bananas.

4 Spoon the mixture into the paper cases. Bake for about 20 minutes until golden. Cool on a wire rack.

Cook's Tips
• Use ripe bananas for this recipe, and do not peel them before you are ready to use them, or they will discolour. Slice thickly into a bowl before mashing with a fork; do not try to mash them while they are still whole, as they are likely to slide about and fly across the kitchen.
• You can use plain (semisweet) chocolate chips instead of chunks, if you prefer.

Wholemeal Banana Muffins

Wholemeal muffins, with banana for added fibre, make a great treat at any time of the day. If you like, slice off the tops and fill with a teaspoon of jam or marmalade, then replace the tops before serving.

Makes 12
75g/3oz/¾ cup plain (all-purpose) wholemeal (whole-wheat) flour
50g/2oz/½ cup plain (all-purpose) white flour
10ml/2 tsp baking powder
pinch of salt
5ml/1 tsp mixed spice (apple pie spice)
40g/1½oz/scant ¼ cup soft light brown sugar
50g/2oz/¼ cup butter
1 egg, beaten
150ml/¼ pint/²⁄₃ cup semi-skimmed (low-fat) milk
grated rind of 1 orange
1 ripe banana
20g/¾oz/¼ cup rolled oats
20g/¾oz/scant ¼ cup chopped hazelnuts

1 Preheat the oven to 200°C/400°F/Gas 6. Arrange 12 paper cases in a muffin tin (pan).

2 Sift together both flours, the baking powder, salt and mixed spice into a bowl, then tip the bran remaining in the sieve (strainer) into the bowl. Stir in the sugar.

3 Melt the butter in a pan over a very low heat. Remove from the heat and leave to cool slightly, then beat in the egg, milk and grated orange rind. Make a well in the centre of the flour mixture, pour in the butter mixture and beat well to incorporate the dry ingredients.

4 Mash the banana with a fork, then stir it gently into the mixture, being careful not to overmix. Spoon the mixture into the paper cases.

5 Combine the oats and hazelnuts and sprinkle a little of the mixture over each muffin.

6 Bake for 20 minutes until the muffins are well risen and golden, and a skewer inserted in the centre comes out clean. Transfer to a wire rack and serve warm or cold.

Chunky Chocolate Energy 240kcal/1003kJ; Protein 3.7g; Carbohydrate 26.3g, of which sugars 11.6g; Fat 14.1g, of which saturates 8.4g; Cholesterol 59mg; Calcium 47mg; Fibre 1g; Sodium 92mg.
Wholemeal Banana Energy 116kcal/489kJ; Protein 3g; Carbohydrate 15g, of which sugars 6g; Fat 6g, of which saturates 3g; Cholesterol 29mg; Calcium 42mg; Fibre 1.2g; Sodium 151mg.

Apple Loaf

The apple sauce in this loaf makes it beautifully moist – it tastes perfect simply sliced and spread with butter.

**Makes one 23 x 13cm/
9 x 5in loaf**
1 egg
250ml/8fl oz/1 cup
    bottled or home-made
    apple sauce
50g/2oz/¼ cup butter or
    margarine, melted
100g/3¾oz/scant ½ cup soft
    dark brown sugar
45g/1¾oz/scant ¼ cup caster
    (superfine) sugar
275g/10oz/2½ cups plain
    (all-purpose) flour
10ml/2 tsp baking powder
2.5ml/½ tsp bicarbonate of soda
    (baking soda)
2.5ml/½ tsp salt
5ml/1 tsp ground cinnamon
2.5ml/½ tsp freshly grated
    nutmeg
65g/2½oz/½ cup currants
    or raisins
50g/2oz/½ cup pecan nuts
    or walnuts, chopped

1 Preheat the oven to 180°C/350°F/Gas 4. Line the base and sides of a 23 x 13cm/9 x 5in loaf tin (pan) with baking parchment and grease the paper.

2 Break the egg into a bowl and beat lightly. Stir in the apple sauce, butter or margarine, and both sugars. Set aside.

3 In another bowl, sift together the flour, baking powder, bicarbonate of soda, salt, cinnamon and nutmeg. Fold the dry ingredients, including the currants or raisins and the nuts, into the apple sauce mixture in three batches.

4 Pour into the prepared tin and bake in the oven until a skewer inserted in the centre of the loaf comes out clean, about 1 hour. Leave to stand in the tin for 10 minutes, then turn out on to a wire rack to cool completely.

Variations
Ring the changes with this moist loaf by using different nuts and dried fruit. You could try ready-to-eat dried apricots with hazelnuts, for example.

Pear & Sultana Teabread

This is an ideal teabread to make when pears are plentiful. There's no better use for autumn windfalls.

Serves 6 – 8
25g/1oz/3 cups rolled oats
50g/2oz/¼ cup soft light
    brown sugar
30ml/2 tbsp pear or apple juice
30ml/2 tbsp sunflower oil
1 large or 2 small ripe pears
115g/4oz/1 cup self-raising
    (self-rising) flour
115g/4oz/¾ cup sultanas
    (golden raisins)
2.5ml/½ tsp baking powder
10ml/2 tsp mixed (apple pie) spice
1 egg

1 Preheat the oven to 180°C/350°F/Gas 4. Line a 450g/1lb loaf tin (pan) with baking parchment.

2 Put the oats in a bowl with the sugar, and pour over the pear or apple juice and oil.

3 Mix the ingredients together well using a wooden spoon or electric whisk. Leave to stand for 15 minutes.

4 Quarter, core and grate the pear(s). Add to the bowl with the flour, sultanas, baking powder, spice and egg. Using a wooden spoon, mix thoroughly.

5 Spoon the tea bread mixture into the prepared loaf tin. Bake for 55–60 minutes, or until a skewer inserted into the centre comes out clean.

6 Invert the tea bread on a wire rack and remove the lining paper. Leave to cool.

Cook's Tips
• Health-food stores sell concentrated pear juice, ready for diluting as required.
• You will also find some good-quality sultanas there, and organic oats if you want to make a really healthy treat.

Apple Loaf Energy 2558kcal/10777kJ; Protein 42.6g; Carbohydrate 432.4g, of which sugars 222.5g; Fat 85g, of which saturates 30.9g; Cholesterol 297mg; Calcium 586mg; Fibre 15.3g; Sodium 442mg.
Pear and Sultana Energy 184kcal/780kJ; Protein 3.1g; Carbohydrate 36.3g, of which sugars 23.1g; Fat 4g, of which saturates 0.6g; Cholesterol 24mg; Calcium 43mg; Fibre 1.8g; Sodium 16mg.

Orange Wheatloaf

Perfect just with butter as a breakfast teabread, and for banana sandwiches.

Makes one 450g/1lb loaf

275g/10oz/2¹/₂ cups plain (all-purpose) wholemeal (whole-wheat) flour
2.5ml/¹/₂ tsp salt
25g/1oz/2 tbsp butter
25g/1oz/2 tbsp soft light brown sugar
¹/₂ sachet easy-blend (rapid-rise) dried yeast
grated rind and juice of ¹/₂ orange

1 Lightly grease a 450g/1lb loaf tin (pan). Sift the flour into a large bowl and add any wheat flakes from the sieve to the flour. Add the salt and rub in the butter lightly with your fingertips or a pastry cutter.

2 Stir in the sugar, yeast and orange rind. Pour the orange juice into a measuring jug and use hot water to make up to 200ml/7fl oz/scant 1 cup (the liquid should not be more than hand hot).

3 Stir the liquid into the flour mixture and mix to a soft ball of dough. Knead gently on a lightly floured surface until quite smooth and elastic.

4 Place the dough in the tin and leave it in a warm place until nearly doubled in size. Preheat the oven to 220°C/425°F/Gas 7.

5 Bake the bread for 30–35 minutes, or until it sounds hollow when removed from the tin and tapped underneath. Tip out of the tin and cool on a wire rack.

> **Cook's Tip**
> Easy-blend (rapid-rise) yeast is mixed directly with the dry ingredients and is the easiest yeast to use. Don't confuse this with active dried yeast, which needs to be mixed with liquid first and left to become frothy before it is blended in with the dry ingredients.

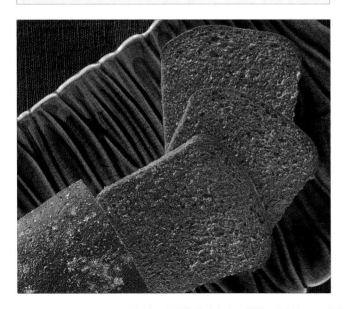

Orange & Honey Teabread

Honey gives a special flavour to this teabread. Serve just with a scraping of butter.

Makes one 23 x 13cm/ 9 x 5in loaf

385g/13¹/₂oz/scant 3¹/₂ cups plain (all-purpose) flour
12.5ml/2¹/₂ tsp baking powder
2.5ml/¹/₂ tsp bicarbonate of soda (baking soda)
2.5ml/¹/₂ tsp salt
25g/1oz/2 tbsp margarine
250ml/8fl oz/1 cup clear honey
1 egg, at room temperature, lightly beaten
25ml/1¹/₂ tbsp grated orange rind
175ml/6fl oz/³/₄ cup freshly squeezed orange juice
115g/4oz/1 cup chopped walnuts

1 Preheat the oven to 160°C/325°F/Gas 3. Line the base and sides of a 23 x 13cm/9 x 5in loaf tin (pan) with baking parchment and grease the paper.

2 Sift the flour, baking powder, bicarbonate of soda and salt together in a bowl.

3 Cream the margarine until soft. Stir in the honey until blended, then stir in the egg. Add the orange rind and combine well.

4 Fold the flour mixture into the honey mixture in three batches, alternating with the orange juice. Stir in the walnuts.

5 Pour into the prepared tin and bake in the oven until a skewer inserted in the centre comes out clean, about 60–70 minutes. Leave for 10 minutes before turning out on to a wire rack to cool completely.

> **Cook's Tip**
> Although you can buy beautifully scented honey with the fragrance of wild flowers and herbs, the scents are usually destroyed in cooking, so for recipes such as this, a less expensive honey will do perfectly well. Clear honey gradually becomes cloudy, but this can be rectified simply by gently heating it.

Wheatloaf Energy 1146kcal/4848kJ; Protein 35.3g; Carbohydrate 204.2g, of which sugars 34.3g; Fat 26.6g, of which saturates 13.8g; Cholesterol 53mg; Calcium 125mg; Fibre 24.8g; Sodium 164mg.
Teabread Energy 3145kcal/13251kJ; Protein 61.3g; Carbohydrate 509.6g, of which sugars 215.4g; Fat 109.9g, of which saturates 8.8g; Cholesterol 190mg; Calcium 707mg; Fibre 16.1g; Sodium 335mg.

Marmalade Teabread

If you prefer, leave the top of this citrus loaf plain, and serve sliced and lightly buttered instead.

Makes one 21 x 12cm/ 8½ x 4½in loaf

200g/7oz/1⅔ cups plain (all-purpose) flour
5ml/1 tsp baking powder
6.5ml/1¼ tsp ground cinnamon

90g/3½oz/7 tbsp butter or margarine
50g/2oz/¼ cup soft light brown sugar
60ml/4 tbsp chunky orange marmalade
1 egg, beaten
about 45ml/3 tbsp milk
60ml/4 tbsp glacé icing and shreds of orange and lemon rind, to decorate

1 Preheat the oven to 160°C/325°F/Gas 3. Lightly butter a 21 x 12cm/8½ x 4½in loaf tin (pan), then line the base with baking parchment and grease the paper.

2 Sift the flour, baking powder and cinnamon together, toss in the butter or margarine, then rub in using your fingertips or a pastry cutter until the mixture resembles coarse breadcrumbs. Stir in the sugar.

3 In a separate bowl, mix together the marmalade, egg and most of the milk, then stir into the flour mixture to make a soft dropping consistency, adding more milk if necessary.

4 Transfer the mixture to the tin and bake for 1¼ hours, or until firm to the touch. Leave the cake to cool in the tin for 5 minutes, then turn on to a wire rack, peel off the lining paper, and leave to cool completely.

5 Drizzle the glacé icing over the top of the cake and decorate with the orange and lemon rind.

> **Cook's Tip**
> To make citrus shreds, pare away strips of orange or lemon rind with a vegetable peeler, then cut into fine shreds with a knife.

Apricot Nut Loaf

Raisins and walnuts combine with apricots to make a lovely light teabread. Full of flavour, it is also ideal for a morning snack or children's lunchboxes.

Makes one 23 x 13cm/ 9 x 5in loaf

115g/4oz/½ cup ready-to-eat dried apricots
1 large orange

75g/3oz/generous ½ cup raisins
150g/5oz/¾ cup caster (superfine) sugar
85ml/5½ tbsp/⅓ cup oil
2 eggs, lightly beaten
250g/9oz/2¼ cups plain (all-purpose) flour
10ml/2 tsp baking powder
2.5ml/½ tsp salt
5ml/1 tsp bicarbonate of soda (baking soda)
50g/2oz/½ cup chopped walnuts

1 Place the apricots in a bowl, cover with lukewarm water and leave to stand for 30 minutes. Preheat the oven to 180°C/ 350°F/Gas 4. Line a 23 x 13cm/9 x 5in loaf tin (pan) with baking parchment and grease the paper.

2 With a vegetable peeler, remove the orange rind, leaving the pith. Chop the strips finely.

3 Drain the softened apricots and chop them coarsely. Place in a bowl with the orange rind and raisins. Squeeze the peeled orange over a bowl. Measure the orange juice and add enough hot water to obtain 175ml/6fl oz/¾ cup liquid.

4 Add the orange juice mixture to the apricot mixture. Stir in the sugar, oil and eggs. Set aside.

5 In another bowl, sift together the flour, baking powder, salt and bicarbonate of soda. Fold the flour mixture into the apricot mixture in three batches, then stir in the walnuts.

6 Spoon the mixture into the prepared tin and bake until a skewer inserted in the centre of the loaf comes out clean, about 55–60 minutes. If the loaf browns too quickly, protect the top with a sheet of foil. Cool in the tin for 10 minutes, then transfer to a wire rack to cool completely.

Marmalade Energy 1725kcal/7238kJ; Protein 49.7g; Carbohydrate 209.3g, of which sugars 55.8g; Fat 82.5g, of which saturates 48.8g; Cholesterol 382mg; Calcium 408mg; Fibre 6.2g; Sodium 3324mg.
Apricot Energy 2904kcal/12229kJ; Protein 51.6g; Carbohydrate 456.8g, of which sugars 265.9g; Fat 109.6g, of which saturates 13.6g; Cholesterol 381mg; Calcium 708mg; Fibre 20.3g; Sodium 227mg.

Raisin Bread

Enjoy this with either
savoury or sweet dishes.

Makes 2 loaves
15ml/1 tbsp active dried yeast
450ml/³/4 pint/1³/4 cups
  lukewarm milk
150g/5oz/1 cup raisins
65g/2¹/2oz/¹/2 cup currants
15ml/1 tbsp sherry or brandy
2.5ml/¹/2 tsp freshly grated nutmeg

grated rind of 1 large orange
60g/2¹/4oz/generous ¹/4 cup
  caster (superfine) sugar
15ml/1 tbsp salt
115g/4oz/¹/2 cup butter, melted
700–850g/1lb 8oz–1lb 14oz/
  6–7¹/2 cups strong white
  bread flour
1 egg beaten with 15ml/1 tbsp
  single (light) cream, to glaze

1 Stir the yeast with 120ml/4fl oz/¹/2 cup of the milk and leave
to stand for 15 minutes to dissolve. Mix the raisins, currants,
sherry or brandy, nutmeg and orange rind together.

2 In another bowl, mix the remaining milk, sugar, salt and half
the butter. Add the yeast mixture. With a wooden spoon, stir
in half the flour, 150g/5oz at a time, until blended. Add the
remaining flour as needed to form a stiff dough. Transfer to a
floured surface and knead until smooth and elastic. This will
take about 10 minutes. Place in a greased bowl, cover and
leave to rise in a warm place until doubled in volume, about
2½ hours.

3 Knock back (punch down) the dough, return to the bowl,
cover and leave to rise in a warm place for 30 minutes. Grease
two 21 × 11cm/8½ × 4½in loaf tins (pans). Divide the dough in
half and roll each half into a 50 × 18cm/20 × 7in rectangle.

4 Brush the rectangles with the remaining melted butter.
Sprinkle over the raisin mixture, then roll up tightly, tucking in
the ends slightly as you roll. Place in the prepared tins, cover,
and leave to rise until almost doubled in volume, about 1 hour.
Preheat the oven to 200°C/400°F/Gas 6. Brush the loaves with
the egg glaze. Bake for 20 minutes. Lower to 180°C/350°F/
Gas 4 and bake until golden, 25–30 minutes more. Cool
on racks.

Swedish Sultana Bread

A lightly sweetened sultana
bread that goes very well
with a selection of cheeses,
and also tastes excellent
when toasted at teatime.

Serves 10
225g/8oz/2 cups strong wholemeal
  (whole-wheat) bread flour
225g/8oz/2 cups strong white
  bread flour
5ml/1 tsp easy-blend (rapid-rise)
  dried yeast

5ml/1 tsp salt
115g/4oz/²/3 cup sultanas
  (golden raisins)
50g/2oz/¹/2 cup walnuts,
  chopped
15ml/1 tbsp clear honey
150ml/¹/4 pint/²/3 cup
  hand-hot water
175ml/6fl oz/³/4 cup
  hand-hot skimmed milk,
  plus extra for glazing

1 Grease a baking sheet. Put the flours in a bowl with the yeast,
salt and sultanas.

2 Set aside 15ml/1 tbsp of the walnuts and add the remainder to
the bowl. Mix the ingredients lightly and make a well in the centre.

3 Dissolve the honey in the water and add the mixture to the
bowl with the milk. Stir from the centre outwards, gradually
incorporating the flour, and mixing to a soft dough, and adding
a little extra water if necessary.

4 Turn the dough on to a floured surface and knead for
5 minutes, or until smooth and elastic. Shape into a 28cm/11in
long sausage shape. Place on the prepared baking sheet.

5 Make diagonal cuts down the length of the loaf. Brush the top
with milk, sprinkle with the remaining walnuts and leave in a
warm place until doubled in size, about 1½ hours. Meanwhile,
preheat the oven to 220°C/425°F/Gas 7.

6 Bake the loaf for 10 minutes, then lower the oven
temperature to 200°C/400°F/Gas 6 and bake for 20 minutes
more or until the loaf sounds hollow when tapped underneath.
Remove to a wire rack to cool.

Raisin Energy 2187kcal/9239kJ; Protein 46.5g; Carbohydrate 388.3g, of which sugars 121.6g; Fat 58.9g, of which saturates 33.9g; Cholesterol 231mg; Calcium 866mg; Fibre 13g; Sodium 3490mg.
Swedish Sultana Energy 225kcal/953kJ; Protein 5.9g; Carbohydrate 43.9g, of which sugars 9.6g; Fat 4.1g, of which saturates 0.4g; Cholesterol 1mg; Calcium 96mg; Fibre 1.8g; Sodium 12mg.

Dried Fruit Loaf

Use any combination of dried fruit you like in this delicious teabread. The fruit is soaked in a bowl of cold tea first, making the loaf superbly moist.

**Makes one 23 x 13cm/
9 x 5in loaf**
*450g/1lb/2¾ cups mixed dried
 fruit, such as currants, raisins,
 chopped ready-to-eat dried
 apricots and dried cherries*
*300ml/½ pint/1¼ cups cold
 strong tea*
*200g/7oz/scant 1 cup soft dark
 brown sugar*
*grated rind and juice of
 1 small orange*
grated rind and juice of 1 lemon
1 egg, lightly beaten
*200g/7oz/1¾ cups plain
 (all-purpose) flour*
15ml/1 tbsp baking powder
1.5ml/¼ tsp salt

1 In a bowl, mix the dried fruit with the cold tea and leave to soak overnight.

2 Preheat the oven to 180°C/350°F/Gas 4. Line the base and sides of a 23 x 13cm/9 x 5in loaf tin (pan) with baking parchment and grease the paper.

3 Strain the soaked fruit, reserving the liquid. In a bowl, combine the dark brown sugar, orange and lemon rind, and strained fruit.

4 Pour the orange and lemon juice into a measuring jug (cup); if the quantity is less than 250ml/8fl oz/1 cup, then top up with the soaking liquid.

5 Stir the citrus juices and lightly beaten egg into the dried fruit mixture until combined.

6 Sift the flour, baking powder and salt together into another bowl. Stir the dry ingredients into the fruit mixture until well blended.

7 Transfer to the tin and bake until a skewer inserted in the centre comes out clean: about 1¼ hours. Leave in the tin for 10 minutes before unmoulding.

Prune Bread

Moist fruit inside, with a tasty, crusty walnut topping.

Makes 1 loaf
225g/8oz/1 cup dried prunes
15ml/1 tbsp active dried yeast
*75g/3oz/⅔ cup strong
 wholemeal (whole-wheat)
 bread flour*
*400–425g/14–15oz/3½–3⅔ cups
 strong white bread flour*
*2.5ml/½ tsp bicarbonate of soda
 (baking soda)*
5ml/1 tsp salt
5ml/1 tsp pepper
*25g/1oz/2 tbsp butter,
 at room temperature*
175ml/6fl oz/¾ cup buttermilk
50g/2oz/½ cup walnuts, chopped
milk, for glazing

1 Simmer the prunes in water to cover until soft, about 20 minutes, or soak overnight. Drain, reserving 60ml/4 tbsp of the soaking liquid. Pit and chop the prunes.

2 Combine the yeast and the reserved prune liquid, stir and leave for 15 minutes to dissolve and so that the yeast becomes frothy.

3 In a large bowl, stir together the wholemeal and white flours, bicarbonate of soda, salt and pepper. Make a well in the centre. Add the prunes, butter and buttermilk. Pour in the yeast mixture. With a wooden spoon, stir from the centre, folding in more flour with each turn, to obtain a rough dough.

4 Transfer to a floured surface and knead until smooth and elastic. This will take about 10 minutes. Return to the bowl, cover with clear film (plastic wrap) and leave to rise in a warm place until doubled in volume, about 1½ hours. Grease a baking sheet.

5 Knock back (punch down) the dough with your fist, then knead in the walnuts. Shape the dough into a long, cylindrical loaf. Place on the baking sheet, cover loosely, and leave to rise in a warm place for 45 minutes. Preheat the oven to 220°C/425°F/Gas 7. With a sharp knife, score the top. Brush with milk and bake for 15 minutes. Lower to 190°C/375°F/Gas 5 and bake for 35 minutes more, or until the base sounds hollow. Cool.

Dried Fruit Energy 2763kcal/11770kJ; Protein 36.6g; Carbohydrate 673.9g, of which sugars 521.5g; Fat 10g, of which saturates 2g; Cholesterol 190mg; Calcium 838mg; Fibre 14.8g; Sodium 156mg.
Prune Energy 2520kcal/10639kJ; Protein 65.6g; Carbohydrate 433.3g, of which sugars 93.2g; Fat 70.4g, of which saturates 19.9g; Cholesterol 70mg; Calcium 915mg; Fibre 33.4g; Sodium 2266mg.

Date & Pecan Loaf

Walnuts may be used instead of pecan nuts to make this luxurious fruity teabread.

**Makes one 23 x 13cm/
9 x 5in loaf**
175g/6oz/1 cup chopped
   stoned (pitted) dates
175ml/6fl oz/³⁄₄ cup boiling water
50g/2oz/¼ cup unsalted
   (sweet) butter, at room
   temperature
50g/2oz/¼ cup soft dark
   brown sugar
50g/2oz/¼ cup caster
   (superfine) sugar
1 egg, at room temperature
30ml/2 tbsp brandy
165g/5½oz/generous 1¼ cups
   plain (all-purpose) flour
10ml/2 tsp baking powder
2.5ml/½ tsp salt
4ml/¾ tsp freshly
   grated nutmeg
75g/3oz/¾ cup coarsely
   chopped pecan nuts

1 Place the dates in a bowl and pour over the boiling water. Set aside to cool. Preheat the oven to 180°C/350°F/Gas 4. Line a 23 x 13cm/9 x 5in loaf tin (pan) with baking parchment and then grease the paper.

2 With an electric mixer, cream the butter and sugars until light and fluffy. Beat in the egg and brandy, then set aside.

3 Sift the flour, baking powder, salt and nutmeg together, at least three times. Fold the dry ingredients into the sugar mixture in three batches, alternating with the dates and water. Fold in the chopped pecan nuts.

4 Pour the mixture into the prepared tin and bake until a skewer inserted in the centre comes out clean, about 45–50 minutes. Leave the loaf to cool in the tin for 10 minutes before transferring it to a wire rack to cool completely.

> **Cook's Tip**
> *Nutmeg is a particularly useful spice for sweet dishes, and is used in small quantities in many recipes, as the spice is poisonous in larger quantities.*

Date & Nut Maltloaf

Choose any type of nut you like to include in this deliciously rich and fruit-packed teabread.

**Makes two 450g/1lb
loaves**
300g/11oz/2²⁄₃ cups strong plain
   (all-purpose) flour
275g/10oz/2½ cups strong
   wholemeal (whole-wheat)
   bread flour
5ml/1 tsp salt
75g/3oz/⅓ cup soft light
   brown sugar
1 sachet easy-blend (rapid-rise)
   dried yeast
50g/2oz/¼ cup butter
   or margarine
15ml/1 tbsp black treacle (molasses)
60ml/4 tbsp malt extract
scant 250ml/8fl oz/1 cup
   lukewarm milk
115g/4oz/²⁄₃ cup chopped dates
75g/3oz/½ cup sultanas
   (golden raisins)
50g/2oz/½ cup chopped nuts
75g/3oz/generous ½ cup raisins
30ml/2 tbsp clear honey,
   to glaze

1 Sift the flours and salt into a large bowl, then tip in the wheat flakes from the sieve. Stir in the sugar and yeast.

2 Put the butter or margarine in a small pan with the treacle and malt extract. Stir over a low heat until melted. Leave to cool, then combine with the milk.

3 Stir the milk mixture into the dry ingredients and knead thoroughly for 15 minutes, or until the dough is elastic.

4 Knead in the chopped dates, sultanas and chopped nuts. Transfer the dough to an oiled bowl, cover with clear film (plastic wrap) and leave in a warm place for about 1½ hours, or until the dough has doubled in size.

5 Grease two 450g/1lb loaf tins (pans). Knock back (punch down) the dough and knead lightly. Divide the dough in half, form into loaves and place in the tins. Cover and leave in a warm place for 30 minutes, or until risen. Meanwhile, preheat the oven to 190°C/375°F/Gas 5.

6 Bake for 35–40 minutes, or until well risen. Cool on a wire rack. Brush with honey while warm.

Loaf Energy 2458kcal/10331kJ; Protein 35.2g; Carbohydrate 356.4g, of which sugars 229.5g; Fat 101.7g, of which saturates 32.4g; Cholesterol 297mg; Calcium 446mg; Fibre 15.6g; Sodium 402mg.
Maltloaf Energy 1939kcal/8200kJ; Protein 43.9g; Carbohydrate 361.7g, of which sugars 162.2g; Fat 45.2g, of which saturates 16.6g; Cholesterol 61mg; Calcium 693mg; Fibre 21.7g; Sodium 308mg.

Fruity Teabread

Serve this orange and berry bread either thinly sliced, toasted or plain, with butter or cream cheese and home-made jam.

**Makes one 23 x 13cm/
9 x 5in loaf**
225g/8oz/2 cups plain
  (all-purpose) flour
115g/4oz/generous ½ cup caster
  (superfine) sugar
15ml/1 tbsp baking powder
2.5ml/½ tsp salt
grated rind of 1 large orange
160ml/5½fl oz/generous ⅔ cup
  fresh orange juice
2 eggs, lightly beaten
75g/3oz/6 tbsp butter or
  margarine, melted
115g/4oz/1 cup fresh cranberries
  or bilberries
50g/2oz/½ cup chopped walnuts

1 Preheat the oven to 180°C/350°F/Gas 4. Then line a 23 x 13cm/9 x 5in loaf tin (pan) with baking parchment and grease the paper.

2 Sift the flour, sugar, baking powder and salt into a mixing bowl. Then stir in the orange rind.

3 Make a well in the centre and add the fresh orange juice, eggs and melted butter or margarine. Stir from the centre until the ingredients are blended; do not overmix. Add the berries and walnuts, and stir until blended.

4 Transfer the mixture to the prepared tin and bake until a skewer inserted in the centre of the loaf comes out clean, about 45–50 minutes. Leave to cool in the tin for 10 minutes before transferring to a wire rack to cool completely.

> **Cook's Tip**
> *Margarine can be used instead of butter for most recipes except those with a high fat content, such as shortbread. Margarine will not, however, produce the same flavour as butter but it is usually less expensive, so can be useful. Block margarines are better than soft margarines for teabreads, buns and muffins.*

Fruit & Brazil Nut Teabread

Mashed bananas are a classic ingredient in teabreads, and help to create a moist texture as well as adding a full fruity flavour.

**Makes one 23 x 13cm/
9 x 5in loaf**
225g/8oz/2 cups plain
  (all-purpose) flour
10ml/2 tsp baking powder
5ml/1 tsp mixed (apple pie) spice
115g/4oz/½ cup butter, diced
115g/4oz/½ cup light soft
  brown sugar
2 eggs, lightly beaten
30ml/2 tbsp milk
30ml/2 tbsp dark rum
2 bananas
115g/4oz/⅔ cup dried
  figs, chopped
50g/2oz/⅓ cup brazil
  nuts, chopped

For the decoration
8 whole brazil nuts
4 whole dried figs, halved
30ml/2 tbsp apricot jam
5ml/1 tsp dark rum

1 Preheat the oven to 180°C/350°F/Gas 4. Grease and base-line a 23 x 13cm/9 x 5in loaf tin (pan). Sift the flour, baking powder and mixed spice into a bowl.

2 Rub in the butter using your fingertips or a pastry cutter until the mixture resembles fine breadcrumbs. Stir in the sugar.

3 Make a well in the centre and work in the eggs, milk and rum until combined. Peel and mash the bananas. Stir in the mashed bananas, chopped figs and brazil nuts and transfer to the prepared loaf tin.

4 To decorate the teabread press the whole brazil nuts and halved figs gently into the mixture, to form an attractive pattern. Bake for 1¼ hours, or until a skewer inserted in the centre comes out clean. Cool in the tin for 10 minutes, then transfer to a wire rack.

5 Heat the jam and rum together in a small pan. Increase the heat and boil for 1 minute. Remove from the heat and pass through a fine sieve. Cool the glaze slightly, brush over the warm loaf, and leave to cool completely.

Fruity Energy 2356kcal/9885kJ; Protein 43.9g; Carbohydrate 317g, of which sugars 145.2g; Fat 110.3g, of which saturates 45.4g; Cholesterol 540mg; Calcium 557mg; Fibre 12.4g; Sodium 630mg.
Fruit and Brazil Energy 3095kcal/12984kJ; Protein 49.5g; Carbohydrate 405.9g, of which sugars 229.5g; Fat 145.6g, of which saturates 72.2g; Cholesterol 628mg; Calcium 874mg; Fibre 19.9g; Sodium 938mg.

Banana Bread

For a change, add 50–75g/
2–3oz/½–¾ cup chopped
walnuts or pecan nuts to
the dry ingredients of this
moist banana bread.

**Makes one 21 x 12cm/
8½ x 4½in loaf**
200g/7oz/1⅔ cups plain
(all-purpose) flour
11.5ml/2¼ tsp baking
powder

2.5ml/½ tsp salt
4ml/¾ tsp ground cinnamon
(optional)
60ml/4 tbsp wheatgerm
65g/2½oz/5 tbsp butter,
at room temperature
115g/4oz/generous ½ cup caster
(superfine) sugar
4ml/¾ tsp grated lemon rind
3 ripe bananas, mashed
2 eggs, beaten

1 Preheat the oven to 180°C/350°F/Gas 4. Grease and flour
a 21 x 12cm/8½ x 4½in loaf tin (pan).

2 Sift the flour, baking powder, salt and cinnamon, if using, into
a bowl. Stir in the wheatgerm.

3 In another bowl, combine the butter with the caster sugar
and grated lemon rind. Beat thoroughly until the mixture is
light and fluffy.

4 Add the mashed bananas and eggs, and mix well. Add the
dry ingredients and blend quickly and evenly.

5 Spoon into the loaf tin. Bake for 50–60 minutes, or until a
skewer inserted in the centre comes out clean.

6 Cool the bread in the tin for 5 minutes, then turn out on to
a wire rack to cool completely.

> **Cook's Tip**
> *Wheatgerm is the heart of the wheat grain, and contains many
> nutrients and important vitamins. It must be used fresh, and
> should be stored in an airtight container. Do not store for long
> periods, as it will become bitter.*

Wholemeal Banana Nut Loaf

With its tasty combination
of banana and chopped
walnuts, this hearty and
filling loaf makes an ideal
winter teatime treat.

**Makes one 23 x 13cm/
9 x 5in loaf**
115g/4oz/½ cup butter,
at room temperature
115g/4oz/generous ½ cup caster
(superfine) sugar

2 eggs, at room temperature
115g/4oz/1 cup plain
(all-purpose) flour
5ml/1 tsp bicarbonate of soda
(baking soda)
1.5ml/¼ tsp salt
5ml/1 tsp ground cinnamon
50g/2oz/½ cup wholemeal
(whole-wheat) flour
3 large ripe bananas
5ml/1 tsp vanilla extract
50g/2oz/½ cup chopped walnuts

1 Preheat the oven to 180°C/350°F/Gas 4. Line the base
and sides of a 23 x 13cm/9 x 5in loaf tin (pan) with baking
parchment and grease the paper.

2 With an electric mixer, cream the butter and sugar together
until light and fluffy. Add the eggs, one at a time, beating well
after each addition.

3 Sift the plain flour, bicarbonate of soda, salt and cinnamon
over the butter mixture, and stir to blend. Then stir in the
wholemeal flour.

4 With a fork, mash the bananas to a purée, then stir into the
mixture. Stir in the vanilla and nuts.

5 Pour the mixture into the prepared tin and spread level.
Bake until a skewer inserted in the centre comes out clean,
about 50–60 minutes. Leave to stand for 10 minutes before
transferring to a wire rack to cool completely.

> **Cook's Tip**
> *Wholemeal (whole-wheat) flour contains the wheat germ and
> bran, giving it a higher fibre, fat and nutritional content than white
> flour. Because of its fat content, it is best stored in a cool larder.*

Banana Energy 2265kcal/9548kJ; Protein 51.9g; Carbohydrate 372.4g, of which sugars 195.9g; Fat 73.6g, of which saturates 38.4g; Cholesterol 519mg; Calcium 461mg; Fibre 18.9g; Sodium 553mg.
Wholemeal Energy 2632kcal/11017kJ; Protein 41.9g; Carbohydrate 313.4g, of which sugars 187.6g; Fat 143.4g, of which saturates 66.5g; Cholesterol 626mg; Calcium 384mg; Fibre 13.1g; Sodium 855mg.

Banana Orange Loaf

For the best banana flavour
and a really good, moist
texture, make sure that the
bananas are perfectly ripe
for this delicious loaf. The
sugar-sprinkled orange slices
make a pretty decoration.

**Makes one 23 x 13cm/
9 x 5in loaf**
90g/3¹/₂oz/³/₄ cup plain
  (all-purpose) wholemeal
  (whole-wheat) flour
90g/3¹/₂oz/³/₄ cup plain
  (all-purpose) flour

5ml/1 tsp baking powder
5ml/1 tsp mixed (apple pie) spice
45ml/3 tbsp flaked (sliced)
  hazelnuts, toasted
2 large ripe bananas
1 egg
30ml/2 tbsp sunflower oil
30ml/2 tbsp clear honey
finely grated rind and juice of
  1 small orange
4 orange slices, halved
10ml/2 tsp icing
  (confectioners') sugar

1 Preheat the oven to 180°C/350°F/Gas 4. Brush a 23 x 13cm/
9 x 5in loaf tin (pan) with sunflower oil and line the base with
baking parchment.

2 Sift the flours with the baking powder and spice into a large
bowl, adding any bran that is caught in the sieve (strainer).
Stir the hazelnuts into the dry ingredients.

3 Peel and mash the bananas in a large bowl. Add the egg,
sunflower oil, honey, and the orange rind and juice to the
mashed bananas and beat together.

4 Add the banana mixture to the dry ingredients and mix to
combine thoroughly.

5 Spoon the mixture into the prepared tin and smooth the
top. Bake in the oven for 40–45 minutes, or until the cake is
firm and golden brown. Remove from the oven and turn out
on to a wire rack to cool.

6 Meanwhile, sprinkle the orange slices with the icing sugar
and place on a grill (broiling) rack. Grill until lightly golden.
Arrange the glazed orange slices on the top of the loaf.

Glazed Banana Spiced Loaf

The lemony glaze perfectly
sets off the warm flavours
of nutmeg and cloves in this
deliciously moist and light
banana teabread.

**Makes one 23 x 13cm/
9 x 5in loaf**
115g/4oz/¹/₂ cup butter,
  at room temperature
165g/5¹/₂oz/³/₄ cup caster
  (superfine) sugar
2 eggs, at room temperature
215g/7¹/₂oz/scant 2 cups plain
  (all-purpose) flour
5ml/1 tsp salt

5ml/1 tsp bicarbonate of soda
  (baking soda)
2.5ml/¹/₂ tsp freshly
  grated nutmeg
1.5ml/¹/₄ tsp mixed spice
1.5ml/¹/₄ tsp ground cloves
175ml/6fl oz/³/₄ cup sour cream
1 large ripe banana, mashed
5ml/1 tsp vanilla extract

For the glaze
115g/4oz/1 cup icing
  (confectioners') sugar
15–30ml/1–2 tbsp lemon juice

1 Preheat the oven to 180°C/350°F/Gas 4. Line a 23 x 13cm/
9 x 5in loaf tin (pan) with baking parchment and grease
the paper.

2 Cream the butter and sugar until light and fluffy. Add the
eggs, one at a time, beating well after each addition.

3 Sift together the flour, salt, bicarbonate of soda, nutmeg,
mixed spice and cloves. Add to the butter mixture and stir
to combine well.

4 Add the sour cream, banana and vanilla extract, and mix to
just blend. Pour this mixture into the prepared tin.

5 Bake until the top springs back when touched lightly, about
45–50 minutes. Cool in the tin for 10 minutes. Turn out on to
a wire rack.

6 To make the glaze, combine the icing sugar and lemon juice
until smooth, then stir until smooth. Place the cooled loaf on a
rack set over a baking sheet. Pour the glaze over the loaf and
allow to set.

Glazed Energy 3293kcal/13836kJ; Protein 41.1g; Carbohydrate 490.2g, of which sugars 324.1g; Fat 143.6g, of which saturates 85.4g; Cholesterol 731mg; Calcium 696mg; Fibre 7.8g; Sodium 933mg.
Banana Orange Energy 1483kcal/6238kJ; Protein 35.3g; Carbohydrate 214.3g, of which sugars 84.6g; Fat 59.9g, of which saturates 7g; Cholesterol 190mg; Calcium 276mg; Fibre 16.1g; Sodium 89mg.

Banana & Cardamom Bread

The combination of banana
and fragrant cardamom
is delicious in this soft-
textured moist loaf.

Serves 6
10 cardamom pods
400g/14oz/3½ cups strong
   white bread flour
5ml/1 tsp salt

5ml/1 tsp easy-blend (rapid-rise)
   dried yeast
150ml/¼ pint/⅔ cup
   hand-hot water
30ml/2 tbsp malt extract
2 ripe bananas, mashed
5ml/1 tsp sesame seeds

1 Grease a 450g/1lb loaf tin (pan). Split the cardamom pods, and remove the seeds and then chop the pods finely.

2 Sift the flour and salt into a large bowl, add the yeast and make a well in the centre. Add the water with the malt extract, chopped cardamom pods and bananas. Stir from the centre outwards, gradually incorporating the flour and mixing to a soft dough, and adding a little extra water if necessary.

3 Turn the dough on to a floured surface and knead for 5 minutes until smooth and elastic. Shape into a braid and place in the prepared tin. Cover loosely with clear film (plastic wrap) (ballooning it to trap the air) and leave in a warm place until well risen, about 1½ hours. Meanwhile, preheat the oven to 220°C/425°F/Gas 7.

4 Brush the braid lightly with water and sprinkle with the sesame seeds. Bake for 10 minutes, then lower the oven temperature to 200°C/400°F/Gas 6. Cook for 15 minutes more, or until the loaf sounds hollow when tapped underneath. Remove to a wire rack to cool.

> **Cook's Tip**
> *Cardamom is a green or white seed pod containing tiny black seeds. It has a distinctive warm and pronounced scent that really works well in cakes, pastries and desserts.*

Banana & Ginger Teabread

The creaminess of the
banana is given a delightful
lift with chunks of stem
ginger in this tasty teabread.
If you like a strong ginger
flavour, add 5ml/1 tsp
ground ginger with the flour.

40g/1½oz/3 tbsp soft margarine
50g/2oz/¼ cup soft light
   brown sugar
50g/2oz/⅓ cup drained
   preserved stem ginger, chopped
60ml/4 tbsp skimmed milk
2 ripe bananas

Serves 6–8
175g/6oz/1½ cups self-raising
   (self-rising) flour
5ml/1 tsp baking powder

1 Preheat the oven to 180°C/350°F/Gas 4. Line and grease a 450g/1lb loaf tin (pan).

2 Sift the flour and baking powder into a large bowl.

3 Using your fingertips or a pastry cutter rub the margarine into the dry ingredients until the mixture resembles breadcrumbs, then stir in the sugar.

4 Peel and mash the bananas in a separate bowl.

5 Add the preserved stem ginger, milk and mashed bananas to the mixture and mix to a soft dough. Spoon into the prepared tin and bake for 40–45 minutes.

6 Run a metal spatula around the edges of the cake to loosen them, then turn the teabread on to a wire rack and leave to cool completely.

> **Variation**
> *To make Banana and Walnut Teabread, add 5ml/1 tsp mixed (apple pie) spice and omit the chopped stem ginger. Stir in 50g/2oz/½ cup chopped walnuts and add 50g/2oz/⅓ cup sultanas (golden raisins).*

Banana Bread Energy 279kcal/1185kJ; Protein 6.8g; Carbohydrate 63.5g, of which sugars 11.9g; Fat 1.5g, of which saturates 0.2g; Cholesterol 0mg; Calcium 102mg; Fibre 2.5g; Sodium 16mg.
Banana Teabread Energy 162kcal/685kJ; Protein 2.7g; Carbohydrate 29.7g, of which sugars 12.5g; Fat 4.5g, of which saturates 0.1g; Cholesterol 0mg; Calcium 45mg; Fibre 1g; Sodium 45mg.

Apple Strudel

Ready-made filo pastry makes a good substitute for paper-thin strudel pastry in this classic Austrian dish.

Serves 10–12
75g/3oz/generous ½ cup raisins
30ml/2 tbsp brandy
5 eating apples
3 large cooking apples
90g/3½oz/scant ½ cup soft dark brown sugar
5ml/1 tsp ground cinnamon
grated rind and juice of 1 lemon
25g/1oz/scant ½ cup dry breadcrumbs
50g/2oz/½ cup chopped pecan nuts or walnuts
12 sheets of filo pastry, thawed if frozen
175g/6oz/¾ cup butter, melted
icing (confectioners') sugar, for dusting

1 Soak the raisins in the brandy for 15 minutes.

2 Peel, core and thinly slice the apples. Combine with the dark brown sugar, cinnamon, lemon rind and juice, half the breadcrumbs, and pecan nuts or walnuts.

3 Preheat the oven to 190°C/375°F/Gas 5. Grease two baking sheets. Unfold the filo pastry and cover with a damp dish towel. One by one, butter and stack the sheets to make two six-sheet piles.

4 Sprinkle half the reserved breadcrumbs over the last sheet and spoon half the apple mixture along the bottom edge. Roll up from this edge, Swiss roll (jelly roll) style. Place on a baking sheet, seam side down, and fold the ends under to seal. Repeat to make a second strudel. Brush both with butter.

5 Bake in the oven for 45 minutes, cool slightly, then dust with icing sugar.

Cook's Tip
Filo pastry is extremely delicate and needs to be kept covered with a damp dish towel when out of the packet and waiting to be used. Otherwise, it will dry out and crack before you are able to use it.

Greek Fruit & Nut Pastries

Aromatic Greek pastries are packed with candied citrus peel and walnuts, soaked in a coffee syrup.

Makes 16
450g/1lb/4 cups plain (all-purpose) flour, plus extra for dusting
2.5ml/½ tsp ground cinnamon
2.5ml/½ tsp baking powder
pinch of salt
150g/5oz/10 tbsp unsalted (sweet) butter
30ml/2 tbsp caster (superfine) sugar
1 egg
120ml/4fl oz/½ cup milk, chilled

For the filling
60ml/4 tbsp clear honey
60ml/4 tbsp strong freshly brewed coffee
75g/3oz/½ cup mixed candied citrus peel, finely chopped
175g/6oz/1½ cups walnuts, chopped
1.5ml/¼ tsp freshly-grated nutmeg
milk, to glaze
caster (superfine) sugar, for sprinkling

1 Preheat the oven to 180°C/350°F/Gas 4. To make the dough, sift the flour, ground cinnamon, baking powder and salt into a bowl. Rub in the butter until the mixture resembles fine breadcrumbs. Stir in the sugar. Make a well in the middle.

2 Beat the egg and milk together and add to the well in the dry ingredients. Mix to a soft dough. Divide the dough into two and wrap in clear film (plastic wrap). Chill for 30 minutes.

3 To make the filling, mix the honey and coffee. Add the peel, walnuts and nutmeg. Stir well and leave to soak for 20 minutes.

4 Roll out a portion of dough on a lightly floured surface to about 3mm/⅛in thick. Stamp out 10cm/4in rounds.

5 Place a heaped teaspoonful of filling on one side of each round. Brush the edges with milk, then fold over and press the edges together to seal. Repeat until all the filling is used.

6 Put the pastries on non-stick baking sheets, brush with milk and sprinkle with caster sugar. Prick each with a fork and bake for 35 minutes. Cool on a wire rack.

Apple Strudel Energy 231kcal/966kJ; Protein 2.3g; Carbohydrate 21.3g, of which sugars 8.6g; Fat 15.2g, of which saturates 7.9g; Cholesterol 31mg; Calcium 33mg; Fibre 1.5g; Sodium 109mg.
Greek Fruit Energy 278kcal/1162kJ; Protein 5g; Carbohydrate 30.2g, of which sugars 8.7g; Fat 16.1g, of which saturates 5.7g; Cholesterol 32mg; Calcium 69mg; Fibre 1.5g; Sodium 80mg.

Baked Lattice Peaches

You could use nectarines for this recipe, left unpeeled.

beaten egg, to glaze
caster (superfine) sugar, for sprinkling

Makes 6
3 peaches
juice of ½ lemon
75g/3oz/scant ½ cup white marzipan
375g/13oz ready-rolled puff pastry, thawed if frozen
a large pinch of ground cinnamon

For the sauce
50g/2oz/¼ cup caster (superfine) sugar
30ml/2 tbsp cold water
150ml/¼ pint/⅔ cup double cream

1 Preheat the oven to 190°C/375°F/Gas 5. Place the peaches in a bowl and pour over boiling water. Leave for 60 seconds, drain, then peel off the skins. Toss the fruit in the lemon juice.

2 Divide the marzipan into six pieces and shape each to form a small round. Cut the peaches in half and remove their stones. Fill the stone cavity in each with a marzipan round.

3 Unroll the puff pastry and cut it in half. Set one half aside, then cut out six rounds from the rest, making each round slightly larger than a peach half. Sprinkle a little cinnamon on each pastry round, then place a peach half, marzipan side down, on the pastry. Cut small slits in rows all over the remaining pastry, starting each row lower than the last. Cut the lattice pastry into six equal squares.

4 Dampen the edges of the pastry rounds with water, then drape a lattice pastry square over each peach half. Press around the edge to seal, then trim off the excess pastry and decorate with peach leaves made from the trimmings. Transfer the peach pastries to a baking sheet. Brush with the beaten egg and sprinkle with the caster sugar. Bake for 20 minutes, until golden.

5 Meanwhile, make the caramel sauce. Heat the sugar with the water in a small pan until it dissolves. Bring to the boil and continue to boil until the syrup turns a dark golden brown. Stand back and add the cream. Heat gently, stirring until smooth. Serve the peach pastries with the sauce.

Baked Sweet Ravioli

These rich pastries are flavoured with lemon and filled with ricotta cheese, fruit and chocolate, for a sweet and rich treat.

Serves 4
225g/8oz/2 cups plain (all-purpose) flour
65g/2½oz/⅓ cup caster (superfine) sugar
90g/3½oz/scant ½ cup butter, diced
2 eggs
5ml/1 tsp finely grated lemon rind, plus extra for sprinkling

For the filling
175g/6oz/¾ cup ricotta cheese
50g/2oz/¼ cup caster (superfine) sugar
4ml/¾ tsp vanilla extract
1 egg yolk, beaten
15ml/1 tbsp mixed candied fruits
25g/1oz dark (bittersweet) chocolate, finely chopped
icing (confectioners') sugar, for sprinkling
grated dark (bittersweet) chocolate, for sprinkling

1 For the dough, process the flour, sugar and butter in a food processor. Add one egg and the lemon rind and process to form a dough. Wrap in clear film (plastic wrap) and chill.

2 Press the cheese through a sieve (strainer) into a bowl. Stir in the sugar, vanilla, egg yolk, fruits and chocolate.

3 Halve the dough and roll out each half between sheets of clear film to a 15 x 56cm/6 x 22in rectangle.

4 Preheat the oven to 180°C/350°F/Gas 4. Lightly grease a baking sheet.

5 Place mounds of filling, 2.5cm/1in apart, in two rows on one dough strip. Beat the remaining egg and brush between the mounds. Top with the second dough strip and press to seal. Stamp out ravioli around each mound with a 6cm/2½in cookie cutter. Gently pinch to seal the edges.

6 Place on the baking sheet and bake for 15 minutes, until golden. Sprinkle with lemon rind, icing sugar and chocolate.

Baked Sweet Energy 628kcal/2636kJ; Protein 13.1g; Carbohydrate 81.4g, of which sugars 38.5g; Fat 30.1g, of which saturates 17.7g; Cholesterol 162mg; Calcium 119mg; Fibre 2.1g; Sodium 186mg.
Baked Lattice Energy 472kcal/1971kJ; Protein 6g; Carbohydrate 45g, of which sugars 23g; Fat 31g, of which saturates 9g; Cholesterol 73mg; Calcium 70mg; Fibre 3.1g; Sodium 217mg.

Apricot & Pear Filo Roulade

A truly delicious mix of dried and fresh fruit and almonds, all wrapped up in light-as-a-feather filo pastry, makes a really great dessert. This dish is also amazingly quick to prepare and cook. Use your imagination and vary the fruits you use, depending on what is in season or what you have readily to hand.

Serves 4–6
115g/4oz/½ cup ready-to-eat
    dried apricots, chopped
30ml/2 tbsp apricot jam
5ml/1 tsp freshly squeezed
    lemon juice
50g/2oz/¼ cup soft brown sugar
2 medium pears, peeled, cored
    and chopped
50g/2oz/½ cup ground almonds
30ml/2 tbsp slivered almonds
25g/1oz/2 tbsp butter
8 sheets of filo pastry
icing (confectioners') sugar,
    to dust

1 Put the dried apricots, apricot jam, lemon juice, brown sugar and prepared pears into a pan and heat gently, stirring all the time, for 5–7 minutes.

2 Remove the pan with the fruit mixture from the heat and cool. Mix in the ground and slivered almonds. Preheat the oven to 200°C/400°F/Gas 6. Melt the butter in a pan.

3 Lightly grease a baking sheet. Layer the filo pastry on the baking sheet, brushing each separate layer carefully with the melted butter.

4 Spoon the fruit-and-nut filling down the pastry, placing the filling just to one side of the centre and within 2.5cm/1in of each end.

5 Lift the other side of the pastry up by sliding a metal spatula underneath. Fold this pastry over the filling, tucking the edge under. Seal the ends neatly and brush all over with melted butter again.

6 Bake for 15–20 minutes, until golden. Dust with icing sugar and serve immediately.

Apricot Triangles

These quite substantial pastries have a luscious filling of dried apricots poached with cinnamon, but a variety of other fillings are also popular. If serving them as snacks, you can make the pastry cases smaller and more delicate.

Makes about 24
115g/4oz/½ cup unsalted
    (sweet) butter, softened
250g/9oz/generous 1 cup sugar
30ml/2 tbsp milk
1 egg, beaten
5ml/1 tsp vanilla extract
pinch of salt
200–250g/7–9oz/1¼–2¼ cups
    plain (all-purpose) flour,
    plus extra for dusting
icing (confectioners') sugar,
    for dusting (optional)

For the filling
250g/9oz/generous 1 cup
    dried apricots
1 cinnamon stick
45ml/3 tbsp sugar

1 Beat the butter and sugar until pale and fluffy. In another bowl, mix together the milk, egg, vanilla extract and salt.

2 Add one-third of the flour, stir, then add the rest in batches, alternating with the milk mixture. Cover and chill for 1 hour.

3 To make the filling, put the ingredients in a pan and add enough water to cover. Heat gently, then simmer for 15 minutes, until the apricots are tender and most of the liquid has evaporated. Remove the cinnamon stick, then purée the apricots in a food processor or blender with a little of the cooking liquid until they form a consistency like thick jam.

4 Preheat the oven to 180°C/350°F/Gas 4. On a lightly floured surface, roll out the dough to 5mm/¼in thick, then cut into 7.5cm/3in rounds using a cookie cutter.

5 Place 15–30ml/1–2 tbsp of filling in the centre of each round, then pinch the pastry together to form three corners.

6 Place on a baking sheet and bake for 15 minutes, or until pale golden. Serve warm or cold, dusted with icing sugar.

Apricot Triangles Energy 125kcal/528kJ; Protein 1.6g; Carbohydrate 21.3g, of which sugars 14.9g; Fat 4.4g, of which saturates 2.6g; Cholesterol 18mg; Calcium 28mg; Fibre 0.9g; Sodium 35mg.
Apricot and Pear Energy 212Kcal/890kJ; Protein 3.7g; Carbohydrate 31.3g, of which sugars 24.7g; Fat 8.8g, of which saturates 2.6g; Cholesterol 9mg; Calcium 59mg; Fibre 3.3g; Sodium 34mg.

Filo Fruit Scrunchies

Quick and easy to make, these pretty fruit pastries are ideal to serve at teatime. Eat them warm, or they will lose their crispness.

20ml/4 tsp soft margarine, melted
50g/2 oz/¹⁄₃ cup demerara (raw) sugar
30ml/2 tbsp flaked almonds
icing sugar, for dusting

Makes 6
5 apricots or plums
4 sheets of filo pastry

I Preheat the oven to 190°C/375°F/Gas 5. Halve the apricots or plums, remove the stones and slice the fruit.

2 Cut the filo pastry into twelve 18cm/7in squares. Pile the squares on top of each other and cover with a clean dish towel to prevent the pastry from drying out.

3 Remove one square of filo and brush it with melted margarine. Lay a second filo square on top, then, using your fingers, mould the pastry into folds.

4 Make five more scrunchies in the same way, working quickly so that the pastry does not dry out.

5 Arrange a few slices of fruit in the folds of each scrunchie, then sprinkle generously with the demerara sugar and flaked almonds.

6 Place the scrunchies on a baking sheet. Bake for 8–10 minutes until golden brown, then loosen the scrunchies from the baking sheet with a palette knife and transfer to a wire rack. Dust with icing sugar and serve at once.

> **Cook's Tip**
> Filo pastry dries out very quickly. Keep it covered as much as possible with a dry cloth or clear film (plastic wrap) to limit exposure to the air, or it will become too brittle to use.

Apricot Parcels

These little filo parcels contain a special apricot and mincemeat filling. They are a good way to use up any mincemeat and marzipan that may have been in your cupboard since Christmas.

8 apricots, halved and stoned (pitted)
60ml/4 tbsp luxury mincemeat
12 ratafia biscuits (almond macaroons), crushed
30ml/2 tbsp grated marzipan
icing (confectioners') sugar, for dusting

Makes 8
350g/12oz filo pastry, thawed if frozen
50g/2oz/¹⁄₄ cup butter, melted

I Preheat the oven to 200°C/400°F/Gas 6. Cut the filo pastry into 32 x 18cm/7in squares. Brush four of the squares with a little melted butter and stack them, giving each layer a quarter turn so that the stack acquires a star shape. Repeat this stacking process to make eight stars.

2 Place an apricot half, hollow up, in the centre of each pastry star. Mix together the mincemeat, crushed ratafias and marzipan, and spoon a little of the mixture into the hollow of each apricot.

3 Top with another apricot half, then bring the corners of each pastry star together and squeeze to make a gathered purse.

4 Place the purses on a baking sheet and brush each with a little melted butter. Bake for 15–20 minutes or until the pastry is golden and crisp. Lightly dust with icing sugar, to serve.

> **Cook's Tips**
> • Whipped cream, flavoured with a little brandy, makes an ideal accompaniment to the delicious parcels.
> • If ratafias are not available, use amaretti instead, or simply omit them, as the mincemeat adds plenty of flavour.

Apricot Parcels Energy 214Kcal/902kJ; Protein 3.2g; Carbohydrate 34.9g, of which sugars 15.2g; Fat 7.9g, of which saturates 4.1g; Cholesterol 14mg; Calcium 56mg; Fibre 1.7g; Sodium 83mg.
Filo Fruit Scrunchies Energy 127kcal/534kJ; Protein 2.2g; Carbohydrate 18g, of which sugars 11.5g; Fat 5.7g, of which saturates 0.2g; Cholesterol 0mg; Calcium 33mg; Fibre 1.2g; Sodium 29mg.

Fruit Turnovers

This recipe uses plums, but you could also use apples, rhubarb or a jar of ready-made fruit compote. Butter gives the pastry a good flavour, while the lard makes it crisp.

Makes 8

450g/1lb plums, stones (pits) removed and chopped
25–40g/1–1½oz/2–3 tbsp sugar
350g/12oz/3 cups plain (all-purpose) flour
85g/3oz/6 tbsp lard or white cooking fat, cut into pieces
85g/3oz/6 tbsp butter, cut into pieces
milk and sugar, for brushing and sprinkling
pinch of salt

1 Bring the fruit and the sugar to the boil with 15ml/1tbsp water, then cover and simmer for 5–10 minutes, stirring frequently, until the fruit is soft. You can reduce the liquid by bubbling uncovered and stirring until thick. Leave to cool.

2 Sift the flour and salt into a bowl, add the lard or cooking fat and butter and rub them into the flour until the mixture resembles fine crumbs (alternatively, process in a food processor). Stir in enough cold water until the mixture forms clumps, then gather together to make a smooth dough. Wrap the pastry and chill for 20–30 minutes to allow it to relax.

3 Preheat the oven to 190°C/375°F/Gas 5. Then line a baking sheet with baking parchment. On a lightly floured surface, roll out the dough to 3–5mm/⅛–¼in thick. Using a small upturned bowl or plate as a guide, cut out eight 15cm/6in circles, re-rolling the pastry offcuts as necessary.

4 Place a spoonful of cooled fruit on to each pastry circle and brush the edges with water. Fold the pastry over the fruit, pinching the edges to seal them well. Arrange the pastries on the baking sheet, brush with milk, sprinkle some sugar over and make a small slit in each.

5 Put into the hot oven and cook for 20–30 minutes until golden brown. Sprinkle with a little extra sugar and transfer to a wire rack to cool.

Plum & Marzipan Pastries

These Danish pastries can be made with any stoned fruit. Try apricots, cherries, damsons or greengages, adding a glaze made from clear honey or a complementary jam.

Makes 6

375g/13oz ready-made puff pastry, thawed if frozen
90ml/6 tbsp plum jam
115g/4oz/¾ cup white marzipan, coarsely grated
3 red plums, halved and stoned
1 egg, beaten
50g/2oz/½ cup flaked (sliced) almonds

For the glaze
30ml/2 tbsp plum jam
15ml/1 tbsp water

1 Preheat the oven to 220°C/425°F/Gas 7.

2 Roll out the pastry, cut it into six equal squares and place on one or two dampened baking sheets.

3 Spoon 15ml/1 tbsp jam into the centre of each pastry square. Divide the marzipan among them. Place half a plum, hollow side down, on top of each marzipan mound.

4 Brush the edges of the pastry with beaten egg. Bring up the corners and press them together lightly, then open out the pastry corners at the top.

5 Brush the pastries all over with a little beaten egg to glaze. Divide the flaked almonds between the six pastries and press all over the tops and sides.

6 Bake the pastries for 20–25 minutes, until crisp and golden brown. Keep a close eye on them towards the end of the cooking time as the almonds can scorch quite quickly, spoiling the appearance and flavour of the pastries.

7 To make the glaze, heat the jam and water in a small pan, stirring until smooth. Press the mixture through a sieve (strainer) into a small bowl, then brush it over the tops of the pastries while they are still warm. Leave to cool on a wire rack.

Fruit Turnovers Energy 340kcal/1420kJ; Protein 4.2g; Carbohydrate 38.5g, of which sugars 5.1g; Fat 19.8g, of which saturates 9.9g; Cholesterol 33mg; Calcium 66mg; Fibre 1.5g; Sodium 66mg.
Plum and Marzipan Energy 416kcal/1746kJ; Protein 6.6g; Carbohydrate 51.8g, of which sugars 29.2g; Fat 22.4g, of which saturates 0.6g; Cholesterol 0mg; Calcium 73mg; Fibre 1.2g; Sodium 205mg.

Plum Filo Pockets

Delicate sugar-dusted layers
of filo pastry surround
warm plums and soft cheese
in these delightful fruit-filled
parcels. They make a very
elegant summer dessert,
when plums are plentiful.

15ml/1 tbsp light muscovado
  (brown) sugar
2.5ml/½ tsp ground cloves
8 large, firm plums, halved
  and stoned
8 sheets of filo pastry
sunflower oil, for brushing
icing sugar, to sprinkle

Serves 4
115g/4oz/½ cup skimmed milk
  soft cheese

1 Preheat the oven to 220°C/425°F/Gas 7. Mix together
the cheese, sugar and cloves.

2 Sandwich the plum halves back together in twos with a
spoonful of the cheese mixture.

3 Spread out the pastry and cut into 16 pieces, each about
23cm/9in square. Brush one lightly with oil and place a second
at a diagonal on top.

4 Repeat with the remaining pastry to make eight
double-layer squares.

5 Place a plum on each pastry square, and pinch corners
together. Place on baking sheet. Bake for 15–18 minutes,
until golden, then dust with icing sugar.

> **Cook's Tips**
> • In the summer, you could use large fresh apricots, or small
> peaches or nectarines in place of the plums – make sure that
> any fruit you choose is just ripe.
> • To remove the stones from plums, first slice all the way
> around the outside of the fruit, then twist the two halves to
> break them apart. Give the plum a shake and the stone
> should fall out easily.

Cherry Strudel

Apple is the most common
filling for a strudel, but
sweet cherries in season
mingled with pecan nuts
make this fine, crisp and
light dessert a real luxury.

80g/3¼oz/scant ½ cup caster
  (superfine) sugar, plus extra
  for sprinkling
25g/1oz/½ cup brioche
  breadcrumbs
10 large sheets of filo pastry,
  thawed if frozen
icing (confectioners') sugar,
  to decorate

Serves 6
65g/2½oz/5 tbsp butter, melted,
  plus extra for greasing
30ml/½ tbsp cherry jam
500g/1¼lb fresh cherries,
  pitted
75g/3oz/½ cup pecan nuts,
  roughly chopped

1 Preheat the oven to 200°C/400°F/Gas 6. Butter and line a
baking sheet with baking parchment. Put the cherry jam in
a small pan and heat slowly until just melted.

2 In a large bowl combine the cherries, pecan nuts, sugar
and brioche breadcrumbs.

3 Lay a damp dish towel on your work surface, then take a
sheet of filo pastry and lay on top. (Cover the remaining filo
pastry with a damp dish towel to prevent it from drying out.)
Brush generously with melted butter, then cover with another
sheet of filo and brush that with butter. Add a third sheet,
and brush with the melted cherry jam as well as the butter.
Continue in this way, with the third sheet brushed with jam
and butter, until all the filo is used up.

4 Put the cherry and pecan mixture down the centre of the
pastry and roll the pastry up.

5 Butter the strudel on all sides, sprinkle on some caster sugar
and curl into a horseshoe. Put on the baking sheet and bake
for 20–30 minutes, or until golden brown. Serve warm or cold,
dusted with icing sugar.

Plum Filo Energy 281kcal/1180kJ; Protein 6g; Carbohydrate 37g, of which sugars 15g; Fat 12g, of which saturates 3g; Cholesterol 0mg; Calcium 15 mg; Fibre 2.4g; Sodium 216mg.
Cherry Strudel Energy 370kcal/1553kJ; Protein 3.2g; Carbohydrate 51.2g, of which sugars 33.2g; Fat 18.4g, of which saturates 11.4g; Cholesterol 47mg; Calcium 57mg; Fibre 1.2g; Sodium 197mg.

Chocolate, Date & Almond Filo Coil

Experience the allure of the Middle East with this delectable dessert. Crisp filo pastry conceals a chocolate and rose water filling studded with delicious dates and almonds.

Serves 6
275g/10oz filo pastry, thawed
    if frozen
50g/2oz/¼ cup butter, melted
icing (confectioners') sugar, cocoa
    powder (unsweetened) and
    ground cinnamon, for dusting

For the filling
75g/3oz/6 tbsp butter
115g/4oz dark (bittersweet)
    chocolate, broken up into pieces
115g/4oz/1⅓ cup ground
    almonds
115g/4oz/⅔ cup chopped dates
75g/3oz/⅔ cup icing
    (confectioners') sugar
10ml/2 tsp rose water
2.5ml/½ tsp ground cinnamon

1 Preheat the oven to 180°C/350°F/Gas 4. Grease a 22cm/8½in round cake tin (pan). To make the filling, melt the butter with the chocolate in a heatproof bowl set over a pan of barely simmering water, then remove from the heat and stir in the remaining ingredients to make a thick paste. Leave to cool.

2 Lay one sheet of filo on a clean, flat surface. Brush with melted butter, then lay a second sheet on top and brush with more butter.

3 Roll a handful of the chocolate and almond mixture into a long sausage shape and place along one long edge of the layered filo. Roll up the pastry tightly around the filling to make a roll.

4 Fit the filo roll in the cake tin, in such a way that it sits snugly against the outer edge. Make more filo rolls in the same way, adding them to the tin from the outside towards the centre, until the coil fills the tin.

5 Brush the coil with the remaining melted butter. Bake for 30–35 minutes until the pastry is golden brown and crisp. Transfer the coil to a serving plate. Serve warm, dusted with icing sugar, cocoa and cinnamon.

Fig & Date Ravioli

These irresistible cushions of sweet pastry are filled with a delicious mixture of figs, dates and walnuts and dusted with icing sugar. They are ideal for serving with coffee.

Makes about 20
375g/13oz ready-made sweet
    shortcrust pastry dough,
    thawed if frozen

milk, for brushing
icing (confectioners') sugar,
    sifted, for dusting

For the filling
115g/4oz/⅔ cup ready-to-eat
    dried figs
50g/2oz/scant ½ cup stoned
    (pitted) dates
15g/½oz/1 tbsp chopped walnuts
10ml/2 tsp lemon juice
15ml/1 tbsp clear honey

1 Preheat the oven to 180°C/350°F/Gas 4. To make the filling, put all the ingredients into a food processor and blend to a paste.

2 Roll out just under half of the shortcrust pastry dough on a lightly floured surface to a square. Place spoonfuls of the fig paste on the dough in neat rows at equally spaced intervals.

3 Roll out the remaining dough to a slightly larger square. Dampen all around each spoonful of filling, using a pastry brush dipped in cold water. Place the second sheet of dough on top and press together around each mound of filling.

4 Using a zig-zag pastry wheel, cut squares between the mounds of filling. Place the cookies on non-stick baking sheets and lightly brush the top of each with a little milk. Bake for 15–20 minutes, until golden.

5 Using a metal spatula, transfer the cookies to a wire rack to cool. When cool, dust with icing sugar.

> **Cook's Tip**
> If you don't have a pastry wheel, use a sharp knife to cut out the ravioli, although it will not produce a fluted edge.

Chocolate Energy 543Kcal/2267kJ; Protein 8.2g; Carbohydrate 55.4g, of which sugars 32.4g; Fat 33.6g, of which saturates 15g; Cholesterol 46mg; Calcium 108mg; Fibre 3.2g; Sodium 133mg.
Fig and Date Ravioli Energy 111kcal/464kJ; Protein 1.5g; Carbohydrate 13.9g, of which sugars 5.3g; Fat 5.9g, of which saturates 1.7g; Cholesterol 3mg; Calcium 31mg; Fibre 0.9g; Sodium 79mg.

Lemon Meringue Pie

Crisp on top, soft beneath, and deliciously tangy in the middle, this is a classic dish, the popularity of which never seems to wane.

Serves 8

225g/8oz shortcrust pastry, thawed if frozen
grated rind and juice of
1 large lemon
250ml/8fl oz/1 cup plus
15ml/1 tbsp cold water
115g/4oz/generous ½ cup caster (superfine) sugar plus
90ml/6 tbsp extra
25g/1oz/2 tbsp butter
45ml/3 tbsp cornflour (cornstarch)
3 eggs, separated
a pinch of salt
a pinch of cream of tartar

1 Line a 23cm/9in pie dish with the pastry, folding under a 1cm/½in overhang to give a firm edge. Crimp the edge and chill for 20 minutes.

2 Preheat the oven to 200°C/400°F/Gas 6. Prick the pastry case base, line with baking parchment and fill with baking beans. Bake for 12 minutes.

3 Remove the paper and beans and bake until golden, 6–8 minutes more.

4 In a pan, combine the lemon rind and juice with 250ml/8fl oz/ 1 cup of the water, 115g/4oz/generous ½ cup of the sugar, and the butter. Bring to the boil.

5 Meanwhile, dissolve the cornflour in the remaining water. Add the egg yolks. Beat into the lemon mixture, return to the boil and whisk until thick, about 5 minutes. Cover the surface with baking parchment and leave to cool.

6 For the meringue, beat the egg whites, using an electric hand whisk, with the salt and cream of tartar until stiffly peaking. Add the remaining sugar a spoonful at a time and beat until glossy.

7 Spoon the lemon mixture into the pastry case. Spoon the meringue on top, sealing it with the pastry rim. Bake until golden, 12–15 minutes.

Filo-topped Apple Pie

With its crisp, melt-in-the-mouth filo topping and minimal butter, this is a really light dessert, making it the perfect choice for those trying to combine a sweet tooth with a healthy eating plan. There's certainly no loss of flavour in this tasty variation on a traditional theme, so feel free to serve it to family and friends who will soon discover that it tastes as good as it looks.

Serves 6

900g/2lb cooking apples
75g/3oz/6 tbsp caster (superfine) sugar
grated rind of 1 lemon
15ml/1 tbsp lemon juice
75g/3oz/½ cup sultanas (golden raisins)
2.5ml/½ tsp ground cinnamon
4 large sheets of filo pastry, thawed if frozen
25g/1oz/2 tbsp butter, melted
icing (confectioners') sugar, for dusting

1 Peel, core and dice the apples. Place the apples in a pan with the caster sugar and lemon rind. Drizzle the lemon juice over.

2 Bring to the boil, stir well, then cook for 5 minutes, until the apples have softened.

3 Stir in the sultanas and cinnamon. Spoon the mixture into a 1.2 litre/2 pint/5 cup pie dish; level the top. Allow to cool.

4 Preheat the oven to 180°C/350°F/Gas 4. Place a pie funnel in the centre of the fruit. Brush each sheet of filo with melted butter.

5 Scrunch the filo up loosely and place on the fruit to cover it completely. Bake for 20–30 minutes until the filo is golden.

6 To serve, dust the pie with the icing sugar.

> **Cook's Tip**
> For a delightful change of flavour and texture, substitute flaked (sliced) almonds – plain or toasted – for some or all of the sultanas (golden raisins) in the pie.

Filo-topped Apple Pie Energy 210kcal/893kJ; Protein 2g; Carbohydrate 43g, of which sugars 36g; Fat 4g, of which saturates 2g; Cholesterol 9mg; Calcium 19mg; Fibre 4.1g; Sodium 68mg.
Lemon Meringue Energy 357kcal/1497kJ; Protein 6.8g; Carbohydrate 42.8g, of which sugars 25.1g; Fat 18.9g, of which saturates 9g; Cholesterol 129mg; Calcium 108mg; Fibre 0.7g; Sodium 137mg.

Key Lime Pie

This American classic is ideal for a festive treat.

Serves 10
225g/8oz/2 cups plain
   (all-purpose) flour
115g/4oz/1/2 cup chilled
   butter, diced
30ml/2 tbsp caster
   (superfine) sugar
2 egg yolks
pinch of salt
30ml/2 tbsp cold water
thinly pared lime rind and mint
   leaves, to decorate

For the filling
4 eggs, separated
400g/14oz can sweetened
   condensed milk
grated rind and juice of 3 limes
a few drops of green food
   colouring (optional)
30ml/2 tbsp caster
   (superfine) sugar

For the topping
300ml/1/2 pint/1 1/4 cups double
   (heavy) cream
2–3 limes, thinly sliced

1 Sift the flour and rub in the butter until the mixture resembles breadcrumbs. Add the sugar, egg yolks, salt and water. Mix to a soft dough. Roll out the pastry and use to line a deep 21cm/ 8½in fluted flan tin (pan), allowing the excess pastry to hang over the edge. Prick the pastry base and chill for 30 minutes.

2 Preheat the oven to 200°C/400°F/Gas 6. Trim off the excess pastry from the edge of the pastry case (pie shell) and line the pastry case with baking parchment and baking beans. Bake the pastry case blind for 10 minutes. Remove the paper and beans and return the case to the oven for 10 minutes.

3 Meanwhile, make the filling. Beat the egg yolks in a bowl until light and creamy, then beat in the condensed milk, with the lime rind and juice. Add the food colouring, if using, and beat until the mixture is thick. In a grease-free bowl, whisk the egg whites to stiff peaks. Whisk in the caster sugar, then fold into the filling.

4 Lower the oven to 160°C/325°F/Gas 3. Pour the filling into the pastry case. Bake for 20–25 minutes or until it has set and is browned. Cool, then chill. Before serving, whip the cream and spoon around the edge. Twist the lime slices and arrange between the cream. Decorate with lime rind and mint leaves.

Peach Leaf Pie

Pretty pastry leaves decorate this most attractive spiced summer fruit pie.

Serves 8
1.2kg/2½lb ripe peaches
juice of 1 lemon
90g/3½oz/½ cup caster
   (superfine) sugar
45ml/3 tbsp cornflour (cornstarch)
1.5ml/¼ tsp freshly grated nutmeg
2.5ml/½ tsp ground cinnamon
1 egg beaten with 15ml/1 tbsp
   water, to glaze

25g/1oz/2 tbsp cold
   butter, diced

For the pastry
275g/10oz/2½ cups plain
   (all-purpose) flour
4ml/¾ tsp salt
115g/4oz/½ cup cold
   butter, diced
60g/2¼oz/4½ tbsp cold
   white cooking fat or
   lard, diced
75–90ml/5–6 tbsp iced water

1 To make the pastry, sift the flour and salt into a bowl. Rub in the butter and fat using your fingertips or a pastry cutter until the mixture resembles breadcrumbs. Stir in just enough water to bind the dough. Gather into two balls, one slightly larger than the other. Wrap and chill for at least 20 minutes. Place a baking sheet in the oven and preheat to 220°C/425°F/Gas 7.

2 Drop the peaches into boiling water for 20 seconds, then transfer to a bowl of cold water. When cool, peel off the skins. Slice the flesh and combine with the lemon juice, sugar, cornflour and spices. Set aside.

3 Roll out the larger dough ball to 3mm/⅛in thick. Use to line a 23cm/9in pie plate. Chill. Roll out the remaining dough to 5mm/¼in thick. Cut out leaves 7.5cm/3in long. Mark veins. With the scraps, roll a few balls.

4 Brush the pastry base with egg glaze. Add the peaches and dot with the butter. Starting from the outside edge, cover the peaches with a ring of leaves. Place a second, staggered ring above. Continue until covered. Place the balls in the centre.

5 Brush with glaze. Bake for 10 minutes. Lower the heat to 180°C/350°F/Gas 4 and bake for 35–40 minutes more.

Key Lime Pie Energy 510kcal/2126kJ; Protein 9.2g; Carbohydrate 46.6g, of which sugars 29.4g; Fat 33.2g, of which saturates 19.5g; Cholesterol 196mg; Calcium 182mg; Fibre 0.7g; Sodium 163mg.
Peach Leaf Energy 424kcal/1778kJ; Protein 4.8g; Carbohydrate 54.2g, of which sugars 22.8g; Fat 22.4g, of which saturates 12.2g; Cholesterol 44mg; Calcium 68mg; Fibre 3.1g; Sodium 112mg.

Peach & Blueberry Pie

This colourful lattice pie is bursting with fruit flavours.

Serves 8
225g/8oz/2 cups plain
  (all-purpose) flour
2.5ml/½ tsp salt
5ml/1 tsp granulated (white) sugar
150g/5oz/10 tbsp cold butter
1 egg yolk
30–45ml/2–3 tbsp iced water
30ml/2 tbsp milk, for glazing

For the filling
6 peaches, peeled, stoned (pitted)
  and sliced
225g/8oz/2 cups fresh blueberries
150g/5oz/¾ cup granulated
  (white) sugar
30ml/2 tbsp fresh lemon juice
40g/1½oz/⅓ cup plain
  (all-purpose) flour
pinch of grated nutmeg
25g/1oz/2 tbsp butter,
  cut into pea-size pieces

1 Sift the flour, salt and sugar into a bowl, and rub in the butter. Mix the egg yolk with 30ml/2 tbsp of the iced water and sprinkle over the flour mixture. Combine until the pastry holds together. If the pastry is too crumbly, add a little more water. Gather the pastry into a ball and flatten into a disk. Wrap in clear film (plastic wrap) and chill for at least 20 minutes.

2 Roll out two-thirds of the pastry to a thickness of 3mm/⅛in. Use to line a 23cm/9in fluted tin (pan). Trim all around, leaving a 1cm/½in overhang, then trim the edges. Gather the remaining pastry into a ball, and roll out to a thickness of about 6mm/¼in. Cut strips 1cm/½in wide. Chill the pastry case and the strips for 20 minutes. Preheat the oven to 200°C/400°F/Gas 6.

3 Line the pastry case with baking parchment and fill with dried beans. Bake 12–15 minutes. Remove from the oven and lift out the paper with the beans. Prick the pastry case, then bake for 5 minutes more. Let the pastry case cool slightly before filling.

4 In a bowl, combine the peach slices with the blueberries, sugar, lemon juice, flour and nutmeg. Spoon the fruit mixture evenly into the pastry case. Dot with the pieces of butter. Weave a lattice top with the chilled pastry strips, pressing the ends to the baked pastry-case edge. Brush the strips with the milk. Bake the pie for 15 minutes. Reduce the heat to 180°C/350°F/Gas 4, and continue baking 30 minutes more. Serve the pie warm.

Plum Crumble Pie

Polenta adds a wonderful golden hue and crunchiness to the crumble topping for this luscious fruit-filled pie.

Serves 6–8
115g/4oz/1 cup unbleached plain
  (all-purpose) flour, sifted
115g/4oz/1 cup wholemeal
  (whole-wheat) flour
150g/5oz/¾ cup golden caster
  (superfine) sugar
115g/4oz/1 cup polenta
5ml/1 tsp baking powder

pinch of salt
150g/5oz unsalted (sweet)
  butter, plus extra for greasing
1 egg
15ml/1 tbsp olive oil
25g/1oz/¼ cup rolled oats
15ml/1 tbsp demerara
  (raw) sugar
custard or cream, to serve

For the filling
10ml/2 tsp caster (superfine) sugar
15ml/1 tbsp polenta
450g/1lb dark plums

1 Mix together the flours, sugar, polenta, baking powder and salt in a large bowl. Rub in the butter with your fingers until the mixture resembles fine breadcrumbs. Stir in the egg and olive oil, and enough cold water to form a smooth dough.

2 Grease a 23cm/9in spring-form cake tin. Press two-thirds of the dough evenly over the base and up the sides of the tin. Wrap the remaining dough in clear film (plastic wrap) and chill while you make the filling.

3 Preheat the oven to 180°C/350°F/Gas 4. Sprinkle the sugar and polenta into the pastry case.

4 Cut the plums in half and remove the stones, then place them, cut-side down, on top of the polenta.

5 Remove the remaining dough from the refrigerator and crumble it between your fingers, then combine with the oats. Sprinkle evenly over the the plums, then sprinkle the demerara sugar on top.

6 Bake for 50 minutes or until golden. Leave for 15 minutes before removing the cake from the tin. Allow to to cool on a wire rack. Serve with custard or cream.

Peach and Blueberry Energy 391kcal/1640kJ; Protein 4.7g; Carbohydrate 53g, of which sugars 27.7g; Fat 19.3g, of which saturates 11.7g; Cholesterol 72mg; Calcium 86mg; Fibre 2.9g; Sodium 139mg.
Plum Crumble Pie Energy 398kcal/1682kJ; Protein 6g; Carbohydrate 61g, of which sugars 29g; Fat 16g, of which saturates 8g; Cholesterol 62mg; Calcium 48mg; Fibre 3.8g; Sodium 74mg.

One-crust Rhubarb Pie

The method used for this simple shortcrust pie can be used for all sorts of fruit, and it is completely foolproof. It doesn't matter how rough the pie looks when it goes into the oven; it always comes out looking fantastic.

Serves 6
350g/12oz shortcrust pastry, thawed if frozen
1 egg yolk, beaten
25g/1oz/3 tbsp semolina
25g/1oz/¼ cup hazelnuts, coarsely chopped
30ml/2 tbsp golden granulated sugar

For the filling
450g/1lb rhubarb, cut into 2.5cm/1in pieces
75g/3oz/6 tbsp caster (superfine) sugar
1–2 pieces preserved stem ginger in syrup, drained and finely chopped

1 Preheat the oven to 200°C/400°F/Gas 6. Roll out the pastry to a circle 35cm/14in across. Lay it over the rolling pin and transfer it to a large baking sheet. Brush a little egg yolk over the pastry. Scatter the semolina over the centre, leaving a wide rim all round the edge.

2 Make the filling. Place the rhubarb pieces, caster sugar and chopped ginger in a large bowl and mix well.

3 Pile the rhubarb mixture into the middle of the pastry. Fold the rim roughly over the filling so that it almost covers it. Some of the fruit will remain visible in the centre.

4 Brush the pastry rim with any remaining egg yolk to glaze, then scatter the hazelnuts and golden sugar over the top. Bake the pie for 30–35 minutes or until the pastry is golden brown. Serve hot or warm.

> **Cook's Tip**
> *Egg yolk glaze brushed on to pastry gives it a nice golden sheen. However, be careful not to drip the glaze on the baking sheet, or it will burn and be difficult to remove.*

Rhubarb Meringue Pie

Tangy rhubarb contrasts beautifully with meringue.

Serves 6
675g/1½lb rhubarb, chopped
250g/9oz/1¼ cup caster (superfine) sugar
grated rind and juice of 3 oranges
3 eggs, separated
75ml/5 tbsp cornflour (cornstarch)

For the pastry
200g/7oz/1¾ cups plain (all-purpose) flour
25g/1oz/¼ cup ground walnuts
115g/4oz/½ cup butter, diced
30ml/2 tbsp sugar
1 egg yolk, beaten with 15ml/1 tbsp water

1 To make the pastry, sift the flour into a bowl and add the walnuts. Rub in the butter until the mixture resembles very fine breadcrumbs. Stir in the sugar and egg yolk mixture to make a firm dough. Knead lightly, wrap and chill for 30 minutes.

2 Preheat the oven to 190°C/375°F/Gas 5. Roll out the pastry on a lightly floured surface and use to line a 23cm/9in fluted flan tin (tart pan). Prick the base all over with a fork. Line the pastry with foil and baking beans, then bake for 15 minutes.

3 Meanwhile, to make the filling, put the chopped rhubarb in a large pan with 75g/3oz/6 tbsp of the sugar. Add the orange rind. Cover and cook over a low heat until tender.

4 Remove the foil and beans from the pastry case, then brush all over with a little egg yolk. Bake the pastry case for about 15 minutes, or until the pastry is crisp and golden.

5 Mix together the cornflour and the orange juice in a mixing bowl. Remove the rhubarb from the heat, stir in the cornflour mixture, then return the pan to the heat and bring to the boil, stirring constantly. Cook for 1–2 minutes more. Cool slightly, then beat in the remaining egg yolks. Pour into the pastry case.

6 Whisk the egg whites until they form soft peaks, then whisk in the remaining sugar, 15ml/1 tbsp at a time. Swirl over the filling and bake for 25 minutes until the meringue is golden.

One-crust Energy 389Kcal/1633kJ; Protein 5.6g; Carbohydrate 49.7g, of which sugars 19.6g; Fat 20.1g, of which saturates 5.6g; Cholesterol 42mg; Calcium 139mg; Fibre 2.5g; Sodium 239mg.
Rhubarb Meringue Energy 567Kcal/2388kJ; Protein 8.4g; Carbohydrate 89.5g, of which sugars 52.6g; Fat 22.1g, of which saturates 11.1g; Cholesterol 136mg; Calcium 202mg; Fibre 2.8g; Sodium 168mg.

Boston Banoffee Pie

Simply press this wonderfully biscuity pastry into the tin, rather than rolling it out. Add the fudge-toffee filling and sliced banana topping, and it will prove irresistible.

Serves 6
115g/4oz/½ cup butter, diced
200g/7oz can skimmed, sweetened condensed milk
115g/4oz/½ cup soft brown sugar
30ml/2 tbsp golden (light corn) syrup
2 small bananas, sliced
a little lemon juice

whipped cream, to decorate
5ml/1 tsp grated plain (semisweet) chocolate

For the pastry
150g/5oz/1¼ cups plain (all-purpose) flour
115g/4oz/½ cup butter, diced
50g/2oz/¼ cup caster (superfine) sugar

1 Preheat the oven to 160°C/325°F/Gas 3. In a food processor, process the flour and diced butter until crumbed. Stir in the caster sugar and mix to form a soft, pliable dough.

2 Press into a 20cm/8in loose-based flan tin (quiche pan). Bake for 30 minutes.

3 To make the filling, place the butter in a pan with the condensed milk, brown sugar and syrup. Heat gently, stirring, until the butter has melted and the sugar has completely dissolved.

4 Bring the pan to a gentle boil and cook for 7–10 minutes, stirring constantly, until the mixture thickens and turns a light caramel colour.

5 Pour the hot caramel filling into the pastry case and leave until completely cold. Sprinkle the banana slices with lemon juice and arrange in overlapping circles on top of the filling, leaving a gap in the centre. Pipe a generous swirl of whipped cream in the centre and sprinkle with the grated chocolate.

Mango Pie

This recipe captures all the sunshine flavours of the Caribbean. For the tastiest pie, be sure the mangoes are good and ripe.

Serves 6
175g/6oz/1½ cups plain flour
pinch of salt
75g/3oz/⅓ cup unsalted (sweet) butter, chilled and diced
25g/1oz/2 tbsp white vegetable fat, chilled and diced

15ml/1 tbsp caster (superfine) sugar, plus extra for sprinkling
about 45ml/3 tbsp cold water
beaten egg, to glaze
vanilla ice cream, to serve

For the filling
2 ripe mangoes
45ml/3 tbsp fresh lime juice
115g/4oz/½ cup caster sugar
15ml/1 tbsp arrowroot mixed to a paste with 15ml/1 tbsp water

1 Sift the flour and salt into a mixing bowl. Rub in the butter and white vegetable fat until the mixture resembles fine breadcrumbs, then stir in the caster sugar. Add enough cold water to make a dough. Knead lightly, then roll out two-thirds of the pastry and line a 18cm/7in pie dish. Wrap the remaining pastry in clear film (plastic wrap) and chill both the pastry and the pastry case for 30 minutes.

2 Meanwhile, make the filling. Peel the mangoes and slice the flesh off the stone. Reserve half the sliced mango, and coarsely chop the rest. Place the chopped mango in a pan with the lime juice and caster sugar. Cover and cook for 10 minutes, or until soft. Pour in the arrowroot paste and cook, stirring all the time until thickened. Set the filling aside to cool.

3 Preheat the oven to 190°C/375°F/Gas 5. Pour the cooled mango sauce into the chilled pastry case and top with the reserved mango slices. Roll out the remaining pastry to make a pie lid. Dampen the rim of the pastry case and add the pastry lid. Crimp the edges to seal, then cut a cross in the centre to allow the steam to escape.

4 Glaze the pastry with the beaten egg and sprinkle lightly with caster sugar. Bake for 35–40 minutes until the pastry is golden brown. Cool slightly on a wire rack. Serve warm with a scoop of vanilla ice cream.

Boston Banoffee Energy 672kcal/2810 kJ; Protein 7g; Carbohydrate 80g, of which sugars 60g; Fat 39g, of which saturates 24g; Cholesterol 106mg; Calcium 176mg; Fibre 1.9g; Sodium 307mg.
Mango Pie Energy 353kcal/1494kJ; Protein 4g; Carbohydrate 55g, of which sugars 30g; Fat 70g, of which saturates 58g; Cholesterol 70mg; Calcium 58mg; Fibre 2.5g; Sodium 84mg.

Crunchy Apple & Almond Flan

Don't put sugar with the apples, as this produces too much liquid. The sweetness is in the pastry and topping.

Serves 8
75g/3oz/6 tbsp butter
175g/6oz/1½ cups plain
  (all-purpose) flour
25g/1oz/¼ cup ground almonds
25g/1oz/2 tbsp caster
  (superfine) sugar
1 egg yolk
15ml/1 tbsp cold water
1.5ml/¼ tsp almond extract

675g/1½lb cooking apples
25g/1oz/2 tbsp raisins

For the topping
115g/4oz/1 cup plain
  (all-purpose) flour
1.5ml/¼ tsp mixed
  (apple pie) spice
50g/2oz/¼ cup butter,
  cut into small cubes
50g/2oz/4¼ cup demerara
  (raw) sugar
50g/2oz/½ cup flaked
  (sliced) almonds

1 To make the pastry, rub the butter into the flour using your fingertips or a pastry cutter until it resembles breadcrumbs. Stir in the almonds and sugar.

2 Whisk the egg yolk, water and almond extract together and mix into the dry ingredients to form a soft dough. Knead until smooth, wrap, and leave to rest for 20 minutes.

3 To make the topping, sift the flour and spice into a bowl and rub in the butter. Stir in the sugar and almonds.

4 Roll out the pastry and use to line a 23cm/9in loose-based flan tin (tart pan). Trim the top and chill for 15 minutes.

5 Preheat a baking sheet in the oven at 190°C/375°F/Gas 5. Peel, core and slice the apples thinly. Arrange over the pastry in overlapping, concentric circles, doming the centre. Sprinkle with the raisins.

6 Cover with the topping mixture, pressing it on lightly. Bake on the hot baking sheet for 25–30 minutes, or until the top is golden brown and the apples are tender (test them with a fine skewer). Leave the flan to cool in the tin for 10 minutes before serving.

Pear & Hazelnut Flan

A delicious fruit flan for Sunday lunch. Grind the hazelnuts yourself if you prefer, or use ground almonds instead.

Serves 6–8
115g/4oz/1 cup plain
  (all-purpose) flour
115g/4oz/1 cup plain wholemeal
  (whole-wheat) flour
115g/4oz/½ cup sunflower
  margarine
45ml/3 tbsp cold water

For the filling
50g/2oz/½ cup self-raising
  (self-rising) flour
115g/4oz/1 cup ground hazelnuts
5ml/1 tsp vanilla extract
50g/2oz/¼ cup caster
  (superfine) sugar
50g/2oz/¼ cup butter, softened
2 eggs, beaten
400g/14oz can pears in
  natural juice
45ml/3 tbsp raspberry jam
a few chopped hazelnuts,
  to decorate

1 For the pastry, stir the flours together, then rub in the margarine using your fingertips or a pastry cutter, until the mixture resembles fine breadcrumbs. Mix to a firm dough with the water.

2 Roll out the dough and use to line a 23–25cm/9–10in flan tin (tart pan), pressing it up the sides after trimming, so that the pastry sits a little above the tin. Prick the base with a fork, line with baking parchment and fill with baking beans. Chill for 30 minutes.

3 Preheat the oven to 200°C/400°F/Gas 6. Place the flan tin on a baking sheet and bake blind for 20 minutes. Remove the paper and beans after 15 minutes.

4 To make the filling beat together the flour, hazelnuts, vanilla extract, sugar and eggs. If the mixture is too thick, stir in some of the juice from the canned pears.

5 Reduce the oven temperature to 180°C/350°F/Gas 4. Spread the jam on the pastry case and spoon over the filling.

6 Drain the pears and arrange them, cut side down, in the filling. Sprinkle over the nuts for decoration. Bake for 30 minutes, or until risen, firm and golden brown.

Crunchy Apple Energy 358kcal/1499kJ; Protein 6.2g; Carbohydrate 42.5g, of which sugars 14.6g; Fat 19.3g, of which saturates 8.8g; Cholesterol 59mg; Calcium 86mg; Fibre 3.2g; Sodium 102mg.
Pear and Hazelnut Energy 389kcal/1626kJ; Protein 7.6g; Carbohydrate 40.9g, of which sugars 16g; Fat 22.8g, of which saturates 3.5g; Cholesterol 49mg; Calcium 69mg; Fibre 3.6g; Sodium 138mg.

Poached Pear Tartlets with Chocolate Sauce

The rich chocolate sauce beautifully complements these spicy pear pastries.

Serves 6

3 firm pears, peeled
450ml/³/₄ pint/scant 2 cups water
strip of thinly pared orange rind
1 vanilla pod (bean)
1 bay leaf
50g/2oz/¼ cup granulated
   (white) sugar

350g/12oz puff pastry
40g/1½oz/⅓ cup cocoa
   powder (unsweetened)
75ml/5 tbsp double (heavy)
   cream
15g/½oz/1 tbsp butter, softened
15ml/1 tbsp soft light
   brown sugar
25g/1oz/¼ cup walnuts, chopped
1 egg, beaten
15g/½oz/1 tbsp caster
   (superfine) sugar

1 Cut the pears in half and scoop out the cores. Put the water in a pan with the orange rind, vanilla pod, bay leaf and sugar. Bring to the boil, stirring. Add the pears and water to cover. Cover and cook for about 15 minutes. Remove the pears with a slotted spoon and set aside to cool slightly. Reserve the syrup.

2 Roll out the pastry on a lightly floured work surface and cut out six pear shapes, slightly larger than the pear halves. Place the shapes on greased baking sheets and chill for 30 minutes.

3 Remove the orange rind, vanilla pod and bay leaf from the reserved syrup, then return the syrup to the heat and boil for 10 minutes. Blend the cocoa powder with 60ml/4 tbsp cold water in a separate pan. Stir a few spoonfuls of the syrup into the cocoa paste, then whisk the paste into the syrup in the pan. Cook until reduced to about 150ml/¼ pint/⅔ cup. Remove the pan from the heat and add the cream to the syrup. Stir well.

4 Preheat the oven to 200°C/400°F/Gas 6. Mix together the butter, sugar and walnuts. Pat the pears dry, then spoon a little filling into each cavity. Brush the pastry shapes with beaten egg. Put a pear half, filled side down, in the centre of each pastry shape. Sprinkle the pastries with caster sugar and bake for 12 minutes. Drizzle over some of the warm chocolate sauce and serve.

Pear Tarte Tatin with Cardamom

Cardamom is a spice that is equally at home in sweet and savoury dishes. It is delicious with pears, and brings out their flavour beautifully in this easy-to-make tart.

Serves 4–6

50g/2oz/¼ cup butter,
   softened

50g/2oz/¼ cup caster
   (superfine) sugar
seeds from 10 green
   cardamom pods
225g/8oz fresh ready-made
   puff pastry
3 ripe, large round pears
single (light) cream, to serve

1 Preheat the oven to 220°C/425°F/Gas 7. Spread the butter over the base of an 18cm/7in heavy ovenproof omelette pan. Sprinkle the butter with the sugar, then sprinkle the cardamom seeds evenly over the top.

2 On a lightly floured work surface, roll out the pastry to a circle slightly larger than the pan. Prick the pastry all over with a fork, place on a baking sheet and chill.

3 Peel the pears, cut in half lengthways and remove the cores. Arrange the pears, rounded side down, in the pan. Place over medium heat and cook until the sugar melts and begins to bubble with the juice from the pears.

4 Once the sugar has caramelized, remove the pan from the heat. Carefully place the pastry on top, tucking in the edges with a knife. Bake for 25 minutes.

5 Leave the tart in the pan for about 2 minutes until the juices have stopped bubbling.

6 Invert a serving plate over the pan then, wearing oven gloves to protect your hands, firmly hold the pan and plate together and quickly turn over, gently shaking them to release the tart. It may be necessary to slide a spatula underneath the pears to loosen them. Allow the tart to cool slightly, then serve warm, with a dollop of single cream.

Poached Pear Energy447 kcal/1867kJ; Protein 7g; Carbohydrate 45g, of which sugars 23g; Fat 29g, of which saturates 7g; Cholesterol 61mg; Calcium 70mg; Fibre 1.6g; Sodium 280mg.
Pear Tarte Energy 265Kcal/1106kJ; Protein 2.5g; Carbohydrate 30.1g, of which sugars 16.8g; Fat 16.1g, of which saturates 4.3g; Cholesterol 18mg; Calcium 36mg; Fibre 1.7g; Sodium 170mg.

Pear & Almond Cream Tart

In this sweet tart recipe, fanned pears glazed with brandy rest on a light almond filling. This dish is equally successful made with other orchard fruits, such as nectarines, peaches, apricots or apples.

lemon juice
15ml/1 tbsp peach brandy
    or cold water
60ml/4 tbsp peach jam, sieved

For the filling
90g/3¹/₂oz/generous ¹/₂ cup
    blanched whole almonds
50g/2oz/¹/₄ cup caster
    (superfine) sugar
65g/2¹/₂oz/5 tbsp butter
1 egg, plus 1 egg white
a few drops of almond extract

Serves 6
350g/12oz shortcrust or
    sweet shortcrust pastry,
    thawed if frozen
3 firm pears

1 Roll out the pastry and use to line a 23cm/9in flan tin. Chill in the refrigerator while you make the filling.

2 For the filling, put the almonds and sugar in a food processor or blender and pulse until finely ground but not pasty. Add the butter and process until creamy, then add the egg, egg white and almond extract, and mix well.

3 Preheat a baking sheet in the oven at 190°C/375°F/Gas 5.

4 Peel the pears, halve them, remove the cores and rub with lemon juice. Put the pear halves, cut side down, on a board and slice thinly crossways, keeping the slices together.

5 Pour the filling into the pastry case. Slide a metal spatula under one pear half and press the top to fan out the slices. Transfer to the tart, placing the fruit on the filling like the spokes of a wheel.

6 Bake the tart on the baking sheet for 50–55 minutes, or until the filling is set and well browned. Cool on a wire rack.

7 Heat the brandy or water with the jam. Brush over the top of the hot tart to glaze. Serve at room temperature.

Orange Tart

If you like oranges, this delicious almond-filled dessert is for you.

15ml/1 tbsp plain
    (all-purpose) flour
45ml/3 tbsp apricot jam

Serves 8
200g/7oz/1 cup caster
    (superfine) sugar
250ml/8fl oz/1 cup fresh
    orange juice, strained
2 large navel oranges
165g/5¹/₂oz/scant 1 cup whole
    blanched almonds
50g/2oz/¹/₄ cup butter
1 egg

For the pastry
210g/7¹/₂oz/scant 2 cups plain
    (all-purpose) flour
2.5ml/¹/₂ tsp salt
50g/2oz/¹/₄ cup cold
    butter, diced
40g/1¹/₂oz/3 tbsp cold
    margarine, diced
45–60ml/3–4 tbsp iced water

1 To make the pastry, sift the flour and salt into a bowl. Add the butter and margarine, and rub in using your fingertips or a pastry cutter until the mixture resembles coarse breadcrumbs. Stir in just enough water to bind the dough. Wrap and chill for 20 minutes.

2 Roll out the pastry to a 5mm/¹/₄ in thickness. Use to line a 20cm/8in tart tin. Trim and chill until needed.

3 In a pan, combine 165g/5¹/₂oz/³/₄ cup of the sugar and the orange juice and boil until thick and syrupy. Cut the unpeeled oranges into 5mm/¹/₄in slices. Add to the syrup. Simmer gently for 10 minutes. Put on a wire rack to dry. When cool, cut in half. Reserve the syrup. Place a baking sheet in the oven and heat to 200°C/400°F/Gas 6.

4 Grind the almonds finely in a blender or food processor. Cream the butter and remaining sugar until light and fluffy. Beat in the egg and 30ml/2 tbsp of the orange syrup. Stir in the almonds and flour.

5 Melt the jam over a low heat, then brush over the pastry case. Pour in the almond mixture. Bake on the baking sheet until set, about 20 minutes, then cool. Arrange overlapping orange slices on top. Boil the remaining syrup until thick and brush over the top to glaze.

Pear and Almond Energy 544kcal/2271kJ; Protein 8.4g; Carbohydrate 51.5g, of which sugars 24.4g; Fat 34.7g, of which saturates 11.7g; Cholesterol 63mg; Calcium 106mg; Fibre 3.9g; Sodium 330mg.
Orange Tart Energy 500kcal/2093kJ; Protein 8.6g; Carbohydrate 59.4g, of which sugars 37.4g; Fat 27g, of which saturates 7.7g; Cholesterol 50mg; Calcium 130mg; Fibre 3.1g; Sodium 137mg.

Fresh Lemon Tart

Serve this prettily decorated tart at room temperature to enjoy the zesty lemon flavour to the full.

Serves 6–8
350g/12oz ready-made rich sweet shortcrust pastry

For the filling
3 eggs
115g/4oz/¹⁄₂ cup caster (superfine) sugar
115g/4oz/1 cup ground almonds
105ml/7 tbsp double (heavy) cream
grated rind and juice of 2 lemons

For the topping
2 thin-skinned unwaxed lemons, thinly sliced
200g/7oz/1 cup caster (superfine) sugar
105ml/7 tbsp water

1 Roll out the pastry and line a deep 23cm/9in fluted flan tin (tart pan). Prick the base and chill for 30 minutes.

2 Preheat the oven to 200°C/400°F/Gas 6. Line the pastry with baking parchment and baking beans and bake blind for 10 minutes. Remove the paper and beans and return the pastry case to the oven for 5 minutes more.

3 Meanwhile, make the filling. Beat the eggs, caster sugar, almonds and cream in a bowl until smooth. Beat in the lemon rind and juice. Pour the filling into the pastry case. Lower the oven temperature to 190°C/375°F/Gas 5 and bake for 20 minutes or until the filling has set and the pastry is golden.

4 Make the topping. Place the lemon slices in a pan and pour over water to cover. Simmer for 15–20 minutes or until the skins are tender, then drain. Place the sugar in a pan and stir in the measured water. Heat gently until the sugar has dissolved, stirring constantly, then boil for 2 minutes. Add the lemon slices and cook for 10–15 minutes until the skins become candied.

5 Lift out the candied lemon slices and arrange them over the top of the tart. Return the syrup to the heat and boil until reduced to a thick glaze. Brush this over the tart and allow to cool completely before serving.

Lemon Tart

This tart, a classic of France, has a wonderfully smooth lemon filling with a refreshing tangy flavour.

Serves 8 – 10
350g/12oz shortcrust or sweet shortcrust pastry, thawed if frozen
grated rind of 2 or 3 lemons
150ml/¹⁄₄ pint/²⁄₃ cup freshly squeezed lemon juice
90g/3¹⁄₂oz/¹⁄₂ cup caster (superfine) sugar
60ml/4 tbsp crème fraîche or double (heavy) cream
4 eggs, plus 3 egg yolks
icing (confectioners') sugar, for dusting

1 Preheat a baking sheet in the oven to 190°C/375°F/Gas 5.

2 Roll out the pastry and use to line a 23cm/9in flan tin (tart pan). Prick the base with a fork, line with foil and fill with baking beans.

3 Bake for 15 minutes, or until the edges are dry. Remove the foil and beans, and bake for a further 5–7 minutes, or until golden.

4 Beat together the lemon rind, juice and caster sugar, then gradually add the crème fraîche or double cream, beating after each addition until well blended.

5 Beat in the eggs, one at a time, then beat in the egg yolks.

6 Pour the filling into the baked pastry case. Return it to the oven and bake for about 15–20 minutes, or until the filling is set. If the pastry begins to brown too much, cover the edges with foil.

7 Leave the tart to cool, and dust lightly with icing sugar before serving.

Variation
This citrus tart would also taste great when made with oranges.

Lemon Tart Energy 268kcal/1122kJ; Protein 5.6g; Carbohydrate 27g, of which sugars 10.9g; Fat 16.1g, of which saturates 5.8g; Cholesterol 148mg; Calcium 57mg; Fibre 0.7g; Sodium 173mg.
Fresh Lemon Energy 528Kcal/2212kJ; Protein 7.8g; Carbohydrate 61.7g, of which sugars 42.3g; Fat 29.6g, of which saturates 5.6g; Cholesterol 89mg; Calcium 91mg; Fibre 1.9g; Sodium 104mg.

Chocolate Lemon Tart

The unusual chocolate pastry is simple to make and complements the tangy lemon filling superbly in this rich tart, generously topped with a tempting decoration of chocolate curls.

Serves 8–10
245g/8³/₄oz/1¹/₄ cups caster (superfine) sugar
6 eggs
grated rind of 2 lemons
160ml/5¹/₂fl oz/generous ²/₃ cup fresh lemon juice
160ml/5¹/₂fl oz/generous ²/₃ cup whipping cream
chocolate curls, to decorate

For the pastry
180g/6¹/₄oz/generous 1¹/₂ cups plain (all-purpose) flour
30ml/2 tbsp unsweetened cocoa powder
25g/1oz/¹/₄ cup icing (confectioners') sugar
2.5ml/¹/₂ tsp salt
115g/4oz/¹/₂ cup cold butter, diced
15ml/1 tbsp water

1 Grease a 25cm/10in flan tin (tart pan). To make the pastry, sift the flour, cocoa powder, icing sugar and salt into a bowl. Set aside.

2 Melt the butter or margarine and water in a large pan over a low heat.

3 Pour over the flour mixture and stir until the dough is smooth.

4 Press the dough evenly over the base and sides of the flan tin. Chill while preparing the filling.

5 Place a baking sheet on the top shelf of the oven and preheat to 190°C/375°F/Gas 5.

6 Whisk the sugar and eggs until the sugar is dissolved. Add the lemon rind and juice, and mix well. Add the cream.

7 Pour the filling into the pastry case and bake on the hot baking sheet until the filling is set, about 20–25 minutes.

8 Leave the tart on a wire rack to cool completely, then decorate with chocolate curls.

Lemon & Lime Cheesecake

This tangy cheesecake is truly a citrus sensation.

Makes 8 slices
150g/5oz/1¹/₂ cups digestive biscuits (graham crackers)
40g/1¹/₂oz/3 tbsp butter

For the topping
grated rind and juice of 2 lemons
10ml/2 tsp powdered gelatine
250g/9oz/generous 1 cup ricotta cheese
75g/3oz/6 tbsp caster (superfine) sugar
150ml/¹/₄ pint/²/₃ cup double (heavy) cream
2 eggs, separated

For the lime syrup
pared rind and juice of 3 limes
75g/3oz/6 tbsp caster (superfine) sugar
5ml/1 tsp arrowroot mixed with 30ml/2 tbsp water
green food colouring (optional)

1 Lightly grease a 20cm/8in round springform cake tin (pan). Place the biscuits in a food processor or blender and process until they form fine crumbs. Melt the butter in a large pan, then stir in the crumbs until well coated. Spoon into the prepared cake tin, press the crumbs down well in an even layer, then chill.

2 Make the topping. Place the lemon rind and juice in a small pan and sprinkle over the gelatine. Leave for 5 minutes. Heat gently until the gelatine has dissolved, then set aside to cool slightly. Beat the ricotta cheese and sugar in a bowl. Stir in the cream and egg yolks, then whisk in the cooled gelatine mixture.

3 Whisk the egg whites in a grease-free bowl until they form soft peaks. Fold them into the cheese mixture. Spoon on to the biscuit base, level the surface and chill for 2–3 hours.

4 Meanwhile, make the lime syrup. Place the lime rind and juice and sugar in a small pan. Bring to the boil, stirring, then boil the syrup for 5 minutes. Stir in the arrowroot mixture and continue to stir until the syrup boils again and thickens slightly. Tint pale green with a little food colouring, if you like. Cool, then chill.

5 Spoon the lime syrup over the set cheesecake. Remove from the tin and cut into slices to serve.

Chocolate Lemon Energy 379kcal/1585kJ; Protein 6.1g; Carbohydrate 40.5g, of which sugars 27g; Fat 22.6g, of which saturates 12.9g; Cholesterol 163mg; Calcium 68mg; Fibre 0.7g; Sodium 127mg.
Lemon and Lime Energy 366Kcal/1526kJ; Protein 6g; Carbohydrate 33.8g, of which sugars 23.5g; Fat 23.9g, of which saturates 13.8g; Cholesterol 105mg; Calcium 44mg; Fibre 0.4g; Sodium 166mg.

Yellow Plum Tart

This lovely tart consists of glazed yellow plums arranged on top of a delectable almond filling.

Serves 8
175g/6oz/1½ cups plain
   (all-purpose) flour
pinch of salt
75g/3oz/6 tbsp butter, chilled
30ml/2 tbsp caster (superfine)
   sugar
a few drops of pure
   vanilla extract
45ml/3 tbsp iced water
45ml/3 tbsp apricot jam, sieved
cream or custard, to serve

For the filling
75g/3oz/6 tbsp caster (superfine)
   sugar
75g/3oz/6 tbsp butter, softened
75g/3oz/¾ cup ground almonds
1 egg, beaten
30ml/2 tbsp plain (all-purpose)
   flour
450g/1lb yellow plums or
   greengages, halved and stoned

1 Sift the flour and salt into a bowl, then rub in the butter until the mixture resembles fine breadcrumbs. Stir in the sugar, vanilla extract and enough of the iced water to form a soft dough.

2 Knead the dough gently on a lightly floured surface until smooth. Wrap in clear film (plastic wrap); chill for 10 minutes.

3 Preheat the oven to 200°C/400°F/Gas 6. Roll out the pastry and line a 23cm/9in fluted flan tin (tart pan), allowing any excess pastry to overhang the top. Prick the base with a fork and line with non-stick baking parchment and baking beans.

4 Bake blind for 10 minutes, remove the paper and beans, then return the pastry case to the oven for 10 minutes. Remove and allow to cool. Trim off any excess pastry with a sharp knife.

5 To make the filling, beat together all the ingredients except the plums. Spread on the base of the pastry case. Arrange the plums on top, cut-side down. To make a glaze, heat the jam with 15ml/1 tbsp water, then brush a little over the fruit.

6 Bake the plum tart for about 50 minutes, until the almond filling is cooked and the plums are tender. Warm any remaining jam glaze and brush over the top. Serve with cream or custard.

Alsatian Plum Tart

Fruit and custard tarts, similar to a fruit flan, are typical in Alsace, in the east of France. Sometimes they have a yeast dough base instead of pastry. You can use other seasonal fruits in this tart, or a mixture of fruit, if you like.

Serves 6–8
450g/1lb ripe plums, halved
   and stoned (pitted)
30ml/2 tbsp Kirsch or
   plum brandy
350g/12oz shortcrust or
   sweet shortcrust pastry,
   thawed if frozen
30ml/2 tbsp seedless
   raspberry jam

For the custard filling
2 eggs
25g/1oz/4 tbsp icing
   (confectioners') sugar
175ml/6fl oz/¾ cup double
   (heavy) cream
grated rind of ½ lemon
1.5ml/¼ tsp vanilla extract

1 Preheat the oven to 200°C/400°F/Gas 6. Mix the plums with the Kirsch or brandy and set aside for about 30 minutes.

2 Roll out the pastry thinly and use to line a 23cm/9in flan tin (tart pan). Prick the base of the pastry case all over with a fork, and line with foil. Add a layer of baking beans and bake for 15 minutes, or until slightly dry and set. Remove the foil and the baking beans.

3 Brush the base of the pastry case with a thin layer of jam, then bake for a further 5 minutes.

4 Remove the pastry case from the oven and transfer to a wire rack. Reduce the oven temperature to 180°C/350°F/Gas 4.

5 To make the custard filling, beat the eggs and sugar until well combined, then beat in the cream, lemon rind, vanilla extract and any juice from the plums.

6 Arrange the plums, cut side down, in the pastry case and pour over the custard mixture. Bake for about 30–35 minutes, or until a knife inserted into the centre comes out clean. Serve the tart warm or at room temperature.

Yellow Plum Energy 361kcal/1510kJ; Protein 6g; Carbohydrate 38g, of which sugars 18g; Fat 22g, of which saturates 10g; Cholesterol 69mg; Calcium 72mg; Fibre 2.1g; Sodium 177mg.
Alsatian Plum Energy 375kcal/1563kJ; Protein 4.8g; Carbohydrate 31.7g, of which sugars 11.6g; Fat 25.5g, of which saturates 11.5g; Cholesterol 84mg; Calcium 65mg; Fibre 1.7g; Sodium 200mg.

De Luxe Mincemeat Tart

Fruity home-made mincemeat is the perfect partner to crumbly, nutty pastry in this very special rich and festive pie.

Serves 8
225g/8oz/2 cups plain (all-purpose) flour
10ml/2 tsp ground cinnamon
50g/2oz/½ cup finely ground walnuts
115g/4oz/½ cup butter
50g/2oz/¼ cup caster (superfine) sugar, plus extra for dusting
1 egg
2 drops vanilla extract
15ml/1 tbsp cold water

For the mincemeat
2 eating apples, peeled, cored and grated
225g/8oz/generous 1½ cups raisins
115g/4oz/½ cup ready-to-eat dried apricots, chopped
115g/4oz/⅔ cup ready-to-eat dried figs or prunes, chopped
225g/8oz/2 cups green grapes, halved and seeded
50g/2oz/½ cup chopped almonds
finely grated rind of 1 lemon
30ml/2 tbsp lemon juice
30ml/2 tbsp brandy or port
1.5ml/¼ tsp mixed (apple pie) spice
115g/4oz/½ cup soft light brown sugar
25g/1oz/2 tbsp butter, melted

1 Process the flour, cinnamon, nuts and butter in a food processor or blender to make fine crumbs. Turn into a bowl and stir in the sugar. Beat the egg with the vanilla extract and water, and stir into the dry ingredients. Form a soft dough, knead until smooth, then wrap and chill for 30 minutes.

2 Mix the mincemeat ingredients together. Use two-thirds of the pastry to line a 23cm/9in, loose-based flan tin (tart pan). Trim and fill with the mincemeat.

3 Roll out the remaining pastry and cut into 1cm/½in strips. Arrange the strips in a lattice over the top of the pastry, wet the joins and press them together. Chill for 30 minutes.

4 Preheat a baking sheet in the oven at 190°C/375°F/Gas 5. Brush the pastry with water and dust with caster sugar. Bake the tart on the baking sheet for 30–40 minutes. Cool in the tin on a wire rack for 15 minutes, then remove the tin.

Mince Tarts

Taste the difference in these luxurious pies filled with home-made mincemeat.

Makes 36
425g/15oz/3¾ cups plain (all-purpose) flour
150g/5oz/1¼ cups icing (confectioners') sugar
350g/12oz/1½ cups butter, chilled and diced
grated rind and juice of 1 orange
milk, for glazing

For the filling
175g/6oz/1½ cups finely chopped blanched almonds
150g/5oz/⅔ cup ready-to-eat dried apricots, chopped

175g/6oz/generous 1 cup raisins
150g/5oz/⅔ cup currants
150g/5oz/scant 1 cup glacé (candied) cherries, chopped
150g/5oz/scant 1 cup cut mixed (candied) peel, chopped
115g/4oz/⅔ cup chopped suet
grated rind and juice of 2 lemons
grated rind and juice of 1 orange
200g/7oz/scant 1 cup soft dark brown sugar
4 cooking apples, peeled, cored and chopped
10ml/2 tsp ground allspice
250ml/8fl oz/1 cup brandy
225g/8oz/1 cup cream cheese
30ml/2 tbsp caster (superfine) sugar
icing (confectioners') sugar, for dusting

1 Mix the first 13 filling ingredients together. Cover and leave in a cool place for 2 days.

2 For the pastry, sift the flour and icing sugar into a bowl. Rub in the butter. Stir in the orange rind and enough juice to bind. Chill for 20 minutes.

3 Preheat the oven to 220°C/425°F/Gas 7. Lightly grease two or three bun trays (muffin pans).

4 Roll out the dough, stamp out 36 8cm/3in rounds and put into the trays. Half fill with mincemeat. Beat the cream cheese and sugar and add a teaspoonful to each pie. Roll out the trimmings and stamp out 36 5cm/2in rounds. Brush the edges with milk and cover the pies. Cut a slit in each.

5 Brush lightly with milk. Bake for 15–20 minutes, then leave to cool. Dust with icing sugar.

De Luxe Energy 434kcal/1822kJ; Protein 4.8g; Carbohydrate 63.6g, of which sugars 42.1g; Fat 19.6g, of which saturates 8.1g; Cholesterol 57mg; Calcium 74mg; Fibre 1.8g; Sodium 108mg.
Mince Tarts Energy Energy 301kcal/1258kJ; Protein 2.9g; Carbohydrate 33g, of which sugars 23.5g; Fat 16.8g, of which saturates 8.8g; Cholesterol 29mg; Calcium 58mg; Fibre 1.6g; Sodium 96mg.

Prune Tart with Custard Filling

A great combination of prunes, brandy and custard.

Serves 6–8

225g/8oz/1 cup pitted prunes
50ml/2fl oz/¼ cup brandy
300ml/½ pint/1¼ cups milk
a few drops of vanilla essence
    (extract)
4 egg yolks
45ml/3 tbsp caster (superfine) sugar
30ml/2 tbsp cornflour (cornstarch)
25g/1oz/¼ cup flaked
    (sliced) almonds

icing (confectioners') sugar,
    for dusting
thick cream, to serve

For the pastry

175g/6oz/1½ cups plain
    (all-purpose) flour
pinch of salt
50g/2oz/¼ cup caster
    (superfine) sugar
90g/3½oz/scant ½ cup butter,
    diced
1 egg

1 Place the prunes in a bowl and add the brandy. Set aside in a warm place to soak. Preheat the oven to 200°C/400°F/Gas 6. Place the flour, salt, sugar and diced butter in a food processor. Set aside 5ml/1 tsp of the egg white and add the remaining egg to the food processor. Process until the mixture forms a soft dough. Shape into a ball and leave to rest for 10 minutes. Lightly flour a 28 × 18cm/11 × 7in loose-based tin. Roll out the pastry and use to line the tin. Chill for 30 minutes.

2 Line the pastry case with foil and fill with baking beans, then bake for about 15 minutes. Remove the foil and beans, and bake for 10–15 minutes more. Brush the base of the pastry with the reserved egg white while the pastry is still hot. Set aside to cool.

3 Pour the milk into a pan and add the vanilla. Bring to the boil. In a bowl, whisk the egg yolks and sugar until thick, then whisk in the cornflour. Strain in the milk and whisk. Return to the cleaned pan and bring back to the boil, whisking to remove lumps. Cook for 2 minutes until smooth, then set aside. Press baking parchment on the surface to prevent a skin from forming. Stir any prune liquid into the custard, then spread the custard over the pastry case. Arrange the prunes randomly on top, sprinkle with the almonds and dust with icing sugar. Bake for 10 minutes more. Serve hot or warm with cream.

Date & Almond Tart

Fresh dates are delicious in a tart when teamed with a sponge filling.

Serves 6

90g/3½oz/scant ½ cup butter
90g/3½oz/scant ½ cup caster
    (superfine) sugar
1 egg, beaten
90g/3½oz/scant 1 cup
    ground almonds
30ml/2 tbsp plain (all-purpose)
    flour

30ml/2 tbsp orange flower water
12–13 fresh dates, halved and
    stoned (pitted)
60ml/4 tbsp apricot jam

For the pastry

175g/6oz/1½ cups plain
    (all-purpose) flour
75g/3oz/6 tbsp butter, diced
1 egg
15ml/1 tbsp chilled water

1 Preheat the oven to 200°C/400°F/Gas 6 and place a baking sheet in it. To make the pastry, sift the flour into a bowl, then rub or cut in the butter until the mixture resembles fine breadcrumbs. Add the egg and water, then work to a dough. Wrap in clear film (plastic wrap) and chill for 20 minutes.

2 Roll out the pastry on a lightly floured surface and use to line a 20cm/8in flan tin (quiche pan). Prick the base with a fork, then chill until required.

3 Cream the butter and sugar in a small mixing bowl with a wooden spoon until light, then beat in the egg. Stir in the ground almonds, flour and 15ml/1 tbsp of the orange flower water and mix thoroughly.

4 Spread the almond filling evenly over the base of the pastry case. Arrange the dates, cut side down, on the mixture. Bake the tart on the hot baking sheet for 10–15 minutes, then lower the oven temperature to 180°C/350°F/Gas 4. Bake for 15 minutes more, or until pale golden and set.

5 Transfer the tart to a wire rack to cool. In a small pan, gently heat the apricot jam, then press through a sieve (strainer) into a bowl. Stir in the remaining orange flower water. Lightly brush the apricot glaze over the tart and serve at room temperature.

Prune Tart Energy 329kcal1380 kJ; Protein 7g; Carbohydrate 38g, of which sugars 18g; Fat 16g, of which saturates 8g; Cholesterol 148mg; Calcium 110mg; Fibre 4.8g; Sodium 155mg.
Date and Almond Energy 618kcal/2587kJ; Protein 10g; Carbohydrate 73g, of which sugars 47g; Fat 34g, of which saturates 16g; Cholesterol 136mg; Calcium 117mg; Fibre 5.6g; Sodium 208mg.

Raspberry & Crème Brûlée Tart

Fresh raspberries and a crunchy caramel topping contrast with the thick vanilla-scented custard filling in this lovely summery tart.

Serves 8
1 vanilla pod (bean)
450ml/¾ pint/scant 2 cups
   double (heavy) cream
1 whole egg, plus 3 egg yolks
30ml/2 tbsp caster (superfine) sugar
150g/5oz/scant 1 cup
   fresh raspberries
5 tbsp icing (confectioners') sugar

For the pastry
150g/5oz/1¼ cups plain
   (all-purpose) flour
pinch of salt
25g/1oz/¼ cup icing
   (confectioners') sugar
75g/3oz/6 tbsp butter, diced
2 egg yolks
finely grated rind of 1 orange
15ml/1 tbsp egg white,
   lightly beaten

1 To make the pastry, sift the flour, salt and icing sugar into a mixing bowl. Rub or cut in the butter until the mixture resembles fine breadcrumbs.

2 Mix the egg yolks and orange rind together, add to the dry ingredients and mix to a soft dough. Knead on a lightly floured work surface for a few seconds, until smooth. Wrap in clear film (plastic wrap) and chill for 30 minutes.

3 Roll out the pastry and use to line a fluted 23cm/9in flan tin (quiche pan). Cover and chill for a further 30 minutes. While the pastry case is chilling, put a baking sheet in the oven and preheat to 200°C/400°F/Gas 6.

4 Prick the base of the pastry all over with a fork and line with foil and baking beans. Place on the hot baking sheet and bake blind for 10 minutes. Remove the foil and beans and bake the pastry for 5 minutes more.

5 Lightly brush the base and sides of the pastry case with egg white, then return to the oven for 3–4 minutes. Lower the oven temperature to 160°C/325°F/Gas 3.

6 Halve the vanilla pod lengthways. Place in a small pan with the cream. Slowly bring to the boil, then remove the vanilla pod. In a mixing bowl or pouring jug (pitcher), whisk the egg and egg yolks with the sugar until pale. Slowly whisk in the hot cream.

7 Sprinkle the raspberries over the base of the pastry case, arranging them so that they are fairly evenly distributed. Pour over the custard, then bake the tart for 17–20 minutes, or until very lightly set. Place on a wire rack to cool. Chill for at least 4 hours, or overnight.

8 To add the crunchy caramel topping, first protect the edges of the pastry case with pieces of foil. Dredge a thin layer of icing sugar over the custard, right to the edge of the pastry case. Place under a hot grill (broiler) for 1 minute, or until the sugar melts and turns a dark golden colour. Take care not to over-grill, or the custard will separate. Chill for about 10 minutes, to allow the caramel to harden slightly, then serve the finished tart in slices.

Strawberry Tart

This tart is best assembled just before serving, but you can bake the pastry case and make the filling ahead.

Serves 6
350g/12oz rough-puff or
   puff pastry, thawed if frozen
225g/8oz/1 cup cream cheese
grated rind of ½ orange
30ml/2 tbsp orange liqueur
   or orange juice
45–60ml/3–4 tbsp icing
   (confectioners') sugar,
   plus extra for dusting (optional)
450g/1lb/4 cups ripe
   strawberries, hulled

1 Preheat the oven to 200°C/400°F/Gas 6. Roll out the pastry to about a 3mm/⅛in thickness and use to line a 28 × 10cm/ 11 × 4in rectangular flan tin (tart pan). Trim the edges, then chill for 30 minutes.

2 Prick the base of the pastry all over with a fork. Line with foil, fill with baking beans and bake for 15 minutes. Remove the foil and beans and bake for a further 10 minutes, or until the pastry is browned. Gently press down on the pastry base to deflate, then leave to cool on a wire rack.

3 Beat together the cheese, orange rind, liqueur or orange juice and icing sugar to taste. Spread the cheese filling in the pastry case. Halve the strawberries and arrange them on top of the filling. Dust with icing sugar, if you like.

Rough-puff Pastry
Cut 175g/6oz/¾ cup butter into small pieces. Sift 8oz/225g/ 2 cups plain (all-purpose) flour into a bowl and add the butter, 5ml/1 tsp salt, 5ml/1 tsp lemon juice and 150ml/¼ pint/ ⅔ cup iced water. Mix together with a knife. Turn on to a work surface and gather it together. Roll into a rectangle. Fold up the bottom third to the centre, fold the top third to meet it and then turn the pasty a quarter turn. Repeat the rolling and folding. Wrap and chill for 20 minutes (or put into the freezer for 5 minutes). Roll, fold and chill twice more.

Strawberry Tart Energy 434kcal/1805kJ; Protein 5.2g; Carbohydrate 34.4g, of which sugars 13.5g; Fat 32.2g, of which saturates 11.1g; Cholesterol 36mg; Calcium 87mg; Fibre 0.8g; Sodium 299mg.
Raspberry Energy 469kcal/1646kJ; Protein 5g; Carbohydrate 24g, of which sugars 9g; Fat 40g, of which saturates 24g; Cholesterol 171mg; Calcium 70mg; Fibre 1.9g; Sodium 134mg.

Tofu Berry 'Cheesecake'

Strictly speaking, this summery 'cheesecake' is not a cheesecake at all, as it is based on tofu – but who would ever guess?

Serves 6

50g/2oz/¼ cup margarine
30ml/2 tbsp apple juice
115g/4oz/5¾ cups bran flakes

For the filling

275g/10oz/1½ cups silken tofu
  or low-fat soft cheese
200g/7oz/scant 1 cup natural
  (plain) yogurt

15ml/1 tbsp/1 sachet
  powdered gelatine
60ml/4 tbsp apple juice

For the topping

175g/6oz/1½ cups mixed
  summer soft fruits, such as
  strawberries, raspberries,
  redcurrants and blackberries
30ml/2 tbsp redcurrant jelly
30ml/2 tbsp hot water

1 Place the margarine and apple juice in a pan and heat gently until melted. Crush the cereal and stir it into the pan. Spoon into a 23cm/9in round flan tin (tart pan) and press down firmly. Leave to set.

2 For the filling, place the tofu or low-fat soft cheese and yogurt in a food processor or blender and process until smooth. Dissolve the gelatine in the apple juice and stir into the tofu mixture.

3 Spread the tofu mixture over the chilled base, smoothing it evenly. Chill until set.

4 Remove the flan tin and place the 'cheesecake' on a serving plate. Arrange the soft fruits over the top. Melt the redcurrant jelly with the hot water. Leave it to cool, and then spoon it over the fruit to serve.

> **Cook's Tip**
> *For a vegetarian version of this recipe, use vegetarian gelatine.*

Tia Maria Berry Tarts

The ideal dessert for a tea or coffee break, these mini coffee pastry cases are filled with a chocolate liqueur truffle centre and topped with fresh ripe berries.

Serves 6

300ml/½ pint/1¼ cups
  double cream
225g/8oz/generous ¾ cup seedless
  bramble or raspberry jam
150g/5oz plain chocolate,
  broken into squares

45ml/3 tbsp Tia Maria liqueur
450g/1lb mixed berries, such as
  raspberries, small strawberries
  or blackberries

For the pastry

225g/8oz/2 cups plain flour
15ml/1 tbsp caster (superfine)
  sugar
150g/5oz/10 tbsp butter,
  cubed
1 egg yolk
30ml/2 tbsp very strong
  brewed coffee, chilled

1 Preheat the oven to 200°C/400°F/Gas 6. Put a baking sheet in the oven to heat. To make the pastry, sift the flour and sugar into a large bowl. Rub in the butter. Stir the egg yolk and coffee together, add to the bowl and mix to a stiff dough. Knead lightly on a floured surface for a few seconds until smooth. Wrap in clear film (plastic wrap) and chill for about 20 minutes.

2 Use the pastry to line six 10cm/4in fluted tartlet tins. Prick the bases with a fork and line with baking parchment and baking beans. Put on the hot baking sheet and bake for 10 minutes. Remove paper and beans and bake for 8–10 minutes longer, until cooked. Cool on a wire rack.

3 To make the filling, slowly bring the cream and 175g/6oz/ generous ½ cup of the jam to the boil, stirring continuously until dissolved.

4 Remove from the heat, add the chocolate and 30ml/2 tbsp of the liqueur. Stir until melted. Cool, then spoon into the pastry cases, and smooth the tops. Chill for 40 minutes.

5 Heat the remaining jam and liqueur until smooth. Arrange the fruit on top of the tarts, then brush the jam glaze over it. Chill until ready to serve.

Tofu Berry Energy 204kcal/854kJ; Protein 7.7g; Carbohydrate 23.2g, of which sugars 13.8g; Fat 9.5g, of which saturates 0.5g; Cholesterol 0mg; Calcium 311mg; Fibre 2.8g; Sodium 253mg.
Tia Maria Energy 846kcal/357kJ; Protein 7g; Carbohydrate 81g, of which sugars 52g; Fat 56g, of which saturates 34g; Cholesterol 157mg; Calcium 119mg; Fibre 5.5g; Sodium 180mg.

Baked Cheesecake with Fresh Fruits

Vary the fruit decoration to suit the season for this rich, creamy dessert.

Serves 12
175g/6oz/2 cups crushed
  digestive cookies (graham
  crackers)
50g/2oz/¼ cup unsalted (sweet)
  butter, melted
450g/1lb/2 cups curd
  (farmer's) cheese
150ml/¼ pint/⅔ cup sour cream

115g/4oz/generous ½ cup caster
  (superfine) sugar
3 eggs, separated
grated rind of 1 lemon
30ml/2 tbsp Marsala
2.5ml/½ tsp almond extract
50g/2oz/½ cup ground almonds
50g/2oz/⅓ cup sultanas
  (golden raisins)
450g/1lb prepared mixed
  fruits, such as figs, cherries,
  peaches and strawberries,
  to decorate

1 Preheat the oven to 180°C/350°F/Gas 4. Grease and line the sides of a 25cm/10in round springform tin (pan) with baking parchment. Combine the cookies and butter, and press into the base of the tin. Chill for 20 minutes.

2 For the cake mixture, beat together the cheese, cream, sugar, egg yolks, lemon rind, Marsala and almond extract until smooth and creamy.

3 Whisk the egg whites until stiff and fold into the cheese mixture with the almonds and sultanas until evenly combined. Pour over the cookie base and bake for 45 minutes, until risen and just set in the centre.

4 Leave in the tin until completely cold. Carefully remove the tin and peel away the lining paper.

5 Chill the cheesecake for at least 1 hour before decorating with the prepared fruits, just before serving.

Cook's Tip
Do not add the fruit topping in advance, or it will make the cake soggy.

Red Berry Sponge Tart

When soft berry fruits are in season, serve this delicious tart warm, with scoops of vanilla ice cream.

Serves 4
450g/1lb/4 cups soft berry
  fruits, such as raspberries,
  blackberries, blackcurrants,
  redcurrants, strawberries
  and blueberries
2 eggs

50g/2oz/¼ cup caster
  (superfine) sugar, plus extra
  to taste (optional)
15ml/1 tbsp plain
  (all-purpose) flour
75g/3oz/¾ cup ground almonds
vanilla ice cream, to serve

1 Preheat the oven to 190°C/375°F/Gas 5. Grease and line a 23cm/9in pie plate with baking parchment.

2 Sprinkle the fruit in the base of the plate with a little sugar if the fruits are tart.

3 Beat the eggs and sugar together for 3–4 minutes, or until they leave a thick trail across the surface.

4 Combine the flour and almonds in a bowl, then carefully fold into the egg mixture with a metal spatula, retaining as much air as possible.

5 Spread the sponge mixture evenly on top of the fruit base, bake in the preheated oven for 15 minutes, then turn out on to a serving plate and serve warm.

Variation
For a more substantial tart, line the pie plate, or use a flan tin (tart pan), with 350g/12oz shortcrust pastry. Line the pastry with baking parchment and fill with baking beans. Bake the crust for 15 minutes and then remove the paper and beans, and bake for 10 minutes more. Add the fruit as step 1 and continue with the recipe.

Baked Cheesecake Energy 296kcal/1238kJ; Protein 7.6g; Carbohydrate 27.1g, of which sugars 19g; Fat 18g, of which saturates 9g; Cholesterol 83mg; Calcium 56mg; Fibre 1.1g; Sodium 139mg.
Red Berry Energy 195kcal/816kJ; Protein 6.7g; Carbohydrate 19.2g, of which sugars 16.5g; Fat 10.7g, of which saturates 1.3g; Cholesterol 76mg; Calcium 71mg; Fibre 2.2g; Sodium 36mg.

Bakewell Tart

Although the pastry base makes this a tart, in the English village of Bakewell where it originated, it is traditionally called Bakewell Pudding.

Serves 4
225g/8oz puff pastry
30ml/2 tbsp raspberry or
    apricot jam
2 eggs, plus 2 egg yolks
115g/4oz/generous ½ cup caster
    (superfine) sugar
115g/4oz/½ cup butter, melted
50g/2oz/⅔ cup ground almonds
a few drops of almond extract
icing (confectioners') sugar,
    for dusting

1 Preheat the oven to 200°C/400°F/Gas 6. Roll out the pastry on a lightly floured surface and use to line an 18cm/7in pie plate. Trim the edge.

2 Re-roll the pastry trimmings and cut out wide strips of pastry. Use these to decorate the edge of the pastry case by gently twisting them around the rim, joining the strips together as necessary. Prick the pastry case all over, then spread the jam over the base.

3 Whisk the eggs, egg yolks and sugar together in a bowl until the mixture is thick and pale.

4 Gently stir the melted butter, ground almonds and almond extract into the whisked egg mixture.

5 Pour the mixture into the pastry case and bake for 30 minutes, or until the filling is just set and is lightly browned. Dust with icing sugar before serving hot, warm or cold.

> **Cook's Tip**
> Since this pastry case is not baked blind before being filled, put a baking sheet in the oven while it preheats, then place the tart on the hot sheet. This will ensure that the base of the pastry case cooks right through.

Red Berry Tart with Lemon Cream

This jewel-like flan filled with summer fruits is best filled just before serving, so that the pastry remains mouth-wateringly crisp.

Serves 6–8
200g/7oz/scant 1 cup cream
    cheese, softened
45ml/3 tbsp lemon curd
grated rind and juice of
    1 lemon
icing (confectioners') sugar,
    to taste (optional)
225g/8oz/2 cups mixed
    red berry fruits
45ml/3 tbsp redcurrant jelly

For the pastry
150g/5oz/1¼ cups plain
    (all-purpose) flour
25g/1oz/¼ cup cornflour
    (cornstarch)
30g/1½oz/scant ⅓ cup icing
    (confectioners') sugar
90g/3½oz/7 tbsp cold
    butter, diced
5ml/1 tsp vanilla extract
2 egg yolks, beaten

1 To make the pastry, sift the flour, cornflour and sugar together. Rub in the butter until the mixture resembles breadcrumbs.

2 Beat the vanilla extract into the egg yolks, then stir into the flour mixture to make a firm dough. Add cold water if the dough is too dry.

3 Roll out the pastry and use it to line a 23cm/9in round flan tin (tart pan). Trim the edges. Prick the base with a fork and leave to rest in the refrigerator for 30 minutes.

4 Preheat the oven to 200°C/400°F/Gas 6. Line the flan with baking parchment and fill with baking beans. Place on a baking sheet and bake for 20 minutes, removing the paper and beans after 15 minutes. Leave to cool, then remove the pastry case from the flan tin.

5 Cream the cheese, lemon curd, and lemon rind and juice, adding icing sugar if you wish. Spread the mixture into the base of the flan. Top with the mixed red berry fruits. Warm the redcurrant jelly and trickle over the fruits just before serving.

Bakewell Tart Energy 700Kcal/2919kJ; Protein 10.8g; Carbohydrate 57.1g, of which sugars 36.7g; Fat 49.9g, of which saturates 17.1g; Cholesterol 257mg; Calcium 110mg; Fibre 0.9g; Sodium 394mg.
Red Berry Energy 253kcal/1059kJ; Protein 3.6g; Carbohydrate 30.5g, of which sugars 12g; Fat 13.8g, of which saturates 7.9g; Cholesterol 75mg; Calcium 65mg; Fibre 0.9g; Sodium 87mg.

Summer Berry Tart

A classic vanilla-flavoured custard tart topped with luscious berry fruits and rich raspberry liqueur.

Serves 6–8

3 egg yolks
50g/2oz/¼ cup caster
   (superfine) sugar
30ml/2 tbsp cornflour (cornstarch)
30ml/2 tbsp plain (all-purpose) flour
5ml/1 tsp vanilla essence (extract)
300ml/½ pint/1¼ cups milk
150ml/¼ pint/⅔ cup double
   (heavy) cream

800g/1¾lb/4½–5 cups mixed
   summer berries, such as
   raspberries, blueberries,
   loganberries or boysenberries
60ml/4 tbsp redcurrant jelly
30ml/2 tbsp raspberry liqueur

For the pastry

185g/6½oz/1⅔ cups plain
   (all-purpose) flour
pinch of salt
115g/4oz/½ cup butter, diced
1 egg yolk
30ml/2 tbsp chilled water

1 Sift the flour and salt into a bowl. Rub in the butter. Mix the egg yolk with the chilled water and sprinkle over the dry ingredients. Mix to a firm dough. Put the dough on to a lightly floured surface and knead for a few seconds. Wrap in clear film (plastic wrap) and chill for 30 minutes. Roll out the pastry and use to line a 25cm/10in petal-shaped flan tin (quiche pan) or a 23cm/9in round pan. Wrap in clear film and chill.

2 Put a baking sheet in the oven and preheat to 200°C/400°F/Gas 6. Prick the base of the pastry, line with foil and baking beans and bake for 15 minutes. Remove the foil and beans and bake for 10 minutes more. Leave to cool.

3 Beat the egg yolks, sugar, cornflour, flour and vanilla together. Bring the milk to the boil in a pan. Pour on to the egg mixture, and whisk. Pour the custard into the cleaned pan and cook over a low heat, stirring. Return to a clean bowl, cover with clear film and set aside. Whip the cream until thick, then fold into the custard. Spoon the custard into the pastry case and spread out evenly.

4 Arrange the fruit on top of the custard. Heat the redcurrant jelly and liqueur together until melted. Allow to cool, then brush over the fruit. Serve the tart within 3 hours of assembling.

Wild Berry Tart

Make this simple tart in the summer when wild berries, such as blackberries and redcurrants, are abundant.

Serves 6–8

500g/1¼lb fresh or frozen
   mixed wild berries
200g/7oz/1 cup caster
   (superfine) sugar
whipped double (heavy) cream,
   to serve

For the pastry

300g/10oz/2½ cups plain
   (all-purpose) flour
115g/4oz/½ cup unsalted
   (sweet) butter, diced
50g/2oz/¼ cup caster
   (superfine) sugar
1 egg, beaten

1 To make the pastry, put the flour in a food processor. Add the butter to the flour and then, using a pulsating action, mix together until the mixture resembles fine breadcrumbs.

2 Stir in the sugar and add the egg. Combine to form a dough. Wrap in baking parchment and chill for 1 hour.

3 Preheat the oven to 180°C/350°F/Gas 4. On a floured surface, roll out the pastry thinly and use to line a 20cm/8in flan tin (pan). Put a circle of baking parchment in the case and fill with baking beans. Bake in the oven for 10–15 minutes until the pastry has set. Remove the paper and beans and bake for 5 minutes more.

4 Fill the tart with the berries and sugar. Then return the tart to the oven and bake for a further 5–10 minutes until the pastry is golden brown. Serve warm with whipped cream.

Cook's Tip

Instead of cooking the fruit in the tart, you can make the tart and then fill it with uncooked fresh berries. Bake the pastry case for a further 10 minutes, leave it to cool and then brush the base with melted plain (semisweet) chocolate. Leave to set and then fill with fresh berries. The chocolate will stop the berries from softening the pastry before the tart is served.

Summer Berry Energy 432kcal/1807kJ; Protein 6.7g; Carbohydrate 47.6g, of which sugars 21.8g; Fat 25.7g, of which saturates 14.6g; Cholesterol 160mg; Calcium 130mg; Fibre 2g; Sodium 150mg.
Wild Berry Energy 618kcal/2601kJ; Protein 8g; Carbohydrate 98.1g, of which sugars 43.3g; Fat 24.2g, of which saturates 14.9g; Cholesterol 60mg; Calcium 141mg; Fibre 3.8g; Sodium 177mg.

Blueberry Frangipane Flan

A lemon pastry case is filled with a sweet almond filling, dotted with blueberries.

Serves 6
30ml/2 tbsp ground coffee
45ml/3 tbsp milk
50g/2oz/¼ cup unsalted (sweet) butter
50g/2oz/¼ cup caster (superfine) sugar
I egg
115g/4oz/1 cup ground almonds
15ml/1 tbsp plain (all-purpose) flour, sifted

225g/8oz/2 cups blueberries
30ml/2 tbsp jam
15ml/1 tbsp brandy

For the pastry
175g/6oz/1½ cups plain (all-purpose) flour
115g/4oz/½ cup unsalted (sweet) butter or margarine
25g/1oz/2 tbsp caster (superfine) sugar
finely grated rind of ½ lemon
15ml/1 tbsp chilled water

1 Preheat the oven to 190°C/375°F/Gas 5. To make the pastry, sift the flour into a bowl and rub in the butter. Stir in the sugar and lemon rind, then add the water and mix to a firm dough. Wrap in clear film (plastic wrap) and chill for 20 minutes.

2 Roll out the pastry on a lightly floured work surface and use to line a 23cm/9in loose-based flan tin (tart pan). Line the pastry with baking parchment and baking beans and bake for 10 minutes. Remove the paper and beans and bake for a further 10 minutes. Remove from the oven.

3 Meanwhile, make the filling. Put the ground coffee in a bowl. Bring the milk almost to the boil, then pour over the coffee and leave to infuse for 4 minutes. Cream the butter and sugar until pale. Beat in the egg, then add the almonds and flour. Finely strain in the coffee-flavoured milk and fold in.

4 Spread the coffee mixture into the pastry case. Scatter the blueberries over and push down slightly into the mixture. Bake for 30 minutes, until firm, covering with foil after 20 minutes.

5 Heat the jam and brandy in a small pan until melted. Brush over the flan and remove from the tin.

Blackcurrant Tart

Blackcurrants grow in the wild, are cultivated throughout Europe, and are widely available in North America. This tart makes the most of these exquisite summer fruits, and is quick and easy to prepare using ready-made puff pastry. Serve with whipped cream.

Serves 4
500g/1¼lb/5 cups blackcurrants
115g/4oz/generous ½ cup caster (superfine) sugar
250g/9oz ready-made puff pastry
50g/2oz/½ cup icing (confectioners') sugar
whipped cream, to serve

1 Preheat the oven to 220°C/425°F/Gas 7.

2 Trim the blackcurrants, making sure you remove all the stalks and any hard parts in the middle.

3 Add the caster sugar and mix together well.

4 Roll out the pastry to about 3mm/⅛in thick and cut out four discs roughly the size of a side plate or a large cereal bowl.

5 Then, using a smaller plate (or bowl), use the point of a knife to lightly mark a circle about 2cm/¾in inside each disc.

6 Spread the blackcurrants over the discs, keeping them within the marked inner circle. Bake in the oven for 15 minutes.

7 Dust generously with the icing sugar.

8 Serve hot with a large dollop of whipped cream, or alternatively serve cold as a teatime snack.

> **Cook's Tip**
> If you are picking wild blackcurrants, look for fruits that are dark, juicy and ripe. Avoid any that are mouldy or have insects or snails on them, and those that are broken. Pick them individually so that you do not squash them.

Blueberry Frangipane Energy 523Kcal/2180kJ; Protein 8.9g; Carbohydrate 44.9g, of which sugars 20.2g; Fat 34.8g, of which saturates 15.6g; Cholesterol 91mg; Calcium 132mg; Fibre 3.6g; Sodium 188mg.
Blackcurrant Tart Energy 426kcal/1798kJ; Protein 4.9g; Carbohydrate 73.2g, of which sugars 50.9g; Fat 15.3g, of which saturates 0g; Cholesterol 0mg; Calcium 133mg; Fibre 4.5g; Sodium 200mg.

Fresh Fig Filo Tart

Figs cook wonderfully well and taste superb in this filo pastry tart – the riper the figs, the better.

Serves 6–8
5 sheets of filo pastry, each
  35 x 25cm/14 x 10in,
  thawed if frozen
25g/1oz/2 tbsp butter, melted,
  plus extra for greasing
6 fresh figs, cut into wedges
75g/3oz/²⁄₃ cup plain
  (all-purpose) flour

75g/3oz/6 tbsp caster
  (superfine) sugar
4 eggs
450ml/¾ pint/scant 2 cups
  milk
2.5ml/½ tsp almond extract
15ml/1 tbsp icing (confectioners')
  sugar, for dusting
whipped cream or Greek
  (US strained plain)
  yogurt, to serve

1 Preheat the oven to 190°C/375°F/Gas 5. Grease a 25 x 16cm/ 10 x 6¼in baking tin (pan) with butter. Brush each filo sheet in turn with melted butter and use to line the prepared tin.

2 Using scissors, cut off any excess pastry, leaving a little overhanging the edge. Arrange the figs in the filo case.

3 Sift the flour into a bowl and stir in the caster sugar. Add the eggs and a little of the milk and whisk until smooth. Gradually whisk in the remaining milk and the almond extract. Pour the mixture over the figs; bake for 1 hour or until the batter has set and is golden.

4 Remove the tart from the oven and allow it to cool in the tin on a wire rack for 10 minutes. Dust with the icing sugar and serve with whipped cream or Greek yogurt.

Cook's Tip
Filo pastry dries out quickly, so keep the sheets not currently being used covered under a clean damp dish towel. Also, work as quickly as possible. If the filo should turn dry and brittle, simply brush it with melted butter to moisten.

Surprise Fruit Tarts

Strawberry cream with a dash of orange-flavoured liqueur makes a beautifully sweet and tangy filling. These delicious and simple little tarts are the perfect summer treat.

Serves 6
4 large or 8 small sheets of
  filo pastry, thawed if frozen
65g/2½oz/5 tbsp butter or
  margarine, melted
250ml/8fl oz/1 cup
  whipping cream
45ml/3 tbsp strawberry jam

15ml/1 tbsp Cointreau or other
  orange-flavoured liqueur
115g/4oz/1 cup seedless black
  grapes, halved
115g/4oz/1 cup seedless white
  grapes, halved
150g/5oz fresh pineapple,
  cubed, or drained canned
  pineapple chunks
115g/4oz/²⁄₃ cup raspberries
30ml/2 tbsp icing
  (confectioners') sugar
6 sprigs fresh mint,
  to decorate

1 Preheat the oven to 180°C/350°F/Gas 4. Grease six cups of a bun tray. Stack the filo sheets and cut with a sharp knife or scissors into 24 pieces each 12cm/4½in square.

2 Lay four squares of pastry in each of the six greased cups, rotating them slightly to make star-shaped baskets.

3 Press the pastry firmly into the cups. Brush the pastry baskets lightly with butter or margarine.

4 Bake until the pastry is crisp and golden, about 5–7 minutes. Cool on a wire rack.

5 In a bowl, lightly whip the cream until soft peaks form. Gently fold the strawberry jam and Cointreau into the cream.

6 Just before serving, spoon a little of the cream mixture into each pastry basket. Top with the halved grapes, pineapple and raspberries.

7 Sprinkle with icing sugar, decorate each basket with a small sprig of mint and serve immediately.

Fresh Fig Energy 213Kcal/900kJ; Protein 5.8g; Carbohydrate 36.7g, of which sugars 20g; Fat 5.9g, of which saturates 2.5g; Cholesterol 102mg; Calcium 89mg; Fibre 1.8g; Sodium 65mg.
Surprise Fruit Energy 400kcal/1669kJ; Protein 4g; Carbohydrate 37g, of which sugars 22g; Fat 27g, of which saturates 16g; Cholesterol 67mg; Calcium 41mg; Fibre 2.0g; Sodium 147mg.

Exotic Fruit Tranche

This is a good way to make the most of a small selection of exotic fruit.

Serves 8
175g/6oz/1½ cups plain
  (all-purpose) flour
50g/2oz/¼ cup unsalted
  (sweet) butter
25g/1oz/2 tbsp white
  vegetable fat
50g/2oz/¼ cup caster
  (superfine) sugar
2 egg yolks
about 15ml/1 tbsp water
115g/4oz/scant ½ cup apricot
  jam, strained and warmed

For the filling
150ml/¼ pint/⅔ cup double
  (heavy) cream, plus extra
  to serve
250g/9oz/generous 1 cup
  mascarpone
25g/1oz/2 tbsp icing
  (confectioners') sugar, sifted
grated rind of 1 orange
450g/1lb/3 cups mixed prepared
  fruits, such as mango, papaya,
  star fruit, kiwi fruit and
  blackberries
90ml/6 tbsp apricot jam,
  strained
15ml/1 tbsp white or
  coconut rum

1 Sift the flour into a bowl and rub in the butter and white vegetable fat until the mixture resembles fine breadcrumbs. Stir in the caster sugar. Add the egg yolks and enough cold water to make a soft dough. Thinly roll out the pastry between two sheets of clear film (plastic wrap) and use the pastry to line a 35 × 12cm/14 × 4½in fluted tranche tin or a 23cm/9in flan tin (tart pan). Allow the excess pastry to hang over the edge of the tin, and chill for 30 minutes.

2 Preheat the oven to 200°C/400°F/Gas 6. Prick the base of the pastry case and line with baking parchment and baking beans. Bake for 10–12 minutes. Lift out the paper and beans and return the pastry case to the oven for 5 minutes. Trim off the excess pastry and brush the inside of the case with the warmed apricot jam to form a seal. Cool on a wire rack.

3 Make the filling. Whip the cream to soft peaks, then stir it into the mascarpone with the icing sugar and orange rind. Spread in the cooled pastry case and top with the prepared fruits. Warm the apricot jam with the rum and drizzle or brush over the fruits to make a glaze. Serve with extra cream.

Pomegranate Jewelled Cheesecake

This light cheesecake has a stunning pomegranate glaze.

Serves 8
225g/8oz oat biscuits (crackers)
75g/3oz/6 tbsp unsalted (sweet)
  butter, melted

For the filling
45ml/3 tbsp orange juice
15ml/1 tbsp powdered
  gelatine
250g/9oz/generous 1 cup
  mascarpone
200g/7oz/scant 1 cup full-fat
  soft cheese
75g/3oz/⅔ cup icing
  (confectioners') sugar, sifted
200ml/7fl oz/scant 1 cup
  coconut cream
2 egg whites

For the topping
2 pomegranates, peeled and
  seeds separated
grated rind and juice of 1 orange
30ml/2 tbsp caster (superfine)
  sugar
15ml/1 tbsp arrowroot, mixed
  to a paste with 30ml/2 tbsp
  Kirsch
red food colouring (optional)

1 Grease a 23cm/9in springform cake tin (pan). Crumb the biscuits in a food processor or blender. Add the butter and process briefly. Spoon into the tin, press in well, then chill.

2 Make the filling. Pour the orange juice into a heatproof bowl, sprinkle the gelatine on top and set aside for 5 minutes. Place the bowl in a pan of hot water; stir until the gelatine dissolves.

3 In a bowl, beat together both cheeses and the icing sugar, then gradually beat in the coconut cream. Whisk the egg whites in a grease-free bowl to soft peaks. Quickly stir the melted gelatine into the coconut mixture and fold in the egg whites. Pour over the biscuit base, level and chill until set.

4 Make the topping. Place the pomegranate seeds in a pan and add the orange rind and juice and sugar. Bring to the boil, then lower the heat, cover and simmer for 5 minutes. Add the arrowroot paste and heat, stirring, until thickened. Stir in a few drops of food colouring, if using. Cool, stirring occasionally.

5 Pour the glaze over the top of the set cheesecake, then chill. Remove from the tin and cut into slices to serve.

Exotic Fruit Energy 429Kcal/1801kJ; Protein 6.4g; Carbohydrate 53.3g, of which sugars 36.9g; Fat 22.2g, of which saturates 12.7g; Cholesterol 99mg; Calcium 105mg; Fibre 2.1g; Sodium 136mg.
Pomegranate Energy 407Kcal/1702kJ; Protein 8.2g; Carbohydrate 37.3g, of which sugars 26.1g; Fat 26.1g, of which saturates 15.2g; Cholesterol 56mg; Calcium 57mg; Fibre 1.1g; Sodium 336mg.

Melon Trio with Ginger Cookies

The eye-catching colours of these three different melons really make this dessert, while the crisp biscuits provide a perfect contrast in terms of texture.

Serves 4

¼ watermelon
½ honeydew melon
½ Charentais melon
60ml/4 tbsp stem ginger syrup

For the cookies

25g/1oz/2 tbsp unsalted (sweet) butter
25g/1oz/2 tbsp caster (superfine) sugar
5ml/1 tsp clear honey
25g/1oz/¼ cup plain (all-purpose) flour
25g/1oz/¼ cup luxury glacé mixed fruit, finely chopped
1–1.5cm/½in piece of preserved stem ginger in syrup, drained and finely chopped
30ml/2 tbsp flaked almonds

1 Remove the seeds from the melons, then cut them into wedges and slice off the rind. Cut all the flesh into chunks and mix in a bowl. Stir in the stem ginger syrup, cover and chill until ready to serve.

2 Meanwhile, make the cookies. Preheat the oven to 180°C/350°F/Gas 4. Place the butter, sugar and honey in a pan and heat until melted. Remove from the heat and stir in the remaining ingredients.

3 Line a baking sheet with baking parchment. Space four spoonfuls of the mixture on the paper at regular intervals, leaving plenty of room to allow for the cookies spreading. Flatten the mixture slightly into rounds and bake for 15 minutes or until the tops are golden.

4 Let the cookies cool on the baking sheet for 1 minute, then lift each one in turn, using a metal spatula, and drape over a rolling pin to cool and harden. Repeat with the remaining ginger mixture to make eight curved cookies in all.

5 Transfer the melon chunks and syrup to a large serving dish or individual glasses and serve accompanied by the crisp ginger cookies.

Cool Green Fruit Salad

A stylish yet simple fruit salad for any time of the year. Serve with amaretti or crisp almond cookies.

1 green-skinned apple
1 lime
175ml/6fl oz/¾ cup sparkling grape juice

Serves 6

3 Ogen or Galia melons
115g/4oz seedless green grapes
2 kiwi fruit
1 star fruit

1 Cut the melons in half and remove the seeds. Keeping the shells intact, scoop out the flesh with a melon baller, or scoop it out with a spoon and cut into bitesize cubes. Reserve the melon shells.

2 Remove any stems from the grapes and, if they are large, cut them in half. Peel and chop the kiwi fruit. Thinly slice the star fruit. Core and thinly slice the apple. Place the grapes, kiwi fruit and apple in a mixing bowl with the melon.

3 Thinly pare the rind from the lime and cut it in fine strips. Blanch the lime strips in boiling water for 30 seconds, drain and rinse in cold water. Reserve for garnishing.

4 Squeeze the juice from the lime and toss the juice into the bowl of fruit.

5 Spoon the prepared fruit into the reserved melon shells and chill the shells until required.

6 Just before serving, spoon the sparkling grape juice over the fruit and scatter with the strips of lime rind.

> **Cook's Tip**
> On a hot summer's day, serve the filled melon shells nestling on a platter of crushed ice, to keep them beautifully cool.

Melon Trio Energy 350kcal/1479kJ; Protein 4.8g; Carbohydrate 65g, of which sugars 60.1g; Fat 9.7g, of which saturates 3.8g; Cholesterol 13mg; Calcium 74mg; Fibre 2.5g; Sodium 167mg.
Cool Green Energy 102kcal/436kJ; Protein 1.7g; Carbohydrate 24.4g, of which sugars 24.4g; Fat 0.4g, of which saturates 0g; Cholesterol 0mg; Calcium 46mg; Fibre 1.9g; Sodium 81mg.

Melon & Strawberry Salad

A beautiful and colourful fruit salad, this is equally suitable to serve as a refreshing appetizer or to round off a meal.

225g/8oz/2 cups strawberries
15ml/1 tbsp lemon juice
15ml/1 tbsp clear honey
15ml/1 tbsp chopped
   fresh mint
1 fresh mint sprig (optional)

Serves 4
1 Galia melon
1 honeydew melon
½ watermelon

1 To prepare the melons, cut them in half and discard the seeds. Use a melon baller to scoop out the flesh into balls. Alternatively, use a knife and cut the melon flesh into cubes. Place the melon in a fruit bowl.

2 Rinse and hull the strawberries, cut in half and add to the melon balls or cubes.

3 Mix together the lemon juice and honey and add about 15ml/1 tbsp water to make it easier to spoon over the fruit. Mix into the fruit gently.

4 Sprinkle the chopped mint over the top of the fruit. Serve the fruit salad decorated with the mint sprig, if wished.

Cook's Tip
Do not rinse the strawberries until just before serving, otherwise they will turn mushy. When buying in punnets, remember that a strong scent means a good flavour. Fruit in season is best.

Variation
Use whichever melons are available: replace Galia with cantaloupe or watermelon with Charentais, for example. Try to choose three melons with a variation in colour.

Italian Fruit Salad & Ice Cream

Fresh summer fruits are steeped in fruit juice to make a delicious Italian salad, which is delectable on its own, but can also be turned into a wickedly rich ice cream. Serve some of the fruit salad alongside the ice cream for a glorious fruity experience.

Serves 6
900g/2lb mixed summer
   fruits such as strawberries,
   raspberries, loganberries,
   redcurrants, blueberries,
   peaches, apricots, plums,
   melons and nectarines
juice of 3–4 oranges
juice of 1 lemon
15ml/1 tbsp liquid pear and
   apple concentrate
60ml/4 tbsp whipping cream
fresh mint sprigs,
   to decorate

1 Prepare the fruit according to type and cut into reasonably small pieces. Put the prepared fruit into a serving bowl and pour over enough orange juice to cover. Add the lemon juice and chill for 2 hours.

2 Set half the macerated fruit aside to serve as it is. Purée the remainder in a blender or food processor.

3 Gently warm the pear and apple concentrate and stir into the fruit purée. Whip the cream and fold it in.

4 Churn the mixture in an ice-cream maker. Alternatively, place in a suitable container for freezing. Freeze until ice crystals form around the edge, then beat the mixture until smooth. Repeat the process once or twice, then freeze until firm.

5 Allow to soften slightly in the refrigerator before serving, decorated with sprigs of mint.

Cook's Tip
Add 30ml/2 tbsp orange liqueur to the ice cream or the fruit salad, for an added touch of luxury.

Melon and Strawberry Energy 204kcal/867kJ; Protein 3.9g; Carbohydrate 47.5g, of which sugars 47.5g; Fat 1.2g, of which saturates 0.3g; Cholesterol 0mg; Calcium 66mg; Fibre 2.9g; Sodium 128mg.
Italian Fruit Salad Energy 69kcal/289kJ; Protein 2.2g; Carbohydrate 15.2g, of which sugars 15.2g; Fat 0.2g, of which saturates 0g; Cholesterol 0mg; Calcium 38mg; Fibre 1.7g; Sodium 18mg.

Pistachio & Rose Water Oranges

This light and tangy dessert is perfect to serve after a heavy main course, such as a hearty meat stew or a leg of roast lamb. A simple combination of three favourite Middle-Eastern ingredients, it is delightfully fragrant and refreshing. If you don't have pistachio nuts, use hazelnuts instead.

Serves 4
4 large oranges
30ml/2 tbsp rose water
30ml/2 tbsp shelled pistachio
 nuts, roughly chopped

1 Slice the top and bottom off one of the oranges to expose the flesh. Using a small serrated knife, slice down between the pith and the flesh, working round the orange, to remove all the peel and pith. Slice the orange into six rounds, reserving any juice. Repeat with the remaining oranges.

2 Arrange the oranges in a shallow dish. Mix the reserved juice with the rose water and drizzle over the oranges.

3 Cover the dish with clear film (plastic wrap) and chill for about 30 minutes. Sprinkle the chopped pistachio nuts over the oranges and serve immediately.

Cook's Tips
• *Rose-scented sugar is delicious sprinkled over fresh fruit salads. Wash and thoroughly dry a handful of rose petals and place in a sealed container filled with caster (superfine) sugar for 2–3 days. Remove the petals before using the sugar.*
• *This salad is delicious served with vanilla cream. Put 150ml/¼ pint/⅔ cup double (heavy) cream in a small pan with a vanilla pod (bean). Bring almost to the boil, then leave to cool and steep for 30 minutes. Remove the vanilla pod, then transfer the cream to a bowl. Mix with another 150ml/¼ pint/⅔ cup cream and caster (superfine) sugar to taste. Whip lightly.*

Grapefruit Salad with Campari & Orange

The bitter-sweet flavour of Campari combines especially well with the citrus fruit to produce a refreshing salad for any time of the year.

60ml/4 tbsp Campari
30ml/2 tbsp lemon juice
4 grapefruit
5 oranges
4 fresh mint sprigs, to decorate

Serves 4
150ml/¼ pint/⅔ cup water
45 ml/3 tbsp caster
 (superfine) sugar

1 Bring the water to the boil in a small pan, add the sugar and simmer until dissolved. Transfer to a bowl, allow to cool, then add the Campari and lemon juice. Chill until ready to serve.

2 Slice the top and bottom off one of the grapefruit to expose the flesh. Using a small serrated knife, slice down between the pith and the flesh, working round the grapefruit, to remove all the peel and pith.

3 Release the segments by cutting between the flesh and the membranes, working over a bowl to catch the juices. Repeat with the remaining grapefruit and the oranges.

4 Add the grapefruit and orange segments to the bowl of Campari syrup and chill.

5 Spoon the salad into four dishes, decorate each with a sprig of fresh mint and serve.

Cook's Tips
• *When buying citrus fruit, choose brightly-coloured varieties that feel heavy for their size.*
• *Before you discard the citrus fruit membranes, squeeze as much juice as possible from them into the bowl of juice.*

Pistachio and Rose Water Energy 101kcal/424kJ; Protein 3g; Carbohydrate 13.4g, of which sugars 13.2g; Fat 4.3g, of which saturates 0.6g; Cholesterol 0mg; Calcium 79mg; Fibre 3g; Sodium 47mg.
Grapefruit Salad Energy 181kcal/766kJ; Protein 3g; Carbohydrate 35.4g, of which sugars 35.4g; Fat 0.3g, of which saturates 0g; Cholesterol 0mg; Calcium 113mg; Fibre 4.6g; Sodium 13mg.

Creole Ambrosia

With several colourful layers of sliced orange and fresh coconut, this refreshing fruit dessert makes a change from the more traditional fruit salad.

Serves 6
6 oranges
1 coconut
25g/1oz/2 tbsp caster
   (superfine) sugar

1 Peel the oranges, removing all the white pith, then slice the flesh thinly, picking out any seeds with the point of a knife. Do this on a plate to catch the juice.

2 Pierce the 'eyes' of the coconut and pour away the milk, then crack open the coconut with a hammer. (This is best done outside on a stone surface.)

3 Remove the coconut flesh from the shell with a sharp knife, then grate half the flesh coarsely, either with a hand grater or in a food processor fitted with a grating blade.

4 Layer the grated coconut and orange slices in a glass bowl, starting and finishing with the coconut. After each orange layer, sprinkle on a little sugar and pour over some of the reserved orange juice.

5 Leave to stand for 2 hours, either at room temperature or in the refrigerator in hot weather, before serving.

Cook's Tip
To remove the rind and pith from an orange cleanly, first cut a slice off either end of the fruit with a sharp knife. Stand it on a board and, working downwards, cut off the peel in wide strips.

Variation
For a more exotic flavour, use mangoes instead of oranges. Peel the mangoes, then slice the flesh away from the stone (pit).

Figs with Honey & Wine

Cooled poached figs make a salad with a difference. They are delicious served with sweetened whipped cream flavoured with vanilla extract.

Serves 6
450ml/¾ pint/scant 2 cups dry
   white wine
75g/3oz/⅓ cup clear honey

50g/2oz/¼ cup caster
   (superfine) sugar
1 small orange
8 whole cloves
450g/1lb fresh figs
1 cinnamon stick

1 Put the wine, honey and sugar in a heavy pan and heat gently until the sugar dissolves.

2 Stud the orange with the cloves and add to the syrup with the figs and cinnamon. Cover and simmer gently for 5–10 minutes, until the figs are softened. Transfer to a serving dish and leave to cool completely before serving.

Fruit with Yogurt & Honey

Fresh fruit most commonly follows a meal in Greece, and the addition of yogurt and honey makes it even more delicious.

Serves 4
225g/8oz/1 cup Greek
   (US strained plain) yogurt
45ml/3 tbsp clear honey
selection of fresh fruit for dipping,
   such as apples, pears,
   tangerines, grapes, figs
   and strawberries

1 Beat the yogurt, place in a dish, and stir in the honey, to leave a marbled effect.

2 Cut the fruits into wedges or bitesize pieces, or leave whole.

3 Arrange the fruits on a platter with the bowl of dip in the centre. Serve chilled.

Creole Ambrosia Energy 160Kcal/668kJ; Protein 2.7g; Carbohydrate 14.7g, of which sugars 14.7g; Fat 10.5g, of which saturates 8.9g; Cholesterol 0mg; Calcium 79mg; Fibre 5g; Sodium 13mg.
Figs with Honey Energy 316kcal/1318kJ; Protein 1.8g; Carbohydrate 29.7g, of which sugars 29.7g; Fat 18.4g, of which saturates 11.1g; Cholesterol 46mg; Calcium 101mg; Fibre 2.3g; Sodium 30mg.
Fruit with Yogurt Energy 131kcal/548kJ; Protein 4.7g; Carbohydrate 17.2g, of which sugars 17.2g; Fat 5.9g, of which saturates 2.9g; Cholesterol 0mg; Calcium 105mg; Fibre 1.4g; Sodium 49mg.

Pineapple with Strawberries & Lychees

The sweet, tropical flavours
of pineapple and lychees
combine well with richly
scented strawberries to
create a most refreshing
and colourful fruit salad.
The pineapple shells make
lovely bowls.

Serves 4

2 small pineapples
450g/1lb/4 cups strawberries
400g/14oz can lychees
45ml/3 tbsp Kirsch or
   white rum
30ml/2 tbsp icing
   (confectioners') sugar

1 Remove the crowns from both pineapples by twisting sharply. Reserve the leaves for decoration.

2 Cut both pineapples in half diagonally using a large, serrated knife. Cut around the flesh inside the skin of both pineapples with a small, serrated knife, keeping the skin intact. Remove the core from the pineapple and discard. Chop the flesh and put in a freezerproof bowl. Reserve the skins.

3 Hull the strawberries and gently combine with the pineapple and lychees, taking care not to damage the fruit.

4 Mix the Kirsch or rum with the icing sugar, pour over the fruit and freeze for 45 minutes.

5 Turn out the fruit into the pineapple skin shells, decorate with the reserved pineapple leaves and serve.

Cook's Tips
• A ripe pineapple will resist pressure when squeezed, and will have a sweet, fragrant smell. In winter, freezing conditions can cause the flesh to blacken.
• Make sure you remove all the brown 'eyes' from the pineapple before cutting into pieces.
• The pineapple can be chopped finely to create almost a 'crush' which will coat the other fruit.

Winter Fruit Salad

This attractive dessert is
guaranteed to brighten up
even the coldest days during
the winter months. It tastes
luscious when served with
thick yogurt or cream.

Serves 6

225g/8oz can pineapple cubes
   in fruit juice
200ml/7fl oz/scant 1 cup freshly
   squeezed orange juice
200ml/7fl oz/scant 1 cup
   unsweetened apple juice
30ml/2 tbsp orange or
   apple liqueur

30ml/2 tbsp clear honey
   (optional)
2 oranges
2 green apples
2 pears
4 plums, stoned (pitted)
   and chopped
12 fresh dates, stoned (pitted)
   and chopped
115g/4oz/1/2 cup ready-to-eat
   dried apricots
fresh mint sprigs, to decorate

1 Drain the pineapple, reserving the juice. Put the pineapple juice, orange juice, apple juice, liqueur and honey, if using, in a large serving bowl and stir.

2 To segment the oranges, cut a slice off the top and bottom of each orange to expose the flesh. Place on a board and remove the skin, cutting downwards. Take care to remove all the white pith. Cut between the membranes to release the segments.

3 Put the orange segments and pineapple in the fruit juice mixture. Peel, core and slice the apples and pears and add to the serving bowl.

4 Stir in the chopped plums, dates and dried apricots to combine well. Cover and chill for several hours. Decorate with fresh mint sprigs, and serve.

Variation
Use other unsweetened fruit juices such as pink grapefruit and pineapple juice in place of the orange and apple juice.

Pineapple Energy 235kcal/999kJ; Protein 2.2g; Carbohydrate 52.5g, of which sugars 52.5g; Fat 0.5g, of which saturates 0g; Cholesterol 0mg; Calcium 62mg; Fibre 4.2g; Sodium 13mg.
Winter Fruit Salad Energy 141kcal/603kJ; Protein 1.9g; Carbohydrate 32g, of which sugars 32g; Fat 0.4g, of which saturates 0g; Cholesterol 0mg; Calcium 60mg; Fibre 4.2g; Sodium 12mg.

Fruits-of-the-tropics Salad

This is a creamy, exotic fruit salad flavoured with coconut and spices. It makes a filling and tasty dessert.

Serves 4–6
1 pineapple
400g/14oz can guava halves
  in syrup
2 bananas, sliced
1 large mango, peeled, stoned
  (pitted) and diced
115g/4oz stem ginger and
  30ml/2 tbsp of the syrup
60ml/4 tbsp thick coconut milk
10ml/2 tsp sugar
2.5ml/½ tsp freshly grated
  nutmeg
2.5ml/½ tsp ground cinnamon
strips of coconut, to decorate

1 Peel, core and cube the pineapple, then place in a serving bowl. Drain the guavas, reserving the syrup, and chop. Add the guavas to the bowl with one of the bananas and the mango.

2 Chop the stem ginger and add to the pineapple mixture.

3 Pour the 30 ml/2 tbsp of the ginger syrup and the reserved guava syrup into a blender or food processor and add the remaining banana, the coconut milk and the sugar. Blend to make a smooth, creamy purée.

4 Pour the banana and coconut purée over the fruit and add a little grated nutmeg and a sprinkling of cinnamon on top. Serve chilled, decorated with strips of coconut.

> **Cook's Tip**
> *To dice mango, slice off a piece of flesh on either side of the stone (pit). Cut a cross-hatch pattern in the flesh of the slices, bend back the skin and scrape off the diced flesh.*

> **Variation**
> *Add a sliced kiwi fruit or seeded papaya for extra colour.*

Pineapple Fruit Salad

A mix of exotic fruit served up in attractive pineapple cases makes an impressive dinner party dessert.

Serves 4
75g/3oz/scant ½ cup sugar
300ml/½ pint/1¼ cups water
30ml/2 tbsp stem ginger syrup
2 pieces star anise
2.5cm/1in cinnamon stick
1 clove
juice of ½ lemon
2 fresh mint sprigs
1 mango
2 bananas, sliced
8 lychees, fresh or canned
225g/8oz/2 cups strawberries
2 pieces stem ginger, cut
  into sticks
1 pineapple

1 Place the sugar in a pan and add the water, ginger syrup, spices, lemon juice and mint. Bring to the boil and simmer for 3 minutes. Strain into a large bowl.

2 Remove both the top and bottom from the mango and remove the outer skin. Stand the mango on one end and remove the flesh in two pieces either side of the flat stone. Slice evenly and add to the syrup. Add the bananas, lychees, strawberries and ginger. Chill until ready to serve.

3 Cut the pineapple in half down the centre. Loosen the flesh with a small, serrated knife and remove to form two boat shapes. Cut the pineapple flesh into large chunks and place in the cooled syrup.

4 Spoon the fruit salad carefully into the pineapple halves and bring to the table on a large serving dish or board. There will be enough fruit salad left over to be able to offer refills for second helpings.

> **Variations**
> *A variety of fruits can be used for this salad, depending on what is available. Look out for fresh mandarin oranges, star fruit, papaya, physalis and passion fruit.*

Fruits-of-the-tropics Energy 165kcal/706kJ; Protein 1.5g; Carbohydrate 41.4g, of which sugars 40.5g; Fat 0.5g, of which saturates 0.1g; Cholesterol 0mg; Calcium 46mg; Fibre 4.8g; Sodium 41mg.
Pineapple Fruit Salad Energy 82kcal/348kJ; Protein 1.2g; Carbohydrate 18.3g, of which sugars 18.1g; Fat 1g, of which saturates 0.1g; Cholesterol 0mg; Calcium 33mg; Fibre 3.7g; Sodium 9mg.

Fresh Fruit with Mango Sauce

Fruit coulis became trendy in the 1970s with nouvelle cuisine. It makes a simple fruit dish very special.

Serves 6
1 large ripe mango, peeled, stoned (pitted) and chopped
rind of 1 unwaxed orange
juice of 3 oranges
caster (superfine) sugar, to taste
2 peaches
2 nectarines

1 small mango, peeled
2 plums
1 pear or ½ small melon
25–50g/1–2oz/2 heaped tbsp wild strawberries (optional)
25–50g/1–2oz/2 heaped tbsp raspberries
25–50g/1–2oz/2 heaped tbsp blueberries
juice of 1 lemon
small mint sprigs, to decorate

1 In a food processor fitted with the metal blade, process the large mango until smooth. Add the orange rind, juice and sugar to taste and process again until very smooth. Press through a sieve (strainer) into a bowl and chill the sauce.

2 Peel the peaches, if you like, then slice and stone (pit) the peaches, nectarines, small mango and plums. Quarter and core the pear, or if using, slice the melon thinly and remove the peel.

3 Place the sliced fruits on a large plate, sprinkle the fruits with the lemon juice and chill, covered with clear film (plastic wrap), for up to 3 hours before serving.

4 To serve, arrange the sliced fruits on serving plates, spoon the berries on top, drizzle with a little mango sauce and decorate with mint sprigs. Serve the remaining sauce separately.

Variation
Use a raspberry coulis instead of a mango one: purée raspberries with a little lemon juice and icing (confectioners') sugar to taste, then pass through a sieve (strainer) to remove the pips. You can use frozen raspberries for this, so it can be made at any time of year.

Exotic Fruit Salad with Passion Fruit Dressing

Passion fruit makes a superb dressing for any fruit, but really brings out the flavour of exotic varieties. You can easily double the quantities given in this recipe and serve the rest for breakfast.

Serves 6
1 mango
1 papaya

2 kiwi fruit
coconut or vanilla ice cream, to serve

For the dressing
3 passion fruit
thinly pared rind and juice of 1 lime
5ml/1 tsp hazelnut or walnut oil
15ml/1 tbsp clear honey

1 Peel the mango, cut it into three slices, then cut the flesh into chunks and place it in a large bowl. Peel the papaya and cut it in half. Scoop out the seeds, then chop the flesh.

2 Cut both ends off each kiwi fruit, then stand them on a board. Using a small sharp knife, cut off the skin from top to bottom. Cut each kiwi fruit in half lengthways, then cut into thick slices. Combine all the fruit in a large bowl.

3 Make the dressing. Cut each passion fruit in half and scoop the seeds out into a sieve (strainer) set over a small bowl. Press the seeds well to extract all their juices.

4 Lightly whisk the remaining dressing ingredients into the passion fruit juice, then pour the dressing over the fruit in the bowl. Mix gently to combine. Leave to chill for approximately 1 hour before serving with generous scoops of coconut or vanilla ice cream.

Cook's Tip
A clear golden honey scented with orange blossom or acacia blossom would be perfect for the dressing.

Fresh Fruit with Mango Energy 82kcal/351kJ; Protein 1.9g; Carbohydrate 19.2g, of which sugars 19.1g; Fat 0.3g, of which saturates 0.1g; Cholesterol 0mg; Calcium 22mg; Fibre 3.3g; Sodium 5mg.
Exotic Fruit Salad Energy 64Kcal/270kJ; Protein 1g; Carbohydrate 14.2g, of which sugars 14g; Fat 0.8g, of which saturates 0.1g; Cholesterol 0mg; Calcium 25mg; Fibre 2.8g; Sodium 7mg.

Fruit Salad with Brandy & Coffee

A medley of colourful and exotic fruit, this decadent salad is the perfect dessert for a dinner party.

Serves 6
130g/4½oz/scant ¾ cup sugar
thinly pared rind and juice of
   1 lime
150ml/¼ pint/⅔ cup water
60ml/4 tbsp brandy
5ml/1 tsp instant coffee granules
   or powder dissolved in
   30ml/2 tbsp boiling water
1 small pineapple
1 papaya
2 pomegranates
1 medium mango
2 passion fruit or kiwi fruit
strips of lime rind, to decorate

1 Put the sugar and lime rind in a small pan with the water. Heat gently until the sugar dissolves, then bring to the boil and simmer for 5 minutes. Leave to cool, then strain into a large serving bowl, discarding the lime rind. Stir in the lime juice, brandy and dissolved coffee.

2 Using a sharp knife, cut the plume and stalk ends from the pineapple. Cut off the peel, then remove the central core and discard. Slice the flesh into bitesize pieces and add to the bowl.

3 Halve the papaya and scoop out the seeds. Cut away the skin, then slice the papaya. Halve the pomegranates and scoop out the seeds. Add to the bowl.

4 Cut the mango lengthways into three pieces, along each side of the stone (pit). Peel the skin off the flesh. Cut into chunks and add to the bowl.

5 Halve the passion fruit and scoop out the flesh using a teaspoon, or peel and chop the kiwi fruit. Add to the bowl and serve, decorated with lime rind.

> **Cook's Tip**
> *Allow the salad to stand at room temperature for an hour before serving, so the flavours can blend.*

Pomegranate Salad

Variations of this pretty, decorative salad are prepared throughout the Middle East. It can be offered to guests as a mark of hospitality, or it can be served as a refreshing dish between courses, at the end of a meal, and as an accompaniment to other sweet dishes. Pomegranate is a great seasonal fruit to serve at Christmas time.

Serves 4–6
45–60ml/3–4 tbsp pine nuts
3 ripe pomegranates
30ml/2 tbsp orange
   flower water
15–30ml/1–2 tbsp fragrant
   runny honey
handful of small mint leaves,
   to decorate

1 Place the pine nuts in a bowl, cover with water and leave to soak for 2 hours.

2 Cut the pomegranates into quarters on a plate so that you catch the juice. Extract the seeds, taking care to discard the bitter pith and membrane, and place in a bowl with the juice.

3 Drain the pine nuts and add them to the bowl. Stir gently to mix the fruit and nuts.

4 Stir in the orange flower water and honey, cover the bowl, and chill in the refrigerator. Serve chilled, or at room temperature, decorated with mint leaves.

> **Cook's Tip**
> *The pomegranate is a fruit about the size of a large orange. It has a thin, smooth skin and is tightly packed with many small seeds, which are in sections separated by a pale yellow membrane. The seeds are tiny and are covered with a red clear pulp that has a sweet yet sharp flavour. While the seeds and pulp are edible, the membrane should be discarded when the pomegranate is being prepared. Pomegranates can be used in both sweet and savoury dishes.*

Fruit Salad Energy 218Kcal/930kJ; Protein 1.4g; Carbohydrate 49.8g, of which sugars 49.8g; Fat 0.4g, of which saturates 0g; Cholesterol 0mg; Calcium 60mg; Fibre 4.4g; Sodium 10mg.
Pomegranate Salad Energy 82kcal/344kJ; Protein 1.3g; Carbohydrate 8.2g, of which sugars 8.1g; Fat 5.2g, of which saturates 0.4g; Cholesterol 0mg; Calcium 4mg; Fibre 1.2g; Sodium 2mg.

Old-fashioned Apple Trifle

This traditional dessert is an easy-to-make layered confection of sweetened breadcrumbs, stewed apples and whipped cream. Use a glass bowl to show the different layers, and assemble about an hour before serving so that the breadcrumbs stay crisp. The seasonal apples in this dish are complemented by the deep, warm spices, adding to the autumnal feel of this delicious dessert.

Serves 6
1kg/2¼lb tart eating apples
90g/3½oz/½ cup sugar,
    or to taste
5ml/1 tsp cinnamon
1.5ml/¼ tsp nutmeg
1.5ml/¼ tsp ground cloves
    (optional)
25g/1oz/2 tbsp butter
175g/6oz/3 cups fresh breadcrumbs
25g/1oz/2 tbsp soft brown sugar
250ml/8fl oz/1 cup double
    (heavy) cream
10ml/2 tsp icing
    (confectioners') sugar
5ml/1 tsp vanilla sugar
chopped nuts or grated plain
    (semisweet) chocolate,
    to decorate

1 Peel and core the apples and cut them into chunks. Place them in a heavy pan with 250ml/8fl oz/1 cup of water, the sugar, cinnamon, nutmeg and cloves (if using).

2 Cover the pan and cook over low heat, stirring occasionally, for about 25 minutes, until soft but still chunky. Remove from the heat and leave to cool.

3 Melt the butter in a frying pan. Stir in the breadcrumbs and brown sugar, tossing to coat the crumbs evenly with the butter. Cook, stirring constantly, for about 4–5 minutes until the crumbs are lightly browned and toasted. Remove from the heat and set aside.

4 Beat the double cream until soft peaks form and stir in the icing and vanilla sugars. Place a thin layer of breadcrumbs in the bottom of six serving glasses or bowls, cover the breadcrumbs with a layer of apple, then a layer of cream. Repeat the layers, ending with cream. Chill, then decorate before serving.

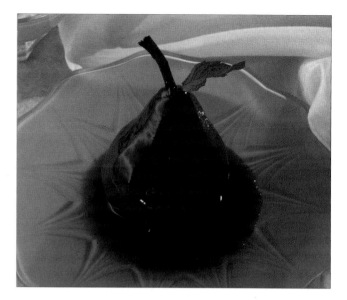

Poached Pears in Red Wine

In this recipe, the pears take on a red blush from the wine and make a very pretty dessert. For best results, use a small slow cooker, which ensures that the pears stay submerged during cooking.

Serves 4
1 bottle fruity red wine
150g/5oz/¾ cup caster
    (superfine) sugar

45ml/3 tbsp clear honey
1 cinnamon stick
1 vanilla pod (bean), split
    lengthways
large strip of lemon or orange rind
2 whole cloves
2 black peppercorns
4 firm ripe pears
juice of ½ lemon
mint leaves, to decorate
whipped cream or sour cream,
    to serve

1 Pour the red wine into the ceramic cooking pot. Add the sugar, honey, cinnamon stick, vanilla pod, lemon or orange rind, cloves and peppercorns. Cover with the lid and cook on high for 30 minutes, stirring occasionally.

2 Meanwhile, peel the pears using a vegetable peeler, leaving the stem intact. Take a very thin slice off the base of each pear so it will stand square and upright. As each pear is peeled, toss it in the lemon juice to prevent the flesh browning when exposed to the air.

3 Place the pears in the spiced wine mixture in the cooking pot. Cover with the lid and cook for 2–4 hours, turning the pears occasionally, until they are just tender; be careful not to overcook them.

4 Transfer the pears to a bowl, using a slotted spoon. Continue to cook the wine mixture, uncovered, for a further hour, until reduced and thickened a little, then turn off the slow cooker and leave to cool. Alternatively, to save time, pour the cooking liquor into a pan and boil briskly for 10–15 minutes.

5 Strain the cooled liquid over the pears and chill for at least 3 hours. Divide the pears between four individual serving dishes and spoon a little of the wine syrup over each one. Garnish with fresh mint and serve with whipped or sour cream.

Old-fashioned Energy 498kcal/2090kJ; Protein 4.7g; Carbohydrate 64.3g, of which sugars 42.5g; Fat 26.5g, of which saturates 16.1g; Cholesterol 66mg; Calcium 79mg; Fibre 3.3g; Sodium 261mg.
Poached Pears Energy 87kcal/367kJ; Protein 0.5g; Carbohydrate 16.6g, of which sugars 16.6g; Fat 0.2g, of which saturates 0g; Cholesterol 0mg; Calcium 19mg; Fibre 3.3g; Sodium 7mg.

Clementine Jelly

Jelly isn't only for children: this adult version has a clean fruity taste and can be made extra special by adding a dash of white rum or Cointreau.

Serves 4
12 clementines
clear grape juice (see method for amount)
15ml/1 tbsp powdered gelatine
25g/1oz/2 tbsp caster (superfine) sugar
whipped cream, to decorate

1 Squeeze the juice from eight of the clementines and pour into a jug (pitcher). Make up to 600ml/1 pint/2½ cups with the grape juice, then strain the mixture through a sieve (strainer).

2 Pour half the juice mixture into a pan. Sprinkle the gelatine on top, leave to stand for 5 minutes, then heat gently until the gelatine has completely dissolved. Stir in the sugar, then the remaining juice; set aside.

3 Pare the rind very thinly from the remaining fruit and set it aside. Using a small sharp knife, cut between the membrane and fruit to separate the citrus segments. Discard the membrane and white pith.

4 Place half the segments in four dessert glasses and cover with some of the liquid fruit jelly. Leave in the refrigerator to set.

5 When the jellies are set, arrange the remaining segments on top. Carefully pour over the remaining liquid jelly and chill until set. Cut the pared clementine rind into fine shreds. Serve the jellies topped with a generous spoonful of whipped cream scattered with clementine rind shreds.

> **Variation**
> Use four ruby grapefruit instead of clementines, if you prefer. Squeeze the juice from half of them and segment the rest, discarding any bitter white pith.

Chocolate Mandarin Trifle

Rich chocolate custard is combined with mandarin oranges to make a colourful and tasty trifle that is too tempting to resist.

Serves 6–8
4 trifle sponges
14 amaretti
60ml/4 tbsp Amaretto di Saronno or sweet sherry
8 mandarin oranges

For the custard
200g/7oz plain (semisweet) chocolate, broken into squares
25g/1oz/2 tbsp cornflour (cornstarch) or custard powder
25g/1oz/2 tbsp caster (superfine) sugar
2 egg yolks
200ml/7fl oz/scant 1 cup milk
250g/9oz/generous 1 cup mascarpone

For the topping
250g/9oz/generous 1 cup mascarpone or fromage frais
chocolate shapes
mandarin slices

1 Break up the trifle sponges and place them in a large glass serving dish. Crumble the amaretti over and then sprinkle with Amaretto or sweet sherry.

2 Squeeze the juice from two of the mandarins and sprinkle into the dish. Segment the rest and put in the dish.

3 Make the custard. Melt the chocolate in a heatproof bowl over hot water. In a separate bowl, mix the cornflour or custard powder, sugar and egg yolks to a smooth paste.

4 Heat the milk in a small pan until almost boiling, then pour in a steady stream on to the egg yolk mixture, stirring constantly. Return to the pan and stir over a low heat until the custard has thickened slightly and is smooth.

5 Stir in the mascarpone until melted, then add the melted chocolate; mix well. Spread over the trifle, cool, then chill to set.

6 To finish, spread the mascarpone or fromage frais over the custard, then decorate with chocolate shapes and the remaining mandarin slices just before serving.

Clementine Jelly Energy 97Kcal/414kJ; Protein 1.3g; Carbohydrate 24.1g, of which sugars 24.1g; Fat 0.2g, of which saturates 0g; Cholesterol 0mg; Calcium 51mg; Fibre 1.5g; Sodium 9mg.
Chocolate Energy 569Kcal/2394kJ; Protein 12.5g; Carbohydrate 80.3g, of which sugars 61.3g; Fat 23.1g, of which saturates 12.8g; Cholesterol 135mg; Calcium 162mg; Fibre 2.9g; Sodium 115mg.

Lemon Mousse

Light and airy, this heavenly
lemon dessert is both easy
to make and very refreshing.

Serves 6–8

50ml/2fl oz/¼ cup apple juice
   or water
30ml/2 tbsp powdered gelatine
15ml/1 tbsp grated lemon rind
90ml/6 tbsp fresh lemon juice

4 eggs, separated
175g/6oz icing (confectioners')
   sugar
250ml/8fl oz/1 cup double
   (heavy) cream

1 Pour the apple juice or water into a small bowl. Add
the gelatine until softened. Add 120ml/4fl oz/½ cup boiling
water and stir to dissolve the gelatine, then stir in the lemon
rind and juice.

2 Combine the egg yolks with 150g/5oz/1¼ cups of the icing
sugar in a bowl, and beat until frothy. Fold the gelatine mixture
into the egg yolks. Refrigerate for at least 1 hour. Beat the egg
whites until stiff, and fold them into the egg yolk mixture.

3 Beat the cream until stiff peaks form, and stir in the remaining
icing sugar. Fold half the cream into the egg and lemon mixture.

4 Spoon the mousse into a deep 2 litre/3½ pint glass bowl or
6 individual bowls. Chill until set. Serve decorated with the
remaining whipped cream and lemon rind.

Note
*Raw eggs are not recommended for very young children and
pregnant women.*

Cook's Tip
*Crumble macaroons into the bottom of dessert glasses and
spoon the mousse over them.*

Lemon Coeur à la Crème
with Cointreau Oranges

This zesty dessert is the
ideal choice to follow all
kinds of main courses, but
in particular a rich dish
such as a meat roast.

Serves 4

225g/8oz/1 cup cottage
   cheese
250g/9oz/generous 1 cup
   mascarpone
50g/2oz/¼ cup caster
   (superfine) sugar

grated rind and juice of 1 lemon
spirals of orange rind, to decorate

For the Cointreau oranges
4 oranges
10ml/2 tsp cornflour (cornstarch)
15ml/1 tbsp icing
   (confectioners') sugar
60ml/4 tbsp Cointreau

1 Put the cottage cheese in a food processor or blender and
process until smooth. Add the mascarpone, caster sugar, lemon
rind and juice and process briefly to mix the ingredients.

2 Line four coeur à la crème moulds with muslin (cheesecloth),
and divide the mixture among them. Level the surface of each,
then place the moulds on a plate to catch any liquid that drains
from the cheese. Cover and chill overnight.

3 Make the Cointreau oranges. Squeeze the juice from two
oranges and pour into a measuring cup. Make the juice up
to 250ml/8fl oz/1 cup with water, then pour into a small pan.
Blend a little of the juice mixture with the cornflour and add to
the pan with the icing sugar. Heat the sauce, stirring until thick.

4 Using a sharp knife, peel the remaining oranges. Cut between
the membrane and fruit to separate the orange segments.
Discard the membrane and white pith. Add the segments to
the pan, stir to coat, then set aside. When cool, stir in the
Cointreau. Cover and chill overnight.

5 Turn the moulds out on to plates and surround with the
oranges. Serve decorated with spirals of orange rind.

Lemon Mousse Energy 278kcal/1159kJ; Protein 3.7g; Carbohydrate 23.4g, of which sugars 23.4g; Fat 19.6g, of which saturates 11.2g; Cholesterol 138mg; Calcium 41mg; Fibre 0g; Sodium 43mg.
Lemon Coeur Energy 333Kcal/1400kJ; Protein 14.3g; Carbohydrate 36.8g, of which sugars 34.5g; Fat 11.4g, of which saturates 7g; Cholesterol 35mg; Calcium 137mg; Fibre 2.1g; Sodium 178mg.

Quince Mousse with Almond Biscuits

Quinces and ginger are perfectly matched flavour partners in the autumn.

Serves 4
450g/1lb quinces, peeled and cored
75g/3oz/⅓ cup caster
  (superfine) sugar
grated rind of ½ lemon
90ml/6 tbsp water
2 pieces stem ginger in syrup,
  finely chopped, plus 15ml/
  1 tbsp syrup from the jar
15ml/1 tbsp powdered gelatine

150ml/¼ pint/⅔ cup double
  (heavy) cream
2 egg whites
mint leaves and blackberries
  dusted with caster (superfine)
  sugar, to decorate

For the biscuits (cookies)
50g/2oz/¼ cup butter
30ml/2 tbsp caster (superfine) sugar
50g/2oz/½ cup plain
  (all-purpose) flour
50g/2oz/½ cup ground almonds
a few drops of almond extract

1 Grease four ramekins and line with baking parchment. Put the quinces in a pan with the sugar, lemon rind and 60ml/4 tbsp of the water. Cover and simmer for 10 minutes or until soft. Remove the lid and cook until the liquid has almost evaporated.

2 Cool the quinces slightly, then purée in a food processor or blender. Press the purée through a sieve (strainer) into a large bowl, then stir in the ginger and syrup and set aside.

3 Pour the remaining 30ml/2 tbsp water into a bowl and sprinkle the gelatine on top. Leave for 5 minutes. Stand the bowl in a pan of hot water until the gelatine has dissolved.

4 Whip the cream. Stir the gelatine into the quince purée, then fold in the cream. Whisk the egg whites to stiff peaks and fold into the quince mixture. Divide among the ramekins, level the tops and chill until firm. Preheat the oven to 190°C/375°F/Gas 5.

5 Make the biscuits. Line a baking sheet with baking parchment. Cream the butter and sugar. Add the flour, almonds and extract and mix to a dough. Roll out and cut into rounds with a 7.5cm/ 3in cutter. Chill on the sheet for 10 minutes. Bake for 12 minutes. Cool slightly on the paper, then lift on to a wire rack to cool. Turn out the mousse on to plates. Decorate and serve.

Steamed Custard in Nectarines

Steaming nectarines or peaches brings out their natural colour and sweetness, so this is a good way of making the most of underripe or less flavourful fruit.

Serves 4–6
6 nectarines
1 large (US extra large) egg
45ml/3 tbsp palm sugar or light
  muscovado (brown) sugar
30ml/2 tbsp coconut milk

1 Cut the nectarines in half. Using a teaspoon, scoop out the stones (pits) and a little of the surrounding flesh.

2 Lightly beat the egg, then add the sugar and the coconut milk. Beat until the sugar has dissolved.

3 Transfer the nectarines to a steamer and carefully fill the cavities three-quarters full with the custard mixture. Steam over a pan of simmering water for 5–10 minutes. Remove from the heat and leave to cool completely before transferring to plates and serving.

> **Cook's Tip**
> Palm sugar, also known as jaggery, is made from the sap of certain Asian palm trees, such as coconut and palmyrah. It is available from Asian food stores. If you buy it as a cake or a large lump, grate it before use.

> **Variations**
> • To add extra colour to this dessert, drizzle the cold fruit with a raspberry sauce. To make the sauce, simply purée fresh raspberries, then press through a sieve (strainer) to remove the seeds. Sweeten with icing (confectioners') sugar to taste.
> • Serve the nectarines with chocolate hazelnut rounds – melt some plain (semisweet) chocolate and spread on to circles drawn on baking parchment. Sprinkle with flaked (sliced) hazelnuts and leave to set. Remove from the paper and serve alongside.

Quince Mousse Energy 534kcal/2226kJ; Protein 6.4g; Carbohydrate 50.3g, of which sugars 40.4g; Fat 37.6g, of which saturates 18.6g; Cholesterol 78mg; Calcium 95mg; Fibre 3.8g; Sodium 145mg.
Steamed Custard Energy 103Kcal/438kJ; Protein 3.2g; Carbohydrate 21.6g, of which sugars 21.6g; Fat 1.1g, of which saturates 0.3g; Cholesterol 32mg; Calcium 21mg; Fibre 1.8g; Sodium 19mg.

Peach Melba Syllabub

If you are making these sophisticated temptations for a dinner party, cook the peaches and raspberries the day before to allow the fruit to chill. Whip up the syllabub at the very last minute, to make a delicious, light-as-a-cloud topping.

Serves 6
4 peaches, peeled, stoned (pitted) and sliced
300ml/½ pint/1¼ cups blush or red grape juice
115g/4oz/⅔ cup raspberries

raspberry or mint leaves, to decorate
ratafia biscuits (almond macaroons) or other small crisp biscuits (cookies), to serve

For the syllabub
60ml/4 tbsp peach schnapps
30ml/2 tbsp blush or red grape juice
300ml/½ pint/1¼ cups double (heavy) cream

1 Place the peach slices in a large pan. Add the grape juice. Bring to the boil, then cover, lower the heat and simmer for 5–7 minutes or until tender.

2 Add the raspberries and remove from the heat. Set aside in the refrigerator until cold. Divide the peach and raspberry mixture among six dessert glasses.

3 For the syllabub, place the peach schnapps and grape juice in a large bowl and whisk in the cream until it forms soft peaks.

4 Spoon the syllabub on top of the fruit and decorate each portion with a fresh raspberry or mint leaf. Serve with ratafias or other crisp biscuits.

Variations
Use pears and sliced kiwi fruit in place of peaches and raspberries. Instead of the syllabub, try topping the fruit with whipped cream flavoured with Advocaat and finely chopped preserved stem ginger.

Peach & Ginger Pashka

A low-fat version of the Russian Easter favourite – a glorious cheese dessert flavoured with peaches and preserved stem ginger.

Serves 4
350g/12oz/1½ cups low-fat cottage cheese
2 ripe peaches or nectarines
90g/3½oz/scant ½ cup low-fat natural (plain) yogurt

2 pieces preserved stem ginger in syrup, drained and chopped, plus 30ml/2 tbsp syrup from the jar
2.5ml/½ tsp vanilla extract
1 peach or nectarine, peeled and sliced, and 10ml/2 tsp slivered almonds, toasted, to decorate

1 Drain the cottage cheese and rub it through a fine sieve (strainer) into a bowl. Remove the stones (pits) from the peaches or nectarines and roughly chop.

2 Mix together the chopped peaches or nectarines in a large bowl with the low-fat cottage cheese, yogurt, preserved stem ginger, syrup and vanilla extract.

3 Line a new, clean flower pot or a sieve (strainer) with a piece of clean, fine cloth, such as muslin (cheesecloth).

4 Add the cheese mixture and wrap over the cloth to cover. Place a saucer on top and weigh down. Stand over a bowl in a cool place and leave to drain overnight.

5 To serve, unwrap the cloth and turn the pashka out on to a serving plate. Decorate the pashka with peach or nectarine slices and toasted almonds.

Cook's Tip
Rather than making one large pashka, line four to six cups or ramekins with the clean cloth or muslin (cheesecloth) and divide the mixture evenly among them.

Peach Melba Energy 329Kcal/1363kJ; Protein 2g; Carbohydrate 17g, of which sugars 17g; Fat 27g, of which saturates 16.7g; Cholesterol 69mg; Calcium 45mg; Fibre 1.6g; Sodium 17mg.
Peach and Ginger Energy 157Kcal/660kJ; Protein 13.3g; Carbohydrate 14.7g, of which sugars 14.6g; Fat 5.1g, of which saturates 2.3g; Cholesterol 14mg; Calcium 165mg; Fibre 1g; Sodium 302mg.

Apricots with Orange Cream

Creamy mascarpone cheese delicately flavoured with orange juice makes a delicious topping for chilled apricots. Here, the apricots themselves are infused with the subtle flavours of orange and cinnamon, with dessert wine added for a rich taste of sweet luxury.

Serves 4
450g/1lb/2 cups ready-to-eat
   dried apricots
strip of orange peel

1 cinnamon stick
45ml/3 tbsp caster (superfine)
   sugar
450ml/¾ pint/scant 2 cups
   water
150ml/¼ pint/⅔ cup sweet
   dessert wine
115g/4oz/½ cup mascarpone
45ml/3 tbsp orange juice
pinch of ground cinnamon
   and fresh mint sprig,
   to decorate

1 Place the apricots, orange peel, cinnamon stick and 15ml/1 tbsp of the sugar in a pan and cover with the water. Bring to the boil, cover and simmer gently for 25 minutes, or until the fruit is tender.

2 Remove from the heat and stir in the dessert wine. Leave until cold, then chill for at least 3–4 hours or overnight.

3 Mix together the mascarpone, orange juice and the remaining sugar in a bowl and beat thoroughly until the mixture is smooth, then chill.

4 Just before serving the dessert, remove the cinnamon stick and orange peel.

5 Serve with a spoonful of the orange cream sprinkled with cinnamon and decorated with a sprig of fresh mint.

> **Cook's Tip**
> The sweet wine Muscat de Beaumes de Venise is a good choice for this recipe, but any sweet muscat wine would do.

Apricots in Marsala

Rich Marsala creates a beautifully flavoured syrup for the apricots. Serve with amaretti to add to the Italian tone of the dish.

Serves 4
12 apricots
50g/2oz/¼ cup caster
   (superfine) sugar
300ml/½ pint/1¼ cups Marsala
2 strips pared orange rind
1 vanilla pod (bean), split

250ml/8fl oz/1 cup water
150ml/¼ pint/⅔ cup double
   (heavy) or whipping cream
15ml/1 tbsp icing
   (confectioners') sugar
1.5ml/¼ tsp ground cinnamon
150ml/¼ pint/⅔ cup Greek
   (US strained plain) yogurt
amaretti, to serve

1 Halve and stone (pit) the apricots, then place in a bowl of boiling water for about 30 seconds. Drain well, then slip off their skins.

2 Place the caster sugar, Marsala, orange rind, vanilla pod and water in a pan. Heat gently until the sugar dissolves. Bring to the boil, without stirring, then simmer for 2–3 minutes.

3 Add the apricot halves to the pan and poach for 5–6 minutes, or until just tender. Using a slotted spoon, transfer the apricots to a serving dish.

4 Boil the syrup rapidly until reduced by half, then pour over the apricots and leave to cool. Cover and chill. Remove the orange rind and vanilla pod.

5 Whip the cream with the icing sugar and cinnamon until it forms soft peaks. Gently fold in the yogurt. Spoon the cream into a serving bowl and chill. Serve with the apricots.

> **Cook's Tip**
> Make sure that the apricots are completely covered by the syrup, so that they don't discolour.

Apricots in Marsala Energy 448Kcal/1870kJ; Protein 4.2g; Carbohydrate 36g, of which sugars 36g; Fat 24.1g, of which saturates 14.5g; Cholesterol 51mg; Calcium 104mg; Fibre 2.1g; Sodium 41mg.
Apricots with Orange Energy 313Kcal/1326kJ; Protein 7.3g; Carbohydrate 56.9g, of which sugars 56.9g; Fat 4.9g, of which saturates 2.6g; Cholesterol 12mg; Calcium 95mg; Fibre 7.1g; Sodium 23mg.

Cherry Syllabub

This recipe follows the style of the earliest syllabubs from the sixteenth and seventeenth centuries, producing a frothy, creamy layer over a liquid one. Ripe cherries sprinkled with fiery Kirsch form the delicious bottom layer.

30ml/2 tbsp Kirsch
2 egg whites
75g/3oz/6 tbsp caster
   (superfine) sugar
30ml/2 tbsp fresh
   lemon juice
150ml/1/4 pint/2/3 cup sweet
   white wine
300ml/1/2 pint/1 1/4 cups double
   (heavy) cream

Serves 4
225g/8oz ripe dark cherries,
   pitted and chopped

1 Divide the chopped cherries among six tall dessert glasses and sprinkle over the Kirsch.

2 In a clean, grease-free bowl, whisk the egg whites until stiff. Gently fold in the sugar, lemon juice and wine.

3 In a separate bowl (but using the same whisk), lightly beat the cream then fold into the egg white mixture.

4 Spoon the cream mixture over the cherries, then chill overnight. Serve straight from the refrigerator.

Cook's Tip
Be careful not to over-beat the egg whites, otherwise they will separate, which will spoil the consistency of the dessert. Whip the cream until it is just forming soft peaks.

Variation
You can use crushed fresh raspberries or chopped ripe peaches or strawberries instead of the cherries. Ratafia biscuits (almond macaroons) make the perfect accompaniment.

Strawberry Snow

Strawberries have a delicate, fragrant taste, and most desserts made from them are best eaten soon after they are made. Dishes like this are generally made from fresh berries in the summer months, such as strawberries and raspberries, but can also be made with apples in the autumn.

Serves 4
120ml/4fl oz/1/2 cup water
15ml/1 tbsp powdered gelatine
300g/11oz/2 3/4 cups strawberries,
   crushed lightly
250ml/8fl oz/1 cup double
   (heavy) cream
4 egg whites
90g/3 1/2oz/1/2 cup caster
   (superfine) sugar
halved strawberries, to decorate

1 Put the water in a small heatproof bowl and sprinkle in the gelatine. Stand the bowl over a pan of hot water and heat gently until dissolved. Remove the bowl from the pan and leave to cool slightly.

2 Put half the crushed strawberries in a pan and bring to the boil. Remove from the heat, then stir in the dissolved gelatine. Chill in the refrigerator for about 2 hours until syrupy.

3 Pour the cream into a bowl and whisk until it holds its shape. Whisk the egg whites until stiff, gradually adding the sugar as they rise.

4 Fold the egg whites into the cooled strawberry mixture, then fold in the remaining crushed strawberries followed by the whipped cream.

5 Turn into individual serving dishes and serve immediately or chill until required. Serve decorated with halved strawberries.

Cook's Tip
Strawberry Snow freezes well and can then be served as an iced strawberry parfait. All you have to do to make this is spoon the mixture into a loaf tin (pan) lined with clear film (plastic wrap) and freeze for a couple of hours, until it is firm.

Cherry Syllabub Energy 514Kcal/2132kJ; Protein 3.3g; Carbohydrate 29.6g, of which sugars 29.6g; Fat 40.3g, of which saturates 25.1g; Cholesterol 103mg; Calcium 60mg; Fibre 0.5g; Sodium 54mg.
Strawberry Snow Energy 443kcal/1841kJ; Protein 7.8g; Carbohydrate 29.1g, of which sugars 29.1g; Fat 33.7g, of which saturates 20.9g; Cholesterol 86mg; Calcium 56mg; Fibre 0.8g; Sodium 81mg.

Raspberry Trifle

This ever-popular dessert looks wonderful served in a glass bowl so that you can see all the layers. Use fresh or frozen raspberries.

Serves 6–8
175g/6oz trifle sponges, or 2.5cm/1in cubes of plain Victoria sponge or coarsely crumbled sponge fingers
60ml/4 tbsp medium sherry
115g/4oz raspberry jam
275g/10oz/1⅔ cups raspberries
450ml/¾ pint/scant 2 cups custard, flavoured with 30ml/2 tbsp medium or sweet sherry
300ml/½ pint/1¼ cups whipping cream
15ml/1 tbsp icing (confectioners') sugar
toasted flaked (sliced) almonds and mint leaves, to decorate

1 Spread half of the sponges, cake cubes or sponge fingers over the bottom of a large serving bowl. (A glass bowl is best for presentation.)

2 Sprinkle half of the sherry over the cake to moisten it. Spoon over half of the jam, dotting it evenly over the cake cubes.

3 Reserve a few raspberries for decoration. Make a layer of half of the remaining raspberries on top.

4 Pour over half of the custard, covering the fruit and cake. Repeat the layers. Cover and chill for at least 2 hours.

5 Before serving, whip the cream with the icing sugar until it forms soft peaks. Spoon the sweetened whipped cream evenly over the top of the custard. To decorate, sprinkle with toasted flaked almonds and arrange the reserved raspberries and the mint leaves on top. Serve as soon as possible.

Variation
Use other ripe summer fruit such as apricots, peaches, nectarines and strawberries in the trifle, with jam and liqueur to complement the fruit.

Meringue Cake with Raspberries

This summer dessert uses a basic meringue mixture. For the best results, avoid very fresh eggs, and ensure they are at room temperature.

Serves 8–10
4 egg whites
225g/8oz/generous 1 cup caster (superfine) sugar

For the filling
300ml/½ pint/1¼ cups whipping cream
caster (superfine) sugar, to taste
3–4 drops of vanilla extract or 2.5ml/½ tsp liqueur, such as Kirsch or Crème de Framboise
450g/1lb/2¾ cups raspberries
icing (confectioners') sugar, for dusting

1 Preheat the oven to 150°C/300°F/Gas 2. Line two baking sheets with baking parchment and draw two circles: one 23cm/9in in diameter and the other 20cm/8in. Fit a piping (icing) bag with a 1cm/½in star nozzle.

2 Whisk the egg whites until stiff peaks form. Add half of the sugar, 15ml/1 tbsp at a time; keep whisking until the mixture stands in stiff peaks. Using a metal spoon, carefully fold in the remaining sugar to mix thoroughly without the loss of volume.

3 Use most of the mixture to pipe inside the prepared circles, then put the remaining meringue into the piping bag and use to pipe nine mini meringues on to the surrounding parchment.

4 Cook in the preheated oven for 50–60 minutes, until lightly coloured and quite dry (the small ones will take less time). Peel off the parchment, cool the meringues on wire racks and, when cold, store immediately in airtight containers.

5 Whip the cream until soft peaks form, sweeten with caster sugar and flavour with a few drops of vanilla extract or liqueur.

6 Lay the larger meringue circle on a serving dish. Spread with three-quarters of the cream and three-quarters of the raspberries, reserving the best berries for the top. Add the smaller meringue circle, spread with the remaining cream, and arrange the small meringues around the edge. Decorate the top with the remaining fruit. Dust lightly with icing sugar.

Raspberry Trifle Energy 330Kcal/1382kJ; Protein 5.1g; Carbohydrate 35.9g, of which sugars 29.1g; Fat 17.7g, of which saturates 9.9g; Cholesterol 90mg; Calcium 102mg; Fibre 1.1g; Sodium 59mg.
Meringue Cake Energy 298kcal/1252kJ; Protein 3.2g; Carbohydrate 39.5g, of which sugars 39.5g; Fat 15.3g, of which saturates 9.5g; Cholesterol 39mg; Calcium 55mg; Fibre 1.4g; Sodium 44mg.

Autumn Fruit Pudding

As its name suggests, this is a tasty seasonal variation of summer fruit pudding, using apples, blackberries and plums – a great combination.

Serves 6
10 slices white or brown bread, at least one day old
1 cooking apple, peeled, cored and sliced
225g/8oz ripe red plums, halved and stoned (pitted)
225g/8oz blackberries
75g/3oz/6 tbsp caster (superfine) sugar
60ml/4 tbsp water
natural (plain) yogurt or Greek (US strained plain) yogurt, to serve

1 Remove the crusts from the bread. Cut a round from one slice of bread to fit in the base of a 1.2 litre/2 pint/5 cup round ovenproof bowl and place in position.

2 Cut the remaining slices of bread in half and use to line the bowl, overlapping the pieces as you work. Save some pieces of bread for the top.

3 Place the apple, plums, blackberries, caster sugar and the water in a pan. Heat gently until the sugar dissolves, then simmer for 10 minutes, until soft. Remove from the heat.

4 Spoon the fruit into the bread-lined bowl, reserving the juice. Cut the remaining bread to fit entirely over the fruit, then gently spoon over the reserved fruit juice.

5 Stand the bowl on a plate and cover with a saucer or small plate that will just fit inside the top of the bowl. Place a heavy weight on top. Chill the pudding overnight. Turn out on to a serving plate and serve with natural or Greek yogurt.

Cook's Tip
Choose good-quality bread, with slices at least 5mm/¼in thick so that it supports the fruit when the pudding is turned out.

Dried Fruit Compote

This dessert uses a mix of frozen fruit and dried fruits. It doesn't take long to prepare, but must be made ahead of time, to allow the dried fruit to plump up and the flavours to blend. It is also good for breakfast.

Serves 4
115g/4oz/½ cup ready-to-eat dried apricots, halved
115g/4oz/½ cup ready-to-eat dried peaches, halved
750ml/1¼ pints/3 cups water
1 pear
1 apple
1 orange
115g/4oz/1 cup frozen mixed raspberries and blackberries, thawed
1 cinnamon stick
50g/2oz/¼ cup caster (superfine) sugar
15ml/1 tbsp clear honey
30ml/2 tbsp lemon juice

1 Place the dried apricots and peaches in a large pan and pour in 600ml/1 pint/2½ cups of the water.

2 Peel and core the pear and apple, then dice. Remove the peel and pith from the orange and cut into wedges. Add all the cut fruit to the pan with the raspberries and blackberries.

3 Pour in the remaining water. Add the cinnamon stick, stir in the sugar and honey, and heat gently, stirring until the sugar and honey have dissolved. Bring to the boil. Cover and simmer for 10 minutes, then remove the pan from the heat.

4 Stir in the lemon or lime juice. Leave to cool completely, then transfer the fruit and syrup to a bowl, cover with clear film (plastic wrap) and chill for 1–2 hours before serving.

Variation
Depending on the season and what is available, you can swap the fruits around, using dried apples and pears and fresh apricots and peaches instead of the combination suggested in the recipe. Seasonal cranberries are a delicious alternative to the raspberries and blackberries.

Autumn Fruit Pudding Energy 182Kcal/775kJ; Protein 4.4g; Carbohydrate 41.5g, of which sugars 20.4g; Fat 1g, of which saturates 0g; Cholesterol 0mg; Calcium 77mg; Fibre 2.6g; Sodium 237mg.
Dried Fruit Compote Energy 190kcal/811kJ; Protein 3.3g; Carbohydrate 46g, of which sugars 46g; Fat 0.5g, of which saturates 0g; Cholesterol 0mg; Calcium 75mg; Fibre 6g; Sodium 13mg.

Red Fruit Jelly

This wonderful bright red dish is a very simple dessert to make. During the summer it can be made with fresh berries, but you can also use frozen fruit. This particular compote recipe comes from the northern region of Germany.

Serves 4

20g/³⁄₄oz caster (superfine) sugar
200ml/7fl oz/scant 1 cup red grape juice
2 pieces of star anise
1 cinnamon stick
15g/¹⁄₂oz/2 tbsp cornflour (cornstarch)
450g/1lb mixed berries (strawberries, blueberries, cranberries, blackberries, raspberries or redcurrants), washed
fresh mint leaves, to decorate
single (light) cream, to serve

1 Heat the sugar in a pan over medium heat until it caramelizes. When it turns golden brown, plunge the base of the pan in a bowl of cold water to stop the sugar burning.

2 Stir in the grape juice, add the spices and return to the heat.

3 Mix the cornflour with a little cold water. When the juice comes to the boil, stir in the cornflour mixture and cook, stirring, for 1 minute to thicken.

4 Halve any large berries, and add them all to the hot juice, bring to the boil again, then remove from the heat and leave to cool.

5 Spoon the cold compote into bowls, decorate with mint leaves and serve with cream.

Cook's Tip
When buying star anise, look for whole, unbroken pieces. They can be stored in a cool, dark place for several months.

Chilled Fruit Pudding

This trifle-like dish is just as good made with frozen fruits, so it is great for making at Christmas time.

Serves 4–6

550g/1lb/4oz mixed soft fruit, such as raspberries, blackberries, blackcurrants and redcurrants
50g/2oz/4 tbsp sugar
large thick slice of bread with crusts removed, about 125g/4¹⁄₄oz without crusts
300ml/¹⁄₂ pint/1¹⁄₄ cups double (heavy) cream
45ml/3 tbsp elderflower cordial
150ml/¹⁄₄ pint/²⁄₃ cup thick natural (plain) yogurt

1 Reserve a few raspberries, blackberries, blackcurrants or redcurrants for decoration, then put the remainder into a pan with the sugar and 30ml/2 tbsp water. Bring just to the boil, cover and simmer gently for 4–5 minutes until the fruit is soft and plenty of juice has formed.

2 Cut the slice of bread into cubes, measuring about 2.5cm/1in, and put them into one large dish or individual serving bowls or dessert glasses.

3 Spoon the fruit mixture over the bread and leave to cool.

4 Whip the cream with the elderflower cordial until stiff peaks begin to form. Gently stir in the yogurt and spoon the mixture over the top of the fruit.

5 Chill in the refrigerator until required. Just before serving, decorate the top with the reserved fruit.

Cook's Tip
Use bread from an unsliced farmhouse loaf for this recipe.

Variation
Instead of mixing yogurt into the topping, try using the same quantity of ready-made custard – it gives a richer result.

Red Fruit Jelly Energy 86kcal/366kJ; Protein 1.1g; Carbohydrate 21.3g, of which sugars 17.8g; Fat 0.2g, of which saturates 0g; Cholesterol 0mg; Calcium 31mg; Fibre 1.3g; Sodium 13mg.
Chilled Fruit Energy 382kcal/1592kJ; Protein 5.2g; Carbohydrate 29.9g, of which sugars 20.2g; Fat 27.8g, of which saturates 16.9g; Cholesterol 69mg; Calcium 124mg; Fibre 2.6g; Sodium 144mg.

Coconut Rice with Fruit Coulis

Desserts similar to this coconut and rice treat are served in countries all over the Far East, often accompanied by fresh tropical fruit, such as mangoes, pineapple and guavas.

Serves 4–6
75g/3oz/scant ½ cup jasmine
  rice, soaked overnight in
  175ml/6fl oz/¾ cup water
350ml/12fl oz/1½ cups
  coconut milk
150ml/¼ pint/⅔ cup single
  (light) cream
50g/2oz/¼ cup caster
  (superfine) sugar
raspberries and fresh mint leaves,
  to decorate

For the coulis
75g/3oz/¾ cup blackcurrants,
  stalks removed
25g/1oz/2 tbsp caster
  (superfine) sugar
75g/3oz/½ cup fresh or
  frozen raspberries

1 Put the rice and its soaking water into a food processor and process for a few minutes until the mixture is soupy.

2 Heat the coconut milk and cream in a non-stick pan. When the mixture is on the point of boiling, stir in the rice mixture. Cook over a very gentle heat for 10 minutes, stirring constantly.

3 Stir the sugar into the coconut rice mixture and continue cooking for a further 10–15 minutes, or until thick and creamy.

4 Line a rectangular tin (pan) with non-stick baking parchment. Pour the coconut rice mixture into the pan, cool, then chill in the refrigerator until the dessert is set and firm.

5 Meanwhile, make the coulis. Put the blackcurrants in a bowl and sprinkle with the sugar. Set aside for 30 minutes. Turn the blackcurrants and raspberries into a sieve (strainer) set over a bowl. Using a spoon, press the fruit so that the juices collect in the bowl. Taste the coulis and add more sugar if necessary.

6 Cut the coconut cream into diamonds. Spoon a little coulis on to individual plates, arrange the diamonds on top and decorate with raspberries and mint leaves. Serve immediately.

Blackcurrant Mousse with Daisies

Here, daisy petals add a simple, carefree topping to this delicious blackcurrant dessert. They look pretty with rhubarb or gooseberry, too. In fact, they are extremely versatile, and can be used with any type of fruit dessert.

Serves 4–6
800g/1lb/12oz fresh or frozen
  blackcurrants
150g/5oz caster (superfine)
  sugar
450ml/¾ pint/scant 2 cups
  natural (plain) yogurt
pink and red daisies, and sprigs
  of blackcurrants, to decorate

1 Strip the blackcurrants off the stalks and put in a pan with 90ml/6 tbsp water and the sugar.

2 Cover tightly and simmer gently for about 10 minutes, until the fruit is pulpy. Blend in a food processor, then press through a sieve and leave to cool.

3 Stir the yogurt into the purée until evenly combined, then spoon the mixture into serving glasses and chill in the refrigerator until ready to serve.

4 Add the blackcurrants to the top of each serving glass, then gently pull the quills from the daisies and scatter over the top.

Cook's Tips
• Edible flowers add both interest and flavour to many dishes, but remember that not all flowers are edible. If uncertain, consult a good reference book prior to consumption.
• If you are lucky enough to have blackcurrants growing in your local area, they can be picked from the wild.
• For a richer flavour, fold the same quantity of lightly whipped cream into the blackcurrant purée instead of the natural (plain) yogurt.

Coconut Rice Energy 165Kcal/696kJ; Protein 2.3g; Carbohydrate 28.7g, of which sugars 18.8g; Fat 5.1g, of which saturates 3.2g; Cholesterol 14mg; Calcium 59mg; Fibre 0.8g; Sodium 73mg.
Blackcurrant Mousse Energy 195kcal/1831kJ; Protein 5g; Carbohydrate 41g, of which sugars 41g; Fat 2g, of which saturates 1g; Cholesterol 8mg; Calcium 233 mg; Fibre 10.4g; Sodium 6.5mg.

Gooseberry & Elderflower Fool

The combination of gooseberries and elderflowers is a match made in heaven, each bringing out the flavour of the other. Serve with amaretti or other dessert biscuits for dipping.

Serves 6

450g/1lb/4 cups gooseberries, trimmed
30ml/2 tbsp water
50–75g/2–3oz/¼–⅓ cup caster (superfine) sugar
30ml/2 tbsp elderflower cordial
400g/14oz fresh ready-made custard
green food colouring (optional)
300ml/½ pint/1¼ cups double (heavy) cream
crushed amaretti, to decorate

1 Put the gooseberries and water in a pan. Cover and cook for 5–6 minutes or until the berries pop open.

2 Add the sugar and elderflower cordial to the gooseberries, then stir vigorously or mash until the fruit forms a pulp. Remove the pan from the heat, spoon the gooseberry pulp into a bowl and set aside to cool.

3 Stir the custard into the fruit. Add a few drops of food colouring, if using. Whip the cream to soft peaks, then fold it into the mixture and chill. Serve the fool in dessert glasses, decorated with crushed amaretti, and accompanied by amaretti.

Cook's Tip
In the summer, you can always make your own elderflower cordial by leaving freshly picked elderflower heads to infuse in water with sugar and lemon for 24 hours. Use immediately.

Variation
Use puréed raspberries, sweetened to taste, instead of the cooked gooseberries, and omit the elderflower cordial.

Rhubarb Fool

This is a quick and simple dessert that makes the most of field-grown rhubarb when it is in season. You could use hothouse rhubarb, but the flavour is inferior. Serve with Scottish shortbread and pass around a dish of heather honey for those with a sweet tooth.

Serves 4

450g/1lb rhubarb, trimmed
75g/3oz/scant ½ cup soft light brown sugar
whipped double (heavy) cream
ready-made thick custard
Scottish shortbread and heather honey (optional), to serve

1 Cut the rhubarb into pieces and wash thoroughly. Stew over a low heat with just the water clinging to it and the sugar. This takes about 10 minutes. Set aside to cool.

2 Pass the rhubarb through a fine sieve (strainer), so you have a thick purée.

3 Use equal parts of the purée, the whipped double cream and thick custard. Combine the purée and custard first, then fold in the cream. Chill in the refrigerator before serving. Serve with pieces of shortbread and a dish of heather honey, if you like.

Cook's Tips
• Rhubarb contains a lot of water, so you just need to barely cover the stalks when cooking it.
• Swirl the ingredients together to create a marbled effect.

Variations
• You can use another fruit if you like for this dessert – try either bramble fruits or apples. Other stewed fruits also work well, such as prunes or peaches. For something a little more exotic, you can use mangoes.
• For a low-fat option, substitute natural (plain) yogurt for the cream.

Gooseberry Energy 333Kcal/1381kJ; Protein 3.4g; Carbohydrate 15.5g, of which sugars 13.1g; Fat 28.4g, of which saturates 16.7g; Cholesterol 70mg; Calcium 107mg; Fibre 1.9g; Sodium 40mg.
Rhubarb Energy 439kcal/1828kJ; Protein 4.6g; Carbohydrate 34.1g, of which sugars 31.8g; Fat 31.7g, of which saturates 18.9g; Cholesterol 80mg; Calcium 233mg; Fibre 1.6g; Sodium 74mg.

Banana & Mascarpone Creams

If you are a fan of cold banana custard, then you'll love this recipe. It is a grown-up version of an old favourite. No one will guess that the secret is simply ready-made custard.

150ml/¼ pint/²/₃ cup Greek (US strained plain) yogurt
4 bananas
juice of 1 lime
50g/2oz/½ cup pecan nuts, coarsely chopped
120ml/4fl oz/½ cup maple syrup

Serves 4–6

250g/9oz/generous 1 cup mascarpone
300ml/½ pint/1¼ cups fresh ready-made custard

1 Combine the mascarpone, custard and yogurt in a large bowl and beat together until smooth. Make this mixture up to several hours ahead, if you like. Cover and chill in the refrigerator, then stir well before using.

2 Slice the bananas diagonally and place in a separate bowl. Pour over the lime juice and toss together until the bananas are coated in the juice.

3 Divide half the custard mixture among four or six dessert glasses and top each portion with a generous spoonful of the banana and lime mixture.

4 Spoon the remaining custard mixture into the glasses and top with the rest of the bananas. Sprinkle the nuts over the top. Drizzle maple syrup over each dessert and chill for 30 minutes before serving.

> **Variations**
> Use clear honey instead of maple syrup and walnuts instead of pecan nuts, if you like. Also, try layering in some crumbled biscuits, such as amaretti or ratafia biscuits (almond macaroons), shortbread crumbs or crushed meringues.

Banana & Apricot Caramel Trifle

Bananas are transformed into a marvellous trifle.

120ml/8 tbsp water
175–225g/6–8oz ginger cake, cubed
3 bananas, sliced, with one reserved for topping
115g/4oz/generous ½ cup granulated (white) sugar
300ml/½ pint/1¼ cups double (heavy) cream
a few drops of lemon juice

Serves 6–8

300ml/½ pint/1¼ cups milk
1 vanilla pod (bean), or 4–5 drops vanilla extract
40g/1½oz/3 tbsp caster (superfine) sugar
20ml/4 tsp cornflour (cornstarch)
3 egg yolks
60ml/4 tbsp apricot jam

1 Pour the milk into a small pan. Carefully split the vanilla pod (if using) down the middle and scrape the seeds into the pan.

2 Add the vanilla pod or extract to the milk and bring just to the boil, then remove the pan from the heat and set aside. When the milk has cooled slightly, remove the vanilla pod.

3 Whisk together the sugar, cornflour and egg yolks until pale and creamy. Whisk in the milk and return the mixture to the pan. Heat to simmering point, stirring constantly, and cook over a low heat until the custard coats the back of a wooden spoon thickly. Leave to cool, covering the surface with clear film (plastic wrap) to prevent a skin forming.

4 Put the apricot jam and 60ml/4 tbsp of the water in a pan and heat gently for 2–3 minutes, stirring. Put the cake in a deep serving bowl and pour on the apricot mixture. Cover with sliced bananas, then the custard. Chill for 1–2 hours.

5 Melt the sugar in a small pan with the remaining water and cook until just turning golden. Immediately pour on to a sheet of foil. Leave to harden, then break the caramel into pieces.

6 Whip the cream, then spread over the custard. Chill the trifle for 2–3 hours, then top with the remaining sliced banana, dipped into lemon juice, and the cracked caramel pieces.

Banana and Mascarpone Energy 457Kcal/1902kJ; Protein 12.4g; Carbohydrate 32.1g, of which sugars 30g; Fat 32.1g, of which saturates 9.1g; Cholesterol 19mg; Calcium 177mg; Fibre 1.2g; Sodium 142mg.
Banana and Apricot Energy 452Kcal/1893kJ; Protein 4.8g; Carbohydrate 53.8g, of which sugars 44.1g; Fat 25.7g, of which saturates 13.6g; Cholesterol 129mg; Calcium 104mg; Fibre 0.7g; Sodium 77mg.

Jamaican Fruit Trifle

This trifle is actually based on a Caribbean fool that consists of fruit stirred into thick vanilla-flavoured cream. This is a lighter version of the original.

Serves 8
1 large sweet pineapple, peeled and cored, about 350g/12oz
300ml/½ pint/1¼ cups double (heavy) cream
200ml/7fl oz/scant 1 cup crème fraîche
60ml/4 tbsp icing (confectioners') sugar, sifted
10ml/2 tsp pure vanilla extract
30ml/2 tbsp white or coconut rum
3 papayas, peeled, seeded and chopped
3 mangoes, peeled, stoned (pitted) and chopped
thinly pared rind and juice of 1 lime
25g/1oz/⅓ cup coarsely shredded or flaked coconut, toasted

1 Cut the pineapple into large chunks, place in a food processor or blender and process briefly until chopped. Turn into a sieve (strainer) placed over a bowl and leave for 5 minutes so that most of the juice drains from the fruit.

2 Whip the double cream to very soft peaks, then lightly but thoroughly fold in the crème fraîche, sifted icing sugar, vanilla extract and rum. Fold in the drained pineapple.

3 Place the papaya and mango in a large bowl and pour over the lime juice. Gently stir to mix. Shred the pared lime rind.

4 Divide the fruit mixture and the pineapple cream between eight dessert plates. Decorate with the lime shreds, toasted coconut and a few small pineapple leaves, if you like.

> **Cook's Tip**
> It is important to let the pineapple purée drain thoroughly, otherwise the pineapple cream will be watery. Don't throw away the drained pineapple juice – mix it with fizzy mineral water for a refreshing drink.

Pineapple Custards

These pineapple crème caramels are the perfect winter dinner party dessert. They are very easy to make, especially if you buy prepared fresh pineapple from the supermarket.

Serves 6
350g/12oz peeled fresh pineapple, chopped
150g/5oz/⅔ cup caster (superfine) sugar
4 eggs, lightly beaten

For the caramel
60ml/4 tbsp granulated (white) sugar
juice of 1 lime

1 Put the pineapple in a blender or food processor and process until smooth. Scrape the purée into a pan and add the sugar. Cook for 5 minutes or until reduced by one-third. The mixture should be thick but not jam-like, so add a little water if it is too thick. Transfer to a bowl and leave to cool.

2 Meanwhile make the caramel. Place the granulated sugar in a heavy pan over medium heat. As the sugar caramelizes around the edges, shake the pan to mix the sugar, but do not stir.

3 Remove the pan from the heat as soon as all the sugar has dissolved and the caramel has become golden brown. Immediately stir in the lime juice, taking care not to burn yourself. The hot caramel will spit when the lime juice is added, but this will stop. Divide the caramel among six ramekins and turn them so that they are coated evenly.

4 Preheat the oven to 180°C/350°F/Gas 4. Stir the eggs into the cool pineapple mixture. Divide the mixture equally among the ramekins. Place the moulds in a roasting pan and pour in warm water to come halfway up their sides. Cover with foil and bake for 45 minutes, until set. Allow to cool.

5 Just before serving, unmould the custards directly on to dessert plates. Loosen the edges of the custards with a knife, invert a dessert plate on top of each mould and quickly turn both over. Serve immediately.

Jamaican Fruit Energy 479kcal/1995kJ; Protein 2.3g; Carbohydrate 41g, of which sugars 40.7g; Fat 34.2g, of which saturates 22.7g; Cholesterol 80mg; Calcium 79mg; Fibre 3.6g; Sodium 27mg.
Pineapple Custards Energy 211kcal/895kJ; Protein 4.6g; Carbohydrate 42.5g, of which sugars 42.5g; Fat 3.8g, of which saturates 1g; Cholesterol 127mg; Calcium 48mg; Fibre 0.7g; Sodium 50mg.

Mango & Chocolate Crème Brûlée

Fresh mangoes topped with a wickedly rich chocolate cream and a layer of crunchy caramel make a fantastic dessert.

Serves 6

2 ripe mangoes, peeled, stoned (pitted) and chopped
300ml/½ pint/1¼ cups double (heavy) cream

300ml/½ pint/1¼ cups crème fraîche
1 vanilla pod (bean)
115g/4oz plain (semisweet) chocolate, chopped into small pieces
4 egg yolks
15ml/1 tbsp clear honey
90ml/6 tbsp demerara (raw) sugar, for the topping

1 Divide the mangoes among six flameproof dishes set on a baking sheet.

2 Mix the cream, crème fraîche and vanilla pod in a large heatproof bowl. Place the bowl over a pan of barely simmering water.

3 Heat the cream mixture for 10 minutes. Do not let the bowl touch the water or the cream may overheat. Remove the vanilla pod and stir in the chocolate, a few pieces at a time, until melted. When smooth, remove the bowl, but leave the pan of water over the heat.

4 Whisk the egg yolks and clear honey in a second heatproof bowl, then gradually pour in the chocolate cream, whisking constantly. Place over the pan of simmering water and stir until the chocolate custard thickens enough to coat the back of a wooden spoon.

5 Remove from the heat and spoon the custard over the mangoes. Cool, then chill in the refrigerator until set.

6 Preheat the grill (broiler) to high. Sprinkle 15ml/1 tbsp demerara sugar evenly over each dessert and spray lightly with a little water. Grill (broil) briefly, as close to the heat as possible, until the sugar melts and caramelizes. Chill again before serving.

Mango & Lime Fool

Canned mangoes are used here for convenience, but the dish tastes even better if made with fresh ones. Choose a good-quality variety such as the voluptuous Alphonso mango, which is wonderfully fragrant and tastes indescribably delicious.

Serves 4

400g/14oz can sliced mango
grated rind of 1 lime
juice of ½ lime
150ml/¼ pint/⅔ cup double (heavy) cream
90ml/6 tbsp Greek (US strained plain) yogurt
fresh mango slices, to decorate (optional)

1 Drain the canned mango slices and put them in the bowl of a food processor. Add the grated lime rind and the lime juice. Process until the mixture forms a smooth purée. Alternatively, mash the mango slices with a potato masher, then press through a sieve (strainer) into a bowl with the back of a wooden spoon. Stir in the lime rind and juice.

2 Pour the cream into a mixing bowl and add the yogurt. Whisk until the mixture is thick, and then quickly whisk in the mango mixture.

3 Spoon into tall glasses and chill for 1–2 hours. Just before serving, decorate each glass with fresh mango slices, if you like.

Cook's Tip
When mixing the cream and yogurt mixture with the mango purée, whisk just enough to combine, so as not to lose the lightness of the whipped cream mixture. If you prefer, fold the mixtures together lightly, so that the finished fool has a pretty rippled effect.

Variation
This fool can also be made with canned apricots, using orange rind and juice in place of the lime.

Mango and Chocolate Energy 670Kcal/2782kJ; Protein 5.2g; Carbohydrate 38.9g, of which sugars 38.4g; Fat 56g, of which saturates 34.6g; Cholesterol 261mg; Calcium 90mg; Fibre 1.8g; Sodium 31mg.
Mango and Lime Energy 289Kcal/1203kJ; Protein 2.4g; Carbohydrate 21.4g, of which sugars 21.3g; Fat 22.4g, of which saturates 13.7g; Cholesterol 51mg; Calcium 62mg; Fibre 0.7g; Sodium 27mg.

Passion Fruit Crème Caramels

Summer is the time when passion fruit are at their best. The fruit has an aromatic flavour that really permeates these crème caramels. Use some of the caramel for dipping the physalis in, to create a unique decoration for these pretty tropical treats.

Serves 4
185g/6½oz/scant 1 cup caster (superfine) sugar
75ml/5 tbsp water
4 passion fruit
4 physalis
3 eggs plus 1 egg yolk
150ml/¼ pint/⅔ cup double (heavy) cream
150ml/¼ pint/⅔ cup creamy milk

1 Place 150g/5oz/⅔ cup of the caster sugar in a heavy pan. Add the water and heat the mixture gently until the sugar has dissolved. Increase the heat and boil until the syrup turns a dark golden colour.

2 Meanwhile, cut each passion fruit in half. Scoop out the seeds from the passion fruit into a sieve (strainer) set over a bowl. Press the seeds against the sieve to extract all their juice. Spoon a few of the seeds into each of four 150ml/¼ pint/⅔ cup ramekins. Set the juice aside.

3 Peel back the papery casing from each physalis and dip the orange berries into the caramel. Place on a sheet of non-stick baking parchment and set aside. Pour the remaining caramel carefully into the ramekins.

4 Preheat the oven to 150°C/300°F/Gas 2. Whisk the eggs, egg yolk and remaining sugar in a bowl. Whisk in the cream and milk, then the passion fruit juice. Strain through a sieve into each ramekin, then place the ramekins in a baking tin (pan). Pour in hot water to come halfway up the sides of the dishes; bake for 40–45 minutes or until just set.

5 Remove the custards from the tin and leave to cool, then cover and chill them for 4 hours before serving. Run a knife between the edge of each ramekin and the custard and invert each in turn on to a dessert plate. Shake the ramekins firmly to release the custards. Decorate each with a dipped physalis.

Passion Fruit Creams

These delicately perfumed creams are light, with a fresh flavour from the seasonal passion fruit. Ripe passion fruit should look purple and wrinkled – choose fruit that are heavy for their size. When halved, the fragrant, sweet juicy flesh with small edible black seeds is revealed. These tasty creams can be decorated with mint or geranium leaves, and served with cream.

Serves 5–6
600ml/1 pint/2½ cups double (heavy) cream, or a mixture of single (light) and double (heavy) cream
6 passion fruits
30–45ml/2–3 tbsp vanilla sugar
5 eggs

1 Preheat the oven to 180°C/350°F/Gas 4. Line the bases of six 120ml/4fl oz/½ cup ramekins with rounds of baking parchment and place them in a roasting pan.

2 Heat the double cream or mix of single and double creams in a small pan to just below boiling point, then remove the pan from the heat.

3 Strain the flesh of four passion fruits through a sieve (strainer), reserving a little for the garnish, and beat together with the vanilla sugar and eggs until well combined. Whisk in the hot cream and then ladle the mixture into the ramekins.

4 Half fill the roasting pan with boiling water. Bake the creams in the preheated oven for 25–30 minutes, or until set, then leave to cool before chilling in the refrigerator for at least 2 hours until set.

5 When ready to serve the desserts, run a knife around the insides of the ramekins, then invert them on to individual serving plates, tapping the bases firmly to release the contents. Carefully peel off the baking parchment and chill in the refrigerator until ready to serve. Spoon on a little passion fruit flesh just before serving.

Passion Creams Energy 585kcal/2414kJ; Protein 7.2g; Carbohydrate 8.5g, of which sugars 8.5g; Fat 58.4g, of which saturates 34.7g; Cholesterol 296mg; Calcium 77mg; Fibre 0.5g; Sodium 84mg.
Passion Crème Caramels 318kcal/1336kJ; Protein 9.8g; Carbohydrate 36.6g, of which sugars 36.6g; Fat 16g, of which saturates 8.2g; Cholesterol 221mg; Calcium 150mg; Fibre 0g; Sodium 108mg.

Apple & Cider Sorbet

This dessert has a subtle apple flavour with just a hint of cider. Because the apple purée is very pale – almost white – you can add just a few drops of green food colouring to echo the pale green of the apple skin.

Serves 6

500g/1¼lb green-skinned
  eating apples
150g/5oz/¾ cup caster
  (superfine) sugar
300ml/½ pint/1¼ cups
  water
250ml/8fl oz/1 cup strong
  dry (hard) cider
few drops of green food
  colouring (optional)
strips of pared lime rind,
  to decorate

1 Quarter, core and roughly chop the apples. Put them in a pan. Add the caster sugar and half the water. Cover and simmer for 10 minutes or until the apples are soft.

2 Press the mixture through a sieve (strainer) placed over a bowl. Discard the apple skins. Stir the cider and the remaining water into the purée. Add a little green colouring, if you like.

3 Pour into a shallow freezer container and freeze for 6 hours, beating with a fork once or twice to break up the ice crystals. Alternatively, churn in an ice cream maker until firm. Scoop into dishes and decorate with strips of lime rind before serving.

Variation
Put 500g/1¼lb/5 cups strawberries in a food processor or blender and process to a purée, then press through a sieve (strainer) into a bowl. Stir in 150g/5oz/¾ cup caster (superfine) sugar and 350ml/12fl oz/1½ cups Champagne or sparkling white wine, mixing well until the sugar has dissolved. Pour into a shallow freezer container and freeze for 3 hours. Stiffly whisk an egg white in a grease-free bowl. Remove the ice from the freezer and beat well with a fork, then fold in the egg white. Return to the freezer for 3 hours more. Serve decorated with mint sprigs.

Spiced Sorbet Pears

Pears poached in wine make an elegant dessert at any time of the year. In this recipe, the cooked pears are hollowed out and filled with a delicious sorbet.

Serves 6

550ml/18fl oz/2½ cups
  red wine
2 cinnamon sticks, halved
115g/4oz/generous ½ cup caster
  (superfine) sugar
6 plump pears

1 Put the wine, cinnamon sticks and sugar in a heavy pan that is big enough for the pears. Heat gently to dissolve the sugar.

2 Peel the pears, leaving the stalks attached, and stand upright in the syrup, taking care not to pack them too tightly. Cover and simmer very gently for 10–20 minutes until just tender, turning so they colour evenly.

3 Lift out the pears with a slotted spoon and set aside to cool. Boil the cooking juice briefly until reduced to 350ml/12fl oz/ 1½ cups. Set aside and leave to cool.

4 Cut a deep 2.5cm/1in slice off the top of each pear and reserve. Use an apple corer to remove the cores. Using a teaspoon, scoop out the centre of each pear, leaving a thick shell. Put the scooped-out flesh in a food processor or blender. Put the hollowed pears and their lids in the freezer.

5 Strain the reduced cooking juice, then set 75ml/5 tbsp aside for serving and add the rest to the food processor. Blend until smooth. Pour the mixture into a freezer container and freeze for 3–4 hours, beating twice as it thickens. Alternatively, use an ice cream maker and churn until the mixture holds its shape.

6 Using a teaspoon, pack the sorbet into the frozen pears, piling it up high. Top with the lids and return to the freezer overnight.

7 Remove the pears from the freezer and leave them to stand for about 30 minutes before serving. The pears should have softened but the sorbet should remain icy. Spoon the reserved syrup around each pear to serve.

Apple and Cider Energy 143kcal/610kJ; Protein 0.4g; Carbohydrate 34.6g, of which sugars 34.6g; Fat 0.1g, of which saturates 0g; Cholesterol 0mg; Calcium 20mg; Fibre 1.3g; Sodium 6mg.
Spiced Sorbet Energy 198Kcal/835kJ; Protein 0.6g; Carbohydrate 35.2g, of which sugars 35.2g; Fat 0.2g, of which saturates 0g; Cholesterol 0mg; Calcium 33mg; Fibre 3.3g; Sodium 12mg.

Pear & Sauternes Sorbet

Based on a traditional sorbet that would have been served between savoury courses, this fruity ice is delicately flavoured with the honied bouquet of Sauternes wine, spiked with brandy.

Serves 6

675g/1½lb ripe pears
50g/2oz/¼ cup caster
  (superfine) sugar

250ml/8fl oz/1 cup water
  plus 60ml/4 tbsp extra
250ml/8fl oz/1 cup Sauternes
  wine, plus extra to serve
30ml/2 tbsp brandy
juice of ½ lemon
1 egg white
fresh mint sprigs, dusted with
  icing (confectioners') sugar,
  to decorate

1 Quarter the pears, peel them and cut out the cores. Slice them into a pan and add the sugar and 60ml/4 tbsp of the measured water. Cover and simmer for 10 minutes, or until the pears are just tender.

2 Transfer the pear mixture into a food processor or blender and process until smooth, then scrape into a bowl. Leave to cool, then chill.

3 Stir the wine, brandy and lemon juice into the chilled pear purée with the remaining water.

4 BY HAND: Pour the mixture into a plastic tub or similar freezerproof container, freeze for about 4 hours, then beat it in a food processor or blender until smooth. Return the sorbet to the tub.
USING AN ICE CREAM MAKER: Simply churn the pear mixture in an ice cream maker until thick.

5 Lightly whisk the egg white with a fork until just frothy. Either add to the sorbet in the ice cream maker, or stir into the sorbet in the tub. Churn or return to the freezer until the sorbet is firm.

6 Serve the sorbet in small dessert glasses, with a little extra Sauternes poured over each portion. Decorate with the sugared mint sprigs.

Watermelon Granita

Pastel pink flakes of ice, subtly blended with the citrus freshness of lime and the delicate flavour of watermelon, make this granita the perfect summer treat for the eye as well as the tastebuds.

Serves 6

150g/5oz/⅔ cup caster
  (superfine) sugar

150ml/¼ pint/¾ cup water
1 whole watermelon, about
  1.75kg/4–4½lb
finely grated rind and juice of
  2 limes, plus lime wedges,
  for serving

1 Bring the sugar and water to the boil in a pan, stirring until all of the sugar has dissolved. Pour into a bowl. Cool, then chill. Cut the watermelon into quarters.

2 Discard most of the seeds, scoop the flesh into a food processor and process briefly until smooth. Alternatively, use a blender, and process the watermelon quarters in small batches.

3 Strain the purée into a large plastic container. Discard the seeds. Pour in the chilled syrup, lime rind and juice and mix well.

4 Cover and freeze for 2 hours until the mixture around the sides of the container is mushy. Mash the ice finely with a fork and return the granita to the freezer.

5 Freeze for 2 hours more, mashing every 30 minutes, until it has a fine slushy consistency. Serve in dishes with extra lime.

Variation
To serve this granita cocktail-style, dip the rim of each glass serving dish in a little water or beaten egg white, then dip it into sugar. Spoon in the granita, pour over a little Cointreau, Tequila or white rum, and decorate with lime wedges or thin strips of lime rind removed with a cannelle knife and twisted around a cocktail stick.

Pear and Sauternes Sorbet Energy 130kcal/549kJ; Protein 1g; Carbohydrate 22.4g, of which sugars 22.4g; Fat 0.1g, of which saturates 0g; Cholesterol 0mg; Calcium 23mg; Fibre 2.5g; Sodium 20mg.
Watermelon Granita Energy 189kcal/808kJ; Protein 1.6g; Carbohydrate 46.8g, of which sugars 46.8g; Fat 0.9g, of which saturates 0.3g; Cholesterol 0mg; Calcium 34mg; Fibre 0.3g; Sodium 7mg.

Orange & Yogurt Ice with Blueberries

With this low-fat fruity ice, you can indulge in a dessert without feeling too guilty.

Serves 6

90ml/6 tbsp water
10ml/2 tsp powdered
  gelatine
115g/4oz/generous ½ cup caster
  (superfine) sugar
250ml/8fl oz/1 cup freshly
  squeezed orange juice from
  a carton or bottle
500ml/17fl oz/generous 2 cups
  bio yogurt
cones or meringue nests,
  blueberries and fresh mint
  sprigs, to serve

1 Put 30ml/2 tbsp of the water in a small bowl and sprinkle the powdered gelatine over the top. Set aside until spongy. Meanwhile, put the sugar in a small pan, add the remaining water and heat through gently until the sugar has dissolved.

2 Remove the pan from the heat, add the gelatine and stir until completely dissolved. Cool, stir in the orange juice and chill for 15–30 minutes.

3 Spoon the yogurt into a bowl, gradually add the chilled orange juice mixture and mix well. Pour the mixture into a freezer container. Freeze for 6 hours or until firm, beating twice with a fork or in a food processor to break up the ice crystals.

4 Alternatively, use an ice cream maker. Freeze the mixture until starting to thicken. Switch off the machine, remove the paddle, if necessary, add the yogurt and mix well. Replace the paddle and continue to churn the ice cream for 15–20 minutes until thick. Scrape it into a freezer container and freeze until firm.

5 Scoop the yogurt ice into cones or meringue nests and decorate with blueberries and mint.

Cook's Tip
Meringue nests are not difficult to make, but if you do not have the time, bought ones are a perfectly acceptable alternative.

Lemon Sorbet

This is probably the most classic fruit sorbet of all. Cooling and deliciously smooth, it literally melts in the mouth.

Serves 6

200g/7oz/1 cup caster
  (superfine) sugar
300ml/½ pint/1¼ cups
  water
4 lemons, well scrubbed
1 egg white

1 Put the sugar and water in a pan and bring to the boil, stirring occasionally until the sugar has just dissolved.

2 Using a swivel vegetable peeler, pare the rind thinly from two of the lemons so that it falls straight into the pan. Simmer for 2 minutes without stirring, then take the pan off the heat. Leave to cool, then chill.

3 Squeeze the juice from all the lemons and add to the syrup.

4 Strain the syrup into a shallow freezer container, reserving the rind. Freeze the mixture for 4 hours until it is mushy.

5 Scoop the sorbet into a food processor and process until smooth. Lightly whisk the egg white with a fork until it is just frothy. Spoon the sorbet back into the container, beat in the egg white and return the mixture to the freezer for 4 hours.

6 Alternatively, use an ice cream maker. Strain the lemon syrup, reserving the rind, and churn until thick. Add the egg white to the mixture and churn for a further 10–15 minutes until firm enough to scoop.

7 Scoop into bowls. Decorate with strips of the reserved rind.

Cook's Tip
Cut one-third off the top of a lemon and reserve as a lid. Squeeze the juice out of the rest. Remove any membrane and use the shell as a ready-made container for the sorbet.

Orange and Yogurt Ice Energy 137Kcal/583kJ; Protein 4.6g; Carbohydrate 30g, of which sugars 30g; Fat 0.9g, of which saturates 0.4g; Cholesterol 1mg; Calcium 173mg; Fibre 0.1g; Sodium 75mg.
Lemon Sorbet Energy 135Kcal/574kJ; Protein 0.7g; Carbohydrate 35.1g, of which sugars 35.1g; Fat 0g, of which saturates 0g; Cholesterol 0mg; Calcium 19mg; Fibre 0g; Sodium 13mg.

Chilli Citrus Sorbet

Served at a dinner party, either as a palate-tingling appetizer or a zingy dessert, this unusual lemon-and-lime sorbet is sure to become a conversational talking point.

Serves 6
1 fresh medium-hot red chilli
finely grated rind and juice of
  2 lemons
finely grated rind and juice of
  2 limes
200g/7oz/1 cup caster
  (superfine) sugar
750ml/1¼ pints/3 cups water
lemon or lime rind,
  to decorate

1 Cut the chilli in half, removing all the seeds and any pith with a small sharp knife. Chop the flesh very finely.

2 Put the chilli, lemon and lime rind, sugar and water in a heavy pan. Heat gently and stir while the sugar dissolves. Bring to the boil, then simmer for 2 minutes without stirring. Leave to cool.

3 Add the lemon and lime juice to the chilli syrup and chill until very cold.

4 Pour the mixture into a freezer container and freeze for 3–4 hours, beating twice as it thickens. Return to the freezer until ready to serve.

5 Alternatively, use an ice cream maker. Freeze the mixture until it holds its shape. Scrape into a freezer container and freeze.

6 Soften slightly at room temperature before spooning into glasses and decorating with thinly pared lemon or lime rind.

> **Cook's Tips**
> • Wash your hands immediately after handling the chilli to avoid getting chilli juice in your eyes, should you rub them.
> • For an added kick to this sorbet, drizzle each portion with a little tequila or vodka before serving.

Elderflower & Lime Yogurt Ice

Fragrant elderflowers have a wonderful flavour, but they are in season for only a very short time. Fortunately, good-quality ready-made elderflower cordial is readily available, and combines beautifully with limes to make a lovely iced dessert.

Serves 6
4 egg yolks
50g/2oz/¼ cup caster
  (superfine) sugar
10ml/2 tsp cornflour (cornstarch)
300ml/½ pint/1¼ cups milk
finely grated rind and juice of
  2 limes
150ml/¼ pint/⅔ cup elderflower
  cordial
200ml/7fl oz/scant 1 cup Greek
  (US strained plain) yogurt
150ml/¼ pint/⅔ cup double
  (heavy) cream
grated lime rind, to decorate

1 Whisk the egg yolks in a bowl with the sugar, cornflour and a little of the milk. Pour the remaining milk into a heavy pan, bring it to the boil, then pour it over the yolk mixture, whisking constantly. Return the mixture to the pan and cook over a very gentle heat, stirring constantly until the custard thickens. Do not let it boil, or it may curdle.

2 Pour the custard into a bowl and add the lime rind and juice. Pour in the elderflower cordial and mix lightly. Cover the surface of the mixture closely with baking parchment. Leave to cool, then chill until very cold.

3 Whip together the yogurt and cream and fold into the custard. Pour the mixture into a freezer container and freeze for 3–4 hours, beating twice as it thickens. Scoop into individual dishes and return to the freezer until ready to serve.

4 Alternatively, use an ice cream maker. Stir the yogurt and cream into the custard and churn until it thickens. Transfer the yogurt ice into individual dishes and freeze until required.

5 Transfer the yogurt ice to the refrigerator 30 minutes before serving. Decorate with the grated lime rind and serve.

Chilli Citrus Sorbet Energy 150Kcal/640kJ; Protein 0.5g; Carbohydrate 39.4g, of which sugars 39.4g; Fat 0.1g, of which saturates 0g; Cholesterol 0mg; Calcium 23mg; Fibre 0g; Sodium 3mg.
Elderflower and Lime Energy 219Kcal/912kJ; Protein 4.3g; Carbohydrate 12.4g, of which sugars 10.9g; Fat 17.7g, of which saturates 10.6g; Cholesterol 37mg; Calcium 125mg; Fibre 0g; Sodium 54mg.

Peach & Cardamom Ice Cream

The velvety texture of this smooth peach ice cream spiced with cardamom suggests it is made with cream rather than yogurt.

6 peaches, about 500g/1¼lb total, halved, and stoned (pitted)
75g/3oz/6 tbsp caster (superfine) sugar
30ml/2 tbsp water
200ml/7fl oz/scant 1 cup natural bio (plain) yogurt

Serves 4

8 cardamom pods

1 Put the cardamom pods on a board and crush them with the bottom of a ramekin, or in a mortar and pestle.

2 Chop the peaches roughly and put them in a pan. Add the crushed cardamom pods, with their black seeds, and the sugar and water. Cover and simmer for 10 minutes or until the fruit is tender. Leave to cool.

3 Transfer the peach mixture into a food processor or blender, process until smooth, then press through a sieve (strainer) placed over a bowl.

4 BY HAND: Add the yogurt to the sieved (strained) purée and mix together in the bowl. Pour into a plastic tub and freeze for 5–6 hours until firm, beating once or twice with a fork, electric whisk or in a processor to break up the ice crystals.
USING AN ICE CREAM MAKER: Churn the purée until thick, then scrape it into a plastic tub or similar container. Stir in the yogurt and freeze until firm enough to hold a scoop shape.

5 Scoop the ice cream into balls and place on to a large platter, and serve immediately.

> **Cook's Tip**
> Use bio natural (plain) yogurt for its extra mild taste. Greek (US strained plain) yogurt or non-bio natural yogurt are both sharper and more acidic, and tend to overwhelm the delicate taste of the peaches.

Apricot & Amaretti Ice Cream

Prolong the very short summer season of fresh apricots by transforming them into this superb ice cream with crushed amaretti cream.

juice of 1 orange
50g/2oz/¼ cup caster (superfine) sugar
300ml/½ pint/1¼ cups whipping cream
50g/2oz amaretti

Serves 4–6

500g/1¼lb fresh apricots, halved and stoned (pitted)

1 Place the apricots, orange juice and sugar in a pan. Cover and simmer for 5 minutes until the fruit is tender. Leave to cool.

2 Lift out one third of the fruit and set it aside on a plate. Transfer the remaining contents of the pan into a food processor or blender and process to a smooth purée.

3 BY HAND: Whip the cream until it is just thick but still soft enough to fall from a spoon. Gradually add the fruit purée, folding it into the mixture. Pour into a plastic tub or similar freezerproof container and freeze for 4 hours, beating once with a fork, electric mixer or in a food processor.
USING AN ICE CREAM MAKER: Churn the apricot purée until it is slushy, then gradually add the cream. Continue to churn until the ice cream is thick, but not firm enough to scoop.

4 BY HAND: Beat for a second time. Crumble in the amaretti.
USING AN ICE CREAM MAKER: Scrape the ice cream into a tub. Crumble in the amaretti.

5 Add the reserved apricots and gently fold into the ice cream. Freeze for 2–3 hours or until firm enough to scoop.

> **Cook's Tip**
> Chill the fruit purée if you have time; this will speed up the churning or freezing process.

Peach Energy 69kcal/296kJ; Protein 3.8g; Carbohydrate 13.3g, of which sugars 13.3g; Fat 0.6g, of which saturates 0.3g; Cholesterol 1mg; Calcium 104mg; Fibre 1.9g; Sodium 43mg.
Apricot Energy 289kcal/1202kJ; Protein 2.3g; Carbohydrate 23.4g, of which sugars 19.8g; Fat 21.3g, of which saturates 13.1g; Cholesterol 53mg; Calcium 58mg; Fibre 1.6g; Sodium 43mg.

Zabaglione Ice Torte with Apricots

For anyone who likes the famous whisked Italian dessert known as zabaglione, this fruity iced version is an absolute must. Its taste and texture are just as good, and there is no last-minute whisking to worry about.

Serves 10
175g/6oz amaretti
115g/4oz/½ cup ready-to-eat dried apricots, finely chopped
65g/2½oz/5 tbsp unsalted (sweet) butter, melted

For the ice cream
65g/2½oz/5 tbsp light muscovado (brown) sugar
75ml/5 tbsp water
5 egg yolks
250ml/8fl oz/1 cup double (heavy) cream
75ml/5 tbsp Madeira or cream sherry
poached fruit, to serve

1 Put the amaretti in a strong plastic bag and crush finely with a rolling pin. Turn into a bowl and stir in the apricots and melted butter until evenly combined.

2 Using a dampened spoon, pack the mixture on to the bottom and up the sides of a 24cm/9½in loose-based flan tin (tart pan) about 4cm/1½in deep. Chill.

3 Make the ice cream. Put the sugar and water in a small, heavy pan and heat, stirring, until the sugar has dissolved. Bring to the boil and boil for 2 minutes without stirring.

4 Whisk the egg yolks in a heatproof bowl until pale, then gradually whisk in the sugar syrup. Put the bowl over a pan of simmering water and continue to whisk for about 10 minutes or until the mixture leaves a trail when the whisk is lifted.

5 Remove from the heat and carry on whisking for a further 5 minutes or until the mixture is cold. In a separate bowl, whip the cream with the Madeira or sherry until it stands in peaks.

6 Using a large metal spoon, fold the cream into the whisked mixture. Spoon it into the lined tin, level the surface, cover and freeze overnight. Serve sliced, with a little poached fruit.

Fruity Indian Ice Cream

In India, kulfi-wallahs (ice cream vendors) have always made kulfi, and actually continue to this day without the assistance of modern freezers. Kulfi is packed into metal cones sealed with dough and then churned in clay pots until set. Try this method with sultanas and glacé cherries – it works extremely well in an ordinary home freezer.

Serves 4–6
3 × 400ml/14fl oz cans evaporated (unsweetened condensed) milk
3 egg whites
350g/12oz/3 cups icing (confectioners') sugar
5ml/1 tsp ground cardamom
15ml/1 tbsp rose water
175g/6oz/1½ cups pistachio nuts, chopped
75g/3oz/½ cup sultanas (golden raisins)
75g/3oz/¾ cup flaked (sliced) almonds
25g/1oz/3 tbsp glacé (candied) cherries, halved

1 Remove the labels from the cans of evaporated milk and lay the cans down in a pan with a tight-fitting cover. Fill the pan with water to reach three-quarters up the cans. Bring to the boil, cover and simmer for 20 minutes. (Don't leave the cans of evaporated milk unattended. Top up the water if necessary; the pan must never boil dry.) When cool, remove the cans and chill in the refrigerator for 24 hours. Chill a large bowl too.

2 Whisk the egg whites in another large bowl until peaks form. Open the cans and empty the milk into the chilled bowl. Whisk until doubled in quantity, then fold in the whisked egg whites and icing sugar.

3 Gently fold in the remaining ingredients, cover the bowl with clear film (plastic wrap) and place in the freezer for 1 hour.

4 Remove the ice cream from the freezer and mix well with a fork. Transfer to a serving container and return to the freezer for a final setting. Remove from the freezer 10 minutes before serving.

Zabaglione Energy 333Kcal/1387kJ; Protein 3.4g; Carbohydrate 25.8g, of which sugars 18.2g; Fat 23.9g, of which saturates 13.6g; Cholesterol 149mg; Calcium 60mg; Fibre 1g; Sodium 110mg.
Fruity Indian Energy 782kcal/3283kJ; Protein 25g; Carbohydrate 92g, of which sugars 91g; Fat 37g, of which saturates 14g; Cholesterol 68mg; Calcium 645mg; Fibre 2.5g; Sodium 511mg.

Mocha, Prune & Armagnac Terrines

This is a sophisticated iced fruit dessert that is perfect for entertaining in style.

Serves 6
115g/4oz/¹/₂ cup ready-to-eat
   pitted prunes, chopped
90ml/6 tbsp Armagnac
90g/3¹/₂oz/¹/₂ cup caster
   (superfine) sugar
150ml/¹/₄ pint/²/₃ cup water
45ml/3 tbsp coffee beans
150g/5oz plain (semisweet)
   chocolate, broken into pieces
300ml/¹/₂ pint/1 ¹/₄ cups
   double (heavy) cream
cocoa powder (unsweetened),
   for dusting

1 Put the prunes in a small bowl. Pour over 75ml/5 tbsp of the Armagnac and leave to soak for at least 3 hours at room temperature, or overnight in the refrigerator. Line the bases of six 100ml/3¹/₂fl oz/scant ¹/₂ cup ramekins with baking parchment.

2 Put the sugar and water in a heavy pan and heat gently until the sugar dissolves, stirring occasionally. Add the soaked prunes and any of the Armagnac that remains in the bowl; simmer the prunes gently in the syrup for 5 minutes.

3 Using a slotted spoon, lift the prunes out of the pan and set them aside. Add the coffee beans to the syrup and simmer gently for 5 minutes.

4 Lift out the coffee beans and put about a third of them in a bowl. Spoon over 120ml/4fl oz/¹/₂ cup of the syrup and stir in the remaining Armagnac.

5 Add the chocolate to the pan containing the remaining syrup and leave until melted. Whip the cream until it just holds its shape. Using a large metal spoon, fold the chocolate mixture and prunes into the cream until just combined. Spoon the mixture into the lined ramekins, cover and freeze for at least 3 hours.

6 To serve, loosen the edges of the ramekins with a knife then dip in very hot water for 2 seconds and invert on to serving plates. Decorate the plates with the coffee bean syrup and a dusting of cocoa powder.

Brandied Fruit & Rice Ice Cream

This alcoholic and fruity ice cream dessert combines spicy rice pudding with a creamy egg custard.

Serves 4–6
50g/2oz/¹/₄ cup ready-to-eat
   pitted prunes, chopped
50g/2oz/¹/₄ cup ready-to-eat
   dried apricots, chopped
50g/2oz/¹/₄ cup glacé (candied)
   cherries, chopped
30ml/2 tbsp brandy
150ml/¹/₄ pint/²/₃ cup single
   (light) cream

For the rice mixture
40g/1¹/₂oz/generous ¹/₄ cup
   pudding (short grain) rice
450ml/³/₄ pint/scant 2 cups milk
1 cinnamon stick, halved,
   plus extra to decorate
4 cloves

For the custard
4 egg yolks
75g/3oz/6 tbsp caster
   (superfine) sugar
5ml/1 tsp cornflour
   (cornstarch)
300ml/¹/₂ pint/1 ¹/₄ cups milk

1 Put the chopped dried fruit in a bowl. Pour over the brandy. Cover and leave to soak for 3 hours or overnight, if possible.

2 Put the rice, milk and spices in a pan. Bring to the boil, then simmer gently for 30 minutes, stirring occasionally until most of the milk has been absorbed. Lift out the spices. Let the rice cool.

3 Whisk the egg yolks, sugar and cornflour in a bowl until thick and foamy. Heat the milk in a heavy pan, then gradually pour it on to the yolks, whisking constantly. Pour back into the pan and cook, stirring until the custard thickens. Leave to cool, then chill.

4 Mix the chilled custard, rice and cream together. Pour into a freezer container and freeze for 4–5 hours until mushy, then beat lightly with a fork to break up the ice crystals.

5 Fold in the fruits then freeze for 2–3 hours until firm enough to scoop. Alternatively, use an ice cream maker. Mix the chilled custard, rice and cream together and churn until thick. Spoon the ice cream into a freezer container and fold in the fruits. Freeze for 2–3 hours until firm.

6 Serve scoops of ice cream decorated with cinnamon sticks.

Mocha Energy 495Kcal/2060kJ; Protein 2.6g; Carbohydrate 38.9g, of which sugars 38.7g; Fat 33.9g, of which saturates 20.9g; Cholesterol 70mg; Calcium 47mg; Fibre 1.7g; Sodium 16mg.
Brandied Fruit Energy 293Kcal/1228kJ; Protein 8g; Carbohydrate 36.7g, of which sugars 30.7g; Fat 13.4g, of which saturates 7.2g; Cholesterol 166mg; Calcium 207mg; Fibre 1.1g; Sodium 73mg.

Iced Christmas Fruit Torte

This makes an exciting
alternative to traditional
Christmas pudding – but
don't feel that you have to
limit it to the festive season.

Serves 8–10
75g/3oz/¾ cup dried cranberries
75g/3oz/scant ½ cup
    pitted prunes
50g/2oz/⅓ cup sultanas
    (golden raisins)
175ml/6fl oz/¾ cup port
2 pieces preserved stem ginger,
    finely chopped

25g/1oz/2 tbsp unsalted
    (sweet) butter
45ml/3 tbsp light muscovado
    (brown) sugar
90g/3½oz/scant 2 cups fresh
    white breadcrumbs
600ml/1 pint/2½ cups
    double (heavy) cream
30ml/2 tbsp icing
    (confectioners') sugar
5ml/1 tsp ground allspice
75g/3oz/¾ cup brazil nuts,
    finely chopped
sugared bay leaves and
    fresh cherries, to decorate

1 Put the cranberries, prunes and sultanas in a food processor
or blender and process briefly. Transfer them to a bowl and add
the port and ginger. Leave to absorb the port for 2 hours.

2 Melt the butter in a frying pan. Add the sugar and heat gently
until the sugar has dissolved. Add the breadcrumbs, stir lightly,
then fry over a low heat for about 5 minutes, until lightly coloured
and turning crisp. Leave to cool.

3 Turn the breadcrumbs into a food processor or blender
and process to finer crumbs. Sprinkle a third into an 18cm/7in
loose-based springform tin (pan) and freeze.

4 Whip the cream with the icing sugar and spice until the
mixture is thick but not yet standing in peaks. Fold in the brazil
nuts with the dried fruit mixture and any port remaining.

5 Spread a third of the mixture over the breadcrumb base
in the tin, taking care not to dislodge the crumbs. Sprinkle
with another layer of the breadcrumbs. Repeat the layering,
finishing with a layer of the cream mixture. Freeze the torte
overnight. Serve immediately decorated with sugared bay
leaves and fresh cherries.

Strawberry & Lavender Sorbet

Delicately perfumed with
just a hint of lavender,
this delightful pastel pink
strawberry sorbet is the
perfect way to finish
a summer dinner party.

Serves 6
150g/5oz/¾ cup caster
    (superfine) sugar
300ml/½ pint/1¼ cups water
6 fresh lavender flowers
500g/1¼lb/5 cups
    strawberries, hulled
1 egg white
lavender flowers, to decorate

1 Bring the sugar and water to the boil in a pan, stirring until
the sugar has dissolved.

2 Take the pan off the heat, add the lavender flowers and leave
to infuse (steep) for 1 hour. Chill the syrup before using.

3 Purée the strawberries in a food processor or blender, then
press the purée through a sieve (strainer) into a bowl.

4 BY HAND: Pour the purée into a plastic tub, strain in the
syrup, then freeze for 4 hours until mushy. Transfer to a food
processor and process until smooth. Whisk the egg white until
frothy, and stir into the sorbet. Spoon the sorbet back into the
tub and freeze until firm.
USING AN ICE CREAM MAKER: Pour the strawberry purée into the
bowl and strain in the lavender syrup. Churn until thick. Add
the whisked egg white to the ice cream maker and continue
to churn until the sorbet is firm enough to scoop.

5 Serve in scoops, piled into tall glasses, and decorate with
sprigs of lavender flowers.

> **Cook's Tip**
> The size of the lavender flowers can vary; if they are very small,
> you may need to use eight. To check, taste a little of the cooled
> lavender syrup. If you think the flavour is a little mild, add two
> or three more flowers, reheat and cool again before using.

Iced Christmas Energy 504kcal/2098kJ; Protein 6.3g; Carbohydrate 38.4g, of which sugars 21g; Fat 36.4g, of which saturates 17.8g; Cholesterol 61mg; Calcium 92mg; Fibre 2.3g; Sodium 209mg.
Strawberry Sorbet Energy 123kcal/523kJ; Protein 1.3g; Carbohydrate 31.1g, of which sugars 31.1g; Fat 0.1g, of which saturates 0g; Cholesterol 0mg; Calcium 27mg; Fibre 0.9g; Sodium 17mg.

Simple Strawberry Ice Cream

Capture the essence of childhood summers with this easy-to-make strawberry ice cream. Whipping cream is better than double cream for this recipe, as it doesn't overwhelm the taste of the fresh fruit.

Serves 4–6

500g/1¼lb/4 cups
   strawberries, hulled
50g/2oz/½ cup icing
   (confectioners') sugar
juice of ½ lemon
300ml/½ pint/1¼ cups
   whipping cream
extra strawberries, to decorate

1 Purée the strawberries in a food processor or blender until smooth, then add the icing sugar and lemon juice and process again to mix. Press the purée through a sieve (strainer) into a bowl. Chill until very cold.

2 BY HAND: Whip the cream until it is just thickened but still falls from a spoon. Fold into the purée, then pour into a plastic tub or similar freezerproof container. Freeze for 6 hours until firm, beating twice with a fork, electric whisk or in a food processor to break up the ice crystals.
USING AN ICE CREAM MAKER: Churn the purée until mushy, then pour in the cream and churn until thick enough to scoop.

3 Scoop the ice cream into serving dishes and decorate each with a few extra strawberries.

Variation
Raspberry or any other summer berry fruit can be used to make this ice cream. Keep your eye out for any berries that may be growing wild in your local neighbourhood.

Cook's Tip
If possible, taste the strawberries before buying them – or picking them, if you are lucky to have a strawberry producer nearby where you can gather your own fruit.

Raspberry Sherbet

Traditional sherbets are made in a similar way to sorbets, but with added milk. This low-fat version is made from raspberry purée blended with sugar syrup and virtually fat-free fromage frais or yogurt.

Serves 6

175g/6oz/scant 1 cup caster
   (superfine) sugar
500g/1¼lb/3½ cups raspberries,
   plus extra, to serve
500ml/17fl oz/2¼ cups
   virtually fat-free fromage frais
   or yogurt

1 Put the sugar in a small pan with 150ml/¼ pint/⅔ cup water and bring to the boil, stirring until the sugar has dissolved completely. Pour into a jug (pitcher) and cool.

2 Put 350g/12oz/2½ cups of the raspberries in a food processor and blend to a purée. Press through a sieve (strainer) into a large bowl and discard the seeds. Stir the sugar syrup into the raspberry purée and chill until very cold.

3 Add the fromage frais or yogurt to the chilled purée and whisk until smooth. Using an ice cream maker, churn the mixture until it is thick but too soft to scoop. Scrape into a freezerproof container, then crush the remaining raspberries between your fingers and add to the ice cream. Mix lightly, then freeze for 2–3 hours until firm. Scoop the ice cream into dishes and serve with extra raspberries.

Cook's Tip
To make the sherbet by hand, pour the raspberry purée into a freezerproof container and freeze for 4 hours, beating once with a fork, electric whisk or in a food processor to break up the ice crystals. Freeze, then beat again.

Variation
Use any fruit – soft fruits can be blended and sieved (strained), but firmer fruits will need poaching in sugar and water first.

Simple Strawberry Energy 244kcal/1012kJ; Protein 2.4g; Carbohydrate 12.2g, of which sugars 10.4g; Fat 20.4g, of which saturates 12.1g; Cholesterol 51mg; Calcium 73mg; Fibre 0.7g; Sodium 32mg.
Raspberry Sherbet Energy 276kcal/1181kJ; Protein 11.6g; Carbohydrate 60g, of which sugars 60g; Fat 0.6g, of which saturates 0.3g; Cholesterol 1mg; Calcium 163mg; Fibre 3.1g; Sodium 48mg.

White Chocolate Raspberry Ripple

A truly luscious fruit treat that always impresses. Note that an ice cream maker is required for this recipe.

Serves 6
250ml/8fl oz/1 cup milk
475ml/16fl oz/2 cups
 whipping cream
7 egg yolks
30ml/2 tbsp granulated
 (white) sugar
225g/8oz good white chocolate,
 chopped into small pieces

5ml/1 tsp vanilla extract
mint sprigs, to decorate

For the sauce
275g/10oz raspberry preserve or
 275g/10oz frozen raspberries
 in light syrup
10ml/2 tsp golden (light corn)
 syrup
15ml/1 tbsp lemon juice
15ml/1 tbsp cornflour
 (cornstarch), if using frozen
 fruit in syrup, mixed with
 15ml/1 tbsp water

1 For the sauce, put the preserve in a pan with the golden syrup, the lemon juice and the water but not the cornflour. If using frozen fruit, press the fruit and its syrup through a sieve (strainer) into a pan and add all the other sauce ingredients. Bring to the boil, stirring. Simmer for 1–2 minutes. Pour into a bowl, cool, then chill.

2 In a pan, combine the milk and 250ml/8fl oz/1 cup of the cream and bring to the boil. In a bowl, beat the yolks and sugar with a hand-held mixer for 2–3 minutes until thick and creamy. Gradually pour the hot milk mixture over the yolks and return to the pan. Cook over a medium heat, stirring constantly, until the custard coats the back of a wooden spoon.

3 Remove the pan from the heat and stir in the white chocolate until melted and smooth. Pour the remaining cream into a large bowl. Strain in the hot custard, mix well, then stir in the vanilla extract. Cool, then freeze in an ice cream maker.

4 When frozen but soft, transfer one-third of the ice cream to a freezerproof bowl. Set aside half the raspberry sauce, spooning a third of the rest over the ice cream. Cover with another third of the ice cream and more sauce. Repeat. With a knife, lightly marble the mixture. Cover and freeze. Let the ice cream soften for 15 minutes. Serve with the rest of the raspberry sauce, and the mint.

Mascarpone & Raspberry Ripple

Creamy mascarpone makes a wonderfully smooth base for ice cream, which is made even more delicious when mixed with a tangy lemon syrup and streaked with raspberry purée.

Serves 8
250g/9oz/1¼ cups caster
 (superfine) sugar

450ml/¾ pint/scant 2 cups
 water
finely grated rind and juice of
 1 lemon
350g/12oz/2 cups raspberries,
 plus extra to decorate
500g/1¼lb/2½ cups
 mascarpone

1 Put 225g/8oz/1 cup of the sugar in a heavy pan. Pour in the water and heat gently until the sugar dissolves. Bring to the boil, add the lemon rind and juice and boil for 3 minutes, without stirring, to make a syrup. Leave to cool.

2 Crush the raspberries lightly with a fork until broken up but not completely puréed, then stir in the remaining sugar.

3 Beat the mascarpone in a large bowl until smooth, gradually adding the lemon syrup.

4 Pour the mascarpone mixture into a freezer container and freeze until it begins to thicken. Beat to break down the ice crystals, then return to the freezer. When beginning to thicken again, repeat the beating process for a second time, then return to the freezer until the ice cream is frozen but still soft.

5 Alternatively, use an ice cream maker. Churn the mixture until thick, then transfer to a freezer container.

6 Spoon the crushed raspberries over the ice cream. Using a metal spoon, fold into the ice cream until rippled, making sure you reach the corners. Freeze for several hours or overnight until firm.

7 To serve, scoop the ice cream into glasses and decorate with the extra raspberries.

White Chocolate Energy 735Kcal/3066kJ; Protein 10.3g; Carbohydrate 63.3g, of which sugars 61g; Fat 50.8g, of which saturates 29.2g; Cholesterol 321mg; Calcium 242mg; Fibre 1.2g; Sodium 110mg.
Mascarpone Energy 217Kcal/916kJ; Protein 10.1g; Carbohydrate 36.9g, of which sugars 36.9g; Fat 5.1g, of which saturates 3.3g; Cholesterol 15mg; Calcium 100mg; Fibre 1.1g; Sodium 277mg.

Blackberry Ice Cream

There could scarcely be fewer ingredients in this deliciously vibrant ice cream. Blackberries are a feature of early autumn, and can often be picked wild on hedges at the side of roads and country paths. You can either use store-bought cookies, or make your own.

Serves 4–6

500g/1¼lb/5 cups blackberries, hulled, plus extra, to decorate
75g/3oz/6 tbsp caster (superfine) sugar
30ml/2 tbsp water
300ml/½ pint/1¼ cups whipping cream
crisp dessert biscuits (cookies), to serve

1 Put the blackberries into a pan, and add the sugar and water. Cover and simmer for 5 minutes until just soft. Place the fruit in a sieve (strainer) over a bowl and press it through using a wooden spoon. Leave to cool, then chill.

2 BY HAND: Whip the cream until it is just thick but still soft enough to fall from a spoon, then mix it with the chilled fruit purée. Pour the mixture into a plastic tub or similar freezerproof container and freeze for 2 hours.
USING AN ICE CREAM MAKER: Churn the chilled purée for 10–15 minutes until it is thick, then gradually pour in the cream. There is no need to whip the cream first.

3 BY HAND: Mash the mixture with a fork, or beat it in a food processor to break up the ice crystals. Return it to the freezer for 4 hours more, beating the mixture again after 2 hours.
USING AN ICE CREAM MAKER: Continue to churn the ice cream until it is firm enough to scoop.

4 Scoop into dishes and decorate with extra blackberries. Serve with crisp dessert biscuits.

> **Variation**
> • Frozen blackberries can be used for the purée. You will need to increase the cooking time to 10 minutes.
> • Blackcurrants can be used instead of blackberries.

Blackcurrant Sorbet

Juicy, ripe blackcurrants produce a vibrant and intensely flavoured sorbet that is ideal for rounding off an *al fresco* summer meal.

120ml/4fl oz/½ cup water
500g/1¼lb blackcurrants
juice of ½ lemon
15ml/1 tbsp egg white
mint leaves, to decorate

Serves 4–6
90g/3½oz/½ cup caster (superfine) sugar

1 Place the sugar and water in a pan over medium-high heat and bring to the boil, stirring until the sugar has dissolved. Continue to boil the syrup for 2 minutes, then remove the pan from the heat and set aside to cool.

2 Remove the blackcurrants from their stalks, by pulling them through the tines of a fork.

3 Put the blackcurrants and lemon juice in a blender or food processor fitted with a metal blade, and process until smooth. Alternatively, chop the blackcurrants coarsely, then add the lemon juice. Mix in the sugar syrup.

4 Press through a sieve (strainer) to remove the seeds.

5 Pour the blackcurrant purée into a non-metallic freezer container. Cover with clear film (plastic wrap) or a lid and freeze until the sorbet is nearly firm, but still a bit slushy.

6 Cut the sorbet into pieces and put in the blender or food processor. Process until smooth, then, with the machine running, add the egg white and process until well mixed. Transfer the sorbet back to the freezer container and freeze until almost firm. Chop the sorbet again and process until smooth. Return to the freezer again until firm.

7 Serve immediately or freeze, tightly covered, for up to one week. Allow to soften for 5–10 minutes at room temperature before serving, decorated with mint leaves.

Blackberry Energy 261kcal/1081kJ; Protein 1.8g; Carbohydrate 18.7g, of which sugars 18.7g; Fat 20.3g, of which saturates 12.6g; Cholesterol 53mg; Calcium 70mg; Fibre 2.6g; Sodium 15mg.
Blackcurrant Energy 84Kcal/361kJ; Protein 1.3g; Carbohydrate 21.2g, of which sugars 21.2g; Fat 0g, of which saturates 0g; Cholesterol 0mg; Calcium 58mg; Fibre 3g; Sodium 14mg.

Gooseberry & Clotted Cream Ice Cream

Often rather neglected fruits, gooseberries conjure up images of the tired grey-looking crumble that used to be served at school or in the works canteen. However, this indulgent ice cream puts gooseberries in a totally different class. The delicious, slightly tart flavour of the fruit goes particularly well with tiny, melt-in-the-mouth meringues.

Serves 4–6
500g/1¼lb/4 cups gooseberries, topped and tailed
60ml/4 tbsp water
75g/3oz/6 tbsp caster (superfine) sugar
150ml/¼ pint/⅔ cup whipping cream
a few drops of green food colouring (optional)
120ml/4fl oz/½ cup clotted cream
fresh mint sprigs, to decorate
meringues, to serve

1 Put the gooseberries in a pan and add the water and sugar. Cover and simmer for 10 minutes or until soft. Transfer into a food processor or blender and process to a smooth purée. Press through a sieve (strainer) over a bowl. Cool, then chill.

2 BY HAND: Chill the purée in a plastic tub or similar container. Whip the cream until it is thick but still falls from a spoon. Fold into the purée with the green food colouring, if using. Freeze for 2 hours, then beat with a fork, electric mixer or in a food processor, to break up. Return to the freezer for 2 hours.

3 BY HAND: Beat the ice cream again, then fold in the clotted cream. Freeze for 2–3 hours.
USING AN ICE CREAM MAKER: Mix the chilled purée with the whipping cream, add a few drops of green food colouring, if using, and churn until thickened and semi-frozen. Add the clotted cream and continue to churn the mixture until thick enough to scoop.

4 To serve, scoop the ice cream into dishes or small plates, decorate with fresh mint sprigs and add a few small meringues to each serving.

Fig, Port & Clementine Sundaes

The distinctive flavours of figs, cinnamon, clementines and port are combined to make a refreshing sundae bursting with taste.

Serves 6
6 clementines
30ml/2 tbsp clear honey
1 cinnamon stick, halved
15ml/1 tbsp light muscovado (brown) sugar
60ml/4 tbsp port
6 fresh figs
about 500ml/17fl oz/2¼ cups orange sorbet

1 Finely grate the rind from two clementines and put it in a small, heavy pan. Using a small, sharp knife, cut the peel away from all the clementines, then slice the flesh thinly.

2 Add the honey, cinnamon, sugar and port to the clementine rind. Heat gently until the sugar has completely dissolved, in order to make a syrup.

3 Put the clementine slices in a heatproof bowl and pour over the syrup. Cool completely, then chill.

4 Slice the figs thinly and add to the clementines and syrup, tossing the ingredients together gently. Leave for 10 minutes, then discard the cinnamon stick.

5 Arrange half the fig and clementine slices around the sides of six serving glasses. Half fill the glasses with scoops of sorbet.

6 Arrange the remaining fruit slices around the sides of the glasses, then pile more sorbet into the centre. Pour over the port syrup and serve.

Cook's Tip
This rich and yet refreshing combination of ingredients creates the ideal dessert for finishing off a hearty winter meal on a light and fruity note.

Gooseberry Energy 278kcal/1152kJ; Protein 1.8g; Carbohydrate 16.7g, of which sugars 16.7g; Fat 23.1g, of which saturates 14.3g; Cholesterol 60mg; Calcium 52mg; Fibre 2g; Sodium 12mg.
Fig Sundaes Energy 282Kcal/1205kJ; Protein 3.7g; Carbohydrate 66.5g, of which sugars 66.5g; Fat 0.9g, of which saturates 0g; Cholesterol 0mg; Calcium 173mg; Fibre 5.4g; Sodium 50mg.

Ginger & Kiwi Sorbet

Freshly grated root ginger gives a lively, aromatic flavour to this exotic sorbet, while the black seeds of the kiwi fruit add interesting texture and colour.

115g/4oz/generous ½ cup caster (superfine) sugar
300ml/½ pint/1¼ cups water
5 kiwi fruit
fresh mint sprigs or chopped kiwi fruit, to decorate

Serves 6
50g/2oz fresh root ginger

1 Peel the ginger and grate it finely. Put the sugar and water in a pan and heat gently until the sugar has dissolved. Add the ginger and cook for 1 minute, then leave to cool. Strain into a bowl and chill until very cold.

2 Peel the kiwi fruit, place in a blender and process to form a smooth purée. Add the purée to the chilled syrup and mix well.

3 Pour the kiwi mixture into a freezer container and freeze until slushy. Beat the mixture, then freeze again. Repeat this beating process one more time, then cover the container and freeze until firm.

4 Alternatively, use an ice cream maker. Freeze the mixture following the manufacturer's instructions, then transfer to a freezer container and freeze until required.

5 Remove the sorbet from the freezer 10–15 minutes before serving, to allow it to soften slightly. Spoon into glass bowls, then decorate with mint sprigs or pieces of chopped kiwi fruit and serve immediately.

> **Cook's Tip**
> Fresh ginger root is widely available and is easy to spot with its knobbly shape and pale brown skin. Look for smooth skin and firm solid flesh. Any left over can be wrapped and stored in the refrigerator for up to three weeks. Use a sharp knife for peeling.

Rhubarb & Ginger Ice Cream

The classic combination of spring rhubarb and root ginger is brought up to date by blending it with mascarpone to make this pretty blush-pink ice cream.

115g/4oz/½ cup caster (superfine) sugar
30ml/2 tbsp water
150g/5oz/⅔ cup mascarpone
150ml/¼ pint/⅔ cup whipping cream
wafer cups, to serve (optional)

Serves 4–6
5 pieces of stem ginger
450g/1lb trimmed rhubarb, sliced

1 Using a sharp knife, roughly chop the stem ginger and set it aside. Put the rhubarb slices into a pan and add the sugar and water. Cover and simmer for 5 minutes until the rhubarb is just tender and still bright pink.

2 Transfer the mixture into a food processor or blender, process until smooth, then leave to cool. Chill if time permits.

3 BY HAND: Mix together the mascarpone, cream and ginger with the rhubarb purée.
USING AN ICE CREAM MAKER: Churn the rhubarb purée for 15–20 minutes until it is thick.

4 BY HAND: Pour the mixture into a plastic tub or similar freezerproof container and freeze for 6 hours or until firm, beating once or twice during the freezing time to break up the ice crystals.
USING AN ICE CREAM MAKER: Put the mascarpone into a bowl, soften it with a wooden spoon, then gradually beat in the cream. Add the chopped ginger, then transfer to the ice cream maker and churn until the ice cream is firm. Serve as scoops in bowls or wafer baskets.

> **Cook's Tip**
> If the rhubarb purée is rather pale, add a few drops of pink colouring when mixing in the cream.

Ginger and Kiwi Energy 100Kcal/426kJ; Protein 0.7g; Carbohydrate 25.3g, of which sugars 25.2g; Fat 0.3g, of which saturates 0g; Cholesterol 0mg; Calcium 23mg; Fibre 1g; Sodium 3mg.
Rhubarb and Ginger Energy 221kcal/924kJ; Protein 3.6g; Carbohydrate 22.1g, of which sugars 22.1g; Fat 13.8g, of which saturates 8.6g; Cholesterol 37mg; Calcium 94mg; Fibre 1.1g; Sodium 10mg.

Mango Sorbet with Sauce

After a heavy meal, this delightful sorbet makes a very refreshing dessert. Mango is said to be one of the oldest fruits cultivated in India, having been presented by Lord Shiva to his beautiful wife, Parvathi.

Serves 4–6
900g/2lb mango pulp
2.5ml/¹/₂ tsp lemon juice
grated rind of 1 orange and
1 lemon
4 egg whites

50g/2oz/¹/₄ cup caster
(superfine) sugar
120ml/4fl oz/¹/₂ cup double
(heavy) cream
50g/2oz/¹/₂ cup icing
(confectioners') sugar

1 In a large, chilled bowl, mix half of the mango pulp with the lemon juice and the grated rind.

2 Whisk the egg whites until peaks form, then gently fold them into the mango mixture, with the caster sugar. Cover with clear film (plastic wrap) and place in the freezer for at least 1 hour.

3 Remove from the freezer and beat again. Transfer to an ice cream container, and freeze until fully set.

4 In a bowl, whip the double cream with the icing sugar and the remaining mango pulp. Cover and chill the sauce for 24 hours.

5 Remove the sorbet 10 minutes before serving. Scoop out individual servings and cover with a generous helping of mango sauce. Serve immediately.

> **Variation**
> *For a delicious change, try this sorbet made with full-flavoured locally grown strawberries, when in season.*

Pomegranate & Orange Flower Water Creams

Take advantage of the availability of fresh pomegranates when in season, to make this wonderfully coloured dessert. The colour of the fruit will range from pastel pink to vibrant cerise, depending on the type of pomegranates used, but whatever shade you achieve, the finished result will always be very impressive.

Serves 6
10ml/2 tsp cornflour
300ml/¹/₂ pint/1¹/₄ cups milk
25g/1oz/2 tbsp caster
(superfine) sugar
2 large pomegranates
30ml/2 tbsp orange
flower water
75ml/5 tbsp grenadine
300ml/¹/₂ pint/1¹/₄ cups
whipping cream
extra pomegranate seeds
and orange flower water,
to serve

1 Put the cornflour in a pan and blend to a paste with a little of the milk. Stir in the remaining milk and the sugar and cook, stirring constantly, until the mixture thickens. Pour it into a bowl, cover the surface closely with baking parchment and leave to cool.

2 Cut the pomegranates in half and squeeze out the juice, using a lemon squeezer. Add the juice to the cornflour mixture, with the orange flower water, grenadine and cream. Stir lightly to mix.

3 BY HAND: Stir to mix, then pour into a container and freeze for 3–4 hours, beating twice as it thickens.
USING AN ICE CREAM MAKER: Churn the mixture until it is thick enough to hold its shape.

4 Spoon the ice cream into one large, or six individual freezerproof serving dishes and freeze for at least 2 hours, or overnight.

5 Transfer the creams to the fridge 30 minutes before serving, to allow them to soften. Top each of them with pomegranate seeds tossed in the extra orange flower water.

Mango Sorbet Energy 258kcal/1088kJ; Protein3g; Carbohydrate 39g, of which sugars 38g; Fat 11g, of which saturates 7g; Cholesterol 27mg; Calcium 30mg; Fibre 4.4g; Sodium 49mg.
Pomegranate Energy 278kcal/1151kJ; Protein 2.8g; Carbohydrate 10.6g, of which sugars 9.1g; Fat 22.1g, of which saturates 13.9g; Cholesterol 60mg; Calcium 101mg; Fibre 0.6g; Sodium 36mg.

Baked Stuffed Apples

The amaretti and apples in this slow-cooker dessert give a lovely almondy and autumnal flavour. Dried cranberries and glacé fruit add sweetness and colour. Choose apples that will stay firm during cooking.

Serves 4

75g/3oz/6 tbsp butter, softened
45ml/3 tbsp orange or apple juice
75g/3oz/scant ½ cup light
   muscovado (brown) sugar

grated rind and juice of
   ½ orange
1.5ml/¼ tsp ground cinnamon
30ml/2 tbsp crushed amaretti
25g/1oz/¼ cup pecan
   nuts, chopped
25g/1oz/¼ cup dried cranberries
   or sour cherries
25g/1oz/¼ cup luxury mixed
   glacé (candied) fruit, chopped
4 large cooking apples,
   such as Bramleys
cream, crème fraîche or vanilla
   ice cream, to serve

1 Grease the ceramic cooking pot with 15g/½oz/1 tbsp of the butter, then pour in the fruit juice and switch the slow cooker to the high setting.

2 Put the remaining butter, the sugar, orange rind and juice, cinnamon and amaretti crumbs in a bowl and mix well.

3 Add the nuts and dried cranberries or sour cherries and glacé fruit to the bowl and mix well, then set aside the filling while you prepare the apples.

4 Wash and dry the apples. Remove the cores using an apple corer, then carefully enlarge each core cavity to twice its size, using the corer to shave out more flesh. Using a sharp knife, score each apple around its equator.

5 Divide the filling among the apples, packing it into the hole, then piling it on top. Stand the apples in the cooking pot and cover with the lid. Reduce the temperature to low and cook for 4 hours, or until tender.

6 Transfer the apples to warmed serving plates and spoon the sauce over the top. Serve immediately, with cream, crème fraîche or vanilla ice cream.

Apple Charlottes

These tempting little fruit Charlottes are a wonderful way to use windfalls, and make ideal-sized desserts to end a meal.

Serves 4

175g/6oz/¾ cup butter
450g/1lb cooking apples
225g/8oz eating apples

60ml/4 tbsp water
130g/4½oz/scant ⅔ cup caster
   (superfine) sugar
2 egg yolks
pinch of grated nutmeg
9 thin slices white bread,
   crusts removed
extra-thick double (heavy) cream
   or custard, to serve

1 Preheat the oven to 190°C/375°F/Gas 5. Put a knob (pat) of the butter in a pan. Peel and core the apples, dice them finely and put them in the pan with the water. Cover and cook for 10 minutes or until the cooking apples have pulped down. Stir in 115g/4oz/½ cup of the caster sugar. Boil, uncovered, until any liquid has evaporated and what remains is a thick pulp. Remove from the heat, beat in the egg yolks and nutmeg and set aside.

2 Melt the remaining butter in a separate pan over a low heat until the white curds start to separate from the clear yellow liquid. Remove from the heat. Leave to stand for a few minutes, then strain the clear clarified butter through a sieve (strainer) lined with muslin (cheesecloth), discarding the curds.

3 Brush four 150ml/¼ pint/⅔ cup individual Charlotte moulds or round tins (pans) with a little of the clarified butter; sprinkle with the remaining caster sugar. Cut the bread slices into 2.5cm/1in strips. Dip the strips into the remaining clarified butter; use to line the moulds or tins. Overlap the strips on the base to give the effect of a swirl and let the excess bread overhang the tops of the moulds or tins.

4 Fill each bread case with apple pulp. Fold the excess bread over the top of each mould or tin to make a lid and press down lightly. Bake for 45–50 minutes or until golden. Run a knife between each Charlotte and its mould or tin, then turn out on to dessert plates. Serve immediately with extra-thick double cream or custard.

Baked Stuffed Apples Energy 347kcal/1457kJ; Protein 1.6g; Carbohydrate 42.4g, of which sugars 41.3g; Fat 20.3g, of which saturates 10.3g; Cholesterol 40mg; Calcium 27mg; Fibre 3g; Sodium 131mg.
Apple Charlottes Energy 686Kcal/2874kJ; Protein 7.5g; Carbohydrate 79.2g, of which sugars 50.8g; Fat 40g, of which saturates 23.6g; Cholesterol 194mg; Calcium 111mg; Fibre 3.6g; Sodium 591mg.

Mini Toffee Apples

Crunchy apple wedges are fried until crisp in a light batter, then dipped in caramel to make a sweet, sticky dessert that is perfect for an autumn festival such as Bonfire Night or Halloween.

10ml/2 tsp baking powder
60ml/4 tbsp cornflour (cornstarch)
4 firm apples
sunflower oil, for deep-frying
200g/7oz/1 cup caster
  (superfine) sugar

Serves 4
115g/4oz/1 cup plain
  (all-purpose) flour

1 In a large mixing bowl, combine the flour, baking powder, cornflour and 175ml/6fl oz/¾ cup water. Stir to make a smooth batter and set aside.

2 Peel and core the apples, then cut each one into 8 thick wedges. Fill a large bowl with ice cubes and chilled water.

3 Fill a wok one-third full of sunflower oil and heat to 180°C/350°F or until a cube of bread, dropped into the oil, browns in 45 seconds. Working quickly, in batches, dip the apple wedges in the batter, drain off any excess and deep-fry for 2 minutes, or until golden brown. Remove with a slotted spoon and place on kitchen paper to drain.

4 Reheat the oil to 180°C/350°F and fry the wedges for a second time, again giving them about 2 minutes. Drain well on kitchen paper and set aside.

5 Very carefully, pour off all but 30ml/2 tbsp of the oil from the wok and stir in the caster sugar. Heat gently until the sugar melts and starts to caramelize. When the mixture is a light brown colour, add a few pieces of apple at a time and toss to coat evenly.

6 Plunge the coated pieces briefly into the bowl of iced water to set the caramel, then remove from the pan with a slotted spoon and serve immediately.

Poor Knights with Apples

This traditional hot apple recipe originally comes from Germany. The title 'poor knights' possibly refers to the fact that making the dish is a way of using up the previous day's bread.

Serves 4
2 eggs
400ml/14fl oz/1²⁄₃ cups milk
grated rind of 1 lemon
2.5ml/½ tsp vanilla extract
pinch of salt
60ml/4 tbsp breadcrumbs

4 thick slices of day-old
  white bread
50g/2oz/4 tbsp butter
25g/1oz/2 tbsp caster
  (superfine) sugar mixed with
  5ml/1 tsp ground cinnamon

For the apple compote
10ml/2 tsp caster
  (superfine) sugar
200ml/7fl oz/scant 1 cup
  apple juice
juice of 1 lemon
4 apples, peeled, cored and diced
5ml/1 tsp raisins

1 Make the apple compote first. Heat the sugar in a pan over medium heat until it caramelizes. When it turns golden brown, plunge the base of the pan into a bowl of cold water to stop the sugar burning.

2 Stir the apple juice and lemon juice into the caramel. Stir in the apples and raisins and cook for 6–7 minutes. Remove from the heat and leave to cool.

3 Beat the eggs lightly and mix in the milk, grated lemon rind, vanilla extract and a pinch of salt. Dip the bread slices into this mixture and then turn them in the breadcrumbs to coat them on both sides.

4 Melt the butter in a frying pan over medium heat and fry the bread slices for 2–3 minutes on each side, until golden. Sprinkle the sugar and cinnamon mix over the top and serve immediately, with the apple compote.

Cook's Tip
Choose any type of tart or dessert apple for this recipe.

Mini Toffee Apples Energy 457kcal/1940kJ; Protein 3.4g; Carbohydrate 97.3g, of which sugars 61.6g; Fat 8.8g, of which saturates 1.1g; Cholesterol 0mg; Calcium 73mg; Fibre 2.5g; Sodium 14mg.
Poor Knights Energy 404kcal/1706kJ; Protein 11.3g; Carbohydrate 58.8g, of which sugars 33.5g; Fat 15.7g, of which saturates 8.7g; Cholesterol 130mg; Calcium 204mg; Fibre 2.5g; Sodium 461mg.

Poached Pears in Scented Honey Syrup

Fruit has been poached in honey since ancient times. The Romans did it, as well as the Persians, Arabs, Moors and Ottomans. The Moroccans continue the tradition today, adding a little orange rind or aniseed, or even lavender, to give a subtle flavouring. Delicate and pretty to look at, these scented pears provide an exquisite finishing touch to a Moroccan meal.

Serves 4
45ml/3 tbsp clear honey
juice of 1 lemon
250ml/8fl oz/1 cup water
pinch of saffron threads
1 cinnamon stick
2–3 dried lavender heads
4 firm pears

1 Heat the honey and lemon juice in a heavy pan that will hold the pears snugly. Stir over a gentle heat until the honey has completely dissolved.

2 Add the water, saffron threads, cinnamon stick and the flowers from 1–2 lavender heads. Bring the mixture to the boil, then reduce the heat and simmer for 5 minutes.

3 Peel the pears, leaving the stalks attached. Add the pears to the pan and simmer for 20 minutes, turning and basting at regular intervals, until they are tender.

4 Leave the pears to cool in the syrup and serve at room temperature, decorated with a few lavender flowers.

Cook's Tips
• When choosing dried lavender for cooking, make sure you buy a culinary variety that has not been sprayed.
• The longer you leave the fruit poaching in the scented mixture, the stronger the flavour.

Pears in Chocolate Fudge Blankets

Warm poached pears coated in a rich chocolate fudge sauce – who could resist?

Serves 6
6 ripe eating pears
30ml/2 tbsp fresh
   lemon juice
75g/3oz/6 tbsp caster
   (superfine) sugar
300ml/½ pint/1¼ cups
   water
1 cinnamon stick

For the sauce
200ml/7fl oz/scant 1 cup
   double (heavy) cream
150g/5oz/scant 1 cup light
   muscovado (brown) sugar
25g/1oz/2 tbsp unsalted
   (sweet) butter
60ml/4 tbsp golden (light corn)
   syrup
120ml/4fl oz/½ cup milk
200g/7oz plain (semisweet)
   chocolate, broken into
   squares

1 Peel the pears thinly, leaving the stalks on. Scoop out the cores from the base. Brush the cut surfaces with lemon juice to prevent browning.

2 Place the sugar and water in a large pan. Heat gently until the sugar dissolves. Add the pears and cinnamon stick with any remaining lemon juice, and, if necessary, a little more water, so that the pears are almost covered.

3 Bring to the boil, then lower the heat, cover the pan and simmer the pears gently for 15–20 minutes.

4 Meanwhile, make the sauce. Place the cream, sugar, butter, golden syrup and milk in a heavy pan. Heat gently until the sugar has dissolved and the butter and syrup have melted, then bring to the boil. Boil, stirring constantly, for about 5 minutes or until thick and smooth.

5 Remove the pan from the heat and stir in the chocolate, a few squares at a time, stirring until it has all melted.

6 Using a slotted spoon, transfer the poached pears to a dish. Keep hot. Boil the syrup rapidly to reduce to 45–60ml/3–4 tbsp. Remove the cinnamon stick and gently stir the syrup into the chocolate sauce. Serve the pears with the sauce spooned over.

Poached Pears Energy 105kcal/447kJ; Protein 1g; Carbohydrate 27g, of which sugars 27g; Fat 0g, of which saturates 0g; Cholesterol 0mg; Calcium 117mg; Fibre 3.2g; Sodium 6mg.
Pears in Chocolate Energy 613Kcal/2570kJ; Protein 3.6g; Carbohydrate 84.8g, of which sugars 84.5g; Fat 31.2g, of which saturates 19.1g; Cholesterol 58mg; Calcium 90mg; Fibre 4.1g; Sodium 77mg.

Baked Quinces in Syrup

Quinces are best enjoyed fresh in season, but can also be preserved for winter use. In this recipe, the fruits are are cooked in quince syrup for a more intense flavour.

Serves 4

6 quinces
juice of 2 lemons

200g/7oz/1 cup caster
    (superfine) sugar
1 vanilla pod (bean),
    split lengthways
300ml/½ pint/1¼ cups water
4 cloves
200ml/7fl oz/scant 1 cup yogurt,
    to serve

1 Peel four of the quinces and cut into quarters. Remove the cores and put the flesh into a large ovenproof dish or casserole with a lid, arranged in a single layer. Pour over the lemon juice.

2 Use the remaining two quinces to make the syrup. Peel, core and chop them coarsely. Put them in a large pan with 115g/4oz/generous ½ cup of the sugar. Scrape out the vanilla seeds and add them to the pan with the pod.

3 Add enough water to cover. Bring to the boil and simmer for 1 hour, or until the quinces are soft and dark red, and the liquid has turned syrupy. Strain the syrup and discard the quince pulp and vanilla pod.

4 Preheat the oven to 120°C/250°F/Gas ½. Pour the syrup over the quince quarters, making sure they are covered. Add the cloves and remaining sugar. Put a piece of baking parchment on top to keep the fruit submerged.

5 Put on the lid and cook in the oven for 1 hour, or until the quinces are soft to the touch and red in colour. To serve, put four quince quarters with some syrup in each dessert bowl, and add a dollop of yogurt.

> **Variation**
> If you are unable to find quinces, pears can be used instead.

Honey-seared Melon with Lavender and Raspberries

This simple dessert is perfect for a summer's evening, with the lavender in flower and a bowl of strongly scented raspberries to hand. The honeycomb is a delicious partner for the melon and raspberries.

Serves 6

1.3kg/3lb melon, preferably
    Charentais
200g/7oz honeycomb
5ml/1 tsp water
a bunch of lavender, plus extra
    flowers for decoration
300g/11oz/2 cups raspberries

1 Cut the melon in half, scoop out the seeds using a spoon, then cut each half into three slices.

2 Put about a third of the honey into a bowl and dilute it by stirring in the water. Make a brush with the lavender and dip it in the honey.

3 Heat a griddle until a few drops of water sprinkled on to the surface evaporate instantly. Lightly brush the melon with the honey mixture.

4 Grill the melon slices for about 30 seconds on each side. Serve with the raspberries, honeycomb and lavender flowers.

> **Cook's Tip**
> Honeycomb has a natural taste, and is usually sold by weight.

> **Variations**
> • Other soft summer fruits can be used in this dessert, if you prefer. Choose whatever is in season and looks best in the store. Strawberries, blueberries or redcurrants will all be delicious in this recipe.
> • You can grill (broil) the melon slices on a barbecue, if you prefer, and if the weather permits.

Baked Quinces Energy 307kcal/1305kJ; Protein 1.1g; Carbohydrate 79.8g, of which sugars 79.8g; Fat 0.3g, of which saturates 0g; Cholesterol 0mg; Calcium 57mg; Fibre 6.1g; Sodium 11mg.
Honey-seared Melon Energy 161kcal/685kJ; Protein 1.9g; Carbohydrate 39.9g, of which sugars 39.9g; Fat 0.4g, of which saturates 0.1g; Cholesterol 0mg; Calcium 42mg; Fibre 2.1g; Sodium 72mg.

Chocolate & Orange Scotch Pancakes

These fabulous mini pancakes are drenched in a rich orange liqueur sauce.

Serves 4
115g/4oz/1 cup self-raising
  (self-rising) flour
30ml/2 tbsp cocoa powder
  (unsweetened)
2 eggs
50g/2oz plain (semisweet)
  chocolate, broken into squares
200ml/7fl oz/scant 1 cup milk
finely grated rind of 1 orange

30ml/2 tbsp orange juice
butter or oil, for frying
60ml/4 tbsp chocolate curls,
  to decorate

For the sauce
2 large oranges
25g/1oz/2 tbsp unsalted
  (sweet) butter
40g/1½oz/3 tbsp light
  muscovado (brown) sugar
250ml/8fl oz/1 cup crème fraîche
30ml/2 tbsp orange liqueur

1 Sift the flour and cocoa into a bowl and make a well in the centre. Add the eggs and beat well, gradually incorporating the surrounding dry ingredients to make a smooth batter.

2 Mix the chocolate and milk in a heavy pan. Heat gently until the chocolate has melted, then beat into the batter until smooth and bubbly. Stir in the grated orange rind and juice.

3 Heat a large heavy frying pan or griddle. Grease with a little butter or oil. Drop large spoonfuls of batter on to the hot surface. Cook over a moderate heat. When the pancakes are lightly browned underneath and bubbling on top, flip them over to cook the other side. Slide on to a plate and keep hot, then make more in the same way.

4 Make the sauce. Grate the rind of 1 of the oranges into a bowl and set aside. Peel both oranges, taking care to remove all the pith, then slice the flesh fairly thinly. Heat the butter and sugar in a wide, shallow pan over a low heat, stirring until the sugar dissolves. Stir in the crème fraîche and heat gently.

5 Add the pancakes and orange slices to the sauce, heat gently for 1–2 minutes, then spoon on the liqueur. Sprinkle with the reserved orange rind. Scatter over chocolate curls and serve.

Lemon Surprise Pudding

This is a much-loved dessert that many of us may remember from our childhoods. The surprise is the unexpected lemon sauce concealed beneath the delectable sponge.

Serves 4
50g/2oz/¼ cup butter,
  plus extra for greasing

grated rind and juice of
  2 lemons
115g/4oz/generous ½ cup
  caster (superfine) sugar
2 eggs, separated
50g/2oz/½ cup self-raising
  (self-rising) flour
300ml/½ pint/1¼ cups milk

1 Preheat the oven to 190°C/375°F/Gas 5. Use a little butter to grease a 1.2 litre/2 pint/5 cup baking dish.

2 Beat the lemon rind, remaining butter and caster sugar in a bowl until pale and fluffy. Add the egg yolks and flour and beat together well. Gradually whisk in the lemon juice and milk (don't be alarmed if the mixture curdles horribly).

3 In a grease-free bowl, whisk the egg whites until they form stiff peaks. Fold the egg whites lightly into the lemon mixture, then pour into the prepared baking dish.

4 Place the dish in a roasting tin (pan) and pour in hot water to come halfway up the side of the dish. Bake for about 45 minutes until golden. Serve immediately.

Cook's Tips
• The uncooked mixture may look like a curdled disaster, but as the dessert cooks, it separates into a top layer of firm sponge, with a luscious lemony sauce beneath.
• Standing the dish in a layer of water in the pan creates a gentle method of cooking – this 'bain-marie' method is often used for custards and other delicate egg dishes.
• For a slightly different accompaniment, whip thick cream with a little vanilla extract and icing (confectioners') sugar.

Chocolate Energy 752Kcal/3131kJ; Protein 12.1g; Carbohydrate 58.1g, of which sugars 35.5g; Fat 53.2g, of which saturates 27g; Cholesterol 185mg; Calcium 282mg; Fibre 3.9g; Sodium 304mg.
Lemon Surprise Energy 319Kcal/1341kJ; Protein 7g; Carbohydrate 43.1g, of which sugars 33.8g; Fat 14.5g, of which saturates 8.1g; Cholesterol 126mg; Calcium 166mg; Fibre 0.4g; Sodium 190mg.

Peach Cobbler

A cobbler is a batter-topped fruit or savoury dish, and this traditional recipe is for a satisfying sweet pudding in which fresh peaches are topped with a hearty almond-flavoured pastry.

Serves 6

about 1.5kg/3lb peaches,
   peeled and sliced
45ml/3 tbsp caster
   (superfine) sugar
30ml/2 tbsp peach brandy
15ml/1 tbsp freshly squeezed
   lemon juice
15ml/1 tbsp cornflour
   (cornstarch)

ice cream or crème fraîche,
   to serve

For the topping

115g/4oz/1 cup plain
   (all-purpose) flour
7.5ml/1½ tsp baking powder
1.5ml/¼ tsp salt
40g/1½oz/¼ cup finely
   ground almonds
50g/2oz/¼ cup caster
   (superfine) sugar
50g/2oz/¼ cup butter or
   margarine
85ml/3fl oz/⅓ cup milk
1.5ml/¼ tsp almond extract

1 Preheat the oven to 220°C/425°F/Gas 7. Place the peaches in a bowl and add the sugar, peach brandy, lemon juice and cornflour. Toss together, then spoon the peach mixture into a 2 litre/3½ pint/8 cup baking dish.

2 Now make the topping. Sift the flour, baking powder and salt into a mixing bowl. Stir in the ground almonds and all but 15ml/1 tbsp of the sugar. With two knives, or a pastry blender, cut in the butter or margarine until the mixture resembles coarse breadcrumbs.

3 Add the milk and almond extract and stir until the topping mixture is just combined.

4 Carefully drop the topping in spoonfuls on to the peaches in the baking dish. Sprinkle the top with the remaining tablespoon of caster sugar.

5 Bake for 30–35 minutes until the cobbler topping is browned. Serve hot with ice cream or crème fraîche, if you prefer.

Stuffed Peaches with Mascarpone Cream

Peaches with an almond-flavoured filling and topped with a rich cream make a delicious Italian-style dessert that is ideal for summer entertaining.

Serves 4

4 large peaches, halved and
   stoned (pitted)
40g/1½oz amaretti, crumbled
30ml/2 tbsp ground almonds
45ml/3 tbsp sugar
15ml/1 tbsp cocoa powder
   (unsweetened)

150ml/¼ pint/⅔ cup sweet
   white wine
25g/1oz/2 tbsp butter

For the mascarpone cream

25g/1oz/2 tbsp caster
   (superfine) sugar
3 egg yolks
15ml/1 tbsp sweet white wine
225g/8oz/1 cup mascarpone
150ml/¼ pint/⅔ cup double
   (heavy) cream

1 Preheat the oven to 200°C/400°F/Gas 6. Using a teaspoon, scoop some of the flesh from the cavities in the peaches, to make a reasonable space for the stuffing. Chop the scooped-out flesh.

2 Mix together the amaretti, ground almonds, sugar, cocoa and peach flesh. Now add enough wine to make the mixture into a thick paste.

3 Place the peaches in a buttered ovenproof dish and fill them with the stuffing. Dot with the butter, then pour the remaining wine into the dish. Bake in the oven for 35 minutes.

4 Make the mascarpone cream. Beat the sugar and egg yolks until thick and pale. Stir in the wine, then fold in the mascarpone. Whip the double cream to form soft peaks and fold into the mixture.

5 Remove the stuffed peaches from the oven and leave to cool completely. Serve at room temperature, along with the mascarpone cream.

Peach Cobbler Energy 299Kcal/1265kJ; Protein 4.9g; Carbohydrate 53.5g, of which sugars 36.6g; Fat 7.6g, of which saturates 4.5g; Cholesterol 19mg; Calcium 72mg; Fibre 4.4g; Sodium 62mg.
Stuffed Peaches Energy 641Kcal/2670kJ; Protein 12.7g; Carbohydrate 40.9g, of which sugars 36g; Fat 45.3g, of which saturates 23.9g; Cholesterol 290mg; Calcium 102mg; Fibre 2.7g; Sodium 132mg.

Baked Sweet Apricots

Hot summers bring abundant stone fruits that are sweet, juicy and full of flavour. This recipe makes the most of apricots, which have a natural affinity with cinnamon and almonds.

Serves 6
600g/1lb/5oz apricots, halved
30ml/2 tbsp caster (superfine)
  sugar
25ml/1½ tbsp ground cinnamon
30ml/2 tbsp honey
45ml/3 tbsp flaked (sliced)
  almonds
icing (confectioners') sugar,
  to dust
200ml/7fl oz/scant 1 cup
  thick natural (plain) yogurt,
  to serve

1 Tightly arrange the apricot halves, cut side up, in a shallow roasting pan.

2 Sprinkle with the sugar and cinnamon, then drizzle with the honey. Cover the roasting pan with foil or a dish towel and allow to rest for 2 hours in the refrigerator.

3 Meanwhile, put the almonds in a dry pan and toast over medium-high heat, tossing regularly, for 1–2 minutes, or until golden brown. Set aside.

4 Preheat the oven to 180°C/350°F/Gas 4. Remove the dish towel from the roasting pan. Add 120ml/4fl oz/½ cup water and roast for 30 minutes, or until the contents are soft and golden brown.

5 Sprinkle the apricots with the toasted almonds and dust the tops with icing sugar. Serve in individual bowls with a portion of yogurt on the side.

> **Variation**
> This simple recipe can be made with plums, peaches and melons. As well as being used fresh while in season, all of these can be preserved for use during the cold winter months.

Caramelized Apricots with Pain Perdu

Pain perdu is a French invention that literally translates as 'lost bread'. Americans call it French toast, while a British version is known as Poor Knights.

Serves 4
75g/3oz/6 tbsp unsalted (sweet)
  butter, clarified
450g/1lb apricots, stoned (pitted)
  and thickly sliced
115g/4oz/½ cup caster
  (superfine) sugar
150ml/¼ pint/⅔ cup double
  (heavy) cream
30ml/2 tbsp apricot brandy

For the pain perdu
600ml/1 pint/2½ cups milk
1 vanilla pod (bean)
50g/2oz/¼ cup caster
  (superfine) sugar
4 large eggs, beaten
115g/4oz/½ cup unsalted
  (sweet) butter, clarified
6 brioche slices, diagonally halved
2.5ml/½ tsp ground cinnamon

1 Heat a heavy frying pan and melt a quarter of the butter. Add the apricot slices and cook for 2–3 minutes until golden. Using a slotted spoon, transfer them to a bowl. Heat the rest of the butter with the sugar, stirring, until golden.

2 Pour in the cream and brandy and cook gently until a smooth sauce forms. Boil for 2–3 minutes until thickened, then pour the sauce over the apricots and set aside.

3 To make the pain perdu, pour the milk into a pan and add the vanilla pod and half the sugar. Heat gently until almost boiling, then set aside to cool. Remove the vanilla pod and pour the milk into a shallow dish. Whisk in the eggs.

4 Heat a sixth of the butter in the clean frying pan. Dip a slice of brioche into the milk mixture and fry until golden brown on both sides. Add the remaining butter as needed. As the pain perdu is cooked, remove the slices and keep hot.

5 Warm the apricot sauce and spoon it on to the pain perdu. Mix the remaining sugar with the cinnamon and sprinkle a little over each portion.

Baked Sweet Apricots Energy 111kcal/470kJ; Protein 2.5g; Carbohydrate 16.8g, of which sugars 16.6g; Fat 4.3g, of which saturates 0.4g; Cholesterol 0mg; Calcium 36mg; Fibre 2.3g; Sodium 4mg.
Caramelized Apricots Energy 1071kcal/4471kJ; Protein 18.5g; Carbohydrate 92.1g, of which sugars 69.2g; Fat 70.9g, of which saturates 41.6g; Cholesterol 353mg; Calcium 343mg; Fibre 3.3g; Sodium 634mg.

Chocolate Crêpes with Plums & Port

The crêpes, fruit filling
and sauce can be made
in advance, and assembled
at the last minute.

Serves 6
50g/2oz plain (semisweet)
  chocolate, broken into squares
200ml/7fl oz/scant 1 cup milk
120ml/4fl oz/½ cup single
  (light) cream
30ml/2 tbsp cocoa powder
  (unsweetened)
115g/4oz/1 cup plain
  (all-purpose) flour
2 eggs

For the filling
500g/1¼lb red or golden
  plums
50g/2oz/¼ cup caster
  (superfine) sugar
30ml/2 tbsp water
30ml/2 tbsp port
oil, for frying
175g/6oz/¾ cup crème fraîche

For the sauce
150g/5oz plain (semisweet)
  chocolate, broken into squares
175ml/6fl oz/¾ cup double
  (heavy) cream
30ml/2 tbsp port

1 Place the chocolate and milk in a heavy pan. Heat gently until the chocolate dissolves. Pour into a blender or food processor and add the cream, cocoa, flour and eggs. Process until smooth. Turn into a jug (pitcher) and chill for 30 minutes.

2 Meanwhile, make the filling. Halve and stone (pit) the plums. Place in a pan with the sugar and water. Bring to the boil, then lower the heat, cover and simmer for about 10 minutes, or until the plums are tender. Stir in the port and simmer for a further 30 seconds. Remove from the heat and keep warm.

3 Have ready a sheet of baking parchment. Heat a crêpe pan, grease lightly with a little oil, then pour in just enough batter to cover the base of the pan, swirling to coat it evenly. Cook until the crêpe has set, then flip it over to cook the other side. Slide on to the paper, then cook 9–11 more crêpes in the same way.

4 Make the sauce. Put the chocolate and cream in a pan. Heat gently, stirring until smooth. Add the port and stir for 1 minute.

5 Divide the plums between the crêpes, add a dollop of crème fraîche to each and roll up. Serve with the sauce spooned over.

Plum Crumble

The crumble is a perennially
popular dessert, and this
comforting plum dish is
sweet, juicy and colourful.

Serves 4
450g/1lb stoned (pitted) plums
50g/2oz/¼ cup soft light
  brown sugar
15ml/1 tbsp water
juice of 1 lemon

For the crumble topping
50g/2oz/½ cup plain
  (all-purpose) flour
25g/1oz/generous ¼ cup coarse
  rolled oats
50g/2oz/¼ cup soft light
  brown sugar
50g/2oz/¼ cup butter, softened

1 Preheat the oven to 200°C/400°F/Gas 6. Place a large pan over a medium heat.

2 Put the plums in the pan and add the sugar, water and lemon juice. Mix thoroughly and bring to the boil, stirring continuously until the sugar dissolves.

3 Cook the plums until they are just beginning to soften. Place the fruit with the juices in a deep pie dish.

4 Place the crumble ingredients in a bowl and mix with your fingers until the mixture resembles breadcrumbs.

5 Sprinkle the crumble topping evenly over the fruit so that it is a good thickness. Bake in the preheated oven for 20 minutes, or until the top is crunchy and brown.

Cook's Tips
• Plums can be divided into three categories – dessert, dual and cooking. Choose whichever dual or cooking plum is available in your local area.
• When buying plums, choose smooth, unbruised fruits.
• If you prefer to remove the skins, drop the plums into boiling water for 15 seconds, then plunge them into cold water immediately. The skins will come away easily.

Chocolate Crêpes Energy 304kcal/1284kJ; Protein 2.9g; Carbohydrate 51.5g, of which sugars 37.4g; Fat 11.1g, of which saturates 6.5g; Cholesterol 27mg; Calcium 53mg; Fibre 2.8g; Sodium 82mg.
Plum Crumble Energy 301kcal/1269kJ; Protein3g; Carbohydrate57g, of which sugars 37g; Fat 11g, of which saturates 7g; Cholesterol 27mg; Calcium 46mg; Fibre 3.4g; Sodium 82mg.

Streusel Plum Cake

This kind of cake, with a shortcrust base and a crumble topping, can be made with various different fruits, depending on the time of year. Plums are harvested from the end of summer until the middle of autumn, and while they are in season, many bakeries sell fresh plum cake.

Makes about 16 pieces
200g/7oz/scant 1 cup butter, softened
150g/5oz/¾ cup caster (superfine) sugar
pinch of salt

1½ tsp vanilla extract or 2 packs vanilla sugar (about 10g/¼oz)
2 eggs
400g/14oz/3½ cups plain (all-purpose) flour
icing (confectioners') sugar, to dust

For the filling
800g/1¾lb plums, halved and stoned (pitted)
100g/3½oz/½ cup caster (superfine) sugar
whipped double (heavy) cream, to serve

1 Preheat the oven to 180°C/350°F/Gas 4. Put the butter in a bowl with the sugar, salt, vanilla, eggs and flour. Rub the mixture with your fingertips until it is crumbly.

2 Use half the crumble dough to line a 40 × 30cm/16 × 12in baking tray, pressing it evenly over the base and up the sides.

3 Put in the halved plums and sprinkle the sugar on top. Scatter the rest of the crumble on top of the plums.

4 Bake the cake in the preheated oven for 45–60 minutes. Dust with icing sugar and cut into squares to serve with a dollop of whipped cream.

Variations
Instead of plums, try making this streusel with other seasonal stone fruits, such as peaches, apricots or nectarines. Choose whatever is available in your local area.

Ice Cream with Hot Cherry Sauce

Hot cherry sauce transforms ice cream into a delicious dessert for any occasion. Serve immediately to ensure that the sauce is still warm to the taste.

Serves 4
425g/15oz can pitted black cherries in juice
10ml/2 tsp cornflour (cornstarch)
finely grated rind of 1 lemon, plus 10ml/2 tsp juice

15ml/1 tbsp caster (superfine) sugar
2.5ml/½ tsp ground cinnamon
30ml/2 tbsp brandy or Kirsch (optional)
400ml/14fl oz/1⅔ cups dark (bittersweet) chocolate ice cream
400ml/14fl oz/1⅔ cups classic vanilla ice cream
drinking chocolate powder, for dusting

1 Drain the cherries, reserving the canned juice. Spoon the cornflour into a small pan and blend to a paste with a little of the reserved juice.

2 Stir in the remaining canned juice with the lemon rind and juice, sugar and cinnamon. Bring to the boil, stirring, until smooth and glossy.

3 Add the cherries, with the brandy or Kirsch, if using. Stir gently, then cook for 1 minute.

4 Scoop the chocolate and vanilla ice cream into shallow dishes. Spoon the sauce around, dust with drinking chocolate powder and serve.

Variation
The hot cherry sauce also makes a delicious filling for pancakes. For a speedy dessert, use heated, ready-made sweet pancakes – just spread a little sauce in the centre of each pancake and fold into a triangle shape or roll up. Then arrange in a serving dish and spoon the rest of the sauce over the top. Finish with spoonfuls of thick yogurt or whipped cream.

Streusel Plum Cake Energy 247kcal/1037kJ; Protein 4g; Carbohydrate 34g, of which sugars 15g; Fat 11g, of which saturates 7g; Cholesterol 56mg; Calcium 49mg; Fibre 2.1g; Sodium 89mg.
Ice Cream Energy 529kcal/2213kJ; Protein 8.4g; Carbohydrate 59.5g, of which sugars 57g; Fat 30.2g, of which saturates 18.1g; Cholesterol 0mg; Calcium 218mg; Fibre 0.7g; Sodium 130mg.

Deep-fried Cherries

Fresh fruit coated with a simple batter and then deep-fried is delicious, and makes an unusual dessert. These succulent cherries are perfect sprinkled with sugar and cinnamon, and served with a scoop of classic vanilla ice cream.

Serves 4–6
450g/1lb ripe red cherries,
  on their stalks
225g/8oz batter mix
1 egg

From the store cupboard
vegetable oil, for deep-frying

1 Gently wash the cherries and pat dry with kitchen paper. Tie the stalks together with fine string to form clusters of four or five cherries.

2 Make up the batter mix according to the instructions on the packet, beating in the egg. Pour the vegetable oil into a deep-fat fryer or large, heavy pan and heat to 190°C/375°F.

3 Working in batches, half-dip each cherry cluster into the batter and then carefully drop the cluster into the hot oil. Fry for 3–4 minutes, or until golden. Remove the deep-fried cherries with a wire-mesh skimmer or slotted spoon and drain on a wire rack placed over crumpled kitchen paper, and serve immediately.

> **Cook's Tip**
> *To check that the oil has come to the required temperature, drop a cube of day-old bread in the oil; if it turns golden brown and crispy in 20 seconds, the oil is hot enough.*

> **Variation**
> *Other fruits can be deep-fried in batter with delicious results. Bananas work well, especially with a little coconut milk in the batter mix. Ready-to-eat pitted prunes, dates or figs can also be used in this recipe*

Black Cherry Clafoutis

It is possible to reproduce this favourite French recipe with all manner of different types of fruit, but you simply can't beat the classic version using slightly tart black cherries.

Serves 6
25g/1oz/2 tbsp butter,
  for greasing
450g/1lb/generous 2 cups
  black cherries, pitted

25g/1oz/¼ cup plain
  (all-purpose) flour
50g/2oz/½ cup icing
  (confectioners') sugar,
  plus extra for dusting
4 eggs, beaten
250ml/8fl oz/1 cup full cream
  (whole) milk
30ml/2 tbsp Kirsch

1 Preheat the oven to 180°C/350°F/Gas 4. Use the butter to thickly grease a 1.2 litre/2 pint/5 cup ovenproof dish. Sprinkle the cherries over the base.

2 Sift the flour and icing sugar together into a large mixing bowl and gradually whisk in the eggs until the mixture is smooth. Whisk in the milk until blended, then stir in the Kirsch.

3 Pour the batter carefully over the cherries, then bake for 35–45 minutes or until just set and lightly golden.

4 Allow the pudding to cool for about 15 minutes. Dust liberally with icing sugar just before serving.

> **Cook's Tip**
> *Traditionally, the cherries are left whole, but you may prefer to pit the fruit first, to make the dish easier to eat.*

> **Variations**
> *Try other liqueurs in this dessert. Almond-flavoured liqueur is delicious teamed with cherries, as is raspberry or orange liqueur.*

Deep-fried Cherries Energy 201kcal/840kJ; Protein 3.7g; Carbohydrate 25.7g, of which sugars 7.3g; Fat 10g, of which saturates 1.3g; Cholesterol 26mg; Calcium 46mg; Fibre 1.3g; Sodium 11mg.
Black Cherry Energy 201kcal/843kJ; Protein 6.7g; Carbohydrate 23.8g, of which sugars 20.7g; Fat 8.9g, of which saturates 4.3g; Cholesterol 142mg; Calcium 89mg; Fibre 0.8g; Sodium 91mg.

Fruity Bread & Butter Pudding

Comfort food suits the festive season well, and desserts do not come more warming and enjoyable than this fruity one. The whiskey sauce is heavenly, but the pudding can also be served with chilled cream or vanilla ice cream – the contrast between the hot and cold is striking and delicious.

Serves 6
8 slices of white bread, buttered
115–150g/4–5oz/³⁄₄–1 cup
  sultanas (golden raisins),
  or mixed dried fruit

2.5ml/½ tsp grated nutmeg
150g/5oz/³⁄₄ cup caster
  (superfine) sugar
2 large (US extra large) eggs
300ml/½ pint/1¼ cups single
  (light) cream
450ml/³⁄₄ pint/scant 2 cups milk
5ml/1 tsp vanilla extract
light muscovado (brown) sugar,
  for sprinkling (optional)

For the whiskey sauce
150g/5oz/10 tbsp butter
115g/4oz/generous ½ cup caster
  (superfine) sugar
1 egg
45ml/3 tbsp Irish whiskey

1 Preheat the oven to 180°C/350°F/Gas 4. Remove the crusts from the bread and put four slices, buttered side down, in the base of an ovenproof dish. Sprinkle with the fruit, some of the nutmeg and 15ml/1 tbsp sugar.

2 Place the remaining four slices of bread on top, buttered side down, and sprinkle again with nutmeg and 15ml/1 tbsp sugar.

3 Beat the eggs lightly, add the cream, milk, vanilla extract and the remaining sugar, and mix well to make a custard. Pour this mixture over the bread, and sprinkle light muscovado sugar over the top, if you like to have a crispy crust.

4 Bake in the preheated oven for 1 hour, or until all the liquid has been absorbed and the pudding is risen and brown.

5 Meanwhile, make the whiskey sauce: melt the butter in a heavy pan, add the caster sugar and dissolve over gentle heat. Remove from the heat and add the egg, whisking vigorously, and then add the whiskey. Serve the pudding on hot serving plates, with the whiskey sauce poured over the top.

Fresh Currant Bread & Butter Pudding

Fresh mixed currants add a tart touch to this scrumptious hot pudding.

Serves 6
8 medium-thick slices day-old
  bread, crusts removed
50g/2oz/¼ cup butter,
  softened
115g/4oz/1 cup redcurrants
115g/4oz/1 cup blackcurrants
4 eggs, beaten

75g/3oz/6 tbsp caster
  (superfine) sugar
475ml/16fl oz/2 cups
  creamy milk
5ml/1 tsp pure vanilla extract
freshly grated nutmeg
30ml/2 tbsp demerara
  (raw) sugar
single (light) cream, to serve

1 Preheat the oven to 160°C/325°F/Gas 3. Generously butter a 1.2 litre/2 pint/5 cup oval baking dish.

2 Spread the slices of bread generously with the butter, then cut them in half diagonally. Layer the slices in the dish, buttered side up, sprinkling the currants between the layers.

3 Beat the eggs and caster sugar lightly together in a large mixing bowl, then gradually whisk in the milk, vanilla extract and a large pinch of freshly grated nutmeg. Pour the milk mixture over the bread, pushing the slices down. Sprinkle the demerara sugar and a little nutmeg over the top.

4 Place the dish in a roasting pan and then add hot water so that the water reaches halfway up the sides of the dish. Bake for 40 minutes, then increase the oven temperature to 180°C/350°F/Gas 4 and bake for 20–25 minutes until golden. Serve with single cream.

> **Variation**
> A mixture of blueberries and raspberries would work very successfully instead of the currants.

Fruity Bread Energy 757kcal/3168kJ; Protein 11.7g; Carbohydrate 82g, of which sugars 65.2g; Fat 40.8g, of which saturates 24.3g; Cholesterol 207mg; Calcium 232mg; Fibre 0.9g; Sodium 472mg.
Fresh Currant Energy 328Kcal/1377kJ; Protein 10.3g; Carbohydrate 42.2g, of which sugars 25.4g; Fat 14.3g, of which saturates 7.4g; Cholesterol 156mg; Calcium 186mg; Fibre 1.9g; Sodium 321mg.

Maple & Sultana Croissant Pudding

This variation of the classic English bread and butter pudding uses rich, flaky croissants topped with a delicious mixture of fruit and pecan nuts. Custard flavoured with maple syrup completes this mouthwatering dessert.

Serves 4

75g/3oz/scant ½ cup sultanas
   (golden raisins)
45ml/3 tbsp brandy
4 large croissants
50g/2oz/¼ cup butter or
   margarine, plus extra
   for greasing
40g/1½oz/⅓ cup pecan nuts,
   roughly chopped
3 eggs, lightly beaten
300ml/½ pint/1¼ cups milk
150ml/¼ pint/⅔ cup single
   (light) cream
120ml/4fl oz/½ cup maple syrup
25g/1oz/2 tbsp demerara
   (raw) sugar
maple syrup and pouring
   (half-and-half) cream,
   to serve

1 Lightly grease the base and sides of a small, shallow ovenproof dish. Place the sultanas and brandy in a small pan and heat gently, until warm. Leave to stand for 1 hour.

2 Cut the croissants into thick slices and spread with butter on one side. Arrange the slices, buttered side uppermost and slightly overlapping, in the greased dish. Sprinkle the brandy-soaked sultanas and the pecan nuts evenly over the croissant slices.

3 In a large bowl, beat the eggs and milk together, then gradually beat in the single cream and maple syrup. Pour the egg custard through a sieve (strainer), over the croissants, fruit and nuts in the dish. Leave the pudding to stand for 30 minutes so that some of the custard is absorbed by the croissants. Meanwhile, preheat the oven to 180°F/350°C/Gas 4.

4 Sprinkle the demerara sugar evenly over the top, then cover the dish with foil. Bake the pudding for 30 minutes, then remove the foil and continue to cook for about 20 minutes, or until the custard is set and the top is golden brown.

5 Leave the pudding to cool for about 15 minutes before serving warm with extra maple syrup and pouring cream.

Christmas Pudding

This rich, slowly steamed fruit pudding is a must for any Christmas feast. Serve with a traditional hot white sauce, flavoured with whiskey, brandy or rum, or simply offer a jug of cream liqueur, to be poured over the pudding as a sauce.

**Makes 2 puddings,
each serving 6–8**

275g/10oz/5 cups fresh
   breadcrumbs
225g/8oz/1 cup light muscovado
   (brown) sugar
225g/8oz/1 cup currants
275g/10oz/2 cups raisins
225g/8oz/1⅓ cups sultanas
   (golden raisins)
50g/2oz/⅓ cup chopped
   (candied) peel
115g/4oz/½ cup glacé
   (candied) cherries
225g/8oz shredded suet
   (US chilled, grated shortening),
   or vegetarian equivalent
2.5ml/½ tsp salt
10–20ml/2–4 tsp mixed
   (apple pie) spice
1 carrot, coarsely grated
1 apple, peeled, cored and
   finely chopped
grated rind and juice of
   1 small orange
2 large (US extra large) eggs,
   lightly whisked
450ml/¾ pint/scant 2 cups
   stout
white sauce, to serve

1 Mix the breadcrumbs, sugar, dried fruit and peel in a bowl. Shred and add the suet, salt, mixed spice, carrot, apple and orange rind. Mix until well combined. Stir in the orange juice, eggs and stout. Leave the mixture overnight, giving it a stir occasionally, if convenient.

2 Well grease and line two 1.2 litre/2 pint/5 cup heatproof bowls with baking parchment. Stir the mixture and turn into the bowls. Cover with buttered circles of baking parchment, then tie pudding cloths over the top, or tightly cover them with several layers of baking parchment and foil, tied under the rim.

3 Steam for about 6–7 hours. Ensure the puddings do not go off the boil, and top up with more water as needed.

4 When cool, re-cover the puddings with paper or foil and store in a cool, dry place for at least a month. When required, steam for another 2–3 hours. Serve hot, with a traditional white sauce.

Maple Energy 738Kcal/3088kJ; Protein 15.1g; Carbohydrate 74.2g, of which sugars 51.3g; Fat 45.6g, of which saturates 19.5g; Cholesterol 226mg; Calcium 218mg; Fibre 1.8g; Sodium 508mg.
Christmas Energy 7171kcal/30,432kJ; Protein 38.8g; Carbohydrate 1596.3g, of which sugars 1479.8g; Fat 112.9g, of which saturates 58g; Cholesterol 321mg; Calcium 1071mg; Fibre 13.8g; Sodium 1965mg.

Prune Rice Pudding

When served as a dessert, rice pudding is traditionally made with rice, milk, sugar and raisins. This recipe uses prunes and a dash of plum brandy, giving the dish a wonderfully rich flavour.

Serves 6

10 large ready-to-eat prunes, stones removed, left whole or roughly chopped

30ml/2 tbsp plum brandy
200g/7oz/1 cup pudding rice
400ml/14fl oz/1²⁄₃ cups double (heavy) cream
700ml/25fl oz/2³⁄₄ cups full-fat (whole) milk
150g/5oz/³⁄₄ cup caster (superfine) sugar
75ml/5 tbsp orange flower water

1 Put the prunes in a shallow dish, cover with the brandy and leave to soak for at least 1 hour.

2 Combine the rice and two-thirds of the cream in a heavy pan. Cook over medium heat for 2–3 minutes. Stir, then add the milk and all but 30ml/2 tbsp of the sugar.

3 Cook the mixture over a low heat, stirring occasionally, for another 10–15 minutes, or until the rice grains are soft and the liquid has been almost totally absorbed into the rice.

4 Add the remaining double cream and the orange flower water and set aside. Preheat the oven to 180°C/350°F/Gas 4.

5 Divide the prunes and the soaking liquid among six small ovenproof dishes and cover with the rice pudding.

6 Bake for 8–10 minutes, or until the tops are golden. Remove from the oven and set aside to cool briefly. Serve while still warm.

> **Cook's Tip**
> The longer you soak the prunes, the less time they take to cook, but you do not have to soak pudding rice before use.

Hot Date Puddings with Toffee Sauce

Fresh dates make this pudding less rich than the conventional dried date version, but it is still a bit of an indulgence. It is preferable to peel the dates, as they can be rather tough – simply squeeze them between your thumb and forefinger and the skins will pop off.

Serves 6

50g/2oz/¼ cup butter, softened
75g/3oz/½ cup light muscovado (brown) sugar
2 eggs, beaten

115g/4oz/1 cup self-raising (self-rising) flour
2.5ml/½ tsp bicarbonate of soda (baking soda)
175g/6oz/1 cup fresh dates, peeled, stoned and chopped
75ml/5 tbsp boiling water
10ml/2 tsp coffee and chicory essence

For the toffee sauce
75g/3oz/½ cup light muscovado (brown) sugar
50g/2oz/¼ cup butter
60ml/4 tbsp double (heavy) cream
30ml/2 tbsp brandy

1 Preheat the oven to 180°C/350°F/Gas 4. Place a baking sheet in the oven to heat up. Grease six individual pudding moulds or tins. Cream the butter and sugar in a mixing bowl until pale and fluffy. Gradually add the eggs, beating well after each addition.

2 Sift the flour and bicarbonate of soda together and fold into the creamed mixture. Put the dates in a heatproof bowl, pour over the boiling water and mash with a potato masher. Add the coffee and chicory essence, then stir the paste into the creamed mixture.

3 Spoon the mixture into the prepared moulds or tins. Place on the hot baking sheet and bake for 20 minutes.

4 Meanwhile, make the toffee sauce. Put all the ingredients in a pan and heat very gently, stirring occasionally, until the mixture is smooth. Increase the heat and boil for 1 minute.

5 Turn the warm puddings out on to individual dessert plates. Spoon a generous amount of sauce over each portion and serve at once.

Prune Rice Pudding Energy 652kcal/2723kJ; Protein 8g; Carbohydrate 68g, of which sugars 39g; Fat 41g, of which saturates 25g; Cholesterol 108mg; Calcium 180mg; Fibre 3.1g; Sodium 70mg.
Hot Date Puddings Energy 418kcal/1752 kJ; Protein 5g; Carbohydrate 51g, of which sugars 37g; Fat 22g, of which saturates 13g; Cholesterol 127mg; Calcium 61mg; Fibre 1.7g; Sodium 228mg.

Monmouth Pudding with Berry Jam

This warming dessert is layered with luscious red berry jam and milk-drenched breadcrumbs, set with eggs.

Serves 4

450ml/¾ pint/scant 2 cups milk
25g/1oz/2 tbsp caster
 (superfine) sugar
finely grated rind of 1 lemon
175g/6oz/3 cups fresh
 white breadcrumbs
2 eggs, separated
60ml/4 tbsp strawberry, raspberry
 or other red jam

1 Pour the milk into a pan, add the sugar and lemon rind and bring to the boil. Pour the hot milk mixture over the breadcrumbs and leave for 15 minutes.

2 Preheat the oven to 150°C/300°F/Gas 2. Lightly butter a 23cm/9in x 15cm/6in ovenproof dish.

3 Stir the egg yolks into the breadcrumb mixture. Whisk the egg whites until stiff peaks form and, with a large metal spoon, fold them into the breadcrumb mixture.

4 Melt the jam (on the hob or in the microwave) and drizzle half of it into the bottom of the prepared dish.

5 Spoon half the breadcrumb mixture on top, gently levelling the surface, and drizzle the jam over it.

6 Spread the remaining breadcrumb mixture over the top of the pudding to make an even layer. Put into the hot oven and cook for about 30–40 minutes or until light golden brown on top and set throughout. Serve warm.

> **Cook's Tips**
> • Cooking the pudding in an ovenproof glass dish shows off the pudding's colourful layers.
> • The jam layers in the pudding could be replaced with lightly cooked summer berries or plums.

Summer Berries in Sabayon Glaze

This luxurious combination of summer berries under a light and fluffy liqueur sauce is lightly grilled to form a crisp, caramelized topping. Fresh or frozen berries can be used in this dessert. If you use frozen berries, defrost them in a sieve over a bowl to allow the juices to drip. Pour a little juice over the fruit before dividing among the dishes.

Serves 4

450g/1lb/4 cups mixed
 summer berries, or soft fruit
4 egg yolks
50g/2oz/¼ cup vanilla sugar
 or caster (superfine) sugar
120ml/4fl oz/½ cup liqueur,
 such as Cointreau or Kirsch,
 or a white dessert wine

1 Arrange the mixed summer berries or soft fruit in four individual flameproof dishes. Preheat the grill (broiler).

2 Whisk the yolks in a large bowl with the sugar and liqueur or wine. Place over a pan of hot water and whisk constantly until the mixture is thick, fluffy and pale. You should be able to form peaks in the sauce that hold their shape.

3 Pour equal quantities of the yolk mixture into each dish. Place under the grill for 1–2 minutes, until just turning brown. Add an extra splash of liqueur, if you like, and serve immediately.

> **Cook's Tip**
> To separate eggs, gently prise the two halves apart with your thumbs. Keep the yolk in one half and allow the white to drop into a bowl below. Slip the yolk from one to the other.

> **Variation**
> If you prefer, you can make a non-alcoholic version of this dish using cranberry juice or pomegranate juice, or any other full-flavoured fruit juice.

Monmouth Pudding Energy 309kcal/1313kJ; Protein 12g; Carbohydrate 57.1g, of which sugars 24.3g; Fat 5.4g, of which saturates 1.9g; Cholesterol 101mg; Calcium 205mg; Fibre 1g; Sodium 418mg.
Summer Berries Energy 219kcal/919kJ; Protein 3.9g; Carbohydrate 29.7g, of which sugars 29.7g; Fat 5.6g, of which saturates 1.6g; Cholesterol 202mg; Calcium 50mg; Fibre 1.2g; Sodium 20mg.

Baked Ricotta Cakes with Red Sauce

These honey-flavoured desserts take only minutes to make from a few ingredients. The fragrant fruity sauce provides a contrast of both colour and flavour. The red berry sauce can be made a day in advance and chilled until ready to use. Frozen fruit doesn't need extra water, as it usually yields its juice easily on thawing.

Serves 4
250g/9oz/generous 1 cup
   ricotta cheese
2 egg whites, beaten
60ml/4 tbsp scented honey,
   plus extra to taste
450g/1lb/4 cups mixed fresh
   or frozen fruit, such as
   strawberries, raspberries,
   blackberries and cherries

1 Preheat the oven to 180°C/350°F/Gas 4. Place the ricotta cheese in a bowl and break it up with a wooden spoon. Add the beaten egg whites and honey, and mix thoroughly until smooth and well combined.

2 Lightly grease four ramekins. Spoon the ricotta mixture into the prepared ramekins and level the tops. Bake for 20 minutes, or until the ricotta cakes are risen and golden.

3 Meanwhile, make the fruit sauce. Reserve about one-quarter of the fruit for decoration. Place the rest of the fruit in a pan, with a little water if the fruit is fresh, and heat gently until softened. Leave to cool slightly and remove any pits if using cherries.

4 Press the fruit through a sieve (strainer), then taste and sweeten with honey if it is too tart. Serve the sauce, warm or cold, with the ricotta cakes. Decorate with the reserved berries.

Variation
You could other soft cheeses for this recipe. Mascarpone would be a good choice, but you could use any fresh, creamy, slightly sweet soft cheese.

Chocolate Fruit Fondue

Fondue originated in Switzerland and is best known as a way of enjoying various cheeses. However, it is also a very simple and tasty way of preparing all kinds of ingredients, and is ideally suited to sweet dishes. This mixed fruit version makes a fun dessert that also looks extremely attractive and appealing.

Serves 6–8
16 fresh strawberries
4 rings fresh pineapple,
   cut into wedges
2 small nectarines, stoned (pitted)
   and cut into wedges
1 kiwi fruit, halved and
   thickly sliced
small bunch of black
   seedless grapes
2 bananas, chopped
1 small eating apple, cored
   and cut into wedges
lemon juice, for brushing
225g/8oz plain
   (semisweet) chocolate
15g/½oz/1 tbsp butter
150ml/¼ pint/⅔ cup single
   (light) cream
45ml/3 tbsp Irish cream
   liqueur
15ml/1 tbsp chopped
   pistachio nuts

1 Arrange the fruit on a serving platter and brush the banana and apple pieces with a little lemon juice. Cover and chill.

2 Place the chocolate, butter, cream and liqueur in a bowl over a pan of simmering water. Stir until smooth.

3 Pour into a warmed serving bowl and sprinkle with the pistachio nuts.

4 To eat, guests should skewer the fruits on to forks, then dip them into the hot chocolate sauce.

Variations
Other delicious dippers for this fondue include: cubes of sponge cake; sweet biscuits (cookies), such as amaretti; miniature marshmallows; ready-to-eat dried fruit, such as apricots; crêpes torn into pieces; and popcorn.

Baked Ricotta Cakes Energy 161kcal/674kJ; Protein 8.1g; Carbohydrate 11.5g, of which sugars 11.5g; Fat 9.6g, of which saturates 5.9g; Cholesterol 26mg; Calcium 23mg; Fibre 0.6g; Sodium 63mg.
Chocolate Fruit Fondue Energy 297kcal/1246kJ; Protein 4g; Carbohydrate 40g, of which sugars 39g; Fat 14g, of which saturates 8g; Cholesterol 16mg; Calcium 49mg; Fibre 3.0g; Sodium 28mg.

Apple & Blackberry Crumble

You could serve this hot fruity dessert with chilled crème fraîche or ice cream.

Serves 6–8
900g/2lb cooking apples
450g/1lb/4 cups blackberries
a squeeze of lemon juice
   (optional)
175g/6oz/scant 1 cup granulated
   (white) sugar

For the crumble topping
115g/4oz/½ cup butter
115g/4oz/1 cup wholemeal
   (whole-wheat) flour
50g/2oz/½ cup fine or medium
   pinhead oatmeal
50g/2oz/¼ cup soft light
   brown sugar
a little grated lemon rind
   (optional)

1 Preheat the oven to 200°C/400°F/Gas 6.

2 To make the crumble topping, rub the butter into the flour, and then add the oatmeal and brown sugar and continue to rub in until the mixture begins to stick together, forming large crumbs. Mix in the grated lemon rind, if using.

3 Peel, core and slice the cooking apples into wedges. Put the apples, blackberries, lemon juice (if using), 30ml/2 tbsp water and the sugar into a shallow ovenproof dish, about 2 litres/3½ pints/9 cups capacity.

4 Cover the fruit with the topping. Sprinkle with a little cold water. Bake in the oven for 15 minutes, then reduce the heat to 190°C/375°F/Gas 5 and cook for another 15–20 minutes until crunchy and brown on top. Serve hot.

> **Cook's Tips**
> • *Choose large, tart cooking apples – they have a firmer flesh than eating apples, and will hold their shape after cooking.*
> • *At the end of summer, it is very satisfying to collect your own blackberries growing wild in hedges. Choose ripe fruits that are shiny, bright and firm, and discard any that are damaged.*
> • *Pinhead oatmeal consists of oats that have been cut into pieces. It gives the dish a nuttier flavour than rolled oats.*

Hot Blackberry & Apple Soufflés

The deliciously tart flavours of blackberry and apple complement each other perfectly to make this surprisingly low-fat dessert.

Serves 6
butter, for greasing
150g/5oz/¾ cup caster
   (superfine) sugar,
   plus extra for dusting

350g/12oz/3 cups fresh
   blackberries
1 large cooking apple, peeled and
   finely diced
grated rind and juice of 1 orange
3 egg whites
icing (confectioners') sugar,
   for dusting

1 Preheat the oven to 200°C/400°F/Gas 6. Generously grease six 150ml/¼ pint/⅔ cup individual soufflé dishes with butter and dust with sugar, shaking out the excess sugar.

2 Put a baking sheet in the oven to heat. Cook the blackberries, diced apple and orange rind and juice in a pan for 10 minutes or until the apple has pulped down well. Press through a sieve (strainer) into a bowl. Stir in 50g/2oz/¼ cup of the sugar. Cool.

3 Put a spoonful of the fruit purée into each prepared dish and smooth the surface. Set the dishes aside.

4 Whisk the egg whites in a large grease-free bowl until they form stiff peaks. Very gradually whisk in the remaining sugar to make a stiff, glossy meringue mixture. Fold in the remaining fruit purée and spoon into the prepared dishes. Level the tops.

5 Place the dishes on the hot baking sheet and bake for 10–15 minutes until the soufflés have risen well and are lightly browned. Dust the tops with icing sugar and serve immediately.

> **Cook's Tip**
> *Run a table knife around the inside edge of the soufflé dishes before baking to help the soufflés rise evenly without sticking to the rim of the dish.*

Apple and Blackberry Energy 470Kcal/1974kJ; Protein 5.1g; Carbohydrate 78.2g, of which sugars 60.3g; Fat 17.2g, of which saturates 10g; Cholesterol 41mg; Calcium 71mg; Fibre 7g; Sodium 128mg.
Hot Blackberry Energy 123Kcal/522kJ; Protein 2.1g; Carbohydrate 30.1g, of which sugars 30.1g; Fat 0.1g, of which saturates 0g; Cholesterol 0mg; Calcium 38mg; Fibre 2g; Sodium 33mg.

Fruit & Honey Pancakes

The batter for these delightfully fluffy pancakes uses yeast to make them extra light. For the topping, you can use a mixture of any berries that are in season. When dusted with white icing sugar, the finished dish is both attractive and irresistible.

Makes 12/Serves 6

165g/5½oz/generous 1¼ cups plain (all-purpose) flour
150ml/¼ pint/⅔ cup warm milk
10ml/2 tsp sugar
5ml/1 tsp salt
2 eggs, separated
10g/¼oz fresh yeast, crumbled
15ml/1 tbsp sour cream
10ml/2 tsp clarified butter

For the topping
60ml/4 tbsp clear honey
115g/4oz/1 cup fresh berries, such as raspberries, blueberries or strawberries
icing (confectioners') sugar, for dusting

1 Put the flour in a large bowl and make a well in the centre. Add the warm milk, sugar and salt, and combine. Stir in the egg yolks and add the yeast. Mix well until you have a smooth batter.

2 Cover and leave in a warm place for 1 hour, or until the batter has doubled in size.

3 Put the egg whites into a clean, grease-free bowl and whisk until they form soft peaks. Fold them into the pancake batter. Stir in the sour cream.

4 Put a heavy, non-stick frying pan, about 18cm/7in in diameter, on medium-high heat. Brush the surface of the pan with a little clarified butter.

5 Pour a ladleful of the pancake mixture into the pan and cook for about 40 seconds, or until golden brown on the underside and the top is set. Flip over and cook the other side until golden.

6 Serve the pancakes hot with a drizzle of honey and some berries, gently dusted with a sprinkling of icing sugar.

Blueberry & Vanilla Crumble

In this heavenly dessert, vanilla ice cream is packed into a buttery crumble case with summer berries, and baked until the ice cream melts over the crumble.

Serves 8

225g/8oz/2 cups plain (all-purpose) flour
5ml/1 tsp baking powder
175g/6oz/¾ cup unsalted (sweet) butter, diced
150g/5oz/¾ cup caster (superfine) sugar
1 egg
75g/3oz/¾ cup ground almonds
10ml/2 tsp natural vanilla extract
5ml/1 tsp ground mixed spice
500ml/17fl oz/2¼ cups vanilla ice cream
175g/6oz/1½ cups blueberries
icing (confectioners') sugar, for dusting

1 Preheat the oven to 180°C/350°F/Gas 4. Put the flour and baking powder in a food processor. Add the butter and process briefly to mix. Add the sugar and process briefly again until the mixture is crumbly. Remove about 175g/6oz/1½ cups of the crumble mixture and set this aside.

2 Add the egg, ground almonds, vanilla extract and mixed spice to the remaining crumble mixture and blend to a paste. Scrape the paste into a 20cm/8in springform tin (pan). Press it firmly on to the base and halfway up the sides to make an even case. Line the case with baking parchment and fill with baking beans.

3 Sprinkle the crumble mixture on to a baking sheet. Bake the crumble for 20 minutes and the case for 30 minutes until pale golden. Remove the paper and beans and bake the case for 5 minutes. Leave both the crumble and the case to cool.

4 Pack the ice cream into the almond pastry case and level the surface. Sprinkle with the blueberries and then the baked crumble mixture. Freeze overnight.

5 About 25 minutes before serving, preheat the oven to 180°C/350°F/Gas 4. Bake the crumble for 10–15 minutes, until the ice cream has started to soften. Dust with icing sugar and serve in wedges.

Fruit and Honey Energy 85kcal/361kJ; Protein 2.9g; Carbohydrate 16g, of which sugars 5.5g; Fat 1.6g, of which saturates 0.6g; Cholesterol 33mg; Calcium 42mg; Fibre 0.5g; Sodium 21mg.
Blueberry Energy 522kcal/2183kJ; Protein 8.1g; Carbohydrate 57.7g, of which sugars 34.4g; Fat 29.7g, of which saturates 15.9g; Cholesterol 86mg; Calcium 142mg; Fibre 2g; Sodium 182mg.

Chocolate & Fruit Puddings

Drenched in a thick chocolate syrup and packed with winter fruit, this slow-cooker pudding is pure indulgence.

2 eggs, lightly beaten
50g/2oz/¹/² cup self-raising (self-rising) flour, sifted
45ml/3 tbsp unsweetened cocoa powder

Serves 4
1 apple, peeled and cored, diced
25g/1oz/¹/⁴ cup cranberries, thawed if frozen
175g/6oz/³/⁴ cup soft dark brown sugar
115g/4oz/¹/² cup soft margarine

For the syrup
115g/4oz plain (semisweet) chocolate, chopped
30ml/2 tbsp clear honey
15g/¹/²oz/1 tbsp unsalted (sweet) butter
2.5ml/¹/² tsp vanilla extract

1 Pour 2.5cm/1in of hot water into the cooking pot and switch the slow cooker to high. Grease four individual heatproof bowls with oil, then line with baking parchment.

2 Place the diced apple in a bowl, and add the cranberries and 15ml/1 tbsp of the sugar. Mix well, then divide among the four bowls, gently patting it down into the base of each one.

3 Place the remaining sugar in a clean mixing bowl and add the margarine, eggs, flour and cocoa. Beat together until smooth. Spoon into the bowls and cover each with a double thickness of greased foil. Place the bowls in the cooking pot and pour in hot water to come two-thirds of the way up the sides of the bowls.

4 Cover with the lid and cook on high for 1½–2 hours, or until the puddings are well-risen and firm. Carefully remove from the slow cooker and leave to stand for 10 minutes.

5 Meanwhile, make the chocolate syrup. Put the chocolate, honey, butter and vanilla extract in a heatproof bowl and place in the hot water in the slow cooker. Leave for 10 minutes, until the butter has melted, then stir until smooth.

6 Run a knife around the edge of the puddings to loosen, then turn over on to plates. Serve immediately, with the syrup.

Warm Autumn Fruit Compote

This delicious compote is an unusual combination of pears, figs and raspberries.

Serves 4
75g/3oz/6 tbsp caster (superfine) sugar
1 bottle red wine
1 vanilla pod (bean), split
1 strip pared lemon rind
4 pears
2 purple figs, quartered
225g/8oz/1¹/³ cups raspberries
freshly squeezed lemon juice, to taste

1 Put the sugar and wine in a large pan and heat gently until the sugar has dissolved. Add the vanilla pod and lemon rind and bring to the boil, then simmer for 5 minutes.

2 Peel and halve the pears, then scoop out the cores, using a melon baller or a teaspoon. Add the pears to the syrup and poach for 15 minutes, carefully turning the pears several times so that they colour evenly. Add the figs to the pan and poach for a further 5 minutes, until the fruits are tender.

3 Transfer the poached pears and figs to a serving bowl using a slotted spoon, then sprinkle over the raspberries.

4 Return the syrup to the heat and boil rapidly to reduce slightly and concentrate the flavour. Add a little lemon juice to taste. Strain the syrup over the fruits and serve warm.

Variation
For Cherry Compote, combine 120ml/4fl oz/¹/² cup red wine, 50g/2oz/¹/⁴ cup light muscovado (brown) sugar, 50g/2oz/¹/⁴ cup granulated (white) sugar, 15ml/1 tbsp honey, two 2.5cm/1in strips of pared orange rind and 1.5ml/¹/⁴ tsp almond extract in a pan with 120ml/4fl oz/¹/² cup water. Stir over medium heat until the sugar dissolves, then increase the heat and boil until the liquid reduces slightly. Add 675g/1¹/²lb pitted sweet fresh cherries and bring back to the boil, skimming off any foam. Reduce the heat slightly and simmer for 8–10 minutes. Serve lukewarm on ice cream.

Warm Autumn Energy 298Kcal/1257kJ; Protein 1.9g; Carbohydrate 42.9g, of which sugars 42.9g; Fat 0.5g, of which saturates 0.1g; Cholesterol 0mg; Calcium 79mg; Fibre 5.5g; Sodium 27mg.
Chocolate Energy 739kcal/3094kJ; Protein 9.1g; Carbohydrate 88.3g, of which sugars 77.2g; Fat 41.3g, of which saturates 14.4g; Cholesterol 124mg; Calcium 103mg; Fibre 3.1g; Sodium 438mg.

Figs & Pears in Honey with Cardamom

Fresh figs picked straight from the tree are so delicious that it seems almost sacrilege to cook them – unless you have so many during the fruit's season that you fancy a change – when you can try this superb recipe.

Serves 4
1 lemon
90ml/6 tbsp clear honey
1 cinnamon stick
1 cardamom pod
350ml/12fl oz/1½ cups water
2 pears
8 fresh figs, halved

1 Pare the rind from the lemon using a cannelle knife (zester) or vegetable peeler and cut the rind into very thin strips.

2 Place the lemon rind, honey, cinnamon stick, cardamom pod and the water in a pan and boil, uncovered, for about 10 minutes, until the liquid is reduced by about half.

3 Cut the pears into eighths, discarding the core. Leave the peel on or discard, as preferred.

4 Place the pear pieces in the syrup; add the figs. Bring the mixture to just near boiling point, then reduce the heat and simmer for about 5 minutes, until the fruit is tender.

5 Transfer the fruit from the pan to a serving bowl with a slotted spoon. Cook the liquid until syrupy, discard the cinnamon stick and pour the sauce over the figs and pears. Serve warm or cold.

> **Cook's Tip**
> The season for fresh figs reaches its peak at the beginning of autumn, so make this dish earlier in the autumn rather than later. Figs are extremely perishable, and should be used as soon after purchase as possible. You can store fresh figs in the refrigerator for about 2–3 days.

Honey Baked Figs with Hazelnut Ice Cream

Figs baked in a lemon grass-scented honey syrup have the most wonderful flavour, especially when served with a good-quality ice cream dotted with roasted hazelnuts. If you prefer to avoid nuts, because you don't like them or because a guest has an allergy, use plain rich vanilla or toffee ice cream instead.

Serves 4
1 lemon grass stalk,
    finely chopped
1 cinnamon stick, roughly broken
60ml/4 tbsp clear honey
200ml/7fl oz/scant 1 cup water
75g/3oz/¾ cup hazelnuts
8 large ripe dessert figs
400ml/14fl oz/1⅔ cups
    good-quality vanilla ice cream
30ml/2 tbsp hazelnut
    liqueur (optional)

1 Preheat the oven to 190°C/375°F/Gas 5. Make the syrup by mixing the lemon grass, cinnamon stick, honey and measured water in a small pan. Heat gently, stirring until the honey has dissolved, then bring to the boil. Simmer for 2 minutes.

2 Meanwhile, spread out the hazelnuts on a baking sheet and grill (broil) under medium heat until golden brown. Shake the sheet occasionally, so that they are evenly toasted.

3 Cut the figs into quarters, leaving them intact at the bases. Stand the figs in a baking dish and pour the syrup over. Cover the dish tightly with foil and bake for 13–15 minutes until the figs are tender.

4 While the figs are baking, remove the ice cream from the freezer and let it soften slightly. Chop the hazelnuts roughly and beat the softened ice cream briefly with an electric beater, then fold in the toasted hazelnuts until evenly distributed.

5 To serve, puddle a little of the syrup from the figs on to each individual dessert plate. Arrange the figs on top and add a spoonful of the nutty ice cream. At the very last moment before serving, spoon a little hazelnut liqueur over the ice cream, if you like.

Figs and Pears Energy 143kcal/606kJ; Protein 1.7g; Carbohydrate 34.4g, of which sugars 34.4g; Fat 0.7g, of which saturates 0g; Cholesterol 0mg; Calcium 109mg; Fibre 4.7g; Sodium 28mg.
Honey Baked Figs Energy 433kcal/1816kJ; Protein 7.8g; Carbohydrate 53.6g, of which sugars 52.1g; Fat 21.2g, of which saturates 7g; Cholesterol 24mg; Calcium 227mg; Fibre 4.2g; Sodium 88mg.

Rhubarb & Raspberry Crumble

A fruit crumble cries out to be eaten on the sofa. It sits beautifully in a bowl, stays where it should – on the spoon and in the mouth – and willingly accepts lashings of cream. The classic fruit to use is rhubarb, preferably the first of the spring, when it is bright pink and tender.

Serves 4
675g/1½lb fresh forced rhubarb, cut into large chunks
a pinch of ground allspice
grated rind and juice of 1 lime
175g/6oz/scant 1 cup golden caster (superfine) sugar
225g/8oz fresh or frozen raspberries
custard or clotted cream, to serve

For the crumble
115g/4oz/1 cup plain (all-purpose) flour
pinch of salt
50g/2oz/½ cup ground almonds
115g/4oz/½ cup cold butter
115g/4oz/1 cup blanched almonds, chopped
50g/2oz/¼ cup golden caster (superfine) sugar

1 Preheat the oven to 200°C/400°F/Gas 6 and put a baking sheet inside to heat up. Put the rhubarb in a pan with the allspice, lime rind and juice and sugar. Cook over a gentle heat for 2 minutes, stirring occasionally, until the chunks of rhubarb are tender but still hold their shape.

2 Pour the rhubarb into a sieve (strainer), set over a bowl to catch the juices. Leave to cool. Reserve the juices for later.

3 To make the crumble, put the flour, pinch of salt, ground almonds and butter into a food processor and process until the mixture resembles fine breadcrumbs. Transfer into a bowl and stir in the blanched almonds and sugar.

4 Spoon the rhubarb into a large ovenproof dish, and stir in the raspberries. Sprinkle the almond mixture evenly over the surface, mounding it up a little towards the centre.

5 Place the dish on the baking sheet in the oven and bake for 35 minutes until crisp and golden on top. Cool for 5 minutes before serving with custard or clotted cream and the warmed, reserved rhubarb juices.

Rhubarb Spiral Cobbler

The addition of orange in both the fruit filling and the topping of this cobbler gives the pudding added zest.

Serves 4
675g/1½lb rhubarb, sliced
50g/2oz/¼ cup caster (superfine) sugar
45ml/3 tbsp orange juice

For the topping
200g/7oz/1¾ cups self-raising (self-rising) flour
30ml/2 tbsp caster (superfine) sugar
about 200g/7oz/scant 1 cup natural (plain) yogurt
grated rind of 1 medium orange
30ml/2 tbsp demerara (raw) sugar
5ml/1 tsp ground ginger
yogurt or fresh ready-made custard, to serve

1 Preheat the oven to 200°C/400°F/Gas 6. Cook the rhubarb, sugar and orange juice in a covered pan until tender. Transfer to an ovenproof dish.

2 Make the topping. Put the flour in a mixing bowl, add the caster sugar and mix together. Stir in enough of the yogurt to bind to a soft dough.

3 Roll out on a floured surface to a 25cm/10in square. Mix together the orange rind, demerara sugar and ginger in a bowl, then sprinkle the mixture evenly over the surface of the dough.

4 Roll up quite tightly, then cut into about ten slices, using a sharp knife. Arrange the slices over the rhubarb.

5 Bake in the oven for 15–20 minutes, or until the spirals are well risen and golden brown. Serve warm, with yogurt or fresh custard.

Variation
For a cinnamon cobbler topping, leave out the orange rind and replace the ginger with ground cinnamon.

Rhubarb Spiral Energy 317Kcal/1355kJ; Protein 8.7g; Carbohydrate 72.6g, of which sugars 35.5g; Fat 1.3g, of which saturates 0.4g; Cholesterol 1mg; Calcium 443mg; Fibre 3.9g; Sodium 229mg.
Rhubarb Crumble Energy 812kcal/3403kJ; Protein 14.2g; Carbohydrate 88.1g, of which sugars 65.1g; Fat 47.4g, of which saturates 16.9g; Cholesterol 61mg; Calcium 345mg; Fibre 7.7g; Sodium 191mg.

Hot Bananas with Rum & Raisins

These sticky, sweet bananas are made in the slow cooker and are utterly moreish. The rich sauce becomes almost toffee-like during the long cooking, and is irresistible.

Serves 4

30ml/2 tbsp seedless raisins
45ml/3 tbsp dark rum
40g/1½oz/3 tbsp unsalted
   (sweet) butter
50g/2oz/¼ cup soft light
   brown sugar
4 slightly under-ripe bananas,
   peeled and halved lengthways
1.5ml/¼ tsp grated nutmeg
1.5ml/¼ tsp ground cinnamon
25g/1oz/¼ cup flaked (sliced)
   almonds, toasted (optional)
whipped cream or vanilla
   ice cream, to serve

1 Put the raisins in a bowl and spoon over 30ml/2 tbsp of the rum. Set aside and leave to soak.

2 Cut the butter into small cubes and place in the ceramic cooking pot with the sugar and remaining 15ml/1 tbsp rum. Switch the slow cooker to high and leave uncovered for 15 minutes, until the butter and sugar have melted.

3 Add the bananas to the butter and sugar mixture, cover with the lid and cook for 30 minutes, or until the fruit is almost tender, turning over the bananas halfway through cooking time.

4 Sprinkle the nutmeg and cinnamon over the bananas, then stir in the rum and raisins. Re-cover and cook for 10 minutes.

5 Carefully lift the bananas out of the ceramic cooking pot and arrange on a serving dish or individual plates. Spoon over the sauce, then sprinkle with almonds, if using. Serve hot with whipped cream or vanilla ice cream.

> **Variation**
> If you don't like the taste of rum, try using an orange liqueur, such as Cointreau, instead. It makes a very good alternative, and is a little less overpowering.

Baked Bananas with Ice Cream

Slowly baked bananas make the perfect partners for delicious vanilla ice cream topped with a toasted hazelnut sauce. This is a quick and easy dessert that looks as good as it tastes.

Serves 4

4 large bananas
15ml/1 tbsp lemon juice
4 large scoops vanilla ice cream

For the sauce

25g/1oz/2 tbsp unsalted
   (sweet) butter
50g/2oz/½ cup hazelnuts,
   toasted and roughly chopped
45ml/3 tbsp golden syrup
30ml/2 tbsp lemon juice

1 Preheat the oven to 180°C/350°F/Gas 4.

2 Place the unpeeled bananas on a baking sheet and brush them with the lemon juice. Bake for about 20 minutes until the skins are turning black and the flesh gives a little when the bananas are gently squeezed.

3 Meanwhile, make the sauce. Melt the butter in a small pan. Add the hazelnuts and cook gently for 1 minute. Add the syrup and lemon juice and heat, stirring, for 1 minute more.

4 To serve, slit each banana open with a knife and open out the skins. Transfer to serving plates and serve with scoops of vanilla ice cream. Pour the sauce over.

> **Cook's Tip**
> Bake the bananas over the dying coals of a barbecue, if you like. Put them on the rack as soon as you have removed all the main course items.

> **Variation**
> Try other nuts in the sauce, such as toasted walnuts or almonds.

Hot Bananas Energy 323kcal/1355kJ; Protein 3g; Carbohydrate 47.1g, of which sugars 44.7g; Fat 12.1g, of which saturates 5.6g; Cholesterol 21mg; Calcium 33mg; Fibre 1.9g; Sodium 72mg.
Baked Bananas Energy 416kcal/1740kJ; Protein 6.3g; Carbohydrate 50.7g, of which sugars 47.2g; Fat 21.1g, of which saturates 9.5g; Cholesterol 35mg; Calcium 117mg; Fibre 1.9g; Sodium 124mg.

Chocolate Chip & Banana Pudding

Hot and steamy, this superb light pudding tastes extra special when served with ready-made fresh chocolate sauce or custard.

Serves 4
200g/7oz/1¾ cups self-raising (self-rising) flour
75g/3oz/6 tbsp unsalted (sweet) butter or margarine
2 ripe bananas
75g/3oz/6 tbsp caster (superfine) sugar
60ml/4 tbsp milk
1 egg, beaten
60ml/4 tbsp plain (bittersweet) chocolate chips or chopped chocolate
whipped cream, to serve

1 Prepare a steamer or half fill a pan with water and bring to the boil. Grease a 1 litre/1¾ pint/4 cup ovenproof bowl.

2 Sift the flour into a mixing bowl and rub in the butter or margarine until the mixture resembles breadcrumbs. Mash the bananas in a bowl. Stir them into the creamed mixture, with the caster sugar.

3 Whisk the milk with the egg in a bowl, then beat into the pudding mixture. Stir in the chocolate.

4 Spoon the mixture into the prepared bowl, cover closely with a double thickness of foil, and steam for 2 hours, topping up the water as required during cooking.

5 Run a knife around the top edge of the pudding to loosen it, then turn it out on to a warm serving dish. Serve hot, with a spoonful of whipped cream.

Cook's Tip
If you have a food processor, make a quick-mix version by processing all the ingredients, except the chocolate, until smooth. Then stir in the chocolate, spoon into the prepared bowl and finish as described in the recipe.

Tapioca with Banana & Coconut

This is the type of traditional dessert that everybody's mother or grandmother makes. Sweet, nourishing and warm, the tapioca pearls are cooked in coconut milk and beautifully sweetened with bananas and sugar.

Serves 4
40g/1½ oz tapioca pearls
550ml/18fl oz/2½ cups coconut milk
90g/3½ oz/½ cup sugar
3 ripe bananas, diced
salt

1 Pour 550ml/18fl oz/2½ cups water into a pan and bring it to the boil. Stir in the tapioca pearls, reduce the heat and simmer for about 20 minutes, until the tapioca is translucent and most of the water is absorbed.

2 Pour in the coconut milk, then add the sugar and a pinch of salt. Cook gently for 30 minutes.

3 Stir in the diced bananas and cook them for 5–10 minutes until soft. Spoon into individual warmed bowls and serve immediately while still hot.

Cook's Tip
A pinch of salt added to this recipe enhances the flavour of the coconut milk and counterbalances the sweetness. You can also make the recipe with sweet potato, taro root, yellow corn or rice.

Variations
Instead of adding the diced bananas to the warm tapioca mixture, try one of the following, adjusting the cooking time as needed so that the fruit is fully cooked:
• *sliced rhubarb*
• *small apple or pear, cut into wedges*
• *nectarine or mango slices*

Chocolate Chip Energy 528Kcal/2220kJ; Protein 8.1g; Carbohydrate 79.3g, of which sugars 40.9g; Fat 22g, of which saturates 13g; Cholesterol 89mg; Calcium 222mg; Fibre 2.5g; Sodium 320mg.
Tapioca Energy 226kcal/964kJ; Protein 1.5g; Carbohydrate 57.2g, of which sugars 45.9g; Fat 0.7g, of which saturates 0.4g; Cholesterol 0mg; Calcium 57mg; Fibre 0.9g; Sodium 154mg.

Grilled Pineapple with Papaya Sauce

Pineapple cooked this way takes on a superb flavour and is quite sensational when served with the tropical papaya sauce.

Serves 6
1 sweet pineapple
melted butter, for greasing
   and brushing
2 pieces drained preserved
   stem ginger in syrup,
   cut into fine matchsticks,
   plus 30ml/2 tbsp of the
   syrup from the jar

30ml/2 tbsp demerara
   (raw) sugar
pinch of ground cinnamon
fresh mint sprigs, to decorate

For the sauce
1 ripe papaya, peeled
   and seeded
175ml/6fl oz/³⁄₄ cup
   apple juice

1 Peel the pineapple and take spiral slices off the outside to remove the eyes. Cut the pineapple crossways into six slices, each 2.5cm/1in thick.

2 Line a baking sheet with a sheet of foil, rolling up the sides to make a rim. Grease the foil with some melted butter. Preheat the grill (broiler).

3 Arrange the pineapple slices on the lined baking sheet. Brush with butter, then top with the ginger matchsticks, sugar and cinnamon. Drizzle over the stem ginger syrup. Grill (broil) for 5–7 minutes or until the slices are golden and lightly charred.

4 Meanwhile, to make the sauce, cut a few slices from the papaya and set aside, then purée the rest with the apple juice in a blender or food processor.

5 Press the purée through a sieve (strainer) placed over a bowl, then stir in any juices from cooking the pineapple. Serve the pineapple slices with sauce drizzled around each plate. Decorate with the reserved papaya slices and the mint sprigs.

Thai Fried Pineapple

This is a very quick and simple Thai dessert – pineapple fried in butter, brown sugar and lime juice, and sprinkled with toasted coconut. The slightly sharp taste of the fruit makes it a very refreshing treat at the end of a meal.

Serves 4
1 pineapple
40g/1¹⁄₂oz/3 tbsp butter
15ml/1 tbsp desiccated
   (dry unsweetened
   shredded) coconut
60ml/4 tbsp soft light
   brown sugar
60ml/4 tbsp fresh lime juice
lime slices, to decorate
thick and creamy natural (plain)
   yogurt, to serve

1 Using a sharp knife, cut the top off the pineapple and peel off the skin, taking care to remove the eyes. Cut the pineapple in half and remove and discard the woody core. Cut the flesh lengthways into 1cm/¹⁄₂in wedges.

2 Heat the butter in a large, heavy frying pan or wok. When it has melted, add the pineapple wedges and cook over a medium heat for 1–2 minutes on each side, or until they have turned pale golden in colour.

3 Meanwhile, dry-fry the coconut in a small frying pan until lightly browned. Remove from the heat and set aside.

4 Sprinkle the sugar into the pan with the pineapple, add the lime juice and cook, stirring constantly, until all of the sugar has dissolved.

5 Divide the pineapple wedges among four bowls, sprinkle each one with the coconut, decorate with the lime slices and serve with the yogurt.

> **Cook's Tip**
> *Choose a golden pineapple with a sweet fragrance, and one in which the base gives a little when pressed.*

Grilled Pineapple Energy 130kcal/558kJ; Protein 1g; Carbohydrate 32.9g, of which sugars 32.9g; Fat 0.4g, of which saturates 0g; Cholesterol 0mg; Calcium 49mg; Fibre 3.4g; Sodium 21mg.
Thai Fried Pineapple Energy 199kcal/833kJ; Protein 1g; Carbohydrate 26g, of which sugars 26g; Fat 11g, of which saturates 7g; Cholesterol 21mg; Calcium 26mg; Fibre 2.1g; Sodium 65mg.

# Tropical Fruit with Maple Butter

This dish turns exotic fruit into warm comfort food.

Serves 4
1 large mango
1 large papaya
1 small pineapple
2 bananas
115g/4oz/½ cup unsalted (sweet) butter
60ml/4 tbsp pure maple syrup
ground cinnamon, for sprinkling

1 Peel the mango and cut the flesh into large pieces. Halve the papaya and scoop out the seeds. Cut into thick slices, then peel. Peel and core the pineapple and slice into thin wedges. Peel the bananas, then halve them lengthways.

2 Cut the butter into small dice and place in a blender or food processor with the maple syrup, then process until creamy.

3 Place the mango, papaya, pineapple and banana on a grill (broiler) rack and brush with the maple syrup butter. Cook under a medium heat for about 10 minutes, until just tender, turning the fruit occasionally and brushing it with the butter. Arrange the fruit on a serving platter and dot with the remaining butter. Sprinkle over a little cinnamon and serve hot.

Variation
For Tropical Fruit in Cinnamon Syrup, sprinkle a third of 450g/1lb/2¼ cups caster (superfine) sugar over the base of a large pan. Add 1 cinnamon stick and half of the following: about 675g/1½lb papayas, peeled, seeded and cut into thin pieces; about 675g/1½lb mangoes, peeled, stoned (pitted) and cut lengthways into thin pieces; about 225g/8oz star fruit, thinly sliced. Sprinkle half the remaining sugar over the fruit pieces. Add the remaining fruit, sprinkled with the remaining sugar. Cover and cook over a medium-low heat for 35–45 minutes, until the sugar melts. Shake the pan occasionally, but do not stir (the fruit will collapse). Simmer, uncovered, for 10 minutes, until the fruit is becoming translucent. Remove from the heat and cool. Transfer to a bowl and chill, covered, overnight. Serve with yogurt or crème frâiche.

Tropical Fruit Gratin

This out-of-the-ordinary gratin is strictly for grown-ups. A colourful combination of fruit is topped with a simple sabayon before being flashed under the grill.

Serves 4
2 tamarillos
½ sweet pineapple
1 ripe mango
175g/6oz/1½ cups blackberries
120ml/4fl oz/½ cup sparkling white wine
115g/4oz/½ cup caster (superfine) sugar
6 egg yolks

1 Cut each tamarillo in half lengthwise and then into thick slices. Cut the rind and core from the pineapple and take spiral slices off the outside to remove the eyes. Cut the flesh into regular chunks. Peel the mango, cut it in half and slice the flesh from the stone.

2 Divide all the fruit, including the blackberries, among four 14cm/5½in gratin dishes set on a baking sheet and set aside. Heat the wine and sugar in a pan until the sugar has dissolved. Bring to the boil and cook for 5 minutes.

3 Put the egg yolks in a large heatproof bowl. Place the bowl over a pan of simmering water and whisk until pale. Slowly pour on the hot sugar syrup, whisking all the time, until the mixture thickens. Preheat the grill (broiler).

4 Spoon the mixture over the fruit. Place the baking sheet holding the dishes on a low shelf under the hot grill until the topping is golden. Serve immediately.

Cook's Tip
Blackberries are widely cultivated from late spring to autumn, and are usually large, plump and sweet. The finest wild blackberries have a bitter edge and a strong depth of flavour – best appreciated with a sprinkling of sugar.

Tropical Fruit Energy 470Kcal/1974kJ; Protein 2.7g; Carbohydrate 64g, of which sugars 62.7g; Fat 24.4g, of which saturates 15.1g; Cholesterol 61mg; Calcium 90mg; Fibre 7.7g; Sodium 229mg.
Tropical Fruit Gratin Energy 300kcal/1270kJ; Protein 6.2g; Carbohydrate 52.8g, of which sugars 52.7g; Fat 8.7g, of which saturates 2.4g; Cholesterol 302mg; Calcium 119mg; Fibre 4.6g; Sodium 22mg.

Grilled Mango Cheeks with Lime Syrup & Sorbet

If you can locate Alphonso mangoes, use them. They have a heady scent and silky texture, which is balanced by the tart lime sorbet and syrup. They ripen in early summer, and are available from specialist greengrocers.

Serves 6
250g/9oz/1¼ cups sugar
juice of 6 limes
3 star anise
6 small or 3 medium to
    large mangoes
groundnut (peanut) oil,
    for brushing

1 Place the sugar in a pan and add 250ml/8fl oz/1 cup water. Heat gently until the sugar has dissolved. Increase the heat and boil for 5 minutes. Cool completely. Add the lime juice and any pulp that has collected in the squeezer. Strain the mixture and reserve 200ml/7fl oz/scant 1 cup in a bowl with the star anise.

2 Pour the remaining liquid into a measuring jug or cup and make up to 600ml/1 pint/2½ cups with cold water. Mix well and pour into a freezerproof container. Freeze for 1½ hours, stir well and return to the freezer for another hour until set.

3 Transfer the sorbet mixture to a processor and pulse to a smooth icy purée. Freeze for 1 hour or longer. Alternatively, make the sorbet in an ice cream maker; it will take 20 minutes, and should then be frozen for at least 30 minutes before serving.

4 Pour the reserved syrup into a pan and boil for 2–3 minutes, or until thickened. Leave to cool. Cut the cheeks from either side of the stone (pit) on each unpeeled mango, and score the flesh on each in a diamond pattern. Brush with a little oil. Heat a griddle until very hot and a few drops of water sprinkled on the surface evaporate instantly. Lower the heat a little and grill (broil) the mango halves, cut side down, for 30–60 seconds until branded with golden grill marks.

5 Invert the mango cheeks on individual plates and serve hot or cold with the syrup drizzled over and a scoop or two of sorbet. Decorate with the reserved star anise.

Exotic Fruit Skewers with Lime Cheese

Lightly charred exotic fruit, served with luscious lime-flavoured cream, make the perfect finale for an *al fresco* meal. The lemon grass skewers impart a subtle citrus tang to the fruit – and they look fun as well.

Serves 4
4 long fresh lemon grass stalks
1 mango, peeled, stoned (pitted)
    and cut into chunks
1 papaya, peeled, seeded and
    cut into chunks
1 star fruit, cut into thick slices
    and halved

8 fresh bay leaves
a nutmeg
60ml/4 tbsp maple syrup
50g/2oz/¼ cup demerara
    (raw) sugar

For the lime cheese
150g/5oz/⅔ cup curd (farmer's)
    cheese or low-fat soft cheese
120ml/4fl oz/½ cup double
    (heavy) cream
grated rind and juice of ½ lime
30ml/2 tbsp icing
    (confectioners') sugar

1 Prepare the barbecue or preheat the grill (broiler).

2 Cut the top of each lemon grass stalk into a point with a sharp knife. Discard the outer leaves, then use the back of the knife to bruise the length of each stalk to release the aromatic oils. Thread each stalk, skewer-style, with a variety of the fruit pieces and bay leaves.

3 Support a piece of foil on a baking sheet and roll up the edges to make a rim. Grease the foil, lay the kebabs on top and grate a little nutmeg over each. Drizzle the maple syrup over and dust liberally with the demerara sugar. Grill (broil) for 5 minutes, until lightly charred.

4 Meanwhile, make the lime cheese. Mix together the cheese, cream, grated lime rind and juice and icing sugar in a bowl.

5 Serve the lightly charred exotic fruit kebabs along with the lime cheese.

Grilled Mango Cheeks Energy 63kcal/272kJ; Protein 2g; Carbohydrate 14.5g, of which sugars 14.3g; Fat 0.2g, of which saturates 0.1g; Cholesterol 0mg; Calcium 12mg; Fibre 2g; Sodium 32mg.
Exotic Fruit Energy 306Kcal/1276kJ; Protein 7.1g; Carbohydrate 28.8g, of which sugars 28.7g; Fat 19.4g, of which saturates 12g; Cholesterol 50mg; Calcium 100mg; Fibre 4.3g; Sodium 180mg.

Papaya Baked with Ginger

Ginger enhances the flavour of papaya in this recipe, which takes no more than ten minutes to prepare. Don't overcook the papaya, or the flesh will become very watery.

Serves 4

2 ripe papayas
2 pieces stem ginger in syrup, drained, plus 15ml/1 tbsp syrup from the jar
8 amaretti or other dessert biscuits (cookies), coarsely crushed
45ml/3 tbsp raisins
shredded, finely pared rind and juice of 1 lime
25g/1oz/¼ cup pistachio nuts, chopped
15ml/1 tbsp light muscovado (brown) sugar
60ml/4 tbsp crème fraîche, plus extra to serve

1 Preheat the oven to 200°C/400°F/Gas 6. Cut the papayas in half and scoop out their seeds. Place the halves in a baking dish and set aside. Cut the stem ginger into fine matchsticks.

2 Make the filling. Combine the crushed amaretti biscuits, stem ginger matchsticks and raisins in a bowl. Stir in the lime rind and juice, two-thirds of the nuts, then add the sugar and the crème fraîche. Mix well.

3 Fill the papaya halves and drizzle with the ginger syrup. Sprinkle with the remaining nuts. Bake for about 25 minutes or until tender. Serve with extra crème fraîche.

> **Cook's Tip**
> If crème fraîche is not available, make your own version. Combine 250ml/8fl oz/1 cup whipping cream and 30ml/2 tbsp buttermilk in a glass bowl. Cover at room temperature for 8–24 hours, or until thick. Stir well, cover and refrigerate for up to 10 days.

> **Variation**
> You can use almonds or walnuts instead of the pistachio nuts.

Exotic Tapioca Pudding

This pudding, made from large pearl tapioca and coconut milk, and served warm, is much lighter than the traditional Western-style version. You can adjust the sweetness to your taste. Serve with lychees or the smaller, similar-tasting longans – also known as 'dragon's eyes'.

Serves 4

115g/4oz/⅔ cup tapioca
475ml/16fl oz/2 cups water
175g/6oz/¾ cup granulated (white) sugar
pinch of salt
250ml/8fl oz/1 cup coconut milk
250g/9oz prepared tropical fruits
finely shredded lime rind and shaved fresh coconut (optional), to decorate

1 Put the tapioca in a bowl and pour over enough warm water to cover completely. Leave to soak for 1 hour so the grains swell. Drain well.

2 Pour the measured water in a large pan and bring to the boil over a medium heat. Add the sugar and salt and stir until completely dissolved.

3 Add the tapioca and coconut milk, reduce the heat to low and simmer gently for 10 minutes, or until the tapioca becomes tender and transparent.

4 Spoon into one large or four individual bowls and serve warm with the tropical fruits. Decorate with the lime rind and coconut shavings, if using.

> **Cook's Tips**
> • Tapioca pearls are a product of cassava, which is a tropical root plant originating from South America. Cassava flour is processed to form the pearls. In the past, tapioca milk pudding was a popular British dessert.
> • For a tropical fruit accompaniment, arrange sliced and peeled pineapple, ripe mango and papaya on a platter with chunks of oranges for added juiciness. Sprinkle with finely grated lime rind.

Papaya Energy 292kcal/1228kJ; Protein 3.6g; Carbohydrate 44.6g, of which sugars 35.7g; Fat 12.3g, of which saturates 5.7g; Cholesterol 17mg; Calcium 84mg; Fibre 4.2g; Sodium 127mg.
Exotic Tapioca Energy 325Kcal/1388kJ; Protein 1g; Carbohydrate 84.9g, of which sugars 57.4g; Fat 0.4g, of which saturates 0.2g; Cholesterol 0mg; Calcium 51mg; Fibre 1.8g; Sodium 74mg.

Rosehip & Apple Jelly

This economical jelly is made with windfall apples and wild rosehips. It is rich in vitamin C, full of flavour, and tastes excellent when spread on freshly toasted crumpets or scones.

Makes about 2kg/4½lb
1kg/2¼ lb windfall apples, trimmed and quartered
450g/1lb firm, ripe rosehips
about 1.3kg/3lb/6½ cups preserving or granulated (white) sugar, warmed

1 Place the quartered apples in a large pan with just enough water to cover, plus 300ml/½ pint/1¼ cups of extra water.

2 Bring the mixture to the boil and cook gently until the apples soften and turn to a pulp. Meanwhile, chop the rosehips coarsely. Add the rosehips to the pan with the apple and simmer for 10 minutes.

3 Remove from the heat and stand for 10 minutes, then pour the mixture into a scalded jelly bag suspended over a non-metallic bowl and leave to drain overnight.

4 Measure the juice into a preserving pan and bring to the boil. Add 400g/14oz/2 cups warmed sugar for each 600ml/1 pint/2½ cups of liquid. Stir until the sugar has completely dissolved. Boil to setting point (105°C/220°F).

5 Pour the jelly into warmed, sterilized jars and seal. Label and store when completely cold.

Cook's Tip
There is no need to remove all the peel from the apples – simply cut out any bruised, damaged or bad areas.

Variation
For grape jelly, add 900g/2lb/6 cups muscat grapes, same quantity sugar, 2 lemons, 30ml/2 tbsp elderflower cordial.

Crab Apple & Lavender Jelly

This fragrant, clear apple jelly can be made in the months before Christmas and stored until needed. It also makes an attractive gift.

Makes about 900g/2lb
900g/2lb/5 cups crab apples
1.75 litres/3 pints/7½ cups water
lavender stems
900g/2lb/4 cups sugar

1 Cut the crab apples into chunks and place in a large pan with the water and two stems of lavender. Bring to the boil, then cover the pan and simmer very gently for 1 hour, stirring occasionally until the fruit is pulpy.

2 Suspend a jelly bag and place a large bowl underneath. Sterilize the jelly bag by pouring through some boiling water. When the bowl is full of water, discard the water and replace the bowl to sit underneath the bag.

3 Pour the pulped fruit mixture from the pan slowly into the jelly bag. Allow the juice from the mixture to drip slowly through for several hours. Do not try to speed up the straining process by squeezing the bag or the jelly will become cloudy.

4 Discard the pulp and measure the quantity of juice gathered in the bowl. To each 600ml/1 pint/2½ cups of juice add 450g/1lb/2 cups of sugar and pour into a clean pan. Sterilize the glass jars and lids required in a very hot oven.

5 Heat the juice gently, stirring occasionally, until the sugar has dissolved. Bring to the boil and boil rapidly for about 8–10 minutes until setting point has been reached. When tested, the temperature should be 105°C/221°F. If you don't have a sugar thermometer, put a small amount of jelly on a cold plate and allow to cool. The surface should wrinkle when you push the jelly. If not yet set, continue to boil and then re-test.

6 Remove from the heat and remove any froth from the surface. Pour the jelly into the warm sterilized jars. Dip the lavender into boiling water and insert a stem into each jar. Cover the jar with a disc of baking parchment and then with cellophane paper and a rubber band.

Rosehip Energy 5684kcal/24,259kJ; Protein 8.4g; Carbohydrate 1505.7g, of which sugars 1505.7g; Fat 0.5g, of which saturates 0g; Cholesterol 0mg; Calcium 761mg; Fibre 7.7g; Sodium 94mg.
Crab Apple Energy 48kcal/205kJ; Protein 0.1g; Carbohydrate 12.7g, of which sugars 12.7g; Fat 0g, of which saturates 0g; Cholesterol 0mg; Calcium 6mg; Fibre 0.1g; Sodium 1mg.

Apple & Sultana Chutney

Use wine or cider vinegar for this stovetop chutney, to give it a subtle and mellow flavour. The fruity chutney is perfect when served with Indian food or cheeses and freshly made bread.

Makes about 900g/2lb
350g/12oz cooking apples
115g/4oz/²/₃ cup sultanas
(golden raisins)

50g/2oz onion
25g/1oz/¼ cup
  almonds, blanched
5ml/1 tsp white peppercorns
2.5ml/½ tsp coriander seeds
175g/6oz/scant 1 cup sugar
10ml/2 tsp salt
5ml/1 tsp ground ginger
450ml/¾ pint/scant 2 cups cider
  vinegar or wine vinegar
1.5ml/¼ tsp cayenne pepper
red chillies (optional)

1 Peel, core and chop the apples. Chop the sultanas, onion and almonds. Tie the peppercorns and coriander seeds in muslin (cheesecloth), using a long piece of string, and then tie to the handle of a preserving pan or stainless steel pan.

2 Put the sugar, salt, ground ginger and vinegar into the pan, with the cayenne pepper to taste. Heat the mixture gently, stirring, until the sugar has completely dissolved.

3 Add the chopped fruit to the pan. Bring the mixture to the boil and then lower the heat. Simmer for about 1½–2 hours, or until most of the liquid has evaporated.

4 Spoon the chutney into warmed sterilized jars and place one whole fresh chilli in each jar, if using. Leave until cold, then cover and seal the jars and attach a label to each one.

5 Store in a cool, dark place. The chutney is best left for a month to mature before eating and will keep for at least 6 months, if it is correctly stored.

> **Variation**
> For a mild chutney, add only a little cayenne pepper. For a spicier one, increase the quantity to taste.

Christmas Chutney

This savoury mixture of spices and dried fruit takes its inspiration from mincemeat, and makes a delicious addition to the Boxing Day buffet.

Makes 900g–1.5kg/2–3½lb
450g/1lb cooking apples, peeled, cored and chopped

500g/1¼lb/3 cups luxury
  mixed dried fruit
grated rind of 1 orange
30ml/2 tbsp mixed
  (apple pie) spice
150ml/¼ pint/²/₃ cup
  cider vinegar
350g/12oz/1½ cups soft
  light brown sugar

1 Place the chopped apples, dried fruit and grated orange rind in a large, heavy pan.

2 Stir in the mixed spice, vinegar and sugar. Heat gently, stirring until all the sugar has dissolved.

3 Bring the mixture to the boil, then lower the heat and simmer for about 40–45 minutes, stirring occasionally, until the mixture has thickened.

4 Ladle the chutney into warm sterilized jars, cover and seal. Keep for 1 month before using.

> **Cook's Tip**
> Watch the chutney carefully towards the end of the cooking time, as it has a tendency to catch on the bottom of the pan. Stir frequently at this stage.

> **Variation**
> If you like, you can use a combination of apples and pears in this recipe. There is a glut of both these fruits over the festive season when they are at their best, so it is an ideal time to make this chutney. Simply replace half the quantity of the apples in the recipe with pears.

Apple and Sultana Energy 1299kcal/5525kJ; Protein 10.9g; Carbohydrate 299.5g, of which sugars 297.7g; Fat 14.9g, of which saturates 1.1g; Cholesterol 0mg; Calcium 254mg; Fibre 10.4g; Sodium 3.97g.
Christmas Energy 1299kcal/5525kJ; Protein 10.9g; Carbohydrate 299.5g, of which sugars 297.7g; Fat 14.9g, of which saturates 1.1g; Cholesterol 0mg; Calcium 254mg; Fibre 10.4g; Sodium 3974mg.

Apple & Leek Relish

Fresh and tangy, this simple relish of sliced leeks and apples with a lemon and honey dressing can be served with a range of cold meats as part of a spring buffet, or for a springtime barbecue when the weather is good enough to eat outdoors. For the best result, make sure you use slim young leeks and tart, crisp apples.

Serves 4

2 slim leeks, white part only, washed thoroughly
2 large apples
15ml/1 tbsp chopped fresh parsley
juice of 1 lemon
15ml/1 tbsp clear honey
salt and ground black pepper, to taste

1 Thinly slice the leeks. Peel and core the apples, then slice the flesh thinly.

2 Place the sliced leek and apple into a large serving bowl and add the fresh parsley, lemon juice and honey. Season to taste with salt and ground black pepper.

3 Toss the ingredients thoroughly with two wooden spoons until they are well combined. Leave the bowl to stand in a cool place for about an hour before serving, to allow the flavours to blend together.

Variation
This relish could also be made with a mixture of pears and apples, if you prefer. The variation in texture between the softer pear slices and the crisp, tart apples will add extra interest to the relish.

Cook's Tip
When buying leeks, look for slim ones with firm white stems and bright green leaves. Avoid those that are discoloured.

Apple & Cider Relish

This relish couldn't be simpler to make. It tastes great with roast pork, duck or goose. It is an ideal way to use cooking apples that appear in the stores in the autumn.

2.5ml/½ tsp cider vinegar
25g/1oz/2 tbsp butter
2 whole cloves
a few sprigs of fresh thyme
15ml/1 tbsp clear honey
10ml/2 tsp Dijon mustard

Makes 450g/1lb
450g/1lb Bramley apples
150ml/¼ pint/⅔ cup sweet cider

1 Peel the apples with a sharp knife or vegetable peeler. Remove the cores and discard, then slice the flesh.

2 Place the apple slices in a large pan. Pour in the sweet cider, cider vinegar, butter, cloves and sprigs of fresh thyme.

3 Bring the mixture to the boil, then reduce the heat and simmer over low heat, stirring occasionally, for about 10 minutes or until the apples are soft and pulpy.

4 Increase the heat and cook over medium heat until most of the liquid has evaporated.

5 Remove the cloves and thyme sprigs and beat in the honey and mustard. Taste and add more honey if necessary, but the sauce is best when slightly tart.

Variation
Other fresh herbs will work as well – try parsley, rosemary or dill.

Cook's Tip
You can press the apple sauce through a sieve (strainer) using a wooden spoon if you prefer it to be perfectly smooth rather than lumpy.

Apple and Leek Energy 59kcal/252kJ; Protein 1.9g; Carbohydrate 12.5g, of which sugars 11.8g; Fat 0.6g, of which saturates 0.1g; Cholesterol 0mg; Calcium 27mg; Fibre 3.4g; Sodium 4mg.
Apple and Cider Energy 453kcal/1909kJ; Protein 2.2g; Carbohydrate 56.4g, of which sugars 56.2g; Fat 21.7g, of which saturates 13.6g; Cholesterol 58mg; Calcium 42mg; Fibre 7.2g; Sodium 504mg.

Chunky Pear & Walnut Chutney

This chutney recipe is ideal for using up hard windfall pears. Its mellow flavour is well suited to being brought out after a festive dinner with a lovely selection of strong cheeses, served with freshly made oatcakes or warm crusty bread.

Makes about 1.8kg/4lb

1.2kg/2½lb firm pears
225g/8oz cooking apples
225g/8oz onions
450ml/¾ pint/scant 2 cups cider vinegar
175g/6oz/generous 1 cup sultanas (golden raisins)
finely grated rind and juice of 1 orange
400g/14oz/2 cups granulated (white) sugar
115g/4oz/1 cup walnuts, roughly chopped
2.5ml/½ tsp ground cinnamon

1 Peel and core the fruit, then chop into 2.5cm/1in chunks. Peel and quarter the onions, then chop into pieces the same size as the fruit chunks. Place in a large preserving pan with the vinegar.

2 Slowly bring to the boil, then reduce the heat and simmer for 40 minutes, until the apples, pears and onions are tender, stirring the mixture occasionally.

3 Meanwhile, put the sultanas in a small bowl, pour over the orange juice and leave to soak.

4 Add the orange rind, sultanas and orange juice, and the sugar to the pan. Heat gently, stirring constantly, until the sugar has completely dissolved, then leave to simmer for 30–40 minutes, or until the chutney is thick and no excess liquid remains. Stir frequently towards the end of cooking to prevent the chutney from sticking to the base of the pan.

5 Gently toast the walnuts in a non-stick pan over low heat for 5 minutes, stirring frequently, until lightly coloured. Stir the nuts into the chutney with the ground cinnamon.

6 Spoon the chutney into warmed sterilized jars, cover and seal. Store in a cool, dark place and leave to mature for at least 1 month. Use within 1 year.

Orange Spoon Preserve

Spoon preserves are made with various types of fruit in a luscious syrup. Make orange peel preserve in late autumn with navel oranges, and in winter use Seville oranges. Orange peel preserve is the easiest type to make, and will happily keep for one or two years.

Makes about 30 pieces

8–9 thick-skinned oranges, total weight about 1kg/2¼ lb, rinsed and dried
1kg/2¼ lb/4½ cups caster (superfine) sugar
juice of 1 lemon

1 Grate the oranges lightly and discard the zest. Slice each one vertically into 4–6 pieces (depending on the size), remove the peel from each segment, keeping it in one piece, and drop it into a bowl of cold water. Use the flesh for another recipe.

2 Have ready a tapestry needle threaded with strong cotton string. Roll up a piece of peel and thread the needle through it. Continue this process until there are 10–12 pieces on the string, then tie the ends together. String the remaining peel in the same way. Put strings in a bowl of cold water and leave for 24 hours, changing the water 3–4 times.

3 Next day, drain the strings of peel and put them in a large pan. Pour in about 2.8 litres/4½ pints/11 cups water. Bring to the boil, partially cover the pan and continue to boil for 15 minutes. Drain. Return the peel to the pan, cover with same amount of water and boil for 10 minutes until the peel feels soft. Transfer into a colander and leave to drain for at least 1 hour.

4 Put the sugar in a large heavy pan and add 150ml/¼ pint/⅔ cup water. Stir over a gentle heat until the sugar dissolves, then boil gently without stirring for about 4 minutes until a thick syrup forms. Remove the fruit from the threads. Simmer for 5 minutes, then take off the heat and leave to stand overnight.

5 Next day, boil the syrup very gently for 4–5 minutes, until it starts to set. Stir in the lemon juice, take the pan off the heat and cool. Pack into sterilized jars. Seal and label when cool.

Chunky Pear Energy 3506kcal/14818kJ; Protein 30.9g; Carbohydrate 705.4g, of which sugars 699.5g; Fat 81.4g, of which saturates 6.4g; Cholesterol 0mg; Calcium 634mg; Fibre 40.7g; Sodium 118mg.
Orange Spoon Preserve Energy 131kcal/560kJ; Protein 0.3g; Carbohydrate 34.8g, of which sugars 34.8g; Fat 0g, of which saturates 0g; Cholesterol 0mg; Calcium 31mg; Fibre 0g; Sodium 3mg.

Three-fruit Marmalade

Seville oranges have a powerful flavour and plenty of setting power to make an excellent preserve. These bitter oranges are usually only available for a short time in winter – but sweet oranges can be used instead.

Makes 2.25kg/5lb
2 Seville (Temple) oranges
2 lemons
1 grapefruit
1.5kg/3lb 6oz/6¾ cups granulated (white) sugar

1 Wash the fruit, halve, and squeeze their juice. Pour into a large heavy pan or preserving pan. Place the pips (seeds) and pulp into a square of muslin (cheesecloth), gather the sides into a bag and tie the neck. Tie the bag to the pan handle so that it dangles in the juice.

2 Remove and discard the membranes and pith from the citrus skins and cut the rinds into slivers. Add to the pan with 1.75 litres/3 pints/7½ cups water. Heat until simmering, then cook gently for 2 hours, or until the rinds are soft and tender.

3 Remove the muslin bag, squeezing the juice into the pan. Discard the bag. Stir the sugar into the pan and heat very gently, stirring occasionally, until the sugar has dissolved.

4 Bring the mixture to the boil and boil for 10–15 minutes, or until the marmalade registers 105°C/220°F on a sugar thermometer. Alternatively, test the marmalade for setting by pouring a small amount on to a chilled saucer. Chill for 3 minutes, then push the marmalade with your finger: if wrinkles form on the surface, it is ready. Cool for 15 minutes.

5 Stir the marmalade and pour it into warm, sterilized jars. Cover with waxed paper discs. Seal and label when cold.

Cook's Tip
Allow the marmalade to cool slightly before potting, so that it is thick enough to stop the fruit from sinking in the jars.

St Clement's Marmalade

This classic preserve made from oranges and lemons has a lovely citrus tang. It has a light, refreshing flavour and is perfect for serving for breakfast, spread on freshly toasted bread.

Makes about 2.25kg/5lb
450g/1lb Seville (Temple) oranges
450g/1lb clementines
4 lemons
1.2kg/2½ lb/5½ cups granulated (white) sugar, warmed

1 Wash the oranges and lemons, then halve and squeeze the juice into a large pan. Tie the pips (seeds) and membranes in a muslin (cheesecloth) bag, shred the orange and lemon rind and add to the pan.

2 Add 1.5 litres/2½ pints/6¼ cups water to the pan, bring to the boil, then cover and simmer for 2 hours. Remove the muslin bag, leave to cool, then squeeze any liquid back into the pan.

3 Add the warmed sugar to the pan and stir over a low heat until completely dissolved. Bring to the boil and boil rapidly for about 15 minutes, or until the marmalade reaches setting point (105°C/220°F).

4 Remove the pan from the heat and skim off any scum from the surface. Leave to cool for about 5 minutes, stir, then pour into warmed sterilized jars and seal. When cold, label, then store in a cool, dark place.

Cook's Tip
Any member of the mandarin family can be used to make this preserve, but clementines tend to give the best result.

Variation
Add 60ml/4 tbsp of Grand Marnier or Cointreau to give the marmalade a potent kick. Serve it, mixed with natural (plain) yogurt, on pancakes for a special breakfast treat.

Three-fruit Energy 6106kcal/26,049kJ; Protein 13.2g; Carbohydrate 1612.4g, of which sugars 1612.4g; Fat 0.6g, of which saturates 0g; Cholesterol 0mg; Calcium 1020mg; Fibre 8.9g; Sodium 115mg.
St Clement's Energy 5061kcal/21,594kJ; Protein 15.9g; Carbohydrate 1330.5g, of which sugars 1330.5g; Fat 0.9g, of which saturates 0g; Cholesterol 0mg; Calcium 1059mg; Fibre 15.3g; Sodium 117mg.

Oxford Marmalade

The characteristic caramel colour and the intensely rich flavour of a traditional Oxford marmalade is obtained by cutting the fruit coarsely and cooking it for several hours before adding the sugar.

Makes about 2.25kg/5lb
*900g/2lb Seville (Temple) oranges
1.3kg/3lb/6½ cups granulated
(white) sugar, warmed*

I Scrub the orange skins, then remove the rind using a vegetable peeler. Thickly slice the rind and put in a large pan.

2 Chop the fruit, reserving the pips (seeds), and add to the rind in the pan, along with 1.75 litres/3 pints/7½ cups water. Tie the orange pips (seeds) in a piece of muslin (cheesecloth) and add to the pan. Bring to the boil, then cover and simmer for 2 hours. Add more water during cooking to maintain the same volume. Remove from the heat and leave overnight.

3 The next day, remove the muslin bag from the oranges, squeezing well, and return the pan to the heat. Bring to the boil, then cover and simmer for I hour.

4 Add the warmed sugar to the pan, then slowly bring the mixture to the boil, stirring until the sugar has dissolved completely. Increase the heat and boil rapidly for about 15 minutes, or until setting point is reached (105°C/220°F).

5 Remove the pan from the heat and skim off any scum from the surface. Leave to cool for about 5 minutes, stir, then pour into warmed sterilized jars and seal. When cold, label, then store in a cool, dark place.

> **Cook's Tip**
> *Traditionalists say that only bitter oranges such as Seville (Temple) should be used to make marmalade. Although this isn't always true, it is certainly the case when making Oxford marmalade.*

Whisky Marmalade

Real home-made marmalade tastes delicious, and flavouring it with whisky makes it a special treat at Christmas time – it is great for spreading on fresh muffins for breakfast.

Makes 3.6–4.5kg/8–10lb
*1.3kg/3lb Seville (Temple) oranges
juice of 2 large lemons
2.75kg/6lb/13½ cups
   sugar, warmed
about 300ml/½ pint/1¼ cups
   Scotch whisky*

I Scrub the oranges thoroughly using a nylon brush and pick off the disc at the stalk end. Cut the oranges in half widthways and squeeze the juice, retaining the pips (seeds). Quarter the peel, cut away and reserve any thick white pith, and shred the peel – thickly or thinly depending on your prefererence.

2 Cut up the reserved pith roughly and tie it up with the pips in a square of muslin (cheesecloth) using a long piece of string. Tie the bag loosely, so that water can circulate during cooking and will extract the pectin from the pith and pips. Hang the bag from the handle of the preserving pan.

3 Add the cut peel, strained juices and 3.5 litres/6 pints/15 cups water to the pan. Bring to the boil and simmer for 1½–2 hours, or until the peel is very tender.

4 Lift up the bag of pith and pips and squeeze it out well between two plates over the pan to extract as much of the juices as possible. Add the sugar to the pan and stir over a low heat until it has completely dissolved.

5 Bring to the boil and boil hard for 15–20 minutes or until setting point is reached. To test, allow a spoonful to cool slightly, and then see if a skin has formed. If not, boil a little longer.

6 Skim, if necessary, and leave to cool for 15 minutes, then stir. Divide the whisky among 8–10 warmed, sterilized jars and swill it around. Using a heatproof jug (pitcher), pour in the marmalade.

7 Cover and seal while still hot. Label when cold, and store in a cool, dark place for up to 6 months.

Oxford Energy 5455kcal/23,275kJ; Protein 16.4g; Carbohydrate 1435g, of which sugars 1435g; Fat 0.9g, of which saturates 0g; Cholesterol 0mg; Calcium 1112mg; Fibre 15.3g; Sodium 123mg.
Whisky Energy 10,736kcal/45,734kJ; Protein 22.8g; Carbohydrate 2657.8g, of which sugars 2657.8g; Fat 1.3g, of which saturates 0g; Cholesterol 0mg; Calcium 1.74g; Fibre 15.6g; Sodium 187mg.

Ruby Red Grapefruit Marmalade

If you like a really tangy marmalade, grapefruit is the perfect choice. To achieve a wonderfully red-blushed preserve, look for the red variety rather than pink. They have a wonderful flavour and make a sweet, jewel-coloured preserve.

Makes about 1.8kg/4lb
900g/2lb ruby red grapefruit
1 lemon
1.3kg/3lb/6½ cups granulated (white) sugar, warmed

1 Wash the grapefruit and lemon and remove the rind in thick pieces using a vegetable peeler. Cut the fruit in half and squeeze the juice into a preserving pan, reserving all the pips (seeds).

2 Put the pips and membranes from the fruit in a muslin (cheesecloth) bag and add to the pan. Discard the grapefruit and lemon shells.

3 Using a sharp knife, cut the grapefruit and lemon rind into thin or coarse shreds, as preferred, and place in the pan.

4 Add 1.2 litres/2 pints/5 cups water and bring to the boil. Cover and simmer for 2 hours, or until the rind is very tender.

5 Remove the muslin bag from the pan, leave to cool, then squeeze it over the pan. Add the sugar and stir over a low heat until it has dissolved. Bring to the boil, then boil rapidly for 10–15 minutes, or to setting point (105°C/220°F).

6 Remove the pan from the heat and skim off any scum using a slotted spoon. Leave to cool for about 10 minutes, then stir and pour into warmed sterilized jars. Seal, then label when cold.

Cook's Tip
Although you can use yellow grapefruit to make this marmalade, it tends to give a very pale result with more tang than the ruby red variety, but a much less fruity flavour.

Pink Grapefruit & Cranberry Marmalade

Cranberries give this glorious marmalade an extra tartness and a full fruit flavour, as well as an inimitable vibrant colour. The resulting preserve makes a lively choice for breakfast, or a brilliant accompaniment for cold roast turkey during the festive season.

Makes about 2.25kg/5lb
675g/1½ lb pink grapefruit
2 lemons
225g/8oz/2 cups cranberries, fresh or frozen
1.3kg/3lb/6½ cups granulated (white) sugar, warmed

1 Wash and quarter the grapefruit, then slice them thinly, reserving the pips (seeds) and any juice that runs out. Juice the lemons, reserving the pips.

2 Tie the grapefruit and lemon pips in a muslin (cheesecloth) bag and place in a large pan with the grapefruit slices and lemon juice.

3 Add 900ml/1½ pints/3¾ cups water and bring to the boil. Cover and simmer gently for 1½–2 hours, or until the grapefruit rind is tender. Remove the muslin bag, leave to cool, then squeeze over the pan.

4 Add the cranberries, then bring to the boil. Simmer for 15–20 minutes, or until the berries have popped and softened.

5 Add the sugar to the pan and stir over a low heat until the sugar has completely dissolved. Bring to the boil and boil rapidly for about 10 minutes, or until setting point is reached (105°C/220°F).

6 Remove the pan from the heat and skim off any scum from the surface using a slotted spoon. Leave to cool for 5–10 minutes, then stir and pour into warmed sterilized jars. Seal, then label when the marmalade is cold.

Lemon Curd

This classic tangy, creamy curd is still one of the most popular of all the curds. It is delicious spread thickly over freshly baked white bread or served with American-style pancakes, and also makes a wonderfully rich, zesty sauce spooned over fresh fruit tarts.

Makes about 450g/1lb
3 unwaxed lemons
200g/7oz/1 cup caster (superfine) sugar
115g/4oz/½ cup unsalted (sweet) butter, diced
2 large (US extra large) eggs
2 large (US extra large) egg yolks

1 Wash the lemons, then finely grate the rind and place in a large heatproof bowl. Using a sharp knife, halve the lemons and squeeze the juice into the bowl. Set over a pan of gently simmering water and add the sugar and butter. Stir until the sugar has dissolved and the butter melted.

2 Put the eggs and yolks in a bowl and beat together with a fork. Pour the eggs through a sieve (strainer) into the lemon mixture, and whisk well until thoroughly combined.

3 Stir the mixture constantly in the bowl over the pan of simmering water until the lemon curd thickens and lightly coats the back of a wooden spoon.

4 Remove the pan from the heat and pour the curd into small, warmed sterilized jars. Cover, seal and label. Store in a cool, dark place, ideally in the refrigerator. Use within 3 months. (Once opened, store in the refrigerator.)

> **Cook's Tip**
> *If you are really impatient when it comes to cooking, it is possible to cook the curd in a heavy pan directly over a low heat. However, you really need to watch it like a hawk to avoid the mixture curdling. If the curd looks as though it's beginning to curdle, plunge the base of the pan in cold water and beat vigorously.*

Preserved Lemons

These richly flavoured fruits are widely used in Middle Eastern cooking. Only the rind, which contains the essential flavour of the lemon, is used in recipes. Traditionally, whole lemons are preserved, but this recipe uses wedges, which can be neatly packed into jars more easily.

Makes about 2 jars
10 unwaxed lemons
sea salt
about 200ml/7fl oz/scant 1 cup fresh lemon juice or a combination of fresh and preserved juice

1 Wash the lemons well and cut each into six to eight wedges. Press a generous amount of salt on to the cut surface of each wedge.

2 Pack the salted lemon wedges into two 1.2 litre/2 pint/5 cup warmed sterilized jars. To each jar, add 30–45ml/2–3 tbsp sea salt and half the lemon juice, then top up with boiling water to cover the lemon wedges. Seal the jars and leave to stand for 2–4 weeks before using.

3 To use, rinse the preserved lemons well to remove some of the salty flavour, then pull off and discard the flesh. Cut the lemon rind into strips or leave in chunks and use as desired.

> **Cook's Tip**
> *The salty, well-flavoured juice that is used to preserve the lemons can be used to give a zingy taste to salad dressings, or it can be added to hot sauces.*

> **Variation**
> *Other acidic citrus fruits can be preserved in a similar way. Try the method with vibrant green limes or their smaller relations, such as kumquats and limequats.*

Preserved Lemons Energy 48kcal/198kJ; Protein 2.5g; Carbohydrate 8g, of which sugars 8g; Fat 0.8g, of which saturates 0.3g; Cholesterol 0mg; Calcium 213mg; Fibre 0g; Sodium 13mg.
Lemon Curd Energy 1927kcal/8056kJ; Protein 20.7g; Carbohydrate 212.1g, of which sugars 212.1g; Fat 116.8g, of which saturates 66.2g; Cholesterol 1029mg; Calcium 294mg; Fibre 0g; Sodium 871mg.

Spiced Poached Kumquats

Warm cinnamon and star anise make a heady combination with the full citrus flavour of kumquats. Star anise is an attractive spice – it is an eight-pointed star that contains tiny aniseed-flavoured, amber-coloured seeds. The kumquats go well with rich meats, such as roast pork or baked ham, or with punchy goat's milk cheese. They are also good with desserts and ice creams.

Serves 6
450g/1lb/4 cups kumquats
115g/4oz/½ cup caster
   (superfine) sugar
1 small cinnamon stick
1 star anise

1 Cut the kumquats in half and discard the pips (seeds).

2 Place the kumquats in a pan with the caster sugar, 150ml/
¼ pint/⅔ cup water and the cinnamon stick and star anise.

3 Cook over a gentle heat, stirring until the sugar has dissolved.

4 Increase the heat, cover the pan and boil the mixture for about 8–10 minutes, until the kumquats are tender.

5 To bottle the kumquats, spoon them into warm, sterilized jars, then seal. Once they are completely cool, label the jars.

6 If you want to serve the spiced kumquats soon after making them, let the mixture cool, then chill it.

Cook's Tips
• *Use half the quantity of kumquats and half of limequats – their green coloured-cousins – in this recipe for a highly decorative preserve.*
• *Kumquats (and limequats) are unusual among the citrus family because they can be eaten whole and do not need to be peeled, although it is advisable to cook or preserve them first. Their thin skins have a pleasantly bitter flavour.*

Squash, Apricot & Almond Chutney

Coriander seeds and ground turmeric add a deliciously spicy touch to this rich, slow-cooker chutney. It is ideal spooned on to little savoury canapés or with melting cubes of mozzarella cheese; it is also good in sandwiches, helping to spice up a variety of fillings.

Makes about 1.8kg/4lb
1 small butternut squash,
   weighing about 800g/1¾lb
400g/14oz/2 cups golden caster
   (superfine) sugar
300ml/½ pint/1¼ cups
   cider vinegar
2 onions, finely chopped
225g/8oz/1 cup ready-to-eat
   dried apricots, chopped
finely grated rind and juice of
   1 orange
2.5ml/½ tsp turmeric
15ml/1 tbsp coriander seeds
15ml/1 tbsp salt
115g/4oz/1 cup flaked
   (sliced) almonds

1 Halve the butternut squash and scoop out the seeds. Peel off the skin, then cut the flesh into 1cm/½in cubes.

2 Put the sugar and vinegar in the ceramic cooking pot of the cooker and switch to high. Heat for 30 minutes, then stir until the sugar has completely dissolved.

3 Add the butternut squash, onions, apricots, orange rind and juice, turmeric, coriander seeds and salt to the slow cooker pot and stir well until the ingredients are well combined.

4 Cover the slow cooker with the lid and cook for about 5–6 hours, stirring occasionally during that time.

5 After about 5 hours the chutney should be a fairly thick consistency with relatively little liquid. If it is still quite runny at this stage, cook uncovered for the final hour. Stir the flaked almonds into the chutney.

6 Spoon the chutney into warmed sterilized jars, cover and seal. Store in a cool, dark place and allow the chutney to mature for at least 1 month before eating. It should be used within 2 years. Once opened, store jars of the chutney in the refrigerator and use within 2 months.

Spiced Poached Kumquats Energy 103kcal/441kJ; Protein 0.8g; Carbohydrate 26.6g, of which sugars 26.6g; Fat 0.1g, of which saturates 0g; Cholesterol 0mg; Calcium 33mg; Fibre 0.9g; Sodium 4mg.
Squash Energy 2770kcal/11,723kJ; Protein 41.7g; Carbohydrate 532.6g, of which sugars 524.1g; Fat 67.3g, of which saturates 5.9g; Cholesterol 0mg; Calcium 807mg; Fibre 31.6g; Sodium 5967mg.

Sweet & Hot Dried-fruit Chutney

This rich, thick and slightly sticky preserve of spiced dried fruit is simple to make in the slow cooker. It is a wonderful way to enliven cold roast turkey left over from your Christmas or Thanksgiving dinner.

Makes about 1.5kg/3lb 6oz

350g/12oz/1½ cups ready-to-eat dried apricots
225g/8oz/1½ cups dried dates, stoned (pitted)
225g/8oz/1⅓ cups dried figs
50g/2oz/⅓ cup glacé (candied) citrus peel
150g/5oz/1 cup raisins
50g/2oz/½ cup dried cranberries
75ml/2½fl oz/⅓ cup cranberry juice
300ml/½ pint/1¼ cups cider vinegar
225g/8oz/1 cup caster (superfine) sugar
finely grated rind of 1 lemon
5ml/1 tsp mixed (apple pie) spice
5ml/1 tsp ground coriander
5ml/1 tsp cayenne pepper
5ml/1 tsp salt

1 Chop the apricots, dates, figs and citrus peel, and put all the dried fruit in the ceramic cooking pot. Pour over the cranberry juice, stir, then cover the slow cooker and switch to low. Cook for 1 hour, or until the fruit has absorbed most of the juice.

2 Add the cider vinegar and sugar to the pot. Turn the slow cooker up to high and stir until the sugar has dissolved.

3 Re-cover and cook for 2 more hours, or until the fruit is very soft and the chutney fairly thick (it will thicken further as it cools). Stir in the lemon rind, mixed spice, coriander, cayenne pepper and salt. Cook, uncovered, for about 30 minutes, until little excess liquid remains.

4 Spoon the chutney into warmed sterilized jars, cover and seal. Store in a cool, dark place. Open within 10 months and, once opened, store in the refrigerator and use within 2 months.

Variation
Pitted prunes can be substituted for the dates, and dried sour cherries for the dried cranberries.

Apricot Chutney

Fruit chutneys can add zest to most meals, and in India you will usually find a selection of different kinds served in tiny bowls for dinner guests to choose from. Dried apricots are readily available from supermarkets and health food shops.

Makes about 450g/1lb/ 2 cups

450g/1lb/2 cups dried apricots, finely diced
5ml/1 tsp garam masala
275g/10oz/1¼ cups soft light brown sugar
450ml/¾ pint/scant 2 cups malt vinegar
5ml/1 tsp grated fresh root ginger
5ml/1 tsp salt
75g/3oz/½ cup sultanas (golden raisins)
450ml/¾ pint/scant 2 cups water

1 Put the dried apricots and garam masala into a medium pan and add the light brown sugar, malt vinegar, ginger, salt, sultanas and water. Mix thoroughly with a spoon.

2 Bring to the boil, then reduce the heat and simmer for 30–35 minutes, stirring occasionally.

3 When the chutney has thickened to a fairly stiff consistency, spoon it into 2–3 clean jam jars and leave to cool. This chutney should be stored in the refrigerator.

Variation
For Orchard Fruit Chutney, put 675g/1½lb peeled, cored and chopped cooking apples into a large pan with 115g/4oz/¼ cup each dried peaches and apricots and 50g/2oz/scant ½ cup raisins. Chop 5 garlic cloves and grate a 5cm/2in piece of fresh root ginger and add them to the pan. Add 350g/12oz soft light brown sugar, 400ml/14fl oz/1⅔ cups malt vinegar, 10ml/2 tsp salt and 5ml/1 tsp cayenne pepper. Bring the mixture to the boil and simmer for 30 minutes, stirring frequently.

Apricot Chutney Energy 2150kcal/9168kJ; Protein 26g; Carbohydrate 537g, of which sugars 535g; Fat 4g, of which saturates 0g; Cholesterol 0mg; Calcium 566mg; Fibre 101.9g; Sodium 2248mg.
Sweet and Hot Energy 2873kcal/12,248kJ; Protein 32g; Carbohydrate 714.3g, of which sugars 703.5g; Fat 6.8g, of which saturates 0.2g; Cholesterol 0mg; Calcium 1075mg; Fibre 52.1g; Sodium 2358mg.

Plum & Apple Jelly

Use dark red cooking plums, damsons or wild plums such as bullaces to offset the sweetness of this deep-coloured fruit jelly. Its flavour complements rich roast meats, such as lamb and pork.

Makes about 1.3kg/3lb
900g/2lb plums
450g/1lb tart cooking apples
150ml/¼ pint/⅔ cup cider vinegar
about 675g/1½ lb/scant 3½ cups preserving or granulated (white) sugar

1 Cut the plums in half along the crease, twist apart, then remove the stones (pits) and roughly chop the flesh. Chop the apples, including the cores and skins. Put the fruit in a large heavy pan with the vinegar and 750ml/1¼ pints/3 cups water.

2 Bring the mixture to the boil, reduce the heat, cover and simmer for 30 minutes, or until the fruit is soft and pulpy.

3 Pour the fruit and juices into a sterilized jelly bag suspended over a large bowl. Leave to drain for at least 3 hours, or until the fruit juices stop dripping.

4 Measure the juice into the cleaned pan, adding 450g/1lb/ 2¼ cups sugar for every 600ml/1 pint/2½ cups juice.

5 Bring the mixture to the boil, stirring occasionally, until the sugar has dissolved, then boil rapidly for about 10 minutes, or until the jelly reaches setting point (105°C/220°F). Remove the pan from the heat.

6 Skim any scum from the surface, then pour the jelly into warmed sterilized jars. Cover and seal while hot. Store in a cool, dark place and use within 2 years.

Cook's Tip
This jelly can be stored for up to 2 years. However, once opened, it should be stored in the refrigerator and eaten within 3 months.

Damson Jam

Dark, plump damsons used only to be found growing in the wild, but today they are available commercially. They produce a deeply coloured and richly flavoured jam that makes a delicious treat when spread on toasted English muffins or warm crumpets at teatime.

Makes about 2kg/4½lb
1kg/2¼lb damsons or wild plums
1kg/2¼lb/5 cups preserving or granulated (white) sugar, warmed

1 Put the damsons in a preserving pan and pour in 1.4 litres/ 2¼ pints/6 cups water. Bring to the boil. Reduce the heat and simmer gently until the damsons are soft, then stir in the sugar.

2 Bring the mixture to the boil, skimming off stones as they rise. Boil to setting point (105°C/220°F). Leave to cool for 10 minutes, then pour into jars. Seal, then label when cool. Store in a cool, dark place.

Cook's Tip
It is important to seal the jars as soon as you have filled them, to ensure the jam remains sterile. However, you should then leave the jars to cool completely before labelling and storing them, to avoid the risk of burns.

Blackcurrant Jam

This jam has a rich, fruity flavour and a wonderfully deep colour. It is punchy and delicious with scones for tea or spread on croissants for a continental-style breakfast. It is the perfect comforting jam on a slice of toast.

Makes about 1.3kg/3lb
1.3kg/3lb/12 cups blackcurrants
grated rind and juice of 1 orange
1.3kg/3lb/6½ cups granulated (white) sugar, warmed
30ml/2 tbsp cassis (optional)

1 Place the blackcurrants, orange rind and juice and 475ml/ 16fl oz/2 cups water in a large heavy pan. Bring to the boil, reduce the heat and simmer for 30 minutes.

2 Add the warmed sugar to the pan and stir over a low heat until the sugar has dissolved.

3 Bring the mixture to the boil and cook for about 8 minutes, or until the jam reaches setting point (105°C/220°F).

4 Remove the pan from the heat and skim off any scum from the surface using a slotted spoon. Leave to cool for 5 minutes, then stir in the cassis, if using.

5 Pour the jam into warmed sterilized jars and seal. Leave the jars to cool completely, then label and store in a cool, dark place.

Plum and Apple Energy 2803kcal/11,963kJ; Protein 5.5g; Carbohydrate 740.7g, of which sugars 740.7g; Fat 0.4g, of which saturates 0g; Cholesterol 0mg; Calcium 401mg; Fibre 6.4g; Sodium 49mg.
Damson Energy 4320kcal/18,430kJ; Protein 10g; Carbohydrate 1141g, of which sugars 1141g; Fat 0g, of which saturates 0g; Cholesterol 0mg; Calcium 770mg; Fibre 18g; Sodium 80mg.
Blackcurrant Energy 5504kcal/23,503kJ; Protein 18.4g; Carbohydrate 1448.7g, of which sugars 1448.7g; Fat 0.1g, of which saturates 0g; Cholesterol 0mg; Calcium 1474mg; Fibre 46.9g; Sodium 122mg.

Greengage & Almond Jam

This is the perfect preserve to make when greengages are readily available in stores, or if you find you have a glut of the fruit. It has a gloriously rich, golden honey colour and a smooth texture that contrasts wonderfully well with the little slivers of almond.

Makes about 1.3kg/3lb
1.3kg/3lb greengages,
    stoned (pitted)
juice of 1 lemon
50g/2oz/½ cup blanched
    almonds, cut into thin slivers
1.3kg/3lb/6½ cups granulated
    (white) sugar, warmed

1 Put the greengages and 350ml/12fl oz/1½ cups water in a preserving pan with the lemon juice and almond slivers. Bring to the boil, then cover and simmer for 15–20 minutes, or until the greengages are really soft.

2 Add the sugar to the pan and stir over a low heat until the sugar has dissolved. Bring to the boil and cook for 10–15 minutes, or until the jam reaches setting point (105°C/220°F).

3 Remove the pan from the heat and skim off any scum from the surface using a slotted spoon.

4 Leave to cool for 10 minutes, then stir gently and pour into warmed sterilized jars. Seal, then leave to cool completely before labelling. Store in a cool place.

Cook's Tip
Greengages look like unripened plums. However, despite their appearance, they have a wonderfully aromatic flavour that is captured perfectly in this delicious jam.

Variation
Coarsely chopped almonds work well with dried apricots to make a deliciously rich jam.

Cherries in Eau de Vie

These potent cherries should be consumed with respect, as they pack quite an alcoholic punch. Serve them with a rich, dark chocolate torte, or as a wicked topping for a creamy rice pudding.

Makes about 1.3kg/3lb
450g/1lb/generous 3 cups
    ripe cherries
8 blanched almonds
75g/3oz/6 tbsp granulated
    (white) sugar
500ml/17fl oz/scant 2¼ cups
    eau de vie

1 Wash and pit the cherries, then pack them into a sterilized, wide-necked bottle along with the blanched almonds.

2 Spoon the sugar over the fruit, then pour in the eau de vie to cover and seal tightly.

3 Store for at least 1 month before serving, shaking the bottle now and then to help dissolve the sugar.

Cook's Tip
Eau de vie actually refers to all spirits distilled from fermented fruits. It is in fact a fruit brandy. Eau de vie is always colourless, with a high alcohol content (sometimes 45% ABV) and a clean, pure scent and the flavour of the founding fruit. This is due to the fast fermenting process used. Popular eaux de vie are made from cherries and strawberries, which go perfectly with the luscious ripe cherries used in this recipe, producing a heady aroma of summer fruit.

Variation
Strawberries, raspberries and blackcurrants are all excellent preserved in eau de vie. They will all produce fine fruity liqueurs and macerated fruit. Orchard fruits, such as apples, pears and plums, are also used to make eau de vie. Use one of these as a base for a preserve of the same type of fruit. The resulting fruit liqueurs, strained, make fabulous Champagne cocktails.

Greengage Energy 5896kcal/25,135kJ; Protein 24.9g; Carbohydrate 1476.3g, of which sugars 1475g; Fat 29.2g, of which saturates 2.2g; Cholesterol 0mg; Calcium 978mg; Fibre 24.5g; Sodium 111mg.
Cherries Energy 1479kcal/6142kJ; Protein 9.3g; Carbohydrate 53.5g, of which sugars 52.8g; Fat 14.4g, of which saturates 1.1g; Cholesterol 0mg; Calcium 119mg; Fibre 5.9g; Sodium 8mg.

Confit of Slow-cooked Onions & Prunes

Onions are caramelized in the slow cooker in sweet-sour balsamic vinegar. This makes a fantastic seasonal accompaniment to cold meats or cheese and chunks of crusty bread.

Serves 6
30ml/2 tbsp extra virgin olive oil
15g/¹⁄₂oz/1 tbsp butter

500g/1¹⁄₄lb onions, thinly sliced
3–5 fresh thyme sprigs
1 bay leaf
30ml/2 tbsp light muscovado (brown) sugar, plus a little extra
30ml/2 tbsp balsamic vinegar, plus a little extra
120ml/4fl oz/¹⁄₂ cup red wine
50g/2oz/¹⁄₄ cup ready-to-eat prunes, chopped
salt and ground black pepper

1 Put the oil and butter in the ceramic cooking pot and heat on high for 15 minutes.

2 Add the onions to the pot and stir to coat the slices in the butter. Cover the cooker with the lid, then place a folded dish towel on top to help retain the heat. Cook the onions for 5 hours, stirring the mixture occasionally.

3 Season with salt and pepper, then add the thyme, bay leaf, sugar, vinegar and wine. Stir until the sugar has dissolved, then stir in the prunes.

4 Cover and cook for 1¹⁄₂–2 hours, until thickened. Adjust the seasoning, adding sugar and/or vinegar to taste.

Cook's Tip
Chopping onions causes tears because of sulfuric compounds in the raw flesh. Most cause this to some extent – ranging from a little sniffle to a torrential downpour. Putting the onion in the freezer for about 20 minutes before chopping helps. If you suffer considerably when chopping onions, you may want to consider safety goggles, even though you may look a little silly wearing them while chopping vegetables.

Strawberry Jam

This is the classic fragrant fruit preserve for English afternoon tea, served with freshly baked scones and clotted cream. It is also extremely good stirred into plain yogurt for breakfast. When selecting strawberries for making jam, choose undamaged, slightly under-ripe fruit if possible – the pectin content will be high, ensuring a good set.

Makes about 1.3kg/3lb
1kg/2¹⁄₄ lb/8 cups small strawberries
900g/2lb/4 cups granulated (white) sugar
juice of 2 lemons

1 Layer the strawberries and sugar in a large bowl. Cover and leave overnight.

2 The next day, scrape the strawberries and their juice into a large, heavy pan. Add the lemon juice. Gradually bring to the boil over a low heat, stirring until the sugar has dissolved completely.

3 Boil steadily for 10–15 minutes, or until the jam registers 105°C/220°F on a sugar thermometer. Alternatively, test for setting by spooning a small amount on to a chilled saucer. Chill for 3 minutes, then push the jam with your finger: if wrinkles form on the surface, it is ready. Cool for 10 minutes.

4 Stir the jam before pouring it into warm sterilized jars, filling them right to the top.

5 Cover with waxed paper discs and seal with lids immediately. Label when cool, and store in a cool, dark place.

Cook's Tip
For best results when making jam, avoid washing the strawberries unless absolutely necessary. Instead, brush off any dirt, or wipe the strawberries with a damp cloth. If you have to wash any, pat them dry and then spread them out on a clean dish towel to dry.

Confit Energy 133kcal/556kJ; Protein 1.2g; Carbohydrate 16.5g, of which sugars 14.6g; Fat 5.9g, of which saturates 1.8g; Cholesterol 5mg; Calcium 26mg; Fibre 1.6g; Sodium 20mg.
Strawberry Energy 3816kcal/16,259kJ; Protein 12.5g; Carbohydrate 1000.5g, of which sugars 1000.5g; Fat 1g, of which saturates 0g; Cholesterol 0mg; Calcium 637mg; Fibre 11g; Sodium 114mg.

Forest Berries in Kirsch

Late summer in a bottle, this preserve captures the essence of the season in its rich, dark colour and flavour. Adding the sweet cherry liqueur Kirsch to the syrup intensifies the flavour of the bottled fruit.

Makes about 1.3kg/3lb
1.3kg/3lb/12 cups mixed
*   prepared summer berries, such*
*   as blackberries, raspberries,*
*   strawberries, redcurrants*
*   and cherries*
225g/8oz/generous 1 cup
*   granulated (white) sugar*
120ml/4fl oz/½ cup Kirsch

1 Preheat the oven to 120°C/250°F/Gas ½. Pack the prepared fruit loosely into sterilized jars. Cover the jars without sealing and place in the oven for 50–60 minutes, or until the juices start to run.

2 Meanwhile, put the sugar and 600ml/1 pint/2½ cups water in a large pan and heat gently, stirring, until the sugar has dissolved. Increase the heat, bring to the boil and boil for 5 minutes. Stir in the Kirsch and set aside.

3 Carefully remove the jars from the oven and place on a dish towel. Use the fruit from one of the jars to top up the rest.

4 Pour the boiling syrup into each jar, twisting and tapping each one to ensure that no air bubbles have been trapped. Seal, allow to cool, then label. Store in a cool, dark place.

> **Cook's Tip**
> *Be careful not to overcook the fruits, because this will cause them to lose their beautiful colour and fresh flavour.*

> **Variation**
> *You can make aromatic blueberries in gin syrup in much the same way, using 1.3kg/3lb/12 cups blueberries, 120ml/4fl oz/ ½ cup gin and the same quantities of sugar and water.*

Blueberry & Lime Jam

The subtle yet fragrant flavour of blueberries can be elusive on its own. Adding a generous quantity of tangy lime juice enhances their flavour and gives this jam a wonderful zesty taste.

Makes about 1.3kg/3lb
1.3kg/3lb/12 cups blueberries
finely pared rind and juice
*   of 4 limes*
1kg/2¼ lb/5 cups preserving sugar
*   with pectin*

1 Put the blueberries, lime juice and half the sugar in a large, non-metallic bowl and lightly crush the berries using a potato masher. Set aside for about 4 hours.

2 Transfer the crushed berry mixture into a pan and stir in the finely pared lime rind together with the remaining preserving sugar. Heat slowly, stirring continuously, until the sugar has completely dissolved.

3 Increase the heat and bring to the boil. Boil rapidly for about 4 minutes, or until the jam reaches setting point (105°C/220°F).

4 Remove the pan from the heat and set aside for 5 minutes. Stir the jam gently, then pour into warmed sterilized jars. Seal the jars, then label when completely cool. Store in a cool, dark place.

> **Cook's Tip**
> *Blueberries are not naturally high in pectin, so extra pectin is needed for a good set. If you prefer, use granulated (white) sugar, and add pectin according to the instruction on the packet in place of the preserving sugar with pectin.*

> **Variation**
> *You can replace the lime juice with lemon juice or the juice of sharp oranges, such as Seville (Temple) oranges, to give a more citrusy zing.*

Forest Berries Energy 1517kcal/6487kJ; Protein 19.3g; Carbohydrate 334.1g, of which sugars 334.1g; Fat 3.9g, of which saturates 1.3g; Cholesterol 0mg; Calcium 444mg; Fibre 32.5g; Sodium 52mg.
Blueberry Energy 4265kcal/18,162kJ; Protein 16.7g; Carbohydrate 1111.3g, of which sugars 1111.3g; Fat 2.6g, of which saturates 0g; Cholesterol 0mg; Calcium 1063mg; Fibre 40.3g; Sodium 86mg.

Cranberry & Claret Jelly

The slight sharpness of cranberries makes this a superb jelly for serving with rich meats, such as lamb or game. Together with claret, the cranberries give the jelly a beautifully festive deep red colour.

Makes about 1.2kg/2½lb
900g/2lb/8 cups fresh or
    frozen cranberries, thawed
350ml/12fl oz/1½ cups water
about 900g/2lb/4½ cups
    preserving or granulated
    (white) sugar
250ml/8fl oz/1 cup claret

1 Wash the cranberries, if fresh, and put them in a large heavy pan with the water. Cover the pan and bring to the boil.

2 Reduce the heat under the pan and simmer for about 20 minutes, or until the cranberries are soft.

3 Pour the fruit and juices into a sterilized jelly bag suspended over a large bowl. Leave to drain for at least 3 hours or overnight, until the juices stop dripping.

4 Measure the juice and wine into the cleaned preserving pan, adding 400g/14oz/2 cups preserving or granulated sugar for every 600ml/1 pint/2½ cups liquid.

5 Heat the mixture gently, stirring occasionally, until the sugar has dissolved, then bring to the boil and boil rapidly for about 10 minutes until the jelly reaches setting point (105°C/220°F). Remove the pan from the heat.

6 Skim any scum from the surface using a slotted spoon and pour the jelly into warmed sterilized jars. Cover and seal. Store in a cool, dark place and use within 2 years. Once opened, keep in the refrigerator and eat within 3 months.

> **Cook's Tip**
> When simmering the cranberries, keep the pan covered until they stop 'popping', as they can occasionally explode and jump out of the pan.

Cranberry & Red Onion Relish

This wine-enriched relish is perfect for serving with hot roast game at a celebratory meal. It is also good served with cold meats or stirred into a beef or game casserole, for a touch of sweetness. It can be made several months in advance.

Makes about 900g/2lb
450g/1lb small red onions
30ml/2 tbsp olive oil

225g/8oz/generous 1 cup soft
    light brown sugar
450g/1lb/4 cups cranberries
120ml/4fl oz/½ cup
    red wine vinegar
120ml/4fl oz/½ cup
    red wine
15ml/1 tbsp yellow
    mustard seeds
2.5ml/½ tsp ground ginger
30ml/2 tbsp orange liqueur
    or port
salt and ground black pepper

1 Halve the red onions and slice them very thinly. Heat the oil in a large pan, add the onions and cook over a very low heat for about 15 minutes, stirring occasionally, until softened.

2 Add 30ml/2 tbsp of the sugar and cook for a further 5 minutes, or until the onions are brown and caramelized.

3 Meanwhile, put the cranberries in another pan with the remaining sugar, and add the vinegar, red wine, mustard seeds and ginger. Stir in well and heat gently, stirring constantly, until the sugar has dissolved, then cover and bring to the boil.

4 Simmer the relish for about 12–15 minutes, then add in the caramelized onions. Stir them into the mixture. Increase the heat slightly and cook the relish uncovered for a further 10 minutes, stirring the mixture frequently, until it is well reduced and nicely thickened.

5 Remove the pan from the heat, then season to taste with salt and pepper. Allow to cool completely before pouring.

6 Transfer the relish to warmed sterilized jars. Spoon a little of the orange liqueur or port over the top of each, then cover and seal. This relish can be stored for up to 6 months. Store in the refrigerator once opened and use within 1 month.

Cranberry and Claret Energy 3821kcal/16,290kJ; Protein 5.7g; Carbohydrate 967.7g, of which sugars 967.7g; Fat 0.3g, of which saturates 0g; Cholesterol 0mg; Calcium 506mg; Fibre 4.8g; Sodium 78mg.
Cranberry Relish Energy 225kcal/933kJ; Protein 1.9g; Carbohydrate 19.7g, of which sugars 16.3g; Fat 16g, of which saturates 7.5g; Cholesterol 29mg; Calcium 43mg; Fibre 2.1g; Sodium 99mg.

Gooseberry & Elderflower Jam

Pale green gooseberries
and fragrant elderflowers
make perfect partners
in this sharp, aromatic,
intensely flavoured jam.
The jam turns a pretty
but unexpected pink
colour during cooking.

Makes about 2kg/4½lb
1.3kg/3lb/12 cups firm
*   gooseberries, topped and tailed*
1.3kg/3lb/6½ cups granulated
*   (white) sugar, warmed*
juice of 1 lemon
2 handfuls of elderflowers
*   removed from their stalks*

1 Put the gooseberries into a large preserving pan, add
300ml/½ pint/1¼ cups water and bring the mixture to the boil.

2 Cover the pan with a lid and simmer gently for 20 minutes
until the fruit is soft. Using a potato masher, gently mash the
fruit to crush it lightly.

3 Add the sugar, lemon juice and elderflowers to the pan and
stir over a low heat until the sugar has dissolved.

4 Boil for 10 minutes, or to setting point (105°C/220°F).
Remove from the heat, skim off any scum and cool for
5 minutes, then stir. Pour into pots and seal, then leave to
cool before labelling.

> **Cook's Tip**
> *The time taken to reach setting point will vary depending*
> *on the ripeness of the gooseberries. The amount of pectin in*
> *gooseberries diminishes as the fruit ripens. The riper the fruit,*
> *the longer the jam will take to reach setting point.*

> **Variation**
> *Poach the gooseberries and elderflowers with a little sugar and*
> *sieve (strain) the resulting mixture to form a purée, then mix it*
> *with whipped cream to make a perfect muscat-flavoured*
> *gooseberry and elderflower fool.*

Rhubarb & Mint Jelly

This delicious jelly is very
pretty, speckled with tiny
pieces of chopped fresh
mint. It has a sharp, tangy
flavour and is fabulous
when spread on toast
or crumpets at teatime.

Makes about 2kg/4½lb
1kg/2¼ lb rhubarb
about 1.3kg/3lb/6½ cups
*   preserving or granulated*
*   (white) sugar, warmed*
large bunch fresh mint
30ml/2 tbsp finely chopped
*   fresh mint*

1 Using a sharp knife, cut the rhubarb into chunks and place
in a large, heavy pan. Pour in just enough water to cover,
cover the pan with a lid and cook until the rhubarb is soft.

2 Remove the pan from the heat and leave the stewed fruit
and juices to cool slightly before pouring into a scalded jelly
bag. Suspend the jelly bag over a non-metallic bowl and leave
to drain overnight.

3 Measure the strained juice into a preserving pan and add
450g/1lb/2¼ cups warmed sugar for each 600ml/1 pint/2½ cups
strained juice.

4 Add the bunch of mint to the pan. Bring to the boil,
stirring until the sugar has dissolved. Boil to setting point
(105°C/220°F). Remove the mint.

5 Leave to stand for 10 minutes, stir in the chopped mint,
then pour into jars and seal. Label when completely cold.
Store in a cool dark place.

> **Cook's Tips**
> • *This recipe is a good way to use up older dark red or*
> *green-stemmed rhubarb, which is usually too tough to use*
> *for desserts.*
> • *As well as serving as a delightful sweet preserve, this jelly*
> *is also very good served with fatty roast meats, such as*
> *lamb and goose.*

Gooseberry Energy 5369kcal/22,906kJ; Protein 20.8g; Carbohydrate 1397.5g, of which sugars 1397.5g; Fat 5.2g, of which saturates 0g; Cholesterol 0mg; Calcium 1053mg; Fibre 31.2g; Sodium 104mg.
Rhubarb Energy 6260kcal/26,715kJ; Protein 13.5g; Carbohydrate 1652.8g, of which sugars 1649.6g; Fat 0.8g, of which saturates 0g; Cholesterol 0mg; Calcium 1301mg; Fibre 5.1g; Sodium 115mg.

Pineapple & Passion Fruit Jelly

This exotic jelly has a wonderful warming glow to its taste and appearance. For the best-flavoured jelly, use a tart-tasting, not too ripe pineapple, rather than a very ripe, sweet one.

Makes about 900g/2lb
1 large pineapple, peeled, topped and tailed and coarsely chopped
4 passion fruit, halved, with seeds and pulp scooped out
about 900g/2lb/4½ cups preserving or granulated (white) sugar, warmed

1 Place the pineapple and the passion fruit seeds and pulp in a large pan with 900ml/1½ pints/3¾ cups water.

2 Bring the mixture to the boil, cover and simmer for 1½ hours. Remove from the heat and leave to cool slightly. Transfer the fruit to a food processor and process briefly.

3 Transfer the fruit pulp and any juices from the pan into a sterilized jelly bag suspended over a non-metallic bowl and leave to drain overnight.

4 Measure the strained juice into a preserving pan and add 450g/1lb/2¼ cups warmed sugar for every 600ml/1 pint/ 2½ cups juice.

5 Heat gently, stirring, until the sugar has dissolved. Increase the heat and boil rapidly, without stirring, for 10–15 minutes, or to setting point (105°C/220°F).

6 Remove the pan from the heat and skim off any scum using a slotted spoon. Ladle the jelly into warmed sterilized jars, cover and seal. When cool, label and store in a cool, dark place.

Cook's Tip
For the best tropical exotic flavour, choose passion fruit with dark purple, wrinkled skins. When cut in half, their heady perfume will permeate the entire room.

Piquant Pineapple Relish

Pineapples are in abundance during the winter, and here is one way of enjoying this delicious fruit. This recipe uses canned pineapples so it can be made all year, but ensure that you use fresh fruit when in season.

Serves 4
400g/14oz can crushed pineapple in natural juice
30ml/2 tbsp light muscovado (brown) sugar
30ml/2 tbsp wine vinegar
1 garlic clove, finely chopped
4 spring onions (scallions), finely chopped
2 red chillies, seeded and chopped
10 fresh basil leaves, finely shredded
salt and ground black pepper

1 Drain the canned pineapple and reserve about 60ml/4 tbsp of the juice.

2 Place the reserved juice in a small pan with the sugar and vinegar, then heat gently, stirring frequently, until all of the sugar has completely dissolved. Remove the pan from the heat and set aside to cool a little. Season with salt and ground black pepper to taste.

3 Place the drained pineapple, chopped garlic, spring onions and chillies in a medium bowl. Mix well and stir in the sugary juice. Allow to cool for about 5 minutes, then stir in the basil and serve immediately.

Cook's Tip
This fruity sweet-and-sour relish is excellent served with grilled (broiled) chicken, gammon (smoked or cured ham) or bacon.

Variation
This relish tastes extra special when made with fresh pineapple. Look out for them in your grocery store or supermarket during the winter months, when they are particularly delicious.

Pineapple Jelly Energy 3633kcal/15,504kJ; Protein 5.7g; Carbohydrate 961.6g, of which sugars 961.6g; Fat 0.5g, of which saturates 0g; Cholesterol 0mg; Calcium 515mg; Fibre 2.9g; Sodium 61mg.
Piquant Pineapple Relish Energy 83kcal/351kJ; Protein 1g; Carbohydrate 21g, of which sugars 21g; Fat 0g, of which saturates 0g; Cholesterol 0mg; Calcium 15mg; Fibre 0.8g; Sodium 101mg.

Mango Chutney

No Indian meal would be complete without this classic chutney, which is ideal for making in a slow cooker. Its gloriously sweet, tangy flavour perfectly complements the warm spices.

Makes 450g/1lb
3 firm mangoes
120ml/4fl oz/½ cup cider vinegar
200g/7oz/scant 1 cup light muscovado (brown) sugar
1 small red finger chilli or jalapeño chilli, split
2.5cm/1in piece fresh root ginger, peeled and finely chopped
1 garlic clove, finely chopped
5 cardamom pods, bruised
1 bay leaf
2.5ml/½ tsp salt

1 Peel the mangoes and cut out the stone (pit), then cut the flesh into small chunks or thin wedges.

2 Put the chopped mangoes in the ceramic cooking pot of the slow cooker. Add the cider vinegar, stir briefly to combine, and cover the slow cooker with the lid. Switch the slow cooker to the high setting and cook for about 2 hours, stirring the chutney halfway through the cooking time.

3 Stir the sugar, chilli, ginger, garlic, bruised cardamom pods, bay leaf and salt into the mango mixture, until the sugar has dissolved completely.

4 Cover and cook for 2 hours, then uncover and let the mixture cook for a further 1 hour, or until the chutney is reduced to a thick consistency and no excess liquid remains. Stir the chutney every 15 minutes during the last hour.

5 Remove and discard the bay leaf and the chilli. Spoon the chutney into hot sterilized jars and seal. Store for 1 week before eating and use within 1 year.

> **Cook's Tip**
> *To make a more fiery chutney, seed and slice two green chillies and stir into the chutney mixture with the other spices.*

Guava Jelly

Fragrant guava makes an aromatic, pale rust-coloured jelly with a soft set and a slightly sweet-sour flavour that is enhanced by lime juice. Guava jelly goes well with goat's cheese.

Makes about 900g/2lb
900g/2lb guavas
juice of 2–3 limes
about 500g/1¼ lb/2½ cups preserving or granulated (white) sugar

1 Thinly peel and halve the guavas. Using a spoon, scoop out the seeds (pips) from the centre of the fruit and discard them.

2 Place the halved guavas in a large heavy pan with 15ml/1 tbsp lime juice and 600ml/1 pint/2½ cups cold water – there should be just enough to cover the fruit. Bring the mixture to the boil, then reduce the heat, cover with a lid and simmer for about 30 minutes, or until the fruit is tender.

3 Pour the fruit and juices into a sterilized jelly bag suspended over a large bowl. Leave to drain for at least 3 hours.

4 Measure the juice into the cleaned preserving pan, adding 400g/14oz/2 cups sugar and 15ml/1 tbsp lime juice for every 600ml/1 pint/2½ cups guava juice.

5 Heat gently, stirring occasionally, until the sugar has dissolved. Boil rapidly for about 10 minutes. When the jelly reaches setting point, remove the pan from the heat.

6 Skim any scum from the surface of the jelly using a slotted spoon, then pour the jelly into sterilized jars. Cover and seal.

7 Store the jelly in a cool, dark place and consume within 1 year. Once opened, keep in the refrigerator and eat within 3 months.

> **Cook's Tip**
> *Do not be tempted to squeeze the jelly bag while the fruit juices are draining from it; this will result in a cloudy jelly.*

Mango Chutney Energy 1045kcal/4465kJ; Protein 4.1g; Carbohydrate 272.5g, of which sugars 271.1g; Fat 0.9g, of which saturates 0.5g; Cholesterol 0mg; Calcium 908mg; Fibre 11.7g; Sodium 1002mg.
Guava Jelly Energy 2090kcal/8912kJ; Protein 3.4g; Carbohydrate 552.5g, of which sugars 552.5g; Fat 0.3g, of which saturates 0g; Cholesterol 0mg; Calcium 298mg; Fibre 6.6g; Sodium 39mg.

Apple-tice

This fabulously fruity and mildly alcoholic tipple is guaranteed to appeal to everyone. Crisp, juicy apples, fresh, cooling mint and sparkling dry cider are perfect partners, and their combination can transform even the plainest juice into a distinctly exciting and fizzy blend that makes an excellent party drink.

Makes 6–8 glasses

25g/1oz/1 cup mint leaves
15g/½oz/1 tbsp caster
 (superfine) sugar
6 eating apples
ice cubes
mint sprigs
1 litre/1¾ pints/4 cups
 dry (hard) cider

1 Roughly snip the mint into a heatproof jug (pitcher). Add the sugar, then pour over 200ml/7fl oz/scant 1 cup boiling water. Stir until the sugar dissolves, then set aside to cool.

2 Chop the apples into chunks and push through a juicer.

3 Drain the mint from the syrup and discard. Mix the apple juice and syrup in a large jug and chill until ready to serve.

4 To serve, add ice cubes and mint sprigs, and top up the remainder of the jug with cider.

Cook's Tips
• Choose any variety of eating apple you like – even the dullest types juice well.
• Because you can choose how much cider you add, it is very easy to control your alcohol consumption with this drink.
• For the best taste, use mint leaves fresh from the garden.

Variation
For a non-alcoholic version, substitute sparkling mineral water or lemonade for the cider.

Vanilla & Apple Snow

While a good-quality vanilla essence is perfectly acceptable for flavouring drinks, a far more aromatic taste will be achieved using a vanilla pod. This simple apple smoothie is deliciously scented, creamy and thick, and well worth the extravagance of using a whole vanilla pod. Its lovely snowy whiteness is delightfully speckled with tiny black vanilla seeds.

Makes 3 glasses

1 vanilla pod (bean)
25g/1oz/2 tbsp caster
 (superfine) sugar
3 eating apples
300g/11oz/1⅓ cups natural
 (plain) yogurt

1 Using the tip of a sharp knife, split open the vanilla pod lengthways. Put it in a small pan with the sugar and 75ml/5 tbsp water.

2 Heat until the sugar dissolves, then boil for 1 minute.

3 Remove from the heat and leave to steep for 10 minutes.

4 Cut the apples into large chunks and push through the juicer, then pour the juice into a large bowl or jug (pitcher).

5 Lift the vanilla pod out of the pan and scrape the tiny black seeds back into the syrup. Pour into the apple juice.

6 Add the yogurt to the bowl or jug and whisk well by hand or with an electric mixer until the smoothie is thick and frothy.

7 Pour the mixture into glasses, chill and serve.

Cook's Tip
Like most smoothies, this one should ideally be served well chilled. Either use apples and yogurt straight from the refrigerator, or you can chill the smoothies briefly before serving. To make thick, icy versions, you could try making the smoothies with frozen yogurt.

Apple-tice Energy 76kcal/322kJ; Protein 0.3g; Carbohydrate 10.9g, of which sugars 10.8g; Fat 0.1g, of which saturates 0g; Cholesterol 0mg; Calcium 20mg; Fibre 1g; Sodium 11mg.
Vanilla and Apple Energy 124kcal/527kJ; Protein 5.4g; Carbohydrate 25.1g, of which sugars 25.1g; Fat 1.1g, of which saturates 0 .5g; Cholesterol 1mg; Calcium 198mg; Fibre 1.6g; Sodium 86mg.

Grape & Apple
Sweet Sharp Shock

The wonderful taste-tingling combination of sweet red grape and tart apple is quite delicious. Grapes are full of natural sugars and, when mixed with apple juice, they will create a seasonal juice that's full of exciting pep and zing. Grapes are also renowned for their healthy cleansing properties, making this an ideal addition to any detox regime. To make a longer drink, top up with sparkling mineral water.

Serves 1
150g/5oz/1¼ cups red grapes
1 green-skinned eating apple
1 small cooking apple
crushed ice

1 Slice some grapes and a sliver or two of the eating apple and set aside to use later for the decoration.

2 Chop the remainder of the eating apple and the cooking apple. Push the pieces through a juicer, followed by the grapes.

3 Pour over crushed ice, decorate with the sliced fruit and serve immediately.

Variation
If you can't find red grapes or green eating apples, then choose another coloured variety of both fruits. The colour may be different, but the taste of the drink will be just as delicious.

Cook's Tip
The simplest flavour combinations are often the most delicious. Sugary grapes together with mouth-puckeringly tart apples is one of those perfect pairings that simply cannot be beaten. The fact that the seasons for the fruits coincide in the autumn months makes this drink an absolute must at this time of year.

Apple Shiner

This refreshing fusion of sweet apple, honeydew melon, red grapes and lemon provides a reviving burst of energy and a feel-good sensation. Serve as a drink, or use to pour over muesli for a quick and healthy breakfast.

Serves 1
1 eating apple
½ honeydew melon
90g/3½ oz red grapes
15ml/1 tbsp lemon juice

1 Quarter the apple and remove the core. Cut the melon into quarters, remove the seeds and slice the flesh away from the skin.

2 Using a juice extractor, juice the apple, melon and grapes. Alternatively, process the fruit in a food processor or blender for 2–3 minutes, until smooth. Pour the juice into a long, tall glass, stir in the lemon juice and serve immediately.

Melon Pick-me-up

Spicy fresh root ginger is delicious with melon and pear in this reviving and invigorating concoction. Charentais or Galia melon can be used instead of the cantaloupe melon. Root ginger can be kept in a cool, dry place for up to a week.

Serves 1
½ cantaloupe melon
2 pears
2.5cm/1in piece of fresh root ginger

1 Quarter the cantaloupe melon, remove the seeds, and carefully slice the flesh away from the skin, reserving any juice. Quarter the pears and reserve any juice.

2 Using a juice extractor, juice the melon flesh and juice, quartered pears and juice and the fresh root ginger. Pour the juice into a tall glass and serve immediately.

Grape and Apple Energy 178kcal/763kJ; Protein 1.4g; Carbohydrate 45.4g, of which sugars 45.4g; Fat 0.4g, of which saturates 0g; Cholesterol 0mg; Calcium 30mg; Fibre 5.1g; Sodium 8mg.
Apple Shiner Energy 197kcal/842kJ; Protein 3.1g; Carbohydrate 47.8g, of which sugars 47.8g; Fat 0.7g, of which saturates 0g; Cholesterol 0mg; Calcium 79mg; Fibre 3.7g; Sodium 158mg.
Melon Pick-me-up Energy 240kcal/1017kJ; Protein 3.4g; Carbohydrate 58g, of which sugars 58g; Fat 0.8g, of which saturates 0g; Cholesterol 0mg; Calcium 98mg; Fibre 8.6g; Sodium 164mg.

Mulled Fruit Claret

This mull is a blend of claret, cider and orange juice. It can be varied to suit the occasion by increasing or decreasing the proportion of fruit juice or, to give the mull more pep, by adding up to 150ml/ ¼ pint/⅔ cup brandy.

Makes 16 × 150ml/ ¼ pints/⅔ cup glasses

1 orange
75ml/5 tbsp clear honey
30ml/2 tbsp seedless raisins
2 clementines
a few cloves
whole nutmeg
60ml/4 tbsp demerara
  (raw) sugar
2 cinnamon sticks
1½ litres/2½ pints/6¼ cups
  inexpensive claret
600ml/1 pint/2½ cups medium
  (hard) cider
300ml/½ pint/1¼ cups
  orange juice

1 With a sharp knife or a vegetable peeler, pare off a long strip of the orange rind.

2 Place the orange rind, honey and raisins in a large heavy pan. Stud the clementines all over with the cloves and add them to the pan with the fruit and honey.

3 Grate a little nutmeg into the sugar and then add it to the pan along with the cinnamon sticks. Pour on the wine and heat over low heat, stirring until the sugar has completely dissolved and the honey has melted.

4 Pour the cider and the orange juice into the pan and continue to heat the mull over low heat. Do not allow it to boil or all the alcohol will evaporate.

5 Warm a punch bowl or other large serving bowl. Remove the clementines and cinnamon sticks from the pan and strain the mull into the bowl to remove the raisins.

6 Add the clementines studded with cloves, and serve the mull hot, in warmed glasses or in glasses containing a silver spoon (to prevent the glass breaking). Using a nutmeg grater, add a little nutmeg over each serving, if you wish.

Vitality Pear Juice

The clue is in the name – this speedy juice really does put a spring in your step. Watercress has a slightly peppery flavour when eaten on its own, but blending it with pear, wheatgerm and yogurt tames the taste while boosting your morning energy levels.

Serves 4

25g/1oz watercress
1 large ripe pear
30ml/2 tbsp wheatgerm
150ml/¼ pint/⅔ cup natural
  (plain) yogurt
15ml/1 tbsp linseeds
  (flax seeds)
10ml/2 tsp lemon juice
mineral water (optional)
ice cubes

1 Roughly chop the watercress (you do not need to remove the tough stalks). Peel, core and roughly chop the pear.

2 Put the watercress and pear in a blender or food processor with the wheatgerm and blend until smooth. Scrape the mixture down from the side of the bowl, if necessary.

3 Add the yogurt, seeds and lemon juice and blend until combined. Thin with a little mineral water if too thick.

4 Put several ice cubes in the bottom of a tall glass.

5 Fill the glass to just below the brim with the Vitality Pear Juice, leaving enough room to decorate with a few sprigs of chopped watercress on top.

Variations
• For a non-dairy version of this delicious, refreshing drink, use yogurt made from goat's milk, sheep's milk or soya.
• A large apple can be used instead of the pear.
• Linseeds are a very useful addition to this juice, as they have abundant levels of omega-3 and omega-6 fatty acids, which are good for strengthening immunity and easing digestive problems. However, they are not to everyone's taste, and three walnuts could be used instead.

Vitality Pear Energy 287kcal/1207kJ; Protein 17.8g; Carbohydrate 39.8g, of which sugars 31.2g; Fat 7.6g, of which saturates 1.6g; Cholesterol 2mg; Calcium 394mg; Fibre 8.8g; Sodium 144mg.
Mulled Fruit Claret Energy 174kcal/728kJ; Protein 0.2g; Carbohydrate 16.3g, of which sugars 16.3g; Fat 0g, of which saturates 0g; Cholesterol 0mg; Calcium 16mg; Fibre 0g; Sodium 11mg.

Pink & Perky Grapefruit Juice

This deliciously refreshing, rose-tinged blend of grapefruit and pear juice will keep you bright-eyed and bushy-tailed. It's perfect for a quick breakfast drink or as a pick-me-up later in the day when energy levels are flagging. If the grapefruit is particularly tart, serve with a little bowl of brown sugar to sweeten, or use brown sugar stirrers.

Serves 2
1 pink and 1 white grapefruit, halved
2 ripe pears
ice cubes

1 Take a thin slice from one grapefruit half and cut a few thin slices of pear.

2 Roughly chop the remaining pear and push through a juicer.

3 Squeeze all the juice from the grapefruit halves. Mix the fruit juices together and serve over ice.

4 Decorate the finished drink with the previously prepared thin slices of grapefruit and pear.

Variation
You can use tart, ripe eating apples instead of pears.

Cook's Tip
Pears are a popular fruit throughout the autumn months. Unlike most fruit, pears improve in texture and flavour after they have been plucked from the tree. This means they can be picked and transported while still hard, preventing damage to the easily bruised fruit. Ripe pears are juicy and, depending on the variety, can range in flavour from spicy to sweet to tart-sweet. When buying, choose specimens that are fragrant and free of any blemishes. Store pears at room temperature until they are ripe, but refrigerate any ripe fruit.

Sparkling Peach Melba

Serve this delightfully fresh and fruity drink during the summer months, when raspberries and peaches are at their sweetest and best. Traditional cream soda gives the drink a really smooth flavour and a lovely fizz, while the optional shot of Drambuie or brandy gives it a definite kick. Serve with long spoons for scooping up any fruit left in the glasses.

Serves 2
300g/11oz/scant 2 cups raspberries
2 large ripe peaches
30ml/2 tbsp Drambuie or brandy (optional)
15ml/1 tbsp icing (confectioners') sugar
cream soda, to serve

1 Pack a few raspberries into six tiny shot glasses, or into six sections of an ice cube tray, and pour over water to cover. Freeze for several hours.

2 Using a small, sharp knife, halve and stone (pit) the peaches and cut one half into thin slices. Reserve 115g/4oz/⅔ cup of the raspberries and divide the rest, along with the peach slices, between two tall stemmed glasses. Drizzle with the Drambuie or brandy, if using.

3 Push the reserved raspberries and the remaining peach flesh through the juicer. Stir the icing sugar into the juice and pour the juice over the fruits.

4 Turn the raspberry-filled ice cubes out of the shot glasses or ice cube tray and add three to each glass. Top up with cream soda and serve immediately.

Cook's Tip
If using shot glasses, dip these into a bowl of warm water for a few seconds to loosen the blocks of frozen raspberries. If using ice cube trays, turn these upside down and hold under warm running water for a few seconds. The ice cubes should then pop out easily.

Pink and Perky Energy 216kcal/910kJ; Protein 3.5g; Carbohydrate 51.8g, of which sugars 51.8g; Fat 0.6g, of which saturates 0g; Cholesterol 0mg; Calcium 107mg; Fibre 10.8g; Sodium 19mg.
Sparkling Peach Melba Energy 100kcal/432kJ; Protein 3.2g; Carbohydrate 22.4g, of which sugars 22.4g; Fat 0.6g, of which saturates 0.2g; Cholesterol 0mg; Calcium 49mg; Fibre 5.3g; Sodium 6mg.

Festive Fruit Liqueurs

These may be made with
a variety of fruits and
spirits. Allow to mature
for 3 months.

**Makes 900ml/1½ pints/
3¾ cups of each liqueur**

For the plum brandy
450g/1lb plums
225g/8oz/1 cup demerara
   (raw) sugar
600ml/1 pint/2½ cups brandy

For the fruit gin
450g/1lb/3 cups raspberries,
   blackcurrants or sloes
350g/12oz/1½ cups sugar
750ml/1¼ pints/3 cups gin

For the citrus whisky
1 large orange
1 small lemon
1 lime
225g/8oz/1 cup sugar
600ml/1 pint/2½ cups
   whisky

1 Sterilize three jars and lids. Wash and halve the plums,
remove the stones (pits) and slice. Place the plums in the
sterilized jar with the sugar and brandy. Crack three of the plum
stones, remove the kernels and chop. Add to the jar and stir in.

2 Place the raspberries, blackcurrants or sloes into the prepared
jar. If using sloes, prick the surface of the berries to extract the
flavour. Add the sugar and gin and stir until well blended.

3 To make the citrus whisky, first scrub the fruit. Using a sharp
knife or vegetable peeler, pare the rind from the fruit, taking
care not to include the white pith. Squeeze out all of the juice
and place in the jar with the fruit rinds. Add the sugar and
whisky, and stir until well blended.

4 Cover the three jars with lids or double-thickness pieces
of plastic tied down. Store in a cool, dark place for 3 months.

5 Shake the Fruit Gin daily for 1 month, and then occasionally.
Shake the Plum Brandy and Citrus Whisky daily for 2 weeks,
then occasionally. Sterilize the bottles and corks or stoppers.

6 When each liqueur is ready to be bottled, strain the liquid,
then pour it into sterilized bottles through a funnel fitted with
a filter paper. Fit the corks or stoppers and label the bottles.

Cherry Berry Trio

Strawberries and grapes
cleanse the system.

Makes 2 large glasses
200g/7oz/1¾ cups strawberries

250g/9oz/2¼ cups red grapes
150g/5oz/1¼ cups red cherries,
   pitted
ice cubes

1 Halve two or three strawberries and grapes and set aside
with a few perfect cherries for decoration. Cut up any large
strawberries, then push through a juicer with the remaining
grapes and cherries. Pour into glasses, top with the halved
fruits, cherries and ice cubes, and serve immediately. For a fun
decoration, skewer a halved strawberry or grape on a cocktail
stick (toothpick) and hang a cherry by its stem.

Cherry Berry Mull

The orange liqueur and
spices add a wonderfully
feisty kick to this drink.

Makes 8 small glasses
2 cinnamon sticks, halved
15ml/1 tbsp whole cloves
15g/½oz/1 tbsp golden caster
   (superfine) sugar
300g/11oz/2¾ cups strawberries

150g/5oz/scant 1 cup raspberries
200g/7oz/scant 1 cup cherries,
   pitted
150g/5oz/1¼ cups redcurrants
60ml/4 tbsp Cointreau or other
   orange-flavoured liqueur
thinly sliced strawberries and
   raspberries, to decorate
extra cinnamon sticks,
   for stirrers

1 Put the cinnamon sticks in a small pan with the cloves, sugar
and 150ml/¼ pint/⅔ cup water. Heat gently until the sugar
dissolves, then bring to the boil. Remove from the heat and
leave to cool.

2 Push the strawberries, raspberries, cherries and redcurrants
through a juicer and pour the juice into a large jug (pitcher).
Strain the cooled syrup through a sieve (strainer) into the fruit
juice, then stir in the liqueur. Add plenty of sliced fruits. Chill
until needed. Serve in small glasses, with cinnamon stirrers.

Simply Strawberry

Nothing evokes a sense of wellbeing more than the scent and flavour of sweet, juicy strawberries. By late spring, local berries should be appearing in the stores, so buy them while you can.

Serves 2
400g/14oz/3½ cups strawberries, plus extra to decorate

30–45ml/2–3 tbsp icing (confectioners') sugar
200g/7oz/scant 1 cup Greek (US strained plain) yogurt
60ml/4 tbsp single (light) cream

1 Hull the strawberries and place them in a blender or food processor with 30ml/2 tbsp of the icing sugar.

2 Blend to a smooth purée, scraping the mixture down from the side of the bowl with a rubber spatula, if necessary.

3 Add the yogurt and cream and blend again until smooth and frothy.

4 Check the sweetness, adding a little more sugar if you find the flavour too sharp. Pour into glasses and serve decorated with extra strawberries.

Cook's Tip
This recipe uses an abundance of fragrant strawberries so, if possible, make it when the season is right and local fruits are at their most plentiful.

Variation
You can replace the strawberries with other fruits, if you wish. Try using raspberries or fresh bananas to make other very popular milkshakes.

Strawberry & Banana Smoothie

The blend of perfectly ripe bananas and strawberries creates a drink that is both fruity and creamy, with a luscious texture. Papaya, mango or pineapple can be used instead of strawberries for a tropical drink. Popular with adults and children alike, this is a great way to get children to enjoy fruit – it is much healthier than commercial milkshakes, too.

Serves 4
200g/7oz/1¾ cups strawberries, plus extra, sliced, to decorate
2 ripe bananas
300ml/½ pint/1¼ cups skimmed milk
10 ice cubes

1 Hull the strawberries. Peel the bananas and chop them into fairly large chunks.

2 Place the fruit in a food processor or blender. Process to a thick, coarse purée, scraping down the sides of the goblet as necessary.

3 Add the skimmed milk and ice cubes, crushing the ice first unless you have a heavy-duty processor. Process until smooth and thick. Pour into tall glasses and top each with strawberry slices to decorate. Serve immediately.

Cook's Tip
For a super-chilled version, use frozen strawberries or a combination of frozen summer berries, such as raspberries, redcurrants and blueberries, instead of fresh. You may need to blend the strawberries and milk slightly longer in order to achieve a really smooth result.

Variation
For a rich and velvety drink, add 120ml/4fl oz/½ cup coconut milk and process as above. Reduce the volume of milk to 175ml/6fl oz/¾ cup.

Simply Strawberry Energy 286kcal/1195kJ; Protein 9.1g; Carbohydrate 30.4g, of which sugars 30.4g; Fat 16.2g, of which saturates 8.9g; Cholesterol 17mg; Calcium 217mg; Fibre 2.2g; Sodium 93mg.
Strawberry and Banana Energy 165kcal/695kJ; Protein 8.4g; Carbohydrate 30.2g, of which sugars 23.6g; Fat 2.1g, of which saturates 0.7g; Cholesterol 2mg; Calcium 255mg; Fibre 1.8g; Sodium 111mg.

Breakfast Fruit in a Glass

This energizing blend
is simply bursting with
goodness and healthy
ingredients – just what you
need when you wake up.

Serves 2
250g/9oz firm tofu
200g/7oz/1¾ cups strawberries

45ml/3 tbsp pumpkin or
    sunflower seeds, plus extra
    for sprinkling
30–45ml/2–3 tbsp clear honey
juice of 2 large oranges
juice of 1 lemon

1 Roughly chop the tofu, then hull and roughly chop the strawberries. Reserve a few strawberry chunks.

2 Put all the ingredients in a blender or food processor and blend until completely smooth, scraping the mixture down from the side of the bowl, if necessary. Pour into tumblers and sprinkle with extra seeds and strawberry chunks.

Apricot & Muesli Smoothie

This divinely smooth drink
has all the goodness of
a nutritious and filling
fruity breakfast muesli, but
none of the lumpy bits.

Serves 2
50g/2oz/¼ cup ready-to-eat
    dried apricots

1 piece preserved stem ginger,
    plus 30ml/2 tbsp syrup from
    the ginger jar
40g/1½oz/scant ½ cup natural
    muesli (granola)
about 200ml/7fl oz/scant 1 cup
    semi-skimmed (low-fat) milk

1 Using a sharp knife, chop the dried apricots into slices or chunks. Chop the preserved ginger.

2 Put the apricots and ginger in a blender or food processor and add the syrup from the ginger jar with the muesli and milk. Process until smooth, adding more milk if necessary, to make a creamy drink. Serve in wide glasses.

Red Defender Fruit Smoothie

Boost your body's defences
with this delicious blend of
red fruits. Watermelon and
strawberries are a good
source of vitamin C, and
the black watermelon seeds,
like all other seeds, are
rich in essential nutrients.
If you really do not like the
idea of blending the seeds,
remove them first.

Serves 2
200g/7oz/1¾ cups strawberries
a small bunch of red grapes,
    about 90g/3½oz
1 small wedge of watermelon

1 Hull the strawberries. Cut any berries in half if they are particularly large.

2 Pull the red grapes from their stalks. Cut away the skin from the watermelon using a knife or a vegetable peeler and chop into a few pieces.

3 Put the watermelon in a blender or food processor and blend until the seeds are broken up.

4 Add the strawberries and grapes and blend the mixture until completely smooth, scraping the mixture down from the side of the bowl, if necessary. Serve in tall glasses.

Variations
• Try this drink with other red summer fruits, such as raspberries or redcurrants.
• Use green grapes, if you prefer, although the colour of the drink won't be quite as dramatic.

Cook's Tip
Decorate this juice with chunks of watermelon or strawberry halves, if you like.

Breakfast Fruit Energy 259kcal/1087kJ; Protein 13.3g; Carbohydrate 30.4g, of which sugars 28.2g; Fat 10.2g, of which saturates 1.1g; Cholesterol 0mg; Calcium 671mg; Fibre 1.8g; Sodium 19mg.
Apricot and Muesli Energy 204kcal/865kJ; Protein 6.6g; Carbohydrate 39.1g, of which sugars 28.8g; Fat 3.4g, of which saturates 1.4g; Cholesterol 6mg; Calcium 150mg; Fibre 3.1g; Sodium 97mg.
Red Defender Energy 85kcal/362kJ; Protein 1.5g; Carbohydrate 20.1g, of which sugars 20.1g; Fat 0.5g, of which saturates 0.1g; Cholesterol 0mg; Calcium 29mg; Fibre 1.5g; Sodium 9mg.

Raspberry & Oatmeal Smoothie

Just a spoonful or so of oatmeal gives substance to this tangy, invigorating drink. It is a sensuously smooth way to enjoy wholesome oats for breakfast.

Makes 1 large glass
22.5ml/1½ tbsp medium oatmeal
150g/5oz/scant 1 cup raspberries
5–10ml/1–2 tsp clear honey
45ml/3 tbsp natural (plain) yogurt
extra raspberries, to decorate

1 Spoon the oatmeal into a heatproof bowl. Pour in 120ml/4fl oz/½ cup boiling water and leave to stand for 10 minutes.

2 Put the soaked oats in a food processor or blender and add the raspberries, honey and about 30ml/2 tbsp of the yogurt. Whizz until smooth and creamy.

3 Pour the raspberry and oatmeal smoothie into a large glass, swirl in the remaining yogurt and top with a few extra raspberries.

4 If you don't like raspberry pips (seeds), press the fruit through a sieve (strainer) to make a smooth purée, then process with the oatmeal and yogurt as before. Alternatively, try making the smoothie with redcurrants.

Berried Treasure

Cranberries and raspberries make a colourful juice classic. This recipe uses raspberry conserve to add sweetness, in place of the more usual sugar or honey.

Makes 2 tall glasses
250g/9oz/1¼ cups raspberries
45ml/3 tbsp raspberry conserve
250g/9oz/1½ cups cranberries
soda water (club soda) or
*   sparkling mineral water*

1 Push all the raspberries through a juicer, then do the same with the raspberry conserve and cranberries.

2 Pour the juice into tall glasses and top up with soda water or sparkling mineral water, and serve immediately.

Purple Haze Blueberry Smoothie

Thick, dark blueberry purée swirled into pale and creamy vanilla-flavoured buttermilk looks stunning and also tastes simply divine. Despite its creaminess, the buttermilk gives this sumptuous smoothie a delicious sharp tang. If you do not like buttermilk or cannot find it in your local supermarket, you could use a mixture of half natural yogurt and half milk instead.

Serves 2
250g/9oz/2¼ cups blueberries
50g/2oz/¼ cup caster
*   (superfine) sugar*
15ml/1 tbsp lemon juice
300ml/½ pint/1¼ cups
*   buttermilk*
5ml/1 tsp vanilla extract
150ml/¼ pint/⅔ cup full cream
*   (whole) milk*

1 Push the blueberries through a juicer and stir in 15ml/1 tbsp of the sugar and the lemon juice.

2 Stir the blueberry mixture well and divide it between two tall glasses.

3 Put the buttermilk, vanilla extract, milk and remaining sugar in a blender or food processor and blend until really frothy. (Alternatively, use a hand-held electric blender and blend until the mixture froths up.)

4 Pour the buttermilk mixture over the blueberry juice so the mixtures swirl together naturally – there is no need to stir them together, as it tastes and looks better if they remain separate to a certain degree. Serve immediately.

> **Cook's Tip**
> *The deep violet blueberry juice in this drink makes a fantastic contrast in both colour and flavour to the buttermilk. If you cannot get hold of blueberries, other slightly tart summer fruits, such as raspberries or blackberries, would also work in this creamy combination.*

Raspberry and Oatmeal Energy 186kcal/793kJ; Protein 7.5g; Carbohydrate 34.6g, of which sugars 16.4g; Fat 3.1g, of which saturates 0.4g; Cholesterol 1mg; Calcium 137mg; Fibre 5.4g; Sodium 51mg.
Berried Treasure Energy 134kcal/576kJ; Protein 2.3g; Carbohydrate 32.4g, of which sugars 32.4g; Fat 0.5g, of which saturates 0.2g; Cholesterol 0mg; Calcium 39mg; Fibre 5.2g; Sodium 13mg.
Purple Haze Energy 274kcal/1157kJ; Protein 9.1g; Carbohydrate 54.2g, of which sugars 49.2g; Fat 3.9g, of which saturates 2.4g; Cholesterol 13mg; Calcium 283mg; Fibre 2.5g; Sodium 99mg.

Very Berry

Tiny crimson redcurrants, glistening like exquisite jewels, make the perfect partner for dark red dried cranberries in this refreshingly tart and sparkling shake. This pretty drink is also the most fantastically tasty dairy-free shake. A low-fat blend, it is packed with natural sugars, essential nutrients and valuable vitamins that are sure to give your system a hard-to-beat boost.

Makes 2 large glasses

25g/1oz/¼ cup dried cranberries
150g/5oz/1¼ cups redcurrants, plus extra to decorate
10ml/2 tsp clear honey
50ml/2fl oz/¼ cup soya milk sparkling mineral water

1 Put the cranberries in a small bowl, pour over 90ml/6 tbsp boiling water and leave to stand for 10 minutes.

2 String the redcurrants by drawing the stems through the tines of a fork to pull off the delicate currants.

3 Put the currants in a food processor or blender with the cranberries and soaking water. Blend well until smooth.

4 Add the clear honey and soya milk to the food processor and whizz briefly to combine.

5 Pour the shake into a large glass. Top with a little sparkling mineral water and drape some redcurrants decoratively over the edge of the glass. Serve immediately.

> **Cook's Tips**
> • Fresh and frozen cranberries are often in short supply, but dried berries are available all year round.
> • If your clear honey has become cloudy during storage, stand the jar in a bowl of very hot water for 15 minutes.

Cranberry & Spice Spritzer

Partially freezing fruit juice gives this drink a refreshingly slushy texture. The fruity combination of cranberry and apple juice is tart and clean. You could add a few fresh or frozen cranberries to decorate each glass.

Serves 4

600ml/1 pint/2½ cups chilled cranberry juice
150ml/¼ pint/⅔ cup clear apple juice
4 cinnamon sticks
about 400ml/14fl oz/1⅔ cups chilled ginger ale

1 Pour the cranberry juice into a shallow freezerproof container and freeze for about 2 hours, or until a thick layer of ice crystals has formed around the edges. Mash the semi-frozen juice with a fork, then return the mixture to the freezer for 2–3 hours, until almost solid.

2 Pour the apple juice into a small pan, add two cinnamon sticks and bring to just below boiling point. Pour into a jug (pitcher) and leave to cool, then remove the cinnamon sticks and set them aside. Cool, then chill the juice.

3 Spoon the cranberry ice into a food processor or blender. Add the cinnamon-flavoured apple juice and process briefly until slushy. Pile the mixture into cocktail glasses, top up with chilled ginger ale, decorate with cinnamon sticks and serve.

Citrus Sparkle

Pink grapefruit have a sweeter flavour than the yellow varieties – in fact, the pinker they are, the sweeter they are likely to be.

Serves 1

1 pink grapefruit
1 orange
30ml/2 tbsp freshly squeezed lemon juice

1 Cut the pink grapefruit and orange in half and squeeze out the juice using a citrus fruit squeezer. Pour the juice into a glass, stir in 15ml/1 tbsp lemon juice, add the remaining lemon juice, if required, and serve.

Very Berry Energy 126kcal/539kJ; Protein 3.8g; Carbohydrate 27.1g, of which sugars 27.1g; Fat 1g, of which saturates 0.1g; Cholesterol 0mg; Calcium 115mg; Fibre 7g; Sodium 25mg.
Cranberry and Spice Energy 86kcal/370kJ; Protein 0.2g; Carbohydrate 22.5g, of which sugars 22.5g; Fat 0.2g, of which saturates 0g; Cholesterol 0mg; Calcium 13mg; Fibre 0g; Sodium 4mg.
Citrus Sparkle Energy 92kcal/391kJ; Protein 2.6g; Carbohydrate 21.1g, of which sugars 21.1g; Fat 0.3g, of which saturates 0g; Cholesterol 0mg; Calcium 93mg; Fibre 4.1g; Sodium 11mg.

Fruity Christmas Spirit

This colourful festive drink has a sharp but sweet taste. It is excellent served as a winter warmer or after a Christmas meal, but it also makes a good summer drink served with crushed ice.

Makes 750g/1¼ pints/3 cups
450g/1lb/2 cups cranberries
2 clementines
450g/1lb/2 cups sugar
1 cinnamon stick
475ml/16fl oz/2 cups vodka

1 Crush the cranberries in a food processor or blender and spoon the purée into a large sterilized jar. Pare the rind from the clementines and add to jar.

2 Squeeze the juice from the clementines and add to the cranberries and pared rind in the jar.

3 Add the sugar, cinnamon stick and vodka to the jar and seal with the lid or a double thickness of plastic, and tie down securely. Shake the jar well to combine all the ingredients.

4 Store the jar in a cool place for 1 month, shaking the jar on a daily basis for 2 weeks, then occasionally.

5 When the drink has matured, sterilize some small decorative bottles and, using a funnel with a filter paper inside, strain the liquid into the bottles and cork immediately. Label the bottles clearly and tie a gift tag around the neck.

Cook's Tip
Sterilize the bottles you are using with a campden tablet, available from wine-making suppliers, dissolved in boiling water.

Variation
Other fruits can be used in this recipe. Try other berries such as raspberries, blackcurrants or blackberries in place of the cranberries, and a lemon or a lime in place of the clementines.

Cranberry Frost

This non-alcoholic cocktail with the colour of holly berries will delight younger and older guests alike at Christmas time. It is the perfect 'one-for-the-road' drink to serve at the end of a festive gathering.

Serves 10
115g/4oz/generous ½ cup caster (superfine) sugar
juice of 2 oranges
still water, enough to dissolve the sugar
120ml/4fl oz/½ cup fresh cranberry juice
1 litre/1¾ pints/4 cups sparkling mineral water
45ml/3 tbsp fresh cranberries, to decorate
handful fresh mint sprigs, to decorate

1 Put the caster sugar, orange juice and still water into a small pan and stir the mixture over a low heat until the sugar has completely dissolved.

2 Bring the mixture to the boil and boil vigorously for about 3 minutes. Set aside to cool.

3 Pour the syrup into a chilled serving bowl, pour on the cranberry juice and mix well to combine.

4 To serve, pour on the mineral water and decorate with cranberries and mint leaves.

Cook's Tip
This is a great drink to make during the festivities because the syrup can be made in advance and stored in a covered container in the refrigerator.

Variation
To make this fabulous non-alcoholic drink the very essence of festive colour, chill with ice cubes made by freezing fresh red cranberries and tiny mint leaves in the water.

Fruity Christmas Energy 2968kcal/12544kJ; Protein 4.1g; Carbohydrate 519.1g, of which sugars 519.1g; Fat 0.6g, of which saturates 0g; Cholesterol 0mg; Calcium 267mg; Fibre 7.3g; Sodium 46mg.
Cranberry Frost Energy 56kcal/237kJ; Protein 0.1g; Carbohydrate 14.6g, of which sugars 14.6g; Fat 0g, of which saturates 0g; Cholesterol 0mg; Calcium 8mg; Fibre 0.1g; Sodium 2mg.

Berry & Grape Juice

Blackcurrants are not only an excellent source of betacarotene and vitamin C, but they are also rich in flavonoids, which help to cleanse the system. Mixed with other dark red fruits, such as blackberries and grapes, they make a highly nutritious and extremely delicious blend that can be refrigerated and enjoyed throughout the day.

Serves 1
*90g/3½ oz/scant 1 cup
    blackcurrants or blackberries
150g/5oz red grapes
130g/4½ oz/generous 1 cup
    blueberries*

1 If you are using blackcurrants, gently pull the stalks through the tines of a fork to remove the fruit.

2 Next, remove the stalks from the grapes.

3 Push all the fruits through a juicer, saving a few for decoration.

4 Place some ice in a medium glass and pour over the juice. Decorate with the reserved fruit and serve.

Hum-zinger Tropical Fruit Drink

Aromatic tropical fruits make a beautifully bright yellow drink that is bursting with both flavour and energy. Enjoy a glass first thing in the morning to kick-start your day.

Serves 1
*½ pineapple, peeled
1 small mango, peeled and
    stoned (pitted)
½ small papaya, seeded
    and peeled*

1 Remove any 'eyes' left in the pineapple, then cut all the fruit into fairly coarse chunks.

2 Using a juice extractor, juice the fruit. Alternatively, use a food processor or blender and process for about 2–3 minutes until smooth. Pour into a glass and serve immediately.

Fruity Sweet Dream

A soothing blend guaranteed to wake you up slowly, this fruity threesome has a naturally sweet taste, so there is no need for any additional sugar. Fresh grapefruit juice marries brilliantly with the dried fruits, and rich creamy yogurt makes a delicious contrast of colour and flavour – simply perfect to sip over a leisurely breakfast while reading the newspaper.

Serves 2
*25g/1oz/scant ¼ cup
    dried figs or dates,
    stoned (pitted)
50g/2oz/¼ cup
    ready-to-eat prunes
25g/1oz/scant ¼ cup sultanas
    (golden raisins)
1 grapefruit
350ml/12fl oz/1½ cups
    full cream (whole) milk
30ml/2 tbsp Greek (US strained
    plain) yogurt*

1 Put the dried fruits in a blender or food processor. Squeeze out the grapefruit juice and add to the machine. Blend until smooth, scraping the mixture down from the side of the bowl, if necessary.

2 Pour the milk into the blender or processor. Blend the mixture until it is completely smooth, scraping down the sides as before.

3 Using a teaspoon, tap a spoonful of the yogurt around the inside of each of two tall glasses so that it runs up in a spiral pattern – don't worry if it isn't too neat. Pour in the fruit mixture and serve immediately.

> **Variations**
> • *To make a dairy-free version of this drink, omit the Greek (US strained plain) yogurt and use soya or rice milk instead of ordinary milk. The consistency of the smoothie will not be as creamy, but it will still be delicious – and perhaps better for those who prefer a lighter drink in the morning. It will also be drinkable by those on a dairy-free diet.*
> • *Other dried fruits can be used as well – try raisins, currants, or ready-to-eat dried apricots.*

Berry and Grape Energy 189kcal/805kJ; Protein 2.7g; Carbohydrate 47.2g, of which sugars 42g; Fat 0.2g, of which saturates 0g; Cholesterol 0mg; Calcium 74mg; Fibre 6.9g; Sodium 6mg.
Hum-zinger Energy 322kcal/1378kJ; Protein 3.7g; Carbohydrate 79.1g, of which sugars 78.7g; Fat 1.3g, of which saturates 0.1g; Cholesterol 0mg; Calcium 136mg; Fibre 13.1g; Sodium 21mg.
Fruity Sweet Energy 246kcal/1033kJ; Protein 8.6g; Carbohydrate 38.3g, of which sugars 38.3g; Fat 7.4g, of which saturates 4.5g; Cholesterol 25mg; Calcium 301mg; Fibre 3.7g; Sodium 103mg.

Banana & Maple Flip

This satisfying drink is packed with so much goodness that it makes a complete breakfast in a glass – great for when you're in a hurry. Be sure to use a really fresh free-range egg. The glass can be adorned with a decorative slice of orange or lime, to serve.

Serves 1
1 small banana, peeled and halved
50ml/2fl oz/¼ cup thick Greek (US strained plain) yogurt
1 egg
30ml/2 tbsp maple syrup

1 Put the peeled and halved banana, thick Greek yogurt, egg and maple syrup in a food processor or blender. Add 30ml/2 tbsp chilled water.

2 Process the ingredients constantly for about 2 minutes, or until the mixture turns a really pale, creamy colour and has a nice frothy texture.

3 Pour the banana and maple flip into a tall, chilled glass and serve immediately. Decorate the glass with an orange or lime slice, if you like.

> **Cook's Tips**
> • To chill the drinking glass quickly, place it in the freezer while you are preparing the drink.
> • If you don't have a heavy-duty food processor or blender, crush the ice before adding it.

> **Variations**
> • For a more exotic tropical fruit flavour, substitute a small, very ripe peeled and stoned mango for the banana.
> • For a hint of sharpness, add 5ml/1 tsp lemon or lime juice, or use a slightly tangy yogurt.
> • Use a fat-free natural (plain) yogurt for a low-fat version.

Thick Banana Smoothie with Rich Chocolate Sauce

The secret of a really good smoothie is to serve it ice cold, and whizzing all the ingredients up in a blender full of ice is the perfect way to ensure this. Keep an ice tray of frozen orange juice at the ready in your freezer for drinks like these.

Serves 2
3 ripe bananas
200ml/7fl oz/scant 1 cup natural (plain) yogurt
30ml/2 tbsp mild honey

350ml/12fl oz/1½ cups orange juice ice cubes, crushed

For the sauce
175g/6oz plain (semisweet) chocolate with more than 60% cocoa solids
60ml/4 tbsp water
15ml/1 tbsp golden (light corn) syrup
15g/½oz/1 tbsp butter

1 Peel and chop the bananas, put them in a bowl, then mash them with a fork.

2 For the sauce, break up the chocolate and put into a bowl over a pan of barely simmering water. Leave undisturbed for 10 minutes until the chocolate has melted, then add the water, syrup and butter and stir until smooth.

3 Place the mashed bananas, yogurt, honey and orange ice cubes in a blender or food processor and blend until smooth, operating the machine in short bursts or pulsing for best results.

4 Pour into large, tall glasses, then pour in some chocolate sauce from a height. The sauce will swirl around the glasses to give a marbled effect. Serve with long-handled spoons.

> **Cook's Tip**
> Pouring chocolate sauce like this cools it slightly on the way down, so that it thickens on contact with the cold smoothie.

Banana and Maple Energy 296kcal/1248kJ; Protein 10.5g; Carbohydrate 43.3g, of which sugars 41.4g; Fat 10.9g, of which saturates 4.2g; Cholesterol 190mg; Calcium 113mg; Fibre 0.9g; Sodium 187mg.
Thick Banana Energy 901kcal/3790kJ; Protein 13.2g; Carbohydrate 148.1g, of which sugars 142.2g; Fat 32.5g, of which saturates 19.4g; Cholesterol 23mg; Calcium 253mg; Fibre 4.9g; Sodium 176mg.

Kiwi & Stem Ginger Spritzer

The delicate, refreshingly tangy flavour of kiwi fruit becomes sweeter and more intense when the flesh is juiced. Choose plump, unwrinkled fruits that give a little when gently pressed, as under-ripe fruits will produce a slightly bitter taste. A single kiwi fruit contains more than the recommended daily intake of vitamin C, so this juice will boost the system.

Serves 1

2 kiwi fruit
1 piece preserved stem ginger, plus 15ml/1 tbsp syrup from the ginger jar
sparkling mineral water

1 Using a sharp knife, roughly chop the kiwi fruit and the piece of preserved stem ginger. (For a better colour, you may wish to peel the kiwi fruit before chopping, but this is not essential.)

2 Push the pieces of stem ginger and kiwi fruit through a juicer and pour the juice into a large jug (pitcher). Add the ginger syrup and stir to combine.

3 Pour the juice into a tall glass, then top up with plenty of sparkling mineral water and serve immediately.

Variation
If you prefer, you can use still mineral water for this smoothie rather than the sparkling variety, although the added fizz makes the drink more refreshing.

Cook's Tip
Kiwis are a subtropical fruit, not a tropical one, so it is best to store them in the refrigerator before using. If you want them to ripen quickly, store in a closed plastic bag together with an apple, pear or banana.

Tropical Fruit Shake

Sweet, fruity and packed with vitamin C, this is a brilliant way to get children to enjoy healthy drinks. If you use really ripe fruit, it shouldn't need any additional sweetening, but taste it to check before serving. Mango makes a thick purée when blended, so top it up with mineral water – or try a good-quality lemonade instead.

Makes 2 glasses

1/2 small pineapple
small bunch seedless white grapes
1 mango
mineral water or lemonade (optional)

1 Using a sharp knife, cut away the skin from the pineapple and halve the fruit. Discard the core and roughly chop the flesh of one half.

2 Add to a blender or food processor with the grapes.

3 Halve the mango either side of the flat stone (pit). Scoop the flesh into the blender.

4 Process thoroughly until really smooth, scraping the mixture down from the side of the bowl, if necessary.

5 Pour into glasses and top up with mineral water or lemonade, if using. Serve immediately.

Cook's Tip
If making this drink for really fussy children, you might want to strain the mixture first. To do this, push it through a fine sieve (strainer), pressing the pulp in the sieve with the back of a spoon to extract as much juice as possible. Follow the recipe as normal, topping up the glasses with mineral water, or lemonade if your children prefer it. To make a novelty decoration, thread pieces of fruit on to straws before you serve the shake.

Kiwi and Stem Ginger Energy 104kcal/439kJ; Protein 1.4g; Carbohydrate 24.6g, of which sugars 24.2g; Fat 0.6g, of which saturates 0g; Cholesterol 0mg; Calcium 32mg; Fibre 2.3g; Sodium 45mg.
Tropical Fruit Energy 129kcal/553kJ; Protein 1.3g; Carbohydrate 32.3g, of which sugars 32g; Fat 0.4g, of which saturates 0.1g; Cholesterol 0mg; Calcium 37mg; Fibre 3.7g; Sodium 5mg.

Pineapple & Rum Crush with Coconut

This thick and slushy tropical cooler is unbelievably rich, thanks to the combination of coconut milk and thick cream. The addition of sweet, juicy, slightly tart pineapple and finely crushed ice offers a refreshing foil, making it all too easy to sip your way through several glasses at a Christmas party.

Serves 4–5
1 pineapple
30ml/2 tbsp lemon juice
200ml/7fl oz/scant 1 cup coconut milk
150ml/¼ pint/⅔ cup double (heavy) cream
200ml/7fl oz/scant 1 cup white rum
30–60ml/2–4 tbsp caster (superfine) sugar
500g/1¼lb finely crushed ice

1 Trim off the ends from the pineapple, then cut off the skin. Cut away the core and chop the flesh. Put the chopped flesh in a blender or food processor with the lemon juice and whizz until very smooth.

2 Add the coconut milk, cream, rum and 30ml/2 tbsp of the sugar. Blend until thoroughly combined, then taste and add more sugar if necessary.

3 Pack the crushed ice into serving glasses and pour the drink over. Serve immediately.

Cook's Tip
This is a great cocktail for making ahead of time. Blend the drink in advance and chill in a jug (pitcher). Store the crushed ice in the freezer, ready for serving as soon as it is required.

Variation
If you prefer, you can use a dark rum or even a spiced rum, such as that made by Morgans, instead of the white rum.

Tropical Fruit Royale

Based on the Kir Royale – a blend of Champagne and crème de cassis – this elegant cocktail is made with tropical fruits and sparkling wine. Delight your guests with this appetizing drink on a balmy summer evening, for a taste of the tropics.

Serves 6
2 large mangoes
6 passion fruit
sparkling wine

1 Peel the mangoes, cut the flesh off the stone (pit), then put the flesh in a food processor or blender. Process until smooth, scraping the mixture down from the sides of the bowl.

2 Fill an ice cube tray with a good half of the mango purée and freeze for 2 hours until solid.

3 Cut six wedges from one or two of the passion fruits and scoop the pulp from the rest into the remaining mango purée. Process until well blended.

4 Spoon the mixture into six stemmed glasses. Divide the mango ice cubes among the glasses, top up with sparkling wine and add the passion fruit wedges. Serve with stirrers.

Cook's Tip
Remember to blend the fruits ahead of time in order to give the mango ice cubes enough time to freeze.

Variation
Make a blackcurrant version of this drink by freezing blackcurrants, washed and stripped from their stems. Half fill each section of the ice cube tray with blackcurrants and top up with water. Put a blackcurrant ice cube in a glass, add some blackcurrant flavoured syrup and top up with sparkling wine.

Pineapple and Rum Energy 336kcal/1400kJ; Protein 1.3g; Carbohydrate 24.9g, of which sugars 24.9g; Fat 16.5g, of which saturates 10.1g; Cholesterol 41mg; Calcium 58mg; Fibre 1.9g; Sodium 54mg.
Tropical Fruit Royale Energy 136kcal/570kJ; Protein 1.2g; Carbohydrate 16.7g, of which sugars 16.5g; Fat 0.2g, of which saturates 0.1g; Cholesterol 0mg; Calcium 21mg; Fibre 2.2g; Sodium 11mg.

Big Breakfast Fruit Smoothie

Very easy to prepare, this energy-packed smoothie makes a great start to the day. Bananas and sesame seeds provide slow-release carbohydrate that will keep you going all morning.

Makes 2 glasses
½ mango
1 banana
1 large orange
30ml/2 tbsp wheatbran
15ml/1 tbsp sesame seeds
10–15ml/2–3 tsp honey

1 Using a small, sharp knife, skin the mango, then slice the flesh off the stone (pit).

2 Peel the banana and break it into lengths, then place it in a blender or food processor with the mango.

3 Squeeze the juice from the orange and add to the blender or food processor, along with the bran, sesame seeds and honey. Whizz until smooth and creamy, then pour into glasses.

Golden Wonder Fruit Drink

Vitamin-rich and energizing, this drink is sure to set you up for the day. Passion fruit has a lovely tangy flavour that goes very well with banana.

Makes 1 large glass
2 passion fruit
2 yellow plums
1 small banana
about 15ml/1 tbsp lemon juice

1 Halve the passion fruit and, using a teaspoon, scoop the pulp into a blender or food processor.

2 Using a small, sharp knife, halve and stone (pit) the plums and add to the blender or food processor.

3 Add the banana and lemon juice, and blend the mixture until smooth, scraping the mixture down from the side of the bowl.

4 Pour into a large glass and check the sweetness. Add a little more lemon juice, if you like.

Grand Marnier, Papaya & Fruit Punch

The term 'punch' comes from the Hindi word panch (five), relating to the five ingredients traditionally contained in the drink – alcohol, lemon or lime, tea, sugar and water. The ingredients may have altered somewhat over the years, but the best punches still combine a mixture of spirits, flavourings and an innocent top-up of fizz or juice. Make a bowl of this drink for a festive gathering of friends and family.

Serves 15
2 large papayas
4 passion fruit
300g/11oz lychees, peeled and stoned (pitted)
300ml/½ pint/1¼ cups freshly squeezed orange juice
200ml/7fl oz/scant 1 cup Grand Marnier or other orange-flavoured liqueur
8 whole star anise
2 small oranges
ice cubes
1.5 litres/2½ pints/6¼ cups soda water (club soda)

1 Halve the papayas and discard the seeds. Halve the passion fruit and press the pulp through a sieve (strainer) into a small punch bowl or a pretty serving bowl.

2 Push the papayas through a juicer, adding 100ml/3½fl oz/ scant ½ cup water to help the pulp through. Juice the lychees.

3 Add the juices to the bowl with the orange juice, liqueur and star anise. Thinly slice the oranges and add to the bowl. Chill for at least 1 hour or until ready to serve.

4 Add plenty of ice cubes to the bowl and top up with soda water. Ladle into punch cups or small glasses, to serve.

Cook's Tip
Cointreau is one of the most famous orange liqueurs, but there are others to choose from. Look out for bottles labelled 'curaçao' or 'triple sec'.

Big Breakfast Energy 172kcal/726kJ; Protein 4.9g; Carbohydrate 27.6g, of which sugars 23.1g; Fat 5.5g, of which saturates 0.9g; Cholesterol 0mg; Calcium 102mg; Fibre 8.5g; Sodium 11mg.
Golden Wonder Energy 108kcal/461kJ; Protein 2.1g; Carbohydrate 25.6g, of which sugars 23.7g; Fat 0.4g, of which saturates 0.1g; Cholesterol 0mg; Calcium 16mg; Fibre 2.8g; Sodium 8mg.
Grand Marnier Energy 65kcal/274kJ; Protein 0.5g; Carbohydrate 11.6g, of which sugars 11.6g; Fat 0.1g, of which saturates 0g; Cholesterol 0mg; Calcium 10mg; Fibre 0.9g; Sodium 6mg.

Passion Fruit Passionata

The combination of ripe passion fruit with sweet caramel is gorgeous in this dreamy milkshake. For convenience, you can easily make the caramel syrup and combine it with the fresh passion fruit juice in advance, so that it's all ready for blending with the milk. For the best results, make sure you use really ripe, crinkly passion fruit.

Makes 4 glasses
90g/3½oz/1/2 cup caster
    (superfine) sugar
juice of 2 large oranges
juice of 1 lemon
6 ripe passion fruit,
    plus extra for garnish
550ml/18fl oz/2½ cups
    full cream (whole) milk
ice cubes

1 Put the sugar in a small, heavy pan with 200ml/7fl oz/ scant 1 cup water. Heat gently, stirring with a wooden spoon until the sugar has dissolved.

2 Bring the mixture to the boil and cook, without stirring, for about 5 minutes until the syrup has turned to a deep golden caramel. Watch closely towards the end of the cooking time because caramel can burn very quickly. If this happens, let the caramel cool, then throw it away and start again.

3 When the caramel has turned deep golden, immediately lower the base of the pan into cold water to prevent it from cooking any further.

4 Carefully add the orange and lemon juice, standing back slightly as the mixture will splutter. Return the pan to the heat and cook gently, stirring continuously, to make a smooth syrup. Transfer the syrup to a small heatproof bowl and set aside until it has cooled completely.

5 Cut the passion fruit in half and, using a teaspoon, scoop out the seeds into a blender or food processor. Add the caramel and milk to the blender and mix until the mixture is smooth and frothy. Pour over ice and serve immediately with a passion fruit garnish.

Pomegranate Plus

With their distinctively exotic flavour, pomegranates are quite delicious. If they have a reddish skin, this is usually a sign that the seeds inside will be vibrant and sweet. Pomegranate juice makes a tasty base for this treat, which is mildly spiced with a hint of ginger.

Serves 2
2 pomegranates
4 fresh figs
15g/½oz fresh root
    ginger, peeled
10ml/2 tsp lime juice
ice cubes and lime wedges,
    to serve

1 Halve the pomegranates. Working over a bowl to catch the juices, pull away the skin to remove the seeds.

2 Quarter the figs and roughly chop the ginger. Push the figs and ginger through a juicer. Push the pomegranate seeds through, reserving a few for decoration. Stir in the lime juice. Pour over ice cubes and lime wedges, then serve.

Ruby Dreamer Fig Smoothie

Figs are now available most of the year round, but they are often at their best in winter, when ruby oranges are also in season – giving you the perfect excuse to make this tasty smoothie.

Makes 2 glasses
6 large ripe figs
4 ruby oranges
15ml/1 tbsp muscovado sugar
    (molasses)
30–45ml/2–3 tbsp lemon juice
crushed ice

1 Cut off the hard, woody tips from the stalks of the figs, then use a sharp knife to cut each fruit in half.

2 Squeeze the oranges and pour the juice into a blender or food processor. Add the figs and sugar. Process well until the mixture is smooth and fairly thick.

3 Add the lemon juice and blend. Pour over the ice and serve.

Passion Fruit Energy 197kcal/828kJ; Protein 5.4g; Carbohydrate 33.2g, of which sugars 33.2g; Fat 5.5g, of which saturates 3.5g; Cholesterol 19mg; Calcium 179mg; Fibre 0.8g; Sodium 67mg.
Pomegranate Plus Energy 224kcal/951kJ; Protein 3.4g; Carbohydrate 52.3g, of which sugars 52.3g; Fat 1.6g, of which saturates 0g; Cholesterol 0mg; Calcium 233mg; Fibre 6.9g; Sodium 58mg.
Ruby Dreamer Energy 417kcal/1776kJ; Protein 7.2g; Carbohydrate 97.8g, of which sugars 97.8g; Fat 2.5g, of which saturates 0g; Cholesterol 0mg; Calcium 443mg; Fibre 13.8g; Sodium 96mg.

Index